Living & working in

AUSTRALIA

David Hampshire

SURVIVAL BOOKS • LONDON • ENGLAND

First published 1998
Second Edition 2003
Third Edition 2005
Fourth Edition 2007
Fifth Edition 2008

Survival Books Limited
26 York Street, London W1U 6PZ, United Kingdom
☎ +44 (0)20-7788 7644, 🖷 +44 (0)870-762 3212
✉ info@survivalbooks.net
🖳 www.survivalbooks.net

British Library Cataloguing in Publication Data.
A CIP record for this book is available
from the British Library.
ISBN 13: 978-905303-68-7

Printed and bound in India by Ajanta Offset

ACKNOWLEDGEMENTS

M sincere thanks to all those who contributed to the successful publication of this book, in particular The Emigration Group, for unravelling the mysteries of the visa system, to Joe Laredo, who was responsible for updating and proofreading the text, to Jim Watson for the superb cover design, cartoons and map, and to the many people who contributed to previous editions, including Alan Allebone, Ruth Barringham, Eugene Benham, James Burton, Graeme Dargi, John Holmes, Adèle Jekgan, Charles King, Pam Miller, Nassem Mohammed, Yolande Pierce-Holmes, Vera Poole, Dianne Rodgers, Ron and Pat Scarborough, Louise Stapleton, Joanna Styles, Ian Wallace and anyone else I've omitted to mention. Finally, a special thank-you to all the photographers who provided the superb photos (see page 478), without which this book would be dull indeed.

THE EDITOR

David Hampshire was born in England and after serving in the Royal Air Force, was employed for many years in the computer industry. His work has taken him around the world and he has lived and worked in many countries, including Australia, France, Germany, Malaysia, the Netherlands, Panama, Singapore, Spain, and Switzerland. David starting working as a technical author in Australia in the '80s and he became a full-time, freelance writer in 1990. He is the author or co-author of some 20 titles, including *Buying a Home in Australia* and *Culture Wise Australia*. David lives with his partner in England and Panama.

WHAT READERS & REVIEWERS

'If you need to find out how France works then this book is indispensable. Native French people probably have a less thorough understanding of how their country functions.'

Living France

'It's everything you always wanted to ask but didn't for fear of the contemptuous put down. The best English-language guide. Its pages are stuffed with practical information on everyday subjects and are designed to compliment the traditional guidebook.'

Swiss News

'Rarely has a 'survival guide' contained such useful advice – This book dispels doubts for first-time travellers, yet is also useful for seasoned globetrotters – In a word, if you're planning to move to the US or go there for a long-term stay, then buy this book both for general reading and as a ready-reference.'

American Citizens Abroad

'Let's say it at once. David Hampshire's Living and Working in France is the best handbook ever produced for visitors and foreign residents in this country; indeed, my discussion with locals showed that it has much to teach even those born and bred in l'Hexagone – It is Hampshire's meticulous detail which lifts his work way beyond the range of other books with similar titles. Often you think of a supplementary question and search for the answer in vain. With Hampshire this is rarely the case. – He writes with great clarity (and gives French equivalents of all key terms), a touch of humour and a ready eye for the odd (and often illuminating) fact. – This book is absolutely indispensable.'

The Riviera Reporter

'A must for all future expats. I invested in several books but this is the only one you need. Every issue and concern is covered, every daft question you have but are frightened to ask is answered honestly without pulling any punches. Highly recommended.'

Reader

'In answer to the desert island question about the one how-to book on France, this book would be it.'

The Recorder

'The ultimate reference book. Every subject imaginable is exhaustively explained in simple terms. An excellent introduction to fully enjoy all that this fine country has to offer and save time and money in the process.'

American Club of Zurich

HAVE SAID ABOUT SURVIVAL BOOKS

'The amount of information covered is not short of incredible. I thought I knew enough about my birth country. This book has proved me wrong. Don't go to France without it. Big mistake if you do. Absolutely priceless!'

Reader

'When you buy a model plane for your child, a video recorder, or some new computer gizmo, you get with it a leaflet or booklet pleading 'Read Me First', or bearing large friendly letters or bold type saying 'IMPORTANT - follow the instructions carefully'. This book should be similarly supplied to all those entering France with anything more durable than a 5-day return ticket. – It is worth reading even if you are just visiting briefly, or if you have lived here for years and feel totally knowledgeable and secure. But if you need to find out how France works then it is indispensable. Native French people probably have a less thorough understanding of how their country functions. – Where it is most essential, the book is most up to the minute.

Living France

A comprehensive guide to all things French, written in a highly readable and amusing style, for anyone planning to live, work or retire in France.

The Times

Covers every conceivable question that might be asked concerning everyday life – I know of no other book that could take the place of this one.

France in Print

A concise, thorough account of the Do's and DONT's for a foreigner in Switzerland – Crammed with useful information and lightened with humorous quips which make the facts more readable.

American Citizens Abroad

'I found this a wonderful book crammed with facts and figures, with a straightforward approach to the problems and pitfalls you are likely to encounter. The whole laced with humour and a thorough understanding of what's involved. Gets my vote!'

Reader

'A vital tool in the war against real estate sharks; don't even think of buying without reading this book first!'

Everything Spain

'We would like to congratulate you on this work: it is really super! We hand it out to our expatriates and they read it with great interest and pleasure.'

ICI (Switzerland) AG

CONTENTS

9. EDUCATION 165

10. PUBLIC TRANSPORT 187

11. MOTORING 211

EDITOR'S NOTES

- All times are shown using am (ante meridiem) for before noon and pm (post meridiem) for after noon. Most Australians don't use the 24-hour clock. All times are local, so check the time difference when making international telephone calls (see **Time Difference** on page 417).

- All prices are in Australian dollars unless otherwise noted (e.g. £ = GB £ sterling). Prices should be taken as estimates only, although they were mostly correct at the time of publication.

- His/he/him also means her/she/her – please forgive me ladies. This is done to make life easier for both the reader and the author, and isn't intended to be sexist.

- Most spelling is (or should be) British English and not American English.

- Warnings and important points are shown in **bold** type.

- The following symbols are used in this book: ☎ (telephone), 📄 (fax), 💻 (Internet) and ✉ (e-mail).

- Lists of **Useful Addresses**, **Further Reading** and **Useful Websites** are contained in **Appendices A**, **B** and **C** respectively.

- For those unfamiliar with the metric system of **Weights & Measures**, Imperial conversion tables are shown in **Appendix D**.

- A communications map of Australia is contained in **Appendix E**.

Great Barrier Reef

INTRODUCTION

Whether you're already living or working in Australia or just thinking about it – this is THE BOOK for you. Forget about those glossy guide books, excellent though they are for tourists; this amazing book was written especially with you in mind and is worth its weight in snags. Furthermore, this updated and fully revised 5th edition is printed in full colour. ***Living and Working in Australia*** is designed to meet the needs of anyone wishing to know the essentials of Australian life – however long your intended stay, you'll find the information contained in this book invaluable.

General information isn't difficult to find in Australia; however, reliable and up-to-date information specifically intended for foreigners living and working in Australia isn't so easy to find, least of all in one volume. Our aim in publishing this book was to help fill this void, and provide the comprehensive, practical information necessary for a relatively trouble-free life. You may have visited Australia as a tourist, but living and working there is a different matter altogether. Adjusting to a different environment and culture and making a home in any foreign country can be a traumatic and stressful experience, and Australia is no exception.

Living and Working in Australia is a comprehensive handbook on a wide range of everyday subjects and represents the most up-to-date source of general information available to foreigners in Australia. It isn't, however, simply a monologue of dry facts and figures, but a practical and entertaining look at life in Australia.

Adjusting to life in a new country is a continuous process, and although this book will help reduce your 'beginner's' phase and minimise the frustrations, it doesn't contain all the answers (most of us don't even know the right questions to ask). What it will do, is help you make informed decisions and calculated judgements, instead of uneducated guesses and costly mistakes. **Most importantly, it will help you save time, trouble and money, and repay your investment many times over!**

Although you may find some of the information a bit daunting, don't be discouraged. Most problems occur only once and fade into insignificance after a short time (as you face the next half a dozen). Most foreigners in Australia would agree that, all things considered, they love living there. A period spent in Australia is a wonderful way to enrich your life, broaden your horizons, and with any luck (and some hard work), also please your bank manager. I trust ***Living and Working in Australia*** will help you avoid the pitfalls of life in Australia and smooth your way to a happy and rewarding future in your new home.

Good luck!

David Hampshire

January 2008

1.

FINDING A JOB

Not surprisingly, Australia is a popular destination among prospective migrants, and few countries offer such an attractive lifestyle and high standard of living, and such good business and employment prospects. Australia has a labour force of just over 10m and a low unemployment rate (see page 22) but there's a worsening skills shortage throughout the country. In mid-2007, Australia was particularly short of railway workers, property (real estate) professionals, and executives in many fields, while a critical shortage of IT workers was predicted for the end of the first decade of the 21st century.

However, if you don't automatically qualify to live or work in Australia (e.g. as a citizen of New Zealand), obtaining a visa is likely to be more difficult than finding a job. Australia is no longer the fabled 'land of opportunity' or 'the lucky country' – at least not for the type of migrant it previously welcomed. It now hopes to become 'the clever country' through the importation of highly educated and skilled workers.

In the early years of the 21st century, the UK was the largest source of 'skilled migrants' (see **Chapter 3**), although only around 20 per cent of the total number of migrants were British). Migrant quotas have risen again after a low of just 85,000 in 2001-02, to 152,800 (including 102,500 places for skilled migrants) in 2007-08. Australian embassies and consulates receive enquiries from around a million people a year, of whom over 400,000 make applications. Of those accepted, almost half have relatives in Australia, around 45 per cent are professionals or skilled workers, and around 10 per cent are refugees.

Australians aren't workaholics (they work to play) and Australian industry is noted for its low productivity. It's estimated that around 15 per cent of companies with five or more employees have between 10 and 25 per cent of their workers absent 'sick' each day. Over 40m working days are lost to sickies each year, costing employers $billions. However, many Australians believe in working (and playing) hard, and they generally work as hard and efficiently as workers in other developed countries. Don't be misled by the informality and casual atmosphere and dress in many companies, as Australian employers can be ruthless when it comes to the bottom line.

Redundancies and cost-cutting in recent years have increased the pressure on all employees, particularly white-collar workers, many of whom now do the work of a number of people. Job dissatisfaction is rife in Australia, one survey showing that (incredibly) over 60 per cent of employees would like a new job.

A number of useful guides for graduate job seekers, including *Graduate Destinations*, *Graduate Course Experience*,

Graduate Salaries, *Postgraduate Destinations* and *Postgraduate Research Experience* are published by Graduate Careers Australia, formerly the Graduate Careers Council of Australia, PO Box 28, Parkville, VIC 3052 (☎ 03-9349 4300, 🖳 www.graduadecareers.com.au). The Australian Bureau of Statistics (ABS, 🖳 www.abs.gov.au) publishes job figures and employment forecasts. Finally, a wealth of job information can be found via the internet (e.g. 🖳 www.jobsearch.com.au). See also **Job Hunting** on page 32.

EMPLOYMENT PROSPECTS

If you want a good job, you must usually be well qualified and speak fluent English (if you're an independent migrant, you won't be accepted without these attributes). Unemployment is high among non-English-speaking adult migrants, particularly those from the Indian subcontinent, the Middle East and North Africa who came to Australia under the Family Reunion Program (although two-thirds have professional qualifications), many of whom believe that they were better off before coming to Australia.

☑ SURVIVAL TIP

You shouldn't plan on obtaining immediate employment in Australia unless you have a firm job offer or special qualifications and experience for which there's a strong local demand, for example in accountancy and medicine.

Most states publish data on current job prospects, indicating occupations with shortages of experienced workers. However, it's important to obtain the latest information concerning jobs (official information sometimes lags behind the real situation); if possible, try to secure a position before your arrival. It's advantageous to make a fact-finding visit to Australia to check your job prospects first hand, although this may not be feasible (a research trip can also help you to judge more accurately whether you're likely to enjoy the Australian way of life). This may also help you find a prospective employer willing to sponsor you, which makes the task of obtaining a visa much easier. If you plan to arrive in Australia without a job, you should have a detailed plan for finding employment on arrival and try to make some contacts before you arrive.

In the last few decades, the country has gone from boom to bust, the prosperous '80s being followed by the worst recession since the Great Depression of the '30s – a recession which hit Australia earlier than most other developed countries. However, the years 1998-2000 saw strong annual economic growth (around 4 per cent), which has dropped slightly in the early 21st century, to around 3 per cent. The Australian job market changed dramatically in the '90s, during which most new jobs shifted from construction, finance and manufacturing to the communications, property and service industries (e.g. retailing and computing). In fact, Australia has undergone an economic revolution, during which many sacred cows have gone (or are going) to the wall, including the power of the unions, protectionism, state ownership and the welfare state.

There has been huge job growth in the white-collar services sector in recent years, particularly in property and business support services, which now employ some 84 per cent of the sector's workforce and are responsible for 25 per cent of export earnings. Agriculture (including fishing, forestry, horses, horticulture and the service industries to agriculture and agribusiness) has also created over 19,500 jobs in the last decade. Retailing is the largest source of jobs in Australia, with some 1.3m workers; property and business services are the second-largest, and manufacturing the third, although its share of national employment has halved to below 15 per cent since the mid-'60s. In recent years, most new jobs have been created in Queensland and Western Australia due to the construction boom in these two states.

Australian manufacturers and the Australian labour market have been relatively slow to embrace new technology and to adjust to the rapidly changing world economy, although there's now an intensive government drive to rectify this.

Many companies depend on (declining) assistance through export incentives, production bounties and import tariffs rather than aiming to eradicate restrictive working practices, improving productivity and reducing costs. Australian productivity is just half that of the US and some 60 per cent of that of many developed countries. Like most developed countries, Australia has found it increasingly difficult to compete with cheap imports from countries (e.g. in Asia) where labour costs are very low.

> There are currently shortages of skilled workers in many sectors, including medicine: it's estimated, for example, that there will be thousands of nursing vacancies by 2010.

The information technology age has spawned a new class of casual, low paid, low skilled, part-time workers, and one of the trade unions' main fears is that new technology will create an 'underclass' and dump thousands of people on the job scrap heap. Although there was major job-shedding by banks and utility companies in the mid-'90s, in recent years economic growth sparked by the 2000 Olympics have led to greater employment. Indeed, although new technology may be putting people out of work in some industries, it's credited with creating jobs overall. Australia's job market, like that of most developed countries, was transformed in the '90s and it's vital for workers in the 21st century to keep their skills up to date in order to stay ahead of the pack.

Although it isn't as easy to find work as it was in the '80s, there's a steady demand for skilled workers in most regions and a shortage in some areas, which has been exacerbated by a sharp reduction in apprenticeships and training in recent years. If you have a choice, compare the job or business opportunities in all states and territories before deciding where to live, as job prospects vary considerably from city to city and state to state (as does the culture, lifestyle and, especially, the weather). Some states (notably South Australia) have a shortage of skilled workers and sometimes offer incentives to migrants such as job-matching schemes, low-interest loans and subsidised accommodation. It's also easier to qualify for immigration if you're willing to settle outside the major cites in a designated 'low-growth' area (in recent years, job prospects

have improved faster in regional centres than in state capitals).

Workforce

The jobs lost in the last decade or so have generally been well paid skilled and semi-skilled manufacturing jobs, which have been replaced by low-paid, part-time or temporary jobs with few benefits (these now comprise some 30 per cent of all jobs in Australia). Labour experts believe that the era of secure, full-time employment with comprehensive employee benefits and lifetime guarantees has gone for ever (not just in Australia, but worldwide).

Today, employees must be flexible, with diverse and up-to-date skills, constantly renewed through further education and training. Australia has a highly mobile labour force (around a quarter of the workforce changes jobs each year), particularly among the young, and even managers and executives often need to change careers or move to another city to stay in a job. An increasing number of people are 'tele-working' (working from home via computer, fax and telephone),

either from choice or because their employers have closed offices to reduce costs. There are around 400,000 home-based workers in Australia – a number which is growing at three times the rate of overall employment – and it's estimated that home workers will comprise some 25 per cent of the workforce in the next decade.

Women

Male chauvinism is alive and positively thriving in Australia, where women employees also face the additional hazard of sexual harassment. See also **Discrimination** on page 57.

Some 55 per cent of Australian women work, and they comprise around 45 per cent of the total Australian workforce, including 35 per cent of full-time employees and 75 per cent of part-time workers (half of employed women work part-time). A woman doing the same or broadly similar work to a man and employed by the same employer is legally entitled to the same pay and terms of employment as a man ('equal pay for work of equal value'). However, as in most developed countries, although there's no **official** discrimination, in practice this is often the case. Despite equal pay legislation (enshrined in the Sex Discrimination Act of 1984), women have found it impossible to close the pay gap between themselves and men, and in the mid-'90s men's wages were increasing at around twice the rate of women's. Women are disadvantaged in terms of pay scales at all levels of employment in all industries and professions, and most employers pay only lip service to equal pay. Women receive an average of around 70 per cent of men's wages (higher in professional jobs) for doing the same work. Women's only advantage is probably that unemployment is lower among women than among men. Careers in which women predominate, such as librarianship, nursery and primary school teaching, nursing, and speech and occupational therapy, are poorly paid compared with those where men dominate. The concentration of women in part-time work is also widening the gap between male and female earnings.

In recent years, women have been moving into male-dominated professions in increasing numbers, including accountancy, auditing and mathematics. However, although more women are breaking into the professions, they don't usually reach the top, where the 'old boy' network thrives. The main discrimination among women professionals isn't in salary or title but in promotion opportunities, as many companies and organisations are loath to elevate women to important positions (ostensibly because of fears that they may leave and start a family or at least take long breaks from work – only around 21 per cent of men take leave from work for family reasons compared with some 40 per cent of women). Employers are (not surprisingly) wary of female employees becoming pregnant, as after one year's employment they're entitled to 12 months' (unpaid) maternity leave, after which they have the right to return to the same job with the same pay.

This invisible barrier is known as the 'glass ceiling'. The saying 'the best man for the job is often a woman' is seldom acknowledged by Australian employers, most of whom prefer male candidates. Although the glass ceiling is less of an obstacle to success than previously (cracks have been appearing in recent years), men are four times more likely than women to be managers and administrators. Women are rare among the directors of major companies and, although 25 per cent of the representatives on government authorities and boards are officially supposed to be women (a figure which should rise to 50 per cent in the long term), in reality it's much lower. According to the

EOWA Australian Census of Women in Leadership, carried out in August 2006 by the Equal Opportunity for Women in the Workplace Agency (EOWA, 🖳 www.eowa. gov.au), women account for 7.4 per cent of executive (line) managers, 8.7 per cent of directors, just 3 per cent of CEOs and a mere 2 per cent of chairs of Australia's 200 top companies. Most successful businesswomen are forced to put their career before their family (most don't have children) and personal life, most female executives working over 50 hours a week.

> ☑ **SURVIVAL TIP**
>
> **Self-employment is the best bet for women who want to get to the top and has increased steadily during the last decade, despite the fact that banks and other financial institutions are usually reluctant to lend women money.**

Industrial Relations

Industrial relations have historically been poor in Australia, with a constant cycle of confrontation between workers, management and the government, but there has been a huge reduction in strikes during the last two decades due, among other things, to legislation: the deal between unions and employers instigated by the Labor Party when it came to power in the early '80s; the Workplace Relations Act of 1996 and the 2005 Amendment, allowing any party affected by a strike to 'apply' for its cessation (previously, this could be done only if Australian industry as a whole was significantly affected); and the present government's 'WorkChoices' programme introduced in 2006. Instead of higher wages, workers now tend to be given better working conditions and benefits, which has helped put a brake on runaway inflation and strengthened the economy, though inevitably at some cost to employee protection, working hours and wages. According to the Australian Bureau of Statistics, since the Act was passed there has been an average annual number of 61 working days lost per 1,000 employees due to disputes; in the decade before the Act, the average was 174.

Unemployment

In August 2007, unemployment in Australia was at a 30-year low of 4.3 per cent (one of the lowest rates in the world). Some commentators regard this figure as less impressive than it appears, however, as the fall in unemployment has resulted mainly from the creation of low-paid jobs.

Unemployment also varies considerably with the region. It's highest in New South Wales (NSW) and Victoria, lowest in Western Australia and Tasmania. It's much higher in rural areas (which is why most migrants head for the cities), among unskilled and semi-skilled workers, and in the younger and older age groups (most long-term unemployed are under 25 or over 45). Age discrimination is widespread in Australia, although it's illegal to specify age limits in job advertisements in some states, but employers are beginning to discover that older people are generally more reliable, making it easier for them to find jobs.

Unemployment is, not surprisingly, much higher than average among migrants who don't speak fluent English. In recent years, many migrants who have been unable to find a job have experienced great hardship, as a recent law means that they can no longer claim social security benefits during their first two years in the country (although some migrants have successfully challenged the law). Would-be working holidaymakers no longer find it easy to find jobs, as unemployed young Australians are snapping up the low-paid temporary and casual jobs which were once the preserve of the itinerant 'backpacker'. In the last few years, the government has introduced a number of job creation schemes, such as 'jobsearch' and 'newstart', in an effort to boost employment, particularly among the young and the long-term unemployed.

SALARY

It can be difficult to determine the salary you should command in Australia, as salaries aren't always stated in job advertisements, except for public sector employees (who are paid according to fixed rates). Salaries may vary considerably for the same job in different parts of Australia. In general, wages are highest in NSW (particularly Sydney, which has the highest cost of living) and Canberra, and lowest in Queensland and South Australia. However, salary variations aren't uniform across Australia and people living in areas with a low cost of living can sometimes earn as much as those in cities with a much higher cost of living. Australia generally has a lower cost of living than most European countries and similar to the US (see page

312). However, although Australians have traditionally been highly paid, some analysts believe that Australia's future may be low-tech, low-pay.

There's a federal minimum wage in Australia, which in 2007 was AS$13.74 per hour (equivalent to AS$522.12 per week) but most job sectors are bound by workplace agreements (see page 44). Overtime rates are usually one-and-a-half times the normal hourly rate but can be twice the normal rate for weekend work.

Many analysts think that the high federal minimum wage is partly responsible for unemployment, although it's in effect undercut by employers hiring part-time and casual workers (many employers, particularly restaurant owners, pay below the legal rate of pay). Many people – including the Australian government – believe that there should be a lower federal minimum wage for unskilled workers, who are currently priced out of jobs. In fact, however, increases in the minimum wage have been minimal in recent years. In 2007 the task of setting it was passed from the Australian Industrial Relations Commission (AIRC) to the newly created Australian FairPay Commission (AFPC, 🖵 www. fairpay.gov.au).

Government surveys of average weekly earnings are published regularly for a wide range of trades and professions, both nationally and for individual states and cities. The government-run organisation Wagenet has a website where you can consult wages and conditions of employment information (🖵 www.wagenet. gov.au). There are also a number of books which detail wages in different occupations, including *What Jobs Pay* by Rod Tilson (Hobsons Press).

Real wages for many workers have fallen over the last decade and many families receive social security payments (e.g. a 'family payment') to top up their incomes. Government employees earn more on average than employees in the private sector (in 2007 an average of around $62,000 per year for federal government employees and $56,000 for local government workers) and receive bigger wage increases. The highest paid private-sector jobs are generally in finance, insurance and mining, while the lowest are in catering, retailing and tourism. As in most other countries, the self-employed are generally the worst off, with an average salary of just $40,400 in 2007. Under a scheme called 'leave loading', full-time employees are paid an extra 17.5 per cent of their normal wage when they're on holiday (usually paid in December).

In September 2007, according to the PayScale research centre (🖵 www. payscale.com), average salaries for various positions were approximately as follows:

Position	Average Annual Salary
Graphic Artist/Designer	$41,400
Administrative/ Office Manager	$42,500
Accountant	$44,300
Personal Assistant	$44,500
Software Developer/ Engineer/Programmer	$57,000
Operations Manager	$67,000
General Manager	$80,000

Not surprisingly, the highest average salaries are in Sydney, followed by Canberra, Melbourne, Perth, Brisbane and Adelaide; bottom of the table is the inappropriately named Gold Coast. There are allowances (called 'tropical loading' or 'remote area allowances') for work in remote parts of the Northern Territory and Western Australia (above the Tropic of Capricorn).

and temporary jobs, where wage growth has been minimal.

Fringe Benefits

For many employees, particularly executives and senior managers, their 'salary' is much more than what they receive in their weekly or monthly pay packets. Many companies offer a number of fringe benefits (or perks) for executives and managers, which may even continue into retirement. These include children's private education, company cars available for private use, expense accounts and private health insurance. However, such benefits have declined considerably in recent years with the introduction of a fringe benefit tax (FBT – see page 306), which is levied at 46.5 per cent on the taxable value of employee fringe benefits. There has also been a tax crackdown on executive pay packages, particularly 'salary sacrifice' schemes, where executives sacrifice part of their pay in return for higher superannuation payments and other benefits.

The most common forms of fringe benefit are allowances for living away from home, subsidised company restaurants or canteens, and superannuation (which is compulsory), all of which are covered by union awards and aren't liable to FBT. Under the mandatory Superannuation Guarantee (introduced in 1992), employers must pay a percentage of your salary into a superannuation fund (see page 269). Most employees consider fringe benefits to be important, particularly childcare on business premises, company cars, 'flexi-days', income protection insurance, life insurance, staff discounts and superannuation. The opportunity to work overtime is also seen as an important 'fringe benefit' by most hourly paid workers, many of whom earn around a quarter of their wages from overtime. Always check whether a quoted salary

Usually, salaries are negotiable, and it's up to you to ensure that you receive a level of salary and benefits commensurate with your qualifications and experience (in other words, as much as you can get!). If you have friends or acquaintances working in Australia or who have worked there, ask them what an average or good salary is for your trade or profession. Salaries paid by some foreign companies (e.g. American or Japanese companies) may be higher on average than those paid by Australian companies, particularly for executives and managers imported from overseas.

Pay increases are often linked to improved productivity and performance, and pay generally rises in line with inflation. The deal between workers, management and the government generally heralded the end of massive pay rises for workers in return for better working conditions and fringe benefits. Women have fallen behind in the pay stakes in recent years, particularly those employed in part-time is salary only or a total salary package, including for example superannuation and a company car.

QUALIFICATIONS

The most important qualification for working in Australia is the ability to speak English fluently (see **Language** on page 38). If you have a degree or a certificate from a recognised educational establishment in an English-speaking country, language usually presents no problems. However, applicants from non-English speaking countries or backgrounds must usually pass an English test and possibly also an occupational English examination, where the pass mark depends on your profession or trade. The failure rate is high.

Once you've overcome this hurdle, you should establish whether your trade or professional qualifications and experience are recognised in Australia. While you may be well qualified in your own country, you may need to pass professional examinations or trade tests to satisfy Australian standards (foreign-trained doctors went on hunger-strike a couple of years ago claiming that they were denied the right to practise by discriminatory qualification tests). If you aren't experienced, Australian employers expect your studies to be in a relevant discipline and to have included work experience.

The points system, on which most immigration is based, depends to a large extent on the skills and qualifications of applicants. Points are awarded for skill levels based on your current or previous employment and whether your qualifications are adequate, including occupational training. Theoretically, qualifications recognised by professional and trade bodies overseas should be recognised in Australia. However, recognition varies with the country and in some cases foreign qualifications aren't recognised by Australian employers or professional and trade associations. All academic qualifications should also be recognised, although they may be given less prominence than equivalent Australian qualifications, depending on the country and the educational institution in which they were obtained.

> ⚠️ **Caution**
>
> **To practise a profession or trade in Australia, you require evidence of an appropriate level of education and practical experience; the usual minimum number of years' experience is three but it can be much higher for some jobs.**

To work in Australia as a licensed tradesman you must have your qualifications assessed by a Vocational Training Board or similar state organisation; you may also need to obtain a licence (or pass an examination) to work in some professions, states or trades. Trades Recognition Australia (TRA, 🖥 www.workplace.gov.au/tra) assesses migrants' experience, qualifications and skills against comparable standards in Australia. For example, the metal and electrical trades have a system whereby overseas-trained tradesmen can be awarded an Australian Recognised Tradesman's Certificate.

The recognition of professional qualifications is usually the responsibility of the relevant professional body, which migrants are normally required to join to practise in Australia. However, a favourable assessment isn't a guarantee that you'll be professionally recognised or able to gain employment in your field of expertise, as some professional bodies require overseas practitioners to pass examinations conducted or supervised by themselves. In some cases, it's necessary for foreign professionals to work under the supervision of a registered professional Australian for a period, e.g. a year, or to undertake further training. Medical practitioners must have studied medicine in Australia or New Zealand to work in some states, and until very recently foreign doctors couldn't work for Medicare (the state healthcare scheme – see page 250). This was reviewed in 2004 – as a result of a shortage of medical staff in parts of Australia – and it's estimated that up to 30 per cent of practising Australian doctors have trained wholly or partly overseas.

The Australian government no longer lists the skills and qualifications necessary for occupations. However, you can check the qualifications required for a particular job in the *Australian Standard Classification of Occupations* (*ASCO*) dictionary, available for reference at Australian High Commission offices and other Australian government offices overseas and at offices of the Department of Immigration and Multicultural and Indigenous Affairs in Australia or on the website of the Australian Bureau of Statistics (⌨ www.abs.gov.au). Additional information can be obtained from the government's 'Australian Education International' (*sic*) service: International Education Group, Department of Education, Science and Training, GPO Box 9880, Canberra ACT 2601 (☎ local call rate 1300-363079 within Australia only, or ☎ +61 3-8341 3611 from abroad, ⌨ http://aei.dest.gov.au/AEI/ QualificationsRecognition/default.htm).

Whatever kind of job you're looking for in Australia, whether temporary or permanent, part or full time, always take proof of your qualifications, training and experience with you, plus copies of references and an up-to-date curriculum vitae.

When leaving a job in Australia, you should ask for a written reference (one isn't usually provided automatically), particularly if you intend to look for further work in Australia or you think your work experience will help you to obtain employment overseas.

GOVERNMENT EMPLOYMENT SERVICE

In Australia, the government authority in charge of employment at federal level is Centrelink. Centrelink offices provide a range of customer services covering education, training and youth affairs; employment; health and family services; primary industries and energy; and social security. Centrelink offices also provide advice and information regarding the government's Jobs, Education and Training (JET) programme; registration and acceptance of new applicants for income support and employment assistance; self-help job-finding facilities, including computer access to a national job vacancies database; and services for disadvantaged groups, including migrants, people with disabilities, single parents and young people. Centrelink has a comprehensive website (⌨ www.

centrelink.gov.au), which provides the latest information on Centrelink services. Centrelink's international service centre can be reached on ☎ 13-1673 (local call rate from anywhere in Australia).

PRIVATE EMPLOYMENT AGENCIES

Private employment agencies abound in all major cities and towns in Australia and find work for almost 100,000 people annually, although nearly two-thirds of them are contracted for casual work. Many large companies are happy to engage agents and consultants to recruit employees, particularly executives, managers, professionals and temporary staff.

There are four main types of private agency in Australia: personnel consultants, labour hire contractors, student employment agencies and 'employment agencies' (see below). Personnel consultants (head-hunters) handle mostly executive, managerial and professional positions (accountants are in demand), although there's some overlap with 'employment agencies'. Labour hire contractors handle jobs for skilled, semi-skilled and unskilled manual workers and tend to be located in industrial areas rather than the main streets of major cities.

The largest number of agencies simply come under the generic term 'employment agencies'. Some specialise in particular fields or industries: accounting; agriculture; au pairing and nannying; banking; care work; computing, engineering and technical; hospitality; industrial and manual; legal; medical and nursing; mining; outback jobs; resort work; sales; secretarial; and tourism. Others deal with a range of industries and professions. Some agencies deal exclusively with temporary workers in a variety of occupations, including baby-sitters, chauffeurs, cleaners, cooks, gardeners, hairdressers, housekeepers, industrial workers, labourers, office staff and security guards. Care, nanny and nursing agencies are common. Many agencies handle both permanent and temporary positions.

Agencies are usually prohibited from charging a fee to job applicants, as they receive their fees from clients, although in some states they may charge a registration fee (check first). For permanent staff, the fee paid by the employer is a percentage of the annual salary (e.g. 10 per cent); for temporary staff, agencies take a percentage of the hourly rate paid by employers. If you take a temporary job through an agency, you're paid by the agency, usually weekly or fortnightly, which may include paid public and annual holidays after a qualifying period. Always obtain a contract and ensure that you know exactly how much you'll be paid and when, and the conditions regarding the termination of a job.

> Agencies must deduct income tax from gross pay and you're required to give an agency your tax file number (see page 353) within a few weeks of starting work; otherwise they must deduct tax at the highest rate.

Salaries vary considerably according to the type of job, but most secretarial jobs pay between $20 and $30 per hour. You usually receive extra pay (loading) for weekend and night work, and there are allowances (called tropical loading or remote area allowances) for jobs in remote areas of the Northern Territory and Western Australia (above the Tropic of Capricorn).

Employment agencies earn a great deal of money from finding people jobs so, provided you have something to offer their clients, they're keen to help you (if you're an experienced accountant, nurse or secretary you may get trampled in the rush). If they cannot help you, they usually

BDS Challenge International, Catalyst Recruitment Systems, Centastaff, Dial-an-Angel, Drake Personnel, Extrastaff (formerly Brook Street), Forstaff, IPA Personnel, Julia Ross Personnel, Kelly Services, Key People, Manpower, Mitier Personnel, Select Appointments, Templine and Western Staff Services. Check the yellow pages for local offices of these and other agencies. If you're travelling around Australia and plan to work in a number of major cities, you may find it advantageous to work for an agency with offices nationwide.

To find local agencies, look in the yellow pages under 'Employment Agencies' and in local newspapers. Employment agencies are increasingly using the internet to advertise job vacancies, which speeds up the response and processing of job applications. Many Australian agencies employing temporary staff advertise overseas in publications (see **Appendix B**) targeted at those with working holiday visas (see page 73). A list of agencies specialising in particular jobs or fields is contained in *Live, Work & Play in Australia* by Sharyn McCullum (Kangaroo Press).

CONTRACT JOBS

Contract or freelance jobs are available through specialist employment agencies in Australia. Contracts are usually full time and for a fixed period, although they may be open-ended. In recent years, many companies have been shifting from full-time employees to contract workers and contracting out jobs such as building maintenance, catering, cleaning, computer installation, construction, and even parts of the manufacturing process. However, the Independent Contractors' Bill, 2006 overrides all state and territory laws and allows independent contractors the right to choose the form of working arrangement that best suits their needs so that they can no longer be deemed to be employees.

tell you immediately and won't waste your time.

When visiting employment agencies, you should dress appropriately for the type of job you're seeking, and take with you your bank details (if you want to get paid!), curriculum vitae (CV), passport (with a visa if applicable), references and tax file number (TFN). Office staff may be given a typing or literacy test (if applicable) and some agencies have in-house training programmes for secretarial staff. You should register with a number of agencies to maximise your chances of finding work. Keep in close contact (ring in every day if possible) and try to provide a telephone number where you can be reached.

There's a plethora of employment agencies in Australia, many operating nationally with offices in all major cities, while others operate in one or two cities only. Among the larger agencies operating nationwide or in most major cities are Accountancy Placements, ADIA,

Penalties now apply to any employer who tries to disguise an offer of employment as an independent contracting arrangement. Employers can be fined up to $33,000 if found to be in breach of this new law.

Many contract positions are for specialists, in fields such as accountancy, computing, electronics, engineering and mining, although there's also a strong market in providing catering, cleaning and maintenance services. Rates vary considerably, e.g. from around $18 per hour for a clerk to $100 or more for a computer specialist. Contractors may work at home or on a client's or contract company's premises. There used to be a lucrative market in contract jobs in Australia, particularly for information technology specialists, although the recession in the '90s put paid to many jobs. Consultant companies (also called bodyshops) specialise in supplying contract staff to major companies. The usual visa regulations apply (see **Chapter 3**) to contract workers, unless you're employed to work outside Australia.

PART-TIME JOBS

A part-time job is generally defined as one for less than 20 hours per week. Part-time jobs are available in most industries and professions in Australia and are most common in cafes, factories, offices, pubs, restaurants and shops. In the last few years the number of part-time workers in Australia has risen considerably, particularly among women, and now totals over 3m – around 30 per cent of the workforce. Over 75 per cent of part-time jobs in larger workplaces (with a minimum of 20 staff) are in the accommodation, cafe and restaurant, education, health and community service, and retail sectors. Part-time jobs apply to all levels (from executives to clerks) and all businesses, many people turning to part-time work for family, health or lifestyle

reasons. Job satisfaction is generally higher among part-time workers than those in full-time employment.

Part-time workers are usually paid on an hourly basis and don't have the same rights as full-time workers, but pay awards normally contain provisions to protect part-time workers' rights. They don't, however, usually receive annual leave, maternity leave, sick pay, or other entitlements of full-time workers, although the balance is being redressed in various industries. Part-time workers are now paid the same (pro rata) as full-time employees.

TEMPORARY & CASUAL JOBS

Temporary and casual jobs differ from part-time jobs in that they're usually for a limited (fixed) period, e.g. from a few hours to a few months, or even intermittent. Casual work usually refers to labouring jobs, whereas a temporary job can be in almost any field.

> Most Australian companies employ temporary or casual staff at some time (around 50 per cent on a regular basis), particularly in clerical positions when staff are sick or on holiday, for special projects and in busy periods.

The temporary job market was hit hard during the recession in the early '90s, but there has been a huge increase in demand in the last few years, particularly in the major cities and in the food, drink and manufacturing sectors. Overall, around 20 per cent of employees identify themselves as casual workers. Downsizing and the cost of making full-time employees redundant (and unfair dismissal claims) have led many companies to employ an army of temporary employees, which is often cheaper and more efficient.

Many people choose 'careers' in temporary and contract work, which provides them with maximum flexibility when it comes to holidays, time off, travel and working hours. Although there's less security than with a full-time job and you don't usually receive any benefits, you're generally compensated by a higher hourly rate of pay. Temporary work also provides an opportunity to try your hand at a range of jobs which you would otherwise probably never do. The easiest way to find temporary work in the major cities is through an agency (see page 32); provided you have a marketable skill (e.g. accountancy, computing or nursing), it's relatively easy to find well paid work. Rates range from around $18 per hour for clerical staff to over $100 for IT professionals.

Casual workers are usually employed on a daily, first-come-first-served basis. The work often entails hard labouring and is therefore usually better suited to men. Pay for casual work is usually low (from $5 per hour) and is usually in cash, although this is illegal.

Working Holidaymakers

Temporary or casual work is often undertaken by foreigners with working holiday visas (see page 73), which permit you to work for any employer for up to three months. It isn't easy to find work in many areas, however, and you often need to hustle to get a job and may require experience or qualifications. It's important to ensure that you have sufficient funds to tide you over until you can find work. You should be prepared to splash out on some smart clothes if a job requires them (or arrange to have some sent to you).

During university holiday periods, there's stiff competition from students so, if you're planning to work in a major city, try to get there before the local students break for their holidays. Most holiday jobs are available in fast food, harvesting, hospitality and retailing. Recruiting is often done a few months before holiday periods,

e.g. companies hire in August to October for the summer period of December to February. The easiest work to find is on farms, usually picking fruit or vegetables (see **Farm Work** below), but well known department and chain stores are generally the best employers. Avoid jobs offering unpaid 'trial' periods, which is illegal and is usually simply a trick to get you to work for nothing. You should also avoid door-to-door selling requiring advance payment (e.g. $200) for sample kits (selling them is how some companies make their money) and jobs which pay only commission.

You may be entitled to a tax rebate when you leave Australia, although claiming it may be more trouble than it's worth.

> ☑ SURVIVAL TIP
>
> **You usually have better job prospects if you plan to stay put for a number of months rather than just a few weeks.**

Visitors to Australia with working holiday visas (see page 73) may be interested in the Visitoz Scheme, which is a work placement scheme designed particularly with working holiday visa holders in mind. Those who are accepted are guaranteed jobs and on-the-spot training during their stay in Australia. Jobs offered are mainly outdoors in the agricultural or rural hospitality industries, although there are jobs available in education, healthcare and maintenance. For more information contact the Visitoz Scheme: in Australia, Springbrook Farm, Goomeri 4601, Queensland (☎ 07-4168 6185, 🖥 www.visitoz.org); in the UK, c/o Will and Julia Taunton-Burnet, 49 Hurst Lane, Oxford OX2 9PR (☎ 01865-861516).

Good sources of information for working holidaymakers are *Live, Work & Play in Australia* by Sharyn McCullum (Kangaroo Press), *Workabout Australia* by Barry Brebner, and the TNT *Australia & New Zealand Travel Planner* (see **Appendix B**), which contains advice on finding casual and temporary work. The British Universities North America Club (BUNAC), 16 Bowling Green Lane, London EC1R 0QH, UK (☎ 020-7251 3472, 🖳 www.bunac.org) has a 'Work Australia' programme which helps graduates with working holiday visas to find temporary work.

Farm Work

One of the most common forms of temporary work in Australia is fruit and vegetable picking, which can be done somewhere in Australia throughout the year (many people manage to stay in work all year). Pay varies considerably (from excellent to poor) and is either an hourly rate or, more often, piece work, where the more you pick the more you earn. Doing piece work you can earn around $700 per week, although you need to work between 50 and 80 hours and possibly every day. You should expect to earn from around $14 to $16 per hour from most harvesting jobs. **Always establish your conditions, hours and pay in advance, as there are unscrupulous employers around who will happily take advantage of you given half a chance.**

Farming is a rough and ready experience and involves hard, often dirty work – definitely not for softies. You must usually have a tent or vehicle to sleep in; some employers provide basic accommodation and food (there may be a charge), but it's usually terrible and it's better to provide your own. It pays to have your own transport, as farms are generally in remote areas. Large farms are sometimes targeted by immigration officials, resulting in the deportation of illegal workers.

The government publication *Harvest Table* carries job advertisements from local fruit-growers' associations and there are harvest labour offices in many country

areas. There's also a Harvest Hotline with the latest information (☎ local call rate 1300-792622). An up-to-date state-by-state harvest guide is included on the *Harvest Trail* link on the Jobsearch website (🖳 www.jobsearch.gov.au).

Wages & Tax

Employers or agencies require your tax file number (see page 301) and when you leave an employer you should receive a group certificate (for tax purposes). If you don't provide a tax file number, your employer must deduct tax at the highest tax rate (45 per cent). If you earn over $450 per month, your employer must pay 9 per cent of your salary into a superannuation fund. This is intended to be rolled over from employer to employer until you reach retirement age but, if it amounts to less than $500, it's usually paid to you in cash. Many employers illegally pay temporary staff in cash without making any deductions for tax or superannuation.

JOB HUNTING

When looking for a job in Australia (or anywhere for that matter), you shouldn't put all your eggs in one basket, as the more job applications you make the better your chances of success. Contact as many prospective employers and employment agencies as possible, by writing to them, telephoning them or calling on them. It's important to find out how your chosen job is normally recruited. For example, the recruitment of executives and senior managers in Australia is usually handled by consultants, who advertise in the Australian national press (and also overseas) and interview all applicants before presenting clients with a shortlist. At the other end of the scale, manual jobs requiring no previous experience may be advertised in local newspapers or in shop windows, where the first suitable able-bodied applicant may be offered the job on the spot. Your method of job hunting obviously depends on your circumstances, experience and qualifications, and the sort of job you're seeking, and may include the following:

- checking the TV teletext job service and other bulletin boards.

- checking employment sites on the internet (which is increasingly being used by Australian agencies and head hunters). Some useful employment websites are:

  - ⌨ www.bluecollar.com.au ('blue-collar' jobs only);

  - ⌨ www.careerone.com.au;

  - ⌨ www.jobsearch.gov.au (this government-run website is one of the largest and most comprehensive, with daily additions);

  - ⌨ www.mycareer.com.au (thousands of jobs from recruitment agencies and employers);

  - ⌨ www.seek.com.au (claims to be Australia's no.1 job-search site);

The Department of Employment and Workplace Relations (DEWR) maintains a regularly updated site with a list of most employment websites (⌨ www.dewr.gov.au). Students can use the Gradlink site, established by the Graduate Careers Council of Australia (⌨ www.graduatecareers.com.au).

- contacting private recruitment consultants and employment agencies (see page 27);

- obtaining copies of Australian daily newspapers (see page 382), all of which contain 'positions vacant' sections (the Saturday editions are the best), including job advertisements dedicated to particular industries or professions on certain days. Most local and national newspapers are available in the reading rooms of local libraries in Australia, so you don't usually need to buy them. Jobs are also advertised in industry and trade newspapers and magazines. Australian newspapers are available in some countries from international news agencies, as well as in Australian embassies and consulates, Australian social clubs, and Australian trade and commercial centres, (although they don't always contain the 'situations vacant' sections);

  In the UK, single copies of the major Australian newspapers can be purchased from Smyth, International Media Representatives, Archgate Business Centre, 825 High Road, London N12 8UB, UK (☎ 020-8446 6400, ⌨ www.smyth-international.com). The 'jobs vacant' sections of major Australian newspapers can sometimes be perused on the internet.

- networking (getting together with like-minded people to discuss business), which is a popular way of making contacts in Australia. It can be particularly successful for executives, managers and professionals when job hunting.

- if you have a professional qualification that's recognised in Australia, writing to an Australian professional organisation for information and advice (addresses are obtainable from Australian chambers of commerce overseas); membership of the organisation may be obligatory to work in Australia. All associations publish journals containing 'positions vacant' advertisements, where members can also offer their services to prospective employers. Information about specific professions, trades and industries, particularly job opportunities in individual states, cities or areas, can be obtained from local chambers of commerce in Australia.

- applying to international and national recruiting agencies acting for Australian companies. Agencies mainly recruit executives and key managerial and technical staff, and some have offices overseas, e.g. in the UK.

- applying to foreign multi-national companies with offices or subsidiaries in Australia and making written applications directly to Australian companies. You can obtain a list of companies working in a particular field from trade directories, copies of which are available at reference libraries in Australia (they can also be consulted at Australian missions and chambers of commerce overseas).

- placing an advertisement in the 'situations wanted' section of a national newspaper in Australia or a local newspaper in the area where you wish to work. If you're a member of a recognised profession or trade, you could place an advertisement in a newspaper or magazine dedicated to your profession or a particular industry.

- asking acquaintances, friends and relatives working in Australia whether they know of an employer looking for someone with your experience and qualifications.

- if you're already in Australia, contacting or joining expatriate groups, professional organisations, social clubs and societies, particularly your country's chamber of commerce.

- applying in person to Australian companies (see **Personal Applications** below).

Always obtain a job offer in writing and a contract; steer clear of an employer who won't provide them. An official job entitles you to accident insurance, protection from discrimination and exploitation, redundancy payments, a state pension and unemployment pay, among other benefits (see also **Working Illegally** on page 47).

Written Applications

When writing for a job, address your letter to the personnel director or manager (try to obtain his name) and include your CV (see below). Writing for jobs from overseas is usually a hit-and-miss affair and it's probably the least successful method of securing employment (although it can be successful for those seeking 'temporary' jobs for up to four years). If you're applying from overseas and are planning to visit Australia, you should tell prospective employers when you're available for interview and should arrange as many interviews as you can fit into your timetable. Visiting Australia for an interview usually convinces prospective employers of your commitment, but note that companies may wish to see a copy of your visa before interviewing you.

Personal Applications

Your best chance of obtaining some jobs (particularly temporary jobs) in Australia is to apply in person, when success is often simply a matter of being in the right place at the right time. Many companies don't advertise but rely on attracting workers by word of mouth and via their own vacancy boards. Always leave your name and address with a prospective employer and (if possible) a telephone number where you can be contacted, particularly if a job may become vacant at short notice.

CURRICULAM VITAE & INTERVIEWS

Curricula vitae (CVs) are important in Australia when looking for work, particularly when jobs are thin on the ground. Don't forget that the purpose of your CV is to obtain an interview, not a job, and it must be written with this in mind. This means that it must be tailored to every job application. If you aren't up to writing a good CV, you can employ a professional writer, who should be able to turn your uneventful working life into something of which Indiana Jones would be proud. A good CV should be: brief (four pages or less); typed/printed on white A4 sheets (one side only); word perfect and user-friendly, e.g. without strange fonts or bizarre layouts; without ego trips, salary demands, unexplained gaps in employment history or verbosity. Include a paragraph on your achievements. Your covering letter also needs to be word perfect and to grab the reader's attention. The government organisation Centrelink offers free advice on the writing of CVs and job applications.

> The standard of many CVs in Australia is poor, so if yours is exceptional you're ahead of the pack already.

Job interviews shouldn't be taken lightly, as making a good impression can be the difference between getting a foot on the ladder of success and standing in the dole queue. Although dress rules in Australia aren't as strict as in some other countries, you should always dress smartly and appropriately when applying for a job (shorts and flip-flops are out). The secret of success is in your preparation, so do your homework on prospective employers and try to anticipate every question that you may be asked, rehearsing your answers. Be prepared to answer questions about why you came to Australia and what you think of the country and its people. Questions may be blunt and to the point, and answers should be positive – you should avoid criticising your home country or former employers (or, needless to say, Australia!).

Employers may require the names of a number of personal or professional

referees, whom they may contact. You should take evidence of your educational, professional and trade qualifications and references from former employers. You'll also be required to produce your passport and visa entitling you to live and work in Australia (if already issued), plus your driving licence. In recent years, Australian employers and recruitment agencies have been increasingly using psychology and personality tests to select staff. Some employers also require prospective employees to complete aptitude and other written tests.

SELF-EMPLOYMENT & RUNNING A BUSINESS

Anyone who is an Australian citizen or a permanent resident can work in a self-employed capacity in Australia, which includes setting up a co-operative, franchise, partnership, private limited company or sole proprietorship. There are numerous opportunities for entrepreneurs in Australia, where everyone (at least in theory) has equal opportunity and is judged on his merits. Although new businesses have a high failure rate within the first few years, working for yourself is still the best way to become (and remain) rich in Australia (and most other countries).

Much of the fall in unemployment in recent years has been due to self-employment or jobs created by small companies. Some 20 per cent of working Australians run their own businesses. Redundancy (and the difficulty of finding full-time employment) is often the spur for those aged over 45 to start a business; around 20 per cent of redundant (retrenched) employees turn to self-employment.

However, if you're planning to enter Australia as a skilled migrant, you must be under 45, have considerable financial resources and pass a points test. In recent years, skilled migrants have brought in over $500,000 each and created an average of seven jobs each; you should regard these figures as a minimum requirement. There's also a considerable amount of red tape for those wishing to start a business in Australia, although it isn't as restrictive as in many other countries; the average small businessman spends as much as four hours per week on government paperwork.

For many people, starting a business is one of the quickest routes to bankruptcy. In fact, many people who start businesses would be better off investing in lottery tickets! **If you're going to work for yourself, you must be prepared to fail (despite your best efforts), as almost two out of three new businesses fail within three to five years.**

Research

The key to starting or buying a successful business is research, research and yet more research (plus innovation, service and value). Bear in mind that choosing the location for a business is vital. Always thoroughly investigate an existing or proposed business (including the catchment area, competition, history and location) before investing a cent. Generally speaking, it isn't wise to run a business in a field in which you have no experience, although obviously this isn't always possible (and some businesses require little experience, specialist knowledge or training). When experience or training is necessary, it's often better to work for someone else in the same line of business to gain experience than to jump in at the deep end. Assistance (including hands-on training) from the seller could be made part of a purchase contract.

⚠ Caution

Like most countries, Australia isn't a place for amateur entrepreneurs, particularly those who don't do their homework and are unfamiliar with the Australian way of doing business.

Potential entrepreneurs should read *Culture Wise Australia* (Survival Books).

Business Structure

There are four main types of business structure to choose from: a limited company, a partnership, a franchise and a sole proprietorship, which can be public or private (proprietary). Because of the ever-changing and complex Australian tax laws, you should consult a tax expert before deciding on the best one for you. Although franchises have a higher success rate than other start-up businesses, it may take years to make a profit (often the only people to get rich are the franchise companies). A *Franchisees Guide* can be obtained from The Franchise Council of Australia (FCA),

PO Box 2195, Malvern East VIC 3145 (☎ local call rate 1300-669030, 🖳 www.franchise.org.au).

Buying a Business

It may be better to buy an established business than to start a business from scratch, as it gives you an immediate client/customer base and cash flow. However, you must thoroughly investigate the financial status, turnover and value of a business (**always** obtain an independent valuation). It's important to engage an accountant and lawyer at the earliest opportunity. A lawyer should be acting solely for you, not for any other parties in a transaction, and shouldn't be receiving commission from anyone involved. **Take care, as there are crooks around who prey on innocent foreigners!**

Businesses for sale are advertised in specialist magazines and some daily newspapers. There are also business migration agents in Australia and overseas who can help you buy a company in Australia, although their fees can be high. The purchase of a business **must** be conditional on obtaining licences, loans and other necessary funding, permits, visas and anything else that's vital to its successful establishment.

Finance & Cash Flow

Most people are far too optimistic about the prospects for a new business, overestimating income levels (it often takes years to make a profit) and disregarding costs. Be realistic or even pessimistic when estimating your income; overestimate the costs and underestimate the revenue (then reduce it by a further 50 per cent!). While hoping for the best, you should plan for the worst and have sufficient funds to last until you're established and profitable. New projects are rarely, if ever, completed within budget. Australian banks are wary of lending to new businesses, especially those run by recent immigrants. If you wish to borrow money for a business venture in Australia, you should carefully consider how and where you plan to raise it. Under-capitalisation is the main reason for small business failures and isn't helped by cash-flow problems caused by late payers.

Grants & Incentives

The Australian government encourages successful business people and investors to apply for residence in Australia, although applicants are generally required to invest at least $500,000 in a business). Business migration schemes provide prospective migrants with a link to professional and commercial advisors. Compare your business prospects in all states and territories, all of which compete to attract foreign investors and business people with incentives such as cash grants, free advice, loan guarantees and tax rebates.

☑ **SURVIVAL TIP**

Some state governments publish lists of business opportunities for migrants.

For information about government-backed finance, contact Austrade (formerly the Australian Trade Commission, ☎ local call rate 13-2878, 🖥 www.austrade.gov.au – a list of office addresses can be found on the site).

Information & Professional Advice

A wealth of free advice and information for budding entrepreneurs is available from Australian chambers of commerce, embassies and high commissions, federal government and state agencies, local councils, professional associations and trade unions. The Australian Securities and Investments Commission (ASIC) has a wealth of free information available from its regional offices and via its website. The

ASIC can be contacted at PO Box 9827, Melbourne, VIC 3001 (☎ local call rate 1300-300630 from Australia only or ☎ +61 3-5177 3988 from abroad, 🖥 www.asic.gov.au).

The Office of Small Business is a government agency with offices in all major cities, offering free advice and assistance to those planning to start a business. It publishes an abundance of information, particularly concerning raising finance for a new business. Centrelink publishes various booklets about starting and running a business. There are Business Enterprise Centres (BECs) in some states and territories (e.g. NSW and the Australian Capital Territory – ACT), where you can obtain free advice and support on a wide range of business-related subjects.

Most international firms of accountants have offices in major cities in Australia (and in many other countries) and are an invaluable source of information (in English and other languages) on a wide range of subjects, including company

law, forming a company, social security and taxation. Many publish free books about doing business in Australia, including *Doing Business in Australia* (Ernst & Young and Price Waterhouse Coopers) and *Establishing a Business in Australia* (Minter Ellison).

Information about starting a small business in Australia can also be obtained from the Department of Fair Trading, PO BOX 972, Parramatta, NSW 2124 (☎ local call rate 13-3220, 🖥 www.fairtrading.[state initials].gov.au, e.g. 🖥 www.fairtrading.nsw.gov.au for the New South Wales office). Australia's major banks have small business centres providing free banking, financial and other advice to new businesses. The Australian Tax Office publishes a number of helpful booklets, including *How to Keep Your Business Records*.

There are many state and local government agencies and departments providing information and advice about starting and running a business. All states operate business advisory, development, industry, investment and technology corporations or departments. One of the best places to start is your local chamber of commerce, which is a mine of information about every aspect of business and relocation to particular towns or areas (many produce relocation and business information packages). Public libraries are also an excellent source of information about starting a business.

LANGUAGE

Surprisingly, an estimated 1m migrants cannot speak English, a huge number in a country of only around 20m people, and some 3m residents (around 15 per cent of the population) speak a language other than English at home. Sydney is Australia's most multicultural city (closely followed by Melbourne), where some 30 per cent of the population doesn't speak English at home (the figure is as high as 65 per cent in some suburbs). Sydney and Melbourne are home to around 65 per cent of all non-English speaking migrants, who together speak a total of some 240 foreign languages. Many

Brisbane, QLD

migrants predominantly use their mother tongue on a day-to-day basis and have only a smattering of English. Australia's failure to train migrants in English is handicapping them in respect of economic, political and social life, and ghettos are emerging where Australian-born children don't speak fluent English.

Nevertheless, if you're planning to live or work in Australia, you need to read, speak and write English well enough to deal with government officials, find your way around the country, shop, and understand and hold conversations with the people you meet. Independent migrants from non-English speaking backgrounds need to take an English test. Your chance of obtaining a good job (or any job) in Australia is greatly diminished if you don't speak English fluently, and many immigrants from non-English speaking backgrounds are unemployed because their lack of English would endanger other employees and reduce workplace efficiency.

> ⚠ Caution
>
> **English proficiency is also important if you have a job requiring a lot of contact with others, or which involves speaking on the telephone or dealing with other foreigners, many of whom speak their own 'dialect' of English.**

It's particularly important for students (unless they're studying English) to have a high standard of English, as they must be able to follow lectures and take part in discussions in the course of their studies. These may require a technical or specialised vocabulary. For this reason, most universities and colleges won't accept students who aren't fluent in English and many require a formal qualification or require students to take a written test. Whether you speak British English, American English or some other variety is irrelevant, although some foreigners have a problem understanding the natives (even Americans and Britons occasionally have problems understanding Australians).

Australian English is similar to British English but has its own colourful vernacular, called 'strine' (from the way 'Australian' is pronounced with a heavy Australian accent), thrown in for good measure. Strine (also called Ozspeak) is Australia's greatest creative product and is full of abbreviations, hyperbole, profanities, vulgar expressions and word-play. Strine is the language of a rebellious subculture and has its origins in the Cockney (London) and Irish slang of the early convicts. The use of strine varies with the state or region and the 'class' of person. The use of expletives is widespread; many of them are used as a sign of familiarity and even affection ('bloody' is in everyday use and no longer considered a swear word in Australia). Absurd comparisons are frequently used for emphasis such as 'as busy as a bricklayer in Beirut' (i.e. idle), 'as useful as a wether at a ram sale' (useless) and 'as straight as a dog's hind leg' (bent). The Australian language also includes many words adopted from Aboriginal languages (see below).

Australians often cannot decide whether to use American or British spelling (program/programme, labor/labour, etc.) and consequently misspellings abound. Many words have a completely different meaning in Australia and other English-speaking countries, such as crook (ill), game (brave), globe (light bulb), knock (criticise), ringer (top performer), shout (round of drinks) and tube (can of beer). Almost any word of more than two syllables is abbreviated in Australia, often with the addition of an o at the end of it, as in derro (derelict), garbo (dustman), reffo (refugee) and rego (car registration), or an ie or y, as in Aussie (Australian), barbie (barbecue), blowie (blowfly), brickie (bricklayer), chrissy (Christmas), cossie (swimming costume), footy (football), mozzie (mosquito), postie (postperson), tinny (can of beer) and truckie (truck driver).

There are slight regional variations in the Australian accent, although foreigners usually find it difficult to detect them. Accents are broader in isolated country areas than among middle-class city dwellers, many of whom are of British ancestry.

Many books have been written about Australian vernacular speech, including the *Aussie Talk-Macquarie Dictionary* by Arthur Delbridge (Macquarie Library), the *Australian Phrasebook* (Lonely Planet), *The Dinkum Dictionary* by Leni Johannsen (Viking O'Neil) and *The Dinkum Aussie Dictionary* by Richard Beckett (Child and Henry). The standard Australian English dictionary is the *Macquarie Dictionary* (compiled by the Macquarie University, Sydney), the bible of Aussie English (2,500 pages!).

Aboriginal Languages

Australian Aboriginal (literally meaning 'indigenous') society has the longest unbroken cultural history in the world, dating back around 60,000 years. When the First Fleet arrived in Australia in 1788, there were estimated to be around 250 Australian languages (all believed to have evolved from a single language family) comprising some 700 dialects. Of the original 250 or so languages, only around 20 survive today, but these are spoken regularly and taught in schools. Kriol, spoken mostly in northern Australia, is the most widely used Aboriginal language and the native language of many young Aboriginals. It contains many English words but the meanings are often different and the spelling is phonetic.

Rainforest, VIC

2.

EMPLOYMENT CONDITIONS

E mployment conditions in Australia are among the best in the developed world and are regulated in most fields of employment at federal or state level, where legislation covers such matters as annual and special leave, discrimination, occupational health and safety, redundancy procedures and payment, and workers' compensation.

In 2005, the Australian government amended the Work Place Relations Act, 1996 and introduced the WorkChoices law, which came into force in March 2006 and is to be implemented over a five-year period. The new legislation, which is the most comprehensive reform of workplace relations in almost a century, was ostensibly designed to 'protect' workers and to encourage more family-friendly working arrangements, and it included provisions for young people, women, outworkers and people from a non-English speaking or indigenous background. In effect, however, it made employment (and dismissal) more 'flexible' and consequently employment less secure.

Among other things, WorkChoices established a body known as the Australian FairPay Commission (AFPC, 🖥 www. fairpay.gov.au) to supersede the Australian Industrial Relations Commission (AIRC), established the Australian Safety and Compensation Council (🖥 www.ascc.gov. au) to oversee occupational health and safety standards and handle workers' compensation claims on a nationwide basis, increased restrictions on industrial action, increased the maximum length of Australian Workplace Agreements (see

below) from three to five years and, most controversially, exempted companies with fewer than 101 employees from unfair dismissal legislation (i.e. allowed them to 'hire and fire' at will).

Before the 2005 Amendment, all new certified agreements (now called collective agreements – see below) were subject to a 'no disadvantage' test, whereby their terms were compared with those of previous agreements applying to the same workers to ensure that they would be no worse off. WorkChoices scrapped the test and introduced the requirement for employers to provide employees with 'five minimum entitlements', covering maximum ordinary working hours, annual leave, parental leave, personal/carer's leave and minimum pay scales. These five minimum entitlements are referred to as the Australian Fair Pay and Conditions Standard. They don't relate to any previous agreements, so in effect employers are free to set their own employment standards.

Not surprisingly, WorkChoices law has met with considerable opposition (over half the Australian population is said to be against it), and the Australian Labor Party, elected to govern in November 2007, has

conditions of employment. These may apply at national, regional or local level. These agreements include awards, collective agreements and Australian Workplace Agreements – described below. Employees in Australia are also protected by a comprehensive federal social security (welfare) system, which includes family payments, pensions, and sickness and disability allowances (see **Chapter 13**).

Awards

Employment conditions and wages in Australia have until recently been decided in negotiations between unions and employers, subject to the approval of the Australian Industrial Relations Commission. The result of this process was termed the 'award' for a particular job or industry. An award specified minimum wages and 'penalty' rates of pay (for overtime and unsociable hours) and regulated such matters as holiday entitlement, redundancy and termination of employment, sick leave and working hours. Since the 2005 Amendment to the Workplace Relations Act, 1996 (see above), however, the determination of such matters has become rather more 'fluid' and awards are being phased out in favour of looser agreements between individual employers and their employees such as Australian Workplace Agreements (see below).

Some awards still apply. These are called either 'transitional awards', which are defined by the government as 'binding those who do not fall within the constitutional scope of the reforms' (it isn't clear who such people might be), or 'pre-reform awards', which are defined even more obscurely as 'an instrument which replaces a former federal award (the original award) that was in force immediately before reform commencement.' Whereas new workers may be brought within the scope of a

vowed to repeal it. In May 2007, the then current government officially abandoned the 'WorkChoices' name, though without proposing a new one – nor any changes to its legislation. (In fact the WorkChoices website, 🖳 www.workchoices.gov.au, was still operational in October 2007!)

Further information about employment conditions and workers' rights can be obtained from the Australian Industrial Registry, Level 42, Nauru House, 80 Collins St, Melbourne, VIC 3000 (postal address: PO Box 19945, Melbourne, VIC 3001, ☎ local call rate 1300-799675, 🖳 www.airc. gov.au) and, with regard to regulations in New South Wales, the Office of Industrial Relations, 1 Oxford Street, Darlinghurst, NSW 2010 (☎ 131-628, 🖳 www. industrialrelations.nsw.gov.au).

WORKPLACE AGREEMENTS

In certain industries, agreements are made between employers and all employees (usually via a union) as to minimum pre-reform award, the same isn't true of transitional awards. Both transitional awards and pre-reform awards, the government warns, are 'subject to a changed list of allowable award matters'.

> Fortunately for employees, many employers' pay and conditions are more generous than the statutory minimum required by industry awards.

COLLECTIVE AGREEMENTS

Collective (formerly certified) agreements are agreements made directly between an employer and a group of employees, or between an employer and a union. All collective agreements must be approved by the AFPC and satisfy certain conditions, e.g. they must meet the approval of the majority of employees and include a dispute settlement procedure and a nominal expiry date, which cannot be more than three years after approval.

Australian Workplace Agreements

Australian Workplace Agreements (AWAs) are fixed-term contracts intended to be used to hire casual workers, contractors, and part-time and temporary workers as required. They are increasingly used, however, to 'use' employees to perform any task within their competence, thus breaking down existing demarcations, and (particularly since the extension of their maximum duration from three to five years under the 2005 legislation) to hire 'permanent' staff. In return for their acceptance of an AWA, workers usually receive guaranteed annual pay rises, performance bonuses and an assurance that AWA pay rates will equal or outstrip wages under any collective agreement negotiated with unions. Like other employment agreements, AWAs must be approved by the AFPC.

CONTRACTS

Under Australian law, a contract of employment exists as soon as an employee proves his acceptance of an employer's terms and conditions of employment, e.g. by starting work, after which both employer and employee are bound by the terms offered and agreed. A contract isn't always in writing (it can be oral and 'sealed' by a handshake), although a company must provide employees who are normally employed in Australia with a WorkChoices Agreement containing certain important terms of employment and additional notes, e.g. regarding discipline and grievance procedures. You should receive a WorkChoices Agreement even for part-time and temporary jobs, although you won't normally receive a contract for casual work such as fruit picking (but you should get written confirmation of your wages and hours).

A contract (which may be called a 'statement of terms and conditions' or an 'offer letter') may consist of a simple sheet of paper or be a comprehensive multi-page document, e.g. from a multi-national company. A contract for a temporary position must state the period of the contract and should guarantee you compensation in the event that employment is terminated without notice.

Your contract of employment usually contains the following details:

- names of the employer and employee;
- date employment begins and whether employment with a previous employer counts as part of the employee's continuous period of employment;
- job title;
- salary details, including bonuses and agreed salary increases or review dates, commission, overtime (penalty) pay and piece rates, and when the salary is to be paid, e.g. weekly, fortnightly or monthly;

- hours of work;
- annual and public holiday entitlements and pay;
- sickness and accident benefits;
- pension (superannuation) scheme details;
- probationary and notice periods (or the expiry date, if employment is for a limited period);
- disciplinary and grievance procedures (which may be contained in a separate document).

Any special arrangements you've made with an employer should also be contained in the contract. If there are no agreed terms under one or more of the above headings, this may be stated in the contract. If all or any of the above particulars are contained in a collective agreement, an employer may refer employees to a copy of this. Similarly, there may be references to other documents, such as the rules relating to flexible working hours and company holidays, sick pay and superannuation scheme conditions, wage regulation orders, and work rules or handbooks.

If you require a visa to work in Australia, your contract may contain a clause stating that the contract is subject to a visa being granted by the authorities. Your employment is usually subject to satisfactory references being received from your previous employer(s) and/or character references. If you're a school-leaver or student, a reference may be required from the head teacher or principal of your last school, college or university.

Unless there's a clause in your contract stating otherwise, your employer cannot change your place of work without your agreement. The place of work usually refers to a town or area of a large city, rather than a specific office or building. If applicable, a contract may state that you

may occasionally be required to work at other company locations.

> **Caution**
>
> For certain jobs, a pre-employment medical examination is required (see Medical Examination on page 59) and periodic examinations may be a condition of employment, e.g. where good health is vital to the safe performance of your duties.

Before signing a contract of employment, you should obtain a copy of any general employment conditions (see below) or documents referred to in the contract and ensure that you understand them. There are usually no hidden surprises or traps for the unwary in an Australian contract of employment, although as with any contract you should know exactly what it contains before signing it. If your knowledge of English is poor, you should ask someone to explain anything you don't understand in simple English (Australian companies rarely provide foreigners with contracts in a language other than English). Employees have the right to review a contract for 14 days before signing it.

You usually receive two copies of your contract, both of which you should sign and date. One copy must be returned to your employer, and the other is for your own records. Employees must usually be notified in writing of any changes in their terms and conditions of employment, e.g. within one month of their introduction. Either party can sue for breach of contract.

Around 10 per cent of employees have individual contracts, which have become an employer's weapon against the union movement and have reduced the cost of labour. However, many workers have rejected individual contracts and stayed with collective agreements negotiated through their union.

RELOCATION & TRAVEL EXPENSES

Your travel and relocation expenses to Australia (or to a new job in another region of Australia) depend on your agreement with your employer and are usually detailed in your contract or your employer's general terms. If you're hired from outside Australia, your air ticket (or other travel) to Australia is usually booked and paid for by your employer. You can usually also claim incidental travel costs, e.g. to and from airports.

Australian employers may also pay your relocation expenses to Australia up to a specified amount. This may be a percentage of your salary or as a set allowance, or cover only specific expenses, such as estate agent's, legal and removal fees. The allowance should be sufficient to move the contents of an average house (castles aren't usually catered for).

Companies may ask you to obtain two or three removal estimates when they're liable for the total cost of removal. If you don't want to bring your furniture to Australia or have only a few belongings to ship, you may be given an allowance to purchase furniture locally (check with your employer). Generally, you're required to organise and pay for the removal yourself. Your employer usually reimburses the equivalent amount in Australian dollars **after** you've paid the bill, although it may be possible to get him to pay the bill directly or make an advance payment.

If you change jobs within Australia, your new employer may pay your relocation expenses when it's necessary for you to move home. Don't forget to ask, as he may not offer to pay (it may depend on how keen he is to employ you). See also **Relocation Consultants** on page 104.

SALARY & BENEFITS

Your salary is stated in your contract, and cost of living increases, overtime rates, piece and bonus rates, planned increases and salary reviews must also be included; only general points, such as the payment of your salary into a bank or other account and the date of salary payments, are usually included in an employer's standard terms. You should receive an itemised pay statement (or wage slip), either with your salary (if it's paid weekly or fortnightly in cash) or separately (when your salary is paid monthly into a bank account).

☑ SURVIVAL TIP

Always ensure that you receive a pay slip containing the legally required information, as it's almost impossible to dispute pay claims without one.

Salaries in Australia are generally reviewed annually, although the salaries of professional employees and all employees

in some businesses may be reviewed every six months. The salaries of new employees may also be reviewed after six months. A percentage of your annual salary increase is usually to compensate for a rise in the cost of living, although some employees receive pay rises below the annual rate of inflation. Annual increases may be negotiated separately by employees on individual contracts, by an independent pay review board or by a union (or unions), when an industry is covered by an award (see page 44 and **Contracts** on page 45). The federal minimum wage in Australia is currently AS$13.74 per hour (equivalent to AS$522.12 per week).

When discussing your salary with a prospective employer, always take into account the total salary package, including bonuses, commission and fringe benefits such as a company car or a low-interest home loan, as well as fringe benefit tax (see page 306).

Commission & Bonuses

Your salary may include commission or bonus payments, calculated on your individual performance (e.g. based on sales) or the company's performance as a whole, which may be paid regularly (e.g. monthly or annually) or irregularly. Some employers pay employees a bonus (in addition to any award holiday bonus) at the end of the year, although this isn't normal practice in Australia. When a bonus is paid, it may be stated in your contract, in which case it's obligatory. If applicable, an annual bonus is usually paid pro rata if you don't work a full calendar year, e.g. in your first and last years of employment with a company. In industry, particularly in small firms, blue-collar workers are often paid bonus or 'piece-work' rates based on their individual productivity. If you're employed on a contract basis for a fixed period, you may be paid an end-of-contract bonus.

Profit-sharing schemes aren't common in Australia, although performance-related bonuses or commissions are common in the finance industry. In some companies, employees are offered company shares at a favourable price, usually well below the market price.

Expenses

Expenses paid by your employer are usually listed in your employment conditions. These may include travel costs from your home to your place of work, e.g. a bus or rail season ticket or the equivalent in cash (paid monthly with your salary). Companies without a company restaurant or canteen may pay employees a lunch allowance or provide luncheon vouchers. Claimable expenses for travel on company business or for training courses may be detailed in your employer's general terms or listed in a separate document. Most companies pay a per-kilometre allowance to staff authorised to use their cars or motorbikes on company business (but you must ensure that business use is covered by your car insurance).

Company Cars

Some employees (e.g. sales reps) are provided with a company car, and many Australian employers give senior employees such as directors and senior managers a car as a fringe benefit. Most companies provide cars under a lease arrangement, which means that employees must pay fringe benefit tax (FBT – see page 306) on the value of a company car that's used privately. If a company car is provided, check whether you're permitted to use it privately and whether, if you leave the company, you're responsible for the balance of the finance. Many companies allow employees to buy second-hand company cars at favourable prices.

If you're provided with a company car, you usually receive details regarding its use and your obligations on starting employment. If you lose your licence (e.g. through drunken driving) and are unable to fulfil the requirements of your job, your employment may be terminated and you may not be entitled to compensation.

Education & Training

The education and training provided by your employer may be stated in your standard terms. It's in your interest to investigate courses of study, lectures and seminars which you feel will be of direct benefit to you and your employer. Most employers give reasonable consideration to a request to attend a course during working time, provided you don't make it a full-time occupation. It's compulsory for companies to provide appropriate and adequate health and safety training for all employees. However, Australian employers are notoriously lax in doing so, and only around half the workforce receives education or training during a year. To encourage employers to improve the quantity and quality of their training programmes, an Industry Training Levy was introduced in 1990 requiring employers to pay a penalty when specified minimum training levels weren't met.

If you need to improve your English, language classes may be paid by your employer. If it's necessary to learn a language other than English in order to perform your job, the cost of language study should be paid by your employer. An allowance may be paid for personal education or hobbies which aren't work related or of direct benefit to your employer (if he really loves you).

In addition to relevant education and training, employers must also provide the essential tools and equipment for a job (although this is open to interpretation).

HOURS

Your working hours in Australia may differ from those in your previous country of residence and vary according to your profession and where you work. A national 38-hour working week was introduced in 1981 and reinforced by the recent WorkChoices law, and the usual working week is 35 to 40 hours for most wage earners (the average in 2006 was just under 38 hours), but overtime is normally available and often 'compulsory' and many employees work up to ten hours a week overtime.

A 2003 survey showed that almost a third of full-time employees work more than 48 hours per week.

Most employees work a five-day week, although over 25 per cent of men work weekends and some 20 per cent work shifts. In the last few years, many companies have switched from eight-hour to 12-hour shifts, which means working only 11 or 12 days per month or ten days every three weeks. Twelve-hour shifts are common in enterprise deals, where the advantage for employers is that they incur no overtime payments. Employees also gain, as they earn around the same as previously (when they worked overtime) and have much more leisure time. Most workers prefer 12-hour shifts after having tried them, although there's a safety risk, particularly in factories, where it's estimated that there's double the risk of accidents due to fatigue. The Australian government is encouraging employers to adopt 'family-friendly practices' whereby employees enjoy more flexible working hours and leave arrangements.

Hourly paid workers are usually paid overtime (see below) for extra hours and higher (penalty) rates for night, shift and weekend work. In contrast, executives, managers and professionals often work over 50 hours per week without extra pay. Twelve-hour days aren't uncommon among managerial and professional staff. In fact, the higher you climb the ladder of success, the harder you're expected to work (burn-out is common among managers and executives).

A standard working day (without overtime) for a blue-collar worker is from 7 or 8am to 3.30 or 4.30pm, while working hours in most offices and shops are from 8.30 or 9.30am until 4.30 or 5.30pm, with an hour's break for lunch.

Tea or coffee breaks may be scheduled at set times mid-morning and mid-afternoon, particularly in factories (employers usually provide free tea and coffee and many also provide biscuits). Long business lunches (two hours or more) are becoming less common, although it's still customary to find employees finishing their lunch late in the afternoon on Thursdays and Fridays.

Your working hours may not be increased above the hours stated in your employment terms without compensation or overtime being paid. Similarly, if you have a guaranteed working week, your hours cannot be reduced (i.e. short-time working) or changed without your agreement, unless there's a clause (sometimes referred to as a 'mobility clause') in your contract. Some employers operate a system of flexible working hours and may also permit employees to job-share or work part of the time at home.

Around a third of Australian workers (usually blue-collar) are required to sign on or clock in and out of work (employees caught cheating may be summarily dismissed).

Flexi-time

A flexi-time system usually requires all employees to be present between certain hours, known as the core or block time – for example, from 9 to 11.30am and from 1.30 to 4pm. Employees may make up their required working hours by starting earlier than the required core time, finishing later or reducing their lunch break. Many business premises are open from around 7am until 6pm or later, and smaller companies may allow employees to work as late as they wish, provided they

don't exceed the maximum permitted daily working hours.

Many Australian companies operate flexi-time working hours or a system of 'rostered days off' (RDO). The conditions and rules relating to flexi-time and RDO schemes vary according to your employer (they're most common in public service); they're more likely to apply to those in administrative, managerial and professional occupations and are standard in construction/labour contracts. At their peak, RDOs applied to almost a third of wage and salary earners. But RDOs were usually taken on a Monday or Friday to provide a long weekend, which proved disruptive to companies' operations. In recent years, therefore, employers have been cutting back on RDOs, e.g. from 12 to 6 per year, converting them to additional holiday, swapping them for superannuation payments or replacing them with time off in lieu on different days of the week.

Overtime

The opportunity to work overtime is seen as a lucrative benefit by most blue-collar workers, many of whom earn around a quarter of their wages from overtime. In some industries there's an ingrained 'overtime culture', although for many workers overtime is a matter of economic necessity. Of the 9.8m people in employment, a third regularly work over 48 hours per week. Overtime (penalty rates) is generally paid at time-and-a-half for the first three hours and double-time thereafter (and on Sundays and public holidays), or as detailed in the award for the trade or industry (workers in some industries receive 2.5 times the normal rate for Sundays). Overtime may be paid at only the standard rate – more likely in non-union workplaces, where workers are three times more likely to have a standard working week longer than 38 hours.

In order to reduce overtime costs, many companies have been extending the normal working week and changing to 12-hour shifts. Many awards stipulate that employees work longer hours at ordinary time (e.g. up to 50 a week) in return for higher wages and bonuses. Some companies pay overtime only when work is urgent and officially approved, and many prefer salaried (i.e. monthly paid) employees to take time off in lieu of payment or expect them to work unpaid overtime. As much as half of all overtime worked is unpaid.

HOLIDAYS & LEAVE

This section covers annual and public holidays, and also time off for other reasons, e.g. for pregnancy, illness and compassionate reasons.

Annual Holidays

All permanent employees in Australia are entitled to at least four weeks' annual holiday and many receive up to six weeks, depending on the award for their trade or industry. Some employers offer four weeks in the first year of employment and six weeks thereafter or after a certain number of years of service; employees in some industries and professions receive as many as nine weeks' paid annual holiday.

Under a scheme called holiday or leave 'loading', full-time employees are paid 17.5 per cent of their normal wage when they take their annual holidays, although this is increasingly being eliminated by AWAs. Some companies pay leave loading only to employees below a certain salary level, e.g. $50,000. In some industries and professions (e.g. teaching), employees are required to take paid holidays at certain times (what a hardship!).

Holidays must usually be taken in the year in which they're earned, although many companies allow employees to carry outstanding annual holiday over to the following year. Employers may also allow employees to take their total annual holiday in one block, rather than split it into periods throughout the year. Holiday entitlement is calculated on a pro rata basis (per completed calendar month of service) if you don't work a full calendar year. Part-time staff may also be entitled to paid holidays on a pro rata basis.

Before starting a job, check that any planned holidays will be approved by your new employer. This is particularly important if they fall within your probationary period (see page 59), when holidays may not be permitted. Holidays may usually be taken only with your manager's permission and in many companies must be booked up to a year in advance.

If you resign or are given notice, most employers pay you in lieu of any outstanding holiday, although this isn't an entitlement and you may be obliged to take the holiday at your employer's convenience.

Public Holidays

The number of statutory public holidays in Australia varies from state to state between 10 and 12. There are eight national public holidays plus state public holidays, the number and dates of which vary according to the state or territory. All states celebrate Labor Day (in addition to the holidays shown below), although the date varies from state to state. Some companies and industries also have their own 'holidays', such as a company outing or a union picnic day. Banks, businesses, schools and most shops are closed on public holidays. All national public holidays are shown below.

If a public holiday falls at a weekend, there's usually a substitute holiday on the following Monday. Some companies close during Christmas and New Year, e.g. from 25th December until 1st January inclusive. To compensate for this shutdown and perhaps other extra holidays during the

Date	Holiday
1st January	New Year's Day
January	Australia Day (the date varies from state to state but is usually on the Monday following 26th January)
March/April	Good Friday (the date changes each year)
March/April	Easter Monday (the Monday after Good Friday)
25th April	Anzac Day (in memory of those who died in the two World Wars)
Second Monday in June	Queen's birthday (except in Western Australia, which celebrates the Queen's birthday in September)
25th December	Christmas Day
26th December	Boxing Day (called Proclamation Day in South Australia)

year, employees may be required to work extra hours throughout the year or to take it as part of their annual holiday entitlement. Part-time staff may be paid for a public holiday only when it falls on a day when they would normally be working.

You aren't required to work on public holidays unless this is stated in your contract. When it's necessary to work on public holidays, you normally receive the same or a higher rate of pay than is paid for working on a Sunday (e.g. double, and often triple, the normal rate) and/or time off in lieu. When a job involves working at weekends and on public holidays (e.g. shift work), you usually receive a penalty rate or are paid a shift allowance.

Pregnancy & Confinement

The new WorkChoices law allows a maximum of 52 weeks' unpaid parental leave, shared between parents, on the birth of a child or the adoption of a child under five years of age (Maternity, Paternity or Adoption Leave). Australia is one of the few countries in the world that has no laws requiring paid benefits in the private sector, although companies are increasingly offering it. A woman has the right to return to her job, or a job with the same status and pay, within 12 months of giving birth.

In addition to the above, time off work for sickness in connection with a pregnancy is usually given without question, but it may not be paid unless authorised by a doctor if it exceeds your annual sick leave allocation (see below).

Sick Leave

Most employees are entitled to take up to two weeks' paid sick leave each year, depending on the award for the trade or industry, and many employees feel that they should take their quota of 'sickies' whether they're sick or not (poor health

is usually the last reason employees take sickies!), particularly those in the public sector. In some states (e.g. New South Wales), up to five days of an employee's sick leave can be used to care for a partner (of either sex) or family member.

Usually, you must have been employed for a minimum period before you're entitled to sick pay, e.g. three or six months, which may coincide with your probationary period. If you're sick during this period, your pay is docked. An employee cannot usually be dismissed when he's sick, although this depends on the number and the frequency of sick days; restrictions should be stipulated in your employment contract or standard terms.

Some employers operate an occupational sick pay (OSP) scheme, under which you receive your full salary for a number of months (depending on your length of service) in the event of sickness or after an accident. OSP may be provided by your employer as part of a company pension scheme.

You're usually required to notify your employer as soon as possible of sickness or an accident that prevents you from working, i.e. within a few hours of your normal starting time. Failure to do so may result in your not being paid for that day. You're required to keep your boss or manager informed about your illness and when you expect to return to work. A doctor's certificate isn't required for sick days taken within your annual allowance, although a certificate is required for additional sick days, for which you may not be paid. (These are quite easy to obtain even if you aren't sick!)

Other Leave

Employees are allowed, by law, to take time off work under certain circumstances, as follows:

- An expectant mother is entitled to 'reasonable' unpaid time off for ante-natal care;

- A trade union official is entitled to paid time off for trade union duties and training for such duties. Employees may also be paid to attend union meetings during working hours. Similarly, a safety representative is allowed paid time off in connection with his safety duties;

- All employees are allowed time off for public duties such as service as a juror or court witness, councillor or school governor, or as a member of a statutory tribunal or authority, although your employer isn't usually required to pay you;

- Parents are usually permitted to leave work for up to an hour at any time to look after children;

- If you're made redundant, you're entitled to take one day off each week to look for a new job or to arrange training in connection with a new job.

Beyond these statutory rights, whether or not you're paid for time off work for compassionate reasons (e.g. a funeral) or time lost through unavoidable circumstances (e.g. public transport strikes or car breakdowns) depends on your employer, on whether you're paid weekly or monthly (e.g. with an hourly rate of pay), and whether you're required to punch a clock. The attitude to paid time off may also depend on your status and position. Executives and managers (who often work much longer hours than officially required) generally have much more leeway regarding time off than blue-collar workers. The conditions for leave should be detailed in your standard employment terms.

Many Australian companies provide paid leave on certain occasions, which may include your own or a family marriage, the birth of a child and the death of a family member or close relative. However, only some 25 per cent of employees have the right to family or carers' leave and only around 20 per cent of awards contain special leave provisions.

> After 10 or 15 years' continuous service with an employer, you may be entitled to up to six months' leave on full or half pay. Some employers also permit unpaid career breaks (sabbaticals) of up to three years.

ACCIDENT & OTHER INSURANCE

All employers in Australia are required to have occupational accident insurance (called workers' compensation insurance or WorkCover) for employees working on their premises, whether in a factory, office, residential accommodation, shop or warehouse. Schemes, many of which operate at a loss, are financed by a levy on salaries, e.g. 2.22 per cent in Victoria. Some states have overhauled their workers' compensation schemes in recent years, e.g. Victoria, where proposed changes in 2001 were met with massive opposition culminating in widespread strikes.

Insurance provision notwithstanding, employees must obey all safety regulations such as those relating to smoking, the use of safety equipment and clothing, the securing of long hair or ties, and the wearing of jewellery. However, unless an employee is grossly negligent and recklessly ignores safety rules and regulations, he's invariably deemed to be entitled to compensation.

A worker is paid compensation (commonly called 'compo') if he's injured or sick as the result of an accident in the workplace or when travelling to or from work or on company business. Compensation covers medical and other expenses and loss of earnings, and a worker's dependants are entitled to compensation if he's killed on the job. Australians tend to claim compo for the slightest injury at work. However, although bogus claims are endemic, particularly concerning the effects of work-related stress, making a claim for compo often carries a stigma and many workers try to avoid claiming (particularly those on contracts).

Occupational health and safety is dealt with by both federal and state governments and at the federal level is determined by the National Occupational Health and Safety Commission. The conditions of payment and the amount of compensation payable are laid down in various state acts, although in some states Workers' Compensation Boards decide on individual claims. If a claim is rejected, a worker can take his case to his union and it's decided by a workers' compensation commission.

Other insurance provided by your employer should be detailed in your employment conditions. This may include free life and health insurance, which may cover travel overseas on company business. Some companies provide free membership of a private health insurance scheme, although this may apply only to executives, managers and 'key' personnel. Where applicable, check whether health insurance includes your family. Companies may also operate a contributory group health insurance scheme, offering reduced subscriptions for members. For information about social security 'insurance' see page 265.

RETIREMENT

Your employment contract may be valid only until the official state retirement age, currently 65 for men and 62 for women (although it's gradually being increased to 65), although in many large companies retirement is possible from the age of 55. If you wish to continue working after you've reached retirement age, you may need to negotiate a new contract of employment (you should also seek psychiatric help). If your employer has a compulsory retirement age, he isn't required to give you notice when you reach it. Many companies present employees with a gift on reaching

retirement age (e.g. the key to your ball and chain), the value of which usually depends on your number of years' service.

UNION MEMBERSHIP

Under the Workplace Relations Act all employees have the right to belong or not to belong to a trade union. Employees can also join an enterprise association, which is a union where the majority of members are employees performing work in the same enterprise. Under WorkChoices legislation, the number of members required to form an enterprise association is 20.

> Trade unions have been active in Australia since the mid-19th century (when many professional agitators were deported from the UK and Ireland) and union membership in Australia is among the highest in the world, at around 30 per cent of the workforce.

Unions earned themselves a terrible reputation during the '60s and '70s, when the country and the economy were frequently crippled by strikes. In recent years, there has again been a series of confrontations between the Liberal/National coalition government and the unions, particularly after the government brought in tougher 'anti-union' laws in an attempt to end 'outdated' restrictive work practices (and the resulting low productivity), which are rampant in industries with strong unions such as mining and the docks. These laws included anti-strike provisions and harsh sanctions against some strikers, and they led to bitter disputes between unions and employers.

Today, there are over 300 trade unions in Australia; 46 are affiliated to the Australian Council of Trade Unions, 393 Swanston St, Melbourne, VIC 3000 (☎ 03-9663 5266, ⌨ www.actu.asn.au), representing around 2m workers. However, in the last few decades the unions have been losing ground and have largely failed to recruit young workers, women, small-business employees and those in growth industries. There was a net loss of around 40 per cent of union membership between 1992 and 2003, and some 60 per cent of workers believe unions are no longer relevant to them (a survey as long ago as 1997 found that non-union members are more likely to be satisfied at work, have more positive attitudes to management and feel more secure than those in unions).

The Workplace Relations Act, 1996 abolished compulsory union membership, and employers aren't allowed to discriminate against an employee because he belongs (or wishes to belong) to a trade union. Nevertheless, despite their reduced membership, unions have a great deal of influence, particularly in companies and industries which previously had 'closed shop' agreements, where all employees had to join a union. The public sector is the most heavily unionised, around 47 per cent of employees being members; membership in the private sector is 19 per cent. Large companies with over 100 employees have the highest rates of unionisation and small businesses with fewer than ten employees the lowest (unions are now active in less than 20 per cent of workplaces).

Whether you're better off as a member of a trade union depends largely on the industry in which you're employed, although there are general benefits to be gained from union membership – especially since the introduction of WorkChoices legislation. In addition to negotiating fair pay and safer working conditions for members, unions offer members legal and medical assistance in work-related disputes. In most industries which recognise trade unions, members' pay and conditions are decided by collective bargaining between employers and trade unions.

OTHER CONDITIONS

Acceptance of Gifts

With the exception of those in the public sector, employees are normally allowed to accept gifts of a limited value from customers or suppliers, e.g. bottles of wine or spirits or other small gifts at Christmas. Generally, any gifts given and received openly and 'above board' aren't considered a bribe or unlawful. Nevertheless, you should declare any gifts received to your immediate superior, who will decide what is to be done with them. Some bosses pool gifts and divide them among all employees. (If you accept a real bribe, make sure it's a big one and that you have a secret Swiss bank account!)

Changing Jobs & Confidentiality

If you disclose any confidential company information, either in Australia or overseas (particularly to competitors), you may be liable to instant dismissal and may also have legal action taken against you. You may not take any secrets or confidential information (e.g. customer mailing lists) from a previous employer, but you may use any contacts, know-how, knowledge and skills acquired during his employ. If you make any inventions while an employee, they remain your property unless you sell or license them to your employer, the invention was made as part of your 'normal duties', or you were specifically employed to invent, e.g. in research and development. Your contract may contain a clause defining the sort of information that the employer considers to be confidential, such as customer and supplier relationships and details of business plans.

You may not compete against a former employer if there's a valid, binding restraint clause in your contract. However, if there's a confidentiality or restraint clause in your contract that's unfair (e.g. inhibits you from changing jobs), it's probably invalid in law and therefore unenforceable. If you're in doubt, consult a solicitor who is an expert in company law about your rights.

If you're a key employee, you may have a legal binding contract preventing you from joining a competitor or starting a company in the same line of business as your employer, and from enticing former colleagues to join your company. However, such a clause is usually valid for a limited period, e.g. a year.

Discrimination

It's illegal under the Racial Discrimination Act, 1975 and Sex Discrimination Act, 1984 for an employer to discriminate against an employee (or job candidate) because of his or her sex (unless a person's sex is an essential qualification for a job), marital status, ethnic or national origin, nationality, race, skin colour or sexual orientation. It's also illegal to discriminate against an employee because he does or doesn't wish to join a trade union. A woman doing the same or broadly similar work to a man or work of equal value is legally entitled to the same salary and other terms of employment as a man. Discrimination applies to appointment, dismissal, promotion, selection and training. Some companies have a policy of employing disabled applicants whenever possible ('positive discrimination').

⚠ Caution

It's difficult to prove discrimination on the grounds of sex and almost impossible on the grounds of race or skin colour, although it's acknowledged that discrimination is widespread.

If you're subjected to sexual harassment (which can happen to both women **and** men) you should report it to your supervisor or manager, as many companies have internal procedures to deal with such matters. However, if you don't receive satisfaction, you can report it to your union (if applicable) or the police and take legal advice. The Human Rights and Equal Opportunities Commission (HREOC) handles sexual harassment and discrimination cases in the utmost confidence and can advise you whether you have legal grounds for a complaint (which must be submitted in writing). The HREOC's national office is in Sydney, Level 8, Piccadilly Tower, 133 Castlereagh Street, Sydney, NSW 2000 (postal address: PO Box 5218, Sydney, NSW 20001, ☎ 02-9284 9600, 🖥 www.hreoc.gov.au) and it has regional offices throughout the country (listed on the website). The 'complaints infoline' is ☎ 1300-656419.

Nevertheless, victims of discrimination who win compensation payments are often left frustrated and empty-handed. Rulings by the HREOC aren't legally enforceable and compensation ordered by it is rarely paid without victims being forced to take further legal action (many just give up). To combat this sense of frustration, since April 2000 the Federal Court has ruled in around 15 per cent of cases where the HREOC hadn't been able to enforce payment. Rulings made by the Federal Court on discrimination are legally enforceable and, as a result, employers are now increasingly aware of their liability. The government has also introduced educational campaigns and workplace training in an attempt to combat discrimination in the workplace and change the general opinion that Australia's discrimination laws are a sham.

If you have a grievance or complaint against a colleague or your boss, there may be an official procedure to be followed in order to obtain redress. If an official grievance procedure exists, it's usually detailed in your general employment terms.

Dismissal & Redundancy

There has been a massive increase in unfair dismissal claims in recent years, running into several thousands annually, as a result of the government's tightening of federal industrial relations laws.

Most large and medium-size companies have comprehensive grievance and disciplinary procedures, which must usually be followed before an employee can be suspended or dismissed. In some cases employees may be suspended with or without pay for certain misdemeanours, e.g. for breaches of contract – usually with pay pending investigation into an alleged offence or impropriety.

Disciplinary procedures usually include both oral and written warnings – e.g. first oral warning, second oral warning, first written warning, second written warning, interview with board, etc. – and official records must be kept by your employer.

These procedures are to protect employees from unfair dismissal and to ensure that dismissed employees cannot (successfully) sue their employer.

It's illegal to dismiss employees on grounds other than those detailed in government and union agreements. In instances where employment was terminated on unjustified grounds, there may be a review by an industrial court, and wrongful dismissal can result in a claim for damages. However, employees dismissed for 'serious misconduct' such as disobedience of management decisions, fraud or any other illegal activity aren't entitled to notice or benefits.

If you believe that you've been unfairly dismissed, you can take your case to the Conciliation and Arbitration Commission. There's a filing fee for a claim for unfair dismissal and provisions allowing costs to be awarded against employees who make frivolous claims.

Medical Examination

Many Australian companies require prospective employees to have a pre-employment medical examination, which is performed by a company doctor (or a doctor nominated by the employer). An offer of employment is usually subject to your being given a clean bill of health. This may be required for employees over a certain age (e.g. 40 years) or for everyone in particular jobs, e.g. where good health is of paramount importance for safety reasons. Thereafter, a medical examination may be required periodically (e.g. every year or two) or when requested by your employer. Medical examinations may be required as a condition of membership of a company health, life insurance or pension scheme. Some companies insist on key employees having regular health screening, particularly senior managers and executives.

Part-time Job Restrictions

Restrictions on part-time employment for an employer other than your regular employer may be detailed in your employment conditions. Many Australian companies don't allow full-time employees to work part-time (i.e. moonlight) for another employer, particularly one in the same line of business. You may, however, be permitted to take a part-time teaching job or similar employment (or you can write a book).

Probationary & Notice Periods

For most jobs there's a probationary period, which may vary from two weeks for weekly paid employees to 13 weeks for permanent employees. Your notice period normally depends on your method of salary payment, your employer, your profession and your length of service, and is detailed in your contract the employer's standard terms. Probationary and notice periods apply equally to employers and employees.

The notice period for weekly paid workers is usually as follows:

Length of Service	Notice Period
Less than 1 year	1 week
1 to 3 years	2 weeks
3 to 5 years	3 weeks
Over 5 years	4 weeks

Most monthly paid employees have a one-month (or four-week) notice period, which takes effect after any probationary period. Employees over 45 with more than two years' service are entitled to an extra week's notice or pay in lieu of notice. The notice period may be longer for executive or key employees, e.g. three or six months, or may be extended after a number of years' service (in which case it's noted in your employment conditions). If an employer doesn't give you the required notice in writing, he's liable to pay you in full for the period of official notice.

If you resign, you must usually do so in writing. If you resign or are given notice, your company may not require you to work your notice period, particularly if you're joining a competitor or your boss feels that you may be a disruptive influence on your colleagues. However, if he doesn't want you to work your notice, he must pay you in full for the notice period, plus any outstanding overtime or holiday entitlement.

If an employer goes bankrupt and cannot pay you, you may terminate your employment without notice, but your employer cannot legally do this. Other valid reasons for an employee **not** to give notice are assault or abuse of him or a colleague by the employer and failure to pay or persistent delay in paying his wages. Nevertheless, employees can usually leave a job for any reason without giving notice and the chances of an employer having any legal rights worth enforcing are negligible, although you may lose any bonuses or other monies owed to you, plus any possibility of receiving a reference.

Redundancy Pay

Redundancy (called retrenchment in Australia) has become a common occurrence in the last dozen or so years. Redundancy is defined as a situation 'where an employer has made a definite decision that he no longer wishes the job that an employee has been doing to be done by anyone, and this isn't due to the ordinary and customary turnover of labour'. Retrenched workers are entitled to severance pay in accordance with the Termination Change and Redundancy (TCR) case in 1984. The amount of severance pay (in terms of normal weeks' pay) for those employed under federal awards depends on the length of service of an employee, as shown below:

Length of Service	Severance Pay
Less than 1 year	0 weeks
1 to 2 years	4 weeks
2 to 3 years	6 weeks
3 to 4 years	7 weeks
4 ot 5 years	8 weeks
5 to 6 years	10 weeks
6 to 7 years	11 weeks
7 to 8 years	13 weeks
8 to 9 years	14 weeks
9 to 10 weeks	16 weeks
Over 10 years	10 weeks*

* discounted by long-service leave

Employees aged over 45 with more than two years' service are entitled to an extra week's notice or pay in lieu of notice. Severance pay is higher in some states, e.g. 16 weeks in New South Wales plus an extra 25 per cent for those over 45. Many awards allow for three or four weeks' pay for each year of service when an employee takes forced redundancy.

Severance pay may not exceed the amount an employee would have earned had he remained in employment until his normal retirement date. If an employee receives a superannuation payment (see page 269), the amount is generally deducted from the severance pay to which he's entitled.

The average severance pay for executives is around six months' salary, although some executives, managers and key personnel have a clause in their contract whereby they receive a generous 'golden handshake' if they're made redundant, e.g. after a take-over.

When an employee has been notified of his redundancy, he's allowed to take a day off each week with pay to look for another job. Employers must contact a Centrelink office and inform them of the number of proposed redundancies, the category of employees affected, and the period over which the redundancies will be made. Some companies provide 'outplacement' consultancy or agency services for employees who are made redundant. This includes advice and counselling on job prospects, investment (for employees fortunate enough to receive large redundancy payments), job hunting, retirement, retraining, setting up in business, and state benefits. Redundant employees are entitled to a 'statement of employment' (reference). It's also possible for employees to take voluntary redundancy or early retirement and receive an early pension, e.g. in the event of ill health.

Australia has no unemployment benefit scheme, but unemployed people receive social security payments under either the jobsearch or the newstart schemes (see page 265).

References

Employers in Australia aren't legally obliged to provide employees with a written reference or 'statement of employment', except in the case of redundancy. However, if you leave an employer on good terms, he will usually provide a written reference on request. If your employer refuses to give you a written reference or gives you an unwarranted 'bad' reference, you should ask your immediate boss or a colleague instead.

In Australia, prospective employers may contact your previous employer (or employers) directly for a reference, either orally or in writing. This can be bad news for employees, as you have no idea what has been said about you and whether it's true or false. However, an employer cannot (legally) maliciously defame you, although should he do so orally, it's almost impossible to sue him successfully.

Hobart, TAS

IMMIGRATION
ARRIVED
−6 AUG 2003
ADELAIDE AIRPORT
088K
AUSTRALIA

346   MALABA   346
KENYA
10. 1. 2003   KENYA
IMMIGRATION OFFICER
346·346·346·346·346·346·346

3.
PERMITS & VISAS

With the exception of New Zealanders, anyone wishing to enter Australia for any purpose requires a visa (see below). New Zealanders receive a 'special category visa' on arrival and nothing is stamped in their passports; there are no formalities and they can live and work in Australia for as long as they wish.

Australia is a nation of migrants and only the Aboriginals represent the indigenous population (2 per cent); everyone else is an immigrant or descended from an immigrant. After the Second World War, Australia instituted a mass immigration policy ('populate or perish') and accepted virtually anybody who applied, even providing assisted passages whereby migrants paid only a small sum (e.g. £10 in the UK) towards their fare to Australia. However, immigration policy has altered dramatically since then and Australia's entry qualifications for independent migrants (those without family in Australia) are now among the most stringent in the world.

⚠ Caution

Before making any plans to live or work in (or even travel to) Australia, you must ensure that you have the appropriate visa, without which you'll be refused permission to enter the country and sent back to your home country at your own expense.

In the '60s, Australia accepted around 140,000 migrants a year, peaking at 172,000 in 1988, but in the '90s the quota was reduced considerably, although a review of immigration policy found that it was too low, particularly regarding skilled migrants, and could stifle economic growth. In the period 2007–08, the migrant allocation was increased to 152,800: 102,500 for skilled migrants, 50,000 for family migrants and 300 for special eligibility migrants (people who applied under the Resolution of Status category and have lived in Australia for 10 years).

Immigration can be a sensitive subject in Australia, where many people are against large-scale immigration (although many also believe that it provides significant benefits for the country and stimulates economic growth). Migrants bring $billions into Australia each year and migration is the country's third-largest foreign currency earner, after tourism and agriculture, to say nothing of the wealth created by migrants. However, over-crowding and over-population, and damage to Australia's culture and environment are among the arguments frequently cited by those opposed to large-scale immigration. Despite its vast size, Australia has a relatively small population (almost 21m) but is nevertheless considered by many Australians to be over-populated owing to its lack of productive land, shortage of water and generally overcrowded cities.

Many Australians feel that migrants are a strain on the economy and take jobs away from native Australians, a view which has become more prominent in recent years. The ethnic background of migrants is also a thorny issue, and although race and ethnic origin aren't officially immigration criteria, almost half of Australians believe that the country accepts too many Asians, and some would also like fewer migrants from the Middle East (settlers from Africa, Asia and the Middle East have borne the brunt of the government's cuts in immigration in recent years).

There's a huge unsatisfied demand for emigration to Australia, which is much more difficult than emigrating to Canada, New Zealand, South Africa or the USA (the regulations are designed to keep people out rather than let them in). It's becoming increasingly difficult to obtain a visa as an independent migrant and it's also more difficult (or impossible) for immigrants who don't speak fluent English. Australian missions receive over 1m enquiries a year and over 400,000 applications, of which around a quarter are accepted for immigration.

The information in this chapter is intended as a guide only, as the rules and regulations regarding visas change frequently, as well as sometimes being ambiguous, confusing and vague. It's important to check the latest regulations with an Australian mission or immigration consultant (such as The Emigration Group – see inside covers) before making a visa application.

VISAS

With the exception of New Zealanders (see above), anyone wishing to enter Australia must obtain a visa before arrival in the country. The type of visa issued depends on the reason for your planned trip to Australia, which may be anything from a few weeks' holiday or a short business trip to permanent residence. Note the following general points:

● There are four main categories of visa: visitor, temporary residence, migration and residence (described in detail below);

● Multiple-entry visas are issued to those who need to visit Australia frequently over a long period, such as businessmen, entertainers, the parents of children living there and sportsmen;

● There are fees for almost all visas, some of which are very high;

● The processing of visa applications in some categories can take a considerable time in some countries owing to the large number of applications to be processed, and approval can take anything from a few weeks to a number of years.

Information about visas, charges and forms can be obtained from offices of the Department of Immigration and Citizenship (DIAC) in Australia (⌨ www.immi.gov.au)

and Australian missions overseas. General information about visa applications is contained in *Making and Processing Visa Applications* (form 1025i).

Applications

It's important to obtain and complete the correct form, pay the correct fee and satisfy other requirements such as being inside or outside Australia, as required.

For most visas where an application is made overseas, you must not be in Australia when a decision is made and for visa applications in Australia, you must be in Australia when the decision is made. If you make a visa application in Australia, you must ensure that you have a visa to return **before** leaving the country; otherwise, if your application is refused, you may have no right of review. If you apply for a visa in Australia, you're usually granted a bridging visa to remain within the law if your current visa expires while a decision is being made.

You must be careful to indicate the visa class under which you wish to be considered, as your application cannot be considered under any class other than the one noted on your application form. There are different application forms for different visa classes, a full list of which can be found on the DIAC website (www.immi.gov.au). Applications must be sent or delivered to the correct DIAC office for the visa class in which you're applying, with all the relevant documentation and the fee.

Family members who apply at the same time can usually apply on the same form and pay just one fee (a child born after an application is made, but before it's decided, is included in the parents' application). In certain circumstances, a spouse or dependent child can be added to an application.

Applications for some visas, such as visitors' visas, may be decided while you wait. In this case, if you're granted a visa you're usually given a visa label in your passport. If your application for a visitors' visa is refused, you're given a notice of refusal. For all other visas, you're notified of the decision by letter. If you're refused a visa, you're notified why and, if applicable, where you can apply for a review of the decision and the time limit for doing so.

> ⚠ **Caution**
>
> If you plan to travel to or from Australia while your visa application is being considered (assuming this is possible), you should inform the DIAC, as a visa will be refused if you're in the 'wrong place' when a decision is made.

Extensions & Restrictions

If your visa expires while you're in Australia and you haven't applied for an extension, you're committing a criminal offence and can be fined, given a suspended prison sentence of up to six months, or even deported. If you're deported, you're usually barred from entering Australia for one to three years. People deported for criminal or security reasons are permanently excluded. If a visa is granted subject to certain conditions, e.g. restrictions on work or study, you must abide by those conditions or your visa can be cancelled. If you wish to change your visa status, e.g. from a visitor to a student, you must seek advice from a local DIAC office in Australia, as your visa may be granted with a 'no further stay' condition.

Visitors

If you're planning a holiday visit or a business trip to Australia, you must apply for a visa (only holders of New Zealand passports are exempt). A tourist visa is normally valid for three to six months, but those on business visits or undergoing medical treatment and the retired parents of an Australian citizen, can obtain a visitor's visa valid for 12 months. If you're applying for a long-stay visitor's visa, you must be able to show that you have access to adequate funds, although the amount is lower if you'll be staying with friends or family in Australia. If applicable, ensure that your visa allows multiple entries within its period of validity, when it should be marked 'multiple travel'.

Nationals of certain countries can obtain a three-month visa on the spot from travel agents (see **Electronic Travel Authority** below) and at Australian missions (if you're applying by post you should allow a minimum of three weeks in most countries). Many travel agents and companies provide a visa application service for visitors, although there's usually a fee in addition to the visa fee levied by the Australian government. If you don't qualify for an ETA (see below), a tourist's visa for stays of up to three months costs $75 and a visa allowing stays of up to a year $215.

Note that your passport must be valid for the period of your proposed stay in Australia.

Electronic Travel Authority

Australia has one of the most efficient visa processing systems in the world for visitors planning to spend up to three months there, called the Electronic Travel Authority (ETA), it's designed to fast-track passengers at airports through immigration and customs processing, and has substantially reduced the time taken to process passengers. An ETA permits you to spend up to three months at a time in Australia during its 12-month validity period or six months in a 12-month period, and can be issued immediately via the internet.

Nationals of the following countries are eligible for an ETA visa: EU countries, Andorra, Brunei, Canada, Hong Kong, Iceland, Japan, Liechtenstein, Malaysia,

Monaco, Norway, San Marino, Singapore, South Korea, Switzerland, the USA and the Vatican City.

> The fee varies depending on the provider, but an ETA costs $20 from the website of the Department of Immigration and Citizenship (see 🖵 www.eta.immi.gov.au).

An ETA cannot be extended, but it's possible to obtain an extension for a visitor's visa under certain circumstances, although you must apply before your visa expires and must have a good reason. **Visitors aren't permitted to engage in any type of employment or formal study**. They may, however, undertake non-formal study involving short-term courses of up to three months, which are recreational or 'personal-enrichment' in nature and aren't subsidised by any government.

The ETA system is eventually intended to replace visa application forms and labels or stamps in passports, although if you require a passport stamp you must complete an *Application to Visit Australia for Tourism* (form 48).

Business Visitors

Business visitors require either a temporary business entry (short stay) or a temporary business entry (long stay) visa, depending on the length of their proposed stay. The latter is classed as a temporary residence visa (see **Business People** on page 69). The business in question must have been agreed by the Australian Government Office, although a business visa also allows you to visit Australia to look for business opportunities, assess business conditions, act as a consultant, attend meetings and sign contracts. Nationals of eligible countries (see the list above) can obtain a business ETA valid for the life of their passport; others must complete form 456, *Application for* *a Temporary Business Entry Visa (for a stay of up to three months).* A temporary business (short stay) visa costs $75.

Medical Treatment

A visitor's visa is required if you're coming to Australia for medical treatment. Two visas are available: for visits of up to three months and for visits from 3 to 12 months. Medical treatment includes either elective or emergency treatment. You must:

- provide documentary evidence that you can pay for medical treatment;

- make arrangements for hospital accommodation and treatment in advance;

- receive significant benefit from such treatment in Australia;

- not pose a public health risk, e.g. because of a contagious disease.

If you're applying for an extension of stay for medical treatment, you need to meet the above criteria and present evidence that:

- arrangements have been made with a doctor and/or hospital to provide you with medical and/or hospital care, i.e. a firm date for treatment must have been made;

- arrangements have been made to pay the full unsubsidised cost of treatment and you can demonstrate you have the means to pay;

- if treatment is in a public hospital, the state or territory medical authorities have agreed to your admission and treatment.

If the purpose of your intended stay in Australia is to provide comfort and support to a person seeking medical treatment, you should also apply for a medical treatment visa.

There's no fee for a short stay medical treatment visa issued outside Australia,

while a long-stay visa costs $45. Both visas cost $185 when issued in Australia.

TEMPORARY RESIDENTS

Certain categories of skilled workers and professionals are permitted to enter Australia for a fixed period (e.g. the duration of a contract) of up to four years to take up employment, where it can be shown that a job cannot be filled by a resident. There are no set quotas for most temporary workers, who may be engaged in a wide range of occupations and include academic staff; domestic staff; entertainers; executive, professional and technical people; foreign government officials; media and film staff; medical practitioners; occupational trainees; religious personnel; retirees; sportsmen/women; and working holidaymakers. Requirements for some of these categories of worker are detailed below. Students must also obtain a temporary residence visa (see page 67).

Applications for temporary residence visas are granted provided that:

- the prospective employer provides sponsorship (see below) and pays the fees (see **Fees** on page 86);
- the required skills are shown to be unavailable in Australia;
- the job is full time;
- the pay and conditions aren't less than the normal pay and conditions for such a job in Australia;
- the employment of a temporary resident isn't a substitute for training Australian or permanent residents for such a position;
- the position isn't for an unskilled or semi-skilled job;
- you meet certain health and character requirements, as for migrants (see page 76).

If you receive a temporary residence visa permitting you to work in Australia and your spouse is named on the application as your dependant, he or she is also permitted to

work in Australia. A temporary residence visa isn't automatically renewable and no change of job or sponsor is allowed after entry into Australia. Anyone in Australia for less than six months must have private health insurance (see page 271) unless their country of citizenship has a reciprocal health agreement with Australia. Information about non-business temporary residence visas is provided in *Temporary Residence in Australia - non-business – General Guide* (form 986i).

Applications are made using form 147 *Application for a Temporary Residence Visa (non-business)*. Applicants may be required to have a medical examination and chest X-ray before a visa is granted, although this isn't usual when the intended stay is 12 months or less. Some types of temporary residence visa require a fee and most require sponsorship (see opposite and **Fees** on page 86).

Applicants are expected to stay for the full period of their planned stay. In most cases, temporary residents are granted a multiple entry visa for the period of their approved stay. Temporary visa holders have no access to social welfare benefits or national public health cover while in Australia.

Sponsorship

Many temporary residents must be sponsored (or require a nomination, written invitation or a sponsor's undertaking to support an application), e.g. by a prospective employer or organisation, as shown in the table opposite, which also indicates whether a sponsorship fee is payable.

Temporary workers seeking to work in Australia for a period of between three months and four years must be sponsored by their prospective employer. The sponsor must lodge a *Sponsorship for Entry to Australia for Temporary Residents* form. Sponsoring employers must have a

Number	Visa Type	Fee	Sponsorship
405	Investor Retirement	Yes	Yes
411	Exchange	No	No
415	Foreign Government Agency	Yes	Yes (1)
416	Special Program	Yes	No
417	Working Holiday	Yes	No
418	Educational/Research	Yes	Yes (1)
419	Visiting Academic	Yes	No
420/421	Cultural & Social Activities	Yes (2)	Yes (1)
422	Medical Practitioner	Yes	Yes
423	Media and Film Staff	Yes	Yes (1)
426	Domestic Worker (Diplomatic/Consular)	Yes	No
427	Domestic Worker (Overseas Executive)	Yes	Yes (3)
428	Religious Worker	Yes	Yes
442	Occupational Trainee	Yes	No
456	Business Entry (Short Stay)	Yes	No
457	Business Entry (Long Stay)	Yes	Yes

NOTES
1. Formal sponsorship is required if the stay in Australia exceeds three months.
2. Fee applies only to professional sportspeople.
3. Must have been included in the sponsorship of the overseas executive.

satisfactory record of training staff and show that there's no resident person available with the required skills. A sponsor must be willing to accept financial and legal responsibility for temporary residents, and is also responsible for their welfare and accommodation. If the sponsor is an employer, any salary paid must be guaranteed and must fall within the industry pay awards for the job.

Business People

The Temporary Business Entry (Long Stay) visa caters for business visits to Australia of between three months and four years for:

- personnel (executives, managers and specialists) of companies operating in Australia;

- personnel of offshore companies seeking to establish a branch in Australia, fulfil a contract awarded to an offshore company or participate in joint ventures;

- personnel coming to Australia under a labour or Invest Australia-supported skills agreement;

Special arrangements exist for employers in regional and low population growth areas across Australia, which help employers who may not otherwise be able to meet minimum salary and skill requirements for employees.

You don't have to be in Australia to apply for a Temporary Business Entry (Long Stay) visa, although you **cannot** apply at an Australian overseas mission. Applications must be made via the internet or in written (hard-copy) form to a departmental office in Australia. Further information and application forms are available on the DIAC website (🖳 www.immi.gov.au).

Cultural & Social Activities

The cultural and social activities visa class applies to the following:

Entertainers

People involved in a wide range of social and cultural events and activities may be eligible for a visa, depending on the availability of Australians to fill the positions. You may not change your employer or change the times or places of engagements in Australia without permission.

Media & Film Staff

This visa applies to correspondents and other professional media staff members posted to Australia by overseas news organisations, and photographers and film and TV crews making documentaries or commercials for overseas consumption. You cannot change your employer without permission.

Religious Workers

For religious workers, including ministers, priests and spiritual leaders, visiting to serve the spiritual needs of people of their particular faith in Australia.

Sports People

Amateur or professional sports people coming to Australia to engage in competition with Australian residents and to improve general sporting standards through

high calibre competition and training. Sponsorship or letters of invitation may be necessary, depending on the activity and length of stay in Australia. Holders must sign a declaration that on arrival in Australia they will have a return or onward ticket and sufficient funds to support themselves (and any family members accompanying them) for the duration of their stay. You cannot change your employer without permission.

Others

People coming to Australia under approved programmes to broaden their work experience and skills (generally youth exchanges or a 'gap' year between secondary and higher education) may be eligible for a visa. This includes young people coming to Australia under a Churchill Fellowship to broaden their experience and understanding of the country, generally in the context of a youth exchange programme, or to take part in a community-based programme of cultural enrichment or community benefit. You may not change your employer or occupation without permission and are permitted to stay in Australia for a maximum of 12 months.

Domestic Workers

A domestic worker's visa class applies to domestic staff for diplomats and consular staff posted to Australia, for whom written approval is required from the Department of Foreign Affairs and Trade (DFAT), and domestic staff of certain holders of a Temporary Business Entry (Long Stay) visa. A visa may be granted only if it can be shown that the entry of domestic staff is necessary for the proper discharge of the executive's representational duties. Domestic workers may not change employers or remain in Australia after the permanent departure of their employer.

Educational Staff

An educational visa applies to the following:

Educational Institution Staff

Full-time staff for educational and research institutions or organisations, to fill academic, research and teaching positions that cannot be filled from within the Australian labour market. You cannot change your employer without permission.

Foreign Government Officials

Foreign government officials who are to conduct official business on behalf of their government for up to three months, when the officials don't have diplomatic or official status in Australia.

Occupational Trainees

THese are people undergoing training in Australia compatible with their employment history. The training should be to upgrade existing skills and be readily usable on return to their home country. Holders may not work in Australia other than in connection with their course of training

Visiting Academics

People whose presence in Australia will contribute to the sharing of research knowledge. You may not receive a salary from the host institution in Australia.

Retirees

The investor retirement visa (formerly the retirement visa) offers a way for retired people with significant assets to live and invest their money in Australia (see form 1248i on the DIAC website, 🖵 www. immi.gov.au, for more information). You can apply for an investor retirement visa provided that you meet the following conditions:

- you are 55 years of age or older;
- are sponsored by an Australian state or territory government agency;
- have no dependants other than a spouse;
- if you're married or in a *de facto* relationship, your partner must have no dependants;
- have minimum assets legally owned and lawfully acquired by you, or you and your spouse, available for transfer to Australia, the amount depending on where you intend to live in Australia (generally between $500,000 and $750,000);
- have a minimum income (e.g. a pension) that can be accessed by you or you and your spouse, the amount depending on where you intend to live in Australia (generally between $50,000 and $65,000 per year);
- are able to make a designated investment in your name or, your own and your spouse's names, in the state or territory in which you've been sponsored. The amount depends on where you intend to live in Australia

and is generally between $500,000 and $750,000;

- have evidence that you and your spouse (if applicable) have adequate health insurance for the period of your intended stay in Australia;

- have no intention of working full time in Australia (you and your spouse will be allowed to work only up to 20 hours per week while in Australia);

- are in good health and of good character.

The visa is initially issued for four years, and before your visa expires you can apply for another four-year visa. The investor retirement visa is temporary only, and doesn't lead to permanent residence or citizenship and confers no right to Medicare or social security benefits. The DIAC website (⌨ www.immi.gov.au) has a full list of those areas of Australia currently deemed to be regional/low population

growth areas, which attract lower financial requirements for this visa.

An investment retirement visa application costs $190, after which, if you're accepted, you must pay a further $8,505 per person!

Students

Although in effect a form of temporary residence visa, student visas are covered by their own eligibility rules. Foreign students require a student visa (costing $430), which is issued after acceptance on a course and payment of at least half the first year's annual fees. There are seven types of student visa:

- **Independent ELICOS** – for overseas students studying English for Overseas Students.

- **Schools** – for students at primary or secondary school.

- **Vocation Education and Training** – for certificate and diploma students.

- **Higher Education** – for students studying for a bachelor degree or a graduate certificate or diploma.

- **Post Graduate Research** – Masters research degree or a doctorate.

- **Non-award Foundation Studies/Other** – for students on courses that don't lead to a degree or other formal award.

- **AusAID or Defence Sponsored**.

To be eligible for a student visa, you must be accepted for full-time study on a registered course. Courses that qualify for a student visa include tertiary level studies at universities or colleges; courses at Technical and Further Education (TAFE) colleges; English-language courses; occupational or religious training; business study or training, e.g. secretarial and business courses; short courses at universities or colleges of advanced education; and study exchange arrangements between Australian and overseas educational establishments.

Students must have the financial resources to meet tuition fees (scholarships are available), return fares to Australia and day-to-day living expenses for the first year of their course – estimated in 2007 to be from $20,000 to $25,000 or more per year for a single person, depending on where you're studying. Students should also have Overseas Student Health Cover (OSCH) or alternative private health insurance. Your assessment level is determined by your nationality and course of study. For more information, see form 1219i on the DIAC website (🖳 www.immi.gov.au).

You and members of your family unit must not work unless you have been granted permission to do so after commencing study in Australia. See the DIAC website for information about the number of hours you and family members can work when (or if) permission is granted.

In order to retain a student visa, there are certain conditions, which include having a satisfactory course attendance and academic results' record.

> Information about student visas is provided in Student Entry to Australia (form 1160i) and Application for a Student (Temporary) Visa (forms 157a).

Working Holidaymakers

The working holiday visa is the largest visa category for temporary residents and accounts for around 45 per cent of the total. Concerns have been voiced in Australia over jobs being taken from Australians by working holidaymakers; however, the farming industry, particularly fruit and vegetable picking, relies to a large extent on working holidaymakers to harvest crops, and many working holidaymakers also work in the hospitality sector. Statistics show that those on working holiday visas inject around $2bn a year into the economy and many businesses in the tourist industry would be hard hit without them. There's no cap on the number of working holiday visas issued.

Eligibility

Working holiday visas are available to single people and childless couples between the ages of 18 and 30, their purpose being to allow young people the opportunity to visit Australia and supplement their travels through casual employment. There are two classes of working holiday visa: subclass 417, which applies to nationals of Belgium, Canada, Cyprus, Denmark, Estonia, Finland, France, Germany, HKSAR, Ireland, Italy, Japan, Korea, Malta, the Netherlands, Norway, Sweden, Taiwan and the UK; and subclass 462, which applies to those with a university education from Chile, Thailand and Turkey.

Applicants must satisfy the following criteria:

- The prime purpose of your visit must be a temporary stay in Australia and you must have no intention of becoming a permanent resident.

- Employment must be incidental to your holiday and to supplement the money that you bring with you.

- Employment mustn't have been arranged in advance except on a private basis and on your own initiative.

- You must have a reasonable prospect of obtaining temporary employment.

- You must have reasonable funds to support yourself for some of your time in Australia and pay for your return air fare. The minimum amount required for British travellers is around £2,000, although it isn't necessary to have a return ticket at the time of your entry into Australia. It helps to have relatives or friends in Australia who can provide extra funds, if necessary.

- You must meet 'normal' character requirements and health standards.

- You mustn't work full time for more than six months with one employer (you may train or study for up to four months).

- You mustn't remain in Australia longer than 12 months and must leave Australia when your working holiday visa has expired (although you can apply for a second working holiday visa – see below).

Applications can be made in person, by post or fax or online (preferred), and can be made inside or outside Australia. You should apply for a working holiday visa at least four weeks before your intended departure date, and, if you're applying by post, should send documents by recorded delivery. The application fees for a working holiday visa are $190 for subclass 417 and $180 for subclass 462.

If your application is approved, your visa is valid for 12 months from the date of your first entry into Australia, during which period there's no limit on the number of times you can leave and re-enter Australia.

You can apply for a second working holiday visa if you've completed three months' seasonal work in Australia on your first working holiday visa. If you successfully apply for a second working holiday visa while in Australia, you're allowed to remain in Australia for 24 months from the date you entered Australia on your **first** working holiday visa.

MIGRANTS

Applying for a visa as a migrant (i.e. for permanent residence) is confusing, difficult, expensive and time consuming – factors which have spawned a wealth of migration consultants and keep thousands of civil servants in 'employment'.

To be accepted for migration to Australia you must meet the personal and occupational requirements of the category for which you're applying, and be of good health and character. The Australian migration programme (often spelled program) is divided into two main categories: migration and humanitarian migration (see page 86). Migration is split into the following 'streams':

- **Family migration** – where migrants can be 'sponsored' by a relative who is an Australian citizen, a permanent resident or an eligible New Zealand citizen.

- **Skilled migration** – for people with particular business or work skills or 'outstanding talents', with a separate quota for states or territories with particular skill shortages.

- **Special eligibility migration** – covering former citizens or residents wanting to return to Australia, and also certain New Zealanders (not covered in detail in this book).

⚠️ Caution

The Australian government is constantly changing the rules for migrants and sometimes introduces retrospective changes that apply to applications already lodged, but not processed. Even when new requirements have been announced, they may not be introduced for many months or even years, and could even be rejected by the upper house (Senate) of the Australian parliament after being passed by the lower house. Before making an application, check the latest regulations and criteria for visa applications.

The Department of Immigration and Citizenship provides an enquiry service (☎ local call rate 13-1881 or 🖥 www.immi. gov.au) for further information. The form *Migrating to Australia – Who can migrate?* (957i) contains general information about migration and the various categories.

There are different forms for the different visa classes. There's a fee (e.g. around £5 in the UK) for the printed forms and the information package, or you can download them free from the DIAC website (see above). You may telephone the DIAC and enquire about the progress of your application (although this can delay the processing), but detailed enquiries must be made in writing, quoting your DIAC file number.

Application fees for migrant visas are high (see **Fees** on page 86) and aren't refundable, so you should ensure that you have a **very** good chance of being accepted before making an application.

Never make any firm plans or arrangements (such as booking flights, selling your home or resigning your job) in the expectation that your visa application will be granted. Even when an application appears to be going smoothly, it can be delayed or even rejected at the last minute, e.g. on health grounds.

Waiting Period

The processing time for migration applications varies depending on the country where you're applying, the number of applicants and your migrant category; for example, skilled migrants are given priority. In certain circumstances, e.g. for compassionate reasons, an application can be expedited, although no guarantees are given. It can take a long time to receive a migrant visa – you should be prepared for a lot of questions and demands for additional paperwork from immigration officials – and a two-year waiting period has been introduced in recent years before most migrants can claim social security benefits, which has caused many unemployed migrants to become destitute. However, if you're really keen to go and you meet the criteria for the category of visa for which you're applying (see below), you'll usually get your visa in the end. On the other hand,

if your application is pooled (which applies to visas in categories subject to a 'points test') or if processing of the class of visa is suspended, your application will be delayed indefinitely and may eventually be refused.

Quotas

The Australian migration year runs from 1st July to 30th June (the same as the Australian financial year) and each year the federal government announces the quotas for the coming year, although these aren't set in stone. All applications for categories where a quota (or capping) applies are processed on a 'first come, first served' basis. When a cap is reached for the current immigration year, the granting of visas is suspended, although processing continues and applicants are granted visas when the new immigration year commences (and a new quota is allocated). The following quotas were for the year 2007-08.

In any case, migration planning figures can never be exact, as some categories (particularly within the skilled stream) are demand-driven and there's no upper limit placed on the number of migrants who can qualify; if you meet the criteria, you're accepted.

Stream	Quota
Family	50,000
Skilled	102,500
Special Eligibility	300

Health & Character Checks

Applicants for migration visas must pass health and character checks before they're granted a visa.

Medical and police certificates are valid for only 12 months, and you're therefore required to make your initial entry into Australia within 12 months of your medical or police clearance date, whichever occurs first.

Medical Examination

All applicants (and their family members) for permanent or long-term temporary residence (over 12 months), plus short-term temporary applicants if their health is of 'special significance', are required to undergo a medical examination. This includes an X-ray for those aged 11 or older, an HIV/AIDS test for those aged 15 or over, and TB screening for those aged 11 or over (and for those under 11 if it's suspected that they have, or have had, TB). Hepatitis B screening is compulsory if the applicant is pregnant, a child for adoption or an unaccompanied refugee minor. Pregnancy must be declared by prospective migrants. A long-term or serious illness or condition suffered by you or a dependent could void your application, e.g. if you have a child who requires special schooling.

Results of the examination are sent to the Department of Health in Australia and can take around six weeks to be assessed. Your case officer provides you with instructions and forms for your medical examination.

Police Check

One of the requirements for immigrants is that they are 'of good character'. You may be required to provide a police check for each country you've resided in for 12 months or more in the last ten years or since the age of 16.

The procedure for obtaining a police certificate varies from country to country. In the UK, you should visit your local police station and request a 'Personal Record of Prosecution/Criminal History' from the National Identification Service, Subject Access Office, Room 1229, New Scotland Yard, Broadway, London SW1H 0BG. In Australia, a certificate of 'no criminal record' (fee $36 to $130, depending on whether fingerprints need to be taken and processed) can be obtained from the Australian Federal Police, Criminal History Branch, Locked Bag 1, Weston, ACT 2611 (☎ 06-6223 3000, 🖳 www.afp.gov.au).

If you have a criminal record it may jeopardise your application – stringent efforts have been made in recent years to prevent the entry of convicted criminals and other undesirables. Further information is provided in *Character Requirement: Police Certificates* (form 47P).

Application Procedure

All application forms must be completed in English and you must provide originals or certified copies of all documents requested (see below).

Documentation & Interviews

You must usually provide copies of documents such as birth and marriage certificates, educational and trade qualifications, and employer references. Copies must be certified by a legal professional, a Justice of the Peace or other person authorised to witness statutory declarations (e.g. a Commissioner for Declarations in Australia), who must state that the copy is true to the original. Original documents mustn't be sent unless specifically requested.

Additional information concerning your application can be provided at any time (and is taken into account) before a decision is made, and you must keep the DIAC informed of any changes to information provided. If you provide incorrect information or documents, your application or visa can be cancelled.

It's rare for applicants (particularly Britons) to be required to attend an interview with the Department of Immigration and Citizenship about a migration application.

Validity

If you're accepted for immigration, you must send your passport to the appropriate embassy or consulate in your country of residence to be stamped with the appropriate visa. You must usually arrive in Australia within nine or ten months of the date stamped in your passport, known as the 'initial entry date'. If you don't enter Australia by this date, the visa is invalid and you need to re-apply for migration. If you enter Australia by the initial entry date, you'll have used (or validated) your migrant visa and by doing so will have become a permanent resident (if applicable).

Leaving & Returning to Australia

Permanent foreign residents of Australia don't enjoy the same rights as Australian citizens with regard to their freedom to leave and enter Australia.

If you migrated to Australia before 1987, you'll have been issued with either an Authority to Return (ATR) or a Return Endorsement (RE), which are valid provided you haven't been out of Australia for more than three years and you haven't become a citizen.

However, if you migrated to Australia in 1987 or later, your initial visa gives you permission to leave and return to Australia freely during only the three, four or five years after your first entry. After this time, if you choose not to apply for Australian citizenship, you must obtain a 'resident return visa' (RRV) before leaving the country, which allows a permanent resident to leave and return to Australia within a period of either three months or five years. Whether the visa is granted depends on how long you've spent in Australia during the previous five years.

An RRV cannot be extended and you must apply for a new one if required; the amount of time you've spent outside Australia in the five years immediately before your application determines whether you're eligible for a new RRV, and, if so, what type. For example, if you've lived in Australia for at least two years within the last five, you're probably eligible for an RRV which gives you the right to remain outside Australia for up to five years. If you aren't eligible for a five-year RRV, you may be eligible for a three-month RRV. If you choose to return to Australia just before your RRV expires, you're obliged to remain there for at least 12 months before you're eligible for another RRV. If you need to leave because of an emergency during this period, you're allowed to do so only once.

Sponsorship

Applicants in the family category need to be sponsored by a relative, who must be aged at least 18 and an Australian resident. Some family-sponsored classes require that the sponsor is 'settled', which is generally accepted to be the case after two years' continual residence. In spouse and parent classes, a minor child can act as a sponsor under certain circumstances. Your sponsor must undertake to assist you financially and with accommodation during your first two years in Australia, plus, if necessary, attendance at English-language classes.

Family migrants aren't usually eligible to receive unemployment or other welfare benefits for a period of two years or longer, so sponsors must be prepared to accept consequent costs.

Family Migration Classes

There are the following classes of family migrant:

- **Partner** (subclass 309 Provisional, subclass 100 Permanent) – a husband, wife or *de facto* partner, who has been living with the sponsor for at least a year.

- **Interdependency Visa** (subclass 310/110) – generally for same-sex partners and applies in the same way as the Partner visa (above).

- **Dependent Child** (subclass 101) – a natural or adopted child (usually under 18) of the sponsor who is dependent on the sponsor. A child who is married or engaged to be married isn't eligible.

- **Adoption** (subclass 102) – a child under 18 coming to Australia for adoption, where the adoption is supported by the appropriate state or territory welfare authorities in Australia, or a child under 18 who was adopted by Australian citizens or permanent residents while they were resident overseas.

- **Parent** (subclass 103) – a parent of the sponsor. Parents must meet the 'balance of family' criteria outlined on the DIAC website (💻 www.immi.gov.au). There's a surfeit of applicants in this visa class and a low annual quota, and most parents have to wait years before they obtain a visa.

- **Contributory Parent** (subclass 143 – Migrant) – a parent of the sponsor who is willing to provide a ten-year assurance of support (see below) and a $10,000 bond for the primary applicant and $4,000 for each other adult applicant. Balance of family requirements are similar to the parent subclass (see above). A greater number of visas are available than for subclass 103, but a second visa application charge of $31,555 per person applies. There are other parent visas – see the DIAC website (⌨ www.immi.gov.au) for information.

- **Orphan Relative** (subclass 117) – an orphan under 18 who is unmarried and a relative of the sponsor.

- **Carer** (subclass 116) – a relative capable of providing substantial and continuing help to an Australian citizen, permanent resident or eligible New Zealand citizen living in Australia who is in need of such help in cases where this cannot be provided by a relative in Australia or by local community, hospital, nursing or welfare services.

- **Aged Dependent Relative** (subclass 114) – a single, widowed or divorced relative who is old enough to be granted an old age pension under the Social Security Act, 1991 and has been financially dependent on the sponsor for a 'reasonable' period. The sponsor is expected to have lived in Australia for at least two years before lodging the application.

- **Remaining Relative** (subclass 115) – those with a brother, sister, parent (or step equivalent) who is an Australian citizen, permanent resident or eligible New Zealand citizen usually resident in Australia. You and your spouse must have no brothers, sisters, children, parents (or step equivalent) other than those in Australia.

- **Prospective Marriage** (subclass 300 – Temporary) – a prospective spouse planning to marry a sponsor in Australia

receives a temporary visa to stay in Australia for up to nine months. You must marry your sponsor and apply to remain permanently within this period, after which you're granted a two-year provisional (temporary) visa if all the requirements are met. If you're still married at the end of the two-year period, you're granted a permanent visa.

Assurance of Support

In certain family migration visa subclasses (see below), an assurance of support (AOS) is mandatory and must be given before a visa is granted. The person giving the AOS is known as the 'assurer' and the migrant the 'assuree'. An AOS is a legal commitment by the assurer to repay the Australian government if certain welfare benefits are paid to the assuree, which, depending on the type of visa the migrant is granted, can be for a period of two or ten years. Where applicable, a refundable bond is payable (a bond isn't required for orphan relatives). The bond is $3,500 or $5,000 for a couple for a two-year AOS, and $10,000 or $14,000 for a couple for a ten-year AOS, which is refundable after two or ten years, along with the accrued interest. The AOS system is administered by Centrelink in Australia (⌨ www.centrelink.gov.au).

An AOS is mandatory for the following categories of family migration:

- Aged Dependent Relative.
- Aged Parent.
- Carer.
- Contributory Aged Parent.
- Contributory Parent.
- Parent.
- Remaining Relative.

Other visa subclasses may require an AOS if an applicant is assessed as liable to become a drain on Australia's

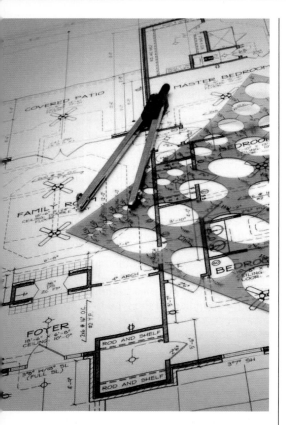

welfare system. Skilled visas with family sponsorship lodged after 1st September 2007 no longer require an AOS.

> For more information about assurances of support, see Fact Sheet 34, Assurance of Support, or the DIAC website (💻 www.immi. gov.au/media/fact-sheets/34aos.htm).

Skilled Migration

The skilled migration category applies to people who are highly skilled, under 45 years of age, have a high level of English and can quickly make a contribution to the Australian economy. There are three categories of visa: permanent, provisional and temporary.

If you're unable to meet the requirements for a permanent visa, a provisional or temporary visa can provide a route to permanent status.

The basic requirements are as follows (if you're unable to satisfy these, it isn't worth applying for a skilled migration category visa):

- **Age** – under 45 when you apply.

- **English ability** – 'competent' or 'vocational' English if you're nominating a trade occupation. There are concessions to English ability if you're applying for a provisional visa.

- **Qualifications/Nominated occupation** – You must have had your skills assessed as suitable for your nominated occupation by the required assessing authority.

- **Recent work experience** – You must have been in paid employment in a skilled occupation on the Skilled Occupations List (see form 1121i) for at least 12 months in the 24 months immediately preceding your application, unless you meet the 'two years' study' requirement.

There are a number of visas and 'schemes' related to the skilled migration programme, each with their own guidelines, which include those listed below and the Business Skills programme (see page 84), Distinguished Talent Visas (see page 85) and Employer Nomination Scheme (see page 85). The following are known as 'offshore' visas, which generally means simply that you and any dependent family members included must be outside Australia when your visa is granted:

- **Skilled Independent** (subclass 175) – Those who meet the basic requirements and pass the points test (see below) for this visa subclass don't need to be sponsored by family or a state or territorial government.

- **Skilled Sponsored** (subclass 176) – You must be sponsored by an eligible relative or have been nominated by a state or territory agency.

- **Skilled Regional Sponsored** (subclass 475 – Provisional) – You require sponsorship by an eligible relative living in a designated area or by a participating state or territory government and must live, work or study in regional Australia or the designated area. This visa is valid for three years.

- **Skilled Recognised Graduate Visa** (subclass 476 – Temporary) – for graduates of a recognised university. You must be under 30 when you make your application and have completed a qualification at a listed university in a field that's in demand in Australia. This visa isn't points tested and is valid for 18 months; you can apply for a permanent skilled visa during this period.

For further details about skilled migration, see Booklet 6, *General Skilled Migration*, and the latest updates (in this ever-changing field) on the DIAC website (⌨ www.immi.gov.au/media/fact-sheets/25skilled_categories.htm).

Points Test

A points test applies to certain categories of skilled migrant. The points test doesn't apply to family applicants, other than those applying under the skilled sponsored visa classes.

The points test aims to ensure that the principal applicant has the skills and other attributes necessary to allow him to quickly enter the Australian workforce and support himself and his family without relying on the Australian government. Only one spouse is assessed and either partner can be considered a principal applicant for the points test, so couples should choose the partner with the better likelihood of scoring sufficient points.

Depending on the visa class applied for, points may be earned for skill, age (or lack of it), ability in English and a designated language, related work experience, Australian qualifications and partner skills, and according to whether your occupation is in demand, whether you've studied and lived in certain parts of Australia, and whether you have state/territory government or designated area sponsorship (see below).

If your score is below the pass mark but equal to or above the pool mark, where these are different (see below), your application is held in reserve (in the pool) for up to two years after assessment. If the pass mark is lowered at any time in the two-year period, and your score is equal to or higher than the new pass mark, your application will be processed further. Current pass and pool marks are shown below.

Note that the following information is a guide to help you estimate your points score; for the latest information, see Booklet 6, *General Skilled Migration*.

Category	Pass Mark	Pool Mark
Skilled Independent (subclass 175)	120	100
Skilled Sponsored (subclass 176)	100	80
Skilled Regional Sponsored (subclass 475)	100	100

Skill: The occupation you nominate must be on the Skilled Occupations List at the time of your application, and it should be one that corresponds to your qualifications and skills. Once the relevant assessment authority has determined that your skills are suitable for your nominated job, points are allocated as shown below (using the exact DIAC wording, which is vague!).

Occupation	Points
Most occupations where training is specific to the occupation	60
More general, professional occupations	50
Other general skilled occupations	40

Age: Points are allocated according to your age at the time of application, as follows:

Age	Points
18 to 29	30
30 to 34	25
35 to 39	20
40 to 44	15

English language ability: Points are allocated for English language ability as shown in the table below.

A UK passport holder scores 15 points automatically but to achieve the maximum of 25 must sit an IELTS test and score at least 7.0 on each of the four components.

Ability	Definition	Points
Proficient	Operational command of English with the ability to use and comprehend complex language well and understand detailed reasoning.	25
Competent	Generally effective command of the English language and the ability to use and understand fairly complex language, particularly in familiar situations.	15
Vocational	A reasonable command of the English language, coping with overall meaning in most situations and the ability to communicate effectively in the nominated field of employment.	15

GONE NEXT DOOR.
BACK IN 3 WEEKS

Experience	Points
If your nominated occupation is worth 60 points (see Skill above) and you've worked in your nominated occupation, or a closely relatedoccupation, for at least three of the four years immediately before you apply.	10
If your nominated occupation is worth at least 40 points and you've worked in any occupation on the Skilled Occupations List for at least three of the four years immediately before you apply.	5

Work experience: The table above shows the points awarded for relevant work experience.

If you've been employed in Australia in your nominated occupation or a closely related occupation for a total of 12 months in the 48 months preceding your application, or have completed a professional year in Australia in your skilled occupation or a closely related occupation in the 48 months preceding your application, you receive 10 points.

Occupation demand: The Migration Occupations in Demand List (MODL, see the DIAC website, ⌨ www.immi.gov.au) identifies occupations and specialisations that are deemed to be in demand in Australia. If your nominated occupation is on the current MODL, you might receive 20 points if you have a job offer or 15 if you don't.

Australian qualifications: Applicants who have Australian qualifications, and are therefore deemed to have a greater chance of securing employment in Australia, are awarded extra points as shown in the table below.

Regional study: Applicants who can claim points for Australian qualifications (see above) may also be eligible to claim five points for having lived and studied for at least two years in 'regional Australia or a low population growth metropolitan area', which means anywhere in Australia **except**

Qualification	Points
An Australian doctorate at an Australian educational institution obtained after at least two academic years' full-time study in Australia.	25
An Australian Master's or Honours degree (to at least upper second level) at an Australian educational institution and, before completing the degree, an Australian bachelor degree after at least one year's full-time study in Australia. The total period of full-time study in Australia must have been at least three years.	15
An Australian Honours bachelor degree at least upper second class level after a period of study of at least two years.	15
Full-time study in Australia towards the award of a degree, diploma or trade qualification for a total of at least two academic years.	5

the Australian Capital Territory (ACT), Brisbane, the Gold Coast, Melbourne, Newcastle, the New South Wales (NSW) Central Coast, Perth, Sydney or Wollongong. The DIAC website (💻 www. immi.gov.au) contains a list of the post codes of relevant areas and a list of educational institutions defined as being in these areas.

Spouse's skills: Five points are awarded if your spouse can satisfy certain requirements as to age, English language ability, occupation, qualifications and recent work experience, and has obtained a suitable skills assessment from the relevant assessing authority for his/her nominated occupation.

Nomination: Ten points are awarded if you've been nominated by a state or territory government (for visa classes 176 and 475).

Designated area sponsorship: If you're applying for a provisional visa, you can earn 25 bonus points if you've been sponsored by an eligible Australian relative living in a designated area.

Designated language: Five points if you have professional-level language skills in a designated language.

Business Skills Programme

The Business Skills programme is administered separately from the Skilled Migrant programme, although the number of visas allocated is included in the overall skilled figure. The Business Skills programme is designed to encourage successful business people to settle permanently in Australia and develop existing or new businesses. It has four subclasses, as follows:

- **Business Owner** – owners or part-owners of successful businesses who intend to establish a business in Australia.

- **Senior Executive** – senior executive employees of a major business who intend to establish a business in Australia.

- **Investor** – successful investors and certain categories of business people who intend to invest in Australia.

- **Business Talent** – people with an outstanding record of success in business and a proposal for a significant investment that will generate exceptional benefits for the sponsoring state.

Visas for the first three subclasses are available either directly through application to the DIAC or via an individual state or territory sponsoring the applicant. The thresholds for eligibility (age, turnover, assets and English ability) are lower if the state sponsorship route is followed.

A two-stage process applies: the initial visa is provisional and valid for four years, after which you can apply for the second stage (permanent residence). To be granted permanent residence, you must show that you've fulfilled the original criteria (level of investment, turnover, job creation, etc.) and resided for at least two years in the sponsoring state.

State sponsorship is mandatory for the Business Talent subclass, but there's no provisional stage and permanent residence is granted immediately.

The DIAC Booklet 7, *Business Skills Entry*, is essential reading for anybody planning to apply under this category.

Distinguished Talent Visas

Distinguished Talent Visas are designed to attract people with an internationally recognised record of exceptional and outstanding achievement who wish to settle permanently in Australia. You can apply within or outside Australia; if you apply within Australia, you must already hold a qualifying visa.

To be eligible for a Distinguished Talent Visa you must:

- demonstrate that you have an internationally recognised record of outstanding achievement in academia, the arts, a profession, research or a sport, are still prominent in your profession, will be an asset to Australia (i.e. contribute culturally, economically or socially), and will have no trouble finding employment or becoming established independently;

- be nominated by an Australian citizen, an Australian permanent resident, an eligible New Zealand citizen or an Australian organisation. The person or organisation nominating you must have a national reputation in your field of expertise;

- meet the mandatory character and health requirements;

- show that you're likely to be of 'exceptional benefit' to the Australian community.

If you're under 18 or over 55, you must also provide evidence that you're financially independent.

Employer Nomination Scheme

The Employer Nomination Scheme (ENS) was developed to allow Australian employers to recruit highly skilled permanent staff from abroad (or among temporary foreign residents of Australia) when they're unable to fill a vacancy from within the Australian labour market or through their own training.

The employer must complete a form (785), *Employer Nomination under the Employer Nomination Scheme*, pay a fee, lodge the nomination at a departmental Business Centre in Australia, and meet certain standards. The position being offered must:

- be full time and available for at least three years;

- be in accordance with the standards for working conditions under Australian industrial laws;

- be a highly skilled occupation on the ENSOL (see form 1121i);

- pay a certain minimum salary (see the *Government Gazette Notice*).

You must complete application form 47ES, *Application for Employer Sponsored Migration to Australia*, pay a fee and lodge the form at the same Departmental Business Centre in Australia as the employer used for his application. You must meet the following requirements:

- be under 45 (except in exceptional circumstances);

- have excellent English language ability (except in exceptional circumstances);

- have worked full time in Australia in the occupation for which you're being nominated for at least two years (including at least the previous year) **or** been nominated to fill a senior executive position with a salary of over $165,000 per annum **or** have had your skills assessed as suitable by the relevant skills assessing authority (published in a *Government Gazette Notice*) **and** (except in exceptional circumstances) have at least three years' experience in the occupation;

- meet any applicable licensing, professional membership and registration requirements;
- meet health and character requirements (also applies to your family).

HUMANITARIAN MIGRANTS

Australia is committed to supporting international humanitarian and refugee programmes. It has become home to over 660,000 refugees in the last 60 years (over 100,000 from South-east Asia since 1975), including large numbers of Afghans, Cambodians, Chileans, Chinese, Czechs, Hungarians, Lebanese, Russians, Timorese, Vietnamese and Yugoslavs.

The Humanitarian Programme consists of two parts: offshore resettlement of people in 'humanitarian need' overseas, and onshore protection for those already in Australia who arrived on temporary visas or illegally and who claim Australia's protection.

In the 2007-08 immigration year, 13,000 places were allocated to humanitarian migrants, which aren't included in the general immigration quotas.

Illegal immigrants can be 'interned' for years to discourage others, and refugees often have a **very** difficult time finding work. Under new laws proposed by the government, humanitarian refugees can be denied social security for up to six years, although a law passed in June 2005 made it illegal for immigrant children to be kept in detention.

Unless your status has already been decided overseas under the terms of the United Nations convention, you're granted refugee status in Australia only if you can prove that you have 'a well-founded fear of persecution in your own country for reasons of race, religion, nationality, or membership of a particular social group or political opinion'.

RESIDENTS

Certain temporary residence visa holders, e.g. 'aged parents' and those with a provisional business visa, are eligible to apply for a residence visa. For information about these, refer to the DIAC website (⌨ www.immi.gov.au) or an Australian mission.

FEES

There are fees for most visas and, although many of these are nominal, those for migrant visas are high (see table below). Fees, which are supposedly intended to cover the costs incurred by the Australian

government in processing your application, aren't refunded if your application is unsuccessful even if you're adversely affected by a change of rules while your application is being processed, such as an increase in the number of points required for a visa.

☑ SURVIVAL TIP

You should ensure that you have a very good chance of being accepted before making an application if you don't want to waste your application fee.

The fees shown below are examples of Australia's visa and migration fees (which sometimes vary according to whether your application is lodged within or outside Australia, as indicated), and were applicable in October 2007 (fees are revised annually on 1st July). **This information is intended as a guide only**; for country-specific charges you should contact an Australian mission.

Payment methods for fees vary depending on the type of application and where it's made. If you're making an internet application, you can pay by credit card or via BPAY (an Australian payment scheme similar to PayPal). If you lodge your application in Australia, you can pay by credit card, by debit card in person, or by bank or money order made payable to DIAC. If you lodge your application outside Australia, check the acceptable methods of payment with the Australian mission where you plan to make your application. Details of these are also given on the DIAC website (💻 www.immi.gov. au), plus a currency converter that shows the visa fees in various currencies.

Type of Application	Fee Outside Australia
Visitor's Visa (Short Stay – up to three months)	$75 ($215 within Australia)
Visitor's Visa (Long Stay – up to a year)	$75 ($215 within Australia)
Business Visa (Short Stay)	$75
Business Visa (Long Stay)	$190
Permission to Work	$60
Working Holiday Visa	$190
Student Visa	$430
Medical Treatment Visa (up to three months' stay)	NIL ($185 within Australia)
Medical Treatment Visa (over three months' stay)	$45 ($185 within Australia)
Retirement Visa	$190 (n/a within Australia)
Sponsorship (one to ten applicants)	$270 each
Sponsorship (11 or more applicants)	$2,700
Employer Nomination	$1,390 ($2,060 within Australia)
Family Migration (most subclasses)	$1,390 to $2,060
Provisional Business Migration	$2,735
Skilled Migration	$2,060

4.

ARRIVAL

On arrival in Australia, your first task is to negotiate immigration and customs, which fortunately presents no problems for most people – provided they have a valid visa! With the exception of New Zealanders, everyone wishing to enter Australia requires a visa (see Chapter 3). If you arrive in Australia without one, you will be refused entry. Australian customs and immigration officials are usually polite and efficient, although they may occasionally be a 'trifle overzealous' in their attempts to deter smugglers and those planning to stay or work illegally.

There are a number of tasks that should be completed on arrival, which are described in this chapter, plus suggestions for finding local help and information.

IMMIGRATION

All arrivals must complete an Incoming Passenger Card (IPC), distributed by airlines and shipping companies (one per person), before their arrival in Australia. The IPC contains your personal details such as address in Australia, name and passport number, and is used by immigration officials to record the reason for your visit. The card is also for customs and quarantine purposes, and contains questions concerning plants and animals and whether you've exceeded the duty-free allowances (see page 386). An IPC card also states that you must list every item of food you are carrying, even if it's only a small packet of sugary sweets it has to be declared on the card and customs **will** inspect it. It is far simpler and quicker not to take any food into Australia.

If you (or anyone over 12 months of age who's travelling with you) have stayed overnight or longer in a yellow fever infected country or area (e.g. Africa or South America) in the six days prior to your arrival in Australia, a yellow fever vaccination certificate is required.

When you disembark, you proceed to the Entry Control Point, where you present your passport and IPC. You may be asked to verify the reason for your visit and provide evidence that you have sufficient funds for your trip and a return or onward ticket. Your IPC is returned to you and must be presented when you arrive at the customs checkpoint (see below).

Australia operates an Advanced Passenger Processing (APP) system at major airports (e.g. Sydney), where passengers can be cleared in the 'express' lane in as little as 20 seconds. It also allows passengers on certain flights (Air New Zealand, Cathay Pacific, Japan Airlines and Qantas) to complete their immigration and customs processing at check-in and be issued with an Express card, which is simply passed through an immigration card reader on arrival.

When you receive your visa from an Australian mission overseas, you usually get a stamp in your passport stating that the visa is valid 'subject to an entry permit on arrival'. This means that you must satisfy the immigration official that you won't infringe the terms of your visa. If you have a visitor's visa, you should present it along with evidence that you have sufficient funds (or access to funds) to last you throughout your stay (e.g. $1,000 per month) and enable you to leave Australia when your visa expires. An airline ticket, bank statements, cash, credit cards and travellers' cheques all help convince immigration officials. If you're staying with friends or relatives in Australia, you usually require fewer funds, but the immigration officer may check with them to verify your statement.

Generally, the onus is on you to **prove** that you're a genuine visitor and won't infringe the immigration laws. The immigration authorities aren't required to establish that you'll violate the immigration laws, and in cases where they believe that you plan to work illegally or overstay your visa, they can refuse you entry or restrict your entry to a shorter period than that permitted by your visa.

⚠ Caution

Take care how you answer seemingly innocent questions (immigration officials never ask innocent questions) , as you could find yourself being refused entry if you give incriminating answers.

The treatment of foreigners by immigration officers varies, but young people in particular may be liable to close scrutiny, especially those travelling light and 'scruffily' dressed or coming from notorious drug areas such as Asia or South America. Like any other visitor, young people should carry evidence of their funds (or access to funds) and proof of why they're entering Australia and why they need to leave (e.g. to return to work or study overseas).

Whatever the question, never imply that you may remain in Australia longer than the period permitted or for a purpose other than that for which you've been granted permission. For example, if you aren't permitted to work in Australia, you could be asked, "Would you like to work in Australia?" If you reply, "Yes", even if you have no intention of doing so, you could be refused entry.

When all is in order and the immigration official is satisfied, he stamps your passport with the official entry permit stating the period that you're permitted to remain in the country. If you decide that this isn't long enough, some visas (e.g. visitor's visas) can be extended, but it's an expensive procedure and you need to convince the authorities that you should be granted an extension. You may find that it's easier to leave the country, e.g. by travelling to New Zealand or Indonesia, and apply for a new visa from there.

CUSTOMS

After you've cleared immigration, you proceed to the luggage claim area to collect your bags. When you have all your bags, you go to the customs checkpoint, where you hand your IPC to a customs officer.

All airports in Australia use a system of red and green 'channels'. Red means you have something to declare and green means you have nothing to declare, i.e. no more than the duty- or tax-free allowances, no goods to sell, and no prohibited or restricted goods. **If you're *certain* that you have nothing to declare, go through the 'green channel'; otherwise go through the red channel.** Customs officers make random checks on people going through

both red and green channels and there are stiff penalties for smuggling. If you're caught trying to smuggle any goods into Australia, they can be confiscated and, if you attempt to import prohibited items (see page 91), you may be liable to criminal charges and/or deportation.

When you enter Australia to take up temporary or permanent residence, you can usually import your belongings duty and tax-free. Personal and household goods that you've owned and used overseas for over 12 months can be imported free of duty and sales tax, although proof of length of ownership may be required and this concession doesn't apply to alcohol, motor vehicles or tobacco products.

Any goods not owned and used overseas for over 12 months may be subject to duty and tax at varying rates, depending on where you've come from, where you purchased the goods, how long you've owned them, and whether duty and tax have already been paid in another country. If you need to pay duty or tax, it must be paid at the time goods are brought into the country. Payment may be made in cash,

by travellers' cheque (in Australian dollars) or by American Express, Bankcard, Diners Club, MasterCard or Visa card.

There's no limit to the amount of Australian or foreign banknotes and coins that can be brought into Australia, but amounts of $10,000 or more (or the equivalent in foreign currency) must be declared on arrival. On the other hand, in accordance with the Anti-Money Laundering and Counter-Terrorism Financing Act 2006, travellers entering or leaving Australia must disclose to a customs or police officer, if asked, whether they're carrying Bearer Negotiable Instruments (BNIs) which include promissory notes, travellers' cheques, cheques, money orders and postal orders. This disclosure will be made by filling out a Cross Border Movement-Bearer Negotiable Instrument (CBM-BNI) form. This is **as well as** declaring the amount of cash carried.

Australian Customs publishes a variety of information for travellers, including a booklet entitled *Customs Information for Travellers*, available from Australian customs offices (see **Appendix A** for a list). General enquiries should be directed to the Australian Customs Service, Customs House, 5 Constitution Ave, ACT 2000 (☎ 1300-363263 within Australia or ☎ 02-6275 6666 from outside Australia, ⌨ www. customs.gov.au). For information regarding duty-free allowances (e.g. alcohol and tobacco), see page 386; the importation of motor vehicles, see page 212; the importation of pets, see page 410.

Prohibited & Restricted Goods

There are strict laws prohibiting or restricting the entry of drugs, firearms, steroids, weapons and certain articles subject to quarantine. If you're carrying any goods which you think may fall into any of the following categories, you must declare them to customs on your arrival in Australia.

Drugs & Other Substances

If you're carrying any prescribed 'drugs of dependence', including medicines containing amphetamines, barbiturates, hallucinogens, narcotics, tranquillisers or vaccines, you must declare them to customs on arrival.

☑ SURVIVAL TIP

If you carry prescription medicines with you, then it is wise to also have a doctor's prescription (or a copy) with you.

If you're uncertain about any drugs or medicines that you're carrying, check with the customs officer on your arrival. **Penalties for drug offences in Australia are severe and can result in imprisonment** (see **Crime** on page 398).

The importation of anabolic steroids, androgenic substances, natural and manufactured growth hormones, and certain other pharmaceutical substances is prohibited unless written approval has been obtained from the Therapeutic Goods Administration, PO Box 100, Woden, ACT 2606 (🖥 www.tga.gov.au).

Weapons

Many weapons are prohibited in Australia, while others require a permit and safety testing. You should contact Australian Customs before you travel if you intend to import any weapons. There are strict rules about carrying firearms and dangerous goods such as fireworks and flammable liquids in aircraft. If you wish to do so, contact your airline for advice before you travel.

Plants & Animals

Australia is free from many of the world's worst animal and vegetable diseases and from pests that afflict many other regions of the world, and it has strict quarantine regulations to ensure that it remains

that way. **All food or goods of plant or animal origin must be declared on your Incoming Passenger Card.** This includes the following:

- gifts and souvenirs made from plants or animals, or that contain plant or animal material (such as feathers, seeds or skin);

- any bottled, dried, fresh or cooked, packaged or tinned food products, e.g. beans, confectionery, eggs and egg products, herbal medicines, herbs and spices, honey and bee products, jams, meat and meat products, milk and dairy products, nuts, sauces, and teas and beverages;

- any food from meals you were served on the aircraft or ship;

- animal products, including bee products, bones, feathers, hair, hunting trophies, rawhide, shells, skins and hides, and wool (see also **Protected Species** below);

- plants and plant products, including bamboo, cane and rattan items, fresh and dried flowers, pine cones, potpourri, seeds, straw objects such as corn dollies, wood carvings and wreaths;

- live animals, which can be imported only with a valid import permit (see page 410).

There are also restrictions on taking fruit and vegetables (produced in Australia) between certain states.

If you have prohibited or unwanted items that you don't wish to declare, you can drop them in the quarantine bin on the way to collect your luggage. Declared goods won't automatically be confiscated and in most cases they're simply inspected by a quarantine officer and returned to you, although some items may require treatment (e.g. fumigation). Quarantine inspections have been strengthened in recent years and on-the-spot fines of up to around $250 are imposed for minor offences.

For further information contact the Australian Quarantine and Inspection Service (AQIS), PO Box 858, Canberra, ACT 2601 (☎ 1800-020504 free within Australia or ☎ 02-6272 3933 from outside Australia, 🖳 www.daff.gov.au/aqis), which publishes information leaflets about what can and cannot be taken into Australia.

Protected species: Australia has laws which strictly regulate the import and export of wildlife and products made from the bones, feathers, shells, skins, etc. of protected species. Wildlife or any accessories, clothing, handbags, ornaments, shoes, souvenirs, trophies, etc. made from protected species are seized by customs on arrival. Travellers are particularly warned of restrictions on items made from alligators and crocodiles (including gavials and caimans), cats (jaguars, leopards, tigers, etc.), elephants (especially ivory and hide products), giant clam shells, hard corals (including black coral), lizards and monitors (goannas), orchids (including live orchids), rhinoceros, snakes, turtles, whales and zebras.

> ### ⚠ Caution
>
> **Some overseas retailers provide certificates and other guarantees stating that their products are made from protected animals specially bred in captivity and legally farmed for by-products, such as their skins. Such certificates aren't recognised in Australia.**

The only document recognised by Australian Customs is an import permit from The Department of the Environment and Water Resources, GPO Box 787, Canberra, ACT 2601 (☎ 02-6274 1111, 🖳 www.environment.gov.au). Import permits may be issued by this Department, provided that export approval has been obtained from the relevant wildlife authority in the country where you made the purchase, and where Australian wildlife import requirements have been met.

Telephones & CB Radios

The importation of cordless telephones and citizen band (CB) radios is prohibited unless they're approved by the Australian Spectrum Management Agency (SMA). Only importers authorised by the SMA and the Australian Telecommunications Authority (AUSTEL) who comply with strict conditions may bring cordless telephones into Australia. Approved cordless telephones must display an approval number and an AUSTEL 'permit to connect' authorisation number. Cellular mobile telephones and facsimile machines can be freely imported – though you should check that they will work in Australia (see **Chapter 7**).

Visitors & Temporary Residents

In addition to the usual duty-free concessions (see page 386), visitors and temporary residents coming to Australia for a limited period may bring most articles into the country duty and tax free, provided customs is satisfied that they're for your personal use and will be taken out of Australia on your departure. Permitted articles include a caravan, motor vehicle, trailer, yacht or other craft to Australia (for up to 12 months, or longer under certain circumstances). However, you may be required to lodge a cash or bank security with customs to the value of the duty and tax otherwise payable. Customs determine the form of security acceptable in each case and, if you don't take the articles with you when you leave Australia, you must pay the duty and tax assessed. Before shipping any articles to Australia which you think will qualify for this concession, you should contact a customs office for advice (see **Appendix A**). This concession isn't available if you're migrating to Australia or a returning resident.

Migrants & Returning Residents

If you're coming to Australia to take up permanent residence for the first time or returning to resume permanent residence, you may import belongings, furniture and household articles that you've owned and used overseas for at least 12 months before your departure for Australia duty and tax free. Migrants may also bring machinery, plant and other equipment to Australia duty and tax free provided certain conditions are met. For example, commercial equipment imported tax and duty free mustn't be hired, mortgaged, sold or otherwise disposed of during your first two years in Australia. Duty-free concessions don't apply to goods arriving

☑ SURVIVAL TIP

Household effects are inspected on arrival in Australia for possible illegal and quarantine risk items. A list of all the items you're importing is required if you pack them yourself.

in Australia as unaccompanied effects (see below).

Unaccompanied Effects

The Australian Customs Service is responsible for the clearance of all unaccompanied effects from overseas. Unaccompanied personal effects can be cleared by the owner, a nominee appointed by the owner or a customs broker (a list of brokers, who charge a fee for their services, is published in the yellow pages). If you don't use a broker, you must contact the local state or territory customs office to arrange clearance and must produce your passport and complete an *Unaccompanied Effects Statement* (form B534).

Your effects can be cleared through customs before your arrival, provided you're arriving in Australia within six months of the arrival of your belongings. If you employ an international company (see **Moving House** on page 102), they handle the associated paperwork and customs clearance for you.

Australian Customs publish an *Unaccompanied Effects* leaflet providing further information.

EMBASSY REGISTRATION

Nationals of some countries are required to register with their local embassy or consulate as soon as possible after arrival in Australia. Even if registration isn't compulsory, most embassies like to keep a record of their nationals resident in Australia (if only to help justify their existence) and it may help to expedite passport renewal or replacement or evacuation in the event of an emergency.

FINDING HELP

One of the biggest difficulties facing new arrivals in Australia is how and where to obtain help with day-to-day problems – for example, finding a home, a school or insurance. This book was written in response to this need. However, in addition to the comprehensive information provided here, you also require detailed local information. How successful you are in finding help depends on your employer, the town or area where you live (e.g. those who live and work in a major city are much better served than those living in rural areas), your nationality and English proficiency, even your sex.

Obtaining information isn't a problem, as there's a wealth of information available in Australia on every conceivable subject (from astronomy to zoology). The problem is sorting the truths from the half-truths, comparing the options available and making the right decisions. Much information isn't intended for foreigners and their particular needs. You may find that your acquaintances, colleagues and friends can help, as they're often able to proffer advice based on their own experiences and mistakes. **But beware!** Although they mean well, you're likely to receive as much irrelevant and conflicting information as helpful advice.

The Department of Immigration and Citizenship, which has at least one office in each state and territory (listed, along with telephone numbers, on its website, 🖳 www.immi.gov.au), provides some basic post-arrival facilities and services, including English-language tuition for adult migrants, migrant community services and a translating and interpreting service (see the website for details), and there's a wealth of settlement programmes for migrants run by individual states and territories. Contact your state or territory government (using the telephone directory) for details. A limited number of hostels (in Melbourne and Sydney) and self-contained apartments are provided for immigrants with nowhere to stay on arrival, although they're drab, depressing places, mostly used by refugees. Government programmes for immigrants include an adult migrant English programme, a grant-in-aid scheme (mainly for refugees), migrant resource centres, telephone interpreter services, translation services and welfare assistance. Some states offer extra help to immigrants.

Many people find their first few weeks or months in Australia stressful, so it helps if you're prepared for a turbulent time. There are over 30 migrant resource centres in major cities and towns, which provide newcomers with counselling and contacts to help them overcome initial problems. The British newspaper *Australian News* (see **Appendix B**) has a 'pen pals' page through which prospective migrants can make contact with recent migrants already in Australia, which helps ease the culture shock.

Telephone interpreter services are available 24 hours a day throughout the country for the cost of a local telephone call (☎ 13-1450). Operators speak several languages and can provide information on accommodation, education, health, insurance, legal and police matters, social welfare and a wide range of other topics. There are also translation units in Canberra, Melbourne and Sydney, and translations can be obtained via the telephone interpreter service (a fee may be charged for documents other than migrant settlement documents).

Citizens' Advice Bureaux (CABs), libraries, local council offices and tourist offices are excellent sources of reliable information on a wide range of subjects. Some companies may have a department or staff whose job is to help new arrivals, or they may contract this job out to a local company. If a woman lives in or near a major town, she's able to turn to many women's clubs and organisations for help (single men aren't so well served).

There are numerous expatriate associations, clubs and organisations in Australia's major cities and large towns (including 'settlers' or 'friendship' associations) for immigrants from most countries, providing detailed local information regarding all aspects of life in Australia, including health services, housing costs, schools, shopping and much more. Many organisations produce booklets, data sheets and newsletters, operate libraries, and organise a variety of social events, which may include day and evening classes ranging from cooking to English classes. For a list of local clubs, look under 'Clubs and Associations' in the yellow pages.

> The Department of Immigration and Multicultural and Indigenous Affairs can put you in touch with clubs and societies in the city or area where you plan to live in Australia.

Most embassies and consulates provide information bulletin boards (accommodation, jobs, travel, etc.) and keep lists of social clubs and societies for their nationals, and many businesses (e.g. banks and building societies) produce books and leaflets containing useful information for newcomers. Libraries and bookshops usually have books about the local area (see also **Appendix B**).

Before Arrival

The following list contains a summary of the tasks that should (if possible) be completed before your arrival in Australia:

- Obtain an international driving permit, if necessary.

- Obtain an international credit card if you don't have one, which will prove invaluable during your first few months in Australia.

- Collect and update your records, including those relating to your family's dental, educational, employment (including job references), insurance (e.g. car insurance), medical and professional history.

Don't forget to bring all the above documents with you, plus bank account and credit card details, birth certificates, death certificate (if a widow or widower), divorce papers, driving licences, educational diplomas and professional certificates, employment references, insurance policies, marriage certificate, medical and dental records, receipts for any valuables you're bringing with you and student ID cards. You also need any documents which were necessary to obtain your visa, plus numerous passport-size photographs.

After Arrival

The following list contains a summary of tasks to be completed after arrival in Australia (if not done before):

- On arrival at an Australian airport or port, have your visa cancelled and passport stamped, as applicable.

- If you don't own a car, you may wish to rent one for a week or two until you buy one locally (see Chapter 11). It's difficult or impossible to get around in rural areas without a car.

- Register with your local embassy or consulate.

- If you plan to work in Australia, you will need to obtain a tax file number (TFN) as soon as possible.

- Obtain a visa (if applicable) for all your family members. Obviously this must be done before arrival in Australia.

- If possible, visit Australia before your move to arrange schooling for your children, compare communities and find a job.

- Arrange temporary or permanent accommodation.

- Arrange for the shipment of your personal effects to Australia.

- Arrange health insurance for your family. This is essential if you won't be covered by Medicare on your arrival in Australia.

- Open a bank account in Australia and transfer some funds (you can open an account with most Australian banks from overseas). You should also obtain some Australian currency before your arrival in Australia, which will save you having to change money immediately on arrival.

● Open a bank account at a local bank and give the details to your employer. This should be done within six weeks of arrival, during which period your passport is sufficient identification (after six weeks other proof of identification is necessary). If you don't have a permanent address, you can pay to use a 'travellers' contact point', which provides post holding and email services; look in the yellow pages under 'mail holding' or 'mail addresses' for companies (e.g. Travellers Contact Point, ▯ www.travellers.com.au) that provide these services.

● Apply for a Medicare Card at a Medicare office.

● Arrange schooling for your children.

● Find a local doctor and dentist.

● Arrange whatever insurance is necessary, including car, health, home contents and personal liability insurance.

Ayers Rock (Uluru), NT

Perth, WA

5.
ACCOMMODATION

Australia is a highly urbanised society, where over 70 per cent of the population lives in the main cities situated on or near the coast, including Adelaide, Brisbane, Canberra, Darwin, Melbourne, Perth and Sydney, all of which have unique characters and attractions. Only some 15 per cent of Australians live in rural areas. The vast majority of Australians live in detached bungalows on individual plots, although apartments are common in inner cities and coastal areas, and townhouses are popular in the suburbs.

The rate of home ownership in Australia is one of the highest in the world, and higher than both the UK and the US: around 68 per cent of householders own their home, subject to a mortgage, and around half of these own outright, while only just over 20 per cent rent (the remainder being in public/social housing or living with relatives, etc.). Most Australians expect to be buying their own homes by the time they reach their 30s, although in recent years more people have been renting and many people under 35 have dropped out of the homeownership market altogether. In an attempt to reverse this trend, the government has introduced housing grants for first-time home buyers.

After fluctuating fortunes in the '80s and '90s, the Australian property market underwent a period of rapidly rising prices until the third quarter of 2003. Several rises in interest rates, combined with an oversupply of property, have since contributed to a market slowdown and falls in some areas and sectors of the market. Sydney has been the worst affected – prices here fell by 0.1 per cent during 2006 while prices nationally rose by 8.3 per cent. On the other hand, homes in Perth increased by nearly 37 per cent and in Darwin by almost 18 per cent. In the first half of 2007, there were still huge regional variations: prices in Brisbane rose by 15.7 per cent and those in Adelaide by 11.7 per cent, but although those in Darwin and Perth increased by 7.4 and 15.3 per cent respectively, both cities saw negative prices rises in the second quarter of the year (Darwin -1.4 per cent and Perth -0.9 per cent). In mid-2007, the average national house price was $431,200 (seven times the average annual wage, compared with just four times in 1996) and those in the capital cities were $525,500 in Sydney, $446,500 in Perth, $428,000 in Canberra, $362,500 in Brisbane, $420,000 in Melbourne, $395,000 in Darwin and $310,000 in Hobart and Adelaide.

Analysts generally agree that the Australian property market is 'recovering', but most don't expect full recovery until late 2008. Some experts are predicting that higher mortgage rates will lead to many forced sales, particularly at the lower end of the market, bringing prices down in many suburban areas. Properties in some cities

– notably Perth – are considered to be over-priced and are therefore expected to fall.

Property price indexes can be found on several websites including 🖳 www.residex.com.au and 🖳 www.homepriceguide.com.au, and there are specialist property magazines such as *Australian Property Investor*, which monitors the latest so-called hotspots (the website 🖳 www.hotspotting.com.au provides a similar service). You can find out the price of homes in any Sydney suburb through the *Sydney Morning Herald Home Price Guide*, which lists all the sales results (both auction and private treaty) in Sydney suburbs for the last 12 months (it can be ordered online from Australian Property Monitors, 🖳 www.apm.com.au). A similar service is provided by newspapers in other major cities, and you can also peruse property advertisements in a number of publications on the internet (e.g. 🖳 www.sydneyproperty.com.au). For more information on the Australian property market, please refer to this book's new sister-publication, *Buying a Home in Australia* (see page 477).

⚠️ Caution

In most cities and regions of Australia there's a wealth of property for sale, so it's a buyer's market, but finding good rental accommodation isn't so easy, particularly in major cities such as Sydney and Melbourne.

In Sydney, rental property at affordable prices is in high demand and short supply, and rents are high. Accommodation generally accounts for around 30 per cent of the average Australian family's budget, but can rise to as much as 50 per cent in major cities. (Around 18 per cent of Australians move house every year and the average person has 11 addresses during his lifetime.) Homelessness is a huge and growing problem in Australia.

MOVING HOUSE

Shipping your belongings to Australia takes just a few weeks from Europe or North America, although it can be two to three months from the time your belongings are collected to the time they arrive at your new home in Australia. Unless you plan well in advance, you'll almost certainly arrive in Australia before your belongings.

A removal company (called a removalist in Australia) usually sends a representative to carry out an inspection and provide an estimate. Obtain at least three written quotes before choosing a company and check what the extra cost is if you need to increase the load later, as it isn't unknown for original estimates to escalate wildly. Some companies routinely increase the price after everything has been packed, ostensibly because more was included than was stated in the estimate. There are numerous advertisements from removal companies in newspapers published specifically for migrants, such as *Australian News* and *Australian Outlook* in the UK (see **Appendix B**).

If possible, always use an international removal company that's a member of an organisation such as the Association of International Removers (AIR), the International Federation of Furniture Removers (FIDI) or the Overseas Moving Network International (OMNI). Members usually subscribe to a payment guarantee scheme, whereby if a member company fails to fulfil its commitments to a customer, the removal is completed at the agreed cost by another company or you receive a full refund. Removal companies also pack your belongings and provide packing cases and containers, although this is naturally more expensive than doing it yourself (ask how they pack fragile and valuable items).

Check whether the cost of insurance and packing cases and materials is included in a quote.

You can send your effects by full container load (FCL) or part load (groupage), which usually takes longer. FCL shipments are loaded into an individual container holding around 1,000ft^3 (28m^3). A shipment of less than around 800ft^3 (22.5m^3) is cheaper to send as groupage. Obtain a separate quote for items that won't fit into a container. If the destination in Australia isn't within 30 miles (48km) of the port of arrival, you may need to pay an extra charge for door-to-door delivery. There may also be extra charges in Australia such as storage (if necessary). Ask about possible extra charges in advance. Most international removers expect to be paid before your goods are shipped, although some allow you to pay when you take delivery. The cost of moving your house contents from your previous country of residence to Australia may be paid for by your Australian employer.

Before shipping any household articles to Australia, check whether they're worth taking, e.g. many people take electrical apparatus that's incompatible and furniture which is unsuitable or simply isn't needed in their new home (see **Household Goods** on page 385). It isn't worthwhile taking cookers (which are usually provided), TVs (incompatible – see page 155) or wardrobes (built-in in most homes) – and it's illegal to import refrigerators. If you're moving from a country with a cold climate, bear in mind that furniture and furnishings must be suitable for a hot climate (unless you're heading for Tasmania). You should carefully consider the cost of packing and shipping large items to Australia, as it may be cheaper to sell them and buy new items on arrival. Good-quality furniture and antiques are worth taking, as are small electrical appliances if they require a 240V supply.

All containers are checked by customs on arrival, but because of the vast number arriving every day, it can take up to 14 days for a container to be checked. If you pack your belongings yourself, you must provide an inventory for Australian customs. If you do your own packing, use paper, wood or wool instead of straw, and don't include any prohibited or illegal items (see page 91), as customs and quarantine checks can be rigorous and penalties severe. On the day of the move, make sure there's room for the removal van or truck to park, if necessary by asking the police to cordon off an area outside your home. Give the shipping company a telephone number and an address in Australia through which you can be contacted, and try to get a relative or friend to handle any problems in the country from which your belongings are being shipped.

Be sure fully to insure your household contents during removal with a well established insurance company – you aren't required to use the one recommended by the removal company, which may not provide the best cover. You should have an all-risks marine insurance policy from domicile to domicile, which is underwritten by an established and solid insurance company. It's wise to make a photographic or video record of any valuables for insurance purposes. If you need to make a claim, be sure to read the small print, as all companies require you to make claims within a limited period. Your insurance cover may differ according to whether items were packed by you or by the shipper. Send a claim by registered post.

☑ SURVIVAL TIP

If you need to put your household effects into storage, it's imperative to have them fully insured, as warehouses have been known to burn down.

Don't forget to insure your home contents from the day you move in (see page 278).

Although most people wouldn't consider doing their own house move, if you have only personal effects to transport locally within Australia, you can hire a van by the hour, half-day or day (see **Car Hire** on page 214). Many removal companies sell packing boxes in various sizes and hire or sell removal equipment (trolleys, straps, etc.) for those who feel up to doing their own house move. See also the checklists in **Chapter 20**.

Relocation Companies

If you're fortunate enough to have your move to (or within) Australia paid for by your employer, he may arrange for a relocation company to handle the details. Relocation companies in Australia generally deal with corporate relocations rather than acting for individuals. In addition to providing school-, job- and house-finding services (see below), many relocation companies find business premises in Australia and relocate complete companies, including plant and machinery. Although you may consider a relocation company's services expensive, particularly if you're footing the bill yourself, most companies and individuals consider it money well spent.

There are relocation companies in all major cities in Australia. You can find one through The International Relocation Associates (*sic*) or TIRA, whose head office is in Geneva (Switzerland ☎ +41 79-406 1817, 🖥 www.tiranetwork.com) or look in your local yellow pages under 'Relocators'. One relocation company with offices throughout Australia is Australiawide Relocations, Abignano House, 19-23 Bridge Street, Pymble, NSW 2073 (☎ 02-9488 9444, 🖥 www.australiawiderelocations. com). Relocation companies provide some or all of the following services:

● **House hunting** – This is usually the main service, covering both rented and bought properties and normally including locating a number of properties matching your requirements and specifications and arranging for you to visit to Australia to view them. You should allow at least two months between your initial visit and moving into a purchased property. Rental properties can usually be found in two to four weeks, depending on the location and your requirements.

● **Negotiations** – Companies usually help and advise you on all aspects of house rental or purchase and may conduct negotiations on your behalf, organise finance (including bridging loans), arrange surveys and insurance, organise your removal to Australia and even arrange quarantine for your pets.

● **School reports** – Consultants usually provide a report on local schools (both state and private) for families with children. If required, the report can include private boarding schools.

- **Local information** – Most companies provide a comprehensive information package for a chosen area, including details of communications (e.g. the availability of cable or broadband internet connection), employment prospects, estate agents, local schools (state and private), public transport, shopping facilities, sports and social facilities, and state and private health services.

- **Other services** – Companies may provide advice and support (particularly for non-working spouses) both before and after a move, counselling for domestic and personal problems, help in finding jobs for spouses, orientation visits for spouses, and even marriage counselling (moving to another country puts a lot of strain on relationships). A relocation company may also find you a suitable car if one isn't provided by your employer.

AUSTRALIAN HOMES

Over three-quarters of Australia's 8m homes are detached houses, some 15 per cent are apartments, and around 10 per cent are semi-detached or 'row homes' (terraced homes or townhouses). The most common Australian family home is a detached, single-storey bungalow (ranch style) on a quarter or third of an acre plot. Typically, it has three or four bedrooms, a combined lounge/dining room, kitchen (possibly eat-in), bathroom (or two), separate toilet, laundry room, possibly a family or 'rumpus' room (which may be an extension of the kitchen), and a garage or car port. Bathrooms usually include a bath and separate shower cubicle and there may also be a shower room. Larger houses usually have two or more bathrooms,

the master bedroom having an en suite bathroom or shower. Larger homes may also have a study and other rooms. The mild climate allows year-round, outdoor living, and most detached homes have terraces or patios with a barbecue, and around half have a swimming pool.

Modern Homes

The quality of modern Australian homes is generally excellent. Construction may be brick (the most expensive material and generally reserved for luxury homes), brick veneer (the most popular), or weatherboard and fibre cement, known as fibro (the cheapest but no longer common). Brick veneer gives the outward appearance of a full brick construction, but the inner frame is made of timber and the inside is lined with plaster board or similar material. It costs less than a full brick home and is particularly suited to Australia's climate. A fibro house is a timber frame covered with fibre cement and weatherboarding on the outside and plasterboard on the inside. Roofs are

generally made of terracotta or cement tiles, although galvanised steel decking or fibre cement sheeting is often used in 'contemporary-style' homes.

In remote country areas, mains electricity, water and sewerage and telephone lines are a luxury, while dirt roads, generators, rain water tanks and septic tanks are common. Houses are raised on stilts in some tropical areas and areas subject to flooding, where the garage may be located below the living area.

When you buy a new home, bathroom, kitchen and light fittings, curtains and fitted carpets are usually included in the price, but wallpaper is rare in Australia, where interior walls are generally painted. Bedrooms normally have built-in wardrobes, and kitchens are fully fitted with a cooker and possibly even a dishwasher.

Fly screens are common on external doors and all windows, and allow you to leave the doors and windows open without inviting insects in. Good insulation helps keep homes cool in summer and warm in winter; in the southern states, homes may have a fireplace or a heating unit in the lounge. Air-conditioning may be fitted as standard in upmarket homes. Most semi-detached and detached houses have single or double garages (included in the price). New properties have a builder's warranty of up to six years from the date of completion.

Period Homes

There are many period homes in the inner suburbs of the major cities, most of which have been modernised and are now quite (or very) expensive. Terraced housing is found in some older inner-city suburbs, e.g. in Sydney, where decorative wrought ironwork is a feature of early homes, particularly in suburbs such as Paddington and Darlinghurst. Federation (early 19th century) houses made of wood and sandstone are also attractive and highly prized. In QLD, there are elevated timber and iron houses with balustrades and verandas (known appropriately as 'Queenslanders'), which allow cooling breezes to permeate homes.

On the other hand, there's also a vast amount of 'period' housing with no architectural merit or heritage value. Many homes built in the '50s and '60s building boom reflect the less sophisticated and enlightened ideas of that era and are entirely unsuited to today's lifestyle. In many cases, the plots they occupy are worth much more than the properties built on them.

Many period homes have problems such as damp, insect infestations, and poor electricity and plumbing installations.

Apartments

Apartments (flats), called units or home units in Australia, are common in inner city and beachside areas because of the high cost of land, although they aren't as widespread as in European cities and resorts. Apartments, particularly older apartments, aren't usually built or designed to the high standards found in North America or many European countries. Many older apartments are tiny, with poor storage and inadequate parking, and are lacking in quality fixtures and fittings. Apartments in Australia are sold freehold (under the Strata Titles Act).

Apartment blocks are usually purpose-built with up to 20 storeys and are rarely conversions of large old houses. Blocks may contain split-level apartments and penthouses (the latter traditionally occupying the whole top floor of a high-rise building) and usually have underground parking.

Many modern apartment blocks have communal pools and other facilities such as gymnasiums, saunas and tennis courts. QLD's Gold Coast has a large number of apartments in retirement villages, which include billiards rooms, bowling greens, croquet lawns, swimming pools and tennis courts, and are served by internal buses.

DUPLEXES

A duplex is the name for a building containing two apartments, one above the other. Duplexes are often the result of conversion of a large house into two dwellings, which tend to be larger than an average apartment. Grounds are shared but the apartments have separate entrances.

Mobile Homes

Mobile homes, also called transportable or manufactured homes because they're factory-built in two or more sections and erected on site, usually in around six weeks are popular in Australia, particularly among retirees. Many mobile homes look like conventional homes and include features such as bay windows, built-in wardrobes, skylights, verandas and even brick finishes. They can cost as little as $50,000 but at the top end of the market aren't much cheaper than conventional homes (i.e. around $300,000). Note that mobile homes are likely to depreciate over the years, rather than appreciate like a conventional home.

Mobile homes are usually sited in caravan parks or 'estates'. Sites must usually be leased, e.g. on a weekly or monthly basis, and you should beware of spiralling rents, which are endemic in most states (although some parks have rent controls). There are also a number of restrictions in parks, e.g. overnight fees for guests, and in some states owners even require the permission of park owners to sell.

For further information contact the Manufactured Housing Industry Association, PO Box H114, Harris Park, NSW 2150, ☎ 02-9615 9999, 🖳 www.mhiansw.com.au), which publishes an information booklet. The Queensland Government Office of Fair Trading publishes Buying or Living in a Manufactured Home, downloadable from 🖳 www.consumer.qld.gov.au.

TEMPORARY ACCOMMODATION

On arrival in Australia, you may find it necessary to stay in temporary accommodation for a few weeks (or even a few months) before moving into permanent accommodation or while waiting for your personal effects and furniture to arrive from overseas. In most large towns and cities, holiday apartments or flats are available, which are usually self-contained and fully furnished with their own bathrooms and kitchens. They're cheaper than hotels (e.g. 25 to 50 per cent less than a standard hotel double room), have over twice the space and are more convenient, particularly for families. Serviced apartments can usually be rented on a weekly basis. Single people and married couples (without children) may be able to find temporary accommodation in hostels.

There are a limited number of government hostels (e.g. in Melbourne and Sydney) and self-contained apartments for migrants with nowhere to stay on arrival, although these are usually drab, depressing places and are mostly used by refugees.

For information about bed and breakfast, hostels, hotels and self-catering, see **Chapter 15**.

RENTED ACCOMMODATION

Renting (rather than buying) a home is usually the better choice for anyone who is staying in Australia for a few years or less, when buying isn't usually practical, as well as the solution for those who don't want the expense and restrictions involved in buying and owning a home. If you're a migrant and intend to buy a property, it's sensible to rent for a period first, particularly if you're unsure where you'll be living or working. There's also the likelihood that you'll change jobs or states within your first few years in Australia or even decide to return home. Renting allows you to become familiar with a neighbourhood, the people and the weather before deciding whether you want to live somewhere permanently.

There isn't as strong a rental market in Australia as in some other countries (although it's becoming more popular in the major cities). Almost 70 per cent of homes are owned, only just over 20 per cent rented, and renters are sometimes made to feel like second-class citizens. However, while renting used to be regarded primarily as a temporary or transitional situation, rising house prices have seen it become an increasingly permanent phenomenon, some 40 per cent of renters doing so for ten years or more and some never being in a position to buy.

Rented accommodation has traditionally been in short supply in most major cities, particularly in Sydney, Brisbane and Melbourne, and the recent stagnation of the property purchase market has seen more people looking for rented accommodation, resulting in a further decline in availability and a rise in rental prices of 10 to 12 per cent per year. Some landlords are cashing in on their luck by auctioning properties to let – the highest bidder gets the rental.

If you're planning to rent for more than a few weeks, it's wise to investigate the rental market in your chosen area before arriving in Australia, e.g. by studying the advertisements in Australian newspapers (which can be done on the internet) and contacting agents. Temporary accommodation (see above) can usually be arranged before arrival, but you shouldn't rent a property long term without inspecting it first; in fact, most estate agents don't allow you to so and you must fill out a pre-rental inspection report before you move in.

Furnished accommodation is naturally more expensive than unfurnished and is even more difficult to find. Some landlords don't allow pets or smokers, so check whether any restrictions apply in advance.

Despite its increasing popularity, renting in Australia is a precarious business. The majority of contracts are short term (often as little as six months), with no guarantee of renewal and no controls or limits on rent increases a landlord can apply. Add to this the fact that you can be evicted at short notice at any time for any reason and you may decide to buy instead.

Finding a Rental Property

Your success or failure in finding a suitable rental property depends on many factors, not least the type of property you're looking for (a one-bedroom apartment is easier to find than a four-bedroom detached house), how much you want to pay and the area where you wish to live. Good rental accommodation is in short supply in major cities, particularly Sydney, Brisbane and Melbourne, with the possible exception of luxury homes with astronomical rents. There are sometimes 20 to 30 applicants for each vacant property in popular suburbs, particularly homes with three or more bedrooms, and you may have to take what you can get – but at least it costs you nothing to apply. Most people settle for something in the outer suburbs and commute to work. However, if you need to travel into a city centre (particularly Sydney) each day, you should be prepared to spend at least an hour or longer travelling each way from the outer suburbs.

There are a number of ways to find a rental property, including the following:

- Ask acquaintances, friends and relatives to spread the word. A lot of rental properties are found by word of mouth, particularly in Sydney and Melbourne, where it's difficult to find somewhere with a reasonable rent unless you have connections (many rental properties change tenants without ever coming onto the market).

- Check the advertisements in local newspapers and magazines (see below). The best day for advertisements is Saturday.

- Visit letting agents and estate agents, who also act as letting agents (all cities and large towns have both – look under 'Real Estate Agents' in the yellow pages).

- Look for advertisements in shop windows and on notice boards in company offices, shopping centres, supermarkets, and universities and colleges.

- Check newsletters published by churches, clubs and expatriate organisations, and their notice boards.

Nobbys Head lighthouse, Newcastle, NSW

To secure accommodation through advertisements in local newspapers, you must be quick off the mark, particularly in the cities.

Buy newspapers as soon as they're published, and start telephoning 'at the crack of dawn'; even then you're likely to find a queue when you arrive to view a property in Sydney, Brisbane or Melbourne. You must be available to inspect properties immediately and at any time. Some people will go to any lengths to secure a rental property, including offering to pay above the asking price (bidding wars sometimes break out), paying six months' rent in advance and signing a contract for two or three years.

Most properties in Australian cities are let through agents, whose main task is to vet prospective tenants. Always dress smartly when visiting properties or agents' offices in order to create a good impression. When registering with an agent, you need two forms of identification (e.g. driving licence and passport), written references from your employer and/or previous landlord, and character references. Agents usually contact all referees and may ask why you left your previous accommodation. If you have a pet, you may need a reference from your previous landlord stating that it was clean and well behaved, but animals aren't usually permitted in rented apartments. You must complete a registration form and should ensure that it's correct in every detail, or you might jeopardise your chances.

Single parents, students, the unemployed and young people have a tough time finding anywhere at an affordable price and, if you're on a low income or are unemployed, you must prove that you can pay the rent. Some people (e.g. Africans and Asians) may encounter discrimination, although it's illegal under the Federal Discrimination Act. If you pass muster, you may be given the keys to view a property in return for a $50 deposit and proof of identity.

⚠️ **Caution**

If you wish to vacate a property before your lease expires, you're liable to pay the rent up to the end of your lease period, although you may be able to find someone to take over the lease and repay your bond (check with your agent or landlord whether this is possible).

Rental Costs & Payment

Rental costs vary considerably according to the size (number of bedrooms) and quality of a property, its age and the facilities provided. Not least, rents depend on the region, city and neighbourhood. Rents are lower in rural than urban areas and, as a general rule, the further a property is from a large city or town, public transport or other essential facilities, the cheaper it is.

Average rents tend to be highest in Sydney, Melbourne and Darwin. Approximate weekly rents for unfurnished properties are shown below:

Type of Property	Weekly Rent
Studio/bedsitter	$150 to $250
1-bedroom apartment	$150 to $500
2-bedroom apartment	$175 to $550
3-bedroom apartment	$200 to $650
2-bedroom house	$300 to $500
3-bedroom house	$250 to $800

The lower rents quoted above apply to modest homes in the less expensive areas in or around cities Adelaide and Perth (or in Tasmania). The upper prices apply to more popular areas in and around Sydney, Melbourne, Brisbane and Darwin. They don't include properties in the central business district (CBD) of major cities or in exclusive residential areas, for which the sky's the limit: you can easily pay $2,000 per week for a swanky two-bedroom apartment in a smart part of Sydney. It may be possible to find older apartments and houses for less than the minimum rents shown above, but they're rare, are generally small and don't contain the standard fixtures and fittings of a modern home.

Rents are controlled in some states, although this doesn't usually extend to new properties or tenancies after a certain date. Your contract may include details of when your rent is to be reviewed or increased, if applicable (the rent for a fixed-term tenancy can be increased only when provision for an increase is included in the lease contract). You must be given notice in writing of any rent increases and a rent tribunal can review excessive rent increases and the existing rent if services are reduced. It's best to pay your rent by cheque or standing order, for which you should (by law) receive a receipt from your landlord.

Fees & Bonds

A fee of two weeks' rent for a one-year lease and one week's rent for a six-month lease are the legal maximum fees, but most agents charge less than this. Usually, you're expected to pay one month's rent in advance, depending on the type of property and the rental agreement, plus a bond (see below) against damage. **Beware of hidden extras such as a fee for connecting the electricity, gas or telephone.**

When renting property in Australia, a bond (deposit) must be paid in advance. The bond is usually equal to between four and six weeks' rent (normally higher for furnished than unfurnished properties), and can be as much as eight months' rent for a luxury furnished property (the bond is unlimited in Queensland on properties costing over $500 per week). If your accommodation is subsidised by your employer, there may be a lower maximum bond. The bond is lodged with the state or territory rental authority, e.g. the Residential Tenancies Authority in Queensland or the Residential Tenancies Tribunal in South Australia, together with a copy of the inspection (condition) report. Information regarding rental bonds can be obtained from ☎ local call rate 13-3220.

Rental Contracts

When you find a suitable house or apartment to rent, you should insist on a written contract with the owner or agent, which is called a tenancy agreement. In some states, such as NSW and Victoria, a standard form must be used by law, and in others there are usually minimum conditions which cannot be reduced by landlords. The tenancy agreement states the responsibilities of both parties.

Although these are fairly balanced between landlord and tenant, you should read an agreement carefully before signing it. Apart from self-catering holiday accommodation (see page 322), renting a house or apartment usually requires a commitment of at least 6 or 12 months with an option to renew.

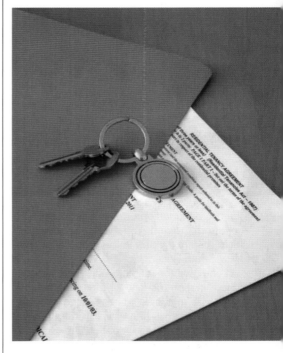

The owner is responsible for property tax (council rates) and unit service charges, and the tenant for utility costs, unless otherwise agreed. If you rent a house with a garden and swimming pool, maintenance costs may be included in the rent. Tenants must take good care of the property, although the landlord is required to maintain it in a habitable condition and ensure that basic services such as water and sewerage are in order. If the landlord refuses to carry out urgent and necessary repairs within a reasonable period, you can arrange to have them done and send him

use or to sell it with vacant possession; he isn't required to state his reason for terminating a contract.

Most states have a Residential Tenancy Tribunal, which handles complaints by landlords and tenants, and disputes over bonds, evictions, excessive rents and repairs, and there may be grounds for a tenant to appeal against termination, e.g. age, lack of alternative accommodation or poor health.

You can obtain advice regarding rental contracts from a citizens' advice bureau, community legal centre, consumer affairs office, legal aid commission or tenants' advice centre. Most large cities also have a tenants' union hotline. The local Office of Fair Trading in many states publishes a *Renting Guide* or *Tenants' Rights Manual* (in NSW see 🖳 www.fairtrading.nsw.gov. au), and similar guides are available from estate agents.

Inspection

One of the most important tasks on moving into a rented house or apartment is to complete (or check) an inventory of the contents and make an inspection report on its condition. This includes the condition of fixtures and fittings, the state of furniture and carpets (if furnished), the cleanliness and state of the decoration, and anything missing or in need of repair. (A rental property should be spotless when you move in, as this is how your landlord will expect you to leave it when you move out.) An inventory is normally provided by your landlord or a letting agent and may include every single item in a furnished property (down to the number of teaspoons).

The inventory and inspection report must usually be completed within seven days of taking possession and you receive a copy signed by you and the agent or landlord. A copy is also lodged with the state or territory rental authority. The property is re-inspected when you leave and, if

the bill, although you mustn't deduct the cost from the rent. You may be required to have a smoke alarm in the property (e.g. in New South Wales).

If you give the landlord adequate notice of termination (usually 21 days), he should attempt to minimise his loss by advertising and re-letting the property. If you have an oral contract (termed a periodic tenancy), renewed on a weekly or monthly basis, a week's or a month's notice is sufficient.

Whether you have an oral or a written agreement, you cannot be evicted or forced to leave unless your landlord obtains an eviction order. In order to be evicted you must be in breach of your lease, e.g. by damaging the property, failing to pay the rent, refusing the landlord entry, renovating without permission or sub-letting. A landlord cannot remove your belongings, change the locks or cut off services in order to force you out. The landlord can terminate a fixed-term agreement by giving 60 days' notice. He may repossess a property for his own necessary, deductions are made from your bond for cleaning and repair, although there's no deduction for ordinary wear and tear.

Note the reading on your meters (electricity, gas and water as applicable) and check that you aren't overcharged on your first bill. Meters should be read by the relevant authorities before you move in, which you may need to organise yourself.

Single Accommodation

Finding accommodation that doesn't break the bank is a huge problem for young single people and students (and anyone not earning a small fortune). For many, the solution is a bedsit (see below), lodgings or shared accommodation. However, young people usually find it harder to find a rental property than mature people, because of the prejudice that the young are grubby, itinerant, noisy, poor, unreliable, untidy, etc.. Particularly when a new term starts and students are looking for housing, there's a huge demand for single accommodation (often from overseas students) in the major cities, especially in Sydney and Melbourne. In some cities, students have saturated the rental market, and foreign students who are prepared (and able) to pay more for accommodation than Australian students have helped drive up rents and exacerbate the problem. Don't expect any luxuries in inexpensive single accommodation, as the standard is generally poor and is usually at its worst in areas with high demand. You must be over 18 to hold a tenancy agreement.

Bedsits & Studios

If you prefer to live on your own but don't want to pay a lot of rent, the solution may be a bedsit or studio apartment. A bedsit usually consists of a furnished room in an old house, where you eat, live, sleep and, in some cases, also cook. If separate cooking facilities are provided, you must usually share them with someone else (or a number of people). You must also usually share a bathroom and toilet, provide your own linen (blankets, sheets and towels), and do your own laundry and cleaning. Bedsits offer privacy but can be lonely and depressing. A bedsit costs from around $150 per week.

Slightly up-market from a bedsit is a studio or flatlet, which may have its own bath or shower and toilet, and sometimes a separate kitchen or kitchenette (a tiny kitchen). The rent for a studio apartment is around 50 per cent more than for a bedsit.

Lodgings & Boarding Houses

Another possibility is to find lodgings in a private home, which is becoming increasingly common, as many people have been forced to take in lodgers to pay their mortgages. This is similar to bed and breakfast accommodation (see page 321) except that you're usually treated as a member of the family and your rent normally includes half-board (breakfast and an evening meal). In lodgings you have less freedom than in a bedsit or studio and are required to eat at fixed times, but at least you have company. Lodgings are often arranged by schools and colleges for foreign students.

A boarding house is similar to lodgings, where the owner takes in a number of lodgers and may provide half-board or cooking facilities. The rent is around the same as for bedsits (see above).

A boarder, lodger or paying guest (i.e. anyone lodging with the owner and sharing the bathroom and kitchen) is termed a 'licensee' in law and has fewer rights than a tenant. If you're a 'licensee', your landlord cannot increase your rent without your consent, although he can ask you to leave at any time (but must give you adequate time to pack and remove your belongings).

Shared Accommodation

Sharing is another answer to high rents, particularly in major towns and cities, and is popular among students and the young. It usually involves sharing the bathroom, dining room, kitchen and living room of a house or apartment, and may even include sharing a bedroom. All bills are usually also shared (in addition to the rent), including electricity, gas and telephone, and in some cases food bills, as well as chores such as cooking and cleaning. Some landlords may include electricity, gas and water in the rent. As always when living with others, there are advantages and disadvantages to shared accommodation, and its success depends on the participants' ability to live together.

If you rent a property with the intention of sharing, make sure that it's permitted in your contract. The law regarding flat-sharing is complicated. It's possible for all sharers to be joint tenants with one tenancy agreement or individual tenants with individual tenancy agreements. However, it's simpler when one person is the tenant and sub-lets to the others. Whatever the arrangement, you should have a single rent book and pay the rent in a lump sum. It's usually the occupants' responsibility to replace flatmates who leave during the tenancy.

The cost of sharing a furnished apartment or house varies considerably according to its size, location and amenities. A rough guide is from $150 (single) to $175 (double) per week with your own bedroom, or up to $250 with your own bathroom.

Sharing is particularly common in major cities, where many newspapers and magazines contain advertisements for flat-sharers, e.g. the *Sydney Morning*

Herald and the *Melbourne Age*. (Note that the phrase 'broad-minded girl/guy' in advertisements is usually code for 'we are lesbian or homosexual'.) There are also agents in major cities who, for a fee of $100 to $200, match sharers with similar interests.

BUYING A HOME

Whether you choose to rent of buy a property in Australia will depend largely on how long you're planning to stay there. Buying a house or apartment has traditionally been a good long-term investment. You shouldn't expect to make a quick profit when buying property in Australia and should look upon it as an investment in your family's future happiness, rather than merely in financial terms. This is particularly true in the current uncertain property market. Property values in Australia increased (sometimes dramatically) in the early years of the 21st century, but the market slowed considerably from 2005 to 2006, with falls in many regions. The 'experts' are predicting that 2007 is the beginning of the end of the general property recession, but recent increases in interest rates mean that mortgage payments now account for over 35 per cent of Australians' household income (the highest ever) and national housing affordability was at a record low in September 2007.

Before making an irrevocable decision regarding buying a home in Australia, you should do extensive research (see page 37), study the possible pitfalls and be prepared to rent for a period before buying (see page 110).

This section contains a summary of information relevant to buying property in Australia; for further details, refer to *Buying a Home in Australia* (Survival Books – see page 477).

Restrictions

Unlike many countries, where foreigners may buy a home without restriction, Australia has strict regulations governing the purchase of a property by foreigners, particularly non-residents. In many cases, foreigners must have approval from the Foreign Investment Review Board (FIRB), The Treasury, Langton Crescent, Parkes, ACT 2600 (▤ 02-6263 2940, ▨ www.firb. gov.au) before they may buy a home. The regulations vary according to your residence status, as described below.

Permanent Residents

The following permanent residents have no restrictions on buying a home in Australia and don't need prior approval from the FIRB:

- Australian and New Zealand citizens;

- holders of permanent resident visas (including new migrants);

- foreigners purchasing a home together with a spouse who is an Australian citizen.

Temporary Residents

Foreigners with a temporary residence visa (which must be valid for a period exceeding 12 months after you plan to buy the property) may buy new property in Australia but require FIRB approval. If you plan to buy a resale home, the FIRB normally approves the purchase under the following conditions:

- the property is to be your permanent residence;

- the property isn't let;

- the property is sold as soon as your visa expires or you leave Australia;

- the property costs under $300,000 (higher-cost purchases are approved under exceptional circumstances).

> ⚠️ **Caution**
>
> **Failure to obtain FIRB approval or meet FIRB requirements is a serious offence and can lead to prosecution and the possibility that you'll be unable to obtain a visa to visit or live in Australia in the future. In some cases, entry into Australia is refused.**

Application Procedure

If you need FIRB approval to buy a home, you should obtain this before committing yourself to a purchase. You may exchange contracts before you obtain permission, but one of the conditional clauses on the contract **must** state that your purchase is subject to FIRB approval.

You must complete R3 Form (available from the FIRB directly and downloadable from the website) and send it by post or fax (see above) together with the appropriate documentation (e.g. copy of passport, visa and information pages from the contract of sale). The FIRB is required to make a decision within 30 days of the application and to convey this to the interested parties within a further ten days.

Cost

Property prices vary considerably throughout the country and in the various suburbs of the major cities. Not surprisingly, the further you are from a town or city, the lower the cost of land and property. Properties in central and beach locations cost anywhere between two and four times as much as similar properties in less fashionable or convenient areas. Apartments are often as expensive as houses and townhouses (or even more so), as they're invariably located in city centres, whereas most houses are in suburbs or in the country. For many buyers it's a choice between a small apartment in an inner city and a large detached family home in the outer suburbs – in recent years the average Aussie battler (commuter) has had to move further and further into the outer suburbs of major cities in order to find affordable accommodation.

Advertised prices are usually around 3 to 8 per cent above a property's 'market value', so you can expect to negotiate a discount of this amount. A two single-storey home in most city outer suburbs is advertised at between $175,000 and $300,000; four-bedroom, two-storey homes cost from around $350,000 to $500,000.

There's a high demand everywhere for waterfront properties, which have generally been an excellent investment, particularly in Sydney, whose 20 most expensive suburbs are all waterfront (harbour or ocean). Waterfront properties in Sydney can be astronomically expensive, and a reasonable two-bedroom apartment in an attractive building with water views costs over $1m ($2m homes are commonplace in Sydney and Melbourne and on the White Sunshine Coast).

The table below shows average house and unit (apartment) selling prices in June 2007 (source: Real Estate Institute of Australia).

A few kilometres can make a huge difference to the price of a property, with apartments in central areas costing up to $2,500 per square metre more than those in harbour-side developments a few kilometres further out. Land prices also reduce considerably from around 15km (9mi) outside a city and are at their lowest around 25km (16mi) from city centres.

City	House/Unit Prices	
	Average Price	
	House	**Unit**
Adelaide	$310,000	$235,000
Brisbane	$362,500	$273,000
Canberra	$428,000	$330,000
Darwin	$395,000	$279,300
Hobart	$310,000	$243,000
Melbourne	$420,000	$350,000
Perth	$446,500	$360,000
Sydney	$525,000	$360,500

The cost of land varies from as little as $50,000 for a plot large enough for an average suburban house at least 25km from cities such as Adelaide, Hobart and Perth to over $400,000 for a similar plot within 15km of central Sydney (if you can find one). Even the cost of building a home varies with the location as well as with the quality of materials used. For example, brick veneer costs from around $800 to $1,000 per m², depending on the location.

Property price indexes can be found on several websites, including 🖳 www.residex. com.au and 🖳 www.homepriceguide. com.au, and there are specialist property magazines such as *Australian Property Investor*, which monitors the latest so-called hotspots (the website 🖳 www.hotspotting. com.au provides a similar service).

Fees

The fees associated with buying a home in Australia are usually lower than in many other countries, the maximum being around 7.5 per cent and the minimum, with stamp duty discounts (see below), as low as 1 per cent or even less in some cases. Total fees are usually between around 4 and 5 per cent. Most fees are calculated as a percentage of the value of the property you're buying, so the more expensive the property, the higher the fees. Even removal costs are higher if you have a large house (unless you have a lot of empty rooms). If you're buying **and** selling, you must consider the cost of both transactions. Bear in mind that fees change regularly and, in the current slow market, there are calls to reduce or abolish some of them, particularly state taxes such as stamp duty.

● **Stamp duty** – Stamp duty (known as transfer duty in QLD and duty in TAS) accounts for the largest slice of the fees involved in a property purchase and is payable on property transactions in all states, although rates and concessions (see below) differ enormously. Rates, which are calculating on a sliding scale in relation to the purchase price of a property, are published by state tax offices, whose websites include stamp duty calculators. Stamp duty must be paid within three months of purchase. The following table shows the stamp duty levied by individual states on properties costing $250,000, $400,000 and $500,000.

Stamp Duty			
State		**Purchase Price**	
	$250,000	**$400,000**	**$500,000**
ACT	$7,265	$13,515	$18,015
NSW	$7,240	$13,490	$17,990
NT	$9,312	$18,800	$26,750
QLD	$7,225	$12,475	$15,975
SA	$8,955	$16,330	$21,330
TAS	$7,550	$13,550	$17,550
VIC	$10,660	$19,660	$25,660
WA	$8,200	$15,700	$20,700

All states offer discounts or concessions on stamp duty for first-home buyers (usually including new arrivals in Australia) and some also offer discounts for the purchase of a principal home (you must usually live in the property for at least six months to qualify).

- **Land transfer registration fee** – This fee is payable to the Land Titles Office for recording a change of owner. It's either a flat fee or a variable fee based on the price paid and varies considerably with the state. The fee on a $200,000 property, for example, is $164 in QLD and $131 in TAS (fixed fees) and around $1,094 in South Australia (variable fee).

- **Legal & conveyancing fees** – Legal and conveyancing fees may vary according to the work involved and do vary considerably from state to state, e.g. from around $550 in Adelaide, Perth and Hobart to around $1,750 in Brisbane for a property costing over $100,000. The fees in most states are within the $550 to $1,100 range. Lawyers and conveyancers are generally free to set their own fees for conveyancing and should provide a written estimate of their fees before you use their services; in WA, however, conveyancers' (settlement agents') fees are set according to a fixed scale (see 🖳 www.sasb.wa.gov.au for details). Always check what's included in the fee and whether a quoted fee is 'full and binding' or just an estimate. A low basic rate may be supplemented by much more expensive 'extras' (called disbursements) such as costs relating to title searches, debt certificates and courier charges.

- **Mortgage fees** – A range of fees is associated with mortgages, including a mortgage application or establishment fee, a valuation fee, legal fees, mortgage stamp duty, maintenance fees and a loan registration fee (for mortgage information see page 294).

- **Inspection or survey fees** – Although it isn't compulsory to have a building inspection or a structural survey carried out, it's often wise, particularly when you're buying an old detached house. You should allow from $400 to $500 for a structural survey. According to Archicentre (🖳 www.archicentre.com.au), for a survey of a one-bedroom apartment you should expect to pay $395, for a two-bedroom apartment or house, $495 and for a four or five-bedroom house, $525. Costs are marginally lower in WA.

A termite and pest inspection costs from around $150 to $250 and may be paid by the vendor or buyer, or shared. Strata inspections cost from around $180 to $250.

- Building Insurance – It's invariably a condition of lenders that properties are fully insured against structural and other damage. It may be necessary to insure a property from the day you sign the purchase contract and you should allow for the cost of this in your calculations (see Building Insurance on page 276).

You also usually need to pay utility connection (or reconnection) fees for electricity, gas, telephone and water supplies. Removal costs must also be taken into account, as must property running costs, which include a caretaker's or management fees if you leave a home empty or let it, maintenance fees for a community property, building and contents insurance (see page 138), property taxes (see page 308), and standing charges for utilities (electricity, gas, telephone, water). Annual running costs usually average around 2 to 3 per cent of the cost of a property.

Estate Agents

Most property in Australia is bought and sold through estate agents (called real estate agents in Australia), who sell property on commission for owners, although you may buy directly from a vendor. When buying property through an agent in Australia, always ensure that he is licensed. The Real Estate and Business Agents Act imposes obligations and requirements on licensed agents, which protect both buyers and sellers by creating a source of legal redress in the event of error, loss, misrepresentation or negligence. The act protects deposits paid by buyers and prevents conduct which could be misleading or prejudicial to buyers, and is backed by disciplinary procedures and a Fidelity Guarantee Fund. The Act doesn't apply to private sales where no agent is involved.

The Real Estate Institute of Australia/ REIA, Level 1, 16 Thesiger Court (PO Box 9068), Deakin, ACT 2600 (☎ 02-6282 4277, 🖳 www.reiaustralia.com. au) is the umbrella organisation for estate agents' associations, e.g. the Real Estate Institute of New South Wales, and you should check with them that an agent is a member. State Offices of Fair Trading also offer help and advise on choosing an estate agent and can tell you if an estate agent is licensed.

In July 2000, the Property Agents and Motor Dealers Act came into force, whereby all estate agents are obliged to adhere to a code of conduct (of which you can request a copy) and incur harsh penalties for false or misleading representation. Estate agents must also have professional indemnity insurance and sign a disclosure form (see below), while clients have access to a Tribunal and Complaints Fund. In 2007, the REIA introduced its 'National Principles of Conduct', designed to encourage better ethics among its members.

Like many countries, estate agents in Australia don't enjoy a particularly good reputation and come tenth on the list of most-complained-about industries. However, the number of complaints received by the Australian Competition and Consumer Commission (the national consumer 'watchdog') about estate agents fell by 16 per cent in 2006.

There's a multi-listing service in all states, whereby homes can be advertised in estate agents' offices throughout the state, which costs vendors nothing until their home is sold. However, some agents may show you only, or at least try to push, properties for which they have an exclusive listing (when they don't need to share the commission with anyone else), so you should specifically ask to see properties that are multi-listed.

> ## ⚠ Caution
>
> Estate agents usually act for the seller and it's their job to obtain the highest price they can for a property, so don't expect impartial advice if you're a buyer. If they offer to make a considerable reduction on the advertised price, it probably means that the property is overpriced and has been on their books for a long time.

An estate agent usually tries to get you to view as many properties as possible (irrespective of whether they fit your requirements or price range), as this makes sellers think he's doing a good job.

Disclosure Form

Under Australian state law, estate agents are required to sign a disclosure form with a buyer **before** a purchase contract is drawn up. The form, known by different names in different states, e.g. a Disclosure Declaration in QLD and an Agency Agreement in NSW, includes information about the estate agent's relationship with the seller of the property (if any); details of the fees, commissions and any other remuneration that the estate agent will receive from the sale; and itemisation of the marketing and advertising costs for the sale. The form must be signed by the estate agent and the buyer.

Buying at Auction

Buying property at auction is popular in Australia, where between 30 and 50 per cent of properties (usually in cities) are brought under the auctioneer's hammer. Auctions have become increasingly popular in the last few years (they're most common in Melbourne and Sydney), as sellers can sell quickly and buyers can usually save money. If you have an eye for a bargain or enjoy the excitement of bidding, you may wish to consider buying a property at auction. However, it's absolutely vital to do your homework before buying at auction. In particular, you should ascertain the true market value of the property, arrange your finance, inspect the property thoroughly, check the conditions of purchase and carry out (or instruct your lawyer to do so on your behalf) checks on the property such as title, registration, debts and planning developments for the area around the property (see **Conveyance** below).

You also need to steel your nerves so that you don't get carried away and bid over your budget!

If you're interested in an auction property, you could consider making a pre-auction bid of around 20 to 30 per cent less than its market value. Prices fetched at auction are notoriously unreliable, and sellers who are 'jittery' may (legally) agree to a deal before the auction, in which case you could have yourself a bargain!

You can engage a buyer's representative to find a house, bid for it at auction and negotiate the sale. Agents may charge as little as a few hundred dollars to bid at an auction or up to 3 per cent of the price if they also conduct searches (regarding title, etc.). However, this can save you a lot of money, time and trouble.

Auction contracts rarely include conditional clauses such as purchase being subject to a favourable building inspection, which means buying at auction is riskier than a conventional purchase. In addition, cooling-off rights (see Contracts below) don't apply when buying at auction.

Contracts

Once a suitable property has been found and a price has been agreed between you and the vendor, both parties sign a contract of sale (also called an offer and acceptance). Contracts are published in standard form by the Law Society and the Real Estate Institute, although it's common for a lawyer or conveyancer to draw up a bespoke contract. Note that developers rarely allow anyone other than themselves to draw up a contract for the purchase of off-plan property. **You should never sign a contract without having it checked by a lawyer or conveyancer.** It's important to check that a property's particulars are complete in every detail and that the terms of sale are correct, including any changes made to the standard terms.

A government warning statement must be attached to the front of a contract of sale. The statement advises (in large, bold print) the buyer to obtain independent legal advice and an independent valuation of the property before signing the contract. It also lists the buyer's rights and explains the terms of the cooling-off period (see below). The buyer and estate agent must sign this statement in front of a witness. An example of a warning statement can be downloaded from the Queensland Government Department of Fair Trading's website (🖳 www.fairtrading.qld.gov.au – go to forms and 'PAMD Form 30c').

Contracts often contain conditional clauses, such as the sale being conditional on a clear survey, on finance being obtained or on approval for purchase from the Foreign Investment Review Board/FIRB (see **Restrictions** on page 115).

Conditions usually apply to events out of the control of the vendor or buyer, although almost anything agreed between the buyer and vendor can be included in a contract. If any conditions aren't met, the contract can be suspended or declared null and void and the deposit returned. However, if you fail to go through with a

purchase and aren't covered by a clause in the contract, you forfeit your deposit or might even be compelled to complete a purchase.

If any fixtures or fittings, such as carpets, curtains or furniture, are included in the purchase price, you should have them listed in an addendum to the contract.

A deposit is payable when you sign the contract of sale and in some cases you must also pay a small holding deposit (e.g. $1,000) as a sign of 'good faith'.

Most states entitle you to a cooling-off period after a contract has been signed, unless the contract specifies otherwise. The amount of time varies with the state: in SA you have two working (business) days, in the ACT and VIC three working days, and in NSW, NT and QLD five. There's no cooling-off period in TAS or WA. Working days are non-bank holidays from Mondays to Fridays from 9am to 5pm so if, for example, you sign a contract of sale in QLD on a Saturday, your cooling-off period is until 5pm on the following Friday.

During the cooling-off period, you have the right to withdraw from the purchase without losing your deposit, although you forfeit 0.25 per cent of the purchase price, known as the termination penalty. If you wish to withdraw from the purchase, you must notify the agent in writing within the cooling-off period. The agent or seller has 14 days to refund the 10 per cent deposit minus the termination penalty.

Note that vendors sometimes refuse to sell unless a certificate waiving the cooling-off period is signed.

CONVEYANCING

Conveyancing (or conveyance) is the legal term for the process of buying and selling property (real estate) and transferring the deed of ownership, a legal document that conveys a property from seller to buyer. There are two main stages of conveyancing: the first takes you up to the exchange of contracts; the second leads to the completion of the sale, when you become the new owner.

Conveyancing in Australia is usually done by a lawyer (solicitor) or a conveyancer (also called a land broker, land agent and settlement agent), although you can also do it yourself. Irrespective of whether you employ a professional or do your own conveyancing, the following should be done before a purchase:

- Verifying that a property belongs to the vendor or that he has legal authority to sell it.

- Checking for the existence of any clauses in the deeds restricting the use, development and possibly appearance of the property (known as restrictive covenants).

- Checking that there are no encumbrances or liens, e.g. mortgages or loans, against the property or any outstanding debts such as local taxes or utility bills – or that these are cancelled by the vendor before

completion (i.e. a conditional clause to that effect is inserted into the contract).

Caution

You must ensure that any debts against a property are cleared before you complete a purchase – a new owner is liable for any debts on a property once it's sold.

- Enquiring about any planned developments that may affect the value of the property (like a new airport runway or motorway at the bottom of the garden).

- Ensuring that planning or building permits are in order (e.g. for water, electricity and sewerage connection). You should also check the drainage or sewerage service diagrams for a home.

- Ensuring that the property has a pest inspection certificate.

- Ensuring that legal title is obtained and arranging the necessary registration of ownership and payment of taxes such as stamp duty.

If you're buying a community property, the following checks should also be carried out:

- In the case of a Company Title property, verifying that the other owners approve of your purchase.

- Verifying that all community levies on the property are up to date and there are no debts.

- Finding out if there's any imminent community expenditure that requires a high one-off payment.

- Checking that your enjoyment of the property won't be adversely affected by any community by-laws.

Inventory

When moving into a property that you've purchased, you should check that the previous owners haven't absconded with anything that was included in the purchase price (and detailed in the contract), such as carpets, curtains, doors, fitted cupboards, kitchen appliances and light fittings, or substituted inferior items. You should also note the reading on your meters (electricity, gas, water, etc.) and check that you aren't overcharged on your first bill. Meters should be read by the relevant authorities before you move in, which you may need to organise yourself.

UTILITIES

This section covers electricity, gas and water connections and supplies. The energy industry is regulated by state governments, and each state and territory has its own Energy Commission. The industry has been deregulated in six states (ACT, NSW, QLD, SA, TAS and VIC) and in these states consumers may choose from a number of energy providers. In NT and WA, the energy industry is still state run and in some cases (e.g. WA), energy companies are owned by state governments. Australia has a non-nuclear policy and has no nuclear power stations, despite being a major producer of uranium.

Immediately after buying or renting a property (unless utilities are included in the rent), you should arrange for meters (if applicable) to be read and services to be switched on.

Electricity

Australia's largest electricity companies (which often provide gas as well) include:

- **Actew AGL** (🖳 www.actewagl.com.au) – based in the ACT, supplying electricity, gas and water.

- **Aurora Energy** (🖳 www.auroraenergy. com.au) – Tasmania's electricity supplier, connected to nearly every household in Tasmania.

- **Australian Gas Limited** (AGL, 🖳 www. agl.com.au) – sells gas and electricity, and has 3m customers across Australia.

- **Energy Australia** (🖳 http://energy.com. au) – one of Australia's larger electricity and gas suppliers, providing energy to over 1.5m Australian homes and businesses. It currently operates in the ACT, NSW, South Australia and Victoria.

- **Ergon Energy** (🖳 www.ergon.com.au) – Queensland's electricity supplier, also operating in the ACT, NSW and Victoria. It has over 500,000 customers.

- **ETSA Utilities** (🖳 www.etsautilities. com.au) – the South Australia electricity distributor, with 765,000 customers.

- **Integral Energy** (🖳 www.integral.com. au) – the second-largest state-owned energy corporation in NSW, distributing electricity to over 2m people.

- **Power & Water** (⌨ www.powerwater.
  com.au) – the Northern Territory's major
  provider of electricity, sewerage and water
  services, with over 70,000 customers.

- **Western Power** (⌨ www.westernpower.
  com.au) – Western Australia's leading
  energy corporation, with around 800,000
  customers.

Power Supply

The electricity supply in Australia is
240/250 volts AC, with a frequency of
50 Hertz (cycles). Power cuts are rare in
most parts of the country, although fairly
frequent in some areas or during bad
weather. In remote areas where there's no
mains electricity, you must usually install a
generator, although some people make do
with gas and oil lamps.

A problem with some electrical
equipment is the frequency rating, which in
some countries, e.g. the US, is designed
to run at 60 Hertz (Hz) and not Australia's
50Hz. Electrical equipment without a
motor is generally unaffected by the
drop in frequency to 50Hz (except TVs).
Equipment with a motor may run with a
20 per cent drop in speed, but clocks,
cookers, record players, tape recorders
and washing machines are unusable if they
aren't designed for 50Hz operation. To find
out, look at the label on the back of the
equipment: if it says 50/60Hz, it should be
safe; if it says 60Hz, you can try it anyway,
but first ensure that the voltage is correct
(see below). If the equipment runs too
slowly, seek advice from the manufacturer
or the retailer.

> ☑ SURVIVAL TIP
>
> Bear in mind that the transformers and
> motors of electrical devices designed to
> run at 60Hz run hotter at 50Hz, so make
> sure that equipment has sufficient space
> around it for cooling.

Converters & Transformers

Electrical equipment rated at 110 volts (e.g.
from the US) requires a converter or a step-
down transformer, although some electrical
appliances (e.g. electric razors and hair
dryers) are fitted with a 110/240 volt switch.
Check for the switch, which may be located
inside the casing, and make sure it's
switched to 240 volts before connecting
it to the power supply. Converters can
be used for heating appliances but
transformers, which are available from
most electrical retailers, are required for
motorised appliances (they can also be
bought secondhand). Add the wattage
of the devices you intend to connect to a
transformer and make sure that its power
rating exceeds this sum.

Generally, all small, high-wattage,
electrical appliances such as heaters,
irons, kettles and toasters need large
transformers. Motors in large appliances
such as cookers, dishwashers, dryers,
refrigerators and washing machines need
replacing or fitting with a large transformer.
In most cases it's simpler to buy new
appliances in Australia, which are of good
quality and reasonably priced.

Plugs, Fuses & Bulbs

Unless you've come to Australia from
New Zealand, all your plugs will require
changing, or you'll need a lot of adapters.
Plug adapters can be difficult to find locally,
so you should bring a number of adapters
with you, although using these isn't
recommended it's better to use extension
leads fitted with local plugs. Australian and
New Zealand plugs have three pins: two
diagonally slanting flat pins above one
straight (earth) pin. Plugs aren't fused.
Some electrical appliances are earthed and
have a three-core flex – you must never
use a two-pin plug with a three-core flex.
Always make sure that a plug is correctly
and securely wired, as bad wiring can
prove fatal.

Most apartments and all houses have fuse boxes, which are usually of the circuit breaker type in modern homes. When a circuit is overloaded, the circuit breaker trips to the OFF position. When replacing or repairing fuses of any kind, if the same fuse continues to blow, contact an electrician and never fit a fuse of a higher rating than specified, even as a temporary measure. When replacing fuses, don't rely on the blown fuse as a guide, as it may have been wrong. If you use an electric lawnmower or power tools outside your home or in your garage, you should have a Residual Current Device (RCD) installed. This can detect current changes of as little as a thousandth of an amp and in the event of a fault (or the cable being cut) it switches off the power in a fraction of a second.

Electric light bulbs (called globes) in Australia are of the Edison type with a bayonet, not a screw fitting. Low-energy light bulbs are also available and, although more expensive than ordinary bulbs, save money due to their longer life and reduced energy consumption. Bulbs for non-standard electrical appliances (i.e.

appliances not made for the local market) such as lamps, refrigerators and sewing machines may be unavailable locally, so you should bring spares with you.

Installation & Registration

If the electricity supply is already connected in your new home, you should contact your local electricity company and have the account transferred to your name. Make sure you have the meter number and the current reading. Meters for an apartment block may be installed in a basement or in a meter 'cupboard' in a stair well or outside a group of properties. You should have free access to your meter and be able to read it.

If the electricity supply needs reconnecting, an electrician from the company must usually visit your home. You need to complete a registration form and should allow at least two days for reconnection, for which there's usually a charge, e.g. $60. If you move into a home without an electricity supply, the installation charge is usually around $750 – higher if the network has to be extended to reach your home.

Most companies require a security deposit (e.g. $80 or $200), although this may not be necessary if you agree to pay your electricity bills by direct debit. Your security deposit is usually refunded after 12 months if all payments have been made on time. You need to contact your electricity company to get a final reading when you vacate your home.

Tariffs

Electricity prices have risen over the last few years throughout Australia, e.g. tariffs increased by 8 per cent in NSW in July 2007 (state Energy Commissions review energy prices in July every year), and further rises are expected. Electricity charges vary considerably with the state and according to the extent of local competition. All tariffs are quoted are exclusive of GST, which is levied at 10 per cent. Most companies offer a range of tariffs which may include peak, off-peak, weekend and 'green' rates (some tariffs require a special meter to be installed). The biggest savings (up to 70 pre cent) can be made when using an off-peak rate for appliances such as washing machines and water heaters.

Bills

Electricity bills usually show meter readings, your consumption (in kWh), charges and your average daily use (shown as a monthly consumption/cost comparison). Customers are billed quarterly and payment can be made at certain banks, by direct debit, by post (by cheque), at post offices, by telephone or online directly to the electricity company (with a credit/debit card). Payment is usually due within 21 days.

Gas

Australia has vast natural gas reserves and mains gas is available in all of Australia's major cities and many other areas. The energy industry has been deregulated in all states with the exception of NT and WA, and in several areas consumers have a choice of mains gas providers, which usually provide electricity as well. For a list of the main companies see Electricity above.

Gas is popular for cooking (it costs less than electricity), although it's less commonly used to provide heating and hot water (though gas heaters are the most popular form of heating in WA). There may be no gas supply in older homes and some modern houses. If you're looking for a rental property and want to cook by gas, make sure it already has a gas supply (some houses have an unused gas service pipe), as it may be impossible

to connect a supply. Bottled gas, known as liquid petroleum gas (LPG), is widely available and comes in 4.5kg, 9kg and 45kg cylinders. When 45kg cylinders are empty, the gas company brings new cylinders to your home or fills up the empty ones from a delivery truck. Smaller empty cylinders must be taken to the gas company's local agency, where they're exchanged for a full cylinder.

Installation & Registration

Mains gas: If a home already has a gas supply, simply contact your local gas company to have the gas supply reconnected or transferred to your name (there's a connection charge). If you buy a house without a gas supply, you can arrange with your local gas company to install a line between your home and a nearby gas main (provided there's one within a reasonable distance, or the cost will be prohibitive). A security deposit (e.g. $120) is usually payable and there may also be a payment to establish an account (e.g. $25).

> **☑ SURVIVAL TIP**
>
> You must contact your local gas company to get a final reading when vacating a property.

Bottled gas: If a home already has a bottled gas supply, contact your local gas company to have the contract transferred to your name. If there's no supply, the gas company can install cylinders, for which there's usually an annual rental charge.

Tariffs

Mains gas tariffs vary tremendously from city to city (or even within a city and its suburbs) and region to region, and are generally more expensive in remote areas. Bottled gas prices also fluctuate widely.

Bills

Customers are billed quarterly and payment can be made at certain banks, by post (by cheque), at post offices or by telephone or online directly to the company (with a credit/debit card).

Water

Water, or rather the lack of it, is a major concern in Australia and the price paid for all those sunny days. Australia is the world's driest country, and many areas are frequently hit by droughts. Since 1870, Australia has suffered ten major droughts and 2006 was the 11th-driest year on record (it was the driest ever in Hobart and Victoria, and the second-driest on record in Adelaide). Climate change is expected to reduce rainfall still further, particularly over southern Australia. Yet despite this lack of water, Australia has one of the highest per capita water consumption rates in the world.

Each major city or state has a water board operated by the local government; the main water boards are as follows:

- ACT – ACTEW (💻 www.actew.com.au);
- NSW – Sydney Water (💻 www.sydneywater.com.au);
- NT – Power & Water (💻 www.powerwater.com.au);
- QLD – Queensland Water Commission (💻 www.qwc.qld.gov.au);
- SA – SA Water (💻 www.sawater.com.au);
- TAS – Hobart Water (💻 www.hobartwater.com.au);
- VIC – Our Water (💻 www.ourwater.vic.gov.au);
- WA – Water Corporation (💻 www.watercorporation.com.au).

Quality

Although Australian drinking water is among the cleanest and safest in the world, the quality varies and it can taste terrible in areas with high mineral deposits. It's possible to have a water purifier fitted to a drinking water tap to improve the taste. Fluoride is added to water in some cities. Australian water doesn't usually contain much lime, so it isn't necessary to use a decalcification liquid to keep your iron,

kettle and other apparatus and utensils clean.

> ⚠ **Caution**
>
> Contaminated water in garden hoses and domestic swimming pools can cause amoebic meningitis, so it's important to clean pools and hoses thoroughly and frequently.

Supply

An important task before renting or buying a home in Australia is to investigate the reliability of the local water supply and the cost. Ask your prospective neighbours and other local residents for information. Many country homes have a bore (well), which comes in handy when there are water restrictions, while many homes have rainwater tanks, which can be used to water gardens and for baths and showers.

When moving into a new home, you should ask where the main stopcock is, so that you can turn off the water supply in an emergency.

Restrictions: During times of drought, there are frequent water restrictions, which are widely publicised and strictly enforced – 'water officers' patrol the streets and report offenders, who are liable for fines of up to $1,500. Water restrictions are graded in 'Stages', Stage 1 being the least restricting. The lower stages might limit sprinkler use (e.g. only between 6 and 8am) and ban car washing and swimming pool filling and topping up, while the higher stages may restrict you to watering your garden only with a watering can and only on certain days of the week, and require you to obtain written permission from the water authorities to top up a pool. In late 2007, all capital cities except Darwin and Hobart had at least Stage 3 water restrictions and in November 2007 Brisbane introduced Stage 6 restrictions.

The water authorities are working hard to reduce water consumption – more desalination plants are planned along with water recycling plants – and to make people more aware of water saving measures such as planting native Australian plants requiring little water and using wood chips or gravel as an alternative to lawns. Comprehensive advice on reducing water use is available on state water board websites (see above). In Australia, water is a precious resource and not something simply to pour down the drain!

Costs & Bills

There were traditionally fixed charges for water in Australia based on the gross rental or rateable value of a property. However, water is now metered in metropolitan areas, and most households pay for their actual consumption (measured in kilolitres/kL) rather than a flat fee. There's usually a low basic charge for a 'reasonable' consumption, and higher charges as consumption increases. Prices vary greatly with the area: for example, Sydney Water charges $1.34 per kL up to 100kL per year and $1.83 per kL for consumption over 100kL; and the Water Corporation (Perth) charges $0.49 per kL for the first 150kL and $0.73 per kL for consumption between 151 and 350kL. There's also a water service charge, which varies substantially, e.g. $14 per quarter in Sydney and $162.60 per year in Perth.

Bills are issued quarterly, three times a year or twice a year and may show your average daily use in kilolitres. Bills can be paid at certain banks (in cash or by cheque), by post (by cheque), at post offices or by telephone or online directly to the company (with a credit/ debit card).

Sewerage

In most parts of Australia, sewerage and drainage are managed by local water boards. Charges may be included on water bills or separately, and are either a fixed rate per household in a particular area or vary according to the rateable value of a property. As with other utilities, charges vary considerably around the country. Examples of current charges are $102 per quarter in Sydney and a minimum charge of $267 per year (around $67 per quarter) in Perth.

New sewerage systems have been installed in many areas, the bulk of the cost being paid for by residents, irrespective of whether they want or need the improvements.

The Twelve Apostles, Marine National Park, VIC

45c

Australian Legends

A. Boyd, Nebuchadnezzar on fire falling over a waterfall

1999

AUSTRALIA

AUSTRALIA

45c

6.
POSTAL SERVICES

Australia Post (AP) handles over 5bn items of post per year (a large percentage of which is junk mail) and provides one of the best services in the world in terms of cost, reliability and speed. AP underwent deregulation in 1994, when parts of the post business were opened to private competitors (AP maintains a monopoly on letters weighing up to 250g). However, it has since gone from strength to strength and is a highly profitable and well run business. There are plans to completely deregulate AP in the future, but a date has yet to be fixed. In major cities, there are other companies, such as Mail Boxes Etc. (⌨ www.mbe. com.au) which provide a wide range of post services (e.g. post boxes), as well as business services, courier, fax and telephone, and there's a thriving courier business in Australia, particularly in the major cities, where 24-hour domestic and international courier services are provided by many companies, including Allied Express, DHL, FedEx, Mayne Nickless and TNT. AP also operates a domestic courier service, Australia Air Express, with Qantas. Many other companies (such as Salmat and Streetfile) just deliver locally, e.g. within a particular city.**

There's a post office in most main towns (a total of around 4,500), offering a wide range of services, most of which are described in this chapter. In rural and outback towns, post services are provided by an AP agency (e.g. a cafe/restaurant, general store or petrol station) licensed to provide most of the services offered by a main post office.

Post offices provide a wide range of services, including 'faxpost', money orders, passport applications, *poste restante* post, stamps and telegrams, gifts (e.g. at Christmas from AP shops or by mail-order), and stationery and office products (listed in a catalogue). AP also operates the country's largest over-the-counter bill payment service, some 160 organisations offering their customers the option of paying their bills at post offices, including credit card companies, councils (for rates), electricity, gas, water and telephone companies, and insurance companies) and some 25 per cent of consumer bills are paid at AP's retail outlets. AP handles over 170m financial transactions per year through its electronic retail network and provides one of the country's largest banking services.

As well as at post offices, stamps can be purchased at hotels, motels, newsagents and shops and from vending machines. Most machines issue fixed-value stamps, although new electronic machines print gummed postage 'labels' to the exact value required. No surcharge is levied by private stamp vendors in Australia.

Post boxes in Australia are red with a white stripe and modern post boxes look like litter bins, although there are still some

Victorian 'receiving pillars' around. In cities and large towns, there are express 'gold' post boxes (see **Express Service** on page 135).

⚠ Caution

Post boxes are scarce in rural areas and you may need to take your post to a post office or agency.

In major towns and metropolitan areas, there are post deliveries once a day, Mondays to Fridays, while in remote areas deliveries may be made just once or twice a week and deliveries can be affected by the weather, as post is usually delivered by air. In the outback, post must usually be collected from a local post office or agency. **There are no weekend deliveries anywhere in Australia.**

AP produces a wealth of free brochures concerning post rates and special services, most of which are available from any post office. A general *Post Charges* booklet contains details of most services and rates, and a comprehensive *Post Guide* ($50) is available for businesses. Information about AP's services is also available on the internet (🖳 www.auspost.com.au).

BUSINESS HOURS

Post office business hours in Australia are usually from 9am to 5pm, Mondays to Fridays, and from 9am to noon on Saturdays. In major cities, general post offices may have slightly longer business hours, e.g. Sydney general post office is open from 8.15am to 5.30pm, Mondays to Fridays, and from 8.30am to noon on Saturdays. Post offices in major towns don't close at lunchtime. In country and outback areas, AP agencies generally keep the same hours as post offices, but may close for an hour during lunch or shut

earlier in the afternoon. They usually open on Saturday mornings and have extended opening hours on some evenings.

LETTER POST

AP's letter handling system is generally efficient and reliable. If you send a letter with insufficient postage, it's usually delivered, although the addressee is charged $1 plus the deficient postage (this also applies to parcels). If the post office is unable to deliver a letter, it's returned to the sender with a note stating the reason it couldn't be delivered.

Domestic Letters

For the standard domestic post service there's a single rate for 'small' letters and three rates for 'large' letters. Small letters must be a maximum size of 130 x 240mm, a maximum thickness of 5mm and a maximum weight of 250g. Large letters must be rectangular, a maximum size of 260 x 360mm, a maximum thickness of 20mm and a maximum weight of 500g. The rates are as follows:

Size & Weight	Rate
Small letters (up to 250g)	$0.50
Large letters:	
Up to 125g	$1.00
125 to 250g	$1.45
250 to 500g	$2.45

Parcel post rates apply to letters over 500g (see page 136). Domestic Christmas greeting cards posted in November and December are charged at a reduced rate of 45 cents. Domestic post charges also apply to the Australian Antarctic Territories, Christmas Island (Indian Ocean), the Cocos (Keeling) Islands and Norfolk Island.

Domestic post is sent by air between states or to remote areas within Australia.

Peel-and-stick 50-cent stamps (no licking) are available in booklets of 10 ($5), 20 ($10), 100 ($50) and 200 ($100 – no quantity reductions with AP!). Pre-paid envelopes are available in various sizes.

Local post is usually delivered the next day and interstate post to major towns and cities in one to two days. However, deliveries to rural locations officially take two days in the same state and up to four days interstate.

Express Service

AP provides an express domestic letter post service with guaranteed next day delivery within states between the capital city and provincial centres. Outside these areas, the fastest possible delivery is provided, but there are no guarantees. No paperwork or forms need be completed, as items are sent in pre-paid envelopes or 'satchels'. There are three sizes of pre-paid envelope: C5 ($4.30), B4 ($5.30) and DL (only available with windows in business packs of 50), which can be used for letters and documents up to 500g and 20mm thick. Express post satchels are available in two sizes (items can be any thickness): up to 500g ($7.40) and up to 3kg ($10.50). Items weighing 3 to 20kg or too large for an express post satchel must be sent as express post parcels (see page 135). All types of envelope (except DL) and satchel are available in packs of 10.

Pre-paid envelopes and satchels can be handed in at post offices or posted in express 'gold' post boxes in cities and major towns. Items must be presented at a post office before close of business or the post closing time in some provincial centres. Items posted by 6pm (earlier in Perth and some provincial centres), Mondays to Fridays, are guaranteed next day delivery to Australia's capital cities and some provincial centres. The cost is

refunded if items aren't delivered the next working day.

Express post must not be used to send cash, gold, jewellery, negotiable securities, precious stones or other valuables, which should be sent by registered post (see page 137).

Australian Addresses

The majority of post is sorted by machine, which is facilitated by the use of full and correct postal addresses (omitting all punctuation). All items of post should have a four-digit postcode (zip code) after the town and state or territory. In major cities, codes indicate whether the town is a suburb of a major city, e.g. 2000 is the central business district (CBD) of Sydney and postcodes from 2001 to 2786 are suburbs. A post office box number (also referred to as a locked or private bag) should prefixed by 'PO Box' or 'GPO Box'. All addresses must contain the name of the state or territory, which are abbreviated as shown overleaf.

State/Territory	Abbr.	First Digit
Australian Capital Territory	ACT	2
New South Wales	NSW	2
Northern Territory	NT	0
Queensland	QLD	4
South Australia	SA	5
Tasmania	TAS	7
Victoria	VIC	3
Western Australia	WA	6

Postcodes are listed at the back of the white pages or you can telephone ☎ 13-1317 for postcode information. You can buy envelopes with pre-printed squares for the postcode. A typical Australian address is shown below:

> Bruce & Sheila Kelly
> 99A Waltzing Matilda Street
> Wooloowollongong
> Sydney
> NSW 2005

You should always put your address on the back of post so that it can be returned if it cannot be delivered.

International Letters

AP provides four services for international letters: airmail, economy airmail, express post international and sea post, detailed below. The fastest way to send post overseas via a post office is by EMS international courier, although this is an expensive option for letters.

Leaflets are published in September listing the latest posting dates for Christmas for surface and airmail, which are some time between the beginning of October (e.g. 6th October for the UK and 8th October for the US by sea post) and the end of November, depending on the country.

If you want to increase your chance of receiving a reply or simply wish to save a correspondent money, you can send them an international reply coupon ($2.50). These are exchangeable at post offices overseas for stamps equivalent to the basic airmail rate anywhere in the world for a letter weighing up to 20g.

Airmail

This is the standard service and is divided into two zones only, as follows:

Airmail Letter Rates		
Weight	**Rate**	
	Asia Pacific (AP)	**Rest of the World (RW)**
Up to 50g	$1.20	$1.80
50 to 125g	$2.40	$3.60
125 to 250g	$3.60	$5.40
250 to 500g	$7.20	$10.80
Postcards cost $1.10 for both zones.		

Most international stamps have a blue strip on the left-hand side with the word 'airmail' in white lettering. Otherwise, airmail letters should have a blue airmail label affixed to the top left hand corner, available from post offices, or 'PAR AVION – BY AIRMAIL' written or stamped on the front. Aerogrammes (pre-printed airmail letters) are available and cost 95 cents to all destinations. They're also sold in packs of ten ($9.50).

The international airmail service is fast and reliable, letters taking a maximum of eight days to most destinations (three to five days to the UK and six to seven days to the US), depending on where they're posted and the destination. Compensation (at AP's discretion) up to $50 is paid for the loss or damage of post upon production of a receipt or other proof of posting.

Economy airmail: For non-urgent international post, AP provides an economy airmail service, where the main part of the journey is made by air. Post takes between 10 and 28 days to most destinations (10 to 14 days to the UK and 14 to 21 days to the US). For most post, however, it isn't worthwhile, as the savings are insignificant unless you're sending a heavy parcel (see page 136).

Express Post International

AP provides an express post international service to over 140 countries, delivering to 54 within three to seven working days.

The service can be used to send letters weighing up to 500g. Envelopes are available in discount packs of ten. As with domestic express post, items can be posted in express post 'gold' posting boxes. Air despatch from Australia is guaranteed the next day from capital cities and other specified areas subject to the availability of flights (otherwise your envelope is replaced free of charge).

Other Services

- Domestic post, including parcels and registered packets, can be sent cash on delivery (COD), where the addressee pays a specified amount to the postman on delivery. It includes insurance cover up to $100 (additional insurance is available for $1 per $100 insured, up to a maximum of $1,500 insured).

- There are reduced rates for bulk local deliveries of a minimum of 50 letters (ten in a small community).

- AP provides a 'print post' service for periodicals sent within Australia.

- Like many countries, Australia provides a range of special services for philatelists. AP produces stamps for the Australian Antarctic Territory, Christmas Island and the Cocos (Keeling) Islands as well as for mainland Australia and

check whether you have any post by telephone). Some general post offices (e.g. Martin Place in Sydney) offer the facility of checking whether you have *poste restante* via the internet. *Poste restante* can be redirected to a suburban post office from a main office for $9 a month.

Most hostels and hotels hold post for guests, and there are also private post and message holding and forwarding services in Australia, e.g. travel agencies, which charge a monthly or annual fee.

> ☑ SURVIVAL TIP
> When using a post holding service, you can telephone from anywhere in Australia to see if there's any post for you and have it redirected.

If you have an American Express card or use American Express travellers' cheques, you can have post sent to any American Express office in Australia. Standard letters are held free of charge, but registered letters and packages aren't accepted. Post, which should be marked 'client post service', is kept for 30 days before being returned to the sender. Post can be forwarded to another office or address, for which there's a charge. Other companies also provide post holding services for customers, e.g. Thomas Cook and Western Union.

PARCEL POST

There are two tariffs for domestic parcels: within the same four-digit postcode area (see **Australian Addresses** on page 133) and to all other areas. Large letters weighing up to 500g can be sent by letter post (see page 132). Important parcels can be sent by registered post (see opposite),

publishes *Stamp Bulletin* magazine (five issues a year), which is available free to Australian residents (see the website for details). AP also operates a Stamp Explorers Club for children aged 6 to 13, who receive a membership card entitling them to discounts and benefits and *Stamp Explorer* magazine (five issues a year).

● You can receive post via post offices throughout Australia through the international *poste restante* service, where post is addressed to a main post office. Post sent to a *poste restante* address is returned to the sender if it's unclaimed after 14 days (a month if sent from overseas). Identification is necessary for collection, e.g. a passport. Post should be addressed as follows: Your Name, c/o Poste Restante, Chief Post Office, Sydney, NSW 2000. Some *poste restante* desks in main cities are hectic and it's often better to send post to a smaller town or a suburb (where you may be able to which provides a signature on delivery and insurance of up to $100. Parcels can also be sent COD.

Parcels are usually delivered the next working day within the metropolitan area of capital cities and certain large towns in the same state, and within two working days to other locations in the same state. Interstate parcels are delivered within two to six working days, depending on the destination. However, AP has a poor reputation for deliveries to rural locations.

AP provides an express domestic parcel service. There's guaranteed next day delivery between Australia's capital cities (except Darwin) and some other major towns (you can claim a refund if a parcel isn't delivered the next day). The service also operates within states between the capital city and provincial centres. Outside these areas, there are no delivery guarantees.

AP provides five services for international parcels: airmail, EMS international courier, express and sea post. Parcels sent to foreign addresses must be accompanied by *Customs/ Douane* form CN22, available from post offices. (No customs form is required for letters.) For items over 2kg or worth over $500 you must also complete form CP72. Items over $2,000 in value must be declared to customs. Press firmly when completing customs forms, some of which have six copies!

Gifts posted to Australia up to the value of $900 are duty-free, except for alcohol and tobacco products. For gifts exceeding $900, duty is calculated on the value in excess of $900. The value of packages that are part of a larger consignment are added for customs purposes. There are restrictions on the sort of goods that can be posted to Australia (see below), and senders of all international parcels and satchels must sign a *Dangerous Goods Declaration*.

A dangerous goods brochure, *Some Things Were Never Meant To Be Posted*, is available from post offices and lists what **cannot** be sent through the post. This includes anything that's alive, corrosive, explosive, flammable, oxidising, radioactive, or likely to deteriorate during its journey through the post (e.g. a cake). Many overseas countries have restrictions on certain items, such as alcohol and medicines.

A leaflet entitled *Packaging Hints* is available from post offices, describing how to pack goods for sending through the post.

> 'Postpak' packaging products, including boxes (or gift boxes), posting tubes and accessories, padded bags and tough bags are available from AP shops and stationery stores.

IMPORTANT DOCUMENTATION

The post office provides a number of services for the delivery of important documents and valuables:

Registered Post

If you're sending jewellery, money or valuable documents, you should use registered post. You're obliged to use pre-paid envelopes for international post not for domestic post. Domestic pre-paid envelopes are available in two sizes: small or DLE (130 x 240mm, 5mm thick) costing $3.20 each and large or B4 (250 x 353mm, 20mm thick) costing $4.30 each. Alternatively, domestic registered post labels for attaching to standard envelopes are available in boxes of 50 ($100). International registered post is available only for letters and documents, using the same size envelopes as the domestic service.

You receive a receipt for registered post, which must be signed for on delivery (although the signatory doesn't need to be the addressee). There's a person-to-person option (fee $5.30 per article), where a registered article must be signed for by the person to whom it's addressed.

Insurance

Domestic and international registered post is insured for $100 against loss or damage. Additional insurance for up to $5,000 is available for domestic registered post for $1.15 per $100 insured but not for international registered post. However, insurance is available for EMS international courier service items; the basic fee is $5.50, to which you must add $2 for each $100 (or part thereof) insured up to a maximum of $5,000 (a lower limit applies to some countries).

Delivery Confirmation

Delivery confirmation is available with registered post, insured items and, for some countries, parcel post. Delivery confirmation costs an additional $1.65 per article for registered post ($5 for addressee confirmation); international delivery confirmation costs $2 per article plus postage. Proof of delivery must be requested at the time of posting. Signed evidence of delivery is returned to the sender, but not from a named individual.

CHANGE OF ADDRESS

When moving house within Australia, you should obtain a 'Change of Address Kit' from a post office containing a *Change of Address Request* form, a brochure describing the service, a moving home checklist and six postcards to inform your relatives and friends about your move (Australians don't have many friends). The change can be permanent or temporary and post can be forwarded, held at your local post office or collected from a nominated post office. Proof of identity must be provided when submitting the

form and a minimum of three working days' notice is required. There's a monthly fee of $38 for businesses and $11 for individuals (there's no charge for certain pensioners and sickness beneficiaries). There's an additional charge for the redirection of parcels.

AP provides a 'priority address notification' service which saves time and effort in informing organisations of your address. Upon receipt of your *Change of Address* form, AP sends you a list of companies which you may wish to notify of your new address. If you're a customer of any of the companies listed on the form, simply tick the box beside the company's name and AP informs them of your change of address free of charge.

Sydney, NSW

7.

TELEPHONE SERVICES

Almost all Australian homes (some 97 per cent) have a telephone, and Australia also has one of the highest per capita rates of mobile telephone ownership in the world. Because of its huge size, telecommunications in Australia have always been a priority and today it has one of the highest standards of telecommunications in the world, employing the latest broadband cable, digital technology, fibre optics and satellite systems. In rural and remote areas, residents will soon receive their telecommunications services via satellite and enjoy the same services that are available in metropilitan centres now. There are also solar-powered public telephone boxes in outback areas requiring no mains electricity.

The telecommunications industry is regulated by the Australian Communications & Media Authority/ACMA (🖳 www.acma.gov.au – the website offers a number of useful factsheets about telephone services) and has its own ombudsman (☎ freecall 1800-062058, 🖳 www.tio.com.au). The ombudsman attempts to resolve complaints concerning telecommunications issues, but only after consumers have attempted to settle them with the company or carrier concerned.

> ☑ SURVIVAL TIP
>
> The general emergency telephone number throughout Australia is ☎ 000

TELEPHONE COMPANIES

The Australian telecommunications market was deregulated on 1st July 1997 and around 30 companies now operate in the country, although the market is still dominated by Telstra (🖳 www.telstra.com.

au), formerly Telecom Australia and two-thirds government-owned. Its main rival, Optus (🖳 www.optus.com.au), established in 1992 and owned by Cable & Wireless, has around a third as many customers. Other major telecommunications companies include Gotalk (🖳 www.gotalk. com.au) and Primus (🖳 www.primus.com. au).

Customers in most regions and major cities can choose their carrier. To use a particular carrier, you must open an account with them and may either pre-select that company or dial an access code before an STD or overseas number. Local number portability (LNP), which allows users to switch between telephone companies without changing their number, has been introduced, although if you sign up with a company you might have a prefix assigned to your telephone number and your calls automatically go through your selected company when you dial. If you make a lot of international calls, it may be beneficial to sign up with a number of companies and 'cherry pick', using the one that offers the lowest rate to the country you're calling.

Since deregulation, international and long-distance telephone charges have been slashed by up to 70 per cent, the price of mobile telephone calls has fallen by 50 per cent and that of local calls by 12 per cent. However, despite the increased competition, deregulation has failed to deliver all the expected benefits to consumers.

Before signing up with a telephone company, check the competition and compare rates. You should continually monitor the market, as new deals are constantly being introduced and what was the best offer last month (or week) is unlikely to remain so for long. Many companies offer a range of services, which may include high speed access to online and interactive services such as the internet, local and long-distance telephone services and pay television (TV). This may be beneficial, as many companies offer attractive package deals if you buy two or more services, such as telephone and pay TV.

ACMA provides comprehensive information on all aspects of choosing a telephone company (🖥 www.toolkit.aca.gov.au).

INSTALLATION & REGISTRATION

Before moving into a new home, check whether there's a telephone line and that the number of lines or telephone points is adequate (most homes already have telephone lines and points in a number of rooms). If a property has a cable system or other telephone network, you don't require a Telstra telephone line. However, if you move into a house or apartment where you aren't the first resident, a telephone line will almost certainly already be installed, although there's usually no telephone. If you're moving into a house or apartment without a telephone connection, e.g. a new house, you must usually apply to Telstra for a line to be installed or connected.

To have a telephone line installed or re-connected, call at any Telstra shop or dial the Telstra Customer Service Centre (☎ local call rate 13-2200). Telstra will arrange a suitable date and time with you to connect your telephone service. Your telephone should be connected within 2 to 20 working days, although if Telstra needs to extend its network to reach your home, connection takes longer.

It costs $59 to have an existing Telstra service reconnected and $299 for a new connection (more if Telstra extends the network when up to $1,540 is charged). The laying of underground cable, known as 'trenching', from your property to the Telstra network is your responsibility and should only be carried out by authorised cablers. Telstra can provide details of registered cablers in your area.

If you're moving house within the same exchange area and call-charging zone, you may retain your old number; otherwise your old number is typically re-allocated to the incoming customer at your old address.

When you register for a telephone line, you're required to provide details of your occupation, credit card and driving licence. Credit assessments are made for all customers and your billing period may depend on your credit assessment. Payment of a security bond may be required (e.g. $250 or $500), which is generally repaid after 12 months when you've established a satisfactory payment record.

> ☑ SURVIVAL TIP
>
> **If your telephone or line has a fault, you must report it to Telstra on ☎ local call rate 13-2203.**

If your health, life, safety or shelter may be at risk without a telephone, you can register for a priority repair service (24 hours, seven days a week). You can take out a maintenance contract with Telstra to maintain equipment and cabling. If you need help in using a Telstra product or service, dial ☎ local call rate 13-2200.

There are 196 (96 company-owned, 100 licensed) Telstra shops in Australia for general enquiries, information about Telstra's products and services, product demonstrations and sales, and telephone bill payments. Shops are open from 9am to 4.30pm, Mondays to Fridays, or longer in many locations. Telstra also has Customer Service Centres in all major cities and towns, open from 8am to 5pm, Mondays to Fridays.

CHOOSING A TELEPHONE

You aren't required to rent a telephone from Telstra and can purchase a telephone from a wide range offered by Telstra and other retailers. You can try the latest Telstra telephones at your local Telstra shop (see your telephone book), where advice and demonstrations are available. Renting a telephone from Telstra doesn't pay, as in one year you'll have paid for the price of a basic (but adequate) telephone. The only advantage of renting a Telstra telephone is that they fix it free of charge if it's faulty and you can change telephones as often as you wish.

A basic, one-piece telephone (with the keys on the handset) costs around $25, while an all-singing, all-dancing model costs from $100. Cordless telephones are popular, and all cordless telephones sold in Australia must have an Austel permit (shown by a sticker), and the import of cordless telephones and citizen band radios without it is prohibited.

USING THE TELEPHONE

Using the telephone in Australia is much the same as in any other country, with a few local eccentricities thrown in for good measure. In some remote areas, for example, there are manual exchanges where you must call the local operator to make a call. Some outback areas in the Northern Territory and Western Australia have radio telephones, where numbers are prefixed by R/T. Calls to R/T numbers can be made via the national network and radio telephone exchanges, although they're expensive. A radio telephone is like using a two-way radio and only one person can speak at a time (you need to say 'over' when you finish speaking and cannot interrupt the other person). Party lines (shared by two or more homes) are common in the outback.

Because of the huge time difference between Australia and many other countries, you should always check the local time when making international calls. If you have a problem obtaining a number, check that it's correct in the white pages or by calling directory enquiries on ☎ 1223 (local and national) or ☎ 1225 (international). An information line, called Easy Info (☎ 12452), provides up to five information searches, e.g. addresses, telephone numbers and time zones, for a single call costing $2.50. For operator assistance dial ☎ 1234 (see **Operator-assisted Calls** on page 145).

You can report line faults 24 hours a day to Telstra on ☎ 13-2203 (for residential lines), ☎ 13-2999 (for business lines) or ☎ 125-111 (for mobile telephones). Telstra aims to repair telephone services within one working day in urban areas, two days in rural areas and three days in remote areas. If you suspect that your telephone is faulty, test the line with another telephone if you have one or test your telephone on another line, e.g. that of a friend or neighbour. A priority repair service is provided for non-commercial emergency and essential service organisations, and to individuals whose life, health, safety or shelter would be at risk without a telephone.

Codes & Numbers

All Australian fixed line numbers have eight digits. The area codes for states and their capital cities are as follows:

Telephone directories usually list the state code in brackets before the subscriber number, e.g. (02) 1234 5678. If you're using a service other than Telstra, you must dial the company's prefix unless you've pre-selected the company in which case the prefix is automatically dialled when you make a call.

Mobile telephone numbers have the prefix 04. When dialling a number within your own exchange area, dial only the

State/Territory	Capital	Code
Australian Capital Territory	Canberra	02
New South Wales	Sydney	02
Northern Territory	Darwin	08
Queensland	Brisbane	07
South Australia	Adelaide	08
Tasmania	Hobart	03
Victoria	Melbourne	03
Western Australia	Perth	08

number, e.g. if you live in New South Wales (NSW) and wish to dial another subscriber in NSW or the Australian Capital Territory (ACT). When dialling anywhere else, the area code must be dialled before the subscriber's number. When telephone numbers are printed, the area code is usually shown in brackets, e.g. (02) 1234 5678. When dialling a number in Australia from overseas, dial the international access code of the country from which you're calling (e.g. 00), followed by Australia's international code (61), the area code **without** the first 0 (e.g. 2 for Sydney) and the subscriber's number. For example, to call Sydney 1234 5678 from the UK, you would dial ☎ 00-61-2-1234 5678.

International Calls

International links are provided by the Overseas Telecommunications Commission (OTC) using undersea cables and satellites (Australia has telephone connections with around 200 countries via Intelsat). All private telephones in Australia are on International Direct Dialling (IDD), allowing calls to be dialled direct to over 250 countries. To make an international call, dial ☎ 0011, the country code, the area code without the first zero, and the subscriber's number. Dial ☎ 0101 for the international operator (☎ 0107 from payphones) to make credit card calls, non-IDD calls, person-to-person and reverse charge calls (which aren't accepted by all countries). Dial ☎ 1225 for international directory enquiries. The international code for most countries is listed at the back of the white pages under 'Telstra 0011 International and Telstra Faxstream 0015 International', as well as the time difference.

Free, Premium Rate & Reduced Rate Numbers

Toll-free numbers, called freecall in Australia, have a prefix of 1800 (note that

mobile phone carriers may charge for 1800 calls).

Numbers with the prefix 13 or 1300 are usually charged at the local call rate from anywhere in Australia, although some numbers are restricted to callers within a city or state.

> ### ⚠ Caution
>
> Calls to numbers with the prefix 190 are charged at premium rate (e.g. $5 a minute). You can instruct Telstra (☎ 13-2200) to restrict access to 190 numbers on your telephone line.

Operator-assisted Calls

There's an extra charge for operator-assisted calls (dial ☎ 1234), and the minimum charge period is three minutes. The following operator services are available:

- **Ring Back Price** – A call can be timed and the charge given at the end of the call. If you want to know the cost of a national or international call, dial ☎ 1222 before the number and the cost is given (for a fee) at the end of your call. Although useful when you aren't using your own telephone and must pay for a call, using 'ring back price' is expensive.

- **Particular Person Call** – You can make an international particular person call (called a personal or person-to-person call in most other countries), where you start paying for the call only when the person required comes on the line, although it may be cheaper to make a brief call to find out whether the person you wish to speak to is available.

- **Reverse Charge Call** – A collect, reverse charge or transferred call, is where the person called agrees to pay for the call. This is useful when you've no change or a payphone won't accept your coins. Making a reverse charge international call is **very** expensive, as it's charged at the operator connected call rate. For reverse charge calls, dial ☎ 12550. These calls cannot be made to mobile telephones.

- **Wake-up Call** – To book a wake-up or reminder call, dial ☎ 12454.

CALL RATES

Telstra offers several telephone packages under its 'Home Phone Plans' with monthly prices ranging from $19.95 to $89.90 plus call costs. Examples of international call costs to the UK, Ireland and North America include $0.18 a minute with Optus and Primus (Desti-Nation plan), and $1 for ten minutes under Telstra's 'Homeline Plus' package. Packages may also include television services and some companies have 'reward schemes' with discounts on call costs when you accumulate a certain number of points. See Telstra's website or call ☎ 13-2200 for details and the latest offers.

Optus offers similar prices and options (some are as obscurely worded and difficult to understand as Telstra's), with a reduction in line rental for 'eligible pensioners'. See Optus's website or call ☎ 1800-501 064 for details.

Most telephone companies offer the option to check your telephone use and cost at any time. To use this service, you must register online and log into your account on the company's website.

TELEPHONE BILLS

Most residential customers are billed quarterly or bi-monthly for calls, line rental and telephone rental (if applicable). Business customers usually receive their bills monthly, although both business and residential customers may be able to choose to be billed monthly, bi-monthly or

quarterly. Telstra also provides a payment card which allows you to pay your account in advance instalments. Where applicable, the telephone connection fee is included in your first bill.

Bills are itemised and show separately local, national and international calls, calls to mobile telephones, Homelink 1800 calls, operator-connected calls, Telecard calls, line and equipment charges, and telephone information services. In late 2003 a new design of bill was introduced as part of a drive to provide bills that are accurate and easy to understand. Telstra also provides email delivery of customer bills and a website where customers can check the status of their account. Optus has an all-in-one billing service with a single bill for all services.

Telstra bills can be paid at any post office, by post to Telstra, PO Box 9901 in all capital cities, at Telstra shops (cash, cheques, credit/charge/EFTPOS cards), with a Telstra payment card, by electronic telephone banking, on the internet and by telephone (with a credit/EFTPOS card). Telstra accepts American Express, Bankcard, Diners Club, MasterCard, Redicard and Visa credit cards.

☑ SURVIVAL TIP

If you have any queries about your Telstra telephone bill, call the Telstra Customer Service Centre (☎ local call rate 13-2200 for residential services) between 8am and 5pm, Mondays to Fridays.

If you believe that your bill is wrong, you need only pay the amount that isn't in dispute while your query is being investigated. If you fail to pay your bill, a reminder or a disconnection notice is issued. If you still fail to pay, your service is disconnected and reconnection takes place only after payment of the account in full plus a reconnection fee has been received.

PUBLIC TELEPHONES

All payphones in Australia (some 85,000) are operated by Telstra (including solar-powered public telephone boxes in outback areas) and are widely available. The company has created a new area of its website that explains the process for requesting the installation of a payphone and is planning an online map to help people to locate payphones in Australia. Telstra Payphone Centres in major cities are usually open from around 9am to 6pm, Mondays to Fridays, and from 10am to 4pm on Saturdays. In addition to Telstra's, there are around 42,000 payphones operated by private businesses.

Payphones can be found at airports, bus and railway stations, in hotels, inside and outside post offices, in streets, pubs, restaurants, service stations, shopping centres, and other private and public buildings. Making non-local calls from hotels is expensive, although free local calls can often be made from telephones in a hotel lobby. Calls made from a payphone are more expensive than from a private telephone, and payphones don't accept incoming calls. Local calls cost 50 cents from a payphone for an unlimited period, although users are requested to limit calls to three minutes when there are people waiting. When making an international call, you should insert at least $3 in coins or a Phonecard (see below) with a minimum of $3 credit.

Payphones accept a range of payment options, including coins, credit cards, Homelink services, Optus Calling Cards, PhoneAway cards, Phonecards, reverse charge calls, and Telstra Telecards. Telstra Telecards and Optus Calling Cards, which are free, can be used to dial direct from

any tone telephone, which includes all payphones and most private telephones, although they cannot be used from mobile telephones. The cost of calls is added to your normal telephone bill. IDD and non-IDD calls (via the international operator) can be made to over 200 countries and to Australia from over 65 countries using the Australia Direct service, although when using a Telecard overseas, you may be charged an astronomical sum. Calls from payphones within Australia are charged at payphone rates.

Telstra Phonecards are available in denominations of $5, $10, $20 and $50 and are available from over 15,000 retail outlets nationally (displaying a 'Phonecard Sold Here' sign), including kiosks, newsagents, pharmacies and shops. An audible signal is given when a Phonecard is nearing the end of its value. Phonecards can store and automatically dial telephone numbers through the use of Autocall features. They're produced in a number of designs on topical themes and (as in other countries) have become collectibles – since their introduction in 1990, many are already fetching high prices among collectors, and Telstra issues a bi-monthly newsletter and catalogue.

Over 98 per cent of Telstra payphones still accept coins. Partly used coins are lost but wholly unused coins are returned when you hang up the receiver. Payphones also have a 'follow on call' button – if you still have unused coins in credit, you can press this button and make another call using the remaining credit. If the display flashes, insert more coins until the flashing stops.

Some phones accept only credit cards (e.g. American Express, Diners Club, MasterCard and Visa), EFTPOS cards, and Telstra and Optus account cards. Credit card telephones are predominantly located in major airports and other transport hubs, and large shopping centres. To use a credit card telephone, swipe the magnetic strip of your card through the telephone's card reader, enter your PIN and dial when you hear the dialling tone.

⚠ Caution

There's usually a high minimum charge when using a credit card payphone, so they should be used only in an 'emergency'.

SMS text messages can be sent from over 40 per cent of Telstra payphones. Around 200 are Teletypewriter (TTY) payphones, which allow people with hearing and communication problems to use the telephone (☎ freecall 1800-068424 for information). Around 1,000 payphones have been modified so that they can be used by people with various other kinds of disability, including those in wheelchairs and those with poor sight. Some payphones also have hands-free operation, hearing aid couplers and volume controls. If you

have difficulties, telephone the operator on ☎ 1234.

International Calls

Not all payphones in Australia can be used to make international calls. Payphones allowing international calls are marked International Subscriber Dialling (ISD), or International Direct Dialling (IDD). These include all gold telephones. You can check by dialling ☎ 0011 (free). If it's an ISD phone, you hear the message 'congratulations, you're connected to ISD'; if not, there's no reply. International calls can also be made from Telstra telephone centres in the major cities and public telephone booths at major post offices.

MOBILE TELEPHONES

The Australians love mobile telephones and in 2007, there were almost as many mobile telephones as people! Services are operated by Telstra (42 per cent of the market), Optus (32 per cent), Vodaphone (17 per cent), Hutchison (6 per cent) and Virgin (3 per cent). The digital network covers some 98 per cent of the population, including all the major population centres and corridors, but only 20 per cent of the country (all operators provide coverage maps). If you live or work in a remote area, you should ensure that a company's coverage includes that area.

In addition to services in the major metropolitan areas, Telstra mobile satellite and radio services provide mobile communications to the aeronautical, marine and remote land area markets. MobileSat allows you to plug a computer, fax machine or satellite navigation equipment into a terminal in an aircraft, boat or car and receive crystal clear communication wherever you are in Australia or up to 200km/124mi off the coast. Australia subscribes to the GSM digital network, which allows the same telephone to be

advertise in magazines and newspapers, where a wide range of special offers is promoted.

Calls to and from mobile telephones, including calls made from a fixed-line telephone, are much more expensive than calls between fixed-line telephones, and calls to 1800 numbers aren't free from mobile telephones. If you choose a phone without a contract, you can 'top up' your credit (up to $100 worth at a time) at post offices, department stores, supermarkets and mobile phone shops – you're given a receipt with an activation number on it – and there's no charge for receiving calls, as there is with some contracts (particularly for international and mobile-to-mobile calls).

Free booklets, *Hold the phone – read this before you buy a mobile*, which is a general guide, with advice on matters such as the different types of contract available, and *Mobile phone etiquette for Australia*, are available from the office of the telecommunications industry ombudsman (☎ freecall 1800-062058, 🖳 www.tio.com. au).

used in around 170 countries worldwide, including most of western Europe and parts of Asia, the Middle East, the Pacific, and central and South Africa (referred to as international roaming).

Buying a mobile telephone is a minefield, as not only are there five networks to choose from, but numerous call charges, connection fees, insurance, monthly subscriptions and tariffs. Before buying a mobile, shop around and compare telephone charge rates, installation and connection charges, prices and features, and rental charges.

Mobile phones are sold by specialist dealers, Telstra shops, and department and chain stores which have arrangements with service providers or networks to sell airtime contracts (along with telephones). Don't rely on getting good or impartial advice from retail staff, some of whom know little or nothing about telephones and networks (it's said that the difference between Clint Eastwood and a mobile telephone seller is that Clint isn't a real cowboy). Retailers

DIRECTORIES

Australian telephone subscribers, both business and private, are listed in directories (also called telephone books) which may be subdivided into white and yellow pages. White pages contain a list of subscribers in alphabetical order and yellow pages a list of businesses classified by business type. In most areas, white and yellow pages are contained in the same volume, while in major cities such as Sydney there are separate volumes.

New editions of telephone books are delivered free to subscribers' homes. If you don't have the latest local telephone book when you move into a new home, you can get one free from your local post office. Directories can be viewed at international telephone directory reference libraries, post offices and public libraries. White and yellow pages are also available on the internet (🖳 www.whitepages.com.au and 🖳 www.yellowpages.com.au), including versions of the white pages in German, Indonesian and Italian.

> Telstra recommend that you recycle your old telephone books (dedicated bins are provided in major cities when new books are issued).

An entry containing your name, address and telephone number is automatically listed in the white pages directory covering your area. You may also purchase an extra entry, e.g. when two people share a telephone, or enhance your listing by having it printed in bold type. Business customers may list an occupation. You can request an unlisted or ex-directory number (called a 'silent line'), for which there's a fee of $2.93 monthly. In this case, your name, address and number won't appear in any directories and won't be made available by directory enquiries (☎ 1223). Around 10 per cent of Australians have silent numbers. If you're bothered by nuisance calls, Telstra run a National Unwelcome Call Service offering advice and solutions (☎ 1899-805996).

A wealth of information is contained in the white pages, including 24-hour emergency numbers, abbreviations of place names (used in directories), community help and welfare services, services for the disabled and aged, telephone information services (190 numbers), telephone prefixes and place names, Telstra information and details of services, including a translation and interpreting service (TIS).

Yellow pages include a calendar of events, emergency and useful local numbers, an entertainment guide, inner city and surroundings maps, local government numbers and public transport information. There are separate business directories

in the major cities such as the Business Information Guide (BIG) in Melbourne.

Directory Enquiries

For directory enquiries (called 'directory assistance' in Australia) you dial ☎ 1223 or ☎ 12456 for local and national numbers, and ☎ 1225 for overseas numbers. All directory assistance calls are usually free, except from mobile telephones. If you want directory enquiries to find a number for you, you must know the town or city of the person or business whose number you require.

EMERGENCY NUMBERS

There's only one national emergency number in Australia, ☎ 000, which is for ambulance, firemen and police as well as cave and mountain rescue services and the coastguard. Emergency calls are free from all telephones, including payphones. When you dial 000, the operator asks you which emergency service you require

("Emergency, which service please?") and you're immediately put through to that service. You must state clearly your name and location, and give a brief description of the emergency.

Lists of other '24-hour Emergency Numbers' and 'Personal Emergency & Help Services' are included at the front of the white pages telephone directory and inside the front cover of the yellow pages. These include aviation search and rescue, chemist emergency prescriptions, child abuse, child protection, city missions, counselling for victims of crime, crime stoppers, crisis centre, customs 'coastwatch', dentists, distress call, doctors, domestic violence, drugs, electricity, gas, hospitals, kids' helpline, lifeline (see below), maritime rescue, Mindwise (mental health), poison information, rape line, state emergency service, translating and interpreting service, veterinary surgeons, water and youth line. Lifeline (☎ local call rate 13-1114) provides a confidential, 24-hour counselling service in times of personal crisis throughout Australia for the cost of a local call. There's also a Women's Information and Referral Services (WIRS, ☎ freecall 1800-817227). See also **Emergencies** on page 150 and **Counselling** on page 259.

INTERNET

Australia has one of the highest interest uses in the world and in 2006 over 70 per cent of the population used internet services. There are internet service providers in all the major cities and many regional towns, and competition for customers is fierce. Broadband connection (ADSL) is popular and promoted by the government who is committed to providing nationwide broadband access – under the programme 'Australia Connected' 99 per cent of the population will have access to broadband by 2009. The programme provides broadband subsidies of up to $2,750 for households in remote areas. 19 companies currently provide broadband access and monthly rates start at around $40 for a speed of 512kbps. Shop around as deals and conditions (e.g. a minimum 12 month contract) vary considerably.

> To help you choose which company and package are best suited to your needs, the government provides an online 'toolkit' (🖳 www.toolkit.aca.gov.au).

Internet Telephony

If you have a broadband internet connection, you can make long-distance and international phone 'calls' for free (or almost-free) to anyone with a broadband connection. Voice over internet protocol (VOIP) is the latest technology which is reshaping the telecoms landscape and will eventually (some say within five years) make today's telephone technology (both land lines and mobile networks) obsolete. The leading company in this field is Skype (🖳 www.skype.com), owned by eBay, which has over 50m users worldwide. There are numerous other companies in the market – a search on 'internet phone' on Google will throw up many other internet phone providers. All you need is access to a local broadband provider and a headset (costing as little as $10) or a special phone, and you're in business. Calls to other computers anywhere in the world are free, while calls to landlines are charged at a few cents a minute.

TELEGRAMS, TELEX & FAX

Telegrams (cables) can be sent by telephone or from any post office. There are three rates: urgent (two to four hour delivery), ordinary (four to six hours) and 'letter' (24 hours), although in some remote areas of Australia deliveries are made just once a week. The cost depends on where a telegram is being sent from, the destination and the speed required.

There are public telex bureaux at all capital city chief telegraph offices and at Telstra offices in many towns.

Faxes can be sent from business offices, hotels and Telstra telephone centres in major towns and cities. Mobile telephone and portable computer users can use a portable fax, which allows fax transmissions to be made from virtually anywhere in Australia and overseas. International faxes can be transmitted to over 90 countries and to any fax machine in the world, provided IDD telephone access is available. When sending an international fax, dial ☎ 0015 (FaxStream Enhanced) instead of 0011, followed by the country code, area code and fax number. FaxStream Enhanced is a network of specially selected lines which provide optimum quality for international fax calls.

FaxPost

Australia Post (AP – see **Chapter 6**) provides a public fax and delivery service (FaxPost), which allows faxes to be sent to virtually anyone in Australia or overseas, irrespective of whether you or the recipient has a fax machine. FaxPost allows delivery of faxed documents to all major centres in Australia within two hours (or the same day) plus fast delivery overseas. To fax a document via FaxPost to someone in Australia without a fax machine, you fax the document to the Fax Centre Post Office nearest the addressee (there are around 2,000 throughout Australia); it's then delivered within two hours, the same day or by post, depending on your instructions. Messages can be delivered to overseas addressees without a fax machine by courier messenger, often on the same day, or can be delivered next day by post. If you don't have a fax machine but the addressee does, you must deliver your document to the nearest Fax Centre, from where it's faxed to the addressee. A document can also be sent to someone when neither party has a fax machine, in which case the document is delivered to the nearest Fax Centre and faxed to the Fax Centre Post Office nearest the addressee, from where it's delivered. The cost for domestic faxes is $4 for the first page and $1 for additional pages, and for international faxes $8 for the first page and $2 for additional pages.

Whitsunday Islands, QLD

8.
TELEVISION & RADIO

Australian television (TV) is poor, but paradoxically still rates among the best in the world. Over half the programmes are purchased from the UK and the US, most local content consisting of current affairs, game shows, soaps and sport. Australian radio is generally excellent. The Australian Broadcasting Corporation (ABC, 🖥 www.abc.net.au), affectionately known as 'Aunty' after the British Broadcasting Corporation (BBC) on which it's modelled, is government-owned and operates both TV and radio stations throughout Australia. Being financed by the government, it carries no advertising. Overall control of Australia's TV and radio services is exercised by the Australian Broadcasting Authority (ABA).

No TV or radio licence is required.

TV programmes are listed in daily newspapers (Saturday newspapers also include Sunday programmes) and weekly guides such as *TV Week*, which is produced in separate editions for each state or territory (because of local time differences). Many Saturday and Sunday newspapers also provide free weekly TV and radio guides. However, few if any pay TV programmes are listed in most publications. Programmes can also be displayed via TV teletext or on the internet. The time difference between the states (see page 417) means that nationwide programmes are broadcast at different times according to where you live in Australia.

TELEVISION

Free terrestrial (known as free-to-air) TV includes both government-owned and commercial stations. In addition, pay TV is provided (via cable) in most major cities, and satellite TV is also available in country and outback areas. WebTV was introduced in 1998, where customers can purchase a set-top box (for around $200) with a built-in modem for internet access (no computer is required), a pay-TV decoder and a CD-ROM drive for games. Digital TV started in early 2001 in Adelaide, Brisbane, Melbourne, Perth and Sydney, and in 2007 was available in all capital cities, many regional areas and some remote areas. To find out if digital TV is available in your area, go to 🖥 www.dba.org.au (click on 'Reception Locator'). Digital TV boxes cost from $70 to $1,200 and TVs with integrated digital boxes start at $900. Analogue TV will be 'switched off' between 2010 and 2012.

Programmes

Australian TV is famous for its soaps, although some have terrible scripts and even worse 'acting'. The most popular Australian soaps include *Flying Doctor*, *Home and Away*, and *Neighbours*, which are sold worldwide and are particularly popular in the UK. British comedy, drama and soaps are also popular in Australia, as are the 'better' American programmes. The choice of films on free-to-air (FTA) TV is usually terrible and you need to subscribe to pay TV to see the latest films. Australian TV isn't as paranoid about nudity as American TV, but you're unlikely to see any explicit sex (except perhaps on pay or satellite TV). News and current affairs programmes are popular, although news tends to be parochial and doesn't include much world news. There are good weather forecasts on all channels.

> There's little good quality Australian produced comedy and drama, mainly because of lack of funds or small audiences.

The best Australian production seems to run to are the so-called 'infotainment' shows, which show you how to update your garden, home, etc. for next to nothing.

Australian TV, particularly commercial stations, shows a surfeit of live sport, particularly at weekends. Coverage includes both local and international events, including American football, athletics, Australian rules football, baseball, basketball, cricket, motor racing, rugby, soccer, swimming and tennis. To protect significant sporting and cultural events from being bought by pay TV, the government introduced an 'anti-siphoning' list of events (11 sports plus the Olympic and Commonwealth Games) which should be televised free to the general public. However, over half the events on the anti-siphoning list have never been shown at all on FTA TV and fewer than a third have been shown live on FTA. Pay TV operators are pushing to have the list reduced or to be permitted to show live sports and events that have been rejected by the FTA stations.

Standards & Equipment

The standards for TV reception in Australia aren't the same as in many other countries, as it uses the PAL-D system. TVs and video recorders manufactured for use in North America (NTSC standard) and for the European PAL B/G or PAL-I systems won't function in Australia. Some foreign TVs can be converted to operate under Australia's PAL-D system, although it usually isn't worth the trouble and expense of shipping a TV (or VCR) to Australia.

The cost of a TV varies considerably according to its features, make, screen size and, not least, the retailer (shop around). The cost of a quality TV ranges from around $200 for a 34cm (14in) portable TV to $1,400 for a state-of-the-art 63cm (24in) TV. You can buy a 42" flat screen plasma TV for around $2,500. Video recorders, which are available only in combination with a TV or DVD player, start at around $200 and DVD players at around $100. All the latest and most sophisticated entertainment systems are available in Australia. If you want a home theatre package it can cost anything from $2,000 to $10,000.

When buying a TV in Australia, it's advantageous to choose one with teletext, which apart from allowing you to display programme listings, also provides a wealth of useful and interesting information, including entertainment, finance, news, shopping, sport, travel and weather. Teletext also provides subtitles for selected programmes for people with hearing problems, which are usually indicated in programme listings. Pay TV and satellite stations also provide teletext services.

There's an active market in second-hand TVs and videos (and most other things) in Australia so, should you wish to sell your old TV to buy one with the latest bells and whistles (or because you're leaving Australia), you'll have no problem. Second-hand colour TVs can be purchased from retailers and rental companies and through advertisements in local newspapers from as little as $50. TV rental is fairly common in Australia and is mostly offered by specialist national rental companies (such as Rentlo), although some local TV and radio shops also rent. It's always cheaper to buy than rent a TV or video, particularly over a long period. Some people are tempted to rent by the ever-changing technology, although you should bear in mind that rental TVs are rarely the latest models and the minimum rental period is usually 12 or 18 months.

Free-to-air Stations

There are five national terrestrial or free-to-air (FTA) networks in Australia: ABC, Nine, SBS, Seven and Ten. ABC (Australian Broadcasting Corporation) and SBS (Special Broadcasting Service) are government-owned, while Nine, Seven and Ten are commercial networks. There are also a number of regional commercial stations (including NBN, Prime, Seven Network, Southern Cross, Ten Network and Win), Imparja Television (an Aboriginal commercial station), plus community, local and student TV.

> Not all areas receive all the national networks: most state capitals can receive between three and five, while in some remote areas ABC may be the only free-to-air station you can receive.

ABC

The name of the local ABC station varies according to the state, e.g. it's called ABN in New South Wales (the N is for NSW) and ABV in Victoria, although it's usually found on channel two. Being non-commercial, it holds the moral high ground with regard to quality programming (almost nothing American is aired!) and its output contains a large percentage of locally produced programmes with the emphasis on comedy, drama, natural history (mostly about Australia), news and current affairs. Comedy and drama programmes are often imported from the UK.

SBS

The Special Broadcasting Service (SBS, ⌨ www20.sbs.com.au) is a government-sponsored, multicultural TV station, established in 1978 to provide multi-lingual radio and TV services that educate, entertain and inform all Australians and reflect Australia's multicultural society. SBS is available in all major cities and a number of regional areas, and is watched by some 8m people per week (according to its website). It's similar to PBS in America, although it screens a large percentage of programmes in foreign languages with subtitles, in addition to English-language programmes. Although mainly funded by the government, it carries advertising. It's usually found on channel eight, although you need a special receiver in some areas.

SBS provides foreign 'culture' unavailable on other channels and excellent world news coverage which is far superior to the more parochial output of ABC and the commercial stations. It also shows foreign sport (e.g. European soccer) that isn't found on commercial TV and is the traditional host channel of the (football) World Cup. It's sometimes criticised, however, as being insensitive to community needs and it also shows a lot of 'trashy' foreign films.

Commercial Television

Australia has three commercial networks: Nine, Seven and Ten, which are available in major cities and offer 24-hour programming. Nine Network has been the leading station for some years, although it's given a close run by Seven Network. Nine is unashamedly populist and produces game shows, lifestyle programmes and news and current affairs programmes, but isn't so good at comedy and drama, although its imported American programmes such as *House* and *King of Queens* rank at the top of the viewing ratings. Its other forte is sport, which dominates programming.

Seven Network is the second-highest rated network (by viewing figures) after Nine and is strong on comedy and drama and more likely to show non-commercial programmes. Its most popular programmes include *The Weakest Link* and recent movies. Seven Network has weaker news and current affairs than Nine.

Ten Network had given up trying to compete with Nine and Seven for the mainstream market and was concentrating on screening popular American shows (*The Simpsons*, *Medium*) for the under 40s, but the success of *Australian Idol* has reversed this trend. It isn't strong on local programmes, although it did come up with *Neighbours* and *Heartbreak High*.

The quality of programmes on commercial TV varies from terrible to excellent. The competition to buy foreign (e.g. British and American) programmes and exclusive rights to sporting events is fierce, particularly with the increased competition from pay TV. It's hoped that this will result in the networks producing more of their own programmes, which, apart from being superior to a lot of the imported drivel, are also a lucrative export product. Commercial TV networks currently produce just over half their programmes.

Advertisements on commercial TV are frequent and irritating, particularly when you're trying to watch a film or sport. Some sports events are ruined by commercial breaks, and advertisements are sometimes even screened during play at the bottom of the screen. Breaks tend to be more frequent and last longer than in many other countries and even exceed those on some American stations (where the advertisements seem to last longer than the programmes). The maximum permitted advertising quota is 13 minutes per hour but, when promotional slots and trailers are included, it's much longer. Commercial stations are huge money-spinners and regularly change owners. Breakfast TV is popular on all commercial stations.

Imparja Television

Imparja Television is an Aboriginal-owned and -run commercial TV station operating out of Alice Springs. It covers a third of the country, mainly in the Northern Territory, South Australia and western NSW. Broadcasts range from soap operas to programmes made especially for Aboriginal people.

Community or Local Television

There are community or local TV stations in all major cities. Community TV stations include ACE-TV (Adelaide), Briz31 (Brisbane), CATV (Canberra), CTS (Sydney), CTV 31 (Perth), LINC TV (NSW) and MCT-31 (Melbourne). There's also

student TV in some cities, such as RMITV in Melbourne.

Pay Television

Pay TV was introduced in Australia in 1995 and shouldn't be confused with pay-per-view, where subscribers pay on a per programme basis (e.g. for a live concert or sports event). With pay TV, viewers pay a monthly fee for a package of stations, delivered via cable or satellite. There are two major pay TV operators in Australia, Foxtel (50 per cent owned by Telstra) and Austar, plus some smaller operators. Pay TV operators have been allowed to broadcast advertisements since 1997.

The installation of cables for pay TV in Australia was one of the largest and fastest such programme undertaken anywhere in the world, and cable currently reaches over 3m homes, mostly in major cities. Most homes in Brisbane, the Gold Coast, Melbourne and Sydney are cabled, plus parts of Adelaide and Perth. Broadband cable is used to deliver FM radio, high-speed internet access, pay TV, telephone, and other interactive services such as community information systems. It also enables operators to offer pay-per-view films and other broadcasts on demand.

Unlike satellite and cable TV in Europe and North America, pay TV in Australia doesn't have sufficient big exclusive sports or entertainment specials to attract the average viewer (Australia's climate also means that many people have better things to do than watch TV). There are two major pay TV operators in Australia, Foxtel (the largest with some 1.4m subscribers) and Austar (640,000 subscribers) as well as other smaller (usually local) companies. Foxtel (🖳 www.foxtel.com.au) covers around 70 per cent of the population in Australia and offers over 100 channels. Austar (🖳 www.austar.com.au) specialises in coverage for regional and rural areas, and offers around 120 channels.

Foxtel and Austar both charge an installation fee of around $100 (but much higher for homes with difficult access) plus a monthly subscription of from around $38, depending on the programme package. You can choose from a range of packages depending on your preferred viewing, e.g. sport or films. Subscriptions can be paid by cash at The Australia & New Zealand Bank (ANZ) branches and post offices and by cheque, credit card, direct debit or money order. Some cable companies offer inexpensive telephone and internet services, in some cases including free local off-peak calls, and it's possible to save enough money on your telephone bill to pay for your cable TV.

Although Brisbane, Melbourne and Sydney have been 'cornered' by Foxtel and Austar, the rest of the country is wide open and being exploited by small companies, such as Northgate Cable in Ballarat and Neighbourhood Cable in Mildura (VIC), who have encroached on the majors' market share by offering internet, telephone and

The latest releases can be rented for around $10 per night and older films can be rented for up to a week for as little as $3. Rental outlets usually have special offers for film buffs such as a free old movie with each new release rented or seven old movies for a week for $10.

Usually, you can take out up to three or four films at any time and must return them up to two hours before closing time the following day. If you're late returning a film, you're charged an extra day's rental for each day overdue. If you lose or damage a film, you're expected to pay for a replacement at retail price. Videos can also be rented from some public libraries. Most video shops sell second-hand videos at reduced prices as well as older videos which are on general sale.

TV services at lower prices, e.g. between $10 and $50 per month for various packages.

Subscribers usually receive free monthly programme guides, which are also available from newsagents. However, most Australian newspapers and TV guides virtually ignore pay TV and don't list any programmes, while some list only selected channels (e.g. Foxtel highlights).

VIDEO & DVD

In the last decade or so, there has been an explosion in the number of video and DVD rental outlets in Australia, which reached saturation point some years ago (they total over 3,000 with an annual turnover of more than $600m). There's also a thriving DVD sales market. Many video shops are open until 8 or 10pm, seven days a week.

To rent a video or DVD you must usually be a member, for which shops insist on proof of address and verification of your signature. A parent is required to stand as a guarantor for those under 18.

RADIO

Australian radio is regulated by the Australian Communications and Media Authority (ACMA). Radio reception is excellent in most parts of the country, including stereo radio, which is clear in all but the most remote areas. Radio is very popular, particularly among the young – three out of four teenagers listen daily. Local stations broadcast on the FM wave band in stereo or on the medium wave (MW) band. High-quality FM radio can also be received via cable or satellite, which provides dozens of stations. The short wave (SW) band is useful for receiving foreign radio stations. Digital radio was introduced in 2001 and allows stations to transmit several channels of sound simultaneously, as well as text and pictures to a small screen attached to receivers.

There are literally hundreds of radio stations in Australia, including ABC, commercial, ethnic, community and university-based stations (operated on a shoe-string and run by volunteers). In the last few decades, dozens of public (community) radio stations have sprung up around Australia, supported by the government and various educational institutions. They often have a limited transmission range and cater for specific community groups within their areas, e.g. there are around 16 community stations in Sydney, which although amateurish are diverse and original.

ABC

The Australian Broadcasting Corporation (ABC) is government-funded and runs metropolitan radio stations in nine cities and 36 regional stations, including ABC Classic FM, Radio National and the Triple-J (JJJ) youth radio network. ABC metropolitan radio includes 702 Sydney and 774 Melbourne. It also operates the 24-hour Parliamentary & News Network, a parliamentary radio service broadcast to all capital cities except Darwin (lucky them!) and to Newcastle. The ABC is also responsible for Radio Australia, an international radio service broadcast via short wave and satellite (in English and eight other languages) to the Asia-Pacific region and worldwide, although services have been reduced in recent years and remain under threat from budget cuts.

ABC Radio National provides excellent news coverage (international news is sent by satellite from the BBC in London) and is broadcast nationwide on both AM and FM. However, in general, ABC stations aren't as popular as commercial stations and are regarded as the thinking person's radio

stations. Triple-J is the one exception and is a good place to hear new music outside the main pop stream and plug into Australia's youth culture. There's no advertising on ABC radio stations.

Commercial Radio

Commercial radio stations are hugely popular in Australia and include large city stations with vast budgets and hundreds of thousands of listeners. The largest radio station networks in Australia are owned by Austereo, the Australian Radio Network and DMG Radio Australia.

Stations provide a comprehensive service of consumer advice, education, local news and information, music and other entertainment, and traffic information. There are also 'talk-back' stations (such as Melbourne's top-rated 3AW), which intersperse music with phone-in discussions. Many stations have star presenters whose 'fame' is often due to their outrageous and insulting behaviour towards their listeners (sports commentators can also be extremely rude about players' performances).

> The location of a station can be determined by its call sign, the first number of which is the same as a state or territory's postcode, e.g. 2UE is a Sydney station and 3CR is in Melbourne.

Stations cater for every musical taste (e.g. classical, easy listening, jazz, pop/rock), although pop stations are the most popular and cater mostly for mainstream tastes. Some stations even change their output (e.g. from easy listening to hard rock or vice versa) at the drop of a hat if their audience figures fall dramatically. Music is usually blended with news updates, traffic and weather reports, although some stations have taken to playing less music and telling jokes, which apparently receive a higher rating than music. Radio stations employ real comedians, not just DJs trying to raise a chuckle, with a down-to-earth sense of humour where anything goes and nothing is sacred.

As their name implies, commercial radio stations in Australia carry advertising, which is their main source of income.

Ethnic Radio

Australians can tune in to local radio broadcasts in over 50 languages, including Aboriginal radio in outback regions. One of these, the Special Broadcasting Service (SBS) was established in 1994 and like SBS TV (see page 157) broadcasts in many languages. It's available in all state and territory capital cities plus some other cities.

BBC World Service

The BBC World Service (the insomniac's station) broadcasts worldwide, in English and around 35 other languages. The BBC World Service is the most famous and highly respected international radio service in the world, with regular listeners estimated at some 120m (give or take a few). Its main aims are to provide unbiased news, project British opinion, and reflect British culture, life and developments in science and industry. News bulletins, current affairs, political commentaries and topical magazine programmes form the bulk of its output, supported by drama, general entertainment, music and a comprehensive sports service. The BBC publishes a monthly magazine *BBC On Air*, giving comprehensive information about BBC radio and TV programmes. A programme guide is also listed on the internet (💻 www.bbc.co.uk/worldservice/programmes).

9.

EDUCATION

Australian educational institutions generally have a good international reputation, particularly universities and tertiary-level colleges, and there are 250,000 foreign students in the Australian higher education sector. Australian schools provide a high standard of teaching and produce good academic results, and the country has a proud record of academic and scientific achievement. In international surveys, Australian students score highly in mathematics and science.

Full-time education was introduced in West Australia in 1871, other states following suit shortly afterwards, and is compulsory between the ages of 6 and 15 (16 in Tasmania). Around 75 per cent of pupils complete 12 years of schooling, although this varies with the state or territory. Primary education lasts for six or seven years up to the age of 12 or 13 and secondary schooling for a further five or six years. Students are encouraged to remain at school until the completion of their 12th year (around the age of 18), although this may depend on the local job market. The government has cut unemployment benefits for young people in recent years to 'encourage' them to stay at school or take up training rather than search for non-existent jobs. This has led to overcrowding in many high schools, where classes are bulging with students who don't want to be there.

Education in Australia is mainly the responsibility of state and territory governments, each of which has its own education system. State and territorial governments have the major responsibility for education and provide most funding, supported by the federal government.

States administer their own primary and secondary schools, and are also responsible for technical and further education. The federal government, via the Department of Education, Science and Training (💻 www.dest.gov.au), is responsible for tertiary education and provides supplementary funding for schools and for technical and further education. It's also responsible for education in the Australian territories of Christmas Island, the Cocos Islands and Norfolk Island.

A national literacy survey in 1997 found that a third of students in primary years three and five couldn't read or write adequately, branded a 'national disgrace' by the federal schools minister. The problem of illiteracy is exacerbated by the thousands of migrant families who don't speak English or where English isn't spoken at home. Aboriginal children also have a low rate of literacy – generally three to four years behind other pupils. It was estimated in 1996 that half of all Australians aged 15 to 74 (over 6m people) had poor or very poor literacy skills, just 2m people (15 per cent) having good literacy skills and a mere 300,000 very good skills. Adults with the poorest skills were (not surprisingly) mostly from non-English speaking backgrounds. A national goal was set for each child starting school from 1998 to achieve an acceptable level of literacy and numeracy through the federal government's Literacy For All programme. As a result, pupils are tested for literacy every two years, in school years 3, 5, 7 and 9 or 10. A National Literacy and Numeracy Week is celebrated annually in early September to help publicise the literacy work in schools, and awards are made to schools and pupils who have made the most impressive progress. The programme has raised the standards of numeracy and literacy right across Australia and in 2006 21 per cent of students achieved a BA degree or higher – a significant increase on the 1996 figure of 13 per cent.

There's no legal obligation for parents to educate their children at school and they may educate them themselves or employ private tutors (with the advent of the internet it's possible for children to be educated almost exclusively at home). Parents educating their children at home don't require a teaching qualification, and in Victoria they aren't even required to inform the Education Department of their decision. In other states, however, they must satisfy the local education authority that a child is receiving full-time education appropriate to his age and aptitude (they check and may test your child). Information can be obtained from the Alternative Education Resources Group in most states.

Many schools have special programmes for children with learning difficulties and for gifted children, and there are also hospital schools, where children who need prolonged hospitalisation are educated, and schools for blind and deaf children. However, whenever possible, children with disabilities attend regular schools in which support is provided for them. Parents can obtain information from the Specific Learning Difficulties Association (SPELD).

The Australian term public school (or government school) refers to a non fee-paying school funded wholly from state and federal government budgets. However, in this book the term state school is used, to avoid confusion with the British English term public school, which means private school.

Australia has around 9,600 primary and secondary schools, some 27 per cent of which are private (mostly Catholic church schools with some Church of England and other parochial schools). Most state schools are co-educational (mixed) day schools, with the exception of a few secondary schools that accept boarders. It's generally considered that private schools are superior to state institutions and, although there's little difference between the best state and private schools, it's true that the worst-performing private schools are generally streets ahead of the worst state schools.

There are many books and magazines for parents choosing between state and private education, including *Choosing a School* magazine (published in separate editions for Victoria and New South Wales), available from Universal Magazines, Unit 5, 6-8 Byfield Street, North Ryde, NSW 2113 (☎ 02-9805 0339, 💻 www. universalmagazines.com.au).

STATE SCHOOLS

Spending on state schools varies from state to state and is a hotly debated subject. Local businesses provide sponsorship and extra funding for schools, plus practical work experience, share resources such as computers and other equipment, and help in creating specialised science courses. In recent years, however, many primary schools have been forced to cut back on computer classes for lack of resources.

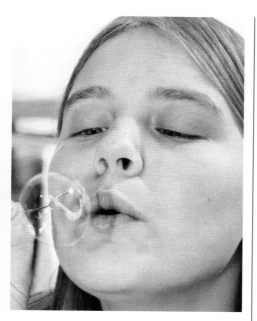

which there has been criticism of the quality of teacher selection and of training and teaching methods – added to which there's an acute shortage of teachers. Many teachers in state schools are demoralised and, according to some reports, around half would give up teaching if they could. Their complaints include having to teach children with little or no English, falling pay compared with other professionals (although teachers are generally well paid), a lack of resources, long hours, low professional standing, large classes, a crowded curriculum, violence and discipline problems (corporal punishment is forbidden in state schools), and poor working conditions, e.g. teaching in portable classrooms in temperatures over 40°C (104°F)!

Most children having a state education attend schools near their homes, although in country areas a long journey may be involved, particularly to secondary school. Usually, primary and secondary schools are separate institutions, but in some country areas there are combined primary and secondary (area or central) schools. School buses may be provided for children in rural areas, while in remote outback regions children do their lessons by correspondence or via the 'school of the air', where lessons are given over the Flying Doctor radio network throughout Australia (both state and private schools participate in programmes). Correspondence lessons use video and audio tapes and are usually supervised by a member of the family and administered by a correspondence school in a state capital. State schools don't have canteens or restaurants, although school 'tuckshops' sell sandwiches, snacks and soft drinks at break and lunchtimes.

A large number of state schools are modern institutions, having been built in the last decade or so, particularly in the outer suburbs of capital cities. Nevertheless, budget restrictions have resulted in school closures and have driven more families to send their children to private schools. In the mid-'90s, there was an unprecedented exodus of students from state to private schools, making it difficult for governments to provide quality state education in some areas (a number of state schools were forced to close by falling enrolments). In recent years, some state schools have been increasingly turning to voluntary levies to raise funds (usually to pay for additional materials) as state and federal funding has been cut. In some states, 'free' state education is fast becoming a misnomer, many parents being forced to pay $1,000 to $2,000 per year (see **Parents & Citizens Committees** below and **Uniforms & Expenses** on page 170).

The state school system has been in almost constant flux in recent years, during

Parents & Citizens Committees

Parents play a vital role in state education in Australia, where each school has a committee comprising parents, student representatives and teachers, called a Parents and Citizens (P&C) committee. Parents can influence decisions such the design and wearing of uniforms, discipline, homework and even the curriculum, and P&C committees (of which parents make up a third) also raise funds for school outings and equipment and assist in running certain aspects of the school such as administration, classroom assistance and school shops.

> **☑ SURVIVAL TIP**
>
> **An enthusiastic and flourishing P&C committee is usually a sign of a good school.**

Curriculum & Homework

The state curriculum contains eight key learning areas: creative and practical arts; English; foreign languages; health and physical education; human society and the environment; mathematics; science; and technology. Although states have a measure of autonomy in setting their own curricula, they must follow guidelines laid down by the federal government, and the curriculum is broadly similar in all states, so children generally experience few problems when moving from one state to another. Individual schools also have a degree of autonomy and can determine their own teaching and learning approaches within the guidelines provided and offer options within the resources available. For example, some schools specialise in languages and place greater emphasis on foreign language study, with imaginative programmes and innovative teaching methods. Where necessary, students from non-English-speaking countries are given extra English classes, and English as a Second Language (ESL) programmes are provided in schools with significant numbers of children from non-English speaking backgrounds.

Computer technology is an increasingly important part of teaching in Australian schools at all levels right across the curriculum. Some schools excel in their use of computers, although the ratio of computers to students is low in most state schools, many of which buy computers (and other equipment) with money raised by parents and sponsors.

Extra-curricular activities are common in Australia and include arts and crafts, camps and other excursions, social events such as discos and barbecues, and sports (an important feature of Australian school life). School bands, choirs, dance troupes, dramatic societies and orchestras are common.

School homework varies considerably, some children doing too little and others doing more than is healthy; the amount is determined largely by individual teachers, although parental influence is important in Australia and parents' views are listened to via P&C committees.

Choosing a School

The quality of state schools, their teaching staff and the education they provide varies considerably according to the state or territory, region, town, city, suburb and individual school. Children have the right to attend their local state school, although they may attend any other state school (in the state or territory where they live) where there's a vacancy. However, priority at any school goes to local children (see **Admissions** below). It's important to research the best schools in a given area and to ensure that your child will be accepted at your chosen school before buying or renting a home. Some high schools (usually in the poorer and more disadvantaged areas) have discipline, drug and violence problems and have had to install video cameras and take other measures to identify offenders. Obviously, these schools are best avoided if possible.

Admissions

Enquiries about admission (enrolment) to a state school should be addressed directly to the headmaster or principal of the school of your choice. Enquiries should be made well in advance of taking up residence in a new area. Most children go to the school nearest their home, particularly at primary level. All children are guaranteed a place at their local state high school, but parents have the option of applying to up to four non-local high schools. Placement outside the local area depends on the availability of places and, if daily travel isn't feasible, accommodation at the school.

When visiting a school, you should take your child's certificates, references and reports from previous schools.

> New pupils are assessed and admitted to the appropriate class for their age and educational level, and it's unusual for a child to be placed with children of more than a year's age difference.

Admission to a state primary school for foreign children is dependent on their parents securing a temporary residence visa (see **Temporary Residents** on page 67) or the child securing a visa sub-class 571 (for secondary exchange school students) – unless they're nationals of Papua New Guinea or certain South Pacific states. Secondary school-age children of any nationality may attend state schools but non-Australians must pay full fees (called the Overseas Students' Charge), which vary from $5,000 to $13,000 annually.

Australia's academic year follows the calendar year from January to December. Starting ages for primary and secondary schools vary with the state or territory and there are at least six different school entry ages across Australia. In South Australia and the Northern Territory there's a continuous intake and children may begin school when they turn five years of age. However, in Western Australia children born after 30th June aren't able to start school until the year they turn seven, and in Victoria they must be aged five by 30th April of the year of enrolment. Such differences can cause problems when children move to a new state, and the federal government has proposed a plan which would ensure that children start school at the same age in all states. All schools prefer children to start at the beginning of a term if possible, and most schools like parents to apply in October for children starting school the following year.

School Hours & Terms

All states have four terms of around ten weeks except Tasmania, which has three. Terms are separated by holidays lasting around two weeks, except the summer break, which is six or seven weeks. There may also be breaks for public holidays. The length and dates of school terms vary

holidays. Children being looked after may spend up to 25 hours a week in care, in addition to normal school hours. Fees vary from almost nothing to $75 per week, rising to $90 for two children and $120 for three.

Uniforms & Equipment

Most state schools encourage pupils to wear uniform and they're compulsory at some schools (although tracksuits or jeans may be permitted during winter). Uniforms are usually optional in primary schools. Uniforms can be expensive (with different uniforms for summer and winter), as each school usually has its own embroidered blazers, caps, jumpers and socks, which means that they must be specially made in small quantities. Uniforms can sometimes be purchased second-hand from school shops.

Hats are an integral part of school uniforms and are designed to protect pupils from the sun. High protection sunscreen is also provided free to pre-school and primary year one pupils in many states, and most schools have a 'hot weather' policy where all children must wear sun hats (with a wide brim to protect the neck) at playtime. Students at some colleges are being encouraged to wear sunglasses with UV400 polycarbonate lenses to protect against eye cancer and other eye problems caused by the sun.

In addition to uniforms, parents can expect to pay for some or all of the following:

● additional clothing such as sportswear and gym shoes, and bags or satchels in which to carry them;

● transport to and from school (local transport authorities may provide concessionary or free travel in some areas);

● calculators, notebooks, pencils, pens, textbooks and writing paper, etc., and arts, crafts and manual work materials;

with the state or territory. School term dates can be found on the Department of Education, Science and Training's website (🖳 www.dest.gov.au). Holiday dates are also published by schools well in advance, thus allowing you plenty of time to schedule family holidays. Normally parents aren't permitted to withdraw children from classes during the school term, except for visits to a doctor or dentist, when the teacher should be informed in advance (if possible).

Classes start at around 9am and continue until 4pm, with breaks mid-morning and mid-afternoon as well as at lunchtime. Some children may need to work longer hours if they need extra tuition, for example in English. The maximum teaching hours are around 22.5 in primary schools and 20 in secondary schools.

Many schools provide care and recreational facilities outside school hours for children whose parents are working, seeking work or studying, for which a fee is levied. Supervision may include before- and after-school care and care during school

Some states provide free books for primary school students; their cost may be subsidised for secondary school students. Many secondary schools operate a text book loan or rental scheme, whereby a refundable deposit is paid by each student at the beginning of secondary schooling. Text books can also be purchased second-hand;

- sports facilities and team matches and trips.

The estimated minimum cost of equipping a child is around $550 per year in primary school and up to $2,250 per year in senior secondary school. Parents are sometimes also asked to contribute to the cost of new books for school libraries.

☑ **SURVIVAL TIP**

Parents of children in the last two years (11 and 12) of secondary school can apply for a means-tested Austudy grant (see page 223).

Pre-school & Day Care

Although attendance at a pre-school for children under five isn't compulsory in Australia, finding a pre-school or day care centre can be difficult, particularly in cities and urban areas. Attendance fees aren't usually charged in states where pre-schools are government-run (although there may be a 'voluntary' levy). However, federal government cuts have resulted in the closure of many non-profit, community-based, child-minding centres in recent years, and those that have remained open have begun to charge for attendance. Fees are around $50 per day at a public day care centre but may depend on the parents' income, better-off parents being asked to contribute more and low income parents exempt.

State pre-schools, also called child-parent centres (or kindergarten for the year prior to primary school), are often incorporated within primary schools and open during school hours. In commercially-run centres, fees are payable to private or voluntary organisations and, in city areas, can cost from $400 to $2,000 per child per term.

Most pre-schools operate from 9am to 2.30pm, Mondays to Fridays. Programmes usually follow the free play approach, with the emphasis on social and emotional development through creative activity. Pre-school doesn't generally provide formal education, although research has shown that children who attend pre-school are generally brighter and usually progress faster than those who don't. After one or two years in pre-school, a child is integrated into the local community and is well prepared for primary school. Pre-school is highly recommended if your child's mother-tongue isn't English.

In Queensland, a trial began in 2007 to replace most state and private pre-schools with 'prep' (short for preparatory) schools. Prep school provides full-time education for all children prior to grade 1. It's provided free in state schools and is non-compulsory. If it proves to be a success, other states will follow suit.

Primary School

Primary education in Australia is compulsory from the age of six – but normally begins at five in some states (see **Admissions** on page 169) – and is almost always co-educational (mixed). Some primary schools also provide nursery or pre-school classes for children under five (see above). Primary education lasts for six or seven years (school years 1 to 6 or 7) up to the age of 12 or 13, depending on the state or territory.

All primary schools must meet broad curriculum and standards guidelines developed by the Board of Studies. The emphasis is on the development of basic language and literacy skills, simple arithmetic, moral and social education, health training and some creative activities. In the higher primary years, lessons include art and craft, English, health, mathematics, music, physical education, science, social studies (e.g. studies of society and environment), and technology and computer studies. Optional subjects may include community studies and foreign languages (called a 'language other than English' or LOTE), instruction on a musical instrument and religious instruction.

In some states (e.g. Victoria) foreign languages are compulsory. Swimming lessons are provided, usually at public swimming pools, as only around 30 per cent of state schools have their own pools. Sex education is also part of the curriculum, though schools can also develop their own programmes to suit local needs and priorities within government guidelines. The school day is generally divided into three or four sessions, daily instruction lasting for around five hours and consisting of 20- or 30-minute lessons.

Parent-teacher interviews are conducted once or twice a year and provide an opportunity for parents to discuss their child's progress. Children are continually assessed and parents periodically receive written reports, e.g. twice a year in Victoria. Under the state-wide literacy and numeracy standards initiative, pupils are assessed in years 3, 5 and 7. Assessment results are usually confidential and are used to identify pupils' needs, e.g. extra help with English.

Pupils in primary schools usually have one teacher for most (if not all) subjects. In large schools, pupils are graded according to age and are moved up each year irrespective of their level of achievement. In rural areas, a primary 'school' may consist of no more than a couple of portable classrooms and two teachers teaching 15 to 30 pupils of various ages in all subjects.

> Many new primary schools are designed on the 'open plan' concept, which allows two or more teachers to supervise up to 70 pupils (team teaching), although pupils are divided into small groups for separate activities, including individual study.

Children progress to a secondary (high) school at school year 7 or 8 (aged 12 or 13).

Secondary School

Secondary school (called high school in Australia) is for children aged from 12 or 13 to 17 or 18 (from school years 7 or 8 to year 12). The minimum school leaving age is 15 (16 in Tasmania), and secondary school lasts for a maximum of five or six years, depending on the state or territory.

Most secondary students complete year 10 (age 16) and a large percentage stay on at school until year 12 (age 18). Completion of year 12 is usually necessary to attend an institution of higher education, such as a university or college of advanced education. Years 11 and 12 are usually taken at separate colleges (also known as senior high schools), offering a range of subjects studied by adults as well as senior students – and sometimes also years 9 and 10.

Secondary schools are usually co-educational, although there are some single-sex schools in capital cities. The most common state secondary school is the comprehensive or multi-purpose high school. In some states there are separate schools for agricultural, commercial and technical subjects, where general academic subjects are combined with practical training, and selective high and grammar schools for academically gifted students (competition for places is stiff). Some secondary schools are further classified as technology or language high schools, or as centres of excellence in certain subjects. At technical high schools, students learn a trade and go on to a TAFE college (see page 229). Most secondary schools have modern facilities for teaching commercial subjects, home economics, manual crafts and other technical disciplines. Most states and territories also provide schools for outstandingly bright or gifted children, where admission is subject to a test and school reports.

Agricultural high schools usually cater for boarders, and some country state schools have hostels for children who are unable to travel to and from school daily.

Students in secondary schools generally have a different teacher for each subject, although variations may occur where open plan or more flexible teaching methods have been adopted. Moving up to the next year is generally automatic on completion of the previous year, although students may be grouped according to ability (streamed)

in some subjects after an initial period in unstreamed classes. However, classes aren't streamed in academic or technically oriented subjects.

Curriculum

In most states, the first one or two years consist of a general programme followed by all students, although there may be some choice of lessons (electives). In the last two years, a basic core of subjects is retained and students are able to select additional subjects, although in some states students select a number of optional subjects from the start of high school.

The core subjects in all schools comprise the eight key learning areas of the arts, English, foreign languages, health, mathematics, science, social studies and the environment, and technology.

Examinations

Individual states and territories set their own examinations, although in most states students take the School Certificate (SC) at the age of 15 or 16 (at the end of year 10) and the Higher School Certificate (HSC) at the age of 17 or 18 (the end of year 12). Most states issue students with certificates after they've completed their compulsory education at the age of 15, and the majority of students who leave at this age go on to do an apprenticeship or other trade training. The SC (replaced by a Junior or Achievement Certificate in some states) is based on school assessment as well as state-wide reference tests in English and mathematics.

The HSC (replaced by a Matriculation Certificate, Senior Certificate or the Tertiary Admission Examination/Certificate of Education in some states) is based on an external examination held in October or November of school year 12 in addition to school assessment based on a student's last two years' work. In order not to disadvantage children who suffer from exam nerves and to reduce cramming and stress, more emphasis is placed on course work and continuous assessment than on the final examinations. In NSW, as part of a radical change in measuring performance in the final years of schooling, HSC students are assessed against a set of standards rather than against each other. Students receive detailed information about their performance in each subject, detailing the skills they've mastered.

> The HSC (or equivalent) is necessary in order to gain entrance to an Australian university. However, a few universities (in NSW) have waived the HSC requirement if families can afford fees of at least $8,000 for a year at a private college undergoing a 'foundation' course.

Twenty-four schools also offer the International Baccalaureate (IB) plus additional courses with state or TAFE accreditation. Senior high schools (see **Secondary School** on page 215) offer tertiary courses such as Open University or TAFE off-campus.

Leaving

Students attaining the minimum school leaving age may leave school and seek employment or enrol in a vocational course at a TAFE college (see page 183) or a private business college. Completion of year 10 of secondary school is the minimum entry requirement for many TAFE courses. Those who continue to year 12 have several options for further study, including TAFE institutions, higher education and other tertiary-level establishments. A student's eligibility for entry to higher education is assessed during or at the end of his final two years in secondary school. Most states use various combinations of school assessment and public examination (see below).

PRIVATE SCHOOLS

Around 30 per cent of Australian children (over 35 per cent in years 11 and 12) attend private schools (officially referred to as independent schools), of which there are some 2,600 in Australia. These range from nursery (kindergarten) schools to secondary schools, from traditional-style schools to those offering 'alternative' methods of education such as Montessori and Rudolf Steiner schools. They include schools sponsored by churches and religious groups (parochial schools – see below), schools for students with learning difficulties or physical disabilities, and schools for gifted children. In addition to mainstream parochial schools (see below), there are schools for religious and ethnic minorities (e.g. Muslim schools, where there's a strict code regarding the segregation of boys and girls). Most private schools are single-sex, although an increasing number have become co-educational in recent years. There are also boarding schools in Australia, although few schools accept boarders only. Children who board usually do so because they live too far from school to travel every day or because their parents work overseas.

The advantages of private schools are manifold, not least their academic record, which is generally much better than that of state schools. Although many private schools have resolutely embraced new technology (the use of computers and the internet to teach pupils is widespread), private schools tend to place the emphasis on traditional teaching, including consideration for others, good manners, hard work, responsibility and, not least, a sense of discipline (values which are sadly lacking in some state schools). They provide a broad-based education (aimed at developing a pupil's character) and generally provide a more varied approach to art, drama, music and sport, and a wider choice of academic subjects than state schools. Their aim is more the development of children as individuals and the encouragement of their unique talents rather than imparting knowledge and skills on a 'production-line' basis. This is made possible by small classes (an average of around 15 to 20 pupils – as little as half that of many state schools), which allow teachers to provide pupils with individually tailored tuition. Don't, however, assume that all private schools are excellent or that they all offer a better education than state schools, which isn't true.

Many private schools are modelled on English schools and generally use the same terminology as them. For example, years are called forms, the first form of secondary school being equivalent to the state school year 7 or 8 at age 12 or 13, while final year students are referred to as sixth-formers. Some private primary schools are called preparatory (prep) schools – not to be confused with the pilot state prep school system.

> There's no snobbery attached to attending a private school in Australia – what's important is a school's academic standing and how well your children perform. Some parents switch their children from the state to the private sector when they progress to secondary school.

Parochial Schools

The Catholic church operates by far the largest number of private schools in Australia, and there are relatively few other parochial schools (e.g. Anglican, Christian Community and Uniting Church). A total of 677,000 children (in 2006) attend some 1,700 Catholic schools, or around two-thirds of all private school students and around 21 per cent of Australia's 3.3m school children. Most Catholic schools are part of a system administered by the Catholic Education Office, and their fees are usually lower than those of other private schools (see below), as between 51 and 56 per cent of their operating costs are met by federal government. Clergy account for almost all teachers in Catholic schools, which (not surprisingly) devote an above average amount of time to religious subjects. Catholic secondary schools accept children from other religious backgrounds, but priority is given to Catholics.

Fees

Private schools are subsidised by the federal government on a 12-point sliding scale: wealthy schools are subsidised at the lowest level (1) and poor schools at the highest level (12). Students at most private schools receive more public funding than those in state schools and there's controversy over the public funding of schools attended by children of affluent parents.

Private school fees vary considerably according to a variety of other factors, including the age of students, the reputation and quality of the school and its location (schools in major cities are usually the most expensive), but especially its denomination. At a parochial day school fees vary from $2,000 to $3,000 per year at primary level and $5,000 to $8,500 per year at secondary level. However, fees at non-denominational schools are up to $9,000 per year for primary schools and over $13,000 per year for 'elite' high schools (fees have risen considerably in recent years). Tuition fees at boarding schools can exceed $27,000 per year, with boarding charges of $7,500 to $14,000 on top. Some schools, particularly secondary schools, publish fees per term (usually four a year), while others are per school year. Some schools offer reduced fees to parents with two or more children attending the school. In addition to the fees, $2,350 or so must be added per year for books, computers, excursion charges, special equipment (e.g. for sports), uniforms and assorted surcharges including 'building levies'.

Most private schools provide scholarships for bright or talented pupils, which vary in value from full fees to a small percentage. Scholarships are awarded as a result of competitive examination, individual talents or skills, and need.

Curriculum

Most private schools provide a similar curriculum to state schools and set the same examinations (see page 173). However, some private schools offer the International Baccalaureate (IB) examination, an internationally recognised university entrance qualification, which may be an important consideration if you plan to stay in Australia only for a short period.

Admissions

If possible, you should apply at least one or two years in advance, which is generally considered to be the best time to book a place. The best and most popular schools have a demanding selection procedure and long waiting lists (perhaps many years), and parents register a child for entry at birth (or even at conception!) at some schools. Don't rely on enrolling your child in a particular school and neglect the alternatives, particularly if the chosen school has a rigorous entrance examination. When applying, you're usually requested to send previous exam results, records and school reports.

☑ **SURVIVAL TIP**

Before enrolling your child in a private school, make sure that you understand the withdrawal conditions in the school contract.

HIGHER EDUCATION

Post-school education in Australia is generally divided into higher and further education. The states and territories are responsible for administering higher education (called tertiary education in Australia), but the federal government provides the funding. Higher education is usually defined as courses of a standard equivalent to or higher than HSC (see **Examinations** on page 173) and usually refers only to first degree courses; further education (see page 183) generally embraces everything except first degree courses, although the distinction is often blurred. Higher education courses may be full-time, part-time or sandwich courses, which have nothing to do with food but are courses that combine periods of full-time study with periods of full-time training and paid work in industry and commerce.

The Department of Education publishes a range of books for students. *The Good Universities Guide* by Dean Ashenden and

Sandra Milligan (💻 www.thegoodguides. com.au) also makes interesting reading, although it has been criticised by some universities; an associated online 'university rating' system can be accessed at 💻 http://ratings.thegoodguides.com.au. A higher education supplement is published in the Wednesday edition of *The Australian* newspaper.

Universities

Australia has one of the highest ratios of universities ('unis') to population in the world, and the number of students in higher education has increased considerably in the last decade, totalling over 600,000. However, disadvantaged students (e.g. Aboriginals and Torres Strait Islanders, the disabled, those from non-English-speaking backgrounds, the poor and rural dwellers) are under-represented at universities, particularly in the elite institutions. Many prospective students cannot afford the high fees, which have led to student protests in the form of occupations and sit-ins

at university buildings in recent years. Universities have been struggling with funding cuts and many have been forced to axe places, cut research budgets and reduce numbers of postgraduate courses.

Australian universities are both teaching and research institutions, and many have world-renowned research programmes funded by industry in the applied science and technology fields. Degree level courses are offered by around 40 universities. The oldest universities are Sydney and Melbourne (established in the 1850s), which, with the universities of Adelaide, Queensland, Tasmania and Western Australia, form the traditional 'sandstone' universities (the Australian equivalent of America's Ivy League). Degrees from these, 'corporate' universities (Monash and UNSW) and universities of technology (UTs) are the most highly rated. Most older universities follow British or American traditions and offer a wide range of courses, although many universities have a multi-campus structure, each campus specialising in a particular discipline, e.g. an agricultural science college linked to the main campus.

The age of admission to university is usually 18 (although most admit exceptional students at a younger age) and courses are normally for three years, although some last for four. This is seen as a big advantage for foreign students from countries where courses last much longer and helps Australian universities attract a large number of overseas students. Most Australian universities have between 10,000 and 30,000 students (the largest, Monash, has nearly 56,000), although they're usually dispersed over a number of campuses. Around a quarter of university students are 'mature' students aged over 30, two-thirds of whom are women.

Competition for students is fierce, and universities have resorted to innovative advertising to lure school-leavers;

some have even lowered their entrance requirements to attract more students. Many universities deliberately over-enrol, partly in order to receive higher government grants, which has led to an increase in student-staff ratios and fears of a reduction in the quality of teaching. In order to compete with private colleges and other degree-level state institutions, many universities have introduced associate degree courses in fields such as applied science, dance, dental therapy, electrical and electronic engineering, and management.

Other Establishments

Australia also has a number of specialist higher education establishments, which include the Australian College of Physical Education (Sydney), the Australian Defence Force Academy (Canberra), the Australian Film, TV and Radio School (North Ryde, NSW), the Australian Institute of Music (Sydney), the Australian International Hotel School (Canberra), the Australian Maritime College (Launceston, Tasmania), the Christian Heritage College (Brisbane), Engineering Education Australia (distance education), the International College of Hotel Management (Adelaide), KvB Institute of Technology (Sydney), Macleay College (Sydney) and the National Institute of Dramatic Art (Sydney).

Overseas Students

All Australian universities accept overseas students and many spend $millions on overseas marketing and student recruitment (the sandstone universities established their own overseas marketing arm in 1997). There are no quotas for foreign students, but all non-resident students must pay full fees (although grants are available). Overseas students, mostly from Asia, are a major source of income for universities, contributing over $3bn to the Australian economy. Many universities also have thousands of 'offshore' students at facilities in Asian countries and in New Zealand. Australian universities enrolled around 100,000 foreign students per year in the early 21st century and the number is expected to increase steadily in the next few years. When students at secondary schools and private colleges are included, the total number of foreign students studying in Australia is well over 200,000.

⚠ Caution

Overseas students require a student visa (see page 91), which is issued after acceptance on a course and payment of at least half the first year's fees.

Students must have the financial resources to meet day-to-day living expenses for the duration of their course, return fares to Australia and tuition fees (see below).

Foreign students must have an adequate knowledge of English (unless studying English!). If English isn't your mother tongue or the language in which you gained your previous qualifications, you must take the Short Selection Test (SST). Private health insurance is required by all students, e.g. Medibank Private overseas student health cove. Students must be attending full-time courses but are permitted to take part-time jobs of up to 20 hours per week to help cover their living costs.

In order to retain their visas, students must have satisfactory attendance and achievement records. On completion of their courses, overseas students must leave Australia when their visas expire (a written undertaking must be made).

Fees & Expenses

Higher education tuition fees for Australian students were introduced in 1990 (prior to

Some students qualify for a 'Commonwealth-supported' place, whereby the government pays the majority of the cost of the course (averaging 73 per cent). Resident students may be eligible for one of two government grants – a Youth Allowance or an Austudy Grant – or another grant or subsidy. Students can pay their tuition fees via a deferred payment arrangement known as the Higher Education Loan Programme (HELP). Further information about student grants, subsidies and loans can be obtained from various Department of Education websites (⊟ www.dest.gov.au, ⊟ www.backingaustraliasfuture.gov.au and ⊟ www.goingtouni.gov.au).

Overseas students must pay in advance full tuition fees, which vary with the course and university between around $10,000 and $16,000 per year. Various scholarships are available which cover tuition fees and living costs or only tuition fees. Information can be obtained from Australian embassies and high commissions overseas and from the website ⊟ www.studyinaustralia.gov.au.

which tuition was free) under the Higher Education Contribution Scheme (HECS). Students' fees are determined by individual institutions but are subject to a legal maximum. Most institutions' charges are at or near the maximums, which depend on the subject(s) studied, 'banded' as follows (approximate figures):

In addition to tuition fees, students can expect to pay between $600 and $1,250 on text books, which are sold at a discount

Band	Max. Annual Fee	Subjects
1	$4,000	National priorities, i.e. education and nursing
	$5,000	Arts, behavioural science, foreign languages, humanities, social studies, and visual and performing arts
2	$7,120	Accounting, agriculture, administration, 'built environment', commerce, computing, economics, engineering, health, maths, science, statistics and surveying
3	$8,330	Dentistry, law, medicine and veterinary science

to students who have proof that they're studying at an Australian educational institution under the Educational Textbook Subsidy Scheme. Books must be bought at a registered bookseller and you must take your current textbook list with you when you go to buy them. Textbooks can also be purchased second-hand and most universities run second-hand book shops.

Annual living costs for students (excluding course fees) are reckoned to be at least $12,000 per year plus a further $6,000 for a spouse and $3,500 for each child (possibly less outside major cities). Many students find it difficult to survive and some choose an educational institution according to where they can more easily manage on meagre resources (or where they can find part-time work), rather than according to the courses it offers. Many students work part-time during terms and holidays to supplement their income, and around half live with their parents to save costs.

Qualifications & Admissions

Admission for Australian students is usually based on results in the Higher School Certificate (HSC) or the equivalent taken in your final year of high school. However, some universities in NSW have waived the HSC requirement if families can afford fees of over $8,000 for a year at a private college doing a 'foundation' course. (This option has been available to overseas students for years).

University admission systems vary considerably, and each state has its own method of ranking students for entry to universities within the state. For year 12 students the following systems are used:

- **ACT & NSW** – The University Admission Index (UAI) is used in these states.

- **NT, SA, Tasmania & WA** – These states give students a numerical 'score' called a Tertiary Entrance Rank (TER), based on exam results compared with a set of standards.

- **Queensland** – Queensland uses an Overall Position (OP) system, which ranks students on a scale of 1 to 25 (out-of-state students are ranked from 1 to 100).

- **Victoria** – Victoria uses the Equivalent National Tertiary Entrance Rank (ENTER).

All Australian universities accept students from other states, when a complicated system of converting marks is used. See the website ▣ www.goingtouni.gov.au for a table giving an indication of the minimum entrance requirements for each of Australia's universities. There are plans to introduce a nationwide system of university entrance marks, although it's expected to be some years before this is instituted (as with many things in Australia, most states think that their way of doing things is best).

Entrance requirements for mature students are usually different from those mentioned above, and most universities operate adult entry admission schemes, which allow applicants over a certain age admission on the basis of work experience and qualifications other than academic ones.

Generally, overseas students' qualifications which would admit them to a university in their own country are taken into consideration. Whatever your qualifications, each application is considered on its merits. All foreign students require a thorough knowledge of English, which is usually examined unless a certificate is provided. Australian universities accept the International Baccalaureate (IB) certificate as an entrance qualification, but an American high school diploma isn't usually sufficient.

Contact individual universities for detailed information or, for general information, the Department of Education, Science and Training, PO Box 9880, Canberra, ACT 2601 (☎ 02-6240 8111, 🖳 www.dest.gov. au).

To apply for a place at university, you should begin by writing to the Tertiary Admissions Centre (TAC) in the state of your choice. The deadline for applications is the end of September. Each state TAC allows you to make one application, on which you list a number of preferences. Acceptance depends on your qualifications (see above) and the number of available places on a course. You should make sure that you spread your preferences to include some courses on which you're almost certain to gain acceptance. It's possible to change preferences once you know your score, e.g. if you score considerably higher or lower than anticipated. Alternatively, you can re-sit your exams or take a year off and re-apply the following year.

Terms & Courses

The university academic year follows the calendar year, courses taking place from February until November or December. The year commences with an orientation week (O-week), during which enrolment takes place for new students. The year is usually divided into two terms (semesters) of around 14 weeks, with a recess of around two weeks in the middle of each semester and a six- to eight-week summer break. However, most universities now offer summer semesters which allow students to catch up on failed or missed subjects. Examinations are in November or December.

Students take a main subject plus one or two subsidiary subjects, concentrating on their main subject for the first one or two years. In some universities, it's possible for students to design their own degree courses. Many students choose a sandwich course, which includes a period spent working in industry or commerce.

Timetables may be flexible and usually include less than ten hours of classes a week in order to maximise reading and research time. Classes are usually very large, some lectures attracting as many as 500 students. Most courses are taught through lectures and tutorials, students being assessed on their work in assignments, essays, examinations (annual and final) and practical work.

Accommodation

After acceptance at university, students are usually advised to apply for a place in a hall of residence or other college accommodation, such as self-catering houses and apartments. However, such accommodation is limited and in high demand, and many universities don't provide student accommodation at all. You should write as soon as possible after acceptance to the accommodation or housing officer, whose job is to help students find suitable accommodation. There's considerable demand for student accommodation (often from overseas students) in the major cities, particularly Sydney and Melbourne, and many universities are looking at ways of providing more student accommodation.

The cost of accommodation in halls of residence ranges from around $90 per week for self-catering to around $280 for full board. Overseas students are usually given priority for housing, although you should investigate the availability and cost of local accommodation before accepting a place at a university. The Coordinating Committee for Overseas Students helps overseas students find accommodation.

 Caution

A large number of students rent privately-owned apartments or houses, which are often shared with other students, although in many areas this kind of accommodation is difficult to find and expensive (see page 324).

Facilities

All universities have a huge variety of clubs, societies and organisations, many run by the students' association or union, which is the centre of social activities. Most campuses are members of the National Union of Students (NUS), which represents students at state and national levels. Most universities also have excellent sports facilities, and all have bars and canteens. Most clubs fall into the categories of cultural, department-based, political, recreational and sporting. During orientation week, most clubs and societies are represented and compete to sign up new members. Fees are payable, although there are a large number of benefits and facilities, many specifically for overseas students. All universities levy a student

amenities or general service fee (anything from $100 to $500 per year), which helps finance the representative council, sports associations and the student union.

Degrees

A diploma is awarded to students who successfully complete a course of at least two years, either full time or the equivalent period part time. The most common degrees awarded in Australia are a Bachelor of Arts (BA) and a Bachelor of Science (BSc). Bachelor's degrees are given a classification, the highest of which is an 'honours' degree, which is granted to students who have undertaken an extra year of specialised study after a three-year course or who perform outstandingly in a four-year course. The highest pass is a first class degree, which is quite rare.

Second-class degrees are average, while a third-class degree is poor. The lowest classification is a 'pass'. Students can request special consideration and be given a second chance by sitting another exam; in some cases they're granted a 'conceded pass'.

Second (postgraduate) degrees are usually a Master of Arts (MA) or a Master of Science (MSc), which are awarded to Bachelors for a one-year course in a subject other than their undergraduate subjects. Students who do postgraduate work in the same subject(s) as their undergraduate work usually undertake a three-year Doctor of Philosophy (PhD) research programme. In addition to the above, qualifications include diploma, advanced diploma, graduate certificate and graduate diploma.

Under the Australia Qualifications Framework, a national system for the recognition of qualifications established in 1995, students can move more easily between private colleges, TAFE colleges (see page 183) and universities, and have their studies and experience classified.

FURTHER EDUCATION

Further education generally embraces everything except first degree courses taken at universities and colleges of higher education, although the distinction between further and higher education (see page 219) is often blurred. Further education courses may be full or part time and are provided by the Adult Migrant Education Service, the Council of Adult Education, evening colleges, technical colleges, technical and further education (TAFE) colleges (see below), universities, the Workers' Education Association and by numerous 'open learning' institutions such as the Open Training and Education Network (OTEN).

Qualifications that can be earned through further education include the School Certificate (SC), the Higher School Certificate (HSC), the International Baccalaureate (IB), trade certificates, Bachelor's and Master's degrees, Master of Business Administration (MBA) degrees, and a range of internationally recognised certificates and diplomas. Around 80 per cent of Australians take a further education course at some time during their lives.

TAFE Colleges

By far the largest provider of further education courses in Australia is the string of over 200 Technical and Further Education (TAFE) colleges, which together have over a million students. TAFE colleges are state run and are similar throughout the country, many having a number of campuses and training centres (including some universities). Many courses have a strong vocational focus and are noted for their practical, hands-on emphasis.

The majority of TAFE courses are at the certificate, diploma and advanced diploma levels, although some degree level courses are offered, and courses can be used as entry to a full-time degree course at university. TAFE courses include pre-apprenticeships and apprenticeships, trade, post-trade and technician courses, plus commercial and general courses to certificate level. TAFE courses are also used to supplement apprenticeships and on-the-job training. Most courses last around two years and can be undertaken on a part-time or full-time basis or combined with a job when the employer allows time off to attend classes.

TAFE colleges offer hundreds of courses, including all major skills in a wide range of artistic, commercial, domestic and industrial occupations. Many courses are specifically designed for school-leavers to upgrade their skills and for adults wishing to get back into the workforce. Courses range from semi-skilled trade training to professional subjects and include correspondence courses and special programmes for disadvantaged groups. Courses for apprentices cover dozens of trades, including the automotive, building, electrical, electronics, farming, fashion, food, gardening, hairdressing, jewellery, metal, plumbing, printing, textiles and watch making industries, to name but a few. Pre-apprenticeship courses allow young people to undertake a substantial part of a trade course before taking up an apprenticeship in an 'advanced' discipline, such as electrical engineering.

> Fees vary with the state or territory, each of which sets its own fees. The average cost of a full-time course in NSW in 2007 was $328 and for a diploma course around $1,086 per year, although some states waive fees for school-leavers who enrol directly in TAFE courses on leaving school.

There are concessionary rates (or no fees) for low-income earners. Resident students are also eligible for Austudy grants.

Open Universities Australia

Open Universities Australia (formerly Open Learning) was set up by the government to offer high quality tertiary education to all Australians. It's owned and operated by a consortium of seven Australian Universities: Curtin University of Technology, Griffith University, Macquarie University, Monash University, RMIT University, Swinburne University of Technology and the University of South Australia. There are no limits on the number of people who may enrol, no educational requirements and, usually, no requirement to attend on-campus or residential seminars. Students can study in any or all of the four study periods each year, beginning in March, June, September and December.

Students have a choice of 700 individual units and 60 undergraduate, postgraduate and TAFE qualifications, and can take up to ten years to complete a course. All units can be studied at home, with the aid of CD-ROMs, on-line learning and video and

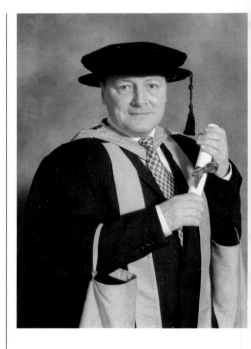

audio cassettes. For further information contact Open Universities Australia, PO Box 5387, Melbourne, VIC 3001 (☎ 03-8628 2500, 🖵 www.open.edu.au).

Private Colleges

Vocational training is offered by private colleges, which are closely aligned to the industries for which they prepare students. Many private colleges offer training in courses such as business, computer studies, hospitality and secretarial skills. Prospective students should check whether a course has been accredited by the relevant body. Some institutions offer distance learning MBA courses for those who cannot (or don't wish to) study on a full- or part-time, locally taught basis. Around 40 business schools and professional organisations offer MBA courses in subjects such as banking, business administration, communications, economics, European languages, information systems, management, marketing, public relations, and social and political studies.

LANGUAGE SCHOOLS

If you don't speak English fluently (or you wish to learn another language) you can enrol on a language course. These are offered by numerous language schools in Australia. Obtaining a working knowledge or becoming fluent in English (or 'strine') while living in Australia is relatively easy, as you're constantly immersed in the English language and have the maximum opportunity to practise. However, if you wish to speak or write English idiomatically, you probably need to attend a language school or find a private tutor. Many thousands of foreign students (mostly from Asian countries) come to Australia each year to learn English, thus ensuring that English-language schools are big business. It's usually necessary to have a recognised qualification in English to be accepted at a college of higher or further education in Australia.

English-language courses are offered at all levels by foreign and international organisations, language schools, local associations and clubs, migrant education colleges, open learning institutions, private colleges, private teachers, universities, and technical and further education (TAFE) colleges. There are English-language schools in all cities and large towns in Australia, most equipped with book shops, computers, libraries and video studios.

Courses range from those for complete beginners, through specialised business or cultural courses, to university-level seminars leading to advanced diplomas. The Department of Immigration, Multicultural and Indigenous Affairs supports Settlement English courses for some migrants, and the cost may be funded by the department. Most language schools offer a variety of classes according to your current language ability, how many hours you wish to study per week, how much money you want to spend and how quickly you wish (or are able) to learn. Language classes generally fall into the following categories: compact (10 to 20 hours per week), intensive (20 to 30 hours), and total immersion (30 to 40 hours or more).

Full-time, part-time and evening courses are offered by most schools, and many also offer residential courses or accommodation with local families (highly recommended to accelerate learning). Courses that include accommodation (often half-board, consisting of breakfast and an evening meal) usually represent good value.

⚠ **Caution**

Bear in mind that, if you need to find your own accommodation, particularly in Sydney or Melbourne, it can be difficult and expensive.

Course fees vary considerably and are usually calculated on a weekly basis. Fees depend on the number of hours' tuition per week, the type of course, and the location and reputation of the school. Expect to pay up to $600 per week for an intensive course and around $400 per week for a compact course. Total immersion or executive courses, which are provided by many schools, can cost $2,000 or more per week, and not everyone is suited to learning at such a fast rate.

Monorail, Sydney, NSW

10.
PUBLIC TRANSPORT

Public transport in Australia varies from region to region and town to town. In most cities and large towns services are good to excellent and relatively inexpensive (see below), although some suburbs and areas are poorly served. Most Australian cities have a relatively small suburban rail network, only New South Wales (NSW) has an extensive rail network, many regions aren't served by trains at all, and bus and rail services in most areas are severely curtailed on Sundays and in some cases on Saturdays as well; these are some of the reasons most Australians are so attached to their cars (only Americans are more devoted to their cars than Australians). However, it isn't always essential to own a car in Australia, particularly if you live in a city (where parking is often impossible). On the other hand, if you live in the country or a suburb off the main rail and bus routes, it's usually essential to have your own transport.

Bear in mind when travelling interstate that Australia is a **huge** country (nearly as big as Europe or the US and over 30 times the size of the UK) with vast distances between capital cities. Flying saves you a lot of time and the loss of sleep associated with long-distance bus and train journeys, although you see little of Australia when flying around the country. Book early if you plan to travel long distance on public holidays or at the beginning or end of school holidays (see page 169). Despite the vast distances involved in travelling in Australia, many Australians prefer to travel by private car.

In cities, trains are much faster than buses, particularly during rush hours, even where new roads have been built. Most cities have an integrated public transport system, and tickets usually allow transfers between buses, ferries, trains and trams (as applicable), fares being calculated on a zone system. Buses and trams carry around 65 per cent of passengers in the major cities, where there's a range of daily, weekly, monthly, quarterly and annual tickets, plus discounted books of ten tickets offering savings on single fares. Many cities have free town centre (downtown) shuttle buses.

> ⚠ Caution
> **Passengers caught travelling without tickets can be fined up to $200.**

Students visiting or living in Australia should obtain an International Student Identity Card (ISIC), which offers a range of travel discounts. STA Travel is the biggest nationwide travel agency and can provide tickets for all domestic and international travel. A number of guides are available for disabled passengers, including the *Accessing City Rail* from City Rail, a guide to access for wheelchairs on trains, and *Easy Access Australia*, available from 🖥 www.easyaccessaustralia.com.au (which also claims to be 'a good general guide to Australia).

CITY TRANSPORT SYSTEM

Most Australian cities have an adequate or good public transport service consisting mainly of buses and a limited suburban rail network, supported by a few ferries and, in Adelaide, a single tram line.

Sydney

Australia's largest city has an integrated service that includes buses, ferries, suburban trains and City Rail's 'underground' system (a conventional railway that runs underground in the city centre). Sydney also has a monorail and a light railway, although they're expensive and mainly a novelty for tourists. Sydney has the most expensive public transport of any Australian city, but it's still relatively cheap by international standards. In 2000, Sydney received some much-needed transport improvements, including expanded rail and ferry lines and a new underground railway linking the airport to the city centre. You can buy a Sydney Pass for three, five or seven days (around $110, $150 and $175 respectively) which is valid for city buses, ferries and suburban trains.

Melbourne

Melbourne has an inexpensive and efficient public transport network (called the 'Met'), consisting of buses, trains and trams, which has recently been privatised. A free *Get around on the Met* map is available (☎ local call rate 13-1638). Trams form the backbone of the public transport system and the city's network is one of the most extensive in the world and the only one remaining in Australia. The network covers 325km (202mi) and is served by some 750

trams operating up to 20km (12mi) outside the city centre. Tickets can be purchased at railway stations, on board buses and trams, and from retail outlets such as newsagents and cafes. An unpopular automated 'Metcard' ticketing system has recently been introduced.

Brisbane

In Brisbane you can buy daily or weekly travel tickets through Translink (☎ local call rate 13-1230). Brisbane is divided into 23 zones, which stretch all the way from Noosa down to Coolangatta. A daily ticket for unlimited travel on any bus, train or ferry in the central zones (including the CityCats) costs around $4.50, a weekly ticket around $17.50. Daily and weekly tickets covering all 23 zones cost around $35 and $115 respectively.

TRAINS

In the mid-19th century, when the first Australian railways were built, the states were independent colonies and governed from London; consequently, Australia's rail network grew piecemeal without any consultation between states. When the Australian federation was formed in 1901, the six colonies all had different gauge lines from their neighbours! This resulted in passengers having to change trains at state borders, often in the middle of the night, a situation which stifled the development of rail travel until the early '60s, when a standard gauge (1,435mm) was introduced on some main lines. However, Australia still has three different railway gauges – 1,067mm, 1,435mm and 1,600mm – and, although the main interstate lines now use the standard gauge, it's only in the last few years that much thought has been given to expanding and updating the local rail network, which by European standards is antiquated and severely limited.

Rail Australia consists of four state-owned rail companies (Countrylink, Queensland Rail, V/Line and Westrail) and the Great Southern Railway (GSR), which was created when the *Ghan*, *Indian Pacific* and *Overland* services were sold by the federal government in 1997. Some states (such as Victoria) have also since privatised their railways.

⚠ Caution

Most Australian cities have only a sparse suburban rail network and many areas of the country aren't served by trains at all.

As in the US, the main task of Australian railways is to haul bulk minerals (particularly coal in NSW and Queensland), grain, petroleum products and other freight over long distances.

Australian trains are more comfortable, leisurely and sociable than buses, but slower (the average speed of Australian trains is around 65kph/40mph), more expensive and sometimes difficult to book. You need to reserve well in advance for the most popular long-distance trains, particularly during the peak holiday season.

Some trains have wheelchair access, including the V/Line Sprinter trains in Victoria and the Countrylink XPT (an abbreviation for Express Passenger Train) and Xplorer trains operating in NSW, Queensland and between Sydney and Melbourne (at speeds of up to 160kph/ 100mph).

Interstate Trains

Australia offers some of the most spectacular rail journeys in the world, although the unchanging scenery in some regions can begin to pall after a few hours (and interstate journeys can be VERY long), unless you're unnaturally keen on flat, red terrain. Interstate rail travel has been overtaken by the age of air travel and (apart from suburban services in the major cities) is mainly of interest to tourists and travellers with plenty of time on their hands. There's an interstate railway service serving all states except Tasmania. Trains don't stop at all intermediate stations, e.g. those within a few hours of major terminals.

Long-distance trains have evocative names such as the *Ghan* (Adelaide-Melbourne-Sydney-Alice Springs-Darwin), the *Great South Pacific Express* (Sydney-Brisbane-Cairns), *Indian Pacific* (Sydney-Adelaide-Perth), the *Prospector* (Perth-Kalgoorlie) and the *Spirit of the Outback* (Brisbane-Longreach). The *Indian Pacific* crosses Australia and takes its name from its route from the Pacific Ocean (Sydney) to the Indian Ocean (Perth), a journey of 4,348km (2,700mi) taking around 65 hours. It includes the longest stretch of straight track (478km/300mi) in the world, across the Nullabor Plain in Western Australia. The *Indian Pacific* is one of the world's longest trains, with up to 25 carriages plus a bar and music room with piano, observation lounge and restaurant. The *Great South Pacific Express* is 'the first five-star hotel on wheels' in Australia and the country's answer to Europe's Orient Express. Cars are carried on the *Queenslander*, the *Spirit of the Outback* and between Adelaide and Alice Springs, Melbourne and Perth, and on the Melbourne-Mildura goods line. The *Prospector* (Perth-Kalgoorlie) provides only first-class, air-conditioned accommodation and maintains the fastest average speed (around 110kph/68mph) of any train in Australia, taking 7.5 hours for the 655km (407mi) journey.

Accommodation

Interstate trains offer a range of accommodation which may include deluxe and first-, holiday-, economy- and coach-class sleeping berths, and economy- and first-class seats. Sleeping berths are available on overnight services (for a surcharge) and are well worth the extra charge on long journeys. In first class there are 'twinette' cabins, which have seats that fold into two sleeping berths and share facilities with adjacent cabins. First-class single 'roomettes' have a private toilet and wash basin, and first-class cabins have hot and cold water, a shower, a socket for an electric shaver, and a toilet and wash basin.

Deluxe cabins and family units are available on the *Ghan* and *Indian Pacific* trains, where meals are included with first-class sleeping berths. In Queensland, economy-class sleepers have three sleeping berths, and each carriage has communal showers and toilets. Where sleeping berths are unavailable, there are reclining seats. Two-berth 'holiday-class' cabins are available on *The Ghan* and the *Indian Pacific* trains. Coach-class cars have reclining seats and, on trains to Alice Springs, Cairns and Perth, coach-

and economy-class sitting cars include showers. All long-distance trains are air-conditioned.

State Services

There are no regular passenger railways in Tasmania, although there's a freight rail service throughout the island and several steam railways for tourists (e.g. Ida Bay to Deep Hole). The main services in the other states are detailed below. A few small private railways serve mainly agricultural and industrial areas, e.g. the iron-ore mining developments in the north-west of Western Australia and an extensive tram network in Queensland connecting the sugar cane fields to the mills in sugar-producing areas.

> State capital cities have more than one railway station, although long-distance trains always arrive and depart from the main interstate station, e.g. Central Station in Sydney and Spencer Street Station in Melbourne.

New South Wales

The NSW Countrylink network (🖥 www.countrylink.info) operates the most comprehensive state rail service in Australia using 'Xplorer' trains, on which seats must be booked. There are commuter trains between Sydney and Goulburn, Katoomba, Lithgow, Newcastle and Wollongong. For information, call ☎ 13-2232 between 6.30am and 10pm any day.

Sydney: Sydney has the most extensive suburban rail network in Australia, although even here many suburbs have no rail service. Most routes are served by old, mostly double-decker trains (Sydney was the first city in the world to introduce double-decker electric trains), on which seats can usually be reversed to face in either direction, but these are being replaced by 'ultra-modern' Tangara trains, on which they cannot.

Yellow stripes on platforms indicate where half-length, four-carriage trains stop (you must stand behind the yellow line). Doors open and close automatically, although the doors on old trains are rarely closed during hot weather, so keep clear of the doorways (or hold on tight).

Trains operate from around 5am until midnight – violence, although rare, has caused the cancellation of trains after midnight on some suburban routes. After dark there are 'Night Safe' areas (marked on the platform in blue) where you can wait for trains. After 8pm, only two carriages are in use (next to the guard's compartment, indicated by a blue light), and a help button is positioned near the door which can be used to alert the guard or driver.

Canberra: Australia's capital city is served by the main Sydney-Melbourne line, which passes through Wodonga to the north-east of Canberra; from there you must take a bus, and the whole journey takes around nine hours. It's usually better to fly when travelling to Canberra.

Northern Territory

Alice Springs: Alice (as it's known) is served by the *Ghan*, which departs from Adelaide at 12.20pm on Sundays and Wednesdays and arrives at 1.45 pm the following day. The return leaves Alice at 9.10am on Thursdays and 11.15am on Sundays and both arrive in Adelaide at 1.30pm the next day (although it's often early). The fare is from around $335 for an adult one way with just your seat to sleep in; cabins are extra. The station in Alice is a 15-minute walk from the edge of the town (taxis meet trains).

Darwin: The north of the Northern Territory has recently joined the rail network, and the *Ghan* (see above) now travels as far as Darwin (already touted as one of the world's great train journeys); the one-way fare is from $690.

Queensland

Queensland has the most extensive rail network of any Australian state, covering over 10,000km (6,200mi) of lines on narrow gauge tracks (trains in Queensland are slower than buses due to the narrow gauge, except tilt trains – see **Brisbane** below). All trains are operated by Queensland Rail (QR, ☎ local call rate 13-1617, 🖥 www.qr.com.au), whose 'flagship' train (in which all passengers travel first class with sleeping berths) is the *Queenslander*, taking a leisurely 30 hours between Brisbane and Cairns. The *Westlander* operates from Brisbane to Charlesville (777km/482mi), taking 16 hours, and the *Inlander* links Townsville with Mount Isa. The only rail link from outside the state is from NSW (served by XPT trains), on which northbound trains run overnight and southbound trains during the day.

Seat or sleeper reservations are compulsory on long-distance trains, known as 'Traveltrains'. Most services are air-conditioned and provide sleeping cars and sitting cars with bar and meal services. Many trains stop at small stations on request and some trains are mixed freight and passenger trains (usually mainly freight with one passenger car). Vehicles can be transported on the *Queenslander* and the *Spirit of the Outback* (Brisbane-Longreach) services.

Local 'tourist' trains include the *Kuranda Scenic Railway* and the *Spirit of the Tropics*, designed for budget travellers and incorporating a non-stop disco car (Club Loco)! The vintage *Gulflander* train operates between Normanton and Croydon in the west of the state. There are plans for a regional rail line on the Sunshine Coast (the existing track is sited 20km/12mi inland from the heavily-populated coastal area).

'Sunshine' rail passes offer unlimited economy class travel on most routes (including the Brisbane suburban network). Ordinary one-way tickets allow unlimited stopovers and 14 days to reach your destination, while return tickets are valid for two months.

> ⚠ **Caution**
>
> **Stop-offs must be stated when buying tickets and bookings made for all journeys. You can change your travel plans, but a re-booking fee may be charged.**

Brisbane: There's a fast Citytrain service in Brisbane with seven lines, and the Airtrain, connecting the airport to the city and the Gold Coast, has recently been opened. The 640km (398mi) stretch between Brisbane and Rockhampton is electrified and served by modern 'tilt' trains (fast trains which run along narrow-gauge lines, sometimes at seemingly precarious angles – hence the name!); the journey costs over $100 one way. 'Rover' tickets for unlimited all-day travel within Brisbane cost around $8.

South Australia

Adelaide: There's a small network of suburban trains in Adelaide operated by the State Transport Authority. Tickets must be purchased before entering platforms or mounting trains.

Long-distance trains depart from the Adelaide Rail Passenger Terminal in Keswick, 2km south-west of the city centre. There's an overnight service to Melbourne taking around 12 hours and a day coach/train service taking 11 hours. The *Ghan* to Alice Springs (19 hours) leaves at 12.20pm on Sundays and Wednesdays, and it carries on to Darwin. There are five weekly trains to Perth (none on Tuesdays and Thursdays) taking around 36 hours, possibly requiring a change of train at Port Pirie.

Victoria

The Victorian State Railway, the V/Line, was recently privatised and is now on lease to the British travel company National

Express. V/Line operates all rail and associated coach routes within Victoria and high-speed (XPT) services to Sydney (Melbourne-Sydney during the day and Sydney-Melbourne overnight) taking 13 hours. V/Line supersaver fares offer a 30 per cent discount when travelling off peak, i.e. on Tuesdays, Wednesdays and Thursdays, arriving in Melbourne after 9.30am and leaving Melbourne at any time except between 4 and 6pm. In recent years, new, air-conditioned, 'high-speed' Sprinter trains have been introduced on some routes. The Canberra Link involves taking a train to Wodonga on the border with NSW and a bus from there to Canberra. There are *Overland* daily night services to Adelaide taking 12 hours (change to the *Indian Pacific* in Adelaide for Perth).

Melbourne: The city centre 'City Loop' forms an underground railway around the centre of Melbourne.

Western Australia

The *Indian Pacific* takes 65 hours to travel from Perth to Sydney and runs twice a week, on Wednesdays and Saturdays. The cheapest adult fare in 2007 was $590. There are also suburban lines (operated by Westrail) between Perth and Armadale, Fremantle, Joondalup and Midland. The only other rail services in Western Australia are the Perth-Bunbury line and the Perth-Kalgoorlie route operated by the *Prospector*. Tickets should be purchased from vending machines at stations before boarding. Multi-ride tickets can be validated at stations. Seven-day advance purchase fares are available in the low season offering a 30 per cent discount. A car-train service is available between Adelaide and Perth.

Vintage Trains

There are a number of 'vintage' trains in Australia, e.g. from Cairns to Kuranda,

taking 90 minutes to cover the 33km (20mi), and there are vintage and tramway museums in all states where you can enjoy excursions on restored steam trains. These include the Ida Bay Railway in Tasmania, the NSW Railway Museum (at Thirlmere near Picton), and the *Puffing Billy* in the Dandenongs Ranges in Victoria. On the first Sunday of the month from March to November, a steam train leaves Sydney Central station for Thirlmere. The Hotham Valley Tourist Railway in WA operates Xplorer trains to various destinations, and restored locomotives operate on short excursions from Alice Springs. The Barossa Wine Train runs from Adelaide to the Barossa wine region on a day trip taking in three wineries and extensive wine tasting.

Train & Station Facilities

The following is a summary of facilities available at Australian stations and on Australian trains:

- **Banks** – Banks or autobanks (ATMs) are located at main railway stations in Brisbane and Melbourne (but surprisingly not in Adelaide, Perth or Sydney).

> ### Bicycles
> In most cities, bicycles can be transported on suburban trains free of charge or for a small fee during off-peak times, although it may not be permitted during peak periods (e.g. 6 to 9am and 3 to 7pm on weekdays) or a permit may be required.

- **Food & drink** – Snacks are served on long-distance and in-state trains (such as XPT and Xplorer trains), and all interstate trains have dining cars offering both formal dining and light meals. There are also lounge and club cars on most services. Railway food is generally good and can be excellent on 'tourist' trains such as the *Ghan*, *Indian Pacific* and *Queenslander*. There are no bar facilities for economy passengers on some long-distance services (e.g. from Adelaide to Melbourne) and there may be a large fine (e.g. $100) for consuming your own alcohol! Taking your own picnic onto a train isn't prohibited but may be frowned upon. There are restaurants and snack bars at main stations, and food and drink machines are provided at many smaller stations.

● **Luggage** – Interstate train passengers are permitted up to 50kg (110lbs) of luggage (two items not exceeding 25kg/55lbs each and a maximum of 180cm/71in in circumference). Medium-size suitcases and hand luggage can be carried in compartments, but larger luggage should be booked in at the luggage desk not less than 30 minutes before departure. Booked luggage is carried in the luggage car and isn't accessible during the journey. There are also luggage storage spaces at the ends of passenger compartments.

Luggage can be sent unaccompanied and can be insured. Many stations and airports have left luggage offices, luggage lockers (from $2 for up to 24 hours) and luggage trolleys. When using a luggage locker, insert the correct money to release the key. It's advisable to make a note the number of the locker in case you lose the key.

● **Smoking** – There's a smoking ban on all trains throughout Australia.

● **Telephones** – Public payphones (which accept Telecards) are available on long-distance train services.

● **Times** – Always check and double-check the departure (and arrival) time of a train (particularly in the outback when the next train may be a week next Thursday and be fully booked), especially when you need to make a flight connection. You may have to undertake part of your journey by air or bus to link with a connecting train. Schedules are liable to change at short notice, particularly at weekends and during holiday periods.

Most long-distance trains operate throughout the year, but local and in-state trains may not run on public holidays (these vary with the state, e.g. many don't operate on holidays such as ANZAC Day (25th April). Christmas Day and Good Friday. It's also important to check that a train actually stops where you want to go, as long-distance trains usually make few stops. See also **Trains** on page 188.

● **Toilets** – Toilets are provided on trains on all but the shortest services but shouldn't be used when a train is in a station.

Tickets

Rail tickets in Australia can be purchased from automatic ticket machines, newsagents (in major cities) and station ticket offices. Most interstate and main state trains have both first-class and standard (economy) seating, although there's little difference between seats on some trains, e.g. XPT trains operating in NSW, Queensland and Victoria. There's no first-class accommodation on the Perth-Bunbury line in Western Australia, most trains in outback Queensland, and all suburban lines.

Many ticket offices in Sydney and other NSW towns are open only for a few hours per day during rush hours, although passengers can buy tickets from ticket machines at other times (see below). Many stations are unmanned for at least half the day during the week and all day at weekends. Tickets can be paid for with major credit cards (e.g. MasterCard and Visa) subject to a $10 minimum charge.

Fare evasion is endemic in Australia, particularly in the major cities, where an estimated 3 per cent of passengers travel without tickets (over 5,000 culprits were discovered in a three-week blitz on Sydney's city loop). **Fare evaders face fines of up to $100 and Sydneysiders have to pay up to $550.**

Ticket Machines

Ticket machines have been introduced in recent years, although there have been a 'few' teething troubles, particularly in Melbourne (where the first machines ate your money, chewed up your tickets and stole your change!). You usually select your destination, choose the type of ticket (e.g. single or return), insert the fare (machines accept coins and notes) and, if you're lucky, a ticket is ejected with your change.

In some cities you must insert your ticket in a ticket barrier with a green arrow (not a red cross) in the direction of the arrow shown on your ticket when leaving a station; a return ticket or multi-day pass is returned if you're on the outward journey, otherwise the ticket is retained.

> ☑ **SURVIVAL TIP**
>
> Whether you buy your ticket from a machine or at a ticket office, you must validate it (stamp it with the current date and time) in a separate machine, without which it's invalid; you must validate a multiple-ride ticket each time you travel.

Bookings

Bookings (reservations) are recommended (at least two months in advance) on all long-distance trains, many of which are fully booked months in advance in the summer season and during school holidays. There's no booking fee on major routes, on which bookings are accepted up to nine months in advance (six months on other long-distance routes). However, if a booking is altered or cancelled, there's a fee of $5 if you make the alteration or cancellation at least 30 days prior to travel; 10 per cent of the fare if you make it 30 days prior to travel; and 20 per cent of the fare if within seven days of travel.

There are no refunds for unused tickets after the departure time and date shown on the ticket. For bookings, call ☎ local call rate 13-2232. On some main routes there are discounts of up to 40 per cent for advance purchase tickets (e.g. seven days), although these aren't applied to the cheapest regular fares (and therefore may not be the cheapest travel option).

Bookings can be made via Rail Australia's website (🖥 www.railaustralia. com.au). Tickets can be booked for any journey throughout the country (apart from local suburban routes) and must be made and paid for at least seven days in advance. The outward journey must start on the date stamped on tickets, and

journeys must be completed within the validity of the ticket. Journeys can usually be broken, except with discount fares. Bookings can be made through Thomas Cook offices in many countries.

Discounts

A variety of discounted tickets are available on Australian railways, including the following:

- **Advance purchase** – On some main routes there are discounts of up to 40 per cent for advance purchase tickets (e.g. seven days), although these aren't applied to the cheapest regular fares (and therefore may not be the cheapest travel option). Only a limited number of discounted seats may be available.

- **Children, students & pensioners** – Children under four travel free, unless they're occupying a separate seat or a sleeping berth on an interstate train (when the under-16 fare applies). Those aged from 4 to 15 travel at a discount (usually half-fare), as

generally do students and pensioners, depending on the state where you're resident.

- **Low season discounts** – Low season is from 1st February to 30th June and the normal season from 1st July to 31st January. Low season fares are around 40 per cent lower than high season fares; standard fares lie in between the two. Low season and standard fares are the same when travelling in economy-class seats and for travel on *Overland* trains between Adelaide and Melbourne.

- **Off-peak travel** – In major cities, off-peak suburban fares are available after 9am on weekdays and any time at weekends, offering savings of up to 60 per cent on return journeys.

- **Season tickets** – There's a range of season tickets (weekly, quarterly and annual) for commuters, providing large discounts over standard fares, which may include travel on suburban buses, ferries, trains and trams (e.g. in Sydney). Weekly passes usually cost around eight times the single fare. A photograph is normally required for a season ticket.

- **Austrail Flexipass** – An Austrail Flexipass provides unlimited travel in economy class anywhere in Australia, either for 15 days in a six-month period (costing around $860) or 22 days in a six-month period (around $1,200). Austrail passes can be purchased from Qantas and offices of Jetabout Tours worldwide. Details of this and similar passes, including the Backtracker Pass, East Coast Discovery Pass, Rail Explorer Pass and Wanderer Rail Pass can be found on the Rail Australia website (🖳 www.railaustralia.com.au).

- **Standby fares** – Standby fares are available on some routes.

Further Information

For further information about Australian railways contact Rail Australia, PO Box 445, Marleston Business Centre, Marleston, SA 5033 (☎ 08-8213 4592, 🖳 www.railaustralia.com.au). Rail Australia has agents in many countries, including Canada, Denmark, France, Germany, Hong Kong, Japan, Korea, the Netherlands, New Zealand, Singapore, South Africa, Sweden, the UK and the US. It publishes a brochure, *Australia By Rail*, which describes the long-distance routes and trains, or you can consult the information on the website.

☑ SURVIVAL TIP

There are rail enquiry numbers in all states which can usually be reached by calling ☎ local call rate 13-2232, although it's often difficult to get through. It's usually easier to visit a rail information office or a station to obtain train information.

BUSES & TRAMS

Buses are the cheapest form of public transport in Australia, both within cities and over long distances, and provide a far more comprehensive network than the railways, reaching almost every corner of Australia. There are comprehensive bus services in Australia's major cities and an extensive network of long-distance, interstate buses, usually referred to as coaches. Bus services in rural areas are less frequent. Melbourne is the only Australian city with an extensive tram network, although other cities are planning new tram lines.

Each city and region of Australia has its own bus companies providing town and country services. In large towns and cities, most bus services start and terminate at a central bus station, which is generally modern and clean. Most are equipped with luggage lockers or a left luggage office, shops, showers, a snack bar or restaurant, and toilets. They have little in common with the seedy places inhabited by drug addicts, drunks and assorted derelicts found in many other countries. Smoking is prohibited on all buses and trams in Australia.

If you need assistance, ask at the bus station information office. Most bus companies provide free timetables and route maps, and in some cities comprehensive timetables and maps are available which include all bus services operating within their boundaries. See also **Timetables & Maps** on page 202.

Long-distance Buses

Greyhound (☎ 13-1499, 🖳 www.greyhound. com.au) is Australia's only national coach operator, formed in 2000 when McCaffertys bought Greyhound Pioneer Australia, but there are several regional operators. The main operator in the southern part of Western Australia is the state rail company, Westrail, while Tasmanian Redline Coaches (☎ 1300-360 000, 🖳 www.tasredline.com. au) provides express services throughout Tasmania.

Long-distance buses are generally cheaper, easier to book and faster than interstate trains, and there's a more comprehensive network. However, they're also less comfortable and more restrictive than trains. Long-distance buses are particularly popular among independent travellers (e.g. backpackers), 80 per cent of whom use them almost exclusively. Travelling by bus is around a third of the cost of travelling by air. There are numerous daily departures on the most popular routes, although some services operate only a few times per week and, in the Northern Territory, northern Queensland and northern parts of Western Australia, some routes are interrupted for weeks at a time during the wet season (November to

May). There are unsociable arrival hours on some long-distance routes.

Buses are usually equipped with air-conditioning, individual reading lights, panoramic windows, reclining seats, toilets, TV and videos with stereo sound, and water fountains. It's wise to get a seat near the front away from the toilet and on the left-hand side away from the lights of approaching traffic at night. Long-distance journeys are tiring and you shouldn't expect to get much (if any) sleep if you're travelling overnight. Frequent stops are made for drinks, food, showers and toilets. There are strict rules concerning what you can eat and drink on buses. No alcohol may be consumed (maximum fine around $500) and smoking is prohibited on all services. **Long-distance buses don't cater for those in wheelchairs.**

Routes & Fares

There's lively competition between the various regional long-distance bus companies, which helps reduce fares.

There's particularly fierce competition on the most popular routes, e.g. Melbourne-Sydney, where fares are around $74, although off the main inter-city routes fares can be high. A 25 per cent discount is provided for students and children on most services. Some companies offer discounts to backpackers on certain services and there are also discounts for students, although the biggest discounts are usually offered on last-minute bookings. Visitors can purchase bus passes overseas in many countries, although you may get a better deal in Australia. Bus passes aren't valid on some local services and a surcharge is usually payable on routes in remote areas. It's always cheaper to buy a through-ticket for a long journey, rather than separate tickets for short stretches, and most tickets allow unlimited stopovers.

The main express routes (on which there are few or no stops) operated by Greyhound include the following:

Route	Journey Time (hours)	Approx. Fare One Way
Adelaide to Alice Springs	20	$250
Alice Springs to Ayers Rock Resort	6	$90
Brisbane to Sydney	18	$120
Brisbane to Melbourne	25	$180
Cairns to Brisbane	18	$235
Darwin to Alice Springs	20	$280
Melbourne to Adelaide	9	$60
Perth to Darwin	35	$720
Sydney to Adelaide	23	$135
Sydney to Canberra	5	$40
Sydney to Melbourne (inland)	12	$75

suburban train, Sydney, NSW

Tickets

Long-distance bus tickets are similar to airline tickets, with destinations shown by a code, such as SYD for Sydney and MEL for Melbourne. When checking your luggage, make sure that the luggage code matches that of your destination (otherwise you may end up in Cairns and your luggage in Perth!).

Bookings can be made online, through travel agents or direct with bus companies. There are also many booking agents in major cities, including Youth Hostel Assocation (YHA) travel offices – see page 324, some of which allow you to book tickets by telephone and pay with a credit card. All bookings are non-refundable and non-transferable to other passengers, but can be transferred to another service up until departure of original service.

Tours

Numerous coach companies offer tours which include accommodation (e.g. bungalow, cabin, camping, hotel or motel) and most meals, ranging in duration from a few days to several months. On camping tours, meals are usually cooked by a travelling cook and prices include meals, sleeping bags, tents and other equipment. Passengers aren't required to erect tents. Some tour companies cater for backpackers and, although they usually offer a 'rough and ready' service, provide good value.

City & Country Buses

In most cities there are a number of local bus companies, sometimes operated by the local railway company or the state or city authorities. There's a comprehensive bus network in all Australian cities, and services are frequent. Buses are slow but are often the only option for getting to most suburbs. Major cities usually have an integrated public transport system, the same ticket being valid on buses, suburban trains, trams (Melbourne) and ferries (Sydney).

City buses on most routes operate from around 6am until 11pm or midnight (but possibly only until 7pm on Sundays). Buses run frequently during the weekday rush hours, e.g. every 10 or 15 minutes on the main routes. Outside rush hours there's usually a half-hour service on most routes during weekdays, although services are often severely restricted at weekends and on public holidays (there may be no service at all on some routes on Sundays and public holidays).

In major cities there's usually an express bus service (called 'rockets' in some cities) operating between the outer suburbs and the major centres on routes to city centres (express bus numbers are usually prefixed with an X). Night services operate in the major cities from around midnight until 6am, some of which have radio links with taxi operators, so that you can arrange to have a taxi meet you at your destination. There are free buses in most major cities covering a circular (loop) route within the city centre.

In stark contrast to the cities, in rural areas there's usually only one bus company and services are sparse and infrequent. In remote areas there may be only school buses, which usually carry other passengers but aren't obliged to.

It's usual to board a bus by the front door and disembark from the centre doors. You must normally ring a bell to inform the driver that you want him to stop at the next stop (a buzzer sounds in the cab) and stand by the centre door. When the bus stops, a green light is illuminated which signals that you must push the handle or press a button to open the door, which doesn't usually open automatically.

In most cities, bus stops have numbers, which are often quoted by people when giving directions, and they may be colour-coded. Buses also display their route number, although in some cities numbers may vary according to whether they're running to or from the city centre. All bus companies publish route maps, and there are comprehensive city guides in most cities, and state bus directories in some states.

Tickets

In the major cities, journeys are based on a zone system whereby the bus network is divided into a number of concentric areas (the central business district and inner suburbs are usually designated zone 1). Tickets are valid for travel within a single zone or a number of zones, and may be colour-coded corresponding to the zones (and modes of transport) for which they're valid. Day Tripper tickets are valid all day with unlimited transfers during this time.

Tickets can be purchased from bus stations, on board buses and trams, and from retail outlets such as newsagents' and cafes in some cities. Automatic ticket machines are provided in some cities, but they may gobble your money and refuse to give you a ticket. You can usually buy a ticket from the driver on boarding a bus, which must then be validated in a machine (to the right of the driver) which stamps your ticket with the date and time of boarding plus the time of expiry of the ticket. **If you have a multi-ride ticket, you must validate it each time you travel.**

All bus companies offer day passes and weekly, monthly and annual tickets for commuters. There are also off-peak tickets that allow you to travel at a reduced rate outside rush hours (e.g. between 9am and 3pm or 3.30pm, Mondays to Fridays and after 7pm until the last service) and at weekends. In most cities you can buy a book of ten tickets (e.g. a TravelTen in Sydney) at a saving of up to 40 per cent compared with buying single tickets. There are concessionary fares for children and pensioners, which are usually half the adult fare.

A day 'rover' ticket is available for around $5 in most cities and allows unlimited bus travel for a whole day; it may also include travel on other modes of city transport.

There are fines of over $100 for anyone discovered travelling without a ticket.

FERRIES

Australia consists of several islands, and most of its inhabited areas are on or near the coast, so sea transport is often a viable alternative to flying or other means.

One of the first things you should do after boarding a ferry or ship is to study the safety procedures, i.e. what to do if it sinks. This is important in Australian waters, which are often full of crocodiles, jellyfish and sharks!

Sydney

Travelling by ferry is one of the joys of living in Sydney, where many people use them to commute to work. The city has eight main ferry routes and 33 ferry wharves, all served from the main Circular Quay ferry terminal. In addition to regular (slow) ferries, there's a catamaran (RiverCat) service from Circular Quay to Parramatta (via the Parramatta River) and a JetCat service to Manly.

Most ferries run from around 6am until midnight, although times vary with the route, and services are restricted at weekends, when ferries may not stop at all wharves. Most services run every 50 minutes during the day and more frequently during rush hours, e.g. every 15 or 20 minutes. Regular commuters can buy a book of ten tickets (called a 'Ferry Ten') or weekly, quarterly and annual commuter tickets, which offer even greater savings and can be combined with other modes of public transport such as buses and suburban trains.

Special tickets are available for trips to major attractions (such as Taronga Zoo), which include the return ferry trip from Circular Quay and the entrance fee, and are cheaper than buying separate tickets. Special ferries are also available to follow sailing races such as the famous Sydney-Hobart race, which starts on Boxing Day (26th December).

Tasmania

The only regular maritime passenger service in Australia is the car ferry operating between Melbourne and Devonport on the north coast of Tasmania. It's served by the *Spirit of Tasmania* (⌨ www.spiritoftasmania.com.au), a luxury 467-cabin ship of 31,356 tonnes, with a capacity of around 1,300 passengers plus vehicles. **The trip is often rough, so poor sailors should take seasickness pills** (or a plane). In fact, the ferry isn't much cheaper than flying and takes around 14 hours, compared with less than an hour by air from Melbourne to Hobart. Ferries run daily during the peak summer season (although there are seasonal variations). Departures are at 8pm or 9pm to Tasmania and at 9am or 8pm in the other direction. Cabins and hostel-style accommodation are available.

There are three fare rates, depending on the time of year: bargain (late April to mid-September), holiday (Christmas to March) and shoulder (the rest of the year). A bargain single costs around $115, including an evening buffet dinner and continental breakfast; shoulder rates are around 30 per cent higher, and holiday rates a similar amount higher still. There's a 25 per cent discount for students in cabin accommodation and occasional mid-week discounts. Vehicle transportation is heavily subsidised by the Tasmanian government and costs between around $70 and $110 (depending on the season) one way. A ferry service also operates from Woodbridge on the south-east coast of Tasmania to Roberts Point on Bruny Island.

Other Ferries

Other regular ferry services in Australia include the following:

- **Brisbane** – Brisbane has a fast and efficient ferry service along and across the Brisbane River operating every 20 minutes from dawn until around 11pm, Mondays to Saturdays (operating hours are reduced on Sundays). There is also a catamaran called the CityCAt with services running every 10 to 20 minutes.

- **Darwin** – Darwin harbour ferries make daily crossings to Mandorah on the Cox peninsula.

- **Fremantle** – Ferries operate from Fremantle to Rottnest Island.

- **Perth** – There's a ferry service across the Swan River from the Barrack Street jetty to the Mends Street jetty.

- **Victoria** – Ferries operate between Cowes on Philip Island and Stony Point on the Mornington Peninsula, from Stony Point to Tankerton on French Island, and from Sorrento to Queenscliff.

TIMETABLES & MAPS

All public transport companies in Australia produce comprehensive guides, route maps and timetables, and many councils publish excellent guides and maps (available from council offices, libraries, newsagents and tourist centres), which include all bus, ferry and rail transport services operating within a city or region. At major airports and railway stations, arrivals and departures are shown on electronic boards and computer screens. Most transport companies use am (before noon) and pm (after noon) in timetables, rather than the 24-hour clock. When am and pm aren't indicated, the general practice is that times printed in light type are before noon and times printed in bold type are after noon. When travelling from east to west (or

vice versa), bear in mind that there may be local time differences, which are usually announced by the conductor (see **Time Difference** on page 417).

Rail

The state rail authorities and the Great Southern Railway all publish free timetables, and Rail Australia publishes a summary of major interstate services (also available online). Suburban timetables are published separately, and leaflets are available concerning particular services from stations. The *Thomas Cook Overseas Timetable* is the nearest thing Australia has to an Australia-wide rail timetable. On interstate timetables, +1, +2 and +3 indicate that the train arrives one, two or three days after departure. **Bear in mind that rail timetables in Australia are usually works of fiction and bear little relation to 'real' time.**

Bus

Bus timetables may be for individual routes, all routes operated by a particular company, or all routes serving a city, town or region. Timetables including all local bus company services are often published by local councils and are available free (or for a nominal price) from bus companies, libraries and tourist information centres. Timetables can be obtained from the relevant bus company (for example, see **Long-distance Buses** on page 197) and from travel agents' and tourist offices.

TAXIS

There are two kinds of taxi in Australia: cabs (short for 'cabriolet') and radio taxis. The main difference from the passenger's point of view is that cabs (which are usually white or yellow) can be hailed in the street (or at taxi ranks, railway stations, airports and hotels – there are courtesy telephones outside main hotels), whereas radio taxis can only be booked by telephone, although cabs can also be booked by telephone. Taxis can be 'officially' shared in some states, e.g. in Darwin there are 'multi-ride' taxis with 12 seats which pick up passengers en route. Wheelchair-accessible taxis are available in most major cities. There are also water taxis in Sydney operating from Circular Quay to most areas on the harbour, which are a novel (but expensive) way of getting around the harbour. The fare depends on the time of day and the number of passengers.

Cabs for hire display a 'Vacant' or 'For Hire' sign or a light on the roof.

⚠ Caution

It's usually fairly easy to find a cab in a city late at night, as there are many 'night' cabs, although they can be difficult to find just after the pubs close because of the strict drink-driving laws in Australia (and between midnight and 6am on Sundays in major cities).

Taxi drivers run a high risk of being mugged in some areas of major cities (e.g. Sydney), which has led to some suburbs being officially classified as 'no-go' areas (and not only for taxi drivers!). Since 1997, taxis in Sydney have been fitted with a protection screen between the passenger compartment and the driver, and a satellite tracking system is installed in taxis to monitor their position and speed (taxis in Melbourne are being fitted with video cameras).

Taxis are relatively inexpensive in Australia, and rates vary little from city to city. In Sydney there's a standing charge (flagfall) of $2.90, plus $1.68 per kilometre. There are a number of surcharges, including a charge of $1.50 when a cab is called by telephone and an extra charge when a bridge toll (e.g. Sydney Harbour Bridge) is included in the journey. There's usually a surcharge for journeys at night and at weekends (in some cities there are three daytime rates). There's usually also a small charge for luggage carried in the boot (trunk). Outside city limits you must pay a higher 'country' rate and possibly a surcharge (befouling fee) of 1 hours waiting time which is about $40 if you dirty a taxi! Many taxis accept credit cards for fares over $5.

Tipping isn't necessary and, although most people round the fare up to the nearest dollar, drivers may actually round the fare down rather than give change and may even refuse tips. Australian taxi drivers are generally honest and helpful (unlike those in many other countries). Complaints about service or hire charges can be made to the local taxi licensing office. Make a note of the taxi's registration number and the date and time of the incident and, if you think you've been overcharged, obtain a receipt.

In addition to taxi services, many taxi companies operate chauffeur and courier services, and private hire (e.g. sightseeing or weddings), and sometimes provide contract and account services, e.g. to take children to and from school.

AIRLINE SERVICES

Australia's national airline is Qantas (Queensland and the Northern Territory Aerial Service), formed in 1920 (only KLM is older) and privatised in 1995. It's one of the best (noted for the excellence of its food and wines) and most profitable airlines in the world. Qantas (🖳 www.qantas.com.au) has a fleet of around 200 aircraft and carries more than 30m passengers per year (over 21m on domestic routes) to 120 destinations in 40 countries. It has partnership agreements with several other international airlines, including American Airlines and British Airways, whereby partners can buy seats on Qantas flights and vice versa. There are Qantas Club lounges at all major airports in Australia and shared lounges in many other countries. Qantas has its own terminals at Australia's major airports, and caters for

disabled passengers and passengers in wheelchairs.

Australian airlines are strict about safety, and it's one of the safest places in the world to fly (Qantas has regularly been rated as one of the safest airlines in the world by IATA, who in 2000 also named Airservices Australia the world's best provider of air traffic control services). Smoking is prohibited on all flights operated by Australian airlines, both domestic and international, with a maximum $500 fine for offenders.

Domestic Flights

Air travel is the fastest way to get around Australia, and around 80 per cent of domestic long-distance trips are made by air. For many years, Qantas and Ansett monopolised the domestic flight market. The 'cooperation' between them meant that domestic air travel remained relatively expensive. But Ansett went into administration in March 2002 and the regional airlines that it owned either went out of business or continued to operate only minor services. This had the effect of shaking up the market, and new airlines have been formed which are taking on Qantas, creating welcome competition (for the consumer).

Regional Express (or Rex, 🖳 www.regionalexpress.com.au) is Australia's largest independent regional airline, connecting 29 metropolitan and regional centres across NSW, South Australia, Tasmania and Victoria. It was formed in August 2002 and currently has a fleet of 69 aircraft. Virgin Blue (🖳 www.virginblue.com.au) is the leading low-cost airline, serving 30 destinations in Australia, two in New Zealand and Fiji, and the Cook Islands and Vanuatu. Other regional airlines include Airlines of South Australia, Skywest (Western Australia) and Sunstate (Queensland). Attempts by other small airlines (e.g. Compass and OzJet) to offer low-cost services have largely been unsuccessful, but a Singapore-based carrier, Tiger Airways, which started services between Singapore and Darwin in 2004, promises to enter the fray. Qantas, which has its own low-cost subsidiary, Jetstar, currently flies to around 57 destinations in Australia.

Flying times between Sydney and other state capitals are: Canberra (236km/147mi) 30 minutes; Brisbane (746km/464mi) and Melbourne (708km/440mi) around one hour 15 minutes; Adelaide (1,166km/725mi) and Hobart (1,039km/646mi) around two hours; and Perth (3,284km/2,041mi) around five hours.

There are many flights each day between Australia's major cities (although some journeys require a number of stops), but on less travelled routes there are just one or two flights a week. You should always book a domestic flight as far in advance as possible, particularly during holiday periods (this also allows you to take maximum advantage of reduced fares). Many regional and local airlines operate small aircraft, which are generally booked up well in advance and consequently don't offer discounts or low fares. Many domestic airlines also offer a variety of air tours lasting from two to 14 days.

Domestic air travel is relatively expensive because of the long distances involved. Random discounting is common, although there are often conditions such as advance booking, flying at weekends only or between fixed dates.

Check-in time is around one hour before departure (sometimes less for first and business class passengers).

International Flights

Australia is served by around 50 international airlines operating scheduled passenger services. Check-in time is around two hours before departure (sometimes less for first and business class passengers).

International Fares

Australia's isolated position in the world means that international air travel is invariably expensive. Air fares are high from most countries, as there's a relatively low volume of traffic on most routes and little competition. The main exception is between the UK and Australia (the 'kangaroo route'), which is one of the more competitive routes in the world. The airlines regularly indulge in a price war, offering cut-price tickets on selected flights.

The return fare from London to Sydney is around GB£600 in low season (April to June), rising to between GB£1,000 and GB£1,500 in high season (December and January), when fares vary little between airlines. Fares during the shoulder season (July to November and February to March) are usually between GB£650 and GB£800. Fares from London to Melbourne or Brisbane are usually higher than to Sydney. Charter flights costing as little as GB£400 return are sometimes available from the UK to Australia between November and April. However, charter flights have severe restrictions, including no stopovers, a minimum stay of two weeks and a maximum of eight.

From Europe, fares vary according to whether you're flying east via Asia or west via North America. It's usually cheaper to fly via America between November and February and via the Far East at other times. Flights from the UK to Australia in the weeks immediately before Christmas are usually fully booked months in advance, and delaying your flight a few days until after the Christmas period can mean a considerable saving. If you fly to Australia from the UK at any time of year with British Airways, Qantas or Singapore Airlines, you usually pay between £100 and

£200 more than with other airlines, but this may be worthwhile if you take advantage of these airlines' domestic deals within Australia (i.e. reduced domestic fares for those flying to and from Australia with the airline). Fares to Australia are higher if you break the journey, although most travellers find that it's worthwhile taking advantage of stopover deals and this helps to avoid or reduce jetlag.

Return fares from Australia to Europe are higher than when travelling in the opposite direction. The best deals are from Sydney, although bargains can be found from Melbourne and Perth (discount fares are advertised in the major daily newspapers). A 'departure tax' of $38 is incorporated into the ticket price for passengers aged 12 or over. Departing passengers must also complete an *Outgoing Passenger Card*.

Fares from the US aren't as good value as from Europe, although excursion and promotional fares are available which are much lower than full fares, e.g. apex and promotional return fares from Los Angeles to Sydney/Melbourne are around US$1,300 in the low season and US$2,000 in the high season. Regular tickets are valid for 12 months, so it may pay to buy your ticket well in advance of your trip. There isn't much choice of flights from the US, from where a limited number of airlines fly non-stop to Australia. Many flights stop at Honolulu, Papeete or Auckland, or a combination of these. An 'open-jaw' ticket (flying into one airport and out of another) is usually no more expensive than an ordinary return.

Major airlines offer economy, business and first class fares. Full fare tickets allow you to change the date and time of travel at a moment's notice and offer a full refund should you decide not to travel. When buying apex and other discounted tickets, always make sure that you fully understand any ticket restrictions.

> ☑ SURVIVAL TIP
>
> **If you're migrating to Australia, you should book as far ahead as possible (but never before you've received your visa!).**

Stopovers & Round-the-world Tickets: When travelling to Australia, you can travel one-stop or take advantage of a number of stopovers, e.g. in Asia, North America and the Pacific. Most return tickets from Europe include 'free' stopover options on outward and return journeys, usually in Asia or the Pacific. Round-the-world tickets to Australia from London via Asia and North America start at around GB£800 for four stops, depending on the season. From Europe you can also fly via South Africa or South America, although these options are more expensive than the usual Asian or North American routes.

Airports

The main airports in Australia are Adelaide, Brisbane, Cairns, Darwin, Melbourne, Perth, Port Hedland, Sydney and Townsville. Sydney and Melbourne are Australia's two largest international airports; Adelaide, Brisbane, Cairns, Darwin, Hobart, Perth and Townsville also have international airports. The capital, Canberra, doesn't have an international airport and is served only by domestic flights from other Australian cities (Sydney is only half an hour away by air). When minor airports and country landing strips are included, Australia has a total of around 445 'airports'.

Most of Australia's major airports are owned and controlled by the Federal Airports Corporation (FAC), although they're gradually being privatised. Most Australian airports are deserted much of the time and come to life for only a few hours a day, when international flights arrive and depart. Terminals may open for only a few hours before arrivals or departures and close for the day after the last flight has arrived or left. International terminals are usually separate from domestic terminals and the two may be located some distance apart. There are bus and taxi services from all major airports to local city centres.

Adelaide

Adelaide airport is just 6km (4mi) south-west of the city centre and has both international and domestic terminals, five minutes' walk apart. It's Australia's fourth-largest domestic airport and sixth-largest international airport, with around 4m passengers per year. Five airlines – Cathay Pacific, Garuda Indonesia, Malaysia Airlines, Qantas and Singapore International – have direct international flights to Adelaide, although many airlines provide free connecting flights to Melbourne, Sydney and even Singapore in order to attract passengers.

Brisbane

Brisbane airport is 10km (6mi) from the city centre and has separate international and domestic terminals some 12 minutes apart by road. There are international flights to Europe, Hong Kong, Japan, New Zealand, North America, Papua New Guinea and Singapore. Brisbane airport handles some 12m passengers a year which is expected to grow to 35m in the next 20 years. The airport is currently undergoing a major extention to it's international terminal which is due for completion in 2008. 2002 also saw the start of a huge 80 hectare business, tourism, retail, entertainment and leisure precinct which is planned to be staged over the next 15 years.

Darwin

Darwin airport (located 8km/5mi south of the city centre) has the longest runway in the country and operates international flights to Bali, Brunei, Dili, Singapore and Timika. There are domestic flights (from the same terminal as international flights) to most major cities once a day or less frequently. Darwin handles around 1.5m passengers per year.

Melbourne

Melbourne's Tullamarine airport is located 23km (14mi) north-west of the city centre and is Australia's second-largest airport (after Sydney), handling around 20m passengers annually. Melbourne has tried (with some success) to attract airlines by reducing airport charges and now serves many more international destinations than previously. The Airtrain rail link joins the airport with the city and to the Gold Coast. Melbourne has a second airport at Essendon, between the city and Tullamarine, which operates local flights within Victoria and to Tasmania.

Perth

Perth airport (21km/13mi east of the city centre) is a gateway for services from

Asia and Europe. It has international and domestic terminals located on opposite sides of the runway some 10km (6mi) apart by road.

⚠ Caution

Changing flights can be a chore, although many international flights arrive after midnight when there are no connecting domestic flights anyway.

Fares to Europe are lower from Perth than elsewhere in Australia and there's a lively market in international tickets. Perth handled over 7m passengers in 2006 and is increasing numbers every year by 12 per cent. The number of domestic passengers is also increasing by 15 per cent per year.

Sydney

Sydney's international airport is called Kingsford-Smith (after Australia's pioneering aviator) and is located in the suburb of Mascot, 10km (6mi) south of the city centre. The international and domestic terminals are located 4km (2.5mi) apart on either side of the runway. It's Australia's busiest airport and handles around 25m passengers per year. It was refurbished and modernised in 1998, when an underground railway link to the city centre was built. A second Sydney airport is planned, although the state government is finding it difficult to find a suitable site.

Other Airports

- **Alice Springs** – Alice airport is 7km (4mi) south of the town centre, from where most flights are to Darwin or Adelaide.

- **Cairns & Townsville** – Cairns and Townsville have international airports which are also connected to Brisbane and other major cities by regular domestic flights.

- **Tasmania** – Tasmania has four main airports: Devonport, Hobart, Launceston and Wynyard (or Burnie), served by domestic flights from the mainland. The only international flights are from Hobart to New Zealand (Christchurch).

Outback Road, Winton, QLD

Q1 Tower, Gold Coast, QLD

11.
MOTORING

Australians are devoted to their cars and (like Americans) rarely go anywhere without them. As a result, public transport provision, especially in rural areas, is poor or non-existent and it's essential to have your own transport in Australia if you live anywhere other than in one of the main cities. Travelling interstate involves vast distances (on the North American scale) and most Australians think nothing of driving hundreds of miles to visit relatives or friends for a few days or even a day out. Almost 80 per cent of all goods in Australia are transported by road, and passenger travel is also dominated by road transport, with over 13m passenger vehicles on the road – virtually one for every person.

Australian cities are often sprawling (particularly Sydney) and even here people are inclined to use their cars rather than public transport. However, Australians haven't learned how to co-exist with the motor car in their cities, where parking problems, traffic jams and vehicle pollution are endemic. Traffic congestion and pollution are chronic in Sydney (where it's estimated they will become six times worse in the next 20 years) and Melbourne, where rush hours should be avoided at all cost. There are 'park and ride' facilities in cities to encourage commuters to use public transport, although they aren't widely used (encouraging car pooling is also a hard slog).

Australia has a high traffic accident rate and around 1,700 people are killed and 200,000 injured (22,000 seriously) on Australian roads each year, although the numbers are falling, partly as a result of the widespread introduction of random breath testing and speed cameras, and a reduction in legal alcohol/blood levels. However, levels of alcohol (and drugs) among those involved in fatal accidents remain high. The risk of young males aged 17 to 25 dying on the roads is around three times that of other age groups, and they're five times more likely to die in a car accident than women of the same age. Public holiday periods are the most dangerous times to be on the roads.

Car theft is rife and on the increase in Australia, where a car is stolen every five minutes on average. Many stolen cars are broken up and sold for spares, while the rest are re-registered and sold. If you regularly park your car in a city street, you have a high chance of having it or its contents stolen, although the favourite spot for thieves (particularly on Fridays and Saturdays) is suburban shopping mall car parks. For peace of mind, particularly in Sydney or Melbourne, you're better off using public transport!

Individual states and territories have jurisdiction over driving licences, the registration of motor vehicles and traffic rules, which therefore vary with the state or territory. For specific information, obtain a copy of a state or territory's 'highway code' (it has various names, such as the *Road Users' Handbook* in New South Wales and *Your Keys To Driving* in Queensland).

☑ SURVIVAL TIP

If you're going to Australia for a short period, don't forget to take your car insurance policy, foreign licence, international driving permit (if applicable), no-claims discount certificate and records of membership of motoring organisations.

IMPORTING A VEHICLE

Before importing a vehicle into Australia, contact the Vehicle Safety Standards Branch of the Department of Transport and Regional Services (🖥 www.dotars.gov. au) to make sure that the vehicle will meet Australia's safety requirements. If it will, there are three stages to importing a motor vehicle privately into Australia:

1. Obtain an Application for Approval to Import a Vehicle from the above office (☎ 1800-815272 or download it from the website – click on 'Importing Vehicles to Australia' on the right)

2. Pay customs duty (see below), goods and services tax/GST (10 per cent) and, where applicable, luxury car tax (usually payable on vehicles valued above around $57,000) and obtain customs clearance at the port of entry.

3. Obtain quarantine clearance from the Australian Quarantine and Inspection Service (AQIS) after the vehicle has arrived at the port of entry (see below for details).

Vehicles manufactured before 1st January 1989 may be imported without restriction. Customs duty varies according to the vehicle's design and value and is subject to change. Contact a customs office before importing a vehicle to enquire how much customs duty it will attract. Tourists and temporary residents can import a motor vehicle for a period of 12 months (longer under certain circumstances) without paying duty, provided that the vehicle is subsequently exported from Australia.

The AQIS inspects all vehicles on arrival in Australia and sometimes requires them to be cleaned (usually steam cleaned) at your expense. This is to prevent the entry of diseases, insect pests and undesirable plant spores into Australia. To avoid this procedure (and the cost of cleaning), you should remove all soil and other matter from your vehicle (including the underside) before bringing it to Australia. See the AQIS website (🖥 www.daff.gov.au/aqis) for further details. You must complete all customs clearance formalities at the port of entry. This is speeded up if you have the following documents to hand: bill of sale, driving licence, insurance documents, log book, passport, registration papers and service record.

TECHNICAL INSPECTION

In most states and territories, vehicles must pass a periodic technical inspection. For example, in New South Wales (NSW) a vehicle over four years old must pass an inspection every year (fee around $30) before its registration can be renewed. In order to sell a car in Australia, you must have the car inspected within one month of the sale and present the inspection certificate to the buyer.

The technical inspection is carried out by authorised garages and includes checking the brakes, horn, lights, seat belts, steering, windscreen wipers and washers, and tyres (which must have at least 1.5mm of tread across the whole surface). If your car passes, you're given an inspection report ('pink slip'), which must be displayed behind the windscreen. If your car fails the test, you're given a defect notice ('black slip') listing the points on which it has failed. You can get a defect notice if your car is too noisy, drips oil or blows out too much smoke; a car can even be failed if the inspector thinks it's too dirty to test! If you get a defect notice, the car must be repaired and officially cleared before you may drive it again; however, you may be permitted to take it home or to a garage for repair. If the police suspect that your car hasn't passed or wouldn't pass a technical inspection, they can affix a yellow sticker (called a 'canary') to your windscreen, which allows you to drive it home or to a garage for repair. If a red sticker is attached to a vehicle, it means that it's considered to be unroadworthy and may not be driven until it's repaired on the spot or towed away for repair.

REGISTRATION

Vehicle registration (often known as 'rego') must be renewed annually. In addition to road tax, the registration fee includes stamp duty (between 2 and 5 per cent of the vehicle's 'market' value depending on the state) and third-party liability insurance, which is compulsory and whose cost is fixed in most states. Registration is the responsibility of the states and territories, and fees vary but are usually $600 to $800 for an average vehicle.

Registration of a vehicle is made with the local state traffic authority, e.g. the Roads and Traffic Authority (RTA) in NSW (see addresses in **Appendix A**). Payment of vehicle registration can be made at the traffic authority's office or at a post office, and a current registration label must be displayed behind your car windscreen; if you lose it, a replacement costs around $20. Motorists who don't pay their rego

within a few weeks of the due date face fines.

The following are required to register a vehicle:

● **Compliance plate** – Before a vehicle can be registered in Australia, it must be fitted with an Australian compliance plate which indicates that it complies with Australian Design Rules (ADR); for details, see the Department of Transport and Regional Services (DOTARS) website (🖳 www.dotars.gov.au). A compliance plate is fitted automatically to a car manufactured in Australia; imported vehicles must be inspected by a state government motor vehicle registration authority. Before a vehicle can be tested, evidence must be shown that import duty and GST have been paid, as applicable (see page 312).

● **Insurance** – It's necessary to have proof of third-party (CTP) insurance (shown by a 'green slip' issued by the insurance company) to register a vehicle in Australia.

Number Plates

Number (registration) plates are issued by state and territory authorities and must be displayed at the front and rear of cars and at the rear of motorcycles. The registration numbers must match those on the vehicle's registration papers. A vehicle may not be parked or driven on a public road without registration, and plates must be returned to the issuing authority when they expire. Each state or territory has coloured plates as shown below.

There are also commercial, diplomatic, official and personalised registration plates with different colours. If you move to another state, you must re-register your vehicle.

Change of Ownership

If you buy a second-hand car, the previous owner must sign the back of the registration document, which you must take with the technical inspection certificate, if applicable, to the motor registry (the state government department concerned with the registration of motor vehicles, listed in the phone book). The change of ownership must be registered with the state authority and a registration transfer fee paid (between around $20 and $30, depending on the state), plus stamp duty of around 2 to 5 per cent, depending on the state. When a vehicle is bought or sold, the CTP insurance transfers to the new owner until the registration expires.

CAR HIRE

The car hire (rental) business is extremely competitive in Australia, with five large companies (Avis, Budget, Hertz, National and Thrifty) and a plethora of smaller companies. The major companies have offices in cities and towns throughout the country and at most major airports. Cars can be hired (rented) from garages and local car hire companies in most towns, which often have much lower rates than the nationals. Look in local newspapers and under 'Car Rentals' in the yellow pages. Shop around for the best rate. Airlines offer fly-drive deals on flights to or within Australia, which must be booked with the flight and don't necessarily represent good value.

Hire companies often offer optional extras such as child seats, a portable telephone and a roof rack, for which some charge a fee. All hire cars from national companies are covered for roadside breakdown assistance from a motoring organisation (see page 238). You can also hire a 4WD vehicle, campervan or motorhome, minibus, prestige luxury car, sports car or a estate car (station wagon), and a choice of manual or automatic gearbox is often available. Most hire companies expect you to have experience

State/Territory	Colour
ACT	Blue on white
NSW	Black on yellow
NT	Red on white
QLD	Green on white
SA	Green on yellow
TAS	Blue on white
VIC	Dark blue on white
WA	Black on yellow

of driving 4WD vehicles before they rent one to you. 'Performance cars' can be hired from a number of specialist rental companies, although if you want to test drive a car for a few days with a view to buying one, you may get a better deal from a garage. Vans and utility vehicles (pick-ups) are available by the hour, half-day or day. You can hire a campervan (motorhome), caravan or trailer from a number of companies (prices vary with the season). Some companies also hire out cars with hand controls for registered disabled drivers. In many cities you can hire a luxury car with a chauffeur – why not?

There's a wealth of companies in Australia hiring out old cars, sporting names such as 'Rent a Ruffy' and 'Rent a Wreck', typically from around $30 per day. You should beware of hiring older cars (cars from major hire companies aren't more than three years old and are usually less than a year old), as they could be dangerous. If you hire a car in an unroadworthy condition, you're responsible if you're stopped by the police or cause an accident. If you need a vehicle for a few months or longer, you may be better off buying one and selling it when you no longer need it.

The rates charged by the national companies in major cities are almost identical, daily rates averaging $50 to $60 for a small family car, $75 for a medium-size car and $100 for a large car. Four-wheel-drive vehicles cost from around $100 per day. Smaller local companies are usually cheaper, although you shouldn't automatically assume that this is so, as the major companies offer deals, including standby, weekend (e.g. three days for the price of two), weekly and monthly rates. You may also be able to negotiate a lower rate if business is slow. In some areas where competition is fierce (such as Tasmania), rates are usually lower, particularly out of season.

Compulsory third-party (CTP) insurance and a collision damage waiver (CDW) are usually included in rates, but check the small print, as even with CDW you may be liable in certain circumstances. If CDW isn't included, you must pay an excess, e.g. $300 to $1,500 (up to $4,000 in the Northern Territory!), if you have an accident. Personal accident insurance is available for an extra charge of around $2.50 per day. Stamp duty of 1 to 2 per cent is payable on all car hire.

You should always check the kilometre restrictions, which may be only 100 to 300km (62 to 186mi) 'free' per day, after which you pay a charge (e.g. 25 cents) per km. In rural and outback areas, there's usually a flat daily charge plus a charge per kilometre. Most companies restrict travel to sealed roads within 100 to 200km (62 to 124mi) of the hire outlet or within the state or territory where the car is rented (although ACT rentals usually cover the whole of NSW). If you breach the rules regarding the operating area, your insurance is automatically cancelled. Major companies usually quote different rates for 'metro' (city), country and 'remote' (outback) driving. Hire car insurance doesn't usually cover travel on dirt roads, with the exception of 4WD vehicles; even then insurance doesn't usually cover off-road travel, i.e. anything that isn't a maintained (sealed or dirt) road. The major companies offer one-way hire, which means you can hire a car at one branch and leave it at another. However, there are a number of conditions, the Northern Territory and Western Australia aren't always included, and it's expensive (around $200 extra).

☑ SURVIVAL TIP

When comparing prices, take into account all the costs, taxes and surcharges, as what initially looks a bargain may not be when you include all the extras. If you're planning to travel in rural areas or interstate, you should make sure that the hire includes membership of a local motoring organisation.

To hire a vehicle in Australia, you require a full national or international driving permit, which must have been held for a minimum of two or three years. You must usually be over 21, although some companies set the minimum age at 23 or 25 for certain vehicles, such as 4WDs. A major credit card is usually necessary for identification and the estimated costs (including a tank of petrol) must be paid in advance. The 'petrol bond' is refunded when a vehicle is returned with a full tank. Without a credit card, the estimated hire charge must be paid in advance plus a bond of around $200, which is returned, less any legitimate deductions.

BUYING A CAR

The cost of labour and parts for even the least expensive family cars is generally high in Australia, so it may pay to buy a car with a long or extended warranty. Popular, locally manufactured cars are best if you don't want high repair bills (spares and servicing for some German and Japanese cars are astronomical).

Air-conditioning is standard on most cars in Australia and is essential for anyone who spends much time behind the wheel. It certainly isn't a luxury when you're stuck in a traffic jam in summer or on long-distance trips in the outback. A basic air-conditioning unit costs from around $2,000 (installed) for a small family car, though many new cars come with air-conditioning as standard.

Information regarding the purchase of both new and used cars is published by Australian motoring organisations (see page 238); the National Roads & Motoring Association (NRMA) website (💻 www. mynrma.com.au) has plenty of information (click on 'Get car buying advice'). New and used car guides are available, including the *New Car Buyer's Guide*, the *Used Car Buyer's Guide* and Universal's *New 4WD Guide*.

New Cars

New cars generally cost slightly more in Australia than in most European countries and up to twice as much as in the US, particularly imported cars, on which there's a hefty import tariff (although it was reduced from 15 per cent to 10 per cent in 2005 and Australia is pledged to reduce or abolish import duty and tax at some time in the future). For example, a small hatchback costs from around $17,000 and a family car from around $33,000.

A number of foreign manufacturers make or assemble cars in Australia, including Ford, Holden (General Motors), Mitsubishi, Nissan and Toyota, which comprise over 75 per cent of the new car market, although other Asian manufacturers are starting to establish a foothold. Ford and Holden models are among the most popular and

to pay from $1,000 for an old 'banger' (which should, however, be mechanically reliable) and from around $5,000 for a decent second-hand car that should last a number of years.

All used cars must be fitted with an immobilizer before transfer of ownership, if they don't already have one. It's important to contact the state Registry of Encumbered Vehicles/REV (☎ 13-3220), which can tell you if a car is under finance or has been stolen or if there are any outstanding fines (e.g. parking) against it (when you buy a car, you assume responsibility for any outstanding fines). This is a free service and for just $12 you can obtain an REV Certificate proving that there are no charges outstanding. As an alternative to buying privately or from a dealer (see below), it's possible to buy at auction, although this isn't recommended unless you're an expert mechanic.

Dealers

The Property Agents and Motor Dealers Act, 2000 came into effect on 1st July 2001, establishing trading standards for used car dealers, who are now required to adhere to a code of conduct.

> All dealers must display a 'statutory warranty', which guarantees that cars are free from serious defects and that any defects occurring during the warranty period will be repaired free of charge.

Warranty periods are three months or 5,000km for cars under ten years old or with under 160,000km on the clock, and one month or 1,000km for cars over ten years old or with more than 160,000km on the clock. Under the new law, buyers have a 'cooling-off' period (until 5pm of the next working day) and may take the car for a test drive and have it independently inspected. They also have the option of a

consequently the cheapest for spares and repairs. Note, however, that local models are often different from those available in other countries, as manufacturers style their cars according to what the local market demands (Australians are proud of their 'unique' cars, particularly old Holden models).

Used Cars

If you want a reliable old car, it's best to buy a Ford Falcon or Holden Commodore, which are engineered to survive Australia's rough outback roads, and have strong six-cylinder engines and relatively inexpensive parts that are easy to obtain. Second-hand parts for most older Australian-made cars can be picked up cheaply from car breakers' yards throughout the country. Estates and panel vans are popular among travellers, as you can put a mattress in the back. Imported cars (e.g. German and Japanese) are generally considered more reliable than Australian-built cars, although they're also much more expensive. Expect

you buy a car in Sydney and break down in Perth the warranty won't be of much use!

A number of dealers in the major cities specialise in selling cars to travellers. Although they may operate from insalubrious premises (they're generally known as car yards), most are honest, as their reputation depends upon it. Many offer to buy vehicles back at an agreed price (provided you don't wreck them), which is usually 50 per cent of the purchase price. However, dealers may try to knock down the buy-back price by finding fault with the car, even when it has been agreed in writing. If this happens, you may get a better deal selling it privately (you should get around two-thirds of the price paid after six to nine months, provided you didn't pay too much). Obviously a buy-back deal is feasible only if you're returning to your starting point.

Buying Privately

Purchasing privately usually means you have less protection (such as a statutory warranty) than when buying through a dealer or at auction. However, to sell a car legally in Australia, the seller must have it inspected (see **Technical Inspection** on page 212) within a month of the sale and present the inspection certificate to the buyer. If you're buying privately, you should therefore only buy a car that has a valid 'pink slip'. It's obviously best to buy a car whose annual registration isn't about to expire. Stamp duty is payable as a percentage (between 2 and 5 depending on the state) of the declared purchase price.

Car markets: Cheap cars can be purchased at car markets in most cities, where owners gather to sell their vehicles. For example, in Sydney you can buy or sell a vehicle at the Kings Cross Car Market, which is dedicated to travellers buying and selling cars and campervans. One of the advantages of buying direct from travellers is that they may include camping

'complaint resolution process'. However, if you decide to use the 'cooling-off' period you must pay a deposit of up to $100, which you lose if you decide not to buy.

It's always best to buy a used car from a dealer who is licensed by the state business licensing authority, who is bound by the Auctioneers and Agents Act, and, preferably, who is a member of a motor traders association; the Motor Trades Association of Australia (MTAA) is the major national body and there are state/territory associations. If there's any question about a car's authenticity or the dealer's right to sell it (e.g. it's stolen or still under finance or has been modified), a licensed dealer must rectify the problem.

When you buy from a car dealer, he usually helps you with the paperwork and provides a technical inspection certificate and warranty, which is compulsory in most states. A dealer may also include free membership of a local motoring organisation. Always carefully check what's included or excluded from a used car warranty, as many contain a number of conditions, which, if you don't adhere to them, make the warranty void. However, if equipment, spares and other useful items in the price. You can also pick up cars registered in a state other than the one where it's being sold, which can be good buys, particularly if you plan to sell in the state where the vehicle is registered.

The best days for car advertisements in local newspapers are Wednesdays and Saturdays. There are also advertisements in publications such as the *Trading Post* (Sydney) and car magazines. You can buy other state newspapers, although it's rarely worth travelling far to inspect a car unless it's a rare model or exceptional value. Deciphering used car advertisements can be difficult unless you speak 'Australian', e.g. a panel van is a van with no rear windows and only front seats, and a ute is a utility or pick-up truck (an open-backed van).

DRIVING LICENCE

The minimum age for driving a car or motorcycle varies between 16 and 18 according to the state or territory and all drivers must have a valid licence. There are heavy penalties in Australia for driving without a licence (or with an expired licence), including fines of between $300 and $4,000, a prison term of up to six months and a ban from driving for a period.

If a foreign licence isn't written in English, an official translation must be obtained. This can be done in Australia by the local state Community Relations Commission or the Department of Immigration and Multicultural and Indigenous Affairs. Your driving licence, translation and passport must be carried when driving.

If you're a resident of Australia, you must have a licence issued by the state or territory where you're resident, and if you move to another state or territory you must obtain (not just apply for) a new licence and return your old licence within three months.

The same applies to foreign licence holders coming to Australia as permanent residents.

☑ **SURVIVAL TIP**

Most foreign licences are valid for a year in Australia, although it's usually worthwhile obtaining an international driving permit, particularly if your national licence doesn't contain your photograph (e.g. an old British driving licence).

The following licence classes apply throughout Australia:

- **Category C** – The basic licence permits you to drive a car or van with a maximum of 12 seats (including the driver's) weighing less than 4.5 tonnes.

- **Category LR** – This licence is required to drive heavy goods vehicles and vehicles with more than 12 seats. You must have held a C licence for at least a year to qualify for an LR licence.

- **Category R-Date** – This type of licence is required to ride a motorcycle of up to 250cc.

- **Category R** – This licence entitles you to ride any motorcycle.

Each class of licence exists in three levels, distinguished by their colour: learner's licence (green); unrestricted licence (silver or gold); provisional licence (red), for those ineligible for an unrestricted licence (see below). A silver licence is issued for one or three years after you first pass your test; after five years, you qualify for a gold licence, which is valid for a further five years. The cost of a driving licence varies with the state but is generally around $45 for one year, $100 for three years or $140 for five years.

To obtain a driving licence, in most states you must:

- pass an eyesight test and, in certain cases (e.g. sufferers from diabetes and epilepsy), a medical examination;

- pass a written road knowledge test (unless you hold a licence from an exempt country, which includes most EU countries, the US, Canada and Japan), costing $34;

- pass a driving test (unless you hold a licence from an exempt country). A driving test costs $42 or around $100 if you use a driving school vehicle (check in advance as fees can be excessive).

Take evidence of the above to the motor registry, along with:

- your foreign licence (with an English translation if necessary), which is photocopied and returned;

- proof of your identity, e.g. with a passport and another document such as a credit card or an account card from a bank, building society or credit union;

- proof of your address;

- the fee (see 🖳 www.rta.nsw.gov.au for an up-to-date list of fees applicable in NSW).

If you fail the road knowledge test, you can take it again (e.g. on the next working day) and you're only asked the questions that you got wrong. If you hold a foreign licence and fail the Australian driving test, you can no longer drive in Australia until you pass it. You must first obtain a learner's licence, which allows you to drive while supervised by a licensed driver with a clean licence (i.e. no demerit points – see below) who has held a licence for at least seven years.

If you pass the test but have held a foreign driving licence for less than a year, you're eligible only for a provisional licence. This means that you must display a 'P' plate (front and rear) on your vehicle at all times and are restricted to lower speeds (maximum 80kph/50mph), a reduced alcohol/blood level (0.02g per 100ml) and are permitted to accumulate a maximum of only three demerit points (see below) during the term of your licence.

If your last licence expired over five years ago, you may be required to return to learner's status. Learners must take a written road knowledge test before taking a practical driving test. They must display an 'L' plate until they've obtained a provisional or unrestricted licence. In some states, learner drivers must keep a logbook (teenagers are supervised by their parents) to prove that they've gained experience driving in a range of conditions and that their training period has extended to a year (a minimum three-month L-plate period applies in many states).

> The state RTAs publish information about obtaining driving licences, e.g. Licence to Drive, and a Guide to DART (Driving Ability Road Test) in NSW, which are available from local motor registries.

Fines & Demerit Points

Fines and 'demerit points' are issued for driving infringements according to the severity of an offence. Demerit points range from one (e.g. failing to dip your headlamps) to six points (exceeding the speed limit by over 45kph/28mph), although most offences carry three demerit points. A list of the infringements and consequent demerit points is provided in a state's Road User's Handbook. If you accumulate a certain number of demerit points within a limited period (usually two years), your licence may be revoked. The number you need to accrue in order to be banned from driving depends on the type of licence you carry. If you accumulate 12 points, your licence is usually cancelled for a minimum of three months. You should check with the RTA for the point limit of the type of licence you carry. Your licence can also be cancelled for up to five years (and you can be imprisoned) for serious offences, such as failing or refusing to take a breath test, failing to stop after an accident in which someone has been injured or killed, and exceeding the speed limit by over 45kph (28mph).

CAR INSURANCE

Car insurance is available from numerous Australian insurance companies (see page 327). Foreign insurance policies aren't valid in Australia, and all vehicles operated there must be insured with an Australian company. Note that it can be difficult to insure some imported vehicles that aren't sold in Australia.

Four categories of car insurance are available in Australia (detailed below). Any insurance policy can include other drivers (either named or unnamed). Separate passenger insurance is usually unnecessary, as passengers are automatically covered by all Australian motor insurance policies. You must ensure that you state any previous accidents or driving offences when applying for car insurance, or your insurer can refuse to pay out in the event of a claim.

Third-party

The minimum insurance cover required by law is third-party, usually referred to as compulsory third-party (CTP) or 'green slip', which is required in all states and territories. CTP covers only bodily injury to third parties (including injuries caused by passengers) and doesn't cover damage done to third-party property (including other vehicles), for which third-party property insurance is required (see below). Under common law, compensation

Woronora bridge, NSW

is paid for both economic loss (medical costs and loss of earnings) and non-economic loss (e.g. pain and suffering), if applicable.

Your 'green slip' must be produced when registering a vehicle. When a vehicle is bought or sold, the CTP transfers to the new owner until the registration expires. CTP is included in a car's annual registration fees, but in the case of imported vehicles (which are exempt from the first year's rego insurance) it must be independently arranged. **Third-party only insurance isn't recommended, as you could be faced with a huge bill if you damage someone else's property.**

Third-party Property

Third-party property (TPP) cover protects you against liability for damage caused to other people's property in an accident, e.g. if you damage another car or knock down a fence. TPP usually includes a provision of up to $3,000 for your own car if it's damaged by an uninsured driver (but you must be able to identify the driver).

Third-party, Fire & Theft

Known in some countries as 'part comprehensive', third-party, fire and theft (TPF&T) cover includes third-party cover (to people and property) and insurance against loss of or damage to your car and anything fitted to it caused by fire, lightning, explosion, theft or attempted theft. It usually covers breakage of glass. The amount you can claim may be limited, e.g. to $5,000, unless otherwise agreed when you take out a policy. Bear in mind that it isn't unusual for a car to overheat and catch fire in Australia so, unless you're driving a worthless heap, it pays you to have TPF&T insurance (and carry a fire extinguisher!). Note also that TPF&T may not cover all your belongings (e.g. if you're travelling around Australia in a camper van containing all your 'worldly possessions').

⚠ Caution

TPF&T insurance is offered by only a few insurance companies in Australia.

Comprehensive

Comprehensive insurance covers you for all the risks listed under the CTP and TPP above, plus breakage of glass (e.g. windscreen replacement), medical expenses and theft of contents. It also usually includes damage due to natural hazards, e.g. storm damage, but not loss or damage due to fire and theft, which are subject to an additional premium. Extra cover may be included free or for an additional fee, e.g. the cost of hiring a car if yours is involved in an accident or stolen, legal assistance, no-claims discount protection, and extra cover for a car stereo or telephone. Clothing and personal effects are usually included in comprehensive policies. Comprehensive insurance may also cover you against loss when your car is in a garage for service or repair.

Check a policy for any restrictions: for example, you may not be covered against theft if your car isn't garaged and locked overnight. Comprehensive insurance can be extended to include other vehicles not belonging to or hired to the policyholder, and it generally covers you for third-party risk when you're driving a car that doesn't belong to you. Most lenders insist on comprehensive insurance for leasing, contract hire and hire purchase agreements.

Premiums

The cost of CTP insurance (which is included in your annual registration fee – see page 213) is fixed in most states, but charges vary from state to state, e.g. $267 in South Australia and $386 in the ACT. The exception is NSW, where the cost can vary considerably (so shop around).

Other insurance premiums vary considerably according to a car's insurance class (although not all insurers place cars in the same class), which is calculated according to the new cost, the cost of spare parts and labour, repair times, and the car's power; your age, occupation and sex (women drivers usually pay lower premiums as they have fewer accidents); what you use your car for (e.g. business or pleasure); the number of miles you cover per year (some policies offer reduced rates for those who do low mileage); your driving experience and driving record (e.g. demerit points or loss of licence); your accident record and no-claims discount (see below); who will drive the car besides the owner; your health (you may be required to pay an excess if you suffer from epilepsy or diabetes); where you live (see below) and whether your car is garaged overnight; and any

your licence for a motoring offence, medical revocation of your licence or being unable to drive owing to injury.

Excess

With comprehensive insurance, you must usually pay an excess (deductible) of $100 to $400 when you make a claim. Drivers under 25, inexperienced drivers (holders of a licence for less than two years) and drivers with a bad accident record must usually pay a larger excess. You're usually also required to pay an excess, e.g. $50, if you make a claim on your windscreen cover (which normally covers all glass), but this doesn't affect your no-claims discount. You may be able to reduce the excess by paying a higher premium.

No-claims Discount

A foreign no-claims discount (or bonus) is usually valid in Australia, although some Australian insurance companies won't accept a no-claims discount earned overseas with a foreign insurance company. You must provide written evidence from your present or previous insurance company, not simply an insurance renewal notice. Some insurance companies offer an introductory discount.

> The no-claims discount offered by insurance companies is typically 20 per cent (after one year), 30 per cent (two years), 44 per cent (three years), 50 per cent (four years) and 60 per cent (five years), which is usually the maximum

extras you require, such as a protected no-claims discount.

Australian cities and states are divided into zones, and premiums are much higher for those living in inner cities than for those in outer suburbs and rural areas. Driving conditions are more hazardous in cities (owing to the high volume of traffic), and there's also usually a high risk of theft. Some insurers insist that a car (particularly a high-risk car) has an engine immobiliser.

For a small extra premium, most insurance companies provide cover for legal costs arising from road accidents (this is also available separately from Australian motoring organisations but is more expensive). If you cannot live without a car, ensure that your policy pays for car hire in the event of an accident or your car being stolen (or that you have separate 'uninsured loss' insurance to cover this). 'Mobility' insurance is available to pay for the cost of alternative transport after losing

Some companies provide an extra no-claims discount for experienced motorists with a clean licence and an accident-free driving record.

Normally, when you make a claim you lose two years' no-claims discount, even if the claim is for fire or theft, so it's sometimes cheaper to pay for minor repairs yourself. Damage to glass doesn't

usually pay in advance, although some companies allow you to pay in instalments either monthly, quarterly or half-yearly by direct debit from a bank account, possibly without incurring an additional charge (if there's an extra charge, check the interest rate). Initially you receive a 'cover note' to prove that you're insured until your insurance certificate is issued. Check that the details in the cover note are correct, particularly the type of cover required and the date and time it commences. Towards the end of your insurance period, you receive a renewal notice.

You can change your insurance company and policy whenever you like in Australia, for example by giving seven days' notice and returning the certificate, whereupon you receive a portion of your premium back, provided you've made no claims. **If you don't renew your policy by the due date, however, your cover ceases automatically.** If you're staying in Australia for a short period, you can usually take out a fixed-period policy, e.g. for three or six months, although this may be more expensive than cancelling an annual policy and obtaining a refund.

MOTOR BREAKDOWN INSURANCE

Breakdown insurance for cars and motorcycles is available from Australian motoring organisations (see page 238), which also offer travel insurance for motoring holidays and other types of insurance.

RULES OF THE ROAD

Each state and territory has its own driving laws, although in general the variations are minor. The road rules detailed below apply in most states of Australia. However, it's essential to familiarise yourself with the local idiosyncrasies in the law by

affect your no-claims discount, but you're usually required to pay the first $50 or $100 of a claim. Most insurance policies offer a protected no-claims discount policy or allow you to insure your no-claims discount. This means that you can usually make one 'at-fault' claim within a certain period (e.g. three years) or two claims within five years, for example, without losing any of your no-claims discount. If you're uninsured (i.e. don't drive) for longer than two years, you usually lose your entire no-claims discount.

If you insure two or more vehicles, you can claim a no-claims discount on only one vehicle, although you may be given a discount on the premium for the other vehicles.

Payment & Terms

Motor insurance policies are valid for a year from the date you're first insured. You must obtaining a copy of a state or territory's 'highway code' (such as the *Road Users' Handbook* in NSW) from the relevant local authority (e.g. the RTA in NSW) or motoring organisation. Handbooks contain advice for all road users, including motorcyclists, motorists and pedestrians. The NSW handbook is available in Arabic, Chinese, Croatian, English, Greek, Korean, Japanese, Serbian, Spanish, Turkish and Vietnamese. A *Heavy Vehicle Drivers' Handbook* and a *Motorcycle Riders' Handbook* are also published in NSW.

The Australian Automobile Association (AAA – see page 295) publishes a free booklet, *Motoring in Australia*, which contains sections in English, French, German, Japanese and Spanish.

Among the many strange habits of Australians is that of driving on the left-hand side of the road, which they inherited from the British. You may find this a shock if you come from a country where people drive on the right; however, it saves a lot of confusion if you do likewise. It may be helpful to have a reminder (e.g. 'think left!') on your car's dashboard. Take extra care when pulling out of junctions and one-way streets and at roundabouts. Remember to look first to the **right** when crossing the road on foot. If you're unused to driving on the left, you should be prepared for some disorientation (or even terror), although most people have few problems adjusting to it.

If you needed spectacles or contact lenses to pass your sight test, you must always wear them when driving. It's wise to carry a spare pair of glasses or contact lenses in your car.

Documents

You're required by law to carry your car or motorcycle registration papers and your driving licence (including an international driving permit if required) when driving in Australia.

Drink & Drugs

In Australia you're no longer considered fit to drive when your blood contains between 0.02g and 0.05g of alcohol (depending on the state and other factors) per 100ml of blood. The limit for experienced drivers is 0.05g (some states are considering lowering it to 0.02g). In most states, the limit is 0.02g for drivers with a learner's or provisional licence, drivers under 25 who have held a licence for less than three years, anyone driving a bus, a car for hire or reward or a taxi, drivers of heavy goods vehicles and anyone carrying a dangerous load. In some states, drivers with a learner's or provisional licence must not drive with any alcohol in their blood. Driving while under the influence of drugs is also illegal.

Junctions

At crossroads and junctions (intersections) in Australia where no right of way is assigned, traffic coming from the right has priority (as in continental Europe). At major junctions, right of way is always indicated by a 'GIVE WAY' (yield) sign or a 'STOP' sign. There are also usually road markings. When faced with a stop sign, you must stop completely before pulling away, even if you can see that no traffic is approaching. At a give way sign, you aren't required to stop, but must give priority to traffic already on the road you're joining. You must also give way to traffic on your right when joining a major road from a slip road. In towns in Queensland (i.e. in 60kph/37mph zones), motorists must give way to buses pulling out.

Lights

Headlights must be used when driving between sunset and sunrise or at any time when there's insufficient daylight to be able to see a person wearing dark clothing at a distance of 100m. It's illegal to drive on side (parking) lights in Australia, and headlights must usually be dipped (low beam) when driving in built-up areas where there's street lighting. Headlights must also be dipped within 200m of an approaching vehicle, immediately an oncoming vehicle has dipped its headlights and when travelling less than 200m behind another vehicle. If you happen to be riding a camel on a road at night in Broome (WA), you must have a rear light!

Headlamp flashing has only one legal use – to warn another vehicle of your presence, although most people use it to give priority to another vehicle, e.g. when someone is waiting to pull out of a side road. It's illegal in some states to warn other vehicles that they're approaching a speed trap or police road block by flashing your lights (although many drivers do it).

Hazard warning lights (all indicators operating simultaneously) should be used to warn other drivers of an obstruction, e.g. an accident or a traffic jam on a main road.

Overtaking

It's usually illegal to overtake on an inside lane unless traffic is being channelled in a different direction. However, overtaking on the inside ('undertaking') is permitted in some states on a highway with three or more lanes in each direction. In Australia, the right-hand lane isn't usually just for overtaking and, although you should keep to the left, it isn't obligatory. Motorists must indicate before overtaking **and** when moving back into an inside lane after overtaking, e.g. on a dual-carriageway or highway.

Pedestrian Crossings

Always approach pedestrian crossings with caution and don't park or overtake another vehicle on the approach to a crossing (usually shown by zigzag lines or a large white diamond). At some crossings, a flashing amber light follows the red light, to warn you to give way to pedestrians before proceeding.

⚠ Caution

Pedestrians have the legal right of way once they've stepped onto a crossing without traffic lights, and you must stop. Motorists who don't are liable to heavy penalties.

Where a road crosses a public footpath, e.g. at the entrance to a property or car park, motorists **must** give way to pedestrians.

Road Markings

White or yellow markings are painted on the road surface in towns and cities, e.g. arrows to indicate the direction traffic must go in a particular lane. White lines mark the separation of traffic lanes. Where there are no lane markings, you should keep to the left side of the road. In many cities, there are 'transit lanes' (indicated by roadside signs) for bicycles, buses, emergency vehicles, motorcycles and taxis during rush hours, e.g. 6 to 10am, Mondays to Fridays. A private vehicle may use these lanes **only** if it's carrying one or two passengers – e.g. in NSW a passenger vehicle in a T2 lane must have at least one passenger and in a T3 lane at least two passengers – or if you intend to make a turn within 100m. There are also 'BUS ONLY' lanes in cities.

A solid single line or two solid lines between opposing lanes means no overtaking in either direction. A solid line to the left of the centre line, i.e. on your side of the road, means that overtaking is prohibited in your direction. You may overtake only when there's a single broken line in the middle of the road or double lines with a broken line on your side of the road.

Double lines may be crossed when making a right turn in some states, but not in others, and U-turns are usually prohibited across any unbroken centre line even if associated with a broken line.

Roundabouts

There are many roundabouts (traffic circles) in Australia, which, although sometimes rather a free-for-all, speed up traffic considerably and are usually preferable to traffic lights, particularly outside rush hours (although some busy roundabouts also have traffic lights). On roundabouts, vehicles on the roundabout (i.e. coming from the right) have priority over those entering it. Traffic flows clockwise round roundabouts and not anti-clockwise, as in countries where traffic drives on the right. Some roundabouts have a filter lane which is reserved for traffic turning left. You should stay in the lane in which you entered the roundabout, follow the lane markings to

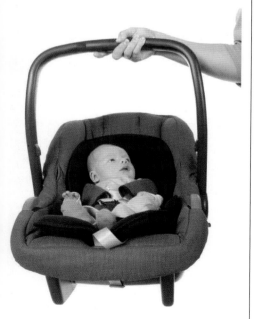

leave and signal as you approach the exit you wish to take.

School Buses

You must drive slowly near school buses and give way to children crossing the road. When loading and unloading children, school buses flash orange lights at the front and rear, and may also display a 'GIVE WAY' sign at the rear. Lights remain flashing for around 30 seconds, after which the doors close and the bus moves off.

Seatbelts

Seatbelts must be worn by all front and rear seat passengers when fitted. In all states, children aged 1 to 13 must use an approved child seat that meets the relevant Australian standard or a firmly adjusted adult seatbelt when available. A child must **never** travel in the front seat without using a child restraint or seatbelt, even when the back seat is full. If all available restraints in a car are in use, children may travel unrestrained (although this is **extremely unwise**).

If you're exempt from using a seatbelt for medical reasons, a safety belt exemption certificate is required from your doctor. More information can be obtained from motoring organisations and motor vehicle authorities.

Signs

Speed limit signs are in kilometres per hour and not miles per hour, e.g. in NSW white rectangular signs indicate the speed limit in black numerals within a red circle. In addition to mandatory speed limits, there are often signs indicating advised limits, e.g. when approaching a sharp bend, which aren't compulsory. Apart from the international octagonal 'STOP' sign (white on red) and the triangular 'GIVE WAY' sign (black on white with a red border), most other Australian road signs don't follow international standards; the different types of sign can usually be distinguished as follows:

- Warning signs telling you that there may be dangers ahead are usually diamond shaped with black or red diagrams (such as a kangaroo) on a yellow background.

- Regulatory signs giving instructions (in words) that must be obeyed are usually rectangular with black letters on a white background (some also have red markings).

- Highway signs giving information about the start, end and exits from highways are of various colours.

- Some parking signs are green on white.

> In Melbourne, to accommodate the city's trams, a local rule applies at certain junctions. Where there's a 'RIGHT TURN FROM LEFT ONLY' sign accompanied by curved broken lines on the road surface, you must keep to the left lane and wait until you get a green light to make a right turn (known locally as a 'hook turn').

Other types of sign include those used in rural areas to indicate where livestock can be expected on or near roads (you must slow or stop as required and can be fined for disobeying signs) and temporary signs used at road works. The most important signs are shown in a state or territory's road users' handbook. Signs may be emphasised by painted warnings on the road.

Speed Limits

The following speed limits are in force for cars and motorcycles throughout Australia, unless indicated otherwise by a sign: 50kph (31mph) in residential areas; 60kph (37mph) in built-up areas and 100kph (62mph) on highways. In Western Australia the speed limit is 110kph (68mph) on country roads and highways, and in the Northern Territory there's no speed limit

outside built-up areas, although speeds are severely limited on most roads by potholes and ruts. Learners and provisional licence holders and drivers towing a caravan, trailer or another vehicle are limited to 80kph (50mph), even when a higher limit is in force.

In some urban areas, there are zones with lower speed limits, including shared traffic zones, where pedestrians, bicycles and other vehicles may all use the road and the limit may be 10kph/6mph (so no running!); school zones, which have reduced speed limits on school days during school hours (e.g. 25kph/15mph or 40kph/25mph); and local traffic zones (40kph/25mph). However, after a court case and intervention by the federal Transport Minister, state governments were declared not to have the power to impose fines for 'speeders' in a 25kph/15mph

speed limit school zone (after thousands had already been fined).

In some residential areas there are speed humps (known as 'sleeping policemen' or 'traffic calmers' – although they certainly don't calm drivers!). They're sometimes indicated by warning signs and, if you fail to slow down, it's possible to damage your suspension or even turn your car over.

Speed limits are rigorously enforced in Australia and police employ radar units and speed cameras to identify speeders. Light planes and helicopters are used to spot speeding vehicles on interstate highways, where white lines may be painted on the road surface to help aerial police calculate speeds (by timing a vehicle between lines). Radar detectors are illegal in all states except Western Australia, and you can be fined up to around $750 for using one (it's also confiscated). However, they're in widespread use throughout Australia. If an oncoming vehicle flashes his headlights at you, it may be that he has spotted a radar trap and is warning you.

Marginal offences are usually dealt with by on-the-spot fines, which can run into $hundreds. You can also 'earn' demerit points on your licence and be disqualified from driving for a period. Despite prosecutions and large fines, speeding is widespread and one of the major causes of accidents; on country roads (where limits are widely ignored) one in three serious injuries is caused by speeding.

Traffic Lights

The sequence of Australian traffic lights is normally red, yellow, green and back to red, although some lights pass through yellow again between green and red. Yellow is a warning light and doesn't mean that you have to stop (or may not go if you're stationary), so most Australian drivers ignore yellow lights! A green filter light may be shown in addition to the normal lights, which means you may go in the direction shown by the arrow, irrespective of other lights showing. Cameras are often installed at busy traffic lights to detect motorists driving through red lights (a favourite pastime of many Australian motorists).

At traffic lights in some states there are 'TURN LEFT AT ANY TIME WITH CARE' or 'LEFT TURN ON RED PERMITTED AFTER STOPPING' signs, permitting vehicles to turn left even when faced with a red light. However, drivers must first stop if indicated and only proceed when they can do so safely.

> ⚠ **Caution**
> **In some cities (e.g. Adelaide) there are flashing 'NO RIGHT TURN' signs at some junctions during business hours.**

Flashing yellow lights and stop signs with three large black dots are used at some junctions to mean that you must stop and give way to all traffic. A sign of a white 'B' on a black background indicates that traffic lights apply to bus lanes, marked 'BUSES ONLY' (you should never drive in bus lanes – unless you're driving a bus).

Tram Lines

In cities with tramways (e.g. Melbourne), tram lines are delineated by yellow lines, which you should remain clear of unless you want a close encounter with a tram; continuous yellow lines may not be crossed, but broken lines may be crossed provided you don't obstruct a tram. When a tram has started to cross a junction, it has right of way over all other vehicles. There are rules concerning the overtaking of trams; for example, you mustn't pass a tram when it stops to pick up or drop off passengers (unless there's a central island). Tram tracks can be slippery when wet; cyclists and motorcyclists should take care.

AUSTRALIAN DRIVERS

Like motorists in all countries, Australians have their idiosyncrasies and customs (many of which run counter to the official rules of the road). Although they aren't considered to be among the best in the world, most Australians are good and careful drivers, who take their driving seriously. On the other hand, Australia has its fair share of seriously crazy drivers. Northern Territorians are reckoned to be Australia's worst drivers, particularly in traffic, and are scornfully referred to as 'bush motorists' as they tend not to bother with the niceties of roadcraft, such as indicating, keeping to lanes, and stopping at stop signs and red lights. Shooting (running) red lights is common practice in Australian cities and the all-red period (when all vehicles are required to stop) has been increased to combat it.

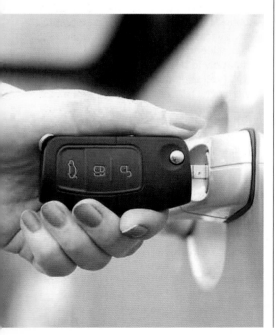

Tempers are rising on Australia's overcrowded streets and in cities, particularly among truck drivers, and it's usually every man for himself, particularly in Sydney. Road rage ('invented' in California – where else?), where drivers blow their tops and attack or drive into other motorists, is becoming more common. It's often provoked by headlight flashing, obscene gestures, obstruction, tailgating and verbal abuse, so take care how you behave when driving in Australia.

Drinking and driving is still fairly commonplace, despite regular spot checks. The macho attitude among young male drivers in particular is a killer and the risk of young people aged 17 to 25 dying on the roads is around three times that of other age groups. However, the once appalling accident rate has fallen in recent years through better driver training and education, improved roads, random breath testing, safer vehicles and stricter laws. Women generally have far fewer accidents than men (particularly the under 25s) and are much less likely to drink and drive. However, young women drivers are increasingly showing aggressive driving behaviour normally associated only with men.

However, don't be discouraged by the tailgaters and road hogs, as driving in Australia is less stressful than in many other countries and can even be enjoyable in country areas (provided you avoid dirt tracks).

AUSTRALIAN ROADS

There are some 813,000km (over 500,000mi) of roads in Australia, varying in quality from eight-lane highways to rutted dirt tracks which are impossible to negotiate in anything other than a four-wheel-drive (4WD) vehicle. Only some 40 per cent of roads are sealed, although this includes the nearly 19,000km (12,000mi) of the National Highway System linking the capital cities plus Brisbane and Cairns in Queensland, and Hobart and Burnie in Tasmania.

Roads are usually classified as primary or secondary routes. Primary routes are the major roads that link the states and territories, together with those serving the principal centres of population and industry within them. Secondary routes include those which allow the carriage of produce from farms and mines, forest roads serving tourist resorts, and most streets in towns and cities. Lighting is good on major urban roads and usually adequate on other urban roads.

Generally, the roads between major cities and state capitals are excellent, with dual-carriageways (divided highways) in metropolitan areas, particularly in the eastern coastal areas of Brisbane, Newcastle and Sydney, although it's generally felt that investment in roads hasn't kept pace with the continued growth of traffic, especially in metropolitan areas. In rural areas, where traffic density isn't high and there are vast distances between towns, roads may have only two lanes, and in the outback dirt roads are common.

> ☑ SURVIVAL TIP
>
> **You should swerve to avoid a kangaroo only when it's safe to do so, as many people kill themselves trying to avoid them.**

Beware of kangaroos and other animals which stray onto country roads, particularly at night. An encounter with a big boomer can seriously damage your vehicle, not to mention the animal itself, which is why most car and truck owners who regularly use country roads fit their vehicles with 'roo bars' (the steel bars commonly seen on 4WD vehicles in countries without kangaroos). Some cars are fitted with an alarm which emits a high-pitched noise to frighten kangaroos ('shu-roo').

Water buffalo are a problem in some northern parts of the country, and grazing cattle can also be a menace in country areas. Many Australians try to avoid travelling when it's dark because of the danger posed by animals (most are nocturnal).

Tasmanian roads are fairly traffic free (a few cars nose-to-tail represents a traffic jam) and driving there is relatively straightforward (except in winter). Take it easy when driving in inclement weather. Ice and snow are rare in most areas except the mountainous regions of NSW, Victoria and Tasmania (which, being farthest south, experiences the worst winter weather). Fog can also make driving extremely hazardous in winter in some regions.

Urban Roads

There are wide roads in most cities, particularly in the suburbs, where they're usually laid out on a grid system (except in Canberra and Sydney). Victoria's roads are the most crowded, followed by urban roads in NSW. Driving in Sydney is to be avoided if possible (finding somewhere to park can be a nightmare), while Melbourne isn't much better, in spite of the new Citylink toll system (see below). Most major cities are choked during rush hours, and Sydney is congested at almost all times, although the Eastern Distributor and M5 and roads built for the 2000 Olympic Games have helped. Sydney Harbour bridge is an infamous bottleneck (a toll is charged when travelling south), although the harbour tunnel has relieved some of the congestion.

Sydney has a 'Metroad' system, which helps make travel into, through and out of the city (a tiny bit) easier, and construction of a western Sydney ring road (the Westlink M7) was completed in December 2005. Driving in Adelaide, Brisbane (with its new Gateway Bridge) and Perth is relatively easy, although rush hours should be avoided.

Toll roads are unpopular with Australians, and the M2 in Sydney has been shunned by many motorists; it carries only around half the number of vehicles forecast. However, despite this setback, more toll roads have been built, including the Melbourne Citylink and the Eastern Distributor in Sydney.

Many Australian cities have tortuous one-way systems, and signposting in cities can be confusing and street names difficult to find.

Rural Roads

Major roads in Australia are variously described as highways, expressways and freeways. The distinctions between these types of road are sometimes blurred, but in general freeways (as their name suggests) are toll-free roads, whereas tolls ($3.50 to $5) are payable at intervals on most highways and expressways.

Expressways usually have fewer junctions and traffic lights than highways, and neither expressways nor freeways allow bicycles. Highway and expressway numbers are sometimes prefixed with an M or an F (which doesn't indicate a freeway!). All major roads are sealed and many have three or four lanes in each direction.

Road numbers are rarely used in Australia and most people refer to roads by their names. Highway 1, which runs right around Australia, mostly hugging the coast, is known by various names in various parts of Australia, such as the Princes Highway between Sydney and Adelaide. It's the country's most dramatic road, some stretches being extremely picturesque, and it passes through many interesting towns.

The most direct route between Sydney and Melbourne is the busier inland Hume Highway (number 31). The most direct route between Melbourne and Adelaide is the Western Highway (number 8), but the Princes Highway (1) offers better views. The main roads between Sydney and Brisbane are the coastal Pacific Highway (1) and the inland New England Highway (15). The quickest route from Sydney to Adelaide is via the Great Western (32), Mid Western (24) and Stuart Highways (20).

On most highways, there are route markers (small shields by the roadside) every 5km (3mi) bearing the initial letter of the last or next major town above the distance in kilometres. There are emergency telephones every kilometre for use in the event of accidents and breakdowns. Some highways have a 'crawler' lane (for slow-moving vehicles) and escape lanes are common on steep downhill stretches to stop vehicles whose brakes fail.

National (i.e. interstate) highways are a federal government responsibility and have been funded from an excise levied on fuel since the early '80s, although it's claimed that far more fuel tax has been collected than spent on the roads.

In some sparsely populated country areas ('back of Bourke') there are long stretches of main road with only one lane paved and wide unsealed shoulders. Even highways such as the Western Australia coastal road (see below) have stretches consisting of a single lane with dirt shoulders. Minor roads can be terrible, consisting mainly of dirt tracks.

☑ **SURVIVAL TIP**

Australia's vast distances and hot sun induce drowsiness in drivers and you should make frequent stops for refreshment and rests on a long journey.

There are plenty of roadside rest areas on main highways, and free coffee is provided at stops on some highways to help reduce driver fatigue. Drivers falling asleep at the wheel are a major cause of accidents on highways, particularly at night (as the sign says, 'Drowsy Drivers Die'!). It's always sensible to have company on long journeys.

Outback Roads

Many outback roads are made of dirt and in varying stages of neglect, although in some outback areas of Western Australia there are sealed roads built privately by mining companies, and visitors may be allowed to use them with a permit. Signposting is virtually non-existent in the outback and can be a bit of a joke (e.g. 'Darwin 2,000km').

There has, however, been a vast improvement in the outback road network in recent years, making it possible for the average motorist to explore the country by car (on main highways) without the need of a 4WD vehicle. However, high ground clearance is necessary on unsealed

outback roads and four-wheel drive is often essential if you don't want to get stuck (although it isn't failsafe).

Outback driving can be hazardous for the inexperienced driver, and thorough preparation is essential. In bygone days it wasn't unusual to come across a vehicle in the outback containing the skeletons of its occupants, although (despite the horror stories) people rarely die in the outback nowadays.

Conditions vary from area to area and season to season. The best time to travel is during the cooler winter months between April and October. Many outback roads are deeply rutted and can be washed away by flash floods and remain impassable for weeks on end during the wet season (some roads in northern Australia are impassable from December until May). Dust can also be a problem during the heat of summer in central Australia (when air-conditioning is practically essential). You should keep a close eye on the temperature gauge in hot weather.

Road conditions and routes must be checked with the local authorities, in addition to weather forecasts and the availability of fuel. On some roads, motorists are required to complete a police destination card giving their expected time of arrival at the next town. It's sensible to carry a two-way UHF radio tuned to the local Royal Flying Doctor Service. Make sure a vehicle is roadworthy, and carry plenty of spares, including a first-aid kit, a plastic windscreen, two spare wheels, tools, a week's supply of food and water (20 litres per person in a number of containers), spare fuel (keep the tank topped up at all times), a workshop manual and maps.

If you break down, it's imperative to stay with your vehicle and wait for assistance. A motorist must (by law) aid someone who has broken down in the outback. As a last resort, burn a tyre, as property owners in the outback never ignore smoke.

On the outback roads of central and northern Australia, you're likely to come across road trains, which are multi-trailer, articulated lorries up to 50m in length and weighing over 100 tonnes, driven by maniacs who don't move over for anyone (except perhaps another road train). It's best to pull over if you see one coming towards you and let it pass. If you come up behind one and want to overtake it (if you can see for dust), allow at least a kilometre.

Many books are published for outback travellers, including *Explore Australia by 4WD* by Peter and Kim Wherrett (Five Mile Press), *The Driving Guide Series* (covering most of Australia's regions) by Ian Read (Cimino Publishing) and *Outback Australia* (Lonely Planet). The Flying Doctor also publishes a booklet, *Outback Travelling*, for visitors planning long-distance trips.

Information

Information about road conditions is provided by motoring organisations and state government roads departments, e.g. in Queensland the Main Roads Department publishes *Queensland Road Conditions*. Information about road conditions throughout Australia can be obtained from the National Roads' and Motorists' Association Limited (NRMA, ☎ local call rate 13-11 22, 🖥 www.mynrma.com.au). The telephone line is open 24 hours a day, offering recorded road reports for the major highways.

TRAFFIC POLICE

Police in Australia don't need a reason to stop motorists and can make spot checks at any time. In recent years, random breath testing has increased considerably as police have cracked down on drinking and driving. Australian state police aggressively enforce all traffic regulations and use a variety of equipment and tactics to catch offenders. Roadblocks with mobile breath-testing units are used to check for drink-driving infringements, and automatic cameras are installed at junctions to identify drivers shooting red lights.

Never antagonise a police officer or make any wisecracks, as this is the fast lane to prosecution; remain courteous and obsequious and you may be let off with a caution. Although you may have read about corrupt Australian police, don't even think about trying to bribe an officer unless you wish to be charged with a much more serious offence! When crossing a state border, your vehicle may be searched for drugs, guns, fresh fruit and vegetables (which may not be transported from one state to another, to prevent the spread of parasites) and pornography.

 Caution

Radar units and hidden speed cameras are employed to identify speeders, and planes and helicopters are used to catch speeding vehicles on rural highways.

You must show your vehicle documents and give a policeman your name and address when requested, although you aren't required to answer questions before obtaining legal advice.

MOTORCYCLES

The minimum age for riding a motorcycle in Australia varies with the state or territory but is usually 17. You may obtain a licence before you reach the required age after passing a written road knowledge test. The following information is based on motorcycle licensing laws in NSW, which are similar to other states'.

A learner must ride a motorcycle with a maximum engine capacity of 250cc, with a power-to-weight ratio of no more than 150kw per tonne. An 'L' plate must be displayed on the back and you mustn't carry a passenger. In some areas, learners must complete a pre-provisional licence course before taking a road knowledge test. The course can be taken at 16 years and six months and allows a learner's licence to be issued at 16 years and nine months.

To obtain a provisional motorcycle licence (class R), you must take a riding test between three and six months after you receive your learner's licence. After passing the test, a 'P' (provisional) plate must be displayed on the back of the motorcycle for a year. If you've held a foreign motorcycle licence for less than a year you're eligible only for a provisional licence, and if you fail the riding test you may be required to undertake further rider training.

Although Australia has an excellent climate for it, biking has declined in popularity in the last decade, and bikes are more a fashion statement nowadays than a transport option, many over-40s buying

them only for leisure riding. Motorcyclists aren't popular with motorists in Australia, particularly in the major cities, where lunatic motorcycle couriers have given bikers a bad name.

The average price of a motorbike is around $5,000, top models costing close to $80,000. If you need a bike only for a short period (e.g. a trip around Australia), some dealers offer buy-back options on second-hand bikes. There's a healthy market in second-hand bikes and you may be able to pick up a bargain from a departing visitor (the best time to buy a bike is at the start of the Australian winter, in May).

Motorcycles can be hired (rented) in Australia, although rates are high and range from $120 to $700 per weekend ($1,000 to $3,000 per week) depending on the engine capacity (there are usually discounts for longer than a week). A deposit of around $1,000 is payable by credit card. One-way rentals are possible with a drop-off fee, although it may be cheaper to buy a second-hand bike and sell it when you arrive.

Large capacity bikes are best for long-distance travel. It's essential to take spares and tools when on a long trip as well as plenty of drinking water, and travelling alone in the outback isn't recommended (see **Outback Roads** on page 233). Contact motorcycle clubs and motoring organisations for information about outback road conditions and the availability of fuel.

A helmet must be worn at all times (but remove it when going into a bank or they may think you're planning to rob it!). Otherwise, laws that apply to cars (see **Rules of the Road** on page 224) also apply to motorcycles. The NSW RTA publishes a *Motorcycle Riders' Handbook*.

ACCIDENTS

If you're involved in (or cause) an accident in Australia, which results in injury to a person or animal, or damage to any third party's vehicle or property, the procedure is as follows:

1. Stop immediately. If possible move your vehicle off the road and keep your passengers and yourself off the road. **Failing to stop after an accident or failure to give particulars or report the accident to the police is a serious offence.**

2. Warn other drivers of any obstruction by switching on your hazard warning lights (particularly on highways) or by placing a warning triangle at the edge of the road at least 50m behind your car on secondary roads and 150m on a highway.

3. If anyone is injured, immediately telephone for an ambulance, the fire brigade (if someone is trapped or oil or chemicals are spilled) or the police (dial ☎ 000). Emergency telephones are provided on highways.

4. If damage worth over $500 or $1,000 (depending on the state) is caused to animals, property or vehicles, the nearest police station must be notified within 24 hours (if the police don't attend the scene). Calling the police to the scene of an accident may result in someone being fined or charged for a driving offence, although you aren't obliged to say anything (apart from giving your name and address).

☑ SURVIVAL TIP

If you injure a wild animal, you should remove it from the road (care should be taken, as many Australian mammals carry their young in pouches), and notify the local Wildlife and Information Rescue Service (WIRES).

If you have an accident involving a domestic animal and are unable to find the owner, it must also be reported to the police or the RSPCA.

5. Report the accident to your insurance company in writing as soon as possible, even if you don't intend to make a claim (but reserve your right to make a claim later). If you're injured and plan to make an insurance claim, you must obtain a doctor's report as soon as possible after the accident to verify your injuries (this is obviously done automatically if you're admitted to hospital).

FUEL

Leaded petrol is being phased out and is available only in a few service stations. Most old cars have been adapted to run on unleaded petrol. Regular unleaded is just 91 octane, but many stations in major cities also sell unleaded of 96 octane rating, and some are now selling 98 octane unleaded. Specially treated petrol is sold in Sydney during the summer months in order to reduce pollution. Diesel is also available at most petrol stations, and two-stroke petrol is available for boats, lawn-mowers, mopeds, etc..

Fuel prices are usually around $1 per litre (or around $4.50 per imperial gallon) for regular unleaded petrol or diesel. Premium unleaded is usually only a few cents more than regular unleaded. Fuel prices vary from area to area, even within cities; in outback areas (where petrol stations are few and far between) and Tasmania, prices are around 15 cents higher than in cities. Petrol is usually cheapest at supermarkets. In recent years, there have been claims of price fixing by the major oil companies, but the big four companies, Ampol, BP, Mobil and Shell, are permitted to own and operate only 4 per cent of the stations carrying their name, where they can fix the prices. The remaining outlets are franchises,

of 24-hour stations is expected to be reduced drastically in future. Some stations have automatic pumps accepting $5 and $10 bills, and possibly credit and debit cards (however, don't rely on finding any outside major towns). Most petrol stations accept major credit and charge cards and Australian debit (EFTPOS) cards.

Most petrol stations provide additional services such as checking oil, water and tyre pressure, and cleaning windscreens. Some also have a car wash and most have a shop selling a wide range of motoring accessories and other goods. Many petrol stations also have workshops and can usually handle minor repairs on the spot.

GARAGES & SERVICING

When buying a car in Australia or importing one, you should bear in mind the local service facilities, as not all cars can be easily serviced. All the major European and Japanese manufacturers are well represented, but garages servicing American and exotic European cars are few and far between. If you drive a 'rare' car, it's wise to carry a basic selection of spare parts, as service stations in Australia may not stock them and you may need to wait several weeks for them to be sent from overseas.

Servicing and repairs at main dealers are expensive, particularly for imported cars. Small garages and workshops are cheaper, although the quality of work is variable and it's best to choose one which has been personally recommended. Ask friends and colleagues if they can recommend a garage close to your home or workplace. If, however, anything goes wrong (and it often does), you have a better chance of redress with a main dealer or a garage that's a member of a trade association or approved by a motoring organisation. When a car is under warranty, it must usually be regularly serviced (at the recommended service

which buy petrol from the oil company at a wholesale price and set their own prices.

Many cars in Australia have been converted to run on liquid petroleum gas (LPG) or propane, including most taxis and buses. Most petrol engines can be converted to use both petrol and LPG (they can be switched between them), although you lose around a third of your boot space to accommodate the gas tank. The advantage is that LPG costs from around 50 cents a litre, although there's a loss of power of around 15 per cent. All urban areas and most large country towns have LPG outlets. However, a word of warning: LPG tanks occasionally explode, often with fatal results!

The trading hours of petrol stations vary considerably. Most open from 7.30am to 6.30pm, Mondays to Saturdays, and on Sunday mornings. Many petrol stations in cities and on highways are open 24 hours a day. However, they run a high risk of robbery and even assaults on staff at night in some cities, and the number intervals) by an approved dealer in order not to invalidate the warranty.

Always obtain a number of quotations for major mechanical work or body repairs and tell the garage if an accident repair is to be paid for privately, as they may increase the price when an insurance company is paying. Quotations for accident repairs usually vary widely, and some garages include the unnecessary replacement of parts. Always get a second opinion if you're quoted a high price for a repair.

⚠ Caution

Poor workmanship and overcharging by garages are the biggest concerns for motorists in Australia and generate the most consumer complaints.

Always instruct a garage what to do in writing and, for anything other than a standard service, get a written estimate that includes labour and parts. Ask the garage to contact you (give them a telephone number) to obtain approval before doing anything that isn't listed or if the cost is likely to exceed the original estimate.

Many garages, including most main dealers, provide a car while yours is being serviced, although you must arrange comprehensive insurance for it. Some garages collect your car from your home or office and deliver it after the service or drop you at a railway station or local town and pick you up there when your car is ready for collection. Most garages are open from around 7.30am to 6.30pm, Mondays to Fridays.

MOTORING ORGANISATIONS

There are motoring organisations in all Australian states and territories, and some 75 per cent of Australian motorists are members of a motoring organisation, one of the highest rates in the world. The Australian Automobile Association/AAA (⌨ www.aaa.asn.au) is the only national motoring organisation and operates as an umbrella organisation for motoring organisations in individual states and territories. It provides no services to individual motorists and any requests must be directed to local organisations. The largest of these is the so-called National Roads and Motoring Association/NRMA (⌨ www.mynrma.com.au) in NSW, with almost 2m members. The AAA publishes a booklet called *Motoring in Australia*.

There are few essential differences between the basic services provided by Australian motoring organisations, although membership costs vary. The primary service of motoring organisations is to provide emergency assistance in the event of an accident or breakdown. Motoring organisations provide a fast and efficient breakdown service, usually arriving within an hour of notification.

Most organisations offer various membership packages providing different levels of service, which may or may not include free public transport or a rental car, home start, legal advice, and towing and vehicle recovery. It's the vehicle that's covered (irrespective of the driver) and not the individual. The most expensive NRMA membership packages provide additional services, including emergency accommodation, passenger transport, a replacement car, and a towing service (up to a maximum cost of $2,000). The larger organisations offer both national and international accident or breakdown cover for no extra charge. All organisations charge a joining fee and an annual membership fee. For example, the NSW NRMA has a joining fee or around $55 and membership fees ranging from around $20 to $150 per year. Fees are similar in other states and territories.

All organisations offer supplementary services, which may include accommodation guides, advice on weather and road conditions, car and household insurance (motoring organisations are among Australia's largest insurers), crash repair centres, driving schools, free publications, holiday centres, international camping cards, international driving permits, road maps and itineraries, technical advice, travel services and vehicle inspection. Some motoring organisations (e.g. the NRMA) are expanding into financial services, including cash management accounts, cheque books, home loans and superannuation.

If you break down, call the local motoring organisation by telephoning a 24-hour number for assistance. Keep your membership card in your car and quote your membership number when calling for help. There are emergency telephones every kilometre on Australian highways for summoning help from local motoring organisations.

Non-members can also get assistance, but it can be expensive. Members of foreign motoring organisations (affiliated to the AAA) who break down anywhere in Australia can obtain free breakdown assistance from Australian organisations, plus free maps and accommodation directories at members' rates (on production of a membership card). Most Australian organisations also have reciprocal arrangements with motoring organisations in other countries (if you take your car overseas).

12.

HEALTH

Australia is among the most advanced countries in the field of medicine and is noted for its highly-trained medical staff and modern hospitals equipped with the latest high-tech apparatus. Two yardsticks widely used to measure the quality of a country's healthcare are the infant mortality rate and life expectancy, both of which rate Australia's – with around five deaths for every 1,000 live births and 82.6 years for women and 77.4 for men respectively – among the best in the world.

Healthcare services are provided by both government (including Commonwealth, state, territory and local governments) and private organisations. Australia has a national health system called Medicare (see page 305), which provides free or subsidised medical care and free hospital treatment in public hospitals for all permanent residents (plus certain visitors) irrespective of their age, health status or income. The public health system is supplemented by a wide variety of private clinics, hospitals and practitioners, plus a range of voluntary agencies and non-profit organisations.

The country spends around 9.5 per cent of its GDP on healthcare (compared with some 15 per cent in the US), which is around average for OECD countries. Despite the rising cost of modern medicine, costs have largely been contained in the last 15 years. Health facilities and doctors are unevenly distributed in Australia, however; the major cities and urban areas have a surplus of GPs, while in most country areas there's a shortage, particularly in the Northern Territory and Western Australia. Trying to persuade

doctors to relocate from the cities to remote country and outback areas is a major difficulty, which the government is circumventing by importing doctors specifically to work in country areas. The Royal Flying Doctor Service provides medical services in remote country areas and evacuates urgent cases to hospital.

Recently, there has been a growing emphasis on preventive medicine and community care, including education programmes to promote a healthy lifestyle. Alternative medicine and natural remedies are popular in Australia, where acupuncture, chiropractic, homeopathy, naturopathy, osteopathy and physiotherapy thrive.

Voluntary euthanasia is a topical subject in Australia, particularly since the world's first voluntary euthanasia law was passed in 1995 in the Northern Territory. This was subsequently overturned in 1997 by the federal government after four people had been medically assisted to die. In most states, patients can refuse life-sustaining treatment, but doctors cannot assist them to die (although in reality many doctors do 'assist' terminally-ill patients).

HEALTH RISKS

Australians are generally healthier than they were 20 years ago, owing to a decrease in smoking and drinking and an improved diet (although Australia's love affair with junk food and red meat is largely undiminished). Nevertheless, the amount of exercise Australians take is generally low, and over half the adult population is overweight; many children have eating disorders, and a quarter are classified as obese. Stress-related problems (often due to over-work or lack of sleep) are on the increase in Australia's cities, and the country has a fairly high suicide rate, particularly among the young and the over 65s.

The biggest killers in Australia are cancer (the cause of some 30 per cent of deaths), heart disease, stroke and smoking-related illnesses. Alcoholism is fairly widespread, as is drug addiction, which is a serious and increasing problem (see **Drug & Alcohol Abuse** on page 319). The country has an unusually high level of diabetes: an estimated 1m sufferers (around 7.5 per cent of the population); information can be found on ⌨ www.diabetesaustralia.com.au.

Virulent flu strains are a widespread problem and directly or indirectly kill some 1,500 people a year and affect as many as 30 per cent of the population (flu vaccinations are recommended for those aged over 65). Miscellaneous health problems in recent years have included outbreaks of dengue fever, hepatitis C (a life-threatening infection transmitted mostly by intravenous drug users), legionnaire's disease, meningococcal disease and salmonella poisoning (from cooked meat).

Air pollution caused by high smog levels is an increasing danger in Australia's cities, particularly Sydney (where pollution is higher than in London, New York or Tokyo) and Melbourne.

> ⚠ Caution
> **Sydney is reportedly the allergy capital of the world on account of the numerous plants that send out pollens on breezy spring days.**

You can safely drink the tap water in Australia, although the wine tastes much better and, taken in moderation, even does you good (if you believe the winemakers!). Water supplies are fluoridated in most parts of Australia in order to help prevent tooth decay.

Smoking

As in most countries, smoking causes a huge loss of life and working days in Australia, although the number of smokers has steadily decreased over the last few decades to around 17 per cent of the population. Action on Smoking and Health (ASH) Australia (www.ashaust.org.au) hopes (ambitiously) to reduce the rate to only 10 per cent by 2010. The dramatic reduction in smoking in recent years is due in part to the massive uptake of the anti-smoking drug Zyban, subsidised by the government since February 2001.

Smokers are increasingly under siege in Australia. Federal law bans smoking in all Commonwealth government buildings, on all public transport, and in airports and international and domestic flights. The National Health and Medical Research Council has recommended a statutory ban in all enclosed public spaces outside the home, but to date further bans have been the responsibility of individual states. Tasmania, Western Australia and the ACT have banned smoking in all enclosed public places, including work places. Queensland has gone even further by banning smoking within 4m (15ft) of the entrance of any non-residential building. In

July 2007 New South Wales and Victoria banned smoking in all enclosed public places and a similar ban will come into force in South Australia by the end of 2007. The Northern Territory, however, has no plans to ban smoking in pubs and nightclubs.

In recent years, there has been increasing concern about passive smoking (sometimes, clumsily, known as 'environmental tobacco smoke'). Although it hasn't generated the paranoia seen in the US, legal history was made in 2001 when a barmaid in NSW who contracted throat cancer as a result of inhaling smoke in the bar where she'd worked for eight years, was awarded more than $300,000 in damages. In January 2007 South Australia banned smoking in cars carrying children.

The anti-smoking group QUIT produces leaflets in 13 languages (National Quit Line ☎ local call rate 13-1848). There are also non-smoking clinics and self-help groups throughout Australia to assist those wishing to stop smoking. Contact your local health authority for information.

Sun

Australia has the highest rate of skin cancer (melanoma) in the world. Although cases are reducing as people take heed of warnings, some 850 people die each year from skin cancer caused by overexposure to the sun. Other problems associated with too much sun include fungal infections, heat exhaustion, prickly heat, sunburn and sunstroke.

Even if you're used to a hot climate, you should limit your exposure to the sun and avoid it altogether during the hottest part of the day (usually between 10am and 3pm), wear protective clothing (including a hat) and use sunscreen. The government's slogan in the battle against skin cancer is 'Slip, Slop, Slap', i.e. slip on a shirt, slop on sunscreen and slap on a hat. This is backed by a 'SunSmart' campaign, which

is particularly targeted at teenagers. It's important to use a sunscreen with a high protection factor, e.g. a pH 15+ broad-spectrum, water-resistant sunscreen (sunscreens with a protection factor of 50+ are now available). Medical experts recommend the wearing of good quality sunglasses, e.g. with UV400 polycarbonate lenses, to protect against eye cancer and other eye problems caused by the sun.

Those with fair skin should take extra care, as you can burn in just 15 minutes on a hot summer day. Children are particularly vulnerable and should wear wide-brimmed hats in the sun and a T-shirt when swimming. Those who live the outdoor life (such as sportsmen) are also especially at risk and should follow the example of Australian cricketers by wearing total-block zinc cream on exposed areas when spending a long time in the sun. Hikers should wear legionnaire or Arab-style hats with neck flaps.

Drink plenty of water when in the sun to prevent dehydration (in extreme heat you should drink a litre every hour), and avoid excessive alcohol consumption and over-exertion, particularly if you're elderly.

Wildlife

Australia has some of the deadliest creatures in the world, including catfish, crocodiles, jellyfish, scorpions, sharks (see **Swimming** on page 442), a plethora of poisonous snakes (e.g. death adder, sea snakes and western taipan), venomous spiders (e.g. the funnel-web, red-back and trap-door), and stonefish, many of which can deliver a fatal bite or sting. Although you're unlikely to have a close encounter with most of Australia's wildlife (unless you venture into the bush or the sea off unprotected beaches), poisonous snakes and spiders can be found in suburban parks and gardens and near watercourses. You should avoid undergrowth and country areas unless you're wearing protective clothing, i.e. not flip flops (thongs) or shorts, and try to avoid disturbing wildlife. Insects (e.g. mosquitoes, ticks and wasps) are also a problem in many areas, although they're unlikely to kill you. Children are taught at school to recognise dangerous wildlife.

Immunisation

Children should have six sets of injections between the age of two months and four years in order to be fully immunised against diphtheria, hepatitis B, measles, mumps poliomyelitis, rubella, tetanus and whooping cough. Children aged between 10 and 19 years also need booster shots for most of these diseases. Immunisations can be provided by your family doctor, an immunisation clinic, local authorities and some public hospitals. There's an Australian Child Immunisation Register (ACIR) where all immunisation details are recorded and which can be accessed by parents and authorities (☎ freecall 1800-65809).

A large percentage of older children aren't fully immunised against diseases such as diphtheria, tetanus and whooping cough, resulting in many unnecessary deaths. Many parents are concerned about the side effects of vaccination, although these are insignificant compared to the effects of the diseases themselves. In an attempt to 'encourage' parents to immunise their children, the government has introduced measures such as the requirement to have children immunised in order to receive family payments such as child care benefit (see page 331). There's also a maternity immunisation allowance

given as a one-off payment ($232.70 in 2007) when the child is 19 months old and is fully immunised. As a result of such campaigns, nearly 90 per cent of children under 18 months are now fully immunised (in some states, such as NSW, the figure is nearer 100 per cent).

EMERGENCIES

The action to take in a medical 'emergency' depends on the degree of urgency. If you're unsure who to call, ask the telephone operator (☎ 1234) or call your local police station. They can tell you who to contact or even call the appropriate service for you. Whoever you call, you should give the approximate age of the patient and, if possible, specify the type of emergency.

☑ SURVIVAL TIP

Keep a record of the telephone numbers of your ambulance service, dentist, doctor, local hospitals and clinics, and other emergency services, next to your telephone.

A mobile telephone can be a lifesaver in a remote area or when you're alone and need help.

Dial ☎ 000 for an ambulance **only in an emergency**. Ambulances generally come without a doctor but usually with a paramedic. Many ambulances are equipped with cardiac, oxygen and other emergency equipment (called intensive care ambulances). Ambulance services aren't covered by Medicare, although private health insurance may include ambulance costs. In Queensland ambulance costs are included in domestic electricity bills.

There are air ambulances (helicopters) in some cities, and remote outback areas are served by the Royal Flying Doctor service,

established as a non-profit organisation in 1927 and funded by the federal government and voluntary contributions. The service covers some 80 per cent of outback areas from 20 bases, ensuring that most people are less than two hours from medical help. Services include regular clinic visits to remote communities, visits by specialists and, in some areas, dental treatment. The service also offers advice on touring and emergency procedures; travellers in remote areas can rent a transceiver with emergency call buttons. For more information, contact the Royal Flying Doctor Service of Australia, Federal Office, Level 8, 15-17 Young Street, Sydney, NSW 2000 (☎ 02-8259 8101, 🖳 www.flyingdoctor.net, ✉ enquiries@frdsno.com) or one of the regional offices listed on the website.

In minor 'emergencies', you should telephone your family doctor if you have one. Failing this you can ask the operator (☎ 1234) for the telephone number of a local doctor or hospital (or consult your telephone book). Police stations keep a list of doctors' and chemists' private telephone numbers in case of emergency. In some cities and regions, there are private, 24-hour doctor services that make house calls (but check the cost before using them). If you have an emergency dental problem outside normal surgery hours, call a dentist providing an emergency service (listed in the yellow pages).

If you're physically able, you can go to the Accident, Casualty or Emergency department of a public hospital, many of which provide a 24-hour service. Check in advance which local hospitals are equipped to deal with emergencies and the quickest route from your home. This information may be of vital importance in the event of an emergency, when a delay could mean the difference between life and death. Emergency cases, irrespective of nationality and the ability to pay, are **never** turned away in Australia, and treatment may be free if you're a national of a country with a reciprocal health agreement with Australia, which currently include Finland, Ireland, Italy, Malta, the Netherlands, New Zealand, Norway, Sweden and the UK (check before travelling to Australia).

THE DISABLED

Australia provides reasonable facilities and services for the disabled. All capital cities and most regional centres produce maps showing accessible parking, paths and toilets for those with mobility difficulties, and nationwide facilities are listed in *Easy Access Australia* (available from 💻 www.easyaccessaustralia.com. au). Many councils provide a directory of services for people with disabilities and for older residents. General information is available from the National Information Communication Awareness Network (NICAN), Unit 5, 48 Brookes Street, Mitchell, ACT, 2911 (☎ 02-6241 1220, 💻 www.nican.com.au).

NATIONAL HEALTH SERVICE

Australia's national health service is called Medicare, which was established in 1984. It provides free treatment in public hospitals and free or subsidised treatment by doctors (including specialists), optometrists and dentists in certain cases. Medicare even covers 75 per cent of the cost of private treatment, so that a private health insurance policy needs to cover only 25 per cent of costs.

As in many countries, the rising cost of healthcare and health insurance has created severe problems for Medicare, which is over-worked, under-resourced and facing a funding crisis. It's also burdened by the increasing life expectancy of Australians (around 13 per cent of the population is aged 65 or older, a figure which is expected to double by the year 2050). In recent

years, the cost of private health insurance, which usually supplements rather than replaces Medicare, has increased sharply and many people have cancelled their policies (thus adding to the burden on Medicare). Before Medicare was introduced in 1984, some two-thirds of Australians had private cover; this has since fallen to less than a third. Many people believe that Australia now has a two-tier health system: a costly private health sector with all the 'bells and whistles' for those who can afford it and a neglected, second-rate public system for those who cannot.

Many public hospitals are cash-starved and cannot cope with the demand; many have a shortage of nursing staff and doctors as well as a lack of new medical equipment.

> **⚠ Caution**
>
> **Although most urgent cases are admitted within 30 days, there are long waiting lists for elective surgery under Medicare, and non-urgent cases may have to wait up to a year for treatment.**

It's generally agreed that vastly increased health expenditure is necessary if Medicare is to continue.

With this in mind, the government has launched the MedicarePlus package, a $2.85bn investment designed to protect the future of Medicare and address the shortage of doctors, nurses and other healthcare professionals, particularly in rural and regional Australia. The scheme should provide an extra 1,500 doctors and 1,600 nurses by the end of 2007, including some who are foreign-trained. Other measures to be introduced include the government paying GPs an extra $7.50 per patient for every bulk-billed service provided to children under 16 and to concession card holders (see page

countries with which Australia has a reciprocal healthcare agreement (see page 304). If you're working in Australia, you're automatically covered by compulsory workers' compensation insurance against injury and illness as a result of an accident (see page 63). Medicare eligibility is immediate upon application (and can even be backdated to your arrival in Australia) but new members may have to wait up to three months to receive refunds. Foreign diplomats and their families aren't covered by Medicare. Medical expenses incurred by men over 55 and women over 51 who have been sponsored in the family reunion migration category are the responsibility of their sponsor for ten years or until they reach retirement age.

Retirees

Foreign retirees with a temporary residence visa aren't covered by Medicare and must take out private health insurance. Permanent resident retirees who aren't in receipt of a social security or veterans' pension and whose income is below a certain amount may qualify for a range of free and concessionary health services. Retirees can apply for a Commonwealth Seniors Health Card (contact Centrelink Retirement Services ☎ local call rate 13-2300) and enjoy various benefits, including bulk-billed GP appointments (see **Bulk Billing** on page 250) and reduced out-of-hospital medical expenses (see **Safety Net** on page 249).

Benefits

The proportion of eligible medical expenses covered by Medicare varies according to the type of service and the medical practitioner providing it.

Medicare covers a percentage of set fees, as specified by the Medicare Benefits

314), and better access to medical care for residents of old people's homes, including a new Medicare payment for doctors who carry out comprehensive health checks of old people's home residents ... It isn't clear, however, where the money to pay for all these improvements is to come from.

General information about Medicare in English is available from the Medicare Information Service (☎ local call rate 13-2011) and information in other languages is available from the Medicare Multilingual Telephone Information Service (☎ 13-1202). Medicare produces a comprehensive booklet *Welcome to Medicare* in a number of languages. The benefit system (see below) was revised in January 2005 and is subject to further change; for further information and the latest developments, see the Medicare Australia website (🖳 www. medicareaustralia.gov.au).

Eligibility

All permanent residents of Australia are eligible to join Medicare, and restricted access is also granted to citizens of certain

- X-rays, pathology and other medical tests, examinations and certain surgical procedures (listed in the *Medicare Benefits Schedule*, available on the website of the Australian Department of Health and Ageing, 🖥 www9.health.gov.au/mbs;

- eye tests performed by an optometrist;

- some surgical procedures performed at a hospital by dentists registered with Medicare and oral surgeons;

- specified items under the Cleft Lip and Palate Scheme.

Medicare provides only partial cover (usually 85 per cent) for medicines (see page 313); procedures and diagnostic tests performed by a general practitioner; referred services, e.g. those provided by consultant physicians, specialists, allied health professionals or dentists; non-referred services in the field of sports medicine or emergency medicine; contraceptives; immunisation; maternity care; psychiatric treatment; and services provided by optometrists.

Medicare **doesn't** cover dental examinations and treatment (although certain essential dental surgery is covered); ambulance services; home nursing; chiropody, occupational therapy, physiotherapy, podiatry, psychology, and speech and eye therapy; acupuncture (unless treatment is provided by a doctor); spectacles and contact lenses; hearing aids, prostheses and other appliances; medical and hospital costs incurred overseas; medical treatment that isn't necessary, including elective or cosmetic surgery; treatment arranged before arriving in Australia; accommodation and medical treatment in a private hospital or as a private patient in a public hospital; medical repatriation or funeral costs; or examinations for life insurance, membership of a friendly society or superannuation.

Schedule (MBS), which is drawn up by the Commonwealth government. These, known as 'schedule fees', are increased annually (on 1st November) at half the rate of inflation. In general terms, Medicare pays for 85 per cent of the schedule fee for hospital outpatient treatment and 100 per cent of the schedule fee for inpatient services (see page 315). Specifically, Medicare normally provides 100 per cent cover for the following:

- doctors' consultation fees, including treatment by specialists when referred by a general practitioner (GP). But when a doctor charges more than the schedule fee (as many do), patients must meet the additional cost (or buy private insurance to cover it);

- most surgical and other therapeutic procedures performed by doctors;

- all treatment costs when you're treated as a Medicare patient in a public hospital;

Medicare also doesn't cover situations where someone else is responsible for medical costs (e.g. a compensation insurer, an employer or a government authority). If you receive treatment under Medicare for an injury or accident which is subject to compensation by a third party, such as an insurance company or workers' compensation fund, the insurer must reimburse Medicare for any benefits related to the injury before making any payments to you. You're usually required to indicate whether this is the position when making a claim.

Safety Net

Those who require frequent treatment not covered 100 per cent by Medicare are protected from high costs by the Medicare 'safety net'. When you (or your family members) have made payments amounting to a total of around $360 (the figure is adjusted annually, on 1st January) in a Medicare financial year (from 1st July to 30th June), cover is increased to 100 per cent. If your GP charges more than the schedule fee, however, the extra amount doesn't count towards the safety net total; extra amounts for hospital services and medicines (see **Concessions** on page 314) also don't count. Similarly, if you require a lot of medicines, you may qualify for the PBS safety net. Further information can be found on 🖳 www.medicareaustralia. gov.au/yourhealth/our_services/msn/about_ msn.htm.

It isn't necessary for individuals to register for the safety net, as Medicare keeps a record of payments and the higher (100 per cent) benefits apply automatically as soon as the limit is reached. However, families (even when all members are listed on a Medicare card) need to complete a *Medicare Safety Net Registration Form* and take or send it to a Medicare customer service centre; or they can register online via the above website page. A family includes a spouse (or *de facto* spouse), children under 16 in your care and dependent full-time students under 25.

> ☑ SURVIVAL TIP
>
> **It's important to submit a registration form as soon as possible, as refunds aren't made retrospectively.**

Contributions

Medicare is funded by a 1.5 per cent levy on taxable income (around $15,900) and by general taxation, deducted at source from employees' wages. In an effort to 'encourage' high earners to take out private health insurance, the government obliges those who don't have private health insurance that at least covers doctors' fees and hospital accommodation to pay a Medicare levy of 2.5 per cent. The higher levy applies to single people earning over $50,000 per year and families earning over $100,000 per year. The taxable threshold increases by $1,500 for the second and each subsequent child. It may be cheaper to buy private insurance than to pay the increased levy (see page 337).

If you're self-employed, the levy is included in your annual income tax charge. Certain people are exempt from paying the levy, including defence force personnel without dependants, pensioners with a concession card (known as a Commonwealth Concession Card or a Commonwealth Seniors Health Card – see **Retirees** on page 306), single people on incomes below around $15,900, and war veterans and widows. Couples and sole parents who earn less than around $31,700 are entitled to a reduction in their Medicare levy. The unemployed and dependants have automatic deductions made from their unemployment benefits or other allowances.

Enrolment

Assuming you plan to stay in Australia for more than a couple of months, you should enrol in Medicare as soon as possible after you arrive, although it isn't necessary until you use the system, as you can join retrospectively, i.e. claim a refund of previous medical expenses after joining Medicare. You can apply in person at a Medicare office or you can call ☎ local call rate 13-2011 and have an application form sent to you. You're required to show proof of eligibility, e.g. your passport with a residence stamp if you're a permanent resident. Applicants must also provide details of their assets, income and residence.

Medicare Card

You receive a plastic Medicare card (green and gold) by post around two to three weeks after applying, which shows your Medicare membership number, the names of all dependants entitled to use the service and the expiry date of the card. Cards are valid for five years, although you must obtain a replacement card if your address or other details change (e.g. you have a baby). The card has a signature strip on the back and must be signed immediately. If you receive treatment before you obtain your card, you must pay in full and claim a refund or delay payment until you receive your card. You must quote your Medicare number when making enquiries or a claim and use your Medicare card to:

- receive a cash benefit at a Medicare customer service centre;

- receive free or subsidised treatment from a doctor or optometrist who bulk bills Medicare (see below);

- obtain free or subsidised treatment in a public hospital;

- obtain free or subsidised prescriptions.

Bulk Billing

Bulk billing (also called direct billing) is where a doctor (or optometrist) doesn't charge the patient, but the patient verifies his entitlement to benefits to the doctor, who bills Medicare directly. Most doctors bulk bill at least some of their patients, particularly pensioners and Commonwealth Seniors Health Card holders. If your doctor bulk bills, you're asked to complete a form after treatment, of which you receive a copy. You don't need to pay anything and aren't required to make a claim to Medicare. However, doctors can bulk bill only if they charge the schedule fee (currently $35 for a standard consultation). But Australian GPs aren't happy with the schedule, which has fallen in real terms in recent years, and want increased payments. As a result, fewer doctors are bulk billing and even fewer are expected to in the future.

Claims

> ☑ SURVIVAL TIP
>
> If your doctor or optometrist doesn't bulk bill, he will give you a bill for his services. You can either pay the bill and claim a refund from Medicare or submit the bill to your local Medicare office with a claim form (a fairly simple choice!).

Bills can be submitted by post (addressed to Medicare, PO Box 9822 in your state's capital city) or in person with a completed claim form and the original bills or receipts for payments. You receive a cheque made out to the practitioner, which you give to him with your own payment for the balance (gap), if any. (Either Australians are incurably honest or Australian doctors spend half their lives chasing patients for payment!)

PRIVATE HEALTH SERVICES

Private health treatment functions both in conjunction with Medicare and independently of it, and most public hospitals admit private patients. In addition to specialist appointments and hospital treatment, people most commonly use private health services to obtain second opinions, health checks and screening, and for complementary medicine such as acupuncture, chiropractic, homeopathy, naturopathy, osteopathy and physiotherapy (which aren't usually covered by Medicare or, indeed, private health insurance). Private patients are usually free to choose their own doctor and hospital, and may be accommodated in a single, hotel-style room with an en suite bathroom, radio, room service, telephone and colour TV – at corresponding expense!

With the deterioration of Medicare services and lengthening waiting lists, you're strongly recommended to consider taking out private health insurance (see page 271), which ensures you always receive the medical treatment you need, when you need it.

DOCTORS

There are excellent family doctors, who are generally referred to as general practitioners (GPs), throughout Australia. However, there's a glut of doctors in most cities and metropolitan areas and an acute shortage (totalling around 1,000 GPs) in rural areas, where the ratio of doctors to population is less than half the national average. Therefore in rural areas and the outback you may need to travel some distance to visit a doctor, although you may be served by the Royal Flying Doctor Service (see page 304).

Your GP can provide advice and information on all aspects of health and medical care, including blood donations,

If you've already paid for treatment and make a claim in person, you receive a refund in cash (although there's a limit to how much you can be paid in cash), by cheque or by direct payment into your bank account. Claims made by post are paid by cheque. Always take your Medicare card when attending a Medicare office.

Telephone claims (☎ local call rate 1300-360460) can by made by anyone living outside Adelaide, Brisbane, Melbourne, Perth and Sydney. These can be made at any time and don't require a form; you simply endorse your claim form with the information the telephone operator gives you and send it to Medicare. Electronic lodgement of Medicare claims was introduced in 2007 in an attempt to reduce delays in payments and improve access to Medicare for those living in rural and remote areas. The system enables members to use their Medicare cards in EFTPOS-style machines (like bank ATMs), but as yet there's no online claims facility.

home medical equipment, preventive medicine and counselling. If you're a Medicare patient, he should also be able to advise you about the range of benefits provided under Medicare (see page 250). Patients in Australia have no legal right to see their medical records.

It isn't necessary to be registered with a doctor in Australia, where you can choose to visit any doctor, either as a Medicare patient (provided the doctor is registered with Medicare) or a private patient. Many doctors in the suburbs of major cities work at public clinics and medical centres, where a number of doctors have a group practice and at least one is usually female (there's an unusually large percentage of women doctors in Australia). Clinics and medical centres usually have an in-house pharmacy, and medical tests, such as blood and urine analysis and X-rays, may also be conducted in-house.

Fees

If you wish to be treated as a Medicare patient, you must check whether a

doctor charges the schedule fee for consultations and bulk bills Medicare or whether he charges more and requires you to pay. Many doctors now charge more than the schedule fee, and in some areas you may have difficulty finding a doctor who doesn't, although pensioners and Commonwealth Seniors Health Card holders are usually exempt from additional fees. If you wish to see a GP privately, you (or your insurance company) must pay the full fee, which is at the doctor's discretion but is usually at least $50 for a routine consultation.

> ⚠️ **Caution**
>
> The low remuneration paid to doctors by Medicare encourages doctors who charge the schedule fee to rush consultations (referred to as 'six-minute' or 'stop-watch' medicine).

If you're concerned that your doctor doesn't allow sufficient time for a thorough examination, you should change doctors, although you may need to choose one who charges a higher fee.

Surgery Hours

Surgery hours vary, but are typically from 8.30am to 6 or 7pm, Mondays to Fridays, with early closing one day per week, e.g. 5 or 5.30pm on Fridays. Evening surgeries may also be held one or two evenings per week. 'Emergency' surgeries may be held on Saturday mornings, e.g. from 8.30 to 11.30am or noon, when you can be treated without an appointment for urgent but not life-threatening problems. Most doctors' surgeries have answering machines outside surgery hours, when a recorded message informs you of the name and telephone number of the doctor on call (or deputising service).

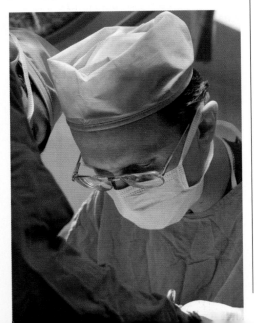

Appointments

An appointment must be made to see a GP, usually one or two days in advance. If you're an urgent case (but not an emergency), your doctor usually sees you immediately, but you should still telephone in advance if possible. Surgeries are often overrun, however, and you may need to wait well past your appointment time to see a doctor. Australian doctors make house calls, although these can be expensive for private patients.

Specialists

Medicare patients must always be referred by a GP to a specialist, e.g. an eye specialist, gynaecologist or orthopaedic surgeon. If you want a second opinion on any health matter, you may ask to see a specialist, although your doctor may refuse to refer you – in which case you can obtain a second opinion from another GP, who may agree to refer you, or you can consult a specialist as a private patient. Patients with private health insurance may be free to make appointments directly with specialists, although most insurance companies prefer patients to be referred by GPs. Most specialists have long waiting lists for Medicare patients.

MEDICINES & CHEMISTS'

Medicines (drugs) are obtained from chemists' (pharmacies), which also provide free advice concerning minor ailments and recommend appropriate medicines. In some isolated areas, e.g. remote parts of Queensland, some doctors act as chemists and dispense a wide range of everyday medicines, including treatment for diabetes and the contraceptive pill. Many medicines in Australia can be prescribed only by a doctor via an official prescription, which is written in a secret language decipherable only by doctors and chemists. Some medicines sold freely in other countries require a doctor's prescription in Australia, while certain medicines that require a prescription in other countries are available over the counter in Australia. To obtain medicines prescribed by a doctor, simply take your prescription to any chemist. Your prescription may be filled immediately if it's available off the shelf, or you may be asked to wait or come back later.

At least one chemist's is open in most towns during the evenings and on Sundays for the emergency dispensing of medicines, and there are 24-hour chemists' in some cities. A roster is posted on the doors of chemists' and published in local newspapers and guides.

Most chemists also sell cleaning supplies, cosmetics, health foods, non-prescription medicines and toiletries. A health food shop sells diet foods, homeopathic medicines and eternal-life/virility/youth pills and elixirs, which are quite popular in Australia (even though their claims are often in the realms of fantasy). Unwanted medicines should be returned to a chemist or dispensing doctor.

Charges

Medicare – via the Pharmaceutical Benefits Scheme (PBS) – subsidises the cost of around 1,700 'necessary and life-saving' medicines but to benefit from the subsidy you must obtain a prescription from a doctor. PBS medicines are available to all Australian residents and to visitors from countries with which Australia has a reciprocal healthcare agreement. Proof of residence or nationality may be required. If you're eligible but unable to provide proof, you may be charged the full price for medicines, although you can obtain a refund at a Medicare customer service centre or by posting your claim (plus the receipt and your Medicare card or proof of eligibility) to Medicare, PO Box 9822 in a state or territory's capital city. If you're eligible, you pay a maximum of around $30 for each PBS medicine; if you qualify for concessions (see below), you pay only around $5.

If medication isn't available under PBS (i.e. is non-prescription), you must pay the entire cost. The cost of non-prescription medicines varies considerably and, if you need medication regularly, it's worth shopping around. If you have private health insurance, you may be able to reclaim the cost of prescriptions from your insurance company.

In recent years, the government has restricted the prescription of expensive medicines in order to control the escalating cost of pharmaceuticals. GPs must now prescribe the cheapest available brand of each type of medicine, and patients wishing to use a more expensive brand must pay a 'therapeutic premium' (the difference between the government subsidy and the actual cost).

It's possible to buy prescription (and other) medicines by post (post free) at savings of up to 50 per cent from Pharmacy Direct, Reply Paid 69380, Silverwater, NSW 2128 (☎ local call rate 1300-347328 or ☎ 02-9648 8888, 💻 www.pharmacydirect. com.au).

Concessions

Once you or your family (which includes your spouse or *de facto* spouse and children under 16 or, if dependent full-time students, under 25) have spent a certain amount – currently $1,039 (adjusted annually on 1st January) – on prescription medicines in a calendar year, you're entitled to receive all additional prescription

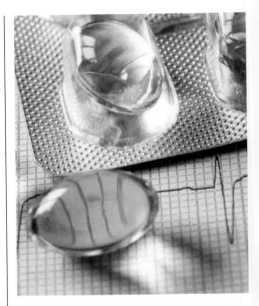

medicines at the concessionary rate of around $5 per item for the remainder of the calendar year. All purchases must be recorded on a *Prescription Record* form by your chemist.

If you have a concession card (issued to low-income families, the unemployed and war widows), you pay the reduced rate per prescription until you've spent a total of around $360, after which there's no charge for the remainder of the year.

Foreign Prescriptions

If you're visiting Australia, you may bring a maximum of four weeks' prescription medicines with you. The brand names for the same medicines vary considerably from country to country so, if you regularly take medication overseas, you should ask your doctor for the generic name. If you wish to match medication prescribed overseas in Australia, you need a current prescription with the chemical name, the dosage, the manufacturer's name and the medication's trade name. This must be endorsed by an Australian-registered doctor before you can take it to an Australian chemist. Most foreign medicines have an equivalent in Australia, although particular brands may be difficult or impossible to obtain.

HOSPITALS & CLINICS

Most Australian towns have a hospital or clinic, signposted by a sign of a white H on a blue background. Australia has a variety of public and private hospitals and clinics, and there are various kinds of public hospital. Major hospitals are called general hospitals and provide treatment and diagnosis for inpatients and outpatients. They may have an infectious diseases unit, maternity department, psychiatric and geriatric facilities, and rehabilitation and convalescent units, and cater for most forms of specialised treatment. Other types of public hospital include including children's hospitals, day hospitals, dental hospitals, district hospitals, psychiatric hospitals, teaching hospitals and veterans' hospitals.

Most of Australia's public hospitals are funded jointly by the federal government and state and territory governments, and administered by state and territory health departments, although some are operated by private companies under a contract.

Public Treatment

If you're eligible for Medicare, it pays for the full cost of accommodation and medical treatment performed by hospital-appointed doctors in public hospitals. Hospital bills for treatment under Medicare are always paid directly by Medicare. However, patients have no choice of doctors or hospital, nor of when they're admitted for treatment or surgery. Patients are usually accommodated in general wards or twin rooms. If you want a TV or a telephone, you must pay extra. When you visit a public hospital, you should take your Medicare card with you (if applicable). The staff may ask whether you wish to be treated under Medicare or as a private patient. Medicare patients also receive free X-rays and pathology tests in public hospitals and free outpatient services in some hospitals.

In recent years, there has been a funding crisis in public hospitals in many states, some of which have chronic shortages of basic medical supplies, including bandages, bed linen, drugs, sterile dressings, swabs and syringes. Some public hospitals also have a lack of diagnostic equipment, e.g. for brain scans. In some over-worked public hospitals, patients are left lying for hours in emergency departments and in corridors waiting for ward beds. Some public hospitals also suffer from a shortage of doctors and nurses, and are forced to recruit casual staff from locum and nursing agencies. Fortunately, there's usually no shortage of life-saving equipment or medicines.

Private Treatment

Even private patients are subsidised by Medicare. If you're a private patient in a public or private hospital, Medicare pays 75 per cent of the schedule fee for medical services and the remaining 25 per cent is paid by your private health insurer, if you have one. When you leave hospital, you're generally asked to pay the difference (if any) between your health insurer's refund and the hospital fees, which you must then reclaim from your insurer.

If you don't have private health insurance, you're asked to pay the estimated costs at the time of admission. The average charge for a private bed is around $250 per day in a public hospital and over $600 per day in a private hospital, where prices have increased greatly in recent years. Patients in private hospitals are usually given one or two bills for the total cost of treatment, although some hospitals still prefer to charge separately for different treatments and care.

Private patients are usually provided with single rooms equipped with all the comforts of home, including ensuite bathroom, radio, room service, telephone and TV. If you're a private patient, you can choose the hospital and your attending doctor and surgeon, although if you want your own doctor to treat you in a public hospital there's a daily 'accommodation' charge.

CHILDBIRTH

Childbirth in Australia usually takes place in a hospital labour ward or birth centre (a small unit normally located in the grounds of a hospital), where a stay of up to five days is usual (although many women leave hospital within three days of giving birth). Public hospitals are under pressure to discharge mothers earlier, and even privately insured mothers are being encouraged to cut their hospital stay in exchange for lower maternity (e.g. obstetrician) bills.

Few people in Australia choose to give birth at home and, if you wish to do so, you must find a doctor or midwife (see below) who's willing to attend you. Some doctors are opposed to home births, in case there are complications requiring specialist equipment or staff. However, you can hire a private midwife to attend you at home throughout and after your pregnancy.

Medicare patients are usually unable to choose the hospital where they have their baby or their obstetrician. If you have a choice, find out as much as possible about local hospital methods and policies concerning childbirth, either directly or from friends or neighbours, before booking a bed. The policy regarding a father's attendance at a birth varies with the hospital.

☑ **SURVIVAL TIP**

A husband or partner doesn't have the right to be present with a woman during labour or childbirth; his presence is at the consultant's discretion.

Women who don't speak English often have problems and are generally dissatisfied with their hospital treatment during pregnancy; interpreters are rarely provided and information isn't usually published in foreign languages.

Antenatal classes must be paid for, although the cost is usually covered by private insurance. There are Maternal and Child Health Centres in some states (e.g. Victoria), funded by the state government or local councils. However, there's a dearth of services for new mothers in many areas and postnatal care may be patchy or even non-existent, new mothers being left to their own devices.

Births must be registered with the Registrar of Births, Deaths and Marriages within 60 days (even when a child is stillborn). When a birth takes place in a hospital, parents are given the relevant form to register the birth. In the case of home births, a form can be obtained from a hospital or from the Registrar of Births. A child born to an unmarried mother is usually registered in her name but can be registered in the father's name if both parents agree. The birth of a child to foreign parents may need to be reported to a consulate or embassy, e.g. to obtain a national birth certificate and passport for a child. If you need to obtain a copy of a birth certificate, the cheapest way is to apply to the registrar in the state or territory where it was registered.

Family planning associations provide free counselling, instruction and other services. There are many publications for mothers, including *New Mother's Handbook* published for Melbourne and Sydney (Universal Magazines, Unit 5, 6-8 Byfield Street, North Ryde, NSW 2113, ☎ 02-9805 0399, 🖳 www.universalmagazines.com.au) and *The New Good Birth Guide* by Sheila Kitzinger (Penguin).

DENTISTS

There are excellent dentists in cities and towns throughout Australia, although they're thin on the ground in rural areas. There are mobile dentists in some country regions, and in remote areas emergency dental services are provided via the Flying Doctor Service. There's no need to register with a dentist, and the best way to find a good one is to ask colleagues, friends or neighbours if they can recommend someone. Dentists are listed under 'Dental Surgeons' in the yellow pages and are permitted to advertise any special services they provide, such as emergency or 24-hour answering services, a dental hygienist, and evening or weekend surgeries. Many family dentists in Australia are qualified to perform treatment such as endodontics or periodontics, which are carried out by specialists in many other countries.

General dental services aren't funded by Medicare, although it pays for 75 per cent of in-hospital medical procedures performed by a Medicare-registered dentist or an oral surgeon. The cost of dental treatment has risen considerably in recent years, though charges vary with the area and the dentist. If you miss a dental appointment without giving 24 hours' notice, your dentist may charge you a standard fee. Most dentists accept payment by credit card (plus bearer bonds, diamonds, gold, etc.). Dental teaching hospitals in the major cities treat patients for less than private dentists, although you may be something of a guinea pig.

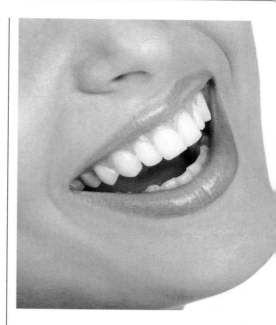

Those with a concession card may be entitled to free general and emergency dental treatment under the Commonwealth Dental Health Program, although there are waiting times of up to two years for treatment! Children in some states receive free school dental care. Information about dental charges can be obtained from the Australian Dental Association, PO Box 520, St Leonards, NSW 1590 (☎ 02-9906 4412, 🖳 www.ada.org.au). .

OPTICIANS

There are three kinds of professional providing eye care in Australia. The most highly qualified is an ophthalmologist, who's a specialist physician trained in diagnosing and treating disorders of the eye. In addition to performing eye surgery and prescribing medicines, he may perform sight tests and prescribe spectacles and contact lenses. You may be referred to an ophthalmologist by an optometrist or your GP. Optometrists are licensed to examine eyes, prescribe corrective lenses, and dispense spectacles and contact lenses. They're also trained to detect eye diseases and may prescribe medicines and treatment.

> ### ▲ Caution
>
> **Medicare pays for 85 per cent of the cost of eye tests by optometrists, but not tests by ophthalmologists.**

In Australian an optician isn't the same as an optometrist and may not examine eyes or prescribe lenses; opticians are licensed to fill prescriptions written by optometrists and ophthalmologists and to fit and adjust spectacles. There are opticians at optical retail chain stores in Australia, where you can have spectacles made within an hour. You aren't required to buy your spectacles or contact lenses from the optometrist who tests your sight, and he must give you your prescription at no extra charge.

As with doctors and dentists, there's no need to register with an optometrist or optician. You simply make an appointment with anyone of your choice, although it's sensible to ask colleagues, friends or neighbours if they can recommend someone. Opticians and optometrists are listed in the yellow pages, where they may advertise their services.

The eye care business is very competitive in Australia and, unless someone is highly recommended, you should shop around for the best deal. Prices for both spectacles and contact lenses vary considerably, so it's wise to compare costs (although make sure you're comparing like with like) before committing yourself to a large bill. Special offers are common, such as 'buy a new pair of spectacles and receive a spare pair free', but the cheapest products aren't necessarily the best value. Always ask about extra charges for adjustments, eye examinations, fittings, follow-up visits, lens-care kits and the cost of replacement lenses (if they're expensive, it may be worthwhile taking out insurance). Many opticians offer insurance against the accidental damage of spectacles for a nominal fee.

Many Australians wear contact lenses. Disposable (one-day) and extended-wear (e.g. one or three months) contact lenses are widely available, although most medical experts believe that extended-wear lenses should be approached with extreme caution, as they greatly increase the risk of potentially blinding eye infections. **Obtain advice from a doctor or eye specialist before buying them.** Soft contact lenses or spectacles (frames and lenses) can be purchased in Australia from around $150 to $200 (usually inclusive of an eye examination).

It's best to have your eyes tested before your arrival in Australia and to bring a spare pair of spectacles or contact lenses with you (also bring a copy of your prescription

in case you need to obtain replacements in a hurry).

COUNSELLING

Counselling and assistance for health and social problems are available under Medicare and from many community groups and volunteer organisations, ranging from national associations to small local groups (including self-help groups). In times of need there's nearly always someone to turn to, and all services are strictly confidential.

Local authorities provide social workers to advise and support those requiring help within their community. If you need to find help locally, you can contact your council or voluntary services or a citizens' advice bureau. A list of 24-hour emergency services (including many counselling services) is included at the front of both white and yellow pages, as are community help and welfare services, and help for young people.

Many colleges and educational establishments provide a counselling service for students, and general hospitals have a psychiatrist on call 24 hours a day. Problems for which help is available are numerous and include alcoholism (e.g. Alcoholics Anonymous); obesity (e.g. Weight Watchers); drug, tobacco and gambling addiction; sexuality-related, marital and relationship problems; rape and battering; suicidal tendencies and other psychiatric disorders; and youth problems.

Trained counsellors provide advice and help for sufferers from various diseases (e.g. muscular dystrophy) and the disabled (e.g. the blind and deaf). They also help terminally ill patients (e.g. AIDS, multiple sclerosis, cancer and leukaemia sufferers) and their families come to terms with their situation. A number of voluntary organisations and local authorities run refuges for battered wives (and their children) or maltreated children, whose conditions have become intolerable (some provide 24-hour emergency telephone numbers).

☑ SURVIVAL TIP

If you or a member of your family are the victims of a violent crime, the police usually put you in touch with a local victim support scheme.

In major towns, counselling may be available in your native language if you don't speak English. If you need help desperately, someone speaking your language can usually be found. Lifeline (☎ 13-1114) provides a confidential, 24-hour counselling service (e.g. for the desperate, lonely and suicidal) throughout Australia for the cost of a local call. There's also a freecall Women's Information Service (☎ 1800-817227). Many councils publish a directory of children's and family services.

DRUG & ALCOHOL ABUSE

Drug abuse is an increasingly serious problem in Australia, where it's estimated that heroin users alone spend around $3.5bn per year on the drug and it costs the country around $2bn per year to deal with its effects. The average drug abuser starts at just 14 and the average time between take-up and death is around ten years. Over 1,000 people die each year from drug abuse, heroin overdoses accounting for three-quarters of drug-related deaths. Cannabis or marijuana is the most widely taken drug, followed by amphetamines, ecstasy and hallucinogens. It's widely grown and smoked throughout Australia, where each state has its own laws regarding the use (or abuse) of drugs (see **Crime** on page 399).

The National Drug Strategy (💻 www. nationaldrugstrategy.gov.au), which is a co-operative venture between national, state and territorial governments and the non-government sector, works to improve the country's economic, health and social situation by preventing harmful drug use. Many other government and voluntary organisations provide drug advice and rehabilitation services, including residential facilities. There are government-run detoxification units in the major cities, where there are also voluntary groups providing counselling and support for drug users, their relatives and friends (see your local white or yellow pages). There's also a national Children's Help Line (☎ freecall 1800-551800). If you can afford to pay for treatment, a number of private clinics and hospitals specialise in treating people for alcohol, drug and substance abuse, and other health problems.

Drunkenness and alcoholism are common in Australia, where it's estimated that more than 6,000 Australians die each year of alcohol-related causes (including some 30 per cent of those who die on the roads); drinking is also a growing problem among children. Alcoholics Anonymous has self-help groups throughout Australia (see your telephone book).

DEATHS

Deaths must be registered with the Registrar of Births, Deaths and Marriages within a certain period, which is usually 21 days. The registrar is normally notified directly by the hospital authorities when a death occurs in a hospital. He decides whether to issue a death certificate after obtaining a medical certificate and other details concerning the deceased. If someone dies accidentally, suddenly, during an operation or in unusual circumstances, or the cause of death is unknown, the registrar notifies the police and/or a coroner, who decides whether an autopsy is necessary to determine the cause of death.

The registrar needs to know the personal details of the deceased, including his date and place of birth and death, marriage details (if applicable) and whether he was receiving a state pension or any welfare benefits. The registrar then issues a death certificate, which authorises the funeral to take place. The certificate must be given to a funeral director (or undertaker) to organise burial or cremation, or you can arrange for the body to be shipped to another country for burial. You may wish to announce a death in a local or national newspaper, giving the date, time and place of the funeral and your wishes concerning flowers or contributions to a charity.

The death of a foreigner may also need to be reported to a consulate or embassy, e.g. to register the death in the deceased's home country. In the event of the death of an Australian resident, all interested parties must be notified (see **Chapter 20**). You need a number of copies of the death certificate, e.g. for financial institutions, insurance companies, pension claims and the proving of the will (probate). If you need to obtain a copy of a death certificate, the cheapest way is to apply to the registrar in the state or territory where it was registered.

A brochure, *What To Do When Someone Dies*, is available from Centrelink (☎ local call rate 13-1021).

Funeral Costs

Traditional funerals are expensive in Australia, where cremation costs an average of around $4,000 and burial around $7,000 (undertakers only get one bite of the cherry and have to make the most of it!). A grave plot (which are in short supply in some cities) can cost anything from $400 to $4,000, plus digging fees of around $400 to $1,000. The tenure on a plot may be indefinite or limited, e.g. from 25 to 99 years, after which you must make an additional payment if you wish to retain the plot. You can pay in advance for your funeral through a variety of pay-now-die-later schemes, although there are no legal safeguards and the pre-paid funeral trade is rife with fraud, mismanagement and over-selling. If you want to have a body buried overseas or have someone who died overseas buried in Australia, the body probably needs to be transported by air, which can be **very** expensive.

Three Sisters, Blue Mountains, NSW

13.
INSURANCE

Australia is a nation of gamblers, which is reflected in the relatively low level of insurance, even for basic contingencies. There are only a few cases in Australia where insurance for individuals is compulsory, including mortgage insurance (because lenders insist on it) and third-party motor insurance (CTP), which is required by law but is included in vehicle registration fees (see page 213). If you're an employee, you must also belong to a pension (superannuation) fund. You may need third-party and accident insurance for high-risk sports. Voluntary insurance includes accident, dental, home contents, income protection, legal expenses, life insurance, motor breakdown, personal liability, private health and travel. For information about motor breakdown insurance and car insurance, see page 221; information on other types of insurance is given in this chapter.

The Australian government and Australian law stipulate various obligatory insurance and benefit schemes, including disability, health, sickness and work injuries insurance, state and private (superannuation) pensions, and maternity and unemployment benefit – some of which are the responsibility of the state (social security or 'welfare'), some of employers. Australia has one of the most comprehensive social security systems in the world in terms of the number of people eligible for benefits, which has engendered widespread welfare dependency, around a third of all Australians relying on welfare payments as their main source of income (half of them pensioners); on the other hand, benefits cover only the most basic needs.

Most Australians and foreign residents and their families receive health treatment under Medicare, the national health service (see page 246). If you don't qualify for Medicare, it's essential to have private health insurance, which is obligatory for some temporary residents; even if you do, you may wish to take out a top-up policy to cover the expenses not reimbursed under Medicare. You'd also be wise to ensure that your family has comprehensive health insurance during the period between leaving your last country of residence and arriving in Australia. This is particularly important if a private health insurance policy in your home country doesn't cover you overseas. One way is to take out a travel insurance policy (see page 280).

However, it's usually better to extend your present health insurance policy, if possible, particularly if you have existing health problems, which may not be covered by a new policy.

It isn't necessary to spend half your income insuring yourself against every eventuality from the common cold to being sued for your last cent, but it's important to be covered for any event which could precipitate a major financial disaster (such as a serious accident or your house falling down). **As with everything to do with finance, it's imperative to shop around when buying insurance.** Just picking up a few brochures from insurance agents and making a few telephone calls could save you a lot of money (enough to pay for this book many times over). Regrettably, you cannot insure yourself against being uninsured or sue your insurance broker for giving you bad advice!

Information in this chapter is intended only as a guide, as the rules regarding insurance matters are constantly changing, particularly health insurance, social security and superannuation. You should therefore obtain the latest information from the appropriate authorities or an insurance company in Australia. It's your responsibility to ensure that your family is legally insured in Australia.

> ### ⚠ Caution
> **Australian law may be very different from that in your home country or your previous country of residence, and you should never assume that it's the same.**

INSURANCE COMPANIES

There are numerous insurance companies in Australia, either providing a range of insurance services or specialising in certain fields. You can buy insurance from many sources, including banks and other financial institutions, direct insurance companies (selling straight to the public instead of via brokers), traditional insurance companies selling through independent agents (brokers), and motoring organisations (see page 238). In recent years, direct insurance companies have enabled consumers to make huge savings, particularly on car,

building and home contents insurance. Direct selling companies give quotations over the telephone; often you aren't even required to complete a proposal form.

The major insurance companies have offices or brokers throughout Australia, including most large towns, and most of them provide a free analysis of your family or business insurance needs. If you choose a broker, you should use one who's independent and sells policies from a wide range of insurance companies. Some brokers or agents and most banks are tied to a particular insurance company and sell policies only from that company.

CONTRACTS

Most insurance policies run for a calendar year from the date on which you take them out. All premiums should be paid punctually, as late payment can affect your benefits or a claim, although if this is so it should be stated in your policy. Before signing an insurance contract, you should take a day or two to think it over, although with some insurance contracts, you may have a 'cooling off' period during which you can cancel a policy without penalty.

Claims

Although insurance companies are keen to take your money, many aren't nearly so happy to settle claims. Like insurance companies everywhere, some Australian insurance companies do almost anything to avoid paying out in the event of a claim and use any available loophole. For example, if you wish to make a claim, you must usually inform your insurance company in writing by registered letter within a number of days of the incident (possibly within 24 hours in the case of theft). **Failure to do so renders your claim void.** Don't send original bills or documents regarding a claim to your insurance company unless it's necessary (you can send certified copies).

financed from general taxation (although there's a specific levy for Medicare). Nevertheless, many people fail to apply for allowances and pensions to which they're entitled. If you apply and your application is rejected, you can ask for the decision to be reviewed by an Authorised Review Officer (ARO); if it's turned down again, you can appeal to the Social Security Appeals Tribunal, and finally to the Administrative Appeals Tribunal.

A range of publications detailing social security allowances, benefits and pensions is available from social security offices and community organisations. Centrelink provides a telephone enquiry service on ☎ 13-1021. Calls are charged at local rates from anywhere in Australia. For more information, contact the Department of Families, Community Services and Indigenous Affairs (FaCSIA), Box 7788, Canberra Mail Centre, ACT 2610 (☎ local call rate 1300-653227, 🖥 www.facs.gov. au), which is a Centrelink service aimed at helping people through the social security maze.

Eligibility

The main beneficiaries of social security are the aged, single parents, the unemployed, those who are disabled, sick or in special need, and families with children.

Eligibility for most social security benefits is subject to an income and/or means test. The poorest 10 per cent of Australians receive some 600 per cent more in government payments than the richest 10 per cent over their lifetime.

Assets which are means tested include most investments (which count as income) but not superannuation pensions or belongings such as cars and antiques. Your assets don't include your principal family home or the land (up to two hectares)

Keep a copy of all bills, correspondence and documents, and always send letters by registered post so that your insurance company cannot deny receipt.

When dealing with insurance companies, perseverance often pays. Don't bank a cheque received in settlement of a claim if you think it's insufficient, as you may be deemed to have accepted it as full and final settlement. Don't accept the first offer made, as many insurance companies try to get away with making a low settlement (if an insurer pays what you've claimed without a quibble, you probably claimed too little!). If you cannot reach agreement, you can contact The Insurance Ombudsman Service Limited (☎ local call rate 1300-363683, 🖥 www.insuranceombudsman. com.au) for independent arbitration or take legal action.

SOCIAL SECURITY

Social security is the name given to state benefits paid to residents in Australia. Social security is non-contributory and is

on which it's built, provided it's used for domestic purposes.

Migrants

Migrants must wait 104 weeks before they can claim most social security payments, although refugees and humanitarian immigrants are exempt from the waiting period. Migrants can, however, claim Medicare benefits, the minimum rate of family tax benefit (see below) and, in exceptional circumstances, special benefit and a widow's allowance (see **Benefits** below) during the two-year waiting period. Some sponsors of migrants need to provide an Assurance of Support, which makes them liable to repay the government if the migrant needs any welfare benefits during his first two years (ten years for children sponsoring a parent who's within ten years of retirement).

According to the Welfare Rights Centre, the two-year waiting period for welfare has caused some migrants to become destitute and homeless, and there have been calls to have it suspended or cancelled, although these have so far been unsuccessful. Migrant service units monitor and review services to migrants and refugees and liaise with ethnic and voluntary groups, and there are also migrant resource centres in the major towns and cities. Settlement support is provided for migrants with genuine financial problems.

Benefits

Social security benefits include a bereavement allowance, carer pension, child disability allowance, disability support pension, double orphan pension, family tax payment, health care card, 'baby bonus', mobility allowance, multiple birth payment (triplets or more), 'jobsearch' and 'newstart' allowances, parenting or guardian allowance (if a single parent), pharmaceutical allowance, rent assistance, sheltered employment and rehabilitation allowances, sickness allowance, widow's allowance and youth training allowance.

The principal benefits of relevance to foreigner residents are outlined below. A discretionary payment (called special benefit) may be paid to those who aren't eligible for other forms of assistance but are unable to support themselves.

The federal and state governments jointly fund a wide range of welfare services relating to home care for the elderly and disabled and their families. Some 1,500 nursing homes and around 1,000 hostels receive federal support to provide residential care for elderly people. A federal programme funds organisations to provide services that help people with disabilities maintain their independence and achieve their potential. The Commonwealth Rehabilitation Service employs a number of specialists to work with disabled people to help them attain economic and social independence.

● **Family Tax Benefit** – administered by the Family Assistance Office (💻 www.

familyassist.gov.au) and available to parents or guardians with dependent children, including those who are full-time students but aren't in receipt of an allowance or grant. The amount paid depends on the age and number of children in the family and the family's total income. The maximum benefit is around $145 per fortnight per child under 13 (reducing to $63 for children aged 16-17), the minimum (for those earning over around $90,000) around $47 per child under 18. A different scale of benefits (Benefit B) applies to single-parent families and those with only one earner. There's also a Large Family Supplement for those with three or more children. Payments are usually made fortnightly into the mother's bank account, although it's possible to receive the payment in a lump sum at the end of the financial year (July). Family tax benefits and other payments for children (e.g. child care benefit – see below) aren't taxable.

- **Child Care Benefit** – available to parents whose children are in registered or approved care while the parents are working, looking for work or studying. Benefit is also available for children in after-school care (between 20 and 50 hours per week), although up to only 85 per cent of the full amount. If your annual income is under around $33,000, you receive full benefit; otherwise the benefit is subject to an income test.

Baby Bonus

A 'baby bonus' is available to all new parents (including those of adopted children) as a lump sum ($4,187 at the end of 2007, but it's index linked and therefore increases twice a year, in March and September).

- **Unemployment Benefits** – Australia's unemployment benefit system takes the form of 'jobsearch' and 'newstart'

schemes. If you're unemployed, under 18 or have been registered with Centrelink for no more than a year, and a permanent resident, you must register for a jobsearch allowance. You must provide proof of identity and your tax file number. If you've been 'terminated' (sacked, made redundant, etc.) from a previous position, you need your Employment Separation Certificate, which states the reason you left work and your final wage. **For immigrants there's a two-year waiting period before payments start.** If you remain unemployed for more than a year, you must apply for a newstart allowance, for which you must be over 21, a permanent resident and unemployed and have been registered with Centrelink for over a year. Rates of payment depend on your circumstances, including your age, income, marital status and number of children. Unemployed people aged 21 to 34 who have been receiving a newstart allowance for six to 12 months can be obliged to do work experience, mainly on local projects or in community service.

State Pensions

As in many other developed countries, there's a worsening crisis in state pension funding in Australia, where fewer and fewer workers must support an increasing number of pensioners. In 2000, 12 per cent of Australians were over the age of 65; by 2050, the figure is expected to be 25 per cent. The Commonwealth government spends around 3 per cent of the country's GDP on retirement benefits and this figure is expected to increase to only 4.5 per cent by 2050. As in many countries, there are plans to transfer the burden from the public to the private sector, which is why the mandatory Superannuation Guarantee Scheme was created in 1992 (see page 269). However, despite the introduction of superannuation, some 75 per cent of people are expected to be eligible for a full or part state pension (known as an Age Pension) for at least the next 25 years.

State retirement pensions are paid to men at 65 years of age and currently (until 1st July 2009) to women at 63.5. The pensionable age for women is gradually being increased to 65; the qualifying age was first raised from 60 to 60.5 on 1st July 1995, and is being further increased by six months at two-year intervals until 1st July 2013, when it will reach 65.

Pensions are pegged at 25 per cent of average male earnings. A full pension is currently $537.70 per fortnight for a single person and $449.10 each for a married couple. State pensions are indexed twice a year in line with changes in the Consumer Price Index (CPI).

You generally need to have lived continuously in Australia for ten years to qualify for a state pension. A full pension is payable after 25 years' residence during your 'working' life (i.e. from the age of 16). However, Australia has reciprocal social security agreements with some countries (including Austria, Canada, Cyprus, Denmark, Ireland, Italy, Malta, the Netherlands, Portugal and Spain), which may enable newcomers to receive a pension as soon as they reach pensionable age, irrespective of their residence period.

⚠ Caution

The UK no longer has a reciprocal social security agreement with Australia (see British Pensioners below).

If you've lived in Australia for less than 25 years and then go to live overseas, you receive an Australian pension proportionate to the number of years spent there, e.g. if you've spent 12.5 years in Australia, you receive half of the full retirement pension. Pensioners who delay their retirement become eligible for a cash bonus equal to 9.4 per cent of their pension entitlement for each year they continue working.

In addition to the basic retirement pension, various other pensions are paid in Australia, including pensions for bereaved people, carers, disabled people, double orphans (i.e. those whose parents are both deceased), single parents, widows and wives. All pensions are paid at the same rates. Other social security payments may be claimed in addition to a pension. The basic retirement pension is taxable but on its own is below the tax threshold.

Australian pensioners are entitled to concessionary dental treatment, optometrist services and prescriptions, concessions on public transport fares in most states and territories, and various other benefits (which vary from state to state) that may include reduced council rates and utility costs (e.g. telephone rental and water rates), free post redirection and reduced registration fees for dogs.

Unlike state pensions in most countries, which are paid irrespective of a person's wealth or income, most Australian pensions are subject to income and assets tests (the test which produces the lower rate of pension applies, although there's no assets test for those over 70). This is the case for all pensions except invalidity pensions for permanently blind people and pensions for war and defence widows. Around 30 per cent of Australians are considered too wealthy to receive a state pension.

You can choose the day on which you want your pension paid. Pensions are usually paid into a bank, building society or credit union account. Australian pensions can be paid overseas, although pensioners going overseas for longer than six months must obtain a pre-departure certificate from social security.

and if you migrated to Australia on or before 1st March 2000, the date on which Australia served notice of termination of the agreement on the UK, you continue to have your British contributions recognised for grants of Australian pensions. Otherwise, you're eligible only for your frozen British pension.

SUPERANNUATION

Superannuation (usually referred to simply as 'super') is the term commonly used in Australia for a private pension fund. As the number of retired workers has increased and the number of young workers has declined (because of falling birth and rising unemployment rates), the pressure on government funds to pay state pensions has increased. In order to reduce the burden, the federal government introduced compulsory employer superannuation funds in 1992 under the Superannuation Guarantee Scheme.

For further information about state pensions in Australia, contact Centrelink (🖳 www.centrelink.gov.au) or the Department of Families, Community Services & Indigenous Affairs (FACSIA, ☎ local call rate 1300-653227, 🖳 www.facs.gov.au).

British Pensioners

British state pensions are frozen at the prevailing rate with no annual adjustments for inflation when the recipients move to certain Commonwealth countries, including Australia, Canada, New Zealand and South Africa. This affects over 350,000 British pensioners. There are some 250,000 British state pensioners in Australia with frozen British state pensions (which may be equivalent to just a few A$). What's more, on 1st March 2001 Australia and the UK ceased their reciprocal social security agreement, whereby British pensioners could receive social security 'top-up' payments from the Australian government. If you were receiving top-up payments under the agreement on 1st March 2001, you continue to receive those payments,

Superannuation doesn't replace the state pension (which continues to be available, subject to eligibility), but is intended to supplement it to ensure an adequate income in retirement.

Since its introduction, superannuation has been extended to include part-time and casual workers and those who leave the workforce for up to two years. Self-employed and non-resident employees paid for work undertaken outside Australia aren't required to belong to a superannuation fund, and resident employees employed by non-resident employers and paid for work undertaken outside Australia also needn't be covered.

Generally, if you earn over around $450 per month (whether as a full- or part-time employee or a casual worker), your employer must make superannuation contributions for you; some awards (see **Chapter 2**) require employers also to pay superannuation for employees earning less than $450 per month. Employees earning between $450 and $900 per month can choose to receive their superannuation as additional salary.

Funds are non-contributory for employees, although voluntary contributions can be made. Employer contributions must be at least the minimum level laid down by the government, termed the Superannuation Guarantee (SG). The minimum contribution employers must make for each employee is 9 per cent of their earnings base. This percentage is, however, generally considered to be too low and it's thought that a savings level of 12 to 15 per cent is necessary to maintain standards of living on retirement.

You aren't obliged to join your employer's fund and may choose your own fund, but must do so within 28 days. There are various types of superannuation fund, including do-it-yourself funds (which hold an increasing share of superannuation assets), financial institution funds and industry funds. Banks, building societies, credit unions and life assurance companies can all provide superannuation funds in the form of Retirement Savings Accounts (RSAs). Repayment of all RSA deposits is guaranteed, but interest is usually modest, e.g. 4 per cent per year. Many people begin with small contributions, particularly casual, part-time and seasonal workers.

There's a huge difference between the best- and worst-performing superannuation funds, so it's wise to shop around and compare fund performance over a five- or ten-year period and the level of fees (smaller industry funds generally don't do as well as larger ones). However, in most cases, you'd be foolish to turn down the opportunity to join an employer's fund if it's a good one, as it usually provides extra benefits. These may include free life and disability insurance and insurance against loss of earnings due to injury or illness. Some funds offer members discounted home and personal loans and private health insurance. It's possible that in future employees will be able to use part of their superannuation funds to buy a home.

Your superannuation payout may be related to your final salary, which is the best option. If it isn't, you should ensure that the fund is invested safely, as you could lose out if the share market or property prices collapse in the years just before retirement. When you join a fund, you have a 14-day 'cooling-off' period, during which you may withdraw your membership. If you change employers or professions, your superannuation benefits can be transferred to another fund.

Since superannuation was introduced in 1992, it has become increasingly complicated and difficult for the layman

(or anyone) to understand. Although successive governments have tinkered with the system (some 2,000 changes have been made), many analysts believe that it needs a complete overhaul. The Association of Superannuation Funds of Australia, PO Box 1485, Sydney, NSW 1005 (☎ 02-9264 9300 or ☎ 1800-812798, 💻 www.superannuation.asn.au) publishes a number of useful information sheets, including *What Information You Should Receive from Your Superannuation Fund*. Information about changes to the superannuation system made in July 2007 can be found on the website of the Australian Taxation Office (ATO, 💻 www. ato.gov.au) and further general informaiton about superannuation on 💻 www. smartersuper.com.au.

Tax & Surcharge

Superannuation is taxed at 12.5 per cent. This applies to both voluntary contributions to a superannuation fund and the income from it, although tax relief can be claimed against superannuation payments. Contributions to superannuation for high earners attract a surcharge.

In order to avoid being taxed on income at the top rate of 45 per cent, some employees negotiate higher superannuation contributions and a reduced salary (called 'salary sacrifice' arrangements). Since the surcharge was announced, many wealthy people have quit superannuation and made alternative investments (over 1.5m superannuation accounts have been closed). Nevertheless, superannuation remains attractive to lower earners.

Withdrawals & Payments

Superannuation fund payments can be taken in an annuity, a lump sum or a regular monthly income (e.g. an allocated or lifetime pension), or a combination of these. The age at which contributions may be withdrawn is called the preservation age, and it depends on your date of birth, as follows:

Date of Birth	Preservation Age
Before 1/7/60	55
1/7/60 to 30/6/61	56
1/7/61 to 30/6/62	57
1/7/62 to 30/6/63	58
1/7/63 to 30/6/64	59
After 30/6/64	60

Those over 55 are obliged to exhaust their superannuation funds before being entitled to unemployment benefit. If you leave Australia permanently, your superannuation benefits won't be released until you reach the required age.

The maximum age for contributing to a superannuation fund is 70, provided you work a minimum of ten hours per week (if you work beyond the age of 65, you should check whether you're still eligible for superannuation – and seek psychiatric help).

PRIVATE HEALTH INSURANCE

The Australian Medicare (see page 250) system provides free or subsidised medical treatment for all permanent residents. Anyone living or working in Australia (even temporarily) who isn't eligible for Medicare treatment and who doesn't like living dangerously should have private health insurance. If you're living or working in Australia and aren't covered by Medicare, it's risky or even foolhardy not to have private health insurance for you and your family. Whether you're covered by an Australian or foreign health insurance policy makes little difference (except perhaps in cost), provided you have the required level of cover, including international cover if necessary (see **International Health Policies** on page 275).

If your stay in Australia is short, you may be covered by a reciprocal healthcare agreement between your home country and Australia (currently in place in Finland, Ireland, Italy, the Netherlands, New Zealand, Norway, Sweden and the UK – but check before travelling), or by a private health insurance scheme, although you should check exactly what this entitles you to. If you aren't adequately insured, you could be faced with some extremely high medical bills.

When changing employers or leaving Australia, you should make sure that you have continuous medical insurance. For example, if you and your family are covered by a company health fund, your insurance probably ceases after your last official day of employment. If you're planning to change your health insurance company, ensure that no important benefits are lost. When changing health insurance companies, you should inform your old insurance company if you have any outstanding bills for which they're liable.

Even if you're covered by Medicare, it may be advantageous to take out private health insurance, as Medicare doesn't cover all healthcare costs (see Benefits on page 266). Private insurance can also be used to cover private treatment, e.g. in order to circumvent Medicare waiting lists for specialist appointments and non-emergency hospital treatment (e.g. elective surgery); but note that Medicare covers 75 per cent of the cost of private treatment, so this is an inexpensive way of obtaining private treatment. Private patients are also usually free to choose their own doctor and hospital. However, despite what insurance companies might say, the quality of private treatment is no higher than that provided by Medicare, and you shouldn't assume that because a doctor (or any other

medical practitioner) is in private practice, he's more competent than his Medicare counterpart. In fact, you're likely to see the same specialist or be treated by the same surgeon under Medicare as privately (but a few years earlier).

Most private health insurance in Australia is provided by health funds, which are regulated by the Commonwealth government and follow the principle of 'community rating' to determine premiums, i.e. premiums don't vary according to age, sex or your state of health. This ensures that high-risk members such as the elderly and the chronically sick aren't required to pay astronomical premiums as in some other countries. However, most health funds are eroding this principle and in recent years have introduced a variety of conditions to exclude expensive treatment (called exclusion policies) and surgery such as joint replacements; there may also be financial limits. Many analysts believe this could be the thin end of the wedge and that insurance companies will abandon 'community rating' by stealth.

Changes to private health insurance have been proposed by the government, although they're strongly contested by the Australian Medical Association, which fears that health funds will dictate clinical practices, i.e. the insurer rather than the doctor will decide the treatment.

Health insurers offer two basic types of insurance: hospital and ancillary. Hospital cover contributes to the cost of inpatient treatment and accommodation as a private patient in a private or public hospital. Ancillary cover contributes to the cost of outpatient services that aren't covered by Medicare, such as acupuncture, chiropractic and other alternative therapies, dental treatment, physiotherapy, and spectacles or contact lenses. Ancillary insurance may also include ambulance cover, home nursing and other services, although there's usually no refund for X-rays or prescriptions. There are payment limits for ancillary cover – both per visit limits and annual limits. Some funds have a policy which pays for gym membership or sports equipment such as running shoes on the basis that these improve your health and so reduce their costs.

Private health insurers are allowed to offer four categories of membership as follows:

- single person;
- couple;
- family, consisting of at least two adults and one or more other, which may include children and grandparents;
- single-parent, consisting of at least one adult (who's the contributor) and one or more dependent children.

⚠ Caution

When taking out family or single-parent membership, always carefully check what constitutes a 'dependent' child, as your children may not be covered.

There are several private health insurers, the largest of which include the Hospital Contribution Fund (HCF), Medibank Private, the Medical Benefit Funds (MBF) and National Mutual Health Insurance. By far the largest insurer is Medibank Private (🖳 www.medibank.com.au), a non-profit health benefits organisation (established in 1976) operated by the state-run Health Insurance Commission, covering some 3m people (one third of all those with private health insurance), with some 100 customer service centres throughout the country. Medibank Private also provides cover for temporary residents of Australia who aren't eligible for Medicare benefits.

It's possible to obtain health insurance from some banks, although they may insure only high earners. Compare the benefits and costs provided by a number of health insurers. Most provide a choice of basic, intermediate and comprehensive cover.

If you're unable to resolve a complaint with your health insurer, you can contact the Private Health Insurance Ombudsman, Level 7, 362 Kent Street, Sydney 2000 (☎ 02-8235 8777 or ☎ 1800-640695, 🖳 www.phio.org.au).

Premiums

Premiums vary considerably according to the state or territory. The average cost of 100 per cent hospital cover for a family is around $1,600 and the average cost of 100 per cent ancillary cover around $1,150. The average costs for a single person are between around $750 and $875 (depending on the level of cover) for hospital cover and $575 for ancillary cover. Premiums can usually be paid monthly, quarterly or annually, and a discount may be given for prompt or annual payment. Alternatively, you can pay weekly or fortnightly through automatic salary deductions.

In 2000, the federal government introduced a 30 per cent rebate on private health insurance premiums. Under the scheme, anyone who pays hospital and/or ancillary premiums to a registered health fund can obtain a 30 per cent reduction on the cost of their health insurance. The rebate isn't means tested but the private health insurance policy must cover people eligible for Medicare. The rebate can be claimed in three ways: from your health fund as a straight premium reduction; from a Medicare office, which reimburses you the 30 per cent; or from the Tax Office on your annual income tax form.

Health insurers have contracts with hospitals and doctors in order to assert some control over costs. You may need to choose a hospital and doctor contracted to your health insurer; otherwise you must pay the 'gap' between what the insurer pays and what your doctor or hospital charges. Some insurers have agreements with relatively few private hospitals, outside which you're limited to a private bed in a public hospital, and you may not be covered outside your home state. You should receive a written quotation for non-emergency hospital treatment, including all extra charges (see below).

Before Medicare was introduced in 1984, over 50 per cent of Australians had private cover; this has since fallen to below a third – the system ceases to be viable at 30 per cent! The government is desperate to encourage people to return to (or remain in) private health cover, as Medicare is facing a funding crisis and its survival in its present form relies heavily on a strong private health sector. **If things go on this way, there could be a collapse of health funds AND Medicare (maybe you'd better insure with a foreign company).**

Additional Costs

The benefits (rebates) provided by health insurers aren't usually 100 per cent and you normally need to make an extra payment or 'co-payment' towards fees, called 'out-of-pocket' costs. This can be very high and can run into $hundreds or even $thousands (and can increase at short notice).

⚠ Caution

If you want your own doctor to treat you in a public hospital, you must pay a daily accommodation charge, and some insurers levy a fee per night (e.g. $80) for private hospital patients.

In addition to out-of-pocket costs, there's usually an annual excess charge (deductible), which can be up to $2,000 for a family and may be applied per person for a couple. When you leave hospital, you're generally asked to pay the difference (if any) between your health insurer's refund and the hospital's fees. **High additional costs are the main reason people have abandoned private health insurance in recent years.**

Waiting Periods

All funds have waiting periods before new members are eligible to make a claim, e.g. a general two-month wait for all treatment, nine months for obstetrics (i.e. you cannot join when pregnant and claim for the costs associated with childbirth) and one year for existing conditions. This is to prevent you from making a claim directly after joining and then dropping your membership. However, accidents are covered from the day you join. Before changing funds, always check the waiting times for treatment, particularly if you have existing health problems. If you already belong to a private health insurance scheme in another country, you may be able to transfer your membership to Australia, in which case you won't be subject to waiting lists. Some insurance companies offer a short-term scheme for people staying in Australia only a few months.

at a surgery, in your home or in hospital, and pathology services such as blood tests and X-rays. Payments are the same as for Medicare members, i.e. 85 per cent of the government schedule fee for outpatient treatment and 100 per cent of the schedule fee for hospital inpatient services and most GP services. If a doctor charges more than the schedule fee, you must pay the difference. If you choose to be treated in a private hospital, Medibank Private contributes towards the cost of treatment and accommodation, but you're responsible for paying the difference between the schedule fee and the actual fee charged. The services that aren't covered by OSHC are much the same as for Medicare (see page 250). If you wish to be covered for excluded services, you need additional private health insurance.

International Health Policies

It's possible to take out an international health insurance policy, which may be of interest to people living in Australia temporarily, or those whose work involves a lot of travel or who work part of the time overseas. Some companies offer a range of policies, from basic to comprehensive. All policies offer at least two fee scales, one covering the whole world, including North America (and possible other high-cost areas), the other excluding North America. Most policies include a full refund of ambulance, emergency dental treatment, home nursing (usually for a limited period), hospital, outpatient and repatriation charges. All policies include an annual overall claims limit, usually from $200,000 to $2m (the higher the better, particularly for North America). Some comprehensive policies provide a fixed amount for general medical costs (including routine doctors' visits) and elective dental, maternity and optical expenses. If you don't require permanent international health insurance, you should consider a policy which

Students

Overseas Student Health Cover (OSHC) is obligatory for foreign students and their dependants in Australia and must cover them for the duration of their visa or 12 months (whichever is shorter). It's provided by a number of insurance companies, including Medibank Private. Your initial premium must be paid before you arrive in Australia. If your student visa is for more than 12 months, a further premium is payable after 12 months. If you're a government-sponsored student (e.g. by the Australian Agency for International Development/AusAID), the agency or department of the Australian government which is sponsoring you pays your premium to Medibank Private. If you're a non-government-sponsored student, your premium is usually paid by the school, college or university at which you'll be studying (in fact, it's usually included in your course fees).

OSHC includes full or partial cover for the fees of doctors (including specialists)

provides limited or optional cover when you're overseas.

Premiums range from around $1,750 to over $5,000 per year, depending on your age, level of cover and the areas covered (if North America is covered, premiums are much higher).

> ☑ **SURVIVAL TIP**
>
> **All bills, particularly those received for treatment outside Australia, must include precise details of treatment received. Terms such as 'dental treatment' or 'consultation' are usually insufficient.**

DENTAL INSURANCE

Routine dental services aren't funded by Medicare, although it pays for 75 per cent of in-hospital medical procedures performed by an oral surgeon, and pensioners qualify for free general and emergency dental treatment under the Commonwealth Dental Health Program. Basic dental treatment is usually provided under a health insurer's ancillary policy (see **Private Health Insurance** on page 271), and most international health insurance policies offer optional dental cover or extra dental cover for an additional premium, although there are many restrictions, and cosmetic treatment is excluded. Where applicable, the amount payable by a health insurance policy for a particular item of dental treatment is fixed and depends on your level of dental insurance. A list of specific refunds is available from insurance companies.

It's unusual to have full dental insurance in Australia, as the cost is prohibitive, though some dentists offer a partial insurance scheme, which usually doesn't cover expensive items such as bridges, crowns and dentures. Patients must be

'dentally fit' and are graded according to the condition of their teeth. If you have healthy teeth and rarely pay for more than an annual check-up and a visit to a hygienist, dental insurance provides poor value.

BUILDING INSURANCE

When buying a home, you're usually responsible for insuring it (building insurance) before you even move in. If you take out a mortgage to buy a property, your lender usually insists that your home (including most permanent structures on your property) has building insurance from the time you sign the contract and legally become the owner. Even when it isn't required by a lender, you'd be extremely unwise not to have building insurance.

Building insurance usually includes loss or damage caused by aircraft or vehicles, animals, falling trees or aerials, theft or malicious damage, or a riot, storm or lightning, subsidence or landslide, earthquake, explosion, fire, flood, oil leakage from a central heating system, or water leakage from pipes or tanks, and may also include cover for temporary homelessness. Some insurance companies offer optional cover to include trees and shrubs damaged maliciously or by storms. The highest (and most expensive) level of cover usually includes damage to glass (e.g. windows and patio doors) and porcelain (e.g. baths, washbasins and WCs), although you may have to pay extra for accidental damage, e.g. when your son blasts a cricket ball through the patio window. Always ask your insurer what **isn't** covered and what it costs to include it (if required).

Building insurance must be renewed each year, and insurance companies are continually updating their policies, so you must ensure that a policy still provides the cover you require when you receive a renewal notice. **Building insurance** doesn't cover damage caused by structural faults that existed when you took out the policy, which is why it's important to have a full structural survey carried out when you buy a property.

Lenders fix the initial level of cover when you first apply for a mortgage and usually offer to arrange the insurance for you, but you're usually free to make your own arrangements. If you arrange your own building insurance, your lender will insist that the level of cover is sufficient. Most people take the easy option and arrange insurance through their mortgage lender (premiums are usually added to your monthly mortgage payments), which is generally the most expensive option, e.g. some direct insurance companies guarantee to cut building insurance costs for the majority of homeowners insured through banks and building societies.

Most lenders provide index-linked building insurance, where premiums increase annually in line with inflation and building costs. It's your responsibility, however, to ensure that your level of cover is adequate, particularly if you carry out improvements or extensions which substantially increase the value of your home. All lenders provide information and free advice. If your level of cover is too low, an insurance company is within its rights to reduce the amount it pays when a claim is made, in which case you may find you cannot afford to have your house rebuilt or repaired should disaster strike.

level of cover – between around $3 to $4 per $1,000 of cover (per year) in an inexpensive area to $10 or more per $1,000 in the most expensive or high-risk areas. Therefore insurance on a property costing $150,000 to rebuild costs from around $450 to $1,500 per year. There's usually no deduction for wear and tear, and the cost of redecoration is usually met in full. Insurance for 'non-standard' homes such as those with thatched roofs or timber construction is usually higher.

In recent years, increased competition (particularly from direct insurers) has reduced premiums. The National Roads and Motoring Association (NRMA, 🖳 www.mynrma.com.au) in New South Wales is the nation's biggest insurer and insures around 1.4m homes.

Premiums can usually be paid monthly (although there may be an extra charge) or annually. There may be an excess, e.g. $50 or $100, for some claims, which is intended to deter policyholders from making small claims. Some policies have an excess

> ☑ **SURVIVAL TIP**
>
> The amount for which your home must be insured isn't the current market value but the cost of rebuilding it if it's totally destroyed.

Premiums vary according to the type of property and the area as well as the

house. Burglary is endemic in Australia, particularly in the major cities. Contents include everything that isn't part of the fixtures and fittings and which you could take with you if you were moving house. If you under-insure your contents, your claim may be reduced by the percentage by which you're under-insured.

A basic home contents policy covers your belongings against the same sort of 'natural disasters' as building insurance (see above). A basic policy doesn't usually include such items as bicycles, cash, credit cards (and their fraudulent use), jewellery, musical instruments, sports equipment and certain other valuables, for which you may need to take out extra cover. A basic policy doesn't usually include accidental damage caused by your family to your own property (e.g. putting your foot through the TV during a political party broadcast) or your home freezer contents (in the event of a breakdown or power failure), although you may be able to add this for an extra premium. A basic policy may include garden contents, loss of oil and metered water, personal liability insurance (see below), replacement locks and temporary accommodation. If they aren't included, these items can usually be covered for an additional premium.

Some policies include legal expenses cover (e.g. up to $100,000) for disputes with employers, neighbours, shops, suppliers and anyone who provides you with a service (e.g. a plumber or builder). Most contents policies include public liability cover, e.g. up to $2m. Items such as computers and mobile telephones may need to be listed individually on your policy, and computers and other equipment used for business aren't usually covered (or may be covered only for a prohibitive extra payment). If you have friends or lodgers living in your home, their property won't be covered by your policy.

only for certain claims, e.g. subsidence or landslip (when your house disappears into a hole in the ground or over a cliff), which is usually $2,000 or $4,000. (Not surprisingly, owners of houses vulnerable to subsidence and those living in flood-prone areas are likely to pay higher premiums.)

Many insurance companies provide emergency telephone numbers for policyholders requiring urgent advice. Should you need to make emergency repairs, e.g. to weather-proof a roof after a storm or other natural disaster, most insurance companies allow work up to a certain limit (e.g. $2,000) to be carried out without an estimate or approval from the insurance company, but check first.

Building insurance is often combined with home contents insurance (see below), when it's called home or household insurance, which is usually cheaper than taking out separate policies.

HOME CONTENTS INSURANCE

Home contents insurance is recommended for anyone who doesn't live in an empty

You can usually insure your property for its second-hand value (indemnity) or its full replacement value (new for old), which covers everything except clothes and linen (for which wear and tear is assessed) at the new cost price. Most Australians take out replacement value insurance, which should be index-linked so that the level of cover is automatically increased by a percentage or fixed amount each year. Most policies have a maximum amount they pay per item and/or a maximum amount per claim, e.g. $1,500 for each item of jewellery or work of art, or a total claim of $7,500.

Some insurance companies offer policies called 'no-sum' or 'fixed-sum', where you aren't required to value all your possessions but are covered for a fixed amount depending on the number of bedrooms in your home. With this type of policy the insurance company cannot scale down a claim because of under-insurance. However, the sums insured can be minimal, and you're usually better off calculating the value of the contents to be insured.

Premiums

Your premium depends largely on where you live and your insurer. All insurance companies assess the risk by location, based on your postcode.

> ☑ SURVIVAL TIP
>
> **Check the insurance cost before buying a home, as the difference between low- and high-risk areas can be considerable.**

Annual premiums, which start at around $400 per annum in low-risk areas, can be several times this amount in high-risk areas. Even if you're willing to forgo theft insurance, insurance companies are reluctant to offer this option, as the risk of theft is a convenient excuse to load premiums.

As with building insurance, it's important to shop around for the lowest premium, as premiums vary considerably with the insurer. If you're already insured, you may find that you can save money by changing insurers. However, watch out for penalties when switching insurers. Combining your home contents insurance with your building insurance (see above) is a common practice and is usually cheaper than insuring each separately. Having your building and contents insurance with the same company also avoids disputes over which company should pay what, which can arise if you have a fire or flood affecting both your home and its contents. Those over 50 or 55 (and possibly first-time homeowners) may be offered a discount, and some companies provide special policies for students in college accommodation or lodgings (ask an insurance broker).

Most insurers offer a no-claims discount or a discount (e.g. 5 or 10 per cent) for homes with burglar alarms and other high-security features. In high-risk areas, good security is usually a condition of insurance. Beware of the small print in policies, particularly those regarding security, which insurers often use to avoid paying claims. You forfeit all rights under your policy if you leave doors or windows open (or the keys under a mat or flower pot), particularly if you've claimed a discount for impregnability. If there are no signs of forced entry, e.g. a broken window, you may be unable to claim for a theft (so break a window!). If you plan to leave your house empty for a long period, e.g. a month or longer, you may need to inform your insurer.

Claims

Claims should be made as soon as possible after loss or damage occurs, and policies may specify a maximum notification period. Some insurers provide a 24-hour emergency helpline for policyholders and assistance for repairs for domestic emergencies, such as a blocked drain or electrical failure, up to a maximum amount for each claim. Take care when completing a claim form, as insurers have tightened up on claims and few people receive a full settlement. Many insurers charge an excess of $50 to $100 per claim (check your policy).

You may need to wait months for a claim to be settled. Generally, the larger the claim, the longer you have to wait for your money, although in an emergency a company may make an interim payment. If you aren't satisfied with the final amount offered, don't accept it and try to negotiate a higher figure. If you still cannot reach agreement, you can contact the Insurance Ombudsman Service Limited (☎ local call rate 1300-780808, 🖥 www.insuranceombudsman.com.au) for independent arbitration or take legal action.

PERSONAL LIABILITY INSURANCE

Personal (or legal) liability insurance covers individuals and their dependants against compensation claims for accidental damage, injury or death caused to third parties or their property. It usually covers anything from spilling wine on your neighbour's Persian carpet to your dog or child biting someone. Although common in Europe and North America (where people sue each other for $millions at the drop of a hat – especially if it falls on your toe), personal liability insurance is unusual in Australia. However, home contents policies (see above) usually include personal liability insurance up to $2m against injury or damage to third parties in your home, and personal liability insurance outside your home may be included in a holiday or travel policy (see below).

HOLIDAY & TRAVEL INSURANCE

Holiday and travel insurance is recommended if you don't wish to risk having your holiday or trip ruined or to arrive home broke. As you know, anything can and something often does go wrong with a holiday, sometimes before you even get on the plane (particularly if you **don't** have insurance). Travel insurance is available from many sources, including airlines, banks, insurance brokers, motoring organisations, tour operators and travel agents.

When you pay for your travel costs with some credit cards, your family (possibly including children under the age of 25) are provided with free travel accident insurance up to a specified amount, e.g. $300,000. **Don't rely on this insurance, as it usually covers only death and serious injury.**

Medical expenses are an important aspect of travel insurance and you shouldn't rely on reciprocal health agreements, cover provided by charge and credit card companies, or private medical insurance, none of which usually provide the necessary cover. The minimum medical insurance recommended by experts is $500,000 for Europe and $2m for North America and the rest of the world. Personal liability should be at least $2m for Europe and $4m for the rest of the world.

⚠ **Caution**

Many travel and holiday insurance policies don't provide the level of cover that most people need.

Always check any exclusion clauses in contracts by obtaining a copy of the full policy document, as all relevant information won't be contained in insurance leaflets.

Cost

The cost of travel insurance varies considerably according to your destination. Many companies have different rates for different areas, e.g. Australia, Europe, North America and worldwide (excluding North America). Generally, the longer the period covered, the cheaper the daily cost, although the maximum period may be limited, e.g. six months. Premiums for travel within Australia are around $28 to $40 per person for two weeks, European destinations are usually from $145 for two weeks, and North America (where medical treatment costs an arm and a leg) and a few other destinations cost from $200 for three weeks. The cheapest policies offer reduced cover which may not be adequate. Premiums may be higher for those aged over 65 or 70, and with some policies an excess (e.g. $50) must be paid for each claim.

Annual Policies

For people who travel overseas frequently, whether for business or pleasure, an annual travel policy is often an excellent

idea, costing around $225 to $350 per year for worldwide cover for an unlimited number of trips. However, always carefully check exactly what is included and read the small print (some insist that travel is by air). Most annual policies don't cover you for travel within Australia and there's a maximum limit on the length of a trip, e.g. one to six months.

Claims

Although travel insurance companies quickly and gladly take your money, they aren't so keen to pay claims, and you may need to persevere before they pay up. Fraudulent claims against travel insurance are common, so unless you can produce evidence to support your claim, insurers may assume that you're trying to cheat them. Always be persistent and make a claim irrespective of any small print, as this may be unreasonable and therefore invalid in law. **Insurance companies usually require you to report any loss (or any incident for which you intend to make a claim) to the local police within 24 hours and to obtain a report. Failure to do this usually means that a claim won't be considered.**

14.

FINANCE

Competition for your money is fierce in Australia, where financial services are provided not only by many Australian and foreign banks, but also by Australia Post, building societies, credit unions, insurance companies, investment brokers, mortgage providers, and even supermarkets and motoring organisations. Banks are facing increasing competition from a shake-up of the country's financial services industry, which it's estimated will eventually save consumers $billions per year (although it's happening very slowly). The country has a sophisticated financial system and in recent years has enjoyed a steady growth rate and low inflation, although the latter climbed to over 3 per cent in 2007 and is expected to remain at that level throughout 2008, as well as falling unemployment. Australia's gross domestic product (GDP) is currently around US$400bn. Sydney is Australia's most important financial market, although it's small in international terms.

Australia is a credit-financed society, and banks and finance companies queue up to lend you money or provide credit (interest rates on credit cards are high). Levels of personal debt are over 40 per cent of spending (similar to the UK and US) and average household debt is over $100,000 (including home loans), Australians owing unprecedented amounts on credit cards and bank overdrafts. Moreover, personal savings in Australia are among the lowest in the developed world. There are fears that, if interest rates rise rapidly (Australia's central bank raised interest rates by a quarter of a percentage point to 6.75 per cent in November 2007), many people will be unable even to pay

Credit and other cards have largely replaced cash and now account for the vast majority of retail purchases.

the interest on their debts; even with low interest rates, bankruptcies have been running at record levels in the last few years.

Illogically, however, your financial 'standing' in Australia is usually decided by the number of cards you have, including cash cards, charge cards, credit cards, Electronic Funds Transfer at Point Of Sale (EFTPOS) debit cards and store cards. A Consumer Credit Code was introduced in 1997 in an attempt to prevent credit providers from publishing misleading information; the Code is detailed in the Department of Fair Trading booklet, *Walking the Credit Tightrope is Now a Lot Less Risky* (don't you believe it!).

Personal finance in Australia is a jungle, and there are plenty of predators waiting to get their hands on your loot. Always shop around for financial services, and never sign a contract unless you know

K TRADING VOLUME
700 ML   800 ML   900 ML

1.15 billion shares
worth $947.84 million

CURRENCIES	BUYING	SELLING
Australian dollar	1.2790	1.2940
Euro	2.1330	2.1580
Sterling pound	3.0910	3.1260
US dollar	1.6320	1.6500
Yen (100 units)	1.5467	1.5640

centrelink.gov.au), and good general information on many aspects of finance is available on the Money Manager website (🖥 http://moneymanager.com.au). For information regarding the Medicare levy, pensions (including superannuation) and life insurance, see **Chapter 13**. Other financial information is contained in this chapter.

AUSTRALIAN CURRENCY

The Australian unit of currency is the Australian dollar (A$), which fell to an 11-year low against the US$ in 1997 owing to the turmoil in Asian money markets and collapsing Asian currencies. It took its time to recover but by 2006 was very strong, particularly against the US$.

The Australian dollar is divided into 100 cents, and coins are minted in values of 5 cents, 10 cents, 20 cents, 50 cents (all silver-coloured cupronickel coins), and $1 and $2 (gold-coloured bronze coins with irregular milling on the edge). The $1 and $2 coins are smaller than the 20-cent coin, which can cause confusion. Although the smallest coin is 5 cents, prices are still shown in single cents but totals are rounded up or down to the nearest 5 cents when you pay. Australian banknotes have lurid designs and are printed in values of $5 (blue/mauve), $10 (blue/green/khaki), $20 (grey/red), $50 (blue/gold/ orange) and $100 (green/orange). The $50 and $100 bills are treated with suspicion by some people and may not be accepted by small businesses, taxi drivers, etc..

Forgery used to be a problem in Australia, but it was the first country in the world to have a complete set of plastic banknotes, which offer much greater security against counterfeiting and last four times as long as conventional, paper notes. According to the Reserve Bank of Australia, the rate of counterfeiting decreased in 2003 to around nine notes for every million in

exactly what the costs and implications are. Although bankers, brokers and financiers don't like to admit it, they aren't doing business with you because they like you, but simply to get their hands on your pile of chips. It's up to you to make sure that their share is kept to a minimum and that you receive the best possible value for your money.

When you arrive in Australia to take up residence, ensure that you have sufficient cash, credit cards, travellers' cheques, gold nuggets, luncheon vouchers, coffee machine tokens, precious stones and silver dollars to last at least until your first pay day, which may be some time after your arrival. Don't, however, carry a lot of cash.

There are numerous books and magazines to help you manage your finances, and articles on personal finance are published in the financial pages of the Saturday and Sunday editions of major newspapers. Centrelink gives free financial advice (☎ local call rate 13-1021, 🖥 www.

circulation, compared to 14 counterfeits per million in 2002.

It's sensible to obtain some Australian coins and banknotes before arriving in Australia and to familiarise yourself and your family with them. Keep a supply of 20- and 50-cent coins handy for parking meters and other machines. You should have some dollars in cash, e.g. $50 to $100 in small bills, when you arrive. This saves you having to change money on arrival at an Australian airport (where exchange rates are usually poor and there are often long queues). It's best to avoid $50 and $100 notes (unless you receive them as a gift!).

> There's no limit to the amount of Australian or foreign currency that can be taken into Australia, but amounts of $10,000 or more (or the equivalent in foreign currency) must be declared on arrival (see below).

FOREIGN CURRENCY

Until recently, there were few restrictions on the amount of currency (i.e. banknotes) you could import and export. However, the Anti-Money Laundering & Counter-Terrorism Financing Act, which came into force in December 2006 and is to be phased in over two years, is set to impose tighter restrictions (e.g. anyone importing large amounts of money will have to account for its provenance), although exactly what these will be isn't yet clear.

Import and export declaration forms are available from customs officers at ports and airports and should be addressed to the Cash Transaction Reports Agency, c/o The Treasury, Langton Crescent, Parkes, ACT 2600 (☎ 02-6263 2111, 🖳 www. treasury.gov.au). For further information contact the Australian Transaction Reports and Analysis Centre, PO Box 5516, West

Chatswood, NSW 1515 (☎ 02-9950 0827 or ☎ 1300-021037, 🖳 www.austrac.gov. au). You must also declare, when asked, if you're carrying any 'bearer negotiable instruments', which include travellers' cheques, cheques, promissory notes, money orders and postal orders.

Buying & Selling Currency

Most banks and building societies buy and sell foreign currency, although you usually need to order it a few days in advance, as only the major branches in capital cities keep foreign currency in stock. Major Australian banks change most foreign banknotes (but not coins) but offer a better exchange rate for travellers' cheques (see below). *Bureaux de change* have longer opening hours than banks or building societies (see **Business Hours** on page 358), including Saturdays and Sundays in tourist areas and large cities, but should be used sparingly, as they don't offer the best exchange rates and often charge a large commission.

When buying or selling foreign currency in Australia, beware of excessive charges. Most banks have a wide margin (e.g. 5 to 10 per cent) between their buying and selling rates for foreign currencies. Apart from the difference in exchange rates, which are posted by all banks and *bureaux de change*, there may be a significant difference in charges. It pays to shop around for the best exchange rates and lowest charges, particularly when changing a lot of money (it's possible to barter over rates in some establishments). The standard A$ exchange rate against major international currencies is listed in banks and in the major daily newspapers.

There isn't much difference in cost between exchanging cash, buying and redeeming travellers' cheques and using a credit card to obtain money in Australia. However, many people simply take cash when travelling overseas, which is asking for trouble, particularly if you have no way of obtaining more cash in Australia, e.g. with travellers' cheques or a credit card. **One thing to bear in mind when travelling anywhere is not to rely on only one source of funds!**

Travellers' Cheques

Travellers' cheques in major international currencies are widely accepted in Australia. The commission for cashing travellers' cheques varies with the bank; for example, among the big four banks, ANZ charges $7, WBC $7.50, the National $5 and the Commonwealth $7 per transaction. Australia Post charges $7.70 for cashing up to ten cheques (with a maximum payment of $1,000 per person per day), and other banks and travel agencies 1.5 to 2 per cent or a flat fee of $5 to $10. Banks in rural areas (if you can find any) usually levy the highest fees for cashing travellers' cheques. Stamp duty is also payable at 20 cents per cheque. No fee is charged when cashing American Express or Thomas Cook travellers' cheques at their own branches. You can cash travellers' cheques at luxury hotels and with some businesses, although exchange rates are usually poor. You need your passport to cash cheques.

Most banks charge a commission of 1 per cent of the face value when you're buying travellers' cheques, sometimes with a minimum charge of around $10. When travelling outside Australia, it's best to buy travellers' cheques in £sterling or US$, which are the most widely accepted (US$ cheques should always be used when visiting the US).

Lost or stolen travellers' cheques can be replaced in Australia and most countries overseas (the easiest to replace are American Express, ☎ freecall 1800-688022, 🖥 www.americanexpress.com/australia, and Thomas Cook, ☎ freecall 1800-127495, 🖥 www.travelex.com.au). You should always keep a record of your cheque numbers separate from your cheques.

Cash Transfers

If you have money transferred to Australia by banker's draft or a letter of credit, bear in mind that it can take up to two weeks to be 'cleared' (i.e. while the bank pockets interest on it). You can also have money sent to you by international money order (via a post office), a cashier's cheque or telegraphic transfer, e.g. via Western Union (the quickest, safest and **most expensive** method). You usually need your passport to collect money transferred from overseas or to cash a banker's draft or other credit note.

Postal orders can be sent from British Commonwealth countries and a giro post office transfer can be made from most countries. If you're sending money overseas, it's best to send it in the local currency, so that the recipient won't need to pay conversion charges. Some countries have foreign exchange controls limiting the amount of money that can be sent overseas. Insured post is the only safe

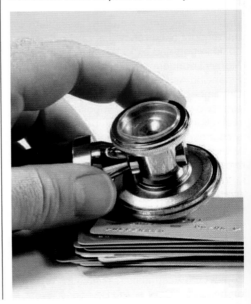

way to send cash, as the insured value is refunded if it's lost or stolen.

You can send money direct from your bank to another bank via an inter-bank transfer. Most banks have a minimum charge for international transfers, which makes it expensive for small sums. Overseas banks may also take a percentage (e.g. 1 or 2 per cent) of the amount transferred (everybody wants a cut!).

CREDIT RATING

Whether you're able to get credit (or how much) in Australia usually depends on your credit rating (or credit score), which is becoming increasingly important in today's credit-driven financial world. Most financial institutions use some kind of credit scoring system and request a credit reference agency report to find out whether you're 'worthy' of having money lent to you (i.e. can afford the exorbitant interest charges!).

⚠️ **Caution**

If you're a new arrival in Australia, a lender may request a report from an agency in your previous country of residence. You may be asked to provide written consent to having your credit rating checked.

Your credit rating depends on many factors, such as your age, occupation and marital status, how long you've held your current job, whether you're a homeowner, where you live, whether you're on the electoral roll, whether you have a telephone and, not least, your credit record. If you're refused credit because of a credit report, you're told and can ask to see the report and challenge anything which is incorrect.

If you have a bad credit rating, it's almost impossible to obtain credit in Australia

unless you're able to provide collateral (i.e. security such as a property). A life assurance policy can be used to provide collateral for a loan. If you're refused credit, look on the bright side: you cannot run up any debts!

You can check the credit rating of a company or person with whom you're planning to do business. Australia's main credit bureau is Veda Advantage (🖥 www.vedaadvantage.com), formerly Baycorp Advantage and before that the Credit Reference Association of Australia and Credit Advantage (perhaps it keeps changing its name to avoid creditors?), which holds records on over 12m people and 1m businesses.

BANKING

Australian banks made huge losses in the '80s and spent the first half of the '90s cost cutting and recovering. The second half of the '90s saw strong growth and a stable credit environment, leading to higher profit margins. Australian banks are currently highly profitable and contribute more in company tax than any other industry to the country's coffers. Nevertheless, many regional (bush or country) banks have closed in recent years (over 2,000 branches have closed in the last decade or so) as banks have slimmed their branch networks. The proliferation of electronic banking (see below) has meant that banks require a much smaller workforce, and they've shed thousands of jobs (bank is a four-letter word with many people in Australia, where they're generally held in low esteem). Consequently, many communities have been left without a local bank, although some towns have successfully fought closures by threatening to withdraw $millions in assets from a bank. In some areas, building societies and credit unions have stepped in to fill the void, but in a small rural town or village, there's likely to be a post office agency, but no bank. A post office account (or an account with one of the banks that allow withdrawals to be made from post offices) is handy for travellers in rural areas.

The major banks have also established low-cost 'kiosk' branches in supermarkets and shopping centres operated by just one or two people and open seven days a week. After initial indifference, supermarket bank kiosks have proved popular and have increased in number.

Banks

The major Australian banks with branches in cities and large towns throughout Australia are the Australia & New Zealand Bank (ANZ, 🖳 www.anz.com.au), the Commonwealth Bank of Australia (🖳 www. commbank.com.au), the National Australia Bank (🖳 nab.com.au), and WBC/Westpac (🖳 www.westpac.com.au), collectively referred to as 'the big four'. These banks also have the widest representation overseas. In addition to the national banks, there are many city, regional and state banks (including drive-in banks).

The major banks offer over 200 'products' (banks no longer provide services), ranging from current accounts (known as transaction accounts) and savings accounts to home insurance and personal superannuation schemes (see page 335). If you do a lot of travelling overseas, you may find the comprehensive range of travel and other services provided by the major banks advantageous. Banks are keen to attract migrants as customers and offer a range of services exclusively to newcomers. The major banks (e.g. the Commonwealth Bank of Australia) provide financial advice and assistance to migrants in a number of countries, and operate a network of Migrant Service Centres in Australia's capital cities. Many services provided by Australian banks are also offered by building societies (see below).

Building Societies & Credit Unions

Building societies and credit unions (collectively referred to here as building societies) compete with banks on a more or less even footing and offer many of the services provided by banks, including cash cards, credit cards, current and savings accounts, insurance, personal loans and travel services. Building societies can also issue cheques in their own name (previously all cheques had to be issued by and cleared through banks). However, building societies don't all offer the same services, types of accounts or rates of interest. If you're looking for a long-term investment, the number of branches may not be of importance, as members of most building societies are linked with the major banks and customers can use their (automated teller machine) ATM networks.

Australian building societies have some 3m members and nearly $13bn in assets, although this represents just 5 per cent of the national financial services market. Added competition in the financial sector in recent years (particularly from mortgage originators) has made life difficult for building societies, many of which are struggling to survive in their present form.

⚠ Caution

Like banks, building societies have been raising their fees to offset smaller margins on home loans.

Building societies don't have an independent dispute scheme but follow a recommended procedure in the event of complaints.

Post Office

GiroPost (styled 'giroPost') is a banking service offered at over 3,000 Australia Post outlets (see **Chapter 6**), involving around ten participating banks and dozens of credit unions.

Business Hours

Normal bank and building society opening hours are from 9 or 9.30am until 4pm, Mondays to Thursdays, and from 9.30am until 5pm on Fridays, with no closure over the lunch period in cities and most towns. Some city branches open from 8am until 6pm, Mondays to Thursdays, and until 8pm on Fridays, while in rural areas banks may open on only one or two days a week. Some banks and building societies open on Saturday mornings, e.g. from 9am until noon. There are bank branches with extended opening hours at international airports and in an increasing number of supermarkets and shopping centres (some open seven days a week). All banks are closed on public holidays. Most banks, building societies and main post offices in Australia have 24-hour ATMs for cash deposits and withdrawals and account balance statements.

Electronic Banking

Australian banks and building societies are in the forefront of electronic banking and over half of all bank transactions are made electronically. Electronic banking includes automated bill payment (BPAY), the use of ATMs (there were over 500,000 in Australia in 2007), smart cards and stored debt cards, electronic funds transfer, telephone and internet banking, and touch-screen customer service terminals. In future, banks will have even fewer branches and it's expected that almost all banking transactions will be done via an ATM, computer or telephone.

Telephone banking (or telebanking) and internet banking are offered by most Australian banks as well as by building societies and credit unions, usually 24 hours a day, seven days a week. Calls may be answered by a recorded message rather

than a real person. Services provided include obtaining account balances, checking interest rates earned/charged, obtaining mortgages and other loans, ordering statements and cheque books, paying bills, providing details of the last five (or more) cheques cleared or the last five transactions, and transferring funds between accounts.

Cheque Accounts

The most common account for day-to-day money management is a cheque account (commonly called a transaction account in Australia), which provides ATM access, a cheque book, an EFTPOS card (see page 363), the facility to pay regular bills by direct debit, telephone banking and possibly other services, such as an overdraft facility. Many people have at least two accounts: a current account for their out-of-pocket expenses and regular transactions, and a savings account (see page 362) for long-term savings. Before opening an account, compare banks' charges and fees (see below), interest rates (e.g. on credit cards and deposits) and the services offered.

If you're planning to work in Australia and are paid fortnightly or monthly, one of your first acts should be to open a current account with a bank, building society or credit union. Your salary is usually paid directly into your account by your employer, and your salary statement is either sent to your home address or given to you at work. Employees who are paid weekly or fortnightly are often paid in cash, in which case it's up to you whether you open an account (although it's difficult to manage without one).

> ☑ **SURVIVAL TIP**
> New arrivals can open an account during their first six weeks in Australia with just a passport.

When opening an account by post, attach a certified photocopy of the pages of your passport showing its number and expiry date, and your signature, photograph and visa (if available). You may also need a copy of your driving licence. If a copy of your passport is sent by post, it must be certified by a professional (such as a doctor, lawyer or teacher) or a person of similar standing with a public position, such as a civil servant, councillor, member of parliament or police officer.

Banks and other financial institutions are required by law (under the Financial Transaction Report Act, 1988) to verify the identity of each signatory to an account. To meet this requirement, you must provide either a reference from a reputable person or specific identification documents.

Most people pay their bills from their current accounts, either by standing order or by cheque. Bills can also usually be paid by telephone.

Bank statements are usually issued monthly (optionally quarterly), and interest is normally calculated daily and paid quarterly. Current accounts pay **very** little interest on account balances, e.g. from 0.1 to 0.5 per cent. If you regularly have $1,000 or more on deposit, you should consider keeping it an account that pays a 'reasonable' interest rate. The minimum opening balance may be nil, although you should bear in mind that you usually need to maintain a much higher balance in order to avoid bank charges (see below).

Bank Charges

Australian banks have increased charges on current account transactions in recent years by as much as 100 per cent (to $4 per transaction in some cases) in an attempt to lure customers away from branches, as electronic banking costs them a fraction of branch transactions, and to recoup their reduced margins on

mortgages and other loans. This caused a public outcry in 2001, when a Parliamentary Commission was set up to investigate bank charges. It was found that customers have little idea what charges are made, and a breakdown of all charges must now be shown on monthly statements.

Charges (often referred to as 'fees', as if they entitled you to a premium service!) commonly levied by banks on current (transaction) accounts include 'account-keeping fees', usually between €2 and €7 per month, irrespective of your account balance, although fees may be waived if you maintain a minimum balance; transaction fees, e.g. 50 cents for a cash withdrawal from an ATM, $1 to clear a cheque, $2 for a counter ('assisted') withdrawal, $6 for cashing a cheque and $15 for stopping a cheque, although some accounts offer a certain number of free transactions (e.g. 5 to 35) each month; and one-off fees of between around $10 are $35 for various other services, such as bank drafts (bank cheques), replacement statements, overdrawing an account and unauthorised cheques. **Few building societies and credit unions impose current account charges.** Debits tax has been abolished.

Banks are increasingly adopting 'user pays' systems, where charges are related to the amount of work involved in processing transactions. This means that there are lower charges for electronic banking than for paper and over-the-counter transactions. Some accounts are exclusively for those who use the electronic banking network to make withdrawals; these levy no charges unless you make over-the-counter withdrawals. Some banks have fee exemptions for customers under the age of 18 or 21, pensioners or tertiary students. Always shop around for the lowest charges. The ABA and Centrelink have produced a joint brochure on how to minimise bank charges.

Cheques

Personal cheques aren't usually accepted as payment in retail outlets in Australia, as they cannot be guaranteed (Australian banks don't issue cheque guarantee cards). Where cheques are accepted, you must usually produce identification, e.g. a driving licence.

Cheques aren't usually crossed, although you can cross your own cheques by drawing two parallel lines across the face. This theoretically provides additional security, because a crossed cheque can be paid only into a bank account and cannot be cashed. There are a number of ways further to safeguard your cheques, one of which is to write 'not negotiable' between the two parallel lines, which means that the cheque cannot be cashed by a third party. Alternatively, you can write 'account payee only' between the lines, which means that the cheque must be paid into the account of the named payee. (For extra security, you can add both 'not negotiable' and 'account payee only' to a cheque.) If you cross out the words 'or bearer' on a cheque, this also prevents anyone except the named person from cashing it. Alternatively, you can arrange with your bank that no cash cheques can be drawn on your account or have the $ limit that can be drawn on any one cheque printed on them.

⚠️ Caution

Take great care when sending cheques by post, particularly for large amounts, as it isn't unknown for cheques to be stolen and paid into another account.

Cheque 'clearing' takes around two to three days (i.e. banks earn interest on your money for this period). Australian cheques are valid for 15 months after the date written on them. **A post-dated cheque can be honoured by your bank before the**

date written on it. To obtain cash from a bank, write the cheque in your own name or write 'cash' alongside 'Pay to' and don't cross it.

Savings Accounts

All banks, building societies and credit unions provide a range of savings accounts, usually referred to as deposit or investment accounts in Australia, many of which are intended for short- or medium-term savings, rather than long-term growth. Other types of savings account include cash management trusts, deeming accounts, mortgage offset accounts and savings investment bonus accounts. Retirement Savings Accounts (RSA) are a kind of superannuation fund (see page 335).

Most banks and building societies offer two basic types of savings account: instant access and term deposit accounts. Instant access accounts, as the name says, allow you access to your money at any time without notification. There's usually a minimum balance, which may be as low as $100 or as high as $5,000. With some high-balance accounts, all deposits and withdrawals must be over $1,000. Interest rates usually depend on the account balance, e.g. $500, $1,000, $5,000 or $10,000.

Non-residents are subject to a withholding tax of 10 per cent on the income earned on bank deposits in Australia (see page 353); this is deducted at source when interest is paid.

Cash Cards

A cash card allows you to withdraw up to around $800 per day from ATMs (see page 366), which are available 24 hours a day, seven days a week (provided they don't run out of money and that you have money in your account). The freedom from queues, bank tellers and bank opening hours provided by cash cards is valuable, and you should think twice before opening an account with a bank or building society which doesn't provide ATMs locally (although most small financial institutions have arrangements with larger banks or building societies). Cash cards can also be used at service stations, supermarkets and other retail outlets throughout Australia, and you can use them to pay for telephone calls in certain public call boxes.

Reloadable 'electronic cash' cards with a stored-value (also known as stored-value cards or SVCs) are being introduced in Australia.

Debit Cards

Most cash cards are also debit cards – known in Australia as Electronic Funds Transfer at Point of Sale (EFTPOS) cards – which are accepted by most retailers and mail-order businesses in Australia and have largely replaced cheques. Half of all card transactions in Australia are made with debit cards. There's no limit to the amount you can pay with a debit card, but you must have the money in your account (or an authorised overdraft).

> ☑ SURVIVAL TIP
>
> **Many retailers, e.g. supermarkets, allow customers to obtain cash (known as 'cash-back') when buying goods with a debit card.**

Many cards can also be used overseas, e.g. Visa or MasterCard EFTPOS cards, to obtain cash and buy goods and services, although there's a charge for obtaining cash.

Credit & Charge Cards

Australia is one of the most credit-oriented societies in the world, and the average Australian owes over $10,000 on credit and charge cards, which are accepted by most retail outlets, whatever their size (although you may have a problem using a credit card in remote areas and small towns or in small shops and restaurants).

The most commonly accepted credit cards in Australia are MasterCard and Visa (and associated cards). Most outlets that accept Bankcard also accept MasterCard and Visa. American Express, Carte Blanche and Diners Club charge cards are also widely accepted. All banks and building societies and many credit unions and major retailers, including most department and chain stores, offer their own credit cards in Australia; some stores don't accept any cards other than their own. Interest rates on store cards are usually **very** high, e.g. up to double what you pay with Visa or MasterCard.

Banks compete fiercely for credit card customers, both on interest rates and the supplementary services attached to cards. The annual fee starts at around $35 for a standard card, around $100 for a 'gold' card and $450 for 'platinum' (ostentation is expensive). The lowest rates are usually offered by credit unions, some of which charge no annual fee, although they may not give you any interest-free credit days. If you spend over a certain sum on your card, e.g. $1,500, the annual fee may be waived. A number of cards can be issued for a single account (a second card is usually issued free). It isn't always necessary to have an account with a financial institution to obtain a credit card.

The annual interest rates charged on credit card balances are between around 11 and 16 per cent. (Banks rarely pass on interest rate cuts to credit card holders.) Most cards offer 15 to 55 days' interest-free credit, although there are no free credit days on some cards.

Credit cards can be used to obtain cash from ATMs (see below) in Australia and overseas, although there's a handling charge and/or commission and a daily

limit, e.g. $500 or $1,000. Interest is levied on cash withdrawals from the date of the withdrawal.

Automated Teller Machines

The big four banks' automated teller machine (ATM) networks are called Autobank (Commonwealth), Flexiteller (National), Handybank (WBC) and Night & Day (ANZ). Some networks are linked so that you can use your cash (and debit and credit) cards in ATMs (commonly known as cash machines) belonging to different banks, giving you access to thousands of cash machines. For example, Commonwealth Bank and WBC are linked, as are ANZ and National Bank. Customers of building societies, credit unions and regional banks also have access to the big four's networks through reciprocal arrangements. Most banks and building societies allow a certain number of free withdrawals per month (e.g. eight) from machines belonging to their own network, but there's a charge (usually at least $1) for

using an ATM belonging to another bank or network.

Other services provided by banks and building societies via ATMs include account balances, mini-statements (usually the last five transactions), cheque book and statement ordering, personal identification number (PIN) changes, deposits (cash and cheques), bill paying (via a bank giro), credit card payments, and transfers between accounts. These services are usually available only via cash machines at branches of your own bank. Some ATMs accept 'smart' cards (i.e. cards with a microchip), which aren't yet standard in Australia.

Complaints

Complaints against banks run into thousands every year, particularly with regard to excessive charges. Most Australian banks are members of the Australian Bankers' Association (ABA), which has a Code of Banking Practice that seeks to foster good relations between banks and their customers (provided it doesn't cost the banks any money), and you should initially make a complaint to the bank.

A banking ombudsman was established in 1989 by the ABA to mediate in disputes between banks and their customers. If you have a dispute with your bank which you're unable to resolve directly, you can take the matter to the Banking and Financial Services Ombudsman, PO Box 3, Melbourne, Victoria 3001 (☎ 1300-780 808, 🖳 www.bfso.org. au). Members agree to abide by the decision of the ombudsman, although if customers disagree with a ruling they aren't obliged to accept it and are free to take it up with a consumer affairs department or office of fair trading, or take legal action.

There's no government- or industry-funded protection scheme for deposits in Australia, as exists in many other countries, and deposit protection varies between banks, building societies and credit unions, none of which provide an explicit guarantee as to the safety of your money. This matter is currently under review by the Commonwealth government and new regulations may be forthcoming.

MORTGAGES

Competition to lend you money is fierce and homebuyers in Australia have a wider variety of home loan finance than is available in many other countries. Mortgages (home loans) in Australia are available from dozens of sources, including banks, building societies, credit unions, finance and insurance companies, mortgage managers, mortgage originators/providers, motoring organisations and state housing authorities. Housing commissions and state banks in some states also provide loans, although eligibility is restricted to low and moderate-income families and there are often long waiting lists. However, despite the increased competition, banks still handle around 80 per cent of new home loans. Westpac bank was the largest lender in 2007, followed by National Australia Bank and ANZ.

> The usual home loan period is 25 years, although it can be anything from 5 to 30 years (or up to the age at which a state pension is paid), while the maximum term for land loans is usually 20 years. Around half of Australian homeowners have a mortgage, the average loan being $225,000 (2007). Many lenders offer extras such as 'free' home insurance and life assurance to attract customers, so it's worth shopping around for the best deal.

The Commonwealth and state governments provide funds for housing loans through the Commonwealth/State Housing Agreement, with interest subsidies provided during the early years of the loan. In most states, the loans are made through co-operative building societies.

After several consecutive interest rate rises, many Australian families are burdened by their loan repayments – figures released in September 2007 show that the proportion of income required by families to meet average loan repayments is over 36 per cent (regional figures vary considerably: 38.5 per cent in NSW, but only 20.6 per cent in ACT). Home loan defaults are on the increase and in some parts of the country, e.g. NSW, financial experts expect a huge rise in the number of defaulters in late 2007/early 2008.

It's usually necessary to have a high income and a secure job to get into and remain in homeownership in Australia. You shouldn't rush into taking out a mortgage, particularly if your income isn't secure. Many people are denied mortgages because of bad credit ratings or insecure employment, which may include the self-employed, who usually need to produce a number of years' tax returns (usually two) unless they choose a 'low-doc' or 'no-doc' mortgage (see page 296). It's possible to take out a mortgage protection policy in case you fall ill, have an accident or are made redundant and are unable to pay your mortgage, although it can be expensive and there are many loopholes. Most lenders offer a 'home loan protection plan', which guarantees repayments in the case of death or permanent disability.

Mortgage Brokers

Almost half of home loans in Australia are secured via the services of a mortgage broker. Using a broker usually means you have access to a wider choice of loans and lenders, and the broker should be able to choose the best loan for your particular circumstances. You should note, however, that brokers earn their living from fees paid by lenders and therefore may not always be impartial. The mortgage broker industry in Australia is currently largely unregulated (the government plans to change this in the near future) and it isn't without its share of 'cowboys'. If you decide to use the services of a mortgage broker, experts recommend you do the following before choosing one:

- Ask around for recommendations.
- Check that your chosen broker is an Accredited Mortgage Consultant and a member of a professional association such as the Mortgage and Finance Association of Australia (MFAA, 🖥 www.mfaa.com.au) or the Financial Brokers Association of Australia (FBAA, 🖥 www.financebrokers.com.au).
- Ensure that the broker has professional indemnity insurance.
- Ask how much the broker is paid and by whom (brokers are usually paid commission by lenders, but some may charge you as well).

Invaluable independent advice and comparative tables of lenders and loans are published in specialist magazines such as *Your Mortgage* in Australia.

Types of Loan

There are numerous types of home loan in Australia, as described below. There's no sub-prime lending on property in Australia.

Fixed Rate & Variable Rate

You can usually choose between a fixed-rate mortgage – at around 7 per cent in mid-2007 – and a variable-rate mortgage – at around 8 per cent in mid-2007. With the latter, the interest rate goes up and down in line with fluctuations in the bank base rate (6.5 per cent in October 2007 – the highest level since 2000). Those who cannot afford an increase in their mortgage repayments are usually better off with a fixed-rate mortgage, where the interest rate is fixed for the term of the loan or a number of years (e.g. one to ten), irrespective of what happens to bank lending rates in the meantime. The longer the fixed-rate period, the lower the interest rate offered. If interest rates go down, you may find yourself paying more than the current mortgage rate, but at least you know exactly what you must pay each month.

Some lenders offer a choice between a 'standard' and a 'basic' variable-rate mortgage. Standard variable-rate loans often include payment flexibility, including:

- additional payments – For example, paying an extra 10 per cent each month can knock five or six years off the repayment term of a 25-year mortgage.

- fixed-variable splits – Most variable-rate loans offer borrowers the option to fix the rate at any time, e.g. when interest rates are rising, and some mortgages combine fixed- and variable-rate loans (sometimes called split fixed/variable rate mortgages), which some analysts recommend as the best compromise. However, this means taking out two loans and incurring higher fees.

- offset accounts – The interest earned on money deposited in an offset account is offset against the interest payable on your loan. This means that a larger part of your repayments goes towards reducing the principal, resulting in significant interest savings and the loan being paid off quicker.

- redraw facilities – These allow you to 're-borrow' money repaid if the need arises.

- variation to payment frequency, e.g. fortnightly instead of monthly – This can help you pay off a loan quicker.

Basic variable-rate loans (known as 'no frills' loans) are usually offer a lower interest rate but are less flexible than standard loans (e.g. they have no offset account or redraw facility).

A small increase or decrease in interest rates makes a significant difference to monthly repayments. For example, a rise or fall of 0.25 per cent on a $300,000 loan over 30 years is equal to $53 a month.

Fixed-rate home loans offer the possibility of fixed interest for the whole loan or part of it for periods of between one and five years, after which time you and your lender review your circumstances and interest rates. Some fixed-rate loans offer benefits such as no fees for lump sum repayments.

To judge whether a fixed-rate mortgage is worthwhile, you must estimate in which direction interest rates are heading (a difficult feat). In October 2007, experts were divided on whether interest rates would continue to go up after two rises in 2007 and three in 2006. In the light of recent increases, however, the number of fixed-rate loans is increasing.

Introductory Rate

Most lenders offer introductory rate (known as 'honeymoon-rate') loans, which offer lower interest rates for a number of months (usually up to 12), meaning lower monthly payments. Once the 'honeymoon' is over, interest rates rise to the standard variable rate. Fees are high for this type of mortgage.

100% Plus

This type of mortgage allows you to borrow 100 per cent of the value of a property plus costs so that a deposit isn't necessary and you need only pay the fees associated with the purchase, such as stamp duty.

Interest rates for this type of loan are usually higher than the standard variable rate and borrowers usually have to take out the lender's mortgage insurance, whose cost can be as high as 2.5 per cent of the amount borrowed.

Low-doc & No-doc

These mortgages are recent additions to the home loan market and were designed for new arrivals in Australia with no credit record and/or little employment history, and the newly self-employed. 'Low-doc' loans, which are available for up to 80 per cent of a property's value, require little documentation to support your claim, e.g. the self-employed need present only three months of business accounts. 'No-doc' loans require no documentation at all and are available for up to 80 per cent of the value. Disadvantages include higher interest rates than the standard variable rate and the fact that you may be tempted to borrow more than you can afford to repay. Low-doc and no-doc mortgages account for less than 10 per cent of the home loan market.

Mortgage experts recommend you reassess your mortgage terms every few years and whenever your circumstances change.

Reverse Mortgages

Known as lifetime mortgages in the UK, reverse mortgages allow the over 60s to borrow between 15 and 45 per cent of the value of their home, the loan being paid in instalments (e.g. monthly) to the homeowner by the bank as a form of income. If you receive a state pension, check that a reverse mortgage doesn't affect (i.e. reduce) your benefits.

Construction Loan

Available for new builds or major renovation work on a property, construction loans are available only at the variable rate of interest. Funds from the loan are withdrawn in stages (you cannot withdraw the whole sum at once) when you need them and you pay interest only on the amount drawn out. Construction loans usually offer various repayment options (e.g. in instalments).

Repayments & Loan Amounts

Your monthly mortgage repayments mustn't usually be more than 30 to 40

80 per cent of the value of a property and is compulsory when the loan is for 100 per cent of the value. The insurance premium is usually between $250 and $500 or 1 per cent of the loan value but is up to 2.5 per cent for 100 per cent loans, and it's normally added to the loan amount. Some lenders insist that you take out their insurance (known as 'captive' insurance), for which you can find yourself paying around 20 per cent above the market rate (shop around for independent mortgage insurance). Mortgage insurance contracts cover the lender and not the borrower.

To get an idea of your potential mortgage repayments, visit 🖥 www. yourmortgage.com.au, where the online calculator provides estimates for repayments depending on the type of mortgage.

Fees & Charges

Mortgages may attract various fees and charges, described below. While mortgage interest rates have generally fallen in recent years, fees have risen. Always make sure that you receive a list of all costs associated with a loan, including discharge fees.

Set-up Fees

Various fees are associated with setting up a mortgage, including:

- legal fees – sometimes waived;
- loan registration fee;
- mortgage application or establishment fee – usually between $0 and $1,650;
- valuation fee – can be up to $300.

Fees vary hugely, so shop around to ensure you obtain the best deal. Some lenders have cut or eliminated fees for setting up mortgages, although they may be clawed back by 'administrative' or 'maintenance' charges, e.g. $60 a month

per cent of your gross basic income – a couple's incomes are combined (some 60 per cent of families paying off a home loan in Australia have two or more wage earners). Sydney owner-occupiers are generally more indebted (or, to use an Aussie euphemism, more highly geared) than Melbourne families. Repayments can be made fortnightly (which can save a considerable amount over the term of a loan) or monthly. Some lenders allow you to reduce your payments by up to 50 per cent for up to six months when taking maternity or paternity leave.

Although it's possible to obtain a loan for the whole cost of a property (i.e. a 100 per cent mortgage), particularly if you're a first-time buyer, most lenders expect borrowers to pay a deposit of 5 to 25 per cent of the purchase price. (The average deposit paid in Sydney is around a third of the value of a property and in Melbourne some 40 per cent.) Housing loan insurance is usually payable when a loan is greater than 75 or or $630 a year, which may apply only to certain types of loan.

Mortgage Stamp Duty

Only three states (NSW, QLD and WA) levy mortgage stamp duty, which will be abolished throughout the country by 1st July 2009. Examples of payments in the three states are as follows:

NSW: $541 on a mortgage of $150,000 and $941 on $250,000. Mortgages on principal residences are exempt. Mortgage stamp duty will be abolished on 1st July 2009.

QLD: $460 on a loan of $150,000 and $860 on $250,000. Mortgage stamp duty will be reduced by 50 per cent from 1st January 2008 and abolished on 1st January 2009.

WA: $300 on a $150,000 mortgage and $500 on a $250,000 mortgage. There are reductions on mortgages for principal residences and mortgages up to $100,000 are exempt. Mortgage stamp duty will be abolished on 1st July 2008.

Discharge Fees

Some mortgages carry discharge (redemption) or exit fees if they're repaid early, e.g. up to $630, plus a state fee ranging from around $50 to $110. While most borrowers never change their lenders, some homeowners re-mortgage every two or three years after shopping around for the best deal available. However, you must do your sums carefully, as changing lenders can be expensive. Some banks offer lower 'loyalty rates' of interest for customers who have maintained a loan for five years or more.

Foreign Currency Mortgages

It's possible to obtain a foreign currency mortgage, e.g. in Japanese yen, Swiss francs or US dollars, all currencies which, with their historically low interest rates, have provided huge savings for some borrowers in the last few decades.

However, you should be cautious about taking out a foreign currency mortgage, as interest rate gains can be wiped out overnight by currency swings. In the '80s many Australians took out Swiss franc loans and were later unable to maintain their payments when the value of the A$ plummeted against the Swiss franc. Most mainstream lenders advise against taking out a foreign currency home loan unless you're paid in that currency.

The conditions for foreign currency loans are much stricter than for local currency loans, e.g. they're generally granted only to high-earners (e.g. those earning a minimum of $100,000 a year) and are usually for a minimum of $200,000 and a maximum of 60 per cent of a property's value. When choosing between a local currency loan and a foreign currency loan, be sure to take into account all costs, fees and possible currency fluctuations. If you have a foreign currency mortgage, you must usually pay commission charges each time you transfer money into a foreign currency to meet your mortgage repayments, although some lenders do this free of charge.

☑ SURVIVAL TIP

Whatever type of home loan you choose, take time to investigate all the options and bear in mind that mortgage advice offered by lenders can be misleading and isn't always to be trusted.

TAXATION

Taxes in Australia vary considerably with the state or territory. Taxes are levied at Commonwealth (federal), state and local government levels. For example, income tax and capital gains tax are levied at federal level. States and territories receive their income from stamp duty on commercial and legal documents (cheques, insurance policies, mortgage transactions, receipts and transfers of land), payroll tax (a state tax imposed on an employer's payroll and the biggest source of income for state governments), taxes on land, spirits (liquor) and motor vehicles, and miscellaneous licence fees. (Since the high court's decision to outlaw state taxes on alcohol, petrol and tobacco, there has been a continuous taxation war between state and federal governments.) The main form of local government tax is property tax, augmented by charges for services such as sewerage and water. There are no gift, inheritance or wealth taxes (Australia is the only OECD country not to have some form of inheritance tax).

The total of direct and indirect taxation is low by international standards, although the government is continually inventing new ways of taxing people, including fringe benefit tax, various taxes on superannuation (private pension) funds, a tax to pay for the public health service, and a tax for not having private health insurance. Australia went through a major reform of the tax system in 2000 and introduced a goods and services tax (GST, a form of value added tax – see page 312) in July 2000, which has been an administrative nightmare for virtually every Australian business.

Among the various Australian eccentricities is the government's financial year, which runs from 1st July to 30th June.

Obtaining Help

Australia has Byzantine tax regulations (the Income Tax Act runs to around 3,300 pages!) and it's possible to receive conflicting information from different tax 'experts' and even from different branches of the Australian Tax Office (ATO). Taxpayers constantly complain of inconsistency in the way the ATO makes its rulings, and you should never trust the

ATO to take only what it should or to credit you all your allowances; although the ATO won't cheat you deliberately, it does make mistakes.

Tax Help is a volunteer service to help certain people complete their tax returns, including Aborigines and Torres Strait Islanders, those on low incomes (including senior citizens), people from non-English-speaking backgrounds, and people with disabilities. The translating and interpreting service (TIS) helps non-English-speaking people with tax questions by setting up a three-way telephone conversation with an interpreter and the tax office (☎ local call rate 13-1450). The languages covered include Arabic, Chinese, Croatian, Greek, Indonesian, Italian, Japanese, Korean, Macedonian, Polish, Serbian, Spanish, Turkish and Vietnamese.

Most TAFE colleges (see page 183), in conjunction with the ATO, run a course explaining the tax system and how to complete tax returns. For general income tax enquiries, contact the ATO's Head

Office, 2 Constitution Avenue, Canberra, ACT 2601 (☎ 13-2861). The ATO runs a comprehensive – if complicated and cumbersome – website (🖥 www.ato.gov.au) where most information is accessible, and there's a 'fax from a tax' information service providing information via fax (☎ 13-2860). A tax appeals system was introduced in 1997 and the ATO also has a problem-resolution service (☎ local call rate 13-2870).

To help you complete your tax return, there are various computer tax programs, such as QuickTax (Reckon Intuit) and SmartTax (Mysterious Pursuit), although they're mainly for 'experts'. Another option is to join Taxpayers Australia, which for an annual fee of around $400 provides you with 24 issues of the latest tax information, a telephone helpline number and a booklet on the current year's tax return (🖥 www.taxpayer.com.au). There are many books published annually about how to reduce your income tax bill, including the *Australian Tax Guide* and the *Australian Master Tax Guide* (Longman).

Using an Accountant

If your tax affairs are complicated and you aren't up to (or haven't time for) 'self-help', you should consider employing an accountant or tax agent (many banks also provide a personal tax service). This applies to most self-employed people, but very few who are on PAYG.

Don't pick an accountant simply by sticking a pin in the telephone book, but ask colleagues or friends if they can recommend someone. If you're self-employed, you should choose an accountant who deals with people in your line of business and who knows exactly what you can and cannot claim.

Accountants' fees vary from around $100 to $400 per hour, so ask in advance what the rates are (they're highest in the major cities). A good accountant usually saves

you more than he charges in fees, but you can reduce these considerably by keeping itemised records of all your business expenses (preferably on a computer), rather than handing over a box of invoices and receipts at the end of each financial year.

Tax File Number

> **☑ SURVIVAL TIP**
> Your tax file number (TFN), consisting of nine digits, is the most important number you will receive in Australia. Without it, you're taxed at the maximum rate (45 per cent) on all your wages (it's that important!).

You also need a TFN to claim sickness and unemployment benefits, to make any investment and to enrol in a fee-free course of higher education. It's required when completing your income tax return and when you start work or change jobs (there are both personal and business tax file numbers).

You can obtain an application form for a TFN from your local ATO. You must produce identification, such as your birth certificate, driving licence or passport with a valid visa, and should receive your TFN around two weeks after making an application. The ATO publishes a brochure, *Applying for Your Tax File Number*, which explains the application procedure. You can also apply online (in 20 minutes) at 🖥 www.ato.gov.au; you need your passport number.

Withholding Tax

When you earn interest income or receive dividends from shares or distributions from unit trust investments, you must ensure that you give your bank your TFN; it isn't compulsory, but Australian banks are required to deduct 'withholding' tax from residents at 45 per cent if you don't! (Your bank is also required to report annually to the ATO the details of interest/dividend income earned and any withholding tax deducted.) If you're a non-resident and don't have a TFN, you'll be charged withholding tax at 10 per cent. However, you may be entitled to a tax refund under double-taxation agreements, so you should include details of withholding tax payments on your tax form.

INCOME TAX

Federal income tax is levied under a two-tier system: the First Class system applies to the self-employed and companies, and the Second Class system, called Pay-As-You-Go (PAYG), is for employees (see page 305). The self-employed pay their tax in arrears, whereas an employee's income tax is deducted at source from his salary by his employer. There's no state income tax

in Australia, although it may be introduced under wide-ranging tax reforms currently under consideration.

The income tax year in Australia runs from 1st July to 30th June (for reasons known only to the tax office), although in certain circumstances an accounting year beginning on a different date may be used for tax purposes. Changes in federal taxation are usually announced in the annual budget in May.

Australian income tax law recognises the following general types of taxpayer: companies, individuals, partnerships and trusts. Specific provisions apply to certain businesses, minors and superannuation funds.

Domicile

Residents of Australia are taxed on their worldwide income and non-residents only on Australian income. You're considered to be resident in Australia for tax purposes if **any** of the following applies:

- you normally reside in Australia;

- you're domiciled in Australia and don't have a permanent place of abode outside the country;

- you spend at least 183 days per financial year in Australia (unless you don't intend to take up Australian residence and have a usual place of abode outside Australia).

Double-taxation Agreements

Despite their name, double-taxation agreements are designed to prevent you paying taxes twice. Under double-taxation agreements, certain foreign residents are exempt from paying Australian tax. Australia has double-taxation agreements with many countries, including Argentina, Austria, Belgium, Canada, China, the Czech Republic, Denmark, Fiji, Finland, France, Germany, Hungary, India, Indonesia, Ireland, Italy, Japan, Kiribati, the Republic of Korea, Malaysia, Malta, the Netherlands, New Zealand, Norway, Papua New Guinea, the Philippines, Poland, Romania, Singapore, the Slovak Republic, South Africa, Spain, Sri Lanka, Sweden, Switzerland, Thailand, the UK, the US and Vietnam. If part of your income is taxed in one of these countries, you won't be required to pay Australian tax on that income.

Foreign employees working in Australia for Australian companies or organisations are subject to Australian tax on their earnings. However, if your stay is for less than six months, you're usually taxed at the (higher) rates applicable to non-residents (see page 304), although double-taxation agreements contain articles dealing with directors, entertainers, government services, professors and teachers, which may alter this position. Income earned by residents from services performed overseas is exempt if you've been employed outside Australia for a continuous period of at least 91 days, provided the income has been taxed overseas.

Depending on your circumstances, you may be required to pay tax on part of your income in your home country and the remainder in Australia. Citizens of most countries are exempt from paying taxes in their home country when they spend a minimum period overseas, e.g. a year. One exception is citizens of the US. American citizens can obtain a copy of a brochure entitled *Tax Guide for US Citizens and Resident Aliens Abroad* from American embassies. If you're in doubt about your tax liability in your home country, contact your embassy or consulate.

Taxable Income

Only a few types of income are exempt from tax, including defence and United Nations payments, education payments, certain pensions, and social security allowances and payments, social security family payments, certain scholarships, bursaries and other educational allowances, and the income of certain non-profit organisations. The tax law makes a basic distinction between income and capital receipts, and generally only income is assessable. However, capital gains made from the sale of assets acquired after 20th September 1985 are included in your taxable income (see **Capital Gains Tax** on page 309). Taxable income also includes certain benefits, dividends and bonuses, foreign income, income from partnerships or trusts, interest, pensions, rental income, salary or wages, and termination payments.

Most government pensions are subject to tax, although a system of rebates ensures that no tax is paid by a pensioner who earns only a small amount of other income. Reductions or exemptions apply to certain other types of income, including lump-sum payments received on retirement, non-cash benefits, irregular income earned by artists, sportsmen, etc., and the income of farmers.

> Those with irregular income are permitted to average their earnings out over five years; the tax payable is calculated according to a complicated formula, taking into account 'normal' income and adding this to one-fifth of your 'abnormal' income over a five-year period.

The profit earned in the operation of a business is added to any other income and you're taxed on the total. Each partner in a partnership is taxed individually on his share of partnership income.

Allowances & Rebates

All taxpayers can claim allowances from their taxable income and rebates in addition to a credit for tax paid during the relevant financial year. Allowances reduce taxable income, but rebates (called credits in some other countries) are subtracted from the tax payable on your taxable income – i.e. rebates are 'worth' the same amount to all taxpayers, irrespective of their tax band.

Most allowances are occupation-specific and must be legitimate expenses incurred in earning your taxable income. They're commonly claimed by employees and include self-education, travel and work expenses. Allowances are also made for certain non-business expenses, such as gifts to approved charities. Allowances must usually be substantiated by documentation, and strict documentation requirements apply where expenses exceed $300 per year. There's a federal government taxation incentive for those who let a property for less than their mortgage repayments, when the loss can be offset against other income. You shouldn't hesitate to claim for anything that you believe is a legitimate business expense. The ATO disallows them if it doesn't agree, but it won't grant you an allowance to which you're entitled but which you've forgotten to claim.

Rebates (also called tax offsets and tax relief) are essentially available only to Australian residents whose dependants also live in Australia. Rebates are made in respect of private health insurance premiums (at 30 per cent provided the insurance is with a registered health fund;

you may choose to claim the rebate as a reduction in your insurance premium) and net medical expenses (including dental, medical and optical aids) over $1,500 that aren't reclaimable from Medicare or private health insurance (at 20 per cent). Rebates don't reduce your Medicare levy (see page 250).

Details of all allowances and rebates for individual taxpayers can be found on the ATO's website (💻 www.ato.gov.au).

Tax Rates

Residents

Australia has four progressive income tax rates for resident taxpayers, which are shown below for the 2007/08 tax year.

Anyone who isn't resident in Australia for a whole financial year receives a pro rata portion of the tax-free allowance ($6,000 per year); for example, if you're resident in Australia for half the tax year, your tax-free allowance is $3,000. Different (usually higher) rates apply to those under the age of 18. There are no reductions for couples in Australia, where the same tax rates apply to married and single individuals.

Non-residents

There's no tax-free allowance for non-residents with business and trading income in Australia, who are taxed as shown opposite. Note that non-residents should obtain a tax file number (see page 301)

Taxable Income	Tax Rate	Cumulative Tax
Up to $6,000	0%	
$6,001 to $30,000	15%	$3,600
$30,001 to $75,000	30%	$17,100
$75,001 to $150,000	40%	$47,100
Over $150,000	45%	

Taxable Income	Tax Rate	Cumulative Tax
Up to $30,000	29%	$8,700
$30,001 to $75,000	30%	$22,200
$75,001 to $150,000	40%	$52,200
Over $150,000	45%	

and quote it to their employer or they will be taxed at the maximum rate of 45 per cent.

PAYG

The Pay-As-You-Go (PAYG) system of tax collection applies to salary and wage earners and includes superannuation and termination payments. Under PAYG, an employee's tax is deducted from his gross salary at source by his employer, who forwards it to the ATO. If you have no income apart from your salary or wages, PAYG covers your entire tax liability. Any additional income, e.g. part-time employment or income from investments or savings, whether tax is deducted at source or not, must be declared to the ATO. Nevertheless, you must lodge a tax return if you received more than $6,000 in taxable income during the financial year. If you have non-salary income to declare, you'll receive a credit for your PAYG payments against any tax due.

You must give your employer your tax file number (see page 301), or you could be taxed at the highest rate. If you want to receive your $6,000 tax-free allowance (and who doesn't?), you must lodge an *Employee Declaration Instalment Form* with your employer; otherwise tax is deducted from **all** your income.

The PAYG scheme is disadvantageous to employees, who in many cases would be entitled to claim larger and more allowances if they were classified as self-employed (they would also have the benefit of paying their tax in arrears). For this reason, many employees disguise themselves as self-employed contractors (the practice is estimated to cost the government at least $100m per year). However, thanks to the recent introduction of WorkChoices legislation, companies are no longer able to pay employees as self-employed 'contractors' to avoid fringe benefit tax, the

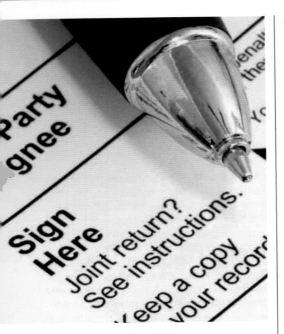

superannuation guarantee and workers' compensation payments.

If your most recent income tax assessment shows more than $2,000 of gross investment or business income or if your most recent income tax return resulted in a tax debt of over $500, you'll receive a letter from the Taxation Office advising you that you must pay PAYG instalments, i.e. advance payments against your next tax bill.

If you pay PAYG tax, make sure that the tax deducted is correct and never hesitate to dispute a tax bill with which you disagree.

Fringe Benefit Tax

Fringe benefit tax (FBT) was introduced in 1986 in order to reduce the amount of non-cash, non-taxable benefits (or 'perks') offered to employees by employers as part of their salary package. FBT is payable by employees on various benefits, including children's private education, company cars for private use, free or subsidised accommodation, free holiday travel, low-interest or interest-free loans, private health insurance, airline transport provided free or at a discount to employees in the travel industry, discounted goods or services provided by an employer in excess of a specified threshold, entertainment expenses, payment or reimbursement of private expenses on behalf of employees, and the waiver of employee loans or debts.

Company cars are taxed at between 7 and 26 per cent depending on the business 'mileage'. However, leases of luxury cars as part of executive salary packages are exempt. A portion of a living-away-from-home allowance paid to employees may also be subject to FBT, although 'reasonable' costs for food and accommodation aren't. Staff canteens, employee share acquisition schemes and superannuation schemes are exempt from FBT. Frequent-flyer schemes aren't taxable, even when your employer pays the membership fees, and childcare provided on 'business premises' or a building controlled by your employer is also exempt (including employer-sponsored/leased places at childcare centres).

FBT is paid at the rate of 46.5 per cent. The FBT tax year is different from the financial year (just to confuse you even further) and runs from 1st April to 31st March. Payments must be made quarterly – by the 28th of July, October, January and April – each payment being equal to 25 per cent of the previous year's liability, the balance being payable when your annual tax return is filed. An employer must usually file an annual FBT return by 28th April each year and fringe benefits are recorded on the employee's payment summary (just in case you forget to declare any of them!).

Self-employed

The business structure you choose when establishing a business is vital in ensuring that you pay no more tax than is necessary (most family businesses operate a family trust in order to reduce taxes). In Australia the self-employed include sole traders and those in a partnership, and not a limited company or trust. If you have a limited company, you must pay corporate or company tax on your profits and need the services of an accountant.

☑ SURVIVAL TIP

It's important to obtain expert legal advice before establishing a business or starting work as a self-employed person in Australia.

Like everything to do with tax law, the regulations applying to the self-employed are complicated and time-consuming and are estimated to cost some $7bn a year in lost time. Not surprisingly, some 90 per cent of the self-employed use a tax agent (see page 375) to complete their tax returns.

From a tax point of view, you're generally better off being self-employed than employed, as you're eligible to claim more allowances in the form of business expenses, including telephone bills, travel to and from work, and work clothes or uniforms. Another advantage for the self-employed is the delay between making profits (if they manage to do so) and paying tax on them, as the self-employed usually pay their tax in arrears.

Recent court cases have declared that, under the current tax laws, airline pilots, bicycle/motorcycle couriers and taxi drivers are independent contractors and are therefore entitled to be treated as self-employed. In the light of these decisions, the ATO sidelined proposals that would have re-classified thousands of self-employed contractors as employees subject to PAYG tax. Nevertheless, an estimated 75,000 people pretend that they're self-employed in order to claim extra allowances.

Company Tax

For taxation purposes, companies include all bodies or associations (corporate and non-corporate), but not partnerships, where partners are taxed individually. In the 2006/07 financial year, companies were liable to pay tax on profits at a flat rate of 30 per cent. Employers are also liable to fringe benefit tax on non-cash benefits made available to employees (such as company cars and low-interest loans – see above). A company has its own tax file number (see page 353) and may also need a GST registration number (see page 312). The date for filing depends on the company's financial year; tax is usually paid in instalments in the year following the year of the tax liability, e.g. tax owed on 2007 income is paid in 2008.

Income Tax Returns

Even if you're an employee on PAYG and have no non-salary income, you must lodge a tax return in Australia if you received more than $6,000 in taxable income during the financial year. Returns must be lodged by 31st October for the previous tax year, e.g. the tax return for the 2007/08 tax year (ending 30th June 2008) must be lodged by 31st October 2008. If you're expecting a refund, the earlier you lodge your return, the quicker you're likely to receive it. If you're unable to meet the deadline because of circumstances beyond your control, you should request permission to lodge at a later date in writing and **before the deadline** to the office where you last lodged.

The ATO provides a comprehensive free *TaxPack* for individual taxpayers, which is available from newsagents', post offices and tax offices (it's also available in some other countries). It contains tax return forms (including spare copies in case you make a mistake!) and instructions on how to complete them. A copy is delivered to all households just before the end of the financial year (30th June).

The tax office where you must lodge your return is determined by your postcode; a list of offices and relevant postcodes is included in the *TaxPack*. You can post your tax return or lodge it personally in the box provided at the office. You can also lodge your tax return electronically by using 'e-tax', a free service provided by the ATO.

☑ SURVIVAL TIP

Keep a copy of your tax form and anything else you send to the ATO. This is useful if your tax form is lost in the post or there are any queries.

Also keep a copy of all documentation (invoices, receipts, statements, etc.) which substantiates claims made in your tax return. Records must be kept for three and a half years for salary and wage earners, and five years for the self-employed (seven years for vehicle- and travel-related expenses). Some tax returns are audited (see page 382), and you may be penalised if the information provided is found to be incorrect. As in most countries, the self-employed are **much** more likely to be audited than employees.

Although tax returns are relatively easy to follow and understand, only 30 per cent of taxpayers complete their own returns and many use a tax agent or accountant (see **Using an Accountant** on page 375), the cost of which is tax deductible. A tax agent has the responsibility for completing your return correctly and is liable for any errors. He will (or should) also ensure that you claim for all the allowances and rebates to which you're entitled. A tax agent usually charges around $100 to complete a tax return for an 'average' taxpayer, although additional fees are charged for extra services; accountants are more expensive. Shop around and obtain a few quotations – some agents offer a free initial consultation.

Payment

After around eight weeks, you receive a *Notice of Assessment* from the ATO, which is an itemised account of the tax you owe. At the bottom of the assessment is your tax debt or, if you're due a refund, your refund cheque (lucky you!). Your notice of assessment tells you when you must pay by in order to avoid incurring a penalty. If you don't agree with the ATO's assessment, you can lodge an appeal.

If the amount owed is over $8,000, you can make the payment in quarterly instalments. Tax can be paid in person at a tax or post office, or by post by cheque or postal order (payable to the Deputy Commissioner of Taxation), which must be sent with the bottom section of your notice of assessment. If you use a tax agent (see above) who lodges returns electronically, your tax bill (or refund) can be paid directly from (or into) a bank, building society or credit union account.

If you're unable to pay your bill on time, contact your tax office and ask for an extension. You need to give a reason for needing an extension (penniless?) and, if it's granted, you're charged interest at a daily rate (equal to 20 per cent per annum) on the amount outstanding after the due date.

PROPERTY & LAND TAXES

Property tax (called council taxes or rates in Australia) is levied by councils on homeowners to pay for local services such as footpaths, health inspections, libraries, parks and recreational facilities, community and welfare services, roads, rubbish collection and disposal (which may be charged separately), and town planning and building control. In some states there's a swimming pool levy to ensure compliance with safety standards and fire service levies are payable in many areas. Tax rates vary with the 'rateable value' of a property, officially called the 'unimproved capital value' (UCV) or the 'capital improved value' (CIV), which is reassessed every two to four years by the Valuer General's Department. When values are reassessed, rates cannot rise more than a certain amount, e.g. 50 per cent (a process known as 'capping') and the increase is usually spread over two or three years.

Rates are levied annually but are often paid quarterly. In some council areas, there's a rebate (e.g. 5 per cent) for prompt payment. Pensioners usually receive a concession, e.g. between 20 and 50 per cent. Council rates vary hugely depending on the state and council, and tend to be higher in large cities, where there are more council services. For a home valued at $250,000, you can pay anything between $500 and $1,500 per year.

Land tax is levied on the ownership of property in all states and territories except the Northern Territory. Its calculation is based on the 'actual unimproved value' (AUV) of land (known simply as the rate) at a prescribed date, e.g. 31st December in NSW, which is determined by a state's Valuer General. Land tax is often expensive and regarded by many as an obstacle to home ownership; the Real Estate Institute of Australia headed a national campaign in 2007 to persuade state governments to abolish all state property taxes, but with land tax revenue

in the tax year 2005/6 amounting to over $2m states are understandably reluctant to scrap it.

Payments are usually made quarterly, but most states offer the option of monthly payment. Many states have a threshold below which no land tax is payable and in some states principal residences are exempt provided you've lived in the property for at least six months. Details of current land tax rates in each state can be found in *Buying a Home in Australia* (Survival Books – see page 477).

CAPITAL GAINS TAX

Australia doesn't have a separate capital gains tax; profits made on the sale of certain assets are included in your income tax liability. The part of a gain that's subject to tax is the difference between the purchase cost and the sale price after the latter has been reduced by indexation and any losses. However, calculating your liability can a complex procedure (see Liability Calculation below) and the amount of tax you pay is calculated by adding 20 per cent of the total gain to your other income, calculating the extra tax due on this portion, and then multiplying it by five (the ATO never makes anything simple). Capital losses can be used to offset gains, either in the current year or in future years without a time limit, but cannot be used to offset other income. The sale of an asset that generates a capital gain or loss is known as a 'capital gains event' in Australia.

Tax may be payable on the sale of equipment and plant, the 'good will' of a business, property (real estate) other than your principal home (see below), shares, and trust distributions. What are termed 'listed personal use assets', including money and works of art and antiques, are also taxable if the purchase price was over $10,000 and they weren't gifts or loans. Exemptions from CGT normally include the following:

- inheritances;

- all assets acquired before 20th September 1985;

- vehicles for personal use;

- collectables valued at less than $500;

- 'personal use assets' valued at less than $10,000;

- main residences if the property has been your home for the entire period of your ownership, has not been let and is on land of less than two hectares.

However, your liability for CGT depends on your residence status, as there are different rules for Australian residents (for tax purposes, temporary residents and foreign residents. Foreign and temporary residents are liable for CGT on fewer assets than permanent residents. Given

the complexity of the rules, if you plan to become a temporary Australian resident or to cease to be an Australian resident, take expert advice as to your possible CGT liability.

Individuals are entitled to a discount of up to 50 per cent on CGT if they use the discount method to calculate their CGT liability (see below). Small businesses (with assets up to $6m) are entitled to four capital gains tax concessions: a 15-year exemption from capital gains tax; a 50 per cent 'active asset' reduction; a retirement exemption, where you're entitled to a lifetime tax-free gain of $500,000 on the sale of a business (if you retire before the age of 55, the amount must be paid into a superannuation or similar fund); and a 'roll-over' (deferral of CGT payment, which is also available to individuals under certain circumstances). All these concessions are subject to certain conditions and you should seek advice from a professional tax adviser.

Liability Calculation

Working out whether you're liable for CGT is only the start of your complications:

there are three methods of calculating your liability (see below) depending on how long you owned each asset and/or when you bought it, and in some cases you have a choice (or you can stick a pin in).

> **☑ SURVIVAL TIP**
>
> **For assets that have been owned for more than 12 months, the tax authorities suggest that you calculate your CGT liability using both the indexation and the discount method to see which is more favourable.**

Indexation Method

This calculation can be used only for assets acquired before 21st September 1999 and assets that have been owned for more than 12 months. The indexation factor (the result of dividing the consumer price index/CPI for the quarter when you sold your asset by the CPI of the quarter when you bought the asset – figures for each quarter are available on the ATO website, 🖥 www.ato.gov.au) is multiplied by your purchase and selling costs. The resulting figure is known as the 'cost base indexed' and you subtract this from your capital proceeds. The final figure is your CGT liability.

Example: A second home is bought in June 1991 for $150,000 plus $7,000 in purchase costs and fees (effective purchase price: $157,000) and sold in October 2006 for $350,000 plus $5,500 in selling costs and fees:

STEP 1 – Calculate the indexation factor: 123.4/106.0 = 1.16

STEP 2 – Multiple the indexation factor by your effective purchase price: 1.16 x $157,000 = $182,120.

STEP 3 – Add selling costs and fees to the above figure: $5,500 + $182,120 = $187,620 (cost base indexed).

STEP 4 – Subtract the cost base indexed from your selling price: $350,000 - $187,620 = $162,380.

You're therefore liable for CGT on $162,380.

Discount Method

This calculation can be used only for assets that have been owned for more than 12 months. The cost base is subtracted from the capital proceeds, then any capital losses are deducted as well as the relevant discount percentage. The resulting figure is your CGT liability.

Example: The same as for the indexation method above:

STEP 1 – Calculate your cost base: $150,000 + $7,000 + $5,500 = $162,500.

STEP 2 – Subtract your cost base from the capital proceeds: $350,000 - $162,500 = $187,500.

STEP 3 – Apply the discount for individuals: $187,500 x 50% = $93,750.

You're therefore liable for CGT on $93,750.

Other Method

The 'other' method (yes, it really is called that!) is only for assets that have been owned for less than 12 months. The cost base is subtracted from the capital proceeds and the result is your CGT liability.

Example: A second home is bought in September 2006 for $350,000 plus $12,000 in purchase costs and fees (effective purchase price: $362,000) and sold in July 2007 for $395,000: $395,000 - $362,000 = $33,000. You're therefore liable for CGT on $33,000.

The ATO has a telephone helpline for CGT queries (13-2861) and the website has comprehensive information on all aspects of CGT including a useful glossary of terms (🖥 www.ato.gov.au – go to 'Individuals' and then 'Capital Gains Tax').

GOODS & SERVICES TAX

Goods and services tax (GST), which was introduced in 2000, is similar to value added tax (VAT) in western European countries and is levied at a flat rate of 10 per cent on most goods and services. GST is included in most quoted prices, although some items are exempt, such as basic foods, cars for the disabled and certain medical aids and appliances. There are also 'compensatory measures' such as the Educational Textbook Subsidy, which the government offered to students when they objected to the 10 per cent increase in the price of books.

Most businesses are required to register for GST and most must lodge a quarterly return to pay or claim GST, although if a company's annual turnover exceeds $20m, a monthly return must be made.

For information about duty and tax on imported vehicles, see **Importing a Vehicle** on page 260. For information on GST refunds for tourists see **GST Refunds** on page 474.

COST OF LIVING

No doubt you'd like to know how far Australian dollars will stretch and how much money (if any) you'll have left after paying your bills. The standard of living in Australia has increased considerably for all income levels in the last 20 years, when incomes have increased much faster for the rich than the poor and, in recent years, many people in 'middle Australia' reckon that life is becoming more expensive.

Australia's consumer price index (CPI) gives an indication of how prices have risen (or fallen) over the past year. The CPI, which sceptics believe stands for 'con people incessantly', is calculated from a basket of basic goods and services, including computer equipment, financial fees and higher education fees but not mortgage interest rates. The CPI increased by 1.9 per cent between September 2006 and September 2007, the highest rises being in the price of housing (up 4.2 per cent), education (4.1 per cent), financial and insurance services (3.2 per cent) and alcohol and tobacco products (3.1 per cent). In the same period, the cost of household goods and services fell by 1.6 per cent and that of transport 0.9 per cent. Australia's central bank raised interest rates by a quarter of a percentage point to 6.75 per cent in November 2007.

Manufactured goods tend to be expensive in Australia, particularly imported goods, including automobiles, clothes and other manufactured items, which are generally more expensive than in Europe or North America. Transport costs between major cities are high owing to the large distances involved, although fuel is cheaper than in Europe.

The price of food is similar to the US and around 25 per cent less than most European countries. Approximately $400 should be sufficient to feed two adults for a month in most areas (excluding alcohol, caviar and fillet steak). The prices of staple foods in Australia's capital cities are listed in the monthly British newspaper *Australian Outlook* (see **Appendix B**) and a free *Property Value Guide* is published annually by the Commonwealth Bank of Australia.

The cost of living in rural areas is, not surprisingly, lower than in the major cities (particularly housing). Sydney is among the most expensive cities in the southern hemisphere, with a similar cost of living to Rome and Vienna. Perth is Australia's second-most expensive city and Melbourne the third. There's little difference in the cost of living between Adelaide, Brisbane and Perth.

Even in the most expensive cities, however, the cost of living needn't be astronomical. If you shop wisely, compare prices and services before buying and don't live too extravagantly, you may be pleasantly surprised at how little you can live on.

Bondi Beach, Sydney, NSW

15.
LEISURE

The leisure and tourist industry is one of Australia's largest, providing direct or indirect employment for over 550,000 people. Australia is one of the world's top tourist destinations, and overseas visitors (mostly, in order of visitor numbers, from New Zealand, Japan, the UK, the US, Singapore, China and South Korea) numbered almost 5.5m in 2005/06 and are growing, accounting for around $20bn of the country's earnings (some 7 per cent of GDP); one of Australia's biggest sources of income is 'frugal' backpackers, who spend an average of around $5,500 each. The 2000 Olympics in Sydney gave a boost to Australia's position as one of the world's leading tourist destinations, and the city is regularly voted among the top three tourist destinations outside Europe, along with Cape Town and San Francisco.

Australia is one of the world's most beautiful countries, with a wide range of unusual landscapes, including magnificent beaches, spectacular countryside and parks, mountains, waterways and the desolate tranquillity of the outback. It's a country of infinite variety, offering something for everyone: warm seas for watersports enthusiasts, historic towns and bustling cosmopolitan cities, a lively nightlife and club scene, superb wines and cuisine, and a wealth of art and serious music.

Until the '70s, Australia was (with some justification) considered to be a cultural desert, the only artistic attraction being the country's 60,000-year Aboriginal heritage. However, the arts have flourished in the last few decades and now match or surpass those found in many 'old world' countries. Australia has a rich history of achievement in arts such as architecture, ballet, drama, film, literature, music, opera, painting and sculpture. The main funding (over 1,700 grants each year) for the arts comes from the Australia Council, and there are further contributions from state and local governments and corporate sponsorship. Nevertheless, Australians' appreciation of the arts still lags far behind their love of sport, which is the country's most popular leisure activity (whether taking part or spectating) – see **Chapter 16**.

The most popular leisure activities apart from sport include visiting animal and marine parks, museums, art galleries and botanical gardens, cinema-going, and watching dance shows, musicals, operas, plays and music concerts. There are modern performing arts centres in the main cities, many of which vie for the title 'arts capital of Australia', while cinemas, concert halls, galleries and theatres abound in the major towns and cities. In addition to the more formal events, a profusion of free concerts and entertainment is staged in public parks, shopping and entertainment centres, including folk, jazz, opera, and rock and classical concerts, plus impromptu shows by an assortment of acrobats, buskers, dancers, fire-eaters, jugglers and mime artists.

> A wealth of festivals and carnivals is held in Australia throughout the year and includes art, beer, folk, food, harvest, music and wine festivals, and agricultural shows and surf carnivals.

Australian cities stage a number of prestigious arts festivals, including the biennial Adelaide Festival (2008, 2010, etc.), which is modelled on the Edinburgh Festival and includes dance, musical and theatrical performances from around the world, with a 'fringe' festival. Other major arts festivals include the Festival of Perth (February), the Melbourne International Comedy Festival (April), the Melbourne International Festival (October) and the National Festival of Australian Theatre (Canberra, October). Most states stage a Royal Agricultural Show, usually in September or October (Sydney's Royal Easter Show is a notable exception), which are much more than 'simply' agricultural shows and include a wide range of displays and entertainment. One of the wackiest events is the Todd River Regatta held in Alice Springs in September, when the Todd River is dry! Tickets for most major entertainment and sporting events can be purchased from BASS, Ticketek and Ticketmaster ticket agencies (they can also be purchased on the internet), which have outlets in all the main towns and cities (there's a surcharge of around $5 per ticket).

Australia offers an abundance of beautiful cities, many of which resemble large country towns. Sydney and Melbourne enjoy an intense rivalry for the title of Australia's premier city. Sydney (Australia's most sophisticated and exciting city) usually wins hands down, thanks largely to its peerless setting ('Venice of the 21st century'), although Melbourne is Australia's cultural and gastronomic capital, and its subtle charms tend to grow on you. The capital, Canberra, is home to the country's foremost art collections, although many people consider it a boring town with little charm. Other major cities include Adelaide, Brisbane, Darwin, Hobart and Perth, all of which have unique attractions.

However, despite the multifarious attractions of its lively cities, Australia's foremost and most enduring appeal is its immense natural beauty, which owes little to man's intervention. Getting away from it all isn't difficult in Australia, with its many lakes and rivers, miles of excellent beaches, and areas of wilderness bigger than many countries. Australia is a country of endless contrasts and colour, with an amazing variety of environments, ranging from bleak, unearthly deserts to lush tropical rain-forests, from palm-fringed sandy beaches and stunning reefs to majestic snowfields, from sparkling blue seas and remote tropical islands to rugged mountains and spectacular rock formations, and from rolling farmlands and vineyards to wild rivers and vast lakes.

All major cities offer sightseeing trips and cruises on local waterways, which may include coffee, lunch and dinner cruises (often including a show). Longer cruises are also available, including trips to the Great Barrier Reef from ports in northern Queensland, many of which use glass-bottomed boats to allow a view of the marine life. There are paddle-wheelers at Echuca-Moama and Mildura in Victoria.

Australia boasts an abundance of natural wonders, many of which are World Heritage Sites, including Ayers Rock (now 'officially' known by its Aboriginal name, Uluru), Bool Lagoon, the Dandenongs, the Ranges, the Flinders Ranges, the Grampians, the Great Barrier Reef (the world's most magnificent

Perth, WA

TOURIST INFORMATION

There are tourist offices, travel centres, visitor centres and visitor information bureaux in all cities, large towns and resorts, although few organisations maintain information desks at airports or major railway stations. All states have Tourist Commissions, which publish a wealth of information and also act as booking agencies for transport companies, hotels and other accommodation. These have offices in state capitals, on major highways at state borders, and in some regional centres. Many smaller towns have tourist offices run by local councils and regional tourist associations.

There are no state-run tourist information offices in Queensland, where tourist offices are often privately operated and act as booking agents for hotels and travel and tour companies.

coral reef), Kakadu National Park, Katherine Gorge, the Murray River, the Naracoorte Caves, the Snowy Mountains, the Tasmanian Wilderness and the Yarra Valley, to name but a few. It's home to a plethora of unique and fascinating flora and fauna, including unusual or unique mammals such as the duck-billed platypus, kangaroos, koala bears, possums, wallabies and wombats.

If you're spending a short time in Australia, bear in mind that it's a vast country; don't try to see it all in a few weeks, which is impossible. If you rush through the outback by train or car, you see little and the country appears to consist of a vast nothingness. However, if you take your time and do a bit of walking, you experience unexpected wonders. There are various organised tours, including 'soft-adventure' holidays (e.g. crocodile or shark watching, rather than a close encounter with the sharp end) and camel safaris.

Tourist offices can provide you with a wealth of information about local accommodation, attractions, car hire, package holidays, public transport, restaurants, sporting events, sports facilities, tours and much more. Offices can provide information on a wide range of leisure activities and sports, so you should mention any special interests when making enquiries. The opening hours of city offices are restricted by international standards, e.g. from 9am until 5pm, Mondays to Fridays, from 9am to between 1 and 4pm on Saturdays, and from 10 or 11am until 4pm on Sundays.

Australia is promoted abroad by Tourism Australia (⌨ www.tourism.australia.com or ⌨ www.australia.com), and most Australian states also maintain tourist offices in a number of countries, including the UK and the US. Tourism Australia has offices in Auckland, Bangkok, Frankfurt, Hong

Kong, Kuala Lumpur, London, Los Angeles, Seoul, Shanghai, Singapore, Taipei and Tokyo.

A plethora of travel guides are dedicated to Australia, including Lonely Planet's *Australia*, which is the most comprehensive guidebook, containing 1,000 pages. Other leading guidebooks include Frommer's *Australia From $50 A Day,* the *Insight Guide to Australia, The Michelin Green Guide to Australia* and *The Rough Guide to Australia.* State motoring organisations (see page 238) also provide tourist and touring information, and leisure information is available on the internet, e.g. CitySearch Sydney (💻 www.sydney.citysearch.com. au).

Most cities and regions publish free entertainment magazines and newspapers (e.g. the *Sydney City Hub*) containing maps and a wealth of useful information about local attractions and events (distributed by hotels, information bureaux, tourist offices and transport companies), and many local councils publish a 'leisure

directory'. Major newspapers publish weekly guides, and there's a variety of commercial entertainment magazines, such as *Entertainment Guide* magazine in Melbourne.

A lot of information is published specifically for backpackers and budget travellers, such as the free magazine *TNT for Backpackers,* available from TNT, Level 4, 46–48 York Street, Sydney, NSW 2000 (☎ 02-9299 4811, 💻 www.tntmagazine. com) or, in the UK, The TNT Group, 14–15 Childs Place, Earl's Court, London SW5 9RX (☎ 020-7373 3377).

ACCOMMODATION

The quality and standard of hotels and other accommodation varies considerably. It includes apartments, bed and breakfast accommodation, boutique hotels, budget hotels, farms, guesthouses, hostels, international five-star luxury hotels, motels and resort hotels. Accommodation other than guesthouses, motels and private hotels must provide a public bar to serve alcohol (guesthouses don't have permits to serve alcohol).

Sydney has a huge range of accommodation, including around 21 five-star hotels (the Regent is rated one of the best in the world). However, the widest choice of accommodation is to be found in Queensland, where tourism is the main industry and there's a wealth of apartments, hostels, luxury hotels, and motels in all resort areas. On the other hand, in country and remote areas, the choice of accommodation is severely restricted, and it's wise to obtain recommendations unless you're prepared to put up with the most basic accommodation.

Motoring organisations (see page 238) publish guides to hotels, motels and other accommodation. These include the *A-Z Australian Accommodation Guide,* the NRMA *Accommodation Directory* and

Weekends for Two, an accommodation guide published bi-annually. The NRMA *Accommodation Directory* lists bed and breakfast accommodation, guesthouses, hotels, motels and serviced apartments throughout Australia. For general information, contact the Australian Hotels Association (☎ 02-6273 4007, 🖳 www.aha. org.au).

In cities there are hotel booking agencies such as the Countrylink New South Wales Travel Centre in Sydney (☎ local call rate 13-2232). There are accommodation information boards at major airports and at railway and bus stations with direct-dial free telephones from which you can book rooms, although these are generally only in up-market hotels.

Hotels

Major groups operating four- and five-star hotels in major cities include Accor, ANA, Beaufort, Hilton, Holiday Inn, Hyatt, InterContinental, Jewel Hotels and Resorts, Matson, Mirvac, Nikko, Parkroyal, Peppers, Radisson, Ramada, Regent, Ritz Carlton, Rydges, Select, Sheraton, Southern Pacific Hotels, Tradewinds, Vista, and Waratah Inns. Most top hotel chains have freecall 1800 booking numbers. Three- to four-star chains include All Seasons Resorts, Best Western, Centra, Country Comfort, Flag, Metro Inn, Quality Pacific and Travelodge.

> The term 'private hotel' is used to denote a hotel which doesn't serve alcohol. Other terms used for an unlicensed hotel are guesthouse (see page 397), inn and lodge.

Confusingly, the term inn is also used to mean motel and, simply, drinking establishment; for this reason, it's avoided in this section. Breakfasts at private hotels are usually huge and excellent. You may come across 'boutique hotels', which are small hotels more like guesthouses, often stylish and aimed at 'trendy' customers. There are old colonial-style hotels in country and outback areas, many of which have been refurbished in recent years. These include National Trust accommodation in pre-1901 buildings, full of character (the bar may also be full of characters) with eccentric owners and bizarre regulations.

Room rates usually vary with the season. The low season is generally from May to November (winter). However, in the centre and tropical north, winter is normally the best time to visit and is therefore the high season; in the summer, rates drop by up to 30 per cent. There's a lack of accommodation in some cities (such as Sydney, where many hotels average over 90 per cent occupancy), particularly budget accommodation, although prices remain reasonable. The busiest period is between November and mid-May, beds being almost impossible to find from mid-December to late January in cities and resorts if you haven't booked. You can obtain discounts of up to 50 per cent for weekly bookings, stand-bys, weekend and low season stays. Travel agents who buy rooms in bulk may be able to offer you a better rate than you can obtain yourself, and motoring organisations also offer member discounts. Many airlines sell vouchers offering reduced rates at motel chains.

The following table is a **rough** guide to per night room prices (prices are usually quoted per room and not per person):

Star Rating	Price Range
1	$20 to $50
2	$55 to $85
3	$80 to $150
4	$150 to $250
5	$230 to $400

Quoted prices generally include all taxes except goods and services tax (GST) at 10 per cent. There's also a 5 per cent accommodation tax in the Northern Territory. Some hotels close on Sundays and public holidays, as they cannot afford to pay staff the high overtime rates demanded.

Budget hotels are in short supply in Australia and, if you're looking for cheap accommodation, your best bet is a bed and breakfast (see page 321), guesthouse (see page 322), hostel (see page 323) or pub (see below). If you don't need to be in the middle of town, suburban hotels offer better value. The cheapest hotel rooms are usually from $20 to $50 for a single and $35 to $70 for a double (some also have suites/triples). Rooms are usually significantly cheaper by the week, e.g. $150 for shared rooms and $230 for doubles. Check whether breakfast is included.

Facilities

A 'double' room usually has twin single beds; if you want a double bed, you should ask for one when booking. Many hotel rooms have a refrigerator stocked with cold drinks (where you can also keep your own drinks cold), and an honour system operates whereby guests are trusted to pay for what they consume. In some hotels a toaster is provided, in which case you're given sliced bread for breakfast. Telephone calls from hotel rooms are expensive and it's best to stock up with 20 cent coins and call from the foyer. When calling from your room, you must usually dial 9 for the hotel operator and 0 to get an outside line. Air-conditioning (or at least ceiling fans) are provided in most hotel rooms, particularly in the Northern Territory, Queensland and Western Australia.

Breakfast in top class hotels is expensive, at around $15 to $20 for a continental buffet breakfast and $18 to $25 for a cooked breakfast. Some luxury hotels

have limited room service and impose surcharges at weekends.

Motels

There's a wide choice of modern, comfortable motels (also called motor hotels, motor inns and inns) throughout Australia. Motels are star-rated in the same way as hotels (see page 319). The major chains are A1, Best Western, Budget, Country Comfort, Flag International, Metro Inns, and Quality Inns. In remote areas there are road stations (similar to motorway rest stops) with motel-type portable rooms called 'demountables'. (Rooms are also called apartments and units.) All motel chains will book you a room at another motel in the same chain free of charge, although you should note that not all motels within a chain are of the same standard.

Motel rooms have a private bath or shower, refrigerator, tea and coffee-making facilities, telephone and a TV. Some luxury motels have a swimming pool or spa. At smaller motels you can park outside your door. Most motels don't have bars, dining rooms or restaurants, although you can usually order breakfast in your room. Some motels have self-catering facilities (particularly in resort areas), although motel rooms usually have small conventional or microwave ovens only.

Single rooms usually start from $40 or $45 per night and doubles from $50 (rising to $170 for a luxury motel). Lower rates are usually available if you're planning to stay for more than a few days. Prices in resort areas are around double those in small towns or country locations. Breakfast isn't usually included in the price. Shared rooms in motels can be economical for a family or a group of three or four, and are popular with Australian families.

Pubs

Pubs used to be called pub hotels or hotels because they originally had to provide accommodation by law, but nowadays many pubs don't offer accommodation. Pubs in country areas, which may be called 'commercials' because guests were traditionally commercial travellers (salesmen), are more likely to offer accommodation than those in cities. Pub hotels are usually basic (so don't expect a bidet or a trouser press) with a bar downstairs and rooms upstairs, which can be noisy (it's best to get a room at the top of the building). Pub hotels in country areas generally charge from around $25 to $35 for a single room, usually with a shared bathroom. Check whether breakfast is included.

Bed & Breakfast

Bed and breakfast (B&B) accommodation consists of a room in a private house or on a university campus, and is found throughout Australia, from cities and large towns to small villages and outback stations. B&B accommodation is more informal than a hotel and often provides a friendly place to meet Australians in their own homes. It encompasses a huge variety of abodes, including conventional family homes, country homesteads, farms, historic houses and inner city townhouses.

B&B is a relatively new concept in Australia but has become popular in the last decade or so, during which an increasing number of Australians have opened their homes to guests (a trend encouraged by the tourist authorities). However, it isn't an inexpensive option (as it is in Europe), single rooms costing from $40 to $100 and doubles from $70 to $100.

 Caution

Most B&Bs don't accept credit cards and only some have permits to serve alcohol.

Bear in mind that some B&Bs have a minimum stay of two or three nights. If you're staying for more than one night, you may be expected to vacate your room for most of the day and to leave by noon (or earlier) on your last day.

There are a number of guide books to B&B accommodation in Australia, including the *Australian Bed & Breakfast Book* (Moonshine Press), *Bed & Breakfast: Australia's Best* by Jane Schonberger (Ten Speed Press) and the *Guide to Bed & Breakfast in Australia & New Zealand* by Jeannie Fairlie (Periplus Editions).

Homestays & Farmstays

Homestays, which are similar to a B&B except that meals are provided, cost from $40 to well over $100 a night, depending on the meals and activities provided. Farmstays are becoming big business (as outback tourism increases in popularity) and accommodation ranges from fairly basic to luxurious, including outback cattle and sheep stations, ranch-style homesteads, small holdings in farming regions and specialist farms. Most are working properties where guests become one of the family and are accommodated in the homestead or in an adjoining cabin or cottage. Prices for full board at an outback farm (station) are from around $70 per day, although some farms offer inexpensive 'backpacker' accommodation in barns (for those who don't mind sleeping with cows and pigs or cannot afford anything better) from around $10 per night.

Guesthouses

A guesthouse is a cross between a B&B and a hotel. Whereas B&Bs tend to consist of one or two rooms in a private house, a guesthouse is more likely to be a building devoted to paying guests; as with homestays (see above), lunch and dinner are usually provided. Guesthouses are normally cheaper than B&Bs, as stays are usually for a minimum of a week.

Rooms in guesthouses usually cost from $20 to $50 for a single and $35 to $70 for a double (some also have suites/triples). Guesthouses don't have permits to serve alcohol.

Self-catering

There's a wide choice of self-catering accommodation in Australia, usually consisting of apartments, although chalets, cottages, houses and mobile homes are also for rent in country and resort areas. An apartment is often a good choice for a family, as it's much cheaper than a hotel room, provides more privacy and freedom, and allows you to prepare your own meals when you please. Standards, while generally high, are variable, and paying a high price doesn't always guarantee a well furnished or appointed apartment (most look wonderful in the brochure). Holiday apartments are generally found in tourist areas and serviced apartments in cities and large towns. Holiday apartments are usually rented on a weekly basis, and prices vary enormously according to standard and location as well as time of year. Serviced apartments, with one to three bedrooms, a bathroom, kitchen, laundry and living area, cost from around $130 to $225 per night (there may be discounts for stays of a week or more). There's usually no low season in major cities, where rates are constant throughout the year.

Holiday apartments are generally well equipped with cooking utensils, crockery and cutlery. However, small studios may have only an electric frying pan and a microwave oven for cooking, while larger apartments usually also have a stove. Check when booking, if you plan to do a lot of cooking. You may need to provide your own linen and towels, although they can usually be hired for an additional fee. Prices vary considerably according to the location and season and are higher during school and public holidays. Before booking self-catering accommodation, check the holiday changeover dates and times, what's included in the rent (e.g. cleaning, linen), whether cots or high chairs are provided and pets allowed, if a garden or parking is provided, access to public transport (if required), and anything you consider essential (such as air-conditioning, heating or a TV).

Self-catering accommodation is listed in guides such as the NRMA *Accommodation Guide* and lists are maintained by tourist offices. If you're seeking long term self-catering accommodation, see **Rented Accommodation** on page 108.

Hostels

One way to stretch limited financial resources is to stay in hostels. Hostels include beach huts and tree houses in Queensland, mountain cabins in Tasmania, disused railway stations, historic renovated buildings, huge purpose-built developments. Some hostels call themselves 'resorts', although facilities remain firmly in the budget bracket. Modern 'chain' hostels generally provide the best facilities, although they lack character and atmosphere, and many people prefer the more intimate, smaller owner-operated hostels. Standards vary enormously, even among hostels operated by the same organisation. One way to discover the best hostels is to ask other travellers.

The competition often leads to a range of extra services and perks being offered to those who turn up on spec, although it's advisable to book during the peak season and on public holidays.

 Caution

If you don't book, it may be difficult to find a bed in cities and at popular tourist spots at any time.

Many hostels have a freecall number. Some city hostels admit only overseas backpackers, as locals tend to treat hostels as dosshouses.

Facilities

The larger hostels have high standards and good facilities, which may include fans or air-conditioning, free tea- and coffee-making facilities, heating in winter, a kitchen (with allotted cupboard space and a shared refrigerator), a laundry room and ironing facilities, lockers or safety deposit boxes, luggage storage, telephones and a travel booking service. In larger cities, hostels usually have an inexpensive cafeteria. Resort hostels may offer a bar, barbecue, billiard table, cafe, gymnasium, launderette, restaurant, sauna, shop, spa, swimming pool, tennis court, TV lounge and a travel shop. Many hostels offer a range of sports equipment on loan or for hire (e.g. bicycles) and may also provide free tuition (e.g. sailing) and organise day trips and tours. Most hostels provide free transport to and from local airports, bus termini, railway stations and towns.

There are few restrictions at hostels in Australia, which generally have no curfews and allow 24-hour access, although YHA hostels (see below) may have more restrictions than private hostels, where the standard of accommodation and facilities may be higher. All hostels provide blankets, pillow cases and sheets (which saves you carrying a sleeping bag and liner), although they may need to be hired. Some hostels are 'party hostels', which stage backpacker party nights, barbecues and other entertainment. If you're looking for a quiet place to stay, these should be avoided!

Theft is common in hostels; if you don't have a safe place for your valuables, never let them out of your sight, even when taking a shower (some travellers live off others and will steal **anything**).

Accommodation & Costs

Accommodation may include single and double rooms, family rooms and dormitories (sleeping up to 24). Most hostels have dormitories for between 4 and 12 people, either single sex or mixed (some hostels advertise separate dormitories but put men and women together!). Dormitories can be noisy and lack privacy.

The cost of a hostel is usually from around $19 per night for a bed in a dormitory to $50 per person per night for a double room. Some hostels have two-bedroom, self-contained units where around six people share a bathroom, kitchen and lounge. Many hostels offer discounts of $10 to $25 for stays of at least four or five days, or weekly rates which usually save you a few dollars per night. Some hostels have limits on the length of stays during peak periods.

Youth Hostel Association

The Youth Hostel Association (YHA) has over 130 hostels in Australia, classified as simple, standard and superior, with a grading of one to five 'backpacks'. Guests don't have to be YHA members but, if you aren't a member, there's an extra charge of around $3 per night. In 2006, the annual membership fee was $52 (renewals $37) for over-18s and $19 for under-18s. There are discounts for two- and three-year memberships. Children under 17 receive free membership when their parents are members (called family membership), and group membership is also available. A range of over 800 discounts is offered to YHA members in Australia, including 10 per cent off Greyhound Pioneer Australia coach passes and up to 30 per cent off car hire.

Sheets and pillows are provided at all YHA hostels except Wilderness Hostels (these can be purchased at hostels or hired for around $3 per night); unlined sleeping bags aren't permitted. Blankets are also provided.

There are few restrictions at YHA hostels, although the length of stays may be limited to a maximum of five to seven days. There are no age restrictions and no rules requiring early check-out.

The YHA has an international booking network through which bookings can be made up to six months in advance (a fee of $2 may apply when booking in Australia). The YHA publishes a free annual *Accommodation and Discounts Guide* plus a free *Australia Visitors Map* showing the location of its hostels. For further information, contact the Australian Youth Hostel Association (💻 www.yha.com.au).

Other Organisations

There are a number of independent hostels in Australia and, in outback areas, Aboriginal hostels (operated by the Aboriginal Hostels Association) which may also take in non-Aboriginals. Rates are from around $20 per night.

YMCAs and YWCAs offer accommodation, although their prices are around double those charged by hostels and they're mainly located in the major cities. They have single rooms and some dormitories.

During summer holidays (i.e. from November to February) and other holiday periods, many university colleges let rooms in their halls of residence to travellers for around $12 to $15 per night for a single room or $20 for bed and breakfast. Rooms must be booked and priority is given to students (others pay a surcharge of 50 to 100 per cent). Many universities are located outside cities and towns.

Publications

There are many publications for hostellers and budget travellers, including the *Australia and New Zealand Travel Planner* (published by TNT Magazine, 14–15 Child's Place, Earls Court, London SW5 9RX, UK), which provides invaluable advice for backpackers and travellers plus a complete hostel directory. TNT also publishes *TNT for Backpackers* magazine. A free monthly magazine, *For Backpackers, By Backpackers*, is available in Sydney, and the YHA publishes a free magazine, *The Hosteller*, available from YHA hostels. The Australian government produces a hostel guide listing over 300 hostels which have been assessed by the Australian Automobile Association (AAA) and given a one to five 'rucksack' rating (a system independent of the YHA's backpack rating). The guide is available from automobile associations, hostel booking offices, hostels, transit points and travel agents in Australia. There are various books for hostellers and backpackers.

Caravanning & Camping

Australia is a great country for camping because of its generally mild climate and minimal camping restrictions. Campsites and caravan parks are common and are available in all major towns and tourist centres (many are on the edge of beaches). However, most campsites near to major cities are well away from the centre, which means that you need your own transport if you want to go sightseeing.

Campsite facilities vary but amenities usually include electricity hook-ups, hot and cold water, laundry facilities, showers and toilets. At large sites, there's usually a range of indoor recreation areas, lock-up storage for valuables, restaurants, shops and a wide variety of sports facilities, which may include boating, canoeing, cycling, fishing, swimming (i.e. a pool), table-tennis, tennis, trampolining and volleyball.

Rates are from around $12 per night for two people. A 'night' is usually from noon to noon. Some sites charge extra to use electricity, showers, sports facilities (such

as tennis courts) and other amenities such as a freezer or iron. Outside peak periods you can usually find a campsite without difficulty on the spot, but don't leave it too late in the day when you're in a popular area (after noon is too late at some sites). It's important to book if you have a caravan and require an electricity hook-up.

Many campsites in Australia are primarily caravan parks, intended more for trailers and motor homes than for tents. Many have gravel surfaces (or hard ground) rather than turf, so pitching a tent can be hard work. Many caravan parks have on-site cabins, caravans, holiday units and villas, which can be hired from around $30 to $35 per night for a caravan and $35 to $45 for a cabin. Linen and blankets can usually be hired, although a portable heater is useful in winter, as many caravans and cabins are unheated.

In the outback you can pitch a tent virtually anywhere you please, although permission is required to camp on private property, but in other areas there may be local regulations restricting camping. For example, in Western Australia, you aren't permitted to camp within 16km (10mi) of a campsite and it's illegal to camp on green areas outside a city centre. In Brisbane, it's illegal to camp within a 22km (14mi) radius of the city centre, although short-term camping is allowed in roadside rest areas in most of the rest of Queensland.

> In most national parks, camping is permitted only in designated areas, but you may camp in 'bush' areas in some of them.

Fees vary from park to park but are usually from around $5 per person per night (whether you camp in a designated area or not); you may need to book at popular campsites in national parks. When spending an extended period in a national park, you should let the park ranger know your route and when you expect to return. You mustn't interfere with the flora and fauna, must observe all fire ban warnings (most camps don't permit open fires, so you need a portable stove), stick to existing camp sites where available rather than creating new ones, take no pets with you, take care not to desecrate Aboriginal sites, take your rubbish with you, use only fallen dead wood for fires (where permitted) and wash well away from lakes, rivers and streams – apart from which, you can do what you like! All states publish information about camping in national parks.

A 'swag' is all you need when camping under the stars in the outback. Many different types are manufactured (e.g. by the Jolly Swag Company of Australia), the best of which include a blanket, mattress, pillow, sheet and down-filled sleeping bag inside a sturdy canvas envelope. You can also buy a tarpaulin cover in case of rain. When camping wild, avoid dried-up river beds in the wet season due to the danger of flash floods.

Camping tours are popular, and many companies offer organised tours in air-conditioned coaches or 4WD vehicles. You can buy or rent a campervan or mobile home throughout Australia; many people purchase a second-hand one from a departing visitor.

Interesting magazines for campers and caravanners include *Outdoor Australia* and *Wild*, both published quarterly. Excellent guide books are available from automobile associations and include the *Camping and Caravan Directory*. For information about driving in the outback see **Outback Roads** on page 233.

PARKS, GARDENS & ZOOS

There are some 2,000 national parks and reserves in Australia, covering an area of over 40m hectares (100m acres – over 5 per cent of Australia's land area), plus a further 38m hectares (95m acres) of marine and estuarine protected areas. Australia has 16 World Heritage Sites, including Uluru-Kata Tjuta (Ayers Rock-Mount Olga),

Fraser Island, the Great Barrier Reef, Kakadu National Park (Northern Territory, where *Crocodile Dundee* was filmed), the Queensland rainforests, and the Tasmanian Wilderness. National parks include every possible habitat, and many are of great scientific interest. Australia was the second country to proclaim a national park, the Royal National Park in Sydney in 1879 (the first was the US with Yellowstone Park).

Each state has its own national parks authority, most of which publish guides detailing park facilities. Some parks charge an entrance fee, e.g. between $10 and $25 for a car in New South Wales (less for motorbikes and pedestrians), although entry to smaller parks is often free and larger parks also allow free entry at weekends. A two-month holiday pass ($50 for a vehicle) and an annual pass ($84) are available in Tasmania. All national parks have information or visitors' centres with leaflets, maps, films and slide shows, and guided tours are organised during peak periods. Some parks provide numbered pegs indicating points of interest, which can be cross-referenced with information sheets. Further information about national parks can be found on the website of the Department of the Environment and Water Resources (🖳 www.environment.gov.au) or the appropriate organisation in each state.

Australia has many excellent aquariums, wildlife parks and zoos. The most famous is the Royal Melbourne Zoological Gardens (Australia's oldest and the third-oldest in the world, dating from 1857), which houses around 4,000 species of animals and birds in 'natural' habitats. Taronga Zoo in Sydney is home to Australia's largest collection of native and exotic animals, and has a peerless setting beside Sydney Harbour (best visited by ferry from Circular Quay) and extensive breeding facilities, some of which are located at its 'sister' zoo (Western Plains Zoo in Dubbo). Other top zoos and wildlife parks include

Adelaide Zoo, the Australia Zoo north of Brisbane (which houses a large collection of Australian wildlife), the Lone Pine Koala Sanctuary near Brisbane and the new Roma Street Parklands in the city, Perth Zoo (16 hectares/40 acres of exotic and native Australian fauna) and the Tidbinbilla Nature Reserve (west of Canberra). There are aquariums in many of Australia's major cities (e.g. Manly Oceanarium, the Melbourne Aquarium, linked with the Yarra river, and the Sydney Aquarium) and tourist resorts (e.g. Sea World on the Gold Coast).

Australia's cities generally have an abundance of green spaces and wide boulevards, with both formal and informal ('native') parks within them or nearby.

All major cities have impressive botanical gardens, such as the Royal Botanic Gardens in Melbourne, the finest in Australia and home to some 12,000 plant species, and the City Botanic Gardens in Brisbane; the Mount Coot-tha Botanic Gardens, 12km (7mi) west of the city are also impressive. Sydney has its own Royal Botanic Gardens, located adjacent to the harbour and the Sydney Opera House, and an exquisite Chinese Garden (Darling Harbour), while Canberra is home to the National Botanic Gardens on Black Mountain, which contain over 6,000 native plants. Some cities, such as Melbourne, publish a *Parks and Gardens* brochure.

The National Trust of Australia (🖳 www.nationaltrust.org.au) is dedicated to preserving historic buildings and parks throughout Australia, and owns a number of properties that are open to the public. Annual membership costs $89 for individuals and $113 for families. There are local National Trust offices in each state.

Further information about aquariums, botanical gardens, national parks and zoos is available from Tourism Australia or any good guide book. All tourist offices and visitors' centres provide information about local attractions.

MUSEUMS & GALLERIES

There are over 1,000 museums and galleries in Australia, visited by more than 7m people annually, including federal and state museums, private galleries, privately-owned collections and regional exhibitions. The most important national collections are in Canberra and include the Australian War Memorial (which houses one of the best military museums in the world), the National Museum of Australia, the National Gallery of Australia, the National Portrait Gallery, the National Library, the National Film and Sound Archive (free admission), the National Science and Technology Centre and the National Aquarium and Wildlife Sanctuary (admission $10).

Elsewhere, major museums and galleries include the Art Gallery of NSW, the Australian Museum, the Museum of Contemporary Art, the National Maritime Museum and the Powerhouse Museum (science, decorative arts and social history) – all in Sydney – the National Museum of Melbourne, the Victorian Arts Centre (housing the National Gallery of Victoria), the Australian Gallery of Sport and Olympic Museum, and the Museum of Australian Art in Melbourne, the Art Gallery of South Australia and the South Australian Museum (both in Adelaide), the National Motor Museum (Birdwood, South Australia), the Western Australian Museum and the Art Gallery of Western Australia (Perth), the Queensland Museum and Queensland Art Gallery (Brisbane), the Tasmanian Museum and Art Gallery (Hobart), the Northern Territory Museum of Arts and Sciences (Darwin), which houses one of the best collections of Aboriginal art in Australia, and the National Museum in Canberra. There are many reminders of Australia's past as

a penal colony and many former prisons have been preserved as museums, notably the Old Melbourne Gaol and the Port Arthur penal colony in Tasmania.

Admission is usually between $5 and $15, and students normally pay half price. Most museums and galleries are open daily from around 9 or 10am until 5pm, although many have reduced opening hours on Sundays.

There's a strong market for contemporary Australian art, particularly Aboriginal art, which has become fashionable in recent years and can be seen in many galleries. It is, however, usually expensive (apart from mass-produced tourist artefacts). Nationally famous Australian painters include Sidney Nolan, Brett Whiteley and Fred Williams.

CINEMA

Cinema-going is the most popular leisure activity (apart from sport) among Australians; ticket sales are over 100m per year. Australian cinemas are split between mainstream ('first run') and 'arthouse' (which show classics, cult, experimental and foreign films). Mainstream cinema is dominated by three chains: Greater Union, Hoyts and Village Roadshow, which together account for around 50 per cent of screens (most in 'multiplexes') and some 60 per cent of tickets sold. Independent operators (indies) control around 30 per cent of Australia's cinemas, although they're being hard hit by the multiplexes, which have as many as 30 screens (but usually between two and ten) and are often owned by the film distributors (film distribution rights are a constant battle for indies). Main cinemas usually have a number of shows a day, including late-night and all-night shows on Friday and Saturday evenings.

At the other extreme, small towns usually have just one single-screen cinema, many of which are ancient. There are private film clubs in the major cities and local film societies in all areas. Films are also shown by cultural organisations, at film festivals and at the State Film Centre (Melbourne). Major film festivals in Australia include the Melbourne International Film Festival (held in July) and the Sydney Film Festival (June). Cinema programmes are published in major national and local newspapers.

Some cinemas (such as Cinema Plus) have giant screens employing IMAX 3-D technology. New centres have air-conditioned auditoriums, wide, comfortable seats and ample leg room, Dolby stereo or THX surround sound, and free parking. Many also have bars, cafes, games rooms and restaurants. Many cinemas (including all new cinemas) have facilities for wheelchair users. Smoking is prohibited in all cinemas.

A few open-air, drive-in cinemas remain, including six in Queensland, four in Victoria and three in New South Wales. Most operate only in summer and some only on Saturday evenings, although some are open in winter (when you may be able to hire an in-car heater!). There's even a Deckchair Cinema in Darwin, where you can watch a film while reclining! The charge is usually per vehicle rather than per passenger.

All films on general release in Australia are given a classification, which denotes any age restrictions, as shown below.

Children (or adults) who look younger than their years may be asked for proof of their age (e.g. a driving licence, school identity card or student card) for admission to age-restricted performances.

Cinema tickets cost around $15 in cities, a little less in country areas. There are

Film Classification

Classification	Signification	Age Restriction
G	General release	None
PG	Parental guidance	Children under 15 must be accompanied by an adult; not recommended for children under 12
M	Mature	Over 15s only
R	Restricted	Over 18s only

reduced prices for matinees, on Tuesday evenings and sometimes also on Mondays. Most cinemas offer reductions for children (e.g. $11 for children under 15), pensioners and students, although you should check in advance, as some reductions apply only to certain performances. Most chains provide discounted passes for multiple visits. Most cinemas take telephone and internet bookings (major credit cards are accepted, although some cinemas charge a booking fee for each seat, e.g. $1.50).

Australia has a thriving film industry which has produced many international hits in the last few decades, including such classics as *Babe, Crocodile Dundee, Gallipoli, Mad Max, Muriel's Wedding, The Piano, Picnic at Hanging Rock, Shine* and *The Year of Living Dangerously*. (The world's first feature film, *Soldiers of the Cross*, was made in Australia in 1900 by the Salvation Army!) The Australian film industry is aided by the Australian Film Commission (AFC), established in 1975 to assist in the development of low budget, innovative film productions. In the industry's heyday, around 40 films per year were produced in Australia. However, in recent years state funding has been reduced and the Australian film industry faces an uncertain future.

Australian film stars include Bruce Beresford, Cate Blanchett, Toni Collette, Russell Crowe (claimed by Australia and New Zealand!), Mel Gibson (also claimed by the US!), Paul Hogan, Nicole Kidman and Jack Thompson; Errol Flynn and Chips Rafferty were also born in Australia. However, like most countries, Australia loses most of its talent to Hollywood.

PERFORMING ARTS

Dance, opera and theatre performance listings are provided in weekly and monthly entertainment guides, available from tourist offices in major cities, and many daily newspapers publish free guides such as the *Metro* on Fridays in the *Sydney Morning Herald* (which includes a theatre directory).

Theatre

Australian theatre is of a high standard and extremely varied, thanks to the country's cosmopolitan and multicultural cities, particularly Brisbane, Melbourne and Sydney. In addition to mainstream traditional theatre – classic plays and international musicals being performed to a very high standard – Australia has a thriving contemporary theatre scene where anything goes. Its wide-ranging performances include outrageous Australian comedy, experimental plays, image-based theatre, outdoor performances and pub and coffee-shop theatre.

Melbourne has the most dynamic theatre scene in Australia and boasts over 70 theatres, including the George Fairfax Studio, Playhouse and State Theatre (all of which are housed in the majestic Victorian Arts Centre), Athenaeum Theatre,

Comedy Theatre, Her Majesty's, Princess Theatre and Russell Theatre (home of the Melbourne Theatre Company). Sydney's main theatres include the Belvoir Street Theatre, Griffin Theatre, New Theatre (boasting the oldest surviving theatre company in Australia – over 65 years old), Opera House, Pilgrim Theatre, Studio (at the Opera House), Seymour Theatre (at Sydney University), Wharf Theatre (home of the Sydney Theatre Company) and York Theatre. Other major Australian theatres include the Canberra Theatre Centre, the Lyric and Cremorne Theatres in Brisbane (within the Queensland Cultural Centre and Performing Arts Complex), and His Majesty's Theatre and the Subiaco Theatre Centre in Perth (home of the State Theatre Company of Western Australia).

Major international productions are regularly staged in Australia's main cities. Most plays performed in Australia have traditionally been written by American and British playwrights. However, Australian playwriting has blossomed in the last few decades and plays such as *The Removalist* (David Williams) and *Stretch of the Imagination* (Jack Hibbert) have become classics.

The Australians excel in comedy and love to send themselves (and everyone else) up. The most famous Australian comedy actor is Barry Humphries, whose larger-than-life characters include Dame Edna Everage, Barry McKenzie, Sir Les Patterson and Sandy Stone.

Melbourne is the comedy capital of Australia and stages the annual International Comedy Festival in April, while Sydney has the Comedy Store, offering a different show each night.

Tickets for most major productions vary considerably in price, but usually cost between $35 and $60, while performances at 'fringe' theatres cost around $15 to $20. Half-price theatre tickets can be purchased on the day of a performance in Sydney from the Halifax kiosk in Martin Place (tickets must be purchased in person and be paid for in cash).

Opera

The Australian Opera was established in 1970 and is largely dependent on government subsidies and sponsorship. The Victoria State Opera and the Australian Opera (Sydney) were merged in 1996 to form a new integrated company, Opera Australia, which performs at the State Theatre in Melbourne and the Sydney Opera House and presents outdoor concerts, such as 'Opera in the Park' in Sydney in January. There are small professional opera companies in some states. The standard of opera produced at Australia's main venues is among the highest in the world, and international stars regularly perform there. Home-grown stars have included John Brownless, Peter Dawson, Joan Hammond, Yvonne Kenny, Dame Nellie Melba and Joan Sutherland.

The Sydney Opera House is one of the architectural landmarks of the 20th century and it has become the symbol of the city since its completion in 1973 after 14 years and at a cost of $102m (it was scheduled to be completed in five years at a cost of $7m – an opera, *Eighth Wonder*, about the building process was even performed there!). In addition to the opera house itself, the building comprises two auditoriums (the larger, for orchestral concerts, seating 2,690, the smaller for song and ballet performances), a cafe, a drama theatre known as The Studio, a small playhouse and three restaurants. Despite its imperfect acoustics (modernisation is to be undertaken), it's often ranked with the world's leading opera houses, including Covent Garden in London, La Scala in Milan and the New York Met.

Most events at the Sydney Opera House are expensive, ranging from around $50 to $200. Information can be obtained from the Box Office, Sydney Opera House, PO Box R239, Royal Exchange, Sydney, NSW 1225 (☎ 02-9251 3943, 🖥 www. sydneyoperahouse.com). The opera season usually runs from July to August and from November to December.

Dance

Ballet is the healthiest art form in Australia, surviving largely on box-office receipts, and there are hundreds of ballet schools. The world-famous Australian Ballet was founded in 1962 and has its headquarters in Melbourne, although it stages a summer and winter season at the Sydney Opera House and also tours Australia. Tickets cost from around $60. Australia also has a number of contemporary dance companies, the most famous of which is the Sydney Dance Company (which performs at the Sydney Opera House).

MUSIC

In addition to the professional music scenes described below, there's a wide variety of amateur music making in Australia, including barbershop singers, choral societies, military bands and orchestras, most of which are constantly on the lookout for new talent. Free music is provided by an army of buskers, some of whom are excellent.

Classical

Classical concerts, music festivals and solo concerts are regularly staged throughout Australia by Australian and foreign musicians and performers. Australia has eight professional orchestras: six symphony orchestras (one in each state capital) run by the Australian Broadcasting Corporation (ABC), the Australian Opera and Ballet Orchestra in Sydney, and

the State Orchestra in Victoria (the last two working with Australian Opera and Australian Ballet). A number of classical music festivals are staged, including the Melbourne Music Festival (February), the Sydney Festival (January) and the Sydney International Music Festival (July). The Sydney Symphony Orchestra performs outdoor concerts, e.g. during the 'Symphony in the Park' season in January. Musica Viva (Sydney) is the best known chamber music society (and the world's largest) and stages a concert series featuring international groups and artists. Regional companies (supported by state governments) perform in state capitals and provincial centres.

Pop

Pop music is an important part of national culture, and Australia has a thriving band scene, most bands performing in pubs, where the best of Australian music is found, and clubs (e.g. Returned Services League and working men's clubs – see **Social**

Clubs on page 334). Many amateur bands are surprisingly good (often performing their own songs), although some are excruciating. Australia is said to be among the hardest training grounds in the world for pop bands, where internationally famous bands and artists such as AC/DC, Air Supply, Nathalie Imbruglia, INXS, Men at Work, Mental as Anything and Kylie Minogue served their apprenticeship. There's usually an admission fee of $5 to $20 to clubs and pubs with live music, although many concerts are free (depending on who's performing).

Major Australian cities, particularly Sydney, Melbourne and Brisbane, are on the itinerary of most international pop stars, many of whom perform in Australia during the Christmas (summer) season. In Sydney, the main venue for pop concerts is the Sydney Entertainment Centre, and the Sydney Town Hall is also an important venue, while in Melbourne it's the Sport and Entertainment Centre on the banks of the Yarra River. Concerts are held in Melbourne at the Kooyong Stadium, the Myer Music Bowl in Alexandra Gardens, and Olympic Park. The big names also play at Brisbane's Entertainment Centre and 52,500-seat Suncorp Stadium, and at the the Perth Entertainment Centre. Free pop concerts are held on summer Sundays in some cities (if it's very hot and the band sounds a bit off key, it may be the result of high humidity, which causes instruments to go out of tune – or it may not!).

Big Day Out is an Australia-wide, popular music festival featuring top bands, staged in January and February.

Concert and 'gig' guides are available in local newspapers, many of which publish a weekly entertainment guide (usually on Fridays). There are free weekly music publications in most cities, which are distributed via bottle shops, pubs and record stores. These include *Beat* and *Inpress* in Melbourne, *Beat*, *3D World* and *Drum Media* in Sydney, *Rave* and *The Scene* in Brisbane, *Son of Barfly* in Cairns and *Pulse* in Darwin. Gig guides are also broadcast on local music radio stations.

Jazz

Jazz has a lively following on the pub circuit, particularly in Sydney, where there are many regular venues (bands also perform in a variety of outdoor venues). A number of jazz festivals are staged in Australia, including the Montsalvat Jazz Festival (Eltham, VIC), held on the Australia Day weekend (January), and the York Jazz Festival in Western Australia in September.

Country & Folk Music

Australian country music has strong local themes, and there are clubs in all major cities; many pubs also feature folk groups. Folk or bush music is popular, having its roots in English, Irish and Scottish folk music, where banjos, fiddles and tin whistles predominate along with a home-grown instrument called the 'lagerphone' (or zob stick), consisting of a wooden frame covered in metal bottle tops which is bashed on the ground, shaken or hit with a stick. The main festivals are the Australasian Country Music Festival in Tamworth (NSW) in January (featuring over 700 events) and the Land of the Beardies Bush Festival (which also includes a long beard competition!) at Glen Innes, NSW in November.

Aboriginal Music

Few people forget the haunting sound of a didgeridoo, which is used in the bush to accompany tribal dances (called corroborees). Busking didgeridoo players (often non-Aboriginal) are common in the main cities, and performances are staged for tourists in northern regions (although they're a pale imitation of real corroborees). It's possible to hear the real thing at an Aboriginal cultural festival, and there are some contemporary Aboriginal bands such as Yothu Yindi, although few have had any commercial success. Other forms of native music are Koori, a cross between traditional Aboriginal music and country music, and 'gum-leaf', in which Aboriginal performers make 'music' by blowing on gum leaves.

SOCIAL CLUBS

If you want to become integrated into your local community or Australian society in general, one of the best ways is to join a social club (even better, join a number of them). There are numerous social clubs and organisations catering for both foreigners and Australians, including Ambassador clubs, Apex clubs, business clubs, church clubs and groups, the freemasons, international men's and women's clubs, Kiwani clubs, Lion and Lioness clubs, Returned Services League (RSL) clubs, Rotary clubs, Round Table clubs, ex-servicemen's clubs, sports clubs, women's clubs, and working men's clubs. RSL clubs (known as 'leagues clubs') are an institution and constitute the main social centre in country towns. They may have nothing to do with the services but be run by a local football club or association. Many have huge halls where a variety of shows are regularly staged, plus ballrooms, bars, discos, poker machines, pay/satellite TV and restaurants. Although ostensibly just for members (and their guests), many admit others.

Expatriates from many countries run a variety of associations, clubs and organisations in major cities (ask at consulates for information). Many clubs organise events such as art and music classes, bridge and chess evenings, local history tours, sports activities, theatre and cinema outings, and whist drives.

There are singles clubs in the major cities that organise a comprehensive range of activities on every day of the week. If you're retired, you may find that your local council publishes a programme of recreational activities for the retired in your area.

> Most councils publish a calendar of local sports and social events, and most libraries provide information about local associations, clubs, groups and organisations.

NIGHTLIFE

There are discotheques (discos) and nightclubs in all cities and major towns. Other nightlife includes cabaret bars, casinos (see **Gambling** below), comedy clubs, dance clubs, karaoke clubs, pool halls and RSL clubs (see above). The differences between a bar, nightclub, pub and restaurant are often minimal in Australian cities, and some establishments are a combination of all four. There's a huge variety of gay clubs in some cities (such as Sydney), where information is published in the gay press such as the *Sydney Star Observer* and *Capital Q*.

Many nightclubs play a combination of live and recorded music. Admission to discos varies, but there's usually a $10 to $25 charge, which may include a drink, though venues with live music may charge as much as $20 for entry and $6 to $12 per drink. Some offer free entry for women on certain days (e.g. Wednesdays) and half-price drinks before 9pm (before the real 'action' starts) on some days. Drinks are usually expensive and even water often costs from $2.50 to $5 per glass. Some up-market discos and dance clubs allow admission only to couples. The dress code is usually smart-casual, which normally excludes jeans, leather, T-shirts and trainers, although in some establishments these may be *de rigueur* (fashion usually dictates, depending on the venue). Dress may also be at the whim of the doorman (bouncer); if he doesn't like the look of you, you're out (or at least not in). Some nightclubs are for members only and have strict dress codes and high prices, which attract an older, more well-to-do clientele. Many discos are open until 3am or later, although some have variable closing times.

Brisbane, Melbourne and Sydney have the most cosmopolitan nightlife, with venues to suit every taste in atmosphere, fashion and music. Melbourne has some of the liveliest nightlife in Australia and a plethora of clubs, including the Metro, which is the largest nightclub in the southern hemisphere. Brisbane has many pubs and nightclubs and the Riverside area boasts dozens of restaurants, some with live entertainment. The main nightlife areas in Sydney are Oxford Street and the sleazy Kings Cross area, where drugs are freely available and violence is never far away.

In the cities, daily newspapers and free entertainment newspapers and information sheets (e.g. *3D World* and *Beat* in Sydney) provide comprehensive lists of entertainment venues and events.

GAMBLING

Gambling is one of Australia's favourite pastimes (for some people it's an occupation) and is a $13bn industry, accounting for 1.5 per cent of annual GDP. It's estimated that 40 per cent of the population gamble regularly and that on average each of them spends (i.e. loses) over $2,000 a year on gambling; the residents of NSW are among the heaviest gamblers, spending over $12m per day on lotteries alone. Gambling revenue is a favourite target of the tax man (around 30 to 40 per cent of the profit on poker machines alone), and taxation raised from gambling accounts for some 12 per cent of state and federal governments' revenue.

Gambling includes bingo (called housie), card games and roulette, football pools, horse, greyhound and camel racing, lotteries, poker machines ('pokies'), raffles and two-up (see page 336). You can even bet on the results of general elections, public appointments, football matches and other sports events. Aussies are compulsive (and impulsive) gamblers and bet on almost anything, even the proverbial two flies climbing a wall; in the outback (where you need to make your own entertainment) you can lose money on cane toad, cockroach, lizard and snail races!

An estimated 2 per cent of the population has a gambling problem (the percentage is lower than those addicted to nicotine or alcohol but higher than the percentage of hard drug addicts). There are a huge number of Gamblers Anonymous groups, and also meetings for the relatives of compulsive gamblers to help them cope with their loved one's addiction. Compulsive gamblers can ban themselves from casinos under the

Casino Control Act. However, you can now gamble at cyberspace casinos on the internet without leaving home, a form of gambling which is set to spiral in coming years. It's totally unregulated, however, and there's no guarantee of getting paid by 'casinos' located overseas (often they're 'based' in offshore jurisdictions).

Casinos

Most states have one or more casinos and there are now around 15 in Australia, including four in Queensland, two in Melbourne, two in Sydney, two in Tasmania (Hobart and Launceston) and one each in Adelaide, Alice Springs, Canberra, Darwin and Perth. New casinos built in recent years have included the Sydney Star City and Sydney Harbour Casinos, the huge Conrad Treasury Casino in Brisbane and the massive Crown Casino in Melbourne (open 24 hours a day). Games on offer include baccarat, blackjack, craps, keno, poker, roulette, Sic Bo and Pai Gow (Chinese card games) and two-up (see below).

> Keno is similar to bingo except that you mark from one to 15 numbers out of 80 on your card and, if your numbers are among the 20 drawn, you win.

Many casinos have a separate Totaliser Agency Board area (see **Racing** below), where you can place bets on horse and greyhound racing.

Casinos require 'smart-casual dress', which usually means a shirt with a collar and no shorts, sports shoes (trainers), T-shirts or flip-flops (thongs); jeans are usually acceptable but some casinos ban jeans and insist on a tie for men, so check in advance. Many casinos are open 24 hours a day. Games usually have a $2 minimum bet, although bets may start at $10 or more. Usually you must pay for drinks. Most casinos publish a free *Casino Gaming Guide*, but don't expect any insider tips on how to break the bank!

Two-up

The national game of chance is called two-up, invented by soldiers in the First World War. It's illegal outside casinos (except on ANZAC Day) and a few licensed two-up schools (not that this discourages many Aussies). Not exactly the most sophisticated of games, it involves two coins being tossed together using a stick called a 'kip'. If one lands heads and the other tails, there's no result and all bets are held for the next throw. If both coins show the same, you win or lose depending on whether you chose heads or tails. Coins must spin when tossed or the arbitrator (called the 'spinner') calls the game void. Bets are placed with the 'boxer'. Casinos keep the stakes when there's a sequence of five identical results (unless you bet on this), which is around a 3 per cent chance.

Football Pools

Football (soccer) pools were traditionally the most common form of gambling in Australia, although they've been overtaken by lotteries and other forms of gambling in recent years. Operated by Australian Soccerpools, the pools offer huge cash prizes if you correctly forecast the results of football matches (Australian in the winter and British in the summer). The most popular bet (oddly known as a treble chance) is where you must guess which matches will be score draws (i.e. not 0-0). If you don't want to fill out a coupon each week, you can have a standing order using the same numbers.

Lotteries

The national lottery ('lotto') is popular in Australia, where you choose six numbers from one to 40. Numbers are drawn once or twice a week and those who select three or more correct numbers win a prize. The minimum stake is $1 and the first prize is usually in the $hundreds of thousands or $millions (the average payout is some 60 per cent of the amount staked). Results are published in the press and are also available via telephone information numbers. In recent years instant lottery tickets, known as 'scratchies', have become one of the most popular forms of gambling.

Gambling Machines

Gambling machines ('pokies' – from poker machines) have spread like wildfire in recent years and are now seen almost everywhere (except Western Australia, where they're banned outside casinos), as state governments have rushed to cash in on Australians' gambling mania and machines now account for over half of gambling revenue.

> There are some 200.000 gambling machines in Australia, the world's second-highest per capita number; NSW leads the way with over 100,000.

Machines are common at leagues and other social clubs, where they're blamed for encouraging gambling among the elderly. Many can be played for as little as 20 cents and some boast jackpots of $25,000 (but not very often). In some states (e.g. Tasmania) there are limits on the amount that can be spent on gambling machines, and in others (e.g. Victoria) there has been a backlash against them, as they've encouraged gambling among the poor in disadvantaged areas.

Racing

Betting on animal racing is a popular form of gambling in Australia. Bets are placed on greyhound racing, harness racing (trotting) and horse racing. Gambling on horse and greyhound racing operates on the tote system (an Australian invention) operated by state Totaliser Agency Boards (TABs). TABs have outlets in all towns and cities (around 1,000 in Sydney alone), where offices (which also accept bets on the football pools) are open from around 11am until 6pm, Mondays to Fridays, and from 10am until 8pm on Saturdays. The TABs' annual turnover exceeds $4bn, including between around $60m and $100m waged on the Melbourne Cup (Australia's premier horse race) alone.

To place a bet, you simply write the name of your horse(s) or dog(s) and the race number on a betting slip and give it to the clerk with your stake. If you win, you can collect your winnings immediately after the race (provided you haven't lost your receipt). There are no off-course 'starting price' (SP) bookmakers in Australia, although there's on-course SP betting where odds are given by bookmakers for each horse and you're given a fixed price. However, illegal telephone bookies flourish, and betting syndicates are active throughout Australia. Betting on harness racing is less organised, and individual bookmakers set their own odds.

BARS & PUBS

It's hard to imagine it today, but some Australian states were originally temperance states. Now, Australia is famous for its pubs (an abbreviation of public house), which are a tradition inherited from the British and are often referred to as hotels, although nowadays most don't provide accommodation. These are among a huge variety of drinking establishments, including hotel bars, lounge bars, cocktail bars, restaurant bars, wine bars (rare), earthy country and outback hotels with sawdust floors (where women aren't made welcome), boisterous barn-like drinking dens, and cabaret, niche and tropical bars. Pubs include music pubs, gay and lesbian pubs, pubs with restaurants and barbies (barbecues), and elegant restored Victorian and Edwardian pubs (many with verandas and balconies). Beer gardens and courtyards are common throughout Australia, and many pubs have live music (jukeboxes are also common).

RSL clubs and other private clubs are popular drinking places and usually have low prices and an inexpensive restaurant. Many RSL clubs are open to all and not just ex-servicemen (of which there's a diminishing number in Australia).

Drinking is a way of life in Australia (known as the 'land of the liquid lunch') and most social activities revolve around a bottle of wine (or three) and a few dozen 'tinnies' (cans of beer). Drinking has even spawned its own language; for example, a state of inebriation is variously described as being full as a tick (or a goog), inked, off your face, on the slops, schicked and stinko. A teetotaler is a waterbag, a round of drinks is called a shout and you won't be popular if you don't when your turn comes around.

Despite their awesome reputation and the plethora of watering holes, many Australians aren't big drinkers. Nevertheless, there's a hardened minority who do their utmost to compensate for this slur on the Australian character, and drunkenness and alcoholism are common: it's estimated that more than 6,000 Australians die each year of alcohol-related causes (the figure includes some 30 per cent of road deaths). Many pubs have a DIY breathalyser which tells you when you're over the limit, although it's wise to go to the pub with a teetotal friend or abstain from driving altogether when you're drinking alcohol. In future, pubs may be forced to provide over-the-bar breath tests before serving customers, in order to protect themselves from negligence claims from drunks and drunken drivers.

> ☑ SURVIVAL TIP
>
> **You usually buy your drinks at the bar and pay when you're served (you cannot run up a tab as in continental Europe and the US). However, some trendy lounge bars insist on serving you at your table (and charging extra for the privilege), although you still pay as you drink.**

Local pub guides are published in some cities, e.g. the *Guide to Melbourne's Pubs* (Melbourne is generally reckoned to have the most varied and interesting pubs in Australia).

Beer

Australia is traditionally a beer-drinking country (Darwin is reputedly the world's

form. The best known Australian beers include Carlton Draught, Foster's and VB (Victoria Bitter) from Victoria, Powers and XXXX from Queensland (pronounced four-ex and said to be so-named because Queenslanders cannot spell beer), Reschs, Toohey's and Tooth's from New South Wales, Emu, Redback and Swan Lager from Western Australia (the last derisively called 'black duck' outside WA), Cooper's (one of Australia's best beers) and West End Bitter from South Australia, and Boag's and Cascade from Tasmania.

Most Australian beers have an alcohol content of around 5 per cent, which is higher than most American and British beers but lower than German and Czech beers. There's also a range of low-alcohol (LA) beers with around 2 to 3.5 per cent alcohol, which include Carlton Cold, Diamond Draught, Foster's Light Ice, Swan Light and Toohey's Blue. The strongest beers (as high as 9 per cent alcohol) are often those brewed by pubs with in-house breweries (called boutique or brew pubs), which are extremely popular. These include the Matilda Bay Brewing Co. in Perth and the Redback Brewery in Melbourne, which makes a German-style *weiss* beer that the locals drink with lemon. Boutique and imported beers are more expensive than standard brands.

Most beer drunk in Australia is of the lager variety, which is generally sweet-tasting, as it's made with sugar. The taste is familiar to Americans but like dishwater to ale or bitter drinkers. Fortunately for them, 'real ales' have become more popular in Australia in the last decade, and a variety of beers that are naturally conditioned (in casks or bottles) are now available from brewers such as Coopers of South Australia. This is the sort of beer generally made by 'boutique' breweries and sold in their in-house pubs for around $6 to $9 per pint.

premier beer-drinking city in terms of per capita consumption) and its beer-related vocabulary is particularly rich: the drink is variously known as amber fluid, amber nectar, brewery broth, neck oil, singing syrup and throat charmer, and a can of beer as a frosty, stubby, tinny or tube. The average Australian consumes around 110 litres (almost 200 pints) of beer per year, although this figure has fallen by some 20 per cent in the last decade or so as wine has become more popular.

Australia boasts one of the widest choices of beers to be found anywhere. Some bars and clubs boast over 100 different types of beer from around the world. The most popular foreign beers include Budweiser and Slitz from the US, Guinness (brewed in Australia), Heineken, Löwenbräu and Stella Artois from Europe, and Dos Equis and Sol from Mexico. But Australia is also known for its own beers, and brewing has been elevated to an art

> ### ⚠ Caution
> Real ale is served warmer than lager but still much colder than similar beer in other countries (e.g. the UK) at between 8 and 12C. Australians drink their lager almost ice cold (around 2C), often in chilled glasses – guaranteed to give you stomach cramp on a hot day.

Not surprisingly, cold-filtered ice beers are gaining in popularity. Beer is usually drunk direct from bottles and cans in country areas. In really hot weather, bottles and cans are kept cool in a foam or polystyrene cooler (stubby holder), and Australians transport their cold beer in an insulated cold box called an 'esky' (after a well known brand name).

Beer is usually served in measures ranging from 115ml/4oz ('small') to 570ml/20oz. Both the names and standard sizes of beer glasses vary considerably from state to state. In Sydney the most common size is 285ml/10oz (a 'handle', 'middy' or 'pot'), while in Melbourne it's 225ml/8oz (a 'glass'). Other measures include 170ml/6oz ('beer six'), 200ml/7oz ('seven') and 425ml/15oz ('schooner' – 285ml/10oz in South Australia). Some pubs serve beer in half-pints (285ml) and pints (570ml). The easiest way to order is to simply ask for a small or large beer, but take care, as what passes for a small beer in one state may be twice as large in another and a large one may be very large indeed: a large beer in Darwin, known as a 'stubby', weighs in at 2.35 litres or over four pints! Bottled beer is sold in 375ml or 750ml bottles (many up-market bars don't sell beer on draught).

Beer is around the same price in Australia as in Europe and North America, a 285ml (half-pint) costing around $3.60 in most pubs, although it can easily be double this in a fancy place. Draught beer is also sold by the jug, which is slightly cheaper than by the glass. Low-alcohol beers are generally slightly cheaper than full strength beers. Some bars and pubs have a 'happy hour' (e.g. from 5pm to 7pm) when drinks are sold at half price or even less, and some watering holes offer half price drinking until 9pm. Many pubs offer women free or low-price drinks, the idea being that where there are women, hard-drinking men will accumulate in large numbers. Needless to say, beer is much cheaper (around half the price) from bottle shops (see **Alcohol** on page 379).

Wine

Australian wines (see page 379) have become world-famous in the last few decades, and wine consumption in Australia is steadily rising at the expense of beer: it's currently around 25 litres per head per year – higher than in any other English-speaking country but still well below the major European wine-producing countries. Nevertheless, there are few wine bars, which haven't yet caught on with the public (although the Casino Wine Bar in Adelaide boasts over 300 wines). Wine is usually reserved for drinking with food (pubs that serve good food generally have a good wine list), although some bars and pubs sell wine by the glass (e.g. $3.50) or the bottle (from around $15). Cheap wine, which may be referred to as bombo, lunatic soup or steam, is best avoided.

Other Drinks

Other popular drinks include alcoholised spring water, such as DNA (containing 5 per cent alcohol), 'alcopops' such as Two Dogs Lemonade (an alcoholised lemonade), Razorback Draught (a shandy), Strongbow White (cider), Sub Zero (alcoholised soda, 5.5 per cent alcohol) and XLR8 (alcoholised cola). Alcoholised soda is often mixed with cranberry juice, grenadine, lime or midori to make a long, cool drink. Cola is drunk in copious quantities in Australia and costs around $3 per glass in a pub. Spirits are rarely drunk in pubs, where a shot of whisky (30ml) or other spirits costs around $3.50 to $7.50. Trendy drinks include (wine) coolers, which are blends of inexpensive wine, sugar and fruit juice or fruit flavouring (they taste like punch).

Licensing Laws

Licensing laws vary from state to state and even from pub to pub but generally aren't as liberal as in most European countries (a legacy of the British, who cannot be trusted with alcohol). Pubs are usually open from 10am until 10pm or 11am until 11pm, Mondays to Saturdays, and from noon until between 8 and 10pm on Sundays. Sunday pub opening is restricted in most states, e.g. to between six and eight hours (the churches still have some clout). In market areas, pubs may open as early as 6 or 6.30am and close at 6 or 6.30pm. In places near the border of two time zones (see page 417), hardened Australian drinkers cross back and forth in order to benefit from extra hours' drinking time!

There are no licensing restrictions in Canberra, where pubs can stay open as long as they wish, and in Tasmania pubs can open virtually when they like, although most close by midnight.

Some pubs stay open until midnight or 1am on Fridays and Saturdays, particularly in tourist areas, and in cities some establishments with a number of bars and a disco serve alcohol for 24 hours. In some cities there are longer opening hours in summer than in winter. Nevertheless, a lot of drinking still takes place after licensing hours, particularly in country areas where the local policeman is likely to be one of the customers, and even when the pubs do close there are usually other places to get a drink (casinos, discos, night-clubs, restaurants, etc.).

There are some odd local laws designed to reduce drunkenness: for example, it's illegal to sell alcohol before 10am in Darwin and in Melbourne it's prohibited to drink at the bar after 10pm, when you must occupy a table (which helps prevent you from falling over). The minimum age for drinking in public places is 18 and, if you look under-age, you may be asked for ID. In some outback towns, pubs have doormen (bouncers) to deter undesirables.

Aboriginals have been ravaged by drunkenness and alcoholism for decades, which has led to the possession and consumption of alcohol being restricted or banned in and around some Aboriginal settlements and towns, where offenders face a large fine (e.g. $1,000), six months' jail or the confiscation of a vehicle used to transport alcohol. As a result, many Aborigine areas are 'dry'.

AUSTRALIAN FOOD

Australians love their food (tucker), and dining out is one of the greatest pleasures of life in Australia (which is why so many Australians are overweight). Australian food is noted for affordability, freshness and variety (most ingredients are caught, grown or reared locally). Many people eat out around three times a week, and Australian households spend over a quarter of their weekly food budget on eating outside the home. The appreciation of good food and wine is universal in Australia and has nothing elitist about it as in some other countries.

The greatest changes in Australia in the last few decades have been in its cuisine, which in the major cities is now among the best and most varied in the world. It wasn't always so. Until the '70s, the staple diet of most Australians consisted of fish and chips, and steak, egg and chips (or over-boiled vegetables) supplemented by burgers, chico rolls (a distant cousin of the Chinese spring roll) and Vegemite (made from yeast slops) sandwiches. 'Real' Australian food still consists largely of barbecued or grilled steaks and chops, curries, fish, roasts, salads and seafood (see below). If there's a national 'dish', however, it has to be the meat pie (which could contain anything from beef or pork to barramundi, buffalo, camel, crocodile or kangaroo). Aussies (mostly males) eat some 2m meat pies a day! A meat pie is eaten swamped in gravy or tomato ketchup. A 'pie floater' is a meat pie floating in a bowl of pea soup – the height of sophistication! At their best, meat pies can be delicious; at their worst, they're rather less tasty than dog food.

In the last few decades, such unwholesome British-derived tastes have been subjected to a culinary revolution led by migrants (Australia's most important gastronomic resource) and a new breed of young Australians who have travelled (and eaten) the world. BYO (see below) and the rapid rise of Australian wines have had a huge impact on the proliferation of good cheap restaurants, and today Australia boasts one of the most cosmopolitan and diverse menus in the world.

Among the few 'native' Australian specialities are pavlova, a combination of meringue and fruit, originally created for the ballerina Anna Pavlova on her Australian tour in 1935; lamingtons, a sponge cake dipped in raspberry jam, covered in chocolate sauce and then rolled in coconut; Peach Melba, a combination of peaches, raspberries and vanilla ice-cream, created (in London) for the Australian soprano Nellie Melba in 1893; and puftaloons, a fried dough scone. Australian ice cream is popular and one of the best is Norgen Vaaz (a take-off of the American Häagen-Dazs). Otherwise, Australian cuisine borrows heavily from various foreign cuisines, with a tendency to make dishes less spicy.

Seafood

Australia is renowned for its excellent seafood (many people reckon it's the best in the world) and each state or city has its specialities. Australia's seas have yet to suffer from widespread over-fishing (although some stocks are threatened) or pollution, so an abundance of fresh fish and other seafood is available, although there isn't the choice found in many traditional fishing countries. Australia's best fish include barramundi (a breed of perch which grows to over a metre in length and is one of the tastiest fish in Australian waters), coral cod/coral trout (Great Barrier Reef), John Dory, King George whiting (South Australia), ocean perch, reef fish (Queensland), shark (called 'flake' when served in fish and chip shops), snapper (or schnapper) and tuna.

> The best and widest choice of fish comes from the waters surrounding Tasmania, including brown, rainbow and sea-run trout, farmed Atlantic salmon, orange roughy, stripey trumpeter, trevally and trevella.

Australia is also famous for its crustaceans and molluscs, which include abalone, crayfish, mussels, oysters and scallops. Specialities include Balmain Bugs (slipper lobsters from Sydney), Coffin Bay oysters (from South Australia), crabs (e.g. sand and mud crabs), Moreton Bay Bugs (a type of lobster caught in the mouth of the Brisbane River), Sydney Rock oysters and yabbies (hard-shelled freshwater shrimps).

Aboriginal Cuisine

Some restaurants specialise in Aboriginal cuisine (bush tucker), which includes emu egg omelettes, pies made from native fruits such as billygoat plums, boabs and quandongs, and witchetty grubs (usually eaten alive!). Other common dishes are camel, crocodile (which tastes like a cross between chicken and pork), emu steaks (from farmed birds), kangaroo (a delicious, almost fat-free meat) and water buffalo steaks. Damper is Australian bush bread (made with flour, salt and water) baked in hot coals (usually on a camp fire). Bush tucker is generally expensive, e.g. $40 per head plus wine.

Vegetarian Food

Australians are ardent carnivores, although not as much as previously, when many people would eat steak and chops for breakfast (a habit still common in the outback). Nowadays there's an increasing number of vegetarians, and vegetarian restaurants are fairly common in the main cities (most restaurants also serve some vegetarian dishes).

RESTAURANTS & CAFES

Melbourne is generally recognised as the gastronomic capital of Australia, followed closely by Sydney, both of which can hold their own with most world capital cities and rate alongside Hong Kong, London, New York and Paris for choice and quality (often ahead of them for value). Each city boasts over 2,000 restaurants (so many in fact, that there's a shortage of good chefs). Perth and Adelaide aren't far behind and have more than enough eateries to satisfy the most demanding gourmet. Brisbane isn't distinguished by its restaurants, although it also has many good places to eat, especially in the attractive Riverside area. Even Darwin isn't bereft of reasonable restaurants, although it's expensive compared to other state capital cities. However, there still isn't much choice in small country and outback towns, where you shouldn't expect to find anything other than basic 'Australian' cooking or an Australianised Chinese restaurant.

Smoking is banned in many restaurants and, if you're a smoker, you should check that it's permitted before booking. Australians don't usually drink water with their meals and, if you want water, you may need to ask a few times before you get it.

Bring Your Own

Rather surprisingly, the majority of Australian restaurants don't have alcohol licences (which are expensive), except in Canberra, where most are licensed. Restaurants without an alcohol licence are known as BYO ('bring your own') or BYOG ('bring your own grog'), where customers bring their own wine and other alcoholic drinks. This is an excellent idea that unfortunately hasn't caught on widely in most other countries, mainly because of the huge profit restaurants make on selling wine. There may be a 'corkage' charge of $1 to $2 (for opening bottles and providing glasses), although many restaurants make no charge. Some up-market restaurants with alcohol licences also allow BYO, but charge around $5 corkage (which still saves you money, unless you choose the cheapest plonk on the wine list).

Regular diners (and drinkers) always carry a few (dozen) bottles of wine in their cars (which isn't illegal in Australia, although it's bad for the wine, which can deteriorate quickly in the heat) so that they're never caught short when visiting a BYO restaurant (although they might be caught by the police on the way home).

> ☑ **SURVIVAL TIP**
>
> Eating at BYO restaurants is excellent value compared with eating out in most of Europe and North America; you can have an excellent meal for $10 to $30 per head (plus the cost of your wine).

Ethnic Restaurants

Most cities have a proliferation of ethnic restaurants, reflecting the countries from which immigrants have come. Indeed, Australia leads the world in ethnic dining, with a huge variety of Asian, European, Middle Eastern and South American restaurants, which include Argentinean, Chinese (many regions are represented), French, Greek, Indian, Indonesian, Italian, Japanese, Korean, Lebanese, Malaysian, Mexican, Mongolian, Polish, Portuguese, Spanish, Russian, Sri Lankan, Thai, Vietnamese and Yugoslavian, to name but a few. For example, Melbourne is known for its Greek and Italian restaurants, Sydney for its Lebanese and Thai restaurants, and Adelaide its German restaurants, while Perth and Darwin have a wealth of Asian restaurants.

Ethnic restaurants in the major cities are often clustered in groups in areas or suburbs where large ethnic communities have been established. There are bustling 'China towns' in Brisbane, Melbourne and Sydney, rivalling those in European and North American cities. In many shopping and entertainment centres there are south-east Asian 'food halls' (also called food markets or food courts), where you can buy food from the surrounding kiosks and eat it at a central seating area, thus allowing you to mix dishes from various countries. But Chinese and other Asian food may be Australianised (i.e. made less spicy) to such a degree that it's unrecognisable, and other foreign cuisine is often 'tailored' to suit Australian tastes and may bear little resemblance to authentic dishes.

Pub Food

The quality of pub food in Australia varies enormously. At its worst it's uninspiring and unappetising, but at its best (it's at its most refined and varied in Sydney) it's delicious and excellent value. However, pub grub is rarely exotic and usually consists of barbecued or grilled steaks and chops, curries, fish, roasts, salads and seafood. Many pubs also serve ethnic food or a

combination of traditional Australian food and ethnic specialities. Outdoor eating is popular (although there's a surprising lack of pavement and garden tables in some Australian cities) and often consists of anything and everything barbecued, including burgers, chicken, chops, fish, sausages (snags), seafood and steak.

Many pubs have large courtyards or gardens in which they operate non-stop, self-service barbies, where you buy a piece of meat and cook it yourself on the barbecue provided (condiments are supplied). You can also buy bread, salad and side dishes. A typical meal costs around $10, although some pubs have special offers and promotions when meals can be had for a little as $3 or $4. Many also have a self-serve salad bar and basic bar meals from $7.50 to $15. Meals are usually served in a dining room or lounge bar from noon to 2pm and from 6 to 8pm, although some pubs serve meals until late evening.

Fast Food

Australians are hooked on fast food and around 75 per cent of the population eats take-away meals at least once every two weeks, spending over $2bn per year in the process (or some 10 per cent of their food budget). Fast food outlets have proliferated in Australia and, at the bottom end of the market, can be as bad as or worse than those found in any country. However, fast or snack food isn't (always) synonymous with junk food, as evidenced by the increasing quality and amazing variety of fast food establishments in Australia. Authentic Australian hamburgers are often much better than the mass-produced variety served in chain restaurants. Australian fast food includes crepes and pancakes, fish and chips, fried or grilled chicken, hamburgers, hot dogs, pies, sandwiches, sausages, seafood, stuffed potatoes and vegetarian snacks, and a huge variety of ethnic snacks such as bagels, calamari, couscous, dim sum, doner or shish kebab, felafel, filled croissants, focaccia, gyros, kosher food, pitta bread, pizza, samosa, sushi, tabouleh, tacos and tortillas. Many places also offer healthy food such as salads, skinless chicken, etc. However, the most popular Australian take-away remains the humble meat pie (see **Australian Food** on page 342). Meat pies are typically served in cafes, milk bars and from mobile food vans (a common sight in major cities and tourist spots).

Common snack outlets include delicatessens, sandwich shops, and milk bars, which are shops selling meat pies, milkshakes, pasties, rolls, sandwiches, snacks and soft drinks. As in all developed (and many undeveloped) countries, American fast food outlets abound, and Hungry Jack's (trading as Burger King in other countries), Kentucky Fried Chicken, McDonald's and Pizza Hut can be found throughout the country. A popular budget restaurant chain is Sizzlers, an American-style restaurant serving chicken, fish and steak and a selection of desserts, pasta dishes and self-serve salads. Take-away barbecued chicken chains include Chicken Treat and Red Rooster.

Some fast food outlets, such as the American-style Fast Eddy's (in Melbourne and Perth), are open 24 hours a day. At most fast food restaurants you should expect to pay from around $6 for a filling meal.

⚠ Caution

Beware of self-serve and other places where food is kept warm for hours on end, which can lead to food poisoning.

Cafes

The Australians take after the British and drink a lot of tea and an increasing amount of coffee. Cafe society (and caffeine culture) is all the rage in Australian cities, where there's a huge variety of trendy and elegant cafes, the best of which are invariably Italian. Most cafes serve food, although it's usually of the snack and fast food variety ('all-day breakfast' is common) rather than à la carte meals. Few cafes have printed menus and you must usually check the blackboard and order from the counter, where you also pay, take a number and display it at your table so that your order can be brought to you. Many people finish their meal in a cafe with coffee and a sweet (e.g. ice cream or pastries). Cafes in capital cities are often open until midnight or early morning and don't usually serve alcohol.

Prices

Eating out is inexpensive in Australia, where a good meal can be had from around $10 per head without wine. Expect to pay between $15 and $40 per head (plus wine) for three courses and coffee in a mid-range restaurant, while for top class restaurants the sky's the limit. If you're on a tight budget, some restaurants offer discounts to 'backpackers' (dress appropriately and preferably don't wash for a few days beforehand) and many employers operate canteens open to the public where food is served buffet-style and you can help yourself (not great food, but cheap and filling). Many restaurants offer lunches which are less expensive than the same meals served in the evening. However, you should avoid tourist-trap restaurants in cities and resorts.

There are usually no additions for tax or service, although a surcharge may be levied at weekends and on public holidays to pay extra staff costs. Few people tip (see page 418) in inexpensive restaurants, although many people leave 5 to 10 per cent in mid-range and top class restaurants. In a busy establishment, it's customary to leave the correct money on the table and leave rather than pay

the waiter/waitress personally. Most restaurants accept payment by credit card, although you should check in advance at budget restaurants, or you may have an embarrassing experience.

In a restaurant with an alcohol licence, wine usually starts at around $20 per bottle, although some restaurants sell wine at bottle shop (retail) prices. In wine-growing areas, there may be a wine tasting room, where you can choose from wines made on the property.

Opening Times

Australians are fairly inflexible about their meal times, and many restaurants have limited hours. For example, dinner (often called tea after the British working class habit) is often served as early as 6 or 7pm and last orders in restaurants may be as early as 9pm (the staff are packing up to go home by around 10pm). In small towns it's usually difficult to find anywhere serving food after 7.30 or 8pm other than a fast food outlet or a fish and chip shop (lunch may also be served for only one hour, e.g. from 12.30 to 1.30pm). However, in the major cities many restaurants stay open late and usually allow diners to circumvent local licensing laws (see page 341). In order to drink legally at a restaurant outside official licensing hours, you must plan to dine, although you can order anything and aren't obliged to eat it (some places may provide a plate of free food to encourage drinkers!). The most common closing day for restaurants is Monday.

Bookings & Dress

Most restaurants accept bookings, and some top restaurants have a 'no show' penalty of around $10 per head for those who don't bother to turn up or who cancel at short notice after booking a table, although many restaurants overbook to compensate for no-shows.

⚠ Caution

Some restaurants have dress rules, although smart-casual is usual, even for the most exclusive establishments, but many ban flip-flops (thongs) and shorts (unless perhaps when worn with shoes and socks – not a common habit in Australia).

Guides

There are many restaurant guides in Australia, including annual *Cheap Eats* guides to budget restaurants in Melbourne and Sydney (each listing over 500 restaurants) and the Lonely Planet *Out to Eat* series, which covers Melbourne and Sydney. There are free magazines in many cities, e.g. the *Adelaide Advertiser*, which feature local restaurants, although these tend to be the more up-market establishments.

16.
SPORTS

Australia is a sporting paradise, thanks largely to its generally mild climate. Sport is an integral part of the nation's culture and the favourite topic of conversation (people even call each other 'sport'); to many Aussies it has the status of a religion. It's both a unifying and divisive pastime (competition is fierce between rival teams), although Australians are generally good sports and appreciate plucky opponents (unless they're Poms). Melbourne is the most sports-mad city (Sydney isn't far behind) and is home to Australia's unique brand of football, Australian Rules. Sports centres abound in all towns and cities and offer facilities for a wide range of sports.

Aerobics is Australia's favourite form of exercise among young people, followed by netball (played only by women but having larger participation than any other sport), basketball, swimming, cricket, soccer and Australian Rules football (the top spectator sport in the country). Other popular sports and activities (in no particular order) are cycling, golf, hiking, horse racing, jogging/running, lawn bowls, martial arts, motorsports, squash, tennis and tenpin bowling. Australia is famous for its beach culture (80 per cent of Australians live within around 30km/18mi of the coast), and watersports are very popular. Australians like their sports tough and love endurance tests such as ironman/ironwoman competitions and triathlons (a 1,500m swim followed by a 40km/25mi bike ride and a 10km/6mi run). However, even these aren't tough enough for 'real' men, who have recently come up with the 'eco-challenge race', which consists of 500km/310mi of bushwalking, canoeing, climbing, cycling, horse-riding, kayaking, rafting and trekking in the outback, rainforests and reef in northern Queensland.

In Australian schools, sports are incorporated into the normal day and aren't extra-curricular activities, as in many other countries. Schools have a wide variety of teams for all sports and participate in inter-school and interstate competitions (most events are held on Saturdays, and parents are called upon to ferry their children around the country to compete). Children come under pressure from coaches, parents and teachers to perform at their highest level, and club scouts scour school sports meetings for talent. Two-thirds of Australian children join a sports club by the age of 11 and almost half the population is registered to participate in sports (over 6m Australians take part in organised sport each year). Children who fail at sport can be made outcasts by their fellow pupils.

There's no such thing as just taking part or engaging in sport merely for fun in Australia, where winning is everything.

The country has some 15 national leagues involving team sports (remarkable when you consider the vast distances involved). As a nation they excel at numerous sports, including cricket, cycling, golf, hockey, horse riding, lawn bowls, motorsports, netball, rowing, rugby, sailing, squash, surfing, swimming, tennis, triathlon and many others. Australians also compete successfully at the World and Olympic Games for the disabled.

> Only the Americans devote more effort, money and time to sports perfection than Australians, who are consumed by sport (although more often than not it's only as gamblers or spectators).

The government and sports bodies promote sport with slogans such as 'sport for all' and 'life be in it'. Sporting talent is nurtured in Australia and given the best possible encouragement through the Australian Institute of Sport (AIS), founded in 1981 in Canberra, and centres of excellence such as the Australian Cricket Academy. There are over 130 national sporting organisations in Australia and thousands of state, regional, city and local club bodies. The government provides financial assistance and coaching for the disabled through the Aussie Able Program. The country received a huge sporting (and economic) boost from hosting the Olympics in the year 2000 in Sydney, where Australian competitors excelled, and Australian spectators will be remembered as among the best and most magnanimous ever. Melbourne hosted the Commonwealth Games in 2006.

However, despite the popular image of Australians as bronzed, muscular lifesavers and bathing beauties, many Australians are overweight and unfit, and the nearest they ever get to working up a sweat is jumping up and down in joy/anger while hurling abuse at TV sport. Fewer than a third of Australians participate in any form of physical activity (Sydneysiders are the biggest slobs).

Sports fans may be interested in visiting the Australian Gallery of Sport and Olympic Museum in Melbourne (open daily from 9.30am until 4.30pm). Tourism Australia (see **Tourist Information** on page 317) publishes a wealth of fact sheets on every conceivable sport. Sports results can be obtained in Australia by telephone or the internet. Local municipal councils may publish a 'leisure directory' listing local sports centres and clubs. An annual *Sport Yearbook* (Gemkit Publishing) is available for those seeking an introduction to Australian sport. The federal government also runs a comprehensive website through the Australian Sports Commission (🖳 www. ausport.gov.au).

AERIAL SPORTS

Most aerial sports have a wide following in Australia (which has an awful lot of airspace), particularly gliding, hang-gliding, hot-air ballooning, microlighting and paragliding. **Most aerial sports or private aviation are specifically excluded from many insurance policies, including, for example, health insurance and mortgage life assurance policies.**

Hang-gliding has become increasingly popular in Australia in the last decade, and there are hang-gliding schools in many areas. Tuition costs round $95 for half an hour to fly in tandem with an instructor; a full course to obtain a pilot's licence, which are issued by the Hang Gliding Federation of Australia, ☎ 02-6559 2713, 🖳 www. hgfa.asn.au, costs around $1,500 and can be undertaken in ten days.

Hot-air ballooning has a small but dedicated band of followers in Australia, although participation is generally limited

Microlight lessons are cheaper in Australia than in most European countries and similar to North America.

AUSTRALIAN RULES FOOTBALL

Australian rules football (called 'Aussie rules' and simply 'footy', although the latter term is also commonly used for rugby and, among expatriates, soccer!) is Australia's leading ball game and considered by most people to be Australia's national sport. However, fans and players of other football codes (and cricket) often disagree and disparagingly refer to Aussie rules as aerial ballet or aerial ping-pong. Its rules were invented in 1858 and are unique, although it was based on Gaelic football (played in Ireland). Aussie rules is an athletic, exciting, fast, skilful game, in which the score can change quickly and the outcome may hinge on the last kick. It's a gruelling, macho game and players are very fit and tough, most spurning any sort of protection (although some players do wear mouthguards, protective head gear and gloves to give them a better grip). They also wear tight shorts and sleeveless shirts to show off their muscles – not surprisingly, it's popular with women, who make up around half the spectators. Players cannot be sent off during a game and consequently there are often scraps on the field (the game is sometimes called 'an excuse for a punch-up' or an 'organised brawl').

to the wealthy on account of the high cost of balloons. A flight in a balloon costs from around $130 ($60 for children) and is a spectacular way to see some of Australia's most stunning landscapes (e.g. Ayers Rock, where balloon operators offer 30- or 60-minute sunrise flights – including 'champagne' breakfast). Alice Springs is the country's ballooning centre.

Aircraft and gliders (sailplanes) can be hired with an instructor or without (provided you have a pilot's licence) from many small airfields in Australia. There are many gliding clubs in Australia, and parachuting and free-fall parachuting (sky-diving) flights can be made from most private airfields. Schools offer tandem jumps for beginners (where you're strapped to an instructor), and a day's course costs around $425. You can take a 'tourist' flight in a small aeroplane from most airfields, and seaplane flights are also offered in some areas, e.g. Sydney harbour.

A match lasts for four quarters of 20 minutes each, but can extend to around three hours when breaks between quarters and stoppages for disputes, injuries and punch-ups are included (plus 'time on', i.e. time added by the umpire).

The goal consists of four tall, evenly-spaced posts, the outer pair of which are slightly shorter than the inner pair. Six points are awarded for kicking the ball between the two central posts (a 'goal') and one point for kicking it through the outer posts (a 'behind'). A typical point score for each team is between 70 and 120 points. The score (goals and behinds) is shown in newspapers for each quarter with the final points total shown in brackets.

The national professional league is the Australian Football League (AFL) comprising 16 teams. Melbourne is the centre of Aussie rules and provides ten of the 16 teams in the AFL, the others coming from Adelaide, Brisbane, Fremantle, Perth, Port Adelaide and Sydney. Aussie rules is the number one sport in five states: the Northern Territory, South Australia, Tasmania, Victoria (where it's a religion) and Western Australia. Matches are played on Friday evenings and Saturday and Sunday afternoons throughout the winter. Crowds are noisy, but there's rarely any trouble. The Grand Final is played in September or October at the Melbourne Cricket Ground before 100,000 fans. It rivals the FA Cup Final in England or the American Super Bowl for atmosphere and passion.

Local, regional and state teams are listed in the phone book. An excellent book on the history of Australian rules is *100 Years of Australian Rules Football* by Ross John.

CLIMBING & CAVING

Those who find walking a bit tame might like to try abseiling, caving, mountaineering, pot-holing (subterranean mountaineering) or rock-climbing. Australia doesn't offer much in the way of mountaineering (Mount Kosciusko in the Snowy Mountains, New South Wales (NSW) is the highest point, at 2,228m/7,307ft), although it has some of the best and most varied rock climbing in the world. Caving is particularly popular in Tasmania, which has some of the most spectacular caves in Australia. Some caves

are open only to experienced cavers, including the Croesus caves, the Exit Cave and the Kubla Khan caves (permits are necessary to enter most caves, many of which are kept locked). There are caving (speleological) clubs and societies in all major cities.

If you're an inexperienced climber, you're recommended to join a climbing club before heading for the hills (an eight-hour beginner's course costs around $295). Contact the Australian School of Mountaineering, 166b Katoomba Street, Katoomba, NSW 2780 (☎ 02-4782 2014, 🖳 www.asmguides.com) for information. There are abseiling and climbing schools in all the major cities, many with indoor training apparatus (e.g. a climbing wall) for aspiring mountaineers. Ask about local clubs at climbing equipment stores.

CRICKET

There are some 500,000 registered cricket players in Australia, where there are leagues at all levels from tots to oldies, for

men and women, indoors and outdoors. Cricket, like footy, dominates its season (from October until March) and attracts big TV audiences. Half of all Australians watch cricket on TV and around 20 per cent go to matches, where tickets for top class games cost $40 for a one-day match and up to $150 for a five-day test match. State cricket is played to a high standard (higher than the English county game), although it isn't a fully professional sport. The main national competition is the interstate Sheffield Shield, in which matches are played over three or four days, and there's also high-quality district cricket.

Australia is the most successful country at international test cricket, although they haven't been so successful at limited-over, one-day matches in the World Cup. Australia is also a top nation in women's cricket and they won the women's World Cup in India in 1997, were runners-up in 2000 and won again in April 2005.

CYCLING

Most people in Australia buy bicycles for getting around town rather than cycling purely for pleasure, exercise or sport (e.g. touring or racing). However, competitive cycling is also popular in Australia and includes bicycle moto-cross, bicycle polo, cross-country racing, cycle speedway, road and track racing, time-trial and touring. Australia has had considerable success in international cycle racing in recent years, particularly track racing at the Olympics and world championships, and is fast becoming a major force in road racing (e.g. the Tour de France).

Cycling is an excellent way to get around most Australian cities, due to their relatively small size. Most cities, except Sydney, have an extensive network of cycle paths and tracks (cycleways): Melbourne's cover 500km (310mi); cyclists in Canberra and Perth can legally ride on footpaths, and pedestrians can use cycle paths. There are children's off-road bicycle circuits in many cities and towns. In most cities, bicycles can be transported on suburban trains free of charge or for a small fee during off-peak times; during peak periods (e.g. 6 to 9am and 3 to 6pm on weekdays) it may not be permitted or a permit may be required. When transporting a bicycle on a plane or bus, you must usually dismantle and box it.

> ☑ SURVIVAL TIP
>
> If you're cycling in Australia's cities, you should note that fresh air is in short supply and you would be wise to wear a face mask to insulate yourself from traffic pollution (although, according to medical experts, they offer little or no protection against carbon monoxide).

The climate and topography (in most regions) of Australia lends itself to cycling, which is a good way to explore coastal areas. You can ride a long way in some regions without encountering any hills, although if you're looking for hills you're also well catered for.

A wide range of bicycles is available to suit all pockets and needs, ranging from a basic 'town' bicycle costing a few hundred dollars to a professional racing cycle costing many thousands. In between these extremes are bicycles with folding frames, BMX bikes, mountain bikes, shopping bicycles, tandems, touring bicycles and tricycles. A new fifteen-speed touring or mountain bike costs from around $300 (you can pay up to $10,000!), a good second-hand one from around $150 (try the weekly *Trading Post* in Sydney). If you're a visitor and need a bicycle for touring, it's cheaper to buy a second-hand bicycle and sell it when you no longer need it (some cycle shops buy back second-hand bicycles at a guaranteed price). **Bicycle theft is** common in Australia, so it's sensible to insure your bicycle if possible and buy a good lock. Most travel insurance companies offer policies for bicycles.

Bicycles can be rented in all cities and large towns, and may include folding bicycles, tandems and tricycles. Ask at the local tourist office for information (see page 317). Touring and mountain bikes can be rented from around $35 per day, $50 for a weekend and around $90 per week (add $10 to these rates in Sydney). They can sometimes also be rented by the hour from around $5 (there may be lower rates for children). Usually a deposit is required or you must leave your passport or a credit card as security. Many hostels provide free bicycles for guests, although you should ensure that a rented or loan bicycle is insured against theft or damage.

Cycling helmets are compulsory in all states and territories, and you can be fined on-the-spot (e.g. $25 to $50) for not wearing one.

Many books are published for cyclists in Australia, including *Cycling Australia: Bicycle Touring Throughout the Sunny Continent* by Ian Duckworth (Van der Plas Publishing), *Cycling Around Sydney*, *Seeing Sydney by Bicycle*, *Discovering Melbourne's Bike Paths* and a series of *Cycling The Bush* (Hill of Content) books by Sven Klinge, which cover a number of states, plus *Cycling The Bush – The Best Rides in Australia*. Free brochures such as *Canberra Cycleways* are also available from tourist offices. Local cycling guides and maps are published by councils and conservation and cycling groups in many areas; many of these organisations also publish safety booklets and brochures for children. Cycling maps are available in the major cities from bookshops and local cycling clubs and organisations (the best are the government series of 1:250,000 scale).

If you're interested in joining a cycling club, your library should have information about local clubs, or you can contact Cycling Australia (☎ 02-9644 3002, 🖳 www.cycling.org.au). There are bicycling organisations in all states, such as Bicycle New South Wales Inc (☎ 02-9281 5400, 🖳 www.bicyclensw.org.au) and Bicycle Victoria, Level 10, 446 Collins Street, Melbourne, VIC 3051 (☎ 03-8636 8888 or ☎ freecall 1800-639634, 🖳 www.bv.com. au).

FISHING

Fishing (or angling) is one of the biggest participant sports in the country. There's good fishing in Australian waters, both inland and offshore, where the main attraction is game fishing (see below). Tasmania's coastal waters are also rich fishing grounds (fishing is permitted all year), where bream, salmon and whiting can all be caught from the shore. Northern Australia is famed for its barramundi ('barra') fishing, found both offshore and inland. Fishing trips are organised from around $275 per day, usually between March and October, including accommodation, all meals, bait, boat rental, equipment, guides and tackle. In the Northern Territory there are limits on catches of barramundi and mud crabs (contact the local fisheries management service for information).

⚠ Caution

You should be wary of eating fish caught in inland waters, as many are polluted, despite $millions spent on cleaning them up (many rivers are used as waste disposal 'pipes' by industry).

Over-fishing of certain species is also an increasing problem for Australia's fishing

industry. There are bag and size limits in most areas for certain species of fish. For example, Victoria limits trout catches to ten a day.

A licence may be required when fishing in inland waters. In Western Australia, for example, fishing licences cost $22 for freshwater angling, $22 for marron, $27 for net fishing, $32 for rock lobster, $38 for abalone or $72 for all of these. Licences are available from the Fisheries Department. In Tasmania, which has Australia's best fresh-water fishing, including superb trout (introduced in 1864 from England), licences cost $59 for the season, $30 for seven days, $47 for twenty eight days and $18 for one day, and are available from post offices, sports stores and state travel and information centres. Some species, such as clams, dugongs (sea cows), triton shells and turtles, are protected and may not be hunted in Australian waters.

The fishing season in most inland waters is from the Saturday nearest to 1st August until the Sunday closest to 30th April. However, there's a shorter season in many areas and in some waters (a *Fishing Code* brochure is available detailing the seasons).

Game Fishing

The main Australian game fishing industry is based in Townsville (Queensland), where game includes black and blue marlin (the prize catch), sailfish, saltfish, Spanish mackerel, tuna and wahoo. The Coral Sea off Cairns is one of the few places in the world where large black marlin are found. Other popular prey include brown trout, eel, English redfin, native blackfish and perch (off the west coast of Tasmania), Australian salmon, crayfish, giant crab, mulloway, shark, trevally and whiting (off South Australia) and bream, crayfish, herring, mulloway, salmon, samson fish, sea pike, Spanish mackerel, tailor and trevally (off the southern coast of Western Australia).

Black and blue marlin are protected by law and **must** be returned to the sea whether dead or alive (often after being tagged) or you risk a fine of up to around $12,500! The main season is from June to November.

Good game fishing is to be had in the waters off Broome (WA), where game includes bronze whale shark, kingfish, hammerhead shark, mackerel, yellowfin tuna, yellowtail and wahoo. There's also good game fishing off NSW (black marlin, marlin, mulloway and tailor fish), Victoria and Tasmania (Australian salmon, bluefin tuna and mulloway), South Australia (tuna), Perth (blue marlin) and Darwin (barracuda, barramundi, queenfish and Spanish mackerel). Fishing on the Great Barrier Reef is particularly popular, and fishing boats depart regularly from Cairns and Townsville for trips lasting 8 to 15 hours.

Game fishing competitions are regularly staged – one of the major events is the Gove Game Classic (NT), which attracts fishermen from all over the world. A game fishing boat for eight can be rented for from around $1,000 per day, although marlin fishing can cost over $1,500 per day for four to six passengers. Bottom fishing boats (for those who like to catch bottom-dwelling fish), carrying up to 30 passengers, are also available for hire.

FOOTBALL

Association football (which the Aussies call soccer) is a minor sport in Australia, where it's played mostly by immigrants (some footy fans insultingly refer to it as 'wogball'). The majority of clubs in the National Soccer League (NSL) or A-League are dominated by Croatians, Dutch, Greeks, Italians, Macedonians, Maltese, Slavs and assorted other 'foreigners' (who represent the ethnic origins of the local populace). The A-League attracts a small following (most fans prefer overseas football), although it's gaining in popularity thanks to the success of the national team (see below). The standard is on a par with top amateur teams in England and other European countries.

The national team (called the 'Qantas Socceroos') has improved beyond all recognition in recent years, as its victory over England in 2003 demonstrated. It qualified for the 2006 World Cup in Germany, having only once before appeared in the elite competition. Australian soccer looks set for a bright future as major sponsorship has been found and some $21m is being invested in the game over the coming years. Further information can be found on the website of Football Federation Australia (⌨ www. footballaustralia.com.au).

GOLF

Golf was introduced to Australia in the 1820s and today there are over 1,400 clubs and around a million golfers, making it one of the most popular participant sports in the country. Melbourne has over 100 golf courses (it claims to have more than any other city in the world) and Sydney has nearly as many. There are many beautiful and spectacularly sited courses throughout the country, many of which are open to the public, although most of the best courses are private. Most private courses allow non-members to play, although you may need to be invited by a member. Many private golf clubs are part of a larger country club or hotel sports complex, where facilities may include a bar, luxury hotel, restaurant, squash and tennis courts, swimming pool and other facilities.

> Golf isn't an expensive sport in Australia, where a round usually costs $12 to $30. Golf clubs can be hired for around $22.

Many golf clubs have nets and covered driving ranges, and most also have professionals to give you lessons. Separate driving ranges are also available in most areas and have all-weather, floodlit bays, and practice bunkers and greens. Crazy golf, miniature golf, pitch and putt, and putting greens (e.g. in public parks) are provided in most areas for those who set their sights a little lower than winning the Australian Open.

When not playing on the European or American circuits, Australia's top professionals play the ANZ PGA Tour of Australasia Order of Merit. The premier event is the Australian Open, staged in November at the Metropolitan Golf Club in Melbourne.

GYMNASIUMS & HEALTH CLUBS

There are gymnasiums and health and fitness clubs in all cities and large towns in

have left annual members out of pocket. This has led to a new law prohibiting gyms from offering annual membership specials that are much cheaper than a monthly payment scheme. Beware of fly-by-night outfits and choose a reputable, long-established club. Many gymnasiums can be used by non-members on payment of an admission fee, where a day ticket usually costs around $30 (monthly membership is also usually available). Some clubs offer reduced rates for couples and family membership.

HIKING

Australians tend to call hiking 'bushwalking', even when it's done far from the outback. Real bushwalking is serious, long-distance walking in the outback, ranging from a day trip to a number of weeks. Australia has a wealth of beautiful, unspoiled hiking country in every state and territory. One of the major trails is the 5,000km (3,000mi) National Trail from Cooktown (north of Cairns) to Melbourne, following the old bush tracks, fire trails and stock routes. Around Sydney, there's the Blue Mountains, Snowy Mountains, Ku-ring-gai Chase National Park and the Royal National Park. A 250km (150mi) walk links Sydney with the Hunter Valley, and in the west of the state the Hume and Hovell Track runs through high country between Albury and Yass. The Snowy Mountains (part of the celebrated Kosciusko National Park in NSW and Victoria) are a Mecca for bushwalkers, and Thredbo is a popular summer hiking resort, with a chair-lift that takes you to the top of Mount Crackenback. One of NSW's most famous parks is the Warrumbungle National Park in the north of the state.

Victoria has some of the country's most spectacular and diverse walking country, including the Australian Alps Walking Track stretching for 655km (405mi) from Walhalla

Australia, including multi-purpose fitness centres with aerobics, fitness machines and swimming pools. Many private health and fitness clubs organise aerobics and keep-fit classes, and may have a Jacuzzi, massage parlour, sauna, solarium and steam bath. Many top class hotels have health clubs and swimming pools, which are usually open to the public, although access to facilities may be restricted to guests at certain times.

A good gymnasium or health club ensures that all members undergo a physical assessment, including a blood pressure test, fat distribution measurements and heart rate checks. All clubs should provide a free trial and produce a personal training programme. Some gyms in major cities (e.g. Sydney) are open 24 hours a day from Mondays to Fridays.

The cost of membership varies considerably according to the city or area, the facilities provided and the local competition. Note that there has been a spate of closures in recent years, which

(145km/90mi east of Melbourne near Mount Baw Baw) to the Brindabella Ranges on the outskirts of Canberra. Other top walking areas in Victoria include the Coastal Walking Track, the Grampians National Park, the Great Dividing Range, Lederderg Gorge, the Little Desert National Park, Mount Bogong, the Snowy River National Park (where the film *The Man From Snowy River* was shot) and Wilsons Promontory National Park.

In South Australia, there's the Flinders Ranges and Mount Lofty, taking in the 1,500km (930mi) Heysen Trail which crosses the state from Cape Jervis to Parachilna Gorge (in the Flinders Ranges).

In Western Australia, there's Porongurup National Park and the Stirling Range (both north of Albany), and the Kalbarri, Karijini and Purnululu national parks. The 640km (400mi) Bibbulman Track runs between Perth and Walpole.

There are also many excellent bushwalking possibilities in Queensland, including Bellenden Ker south of Cairns, Cooloola north of the Sunshine Coast, Lamington in the southern Border Ranges and Main Range in the Great Divide, plus coastal islands such as Fraser and Hinchinbrook.

The Northern Territory provides a wealth of walking areas, including Gregory National Park, Kakadu National Park, the Larapinta Trail in the Western MacDonnell Ranges (near Alice Springs), Trephina Gorge Nature Park in the Eastern MacDonnells and Watarrka (Kings Canyon).

Tasmania has some of the best bushwalking in Australia, including the famous Overland Track from Cradle Mountain to Lake St. Clair (85km/53mi).

A seventh of Tasmania is occupied by national parks, although they're under constant threat from mining and logging interests.

There are marked trails in most national parks and state forests, although some offer tough walking and are only for the seriously fit, and there's generally a lack of marked long-distance trails. You require a national park permit to enter certain parks and reserves; these cost around $10 per day for a vehicle or $50 to $60 per year. Day/night permits are also available in some areas for campers. Tracks are usually marked by coloured triangles on posts, trees, etc. Before setting out on a walk in a national park, you should sign on in the ranger's log book and sign off when you return, so that searches are initiated if you get lost. When on a long walk, it's wise to let someone know your plans and when you expect to return. Some trails are closed in the summer because of fire risks.

It's important to be properly prepared and equipped when going on a long walk and staying out overnight. Many shops sell or rent out bush clothing and equipment, and some hostels rent out equipment. There are bushwalking associations in all states and territories, such as The Confederation of Bushwalking Clubs NSW Inc (☎ 02-9294 6797, 🖳 www. bushwalking.org.au).

Orienteering is popular in Australia and is a combination of hiking and a treasure hunt, or competitive navigation on foot. It isn't necessary to be super fit and the only equipment that's required (in addition to suitable walking attire) is a good map and a compass. There are orienteering clubs in many areas and bushwalking clubs in most towns and regions. In many towns and country areas, guided walks are conducted throughout the year, ranging from sightseeing tours of towns to walks around local beauty spots, for which there may be a small fee. Walks are usually graded, e.g. easy, moderate or strenuous, and dogs can usually be taken unless otherwise stated. Many municipal councils provide local walking guides and there are short guided walks in the major cities. Ask for information at tourist information centres or local libraries.

A wealth of bushwalking books is published in Australia, including *Bushwalking in Australia* by John Chapman (Lonely Planet), *Sydney and Beyond* by Andrew Mevissen, and a series of bushwalking books by Tyrone T. Thomas detailing walks in most states and popular walking areas, including the *20 Best Walks in Australia* (Hill of Content). Bushwalkers may also be interested in the Australian magazines, *Outdoor Australia* and *Wild*.

RACKET SPORTS

There are excellent facilities in Australia for most racket sports, including badminton, racketball, squash and tennis. Some racket clubs cater for both squash and tennis, a few also for badminton. Most private clubs have a resident or visiting coach, providing both individual and group lessons, and many sports clubs and resort hotels hold residential coaching courses and holidays throughout the year. To find the racket clubs in your local area look in the yellow pages, enquire at your local library or contact the appropriate national association.

Tennis

Tennis is the most popular racket sport in Australia and is played outdoors year round in most states. Public (council-owned) courts and those owned by local associations can be hired for around $10 to $15 per hour, although it can be difficult to book a court at popular times. Many hotels have tennis courts, and university courts can be hired during holiday periods for a token fee, e.g. from $3 an hour. Many companies and schools have their own courts. There are many private tennis clubs, although membership fees can be

Mark Philippoussis

high and some have long waiting lists. Indoor courts are rare in Australia, where outdoor courts can be used year round in most regions. Most courts in Australia are hard courts and there are few grass courts left (even the Australia Open is no longer played on grass).

The Australian Open Tennis Championships are held in Melbourne at the National Tennis Centre at Flinders Park, where the main court is unique in that it has a roof which can be closed when it rains or during extreme heat (above 40C/104F). It's staged over two weeks in January and is the first of the world's four 'grand slam' tournaments (with Wimbledon, Roland Garros and the US Open). Anyone can play at the National Tennis Centre (except when the Australian Open is being held) for around $30 per hour indoors and around $25 outdoors. Tours are also available. Further information about tennis in Australia can be found on ⌨ www.tennis.com.au.

Squash & Racketball

Squash is a popular racket sport in Australia and there's an abundance of courts in the major cities and towns. The cost of hiring a court is around $15 per hour, and most clubs have club evenings when members can play for a few dollars. Rackets and balls can be hired. The club standard is among the highest in the world, and competitions are staged at all levels from club and state competitions to the Australian Open.

> Australia is one of the world's top squash nations. However, in the last few years squash has declined in popularity and the number of players has dropped by around 10 per cent.

In some cities (e.g. Sydney), clubs have been closing in increasing numbers in recent years as the cost of maintaining or opening a club increases and property values rise (many former clubs have been redeveloped as apartments, office blocks and shops).

For information about playing squash in Australia contact Squash Australia (☎ 07-3367 3200, 🖥 www.squash.org.au).

Racketball (a variant of squash played on the same court but with slightly different rules, using shorter rackets and a larger, bouncier ball) is played in Australia, and rackets and balls can be hired at some squash clubs.

Badminton & Table Tennis

Badminton is a popular sport, particularly among migrants from China, Indonesia, Malaysia and Singapore, although it lags behind tennis and squash. Most badminton facilities are provided by public sports centres; private clubs are rare. Table tennis is also quite popular and is played both as a serious competitive sport and as a pastime in social and youth clubs. If you want to play seriously, there are clubs in most areas. Costs vary, although it's an inexpensive sport with little equipment necessary.

RUGBY FOOTBALL

Both main codes of rugby football (called 'footy'), rugby league and rugby union, are played in Australia. Rugby is the main football game in Canberra, New South Wales (NSW) and Queensland, where rugby league is the more popular code. Most rugby league teams are based in Sydney (12 of the top 14) with others in Canberra, the Gold Coast of Queensland and Melbourne. Teams from New Zealand also compete in the Australian league. Sydney is the only major city in the world where rugby is more popular than soccer (it's estimated that some 80 per cent of the world's best league players live within 30km/18mi of central Sydney). Local, regional and state teams are listed in the phone book.

Australia is the world's leading rugby league nation (the Winfield Cup is the world's premier rugby league competition), usually easily beating the main opposition (England). The national rugby league team is known as the Kangaroos. National Rugby League (NRL) matches are played on most Friday and Saturday evenings and Sunday afternoons between April and September. League is popular, although attendances are much lower than for NFL (Aussie rules) games. Its popularity has fallen sharply in recent years as a result of continual scandals on and off the pitch. The State-of-Origin series between the Australian states in May/June is the premier interstate competition, although it's poorly supported by the public.

Rugby union was once a strictly amateur code in Australia but is now fully professional at the top level. It's most popular in the Australian Capital Territory

(ACT), NSW, Queensland and Western Australia. The national team (called the Wallabies) play around six internationals a year. The major competition is called the Rugby Super 14s, with Australian state teams competing with teams from New Zealand and South Africa. A few times a year, the ACT Brumbies, the NSW Waratahs and Queensland Reds state teams play each other in a 'state of the union' series. Local, regional and state teams are listed in the phone book.

SKIING

Skiing in Australia dates back to the 1860s and is a popular sport, despite the fact that there's only one proper skiing area: the Australian Alps, straddling the NSW/Victoria border (see below). There are also some small snowfields in Tasmania, which has two minor resorts: Ben Lomond (60km/ 37mi from Launceston) and Mount Mawson

(in Mount Field National Park). These are less developed and even less challenging than the major resorts in NSW and Victoria. However, they're also much cheaper, e.g. a day pass at Mount Field and at Ben Lomond costs just $20.

A lot of money has been spent on improving the infrastructure in recent years, and the facilities and lifts at the larger resorts now compare favourably with the best that Europe and North America have to offer. Australia has unreliable snowfall and in some years there's barely enough natural snow to cover even the highest slopes, and conditions can be hazardous for all but expert skiers. Many Australians ski in New Zealand, which has a more reliable snow record and many more resorts. However, in the last decade snow cannons have been installed in most resorts, which can now guarantee at least some snow for part of the season.

There are artificial snow slopes at Corin Forest Alpine Recreation Area 30 minutes from Canberra, where wheeled bobsleds achieve speeds of up to 80kph (50mph) on a stainless steel slide.

The (snow) ski season normally begins in early June on the Queen's birthday weekend holiday and continues until around October. However, even in a good year there's usually adequate snow cover only in July, August and early September. Ski runs cater for all standards, from beginners to experts, although most long runs are relatively easy, while the more difficult runs are short. Snowboarding is increasingly popular in Australia (the major resorts have purpose-built runs and 'bowls') and equipment can be hired and lessons are available. The conditions are usually excellent for cross-country skiing (also called Nordic or 'langlauf' in Australia) and telemark skiing. The major resorts have ski schools and child-care centres. Ski lessons, including lift tickets cost around $80 per day (less for five or seven days)

Lake Crackenback and Charlotte Pass (1,780m/5,850ft), which is the highest and oldest ski resort in Australia, and only reachable by snowcat from Perisher Valley (8km/5mi). Mount Selwyn (1,492m/4,900ft, 🖥 www.selwynsnow.com.au) is a day resort (no accommodation) with 12 lifts and is ideal for beginners; a one-day lift pass costs $68 and a season pass $390. The NSW snowfields are around four hours by road from Canberra.

> The Perisher Blue resort (1,680m/5,500ft), previously named Blue Cow, is the largest ski resort in the southern hemisphere, with 506 acres of snow terrain, and includes Guthega, Mount Blue Cow, Perisher Valley and Smiggin Holes; it has 30 lifts, some floodlit runs for night skiing and special snowboarding runs.

and the hire of boots and skis around $50 per day (costs are relatively high because of the short season). Major resorts have a reasonable choice of *après ski* entertainment and a selection of mountain restaurants, although there's little nightlife compared with most European and North American resorts.

Thredbo (🖥 www.thredbo.com.au) in NSW is Australia's leading ski resort and is popular with overseas skiers. It has 65 marked runs (including the longest in the country, at 5km/3mi) and a specially designed snowboarding 'park'. A day ticket costs $114 and a five-day pass $485.

Most accommodation is in nearby Jindabyne, which is cheaper as it's a 40-minute drive to the major resorts or a few minutes on the 'Skitube', which links it to the various parts of the Perisher Blue resort. One of the advantages of staying in Jindabyne is that you can travel to whichever area has the best snow conditions each day. Other resorts include

Victoria is home to the vast High Country and the southern end of the Great Dividing Range and the Victorian Alps, which have nine ski resorts. The best are Falls Creek, Mount Baw Baw, Mount Buffalo, Mount Buller, Mount Hotham and Lake Mountain. There's a resort entry fee in winter. Mount Buller is Australia's most popular resort, with 80km (50mi) of runs and an extensive lift system, within easy access of Melbourne's airport and rail and coach stations (from where buses take you directly to the resort). Falls Creek has 30km (18mi) of runs, 23 lifts and a vertical drop of 267m (875ft) – you can also ski directly from the village to the lifts and back; a recent merger with Mount Hotham has created a larger resort with improved facilities. There are also a number of cross-country ski centres in Victoria, e.g. Lake Mountain (🖥 www.lakemountainresort. com.au), which is the closest ski resort to Melbourne (just 100km/62mi away) with around 40km (25mi) of trails. There's a $12 trail fee ($6 for children).

It's possible to travel to the Australian Alps from Sydney or Melbourne for a day's skiing, although it's more practical to ski for at least a weekend or a few days. You can fly to Cooma, from where it's a short trip by road to most resorts. If you drive, snow chains are compulsory (they can be hired) and there are heavy fines for motorists without them, even if there's no snow! Most resorts have a wide choice of accommodation, including hostel dormitories, luxury hotels and self-catering chalets and lodges, many of which are close to ski lifts and runs. The cheapest way to enjoy skiing is to rent a resort lodge or apartment with friends and bring most of your food and drink with you, as prices are high in resorts. Accommodation at a lodge in Thredbo or Perisher costs from around $90 to $500 per person per day sharing a double room, depending on the season. Accommodation is cheaper in Cooma and Jindabyne, from where there's a bus service to the ski slopes.

SWIMMING

There's a wealth of public indoor and outdoor swimming pools in all towns in Australia, where the entrance fee is usually around $5. There are also salt-water, tidal pools on many beaches and Olympic-size pools in all major cities. In the major cities and resorts, there are swimming centres with a number of heated pools, diving area, solarium, sauna, spa and possibly a gymnasium. Many apartment complexes, hostels, hotels and motels have their own swimming pools. Outdoor pools may open only from around October until April in Melbourne and other southern cities.

Australian kids usually learn to swim 'before they can walk'. Children learn to swim at school and regularly swim in the school or local public pool (adult lessons are also given at most pools). Students are divided into classes according to age and swimming ability, and are taught the finer points of swimming by qualified coaches. Students can obtain swimming certificates from junior through intermediate and senior up to lifesaver qualifications (to gold medal standard). Private swimming clubs abound.

Under a law that came into effect in 1997, all private pools in Australia must have fences higher than 1.5m and be inspected by local councils. Legislation is designed to reduce the incidence of drowning among children aged under five, which is the most common cause of death for children in this age group (more than 300 people drown annually).

Sea Swimming

Australia has over 7,000 beaches (many of them long and with white sand) and all Australian coastal cities have a number of beaches, all of which are open to the public. Sydney has miles of ocean beaches (48km/30mi in the Sydney metropolitan area alone) and also many along its harbour (e.g. Balmoral). Sydney's Bondi Beach is one of Australia's (and the world's) most famous beaches, particularly for surfing. Manly (11km/7mi from the city centre) is another famous Sydney beach resort and the TV programme *Home and Away* is filmed at Sydney's Palm Beach.

 Caution

Topless bathing is illegal on most beaches and at all swimming pools and leisure centres.

South Australia was the first Australian state to have a legal nudist beach, and the law was recently changed in NSW to permit nude bathing on selected beaches. Local councils can, however, designate any beach a nudist beach.

There are sunscreen patrols on many beaches in Australia to warn people of the need to protect their skin from the sun. Many beaches have completely lost their sand dunes as a result of beachfront development, and environmental groups believe that urgent action is needed to save what's left of Australia's beaches.

Beach life led to the surf lifesaving movement (which is both a community service and a culture which began in 1906), the surf ski (a cross between a canoe and a waterski) and the surfboat. Australian beaches are among the best guarded and patrolled in the world. All public beaches are patrolled by lifesavers, who may be volunteers (over 50,000) or paid by the local council. They work each day during the summer season and year round in some resorts. When swimming off a protected beach, it's important to stick to the patrolled 'flagged' areas. Protected beaches also have shark and jellyfish nets (Sydney has an 80km/50mi underwater shark net along its coast), although they aren't failsafe. If you get into trouble while swimming off a beach manned by lifesavers, you should raise one arm in the air to alert the lifesavers.

Dangers

There are dangerous riptides (rips), shallow sandbanks and undertows off some beaches, which claim a number of lives each year (particularly on beaches which aren't patrolled by lifesavers). **Swimmers are urged by lifesaving associations never to swim outside patrolled areas (almost all beach drownings are on unpatrolled beaches).**

Efforts are made to keep surfers apart from swimmers on protected beaches. On surfing beaches, swimmers must stay within the swimming area defined by red and yellow flags, which may be hoisted from around 6am until 6 or 7pm in summer (year round on some beaches). They're placed to indicate the safest swimming area in the prevailing conditions and also indicate the area under closest scrutiny by lifesavers.

You should clear the water if a siren sounds, which may signal a shark sighting or a swarm of jellyfish. Shark attacks used to be rare in Australia (although widely reported) and, until recently, on average only one Australian per year was killed by a shark. There's still little risk of being eaten alive by a shark, but the danger is increasing, as a spate of four deaths in the period from July 2004 to March 2005 demonstrated.

Despite this recent increase in the number of shark attacks, the most common problem in Australian waters is jellyfish, particularly box jellyfish (known as sea wasps), whose sting can be fatal (another tiny jellyfish, irukandji, is almost as deadly). During the jellyfish season, warning signs are posted along the Queensland coast from Mackay northwards. However, it's sensible to stay out of the sea during the entire wet season in the Northern Territory

and northern Queensland (from October until May).

Saltwater crocodiles can be a danger near estuaries, and you should also keep a lookout for crocodiles if you're planning to swim in rivers in northern Queensland or the Northern Territory, or in swimming holes in the outback. You're apparently supposed to run away from a crocodile in a zig-zag pattern, as they cannot run that way (unless the croc's had a few beers, in which case you could be in trouble!). Other dangers include catfish, cone shells, poisonous coral, blue-ringed octopus, sea-snakes and stonefish, all of which can kill you.

The water off some Australian beaches is polluted, and many Australian rivers and lakes are too polluted to swim in. Australians don't respect their beaches, and sewage and litter are found on or near many beaches. A recent survey by the Surfrider Foundation showed that around 20 per cent of Australian beaches are within 5km (3mi) of a sewage outlet (over 3bn litres of raw sewage is pumped into the sea every day), a quarter have stormwater pipes draining onto beaches, almost three-quarters have developments within just 250m of the high-tide mark, and around 80 per cent are strewn with litter (including syringes left by drug addicts). If you're after clean sea and sand, go in search of a 'wilderness' beach.

☑ SURVIVAL TIP

Some resorts have a hotline where a recorded message updates callers on pollution from stormwater or sewer outfalls and warns of other hazards, such as stinging jellyfish and dangerous currents.

WATERSPORTS

All watersports, including canoeing, parasailing, power boating, rowing, sailing, sub-aqua, surfing, waterskiing and windsurfing, are popular in Australia, which is hardly surprising considering it has numerous rivers and lakes as well as a coastline of 36,738km (22,826mi) and that some 80 per cent of Australians live within 30km (18mi) of the coast. Boats and equipment can be rented at coastal resorts, lakes and rivers, and instruction is available for most watersports in holiday areas. Jet-skis and 'surf skis' can be hired (around $65 for half an hour) in many beach resorts and on some inland lakes. Parasailing (or parascending or paraflying), where you're attached to a parachute pulled along by a motorboat and float off into the wide blue yonder, is possible in many beach resorts (it's less frightening than jumping out of a plane and you have a softer landing). A ten-minute 'flight' costs from $100.

Every main beach resort stages a surf carnival in summer, in which individuals and teams compete for honours in board-paddling events, swimming and surfboat races, team lifesaving competitions and – the highlight – ironman/ironwoman competitions (a combination of swimming and surf ski riding). There's even a professional ironman circuit which tours Australia in the summer.

Sailing

Boat ownership is among the highest in the world, and boats of all shapes and sizes can be rented from coastal resorts throughout the country. A luxury yacht with up to eight berths costs from around $750 per day (novices can charter a boat with a skipper) but a dinghy can be hired for around $35 per hour. Some companies offer flotilla trips, where you travel in a group with an experienced skipper. Sailing schools abound in resort areas and offer introductory lessons and courses for beginners up to racing standard. Airlie Beach and the Whitsunday Islands are the most popular sailing areas in Queensland, which is the centre of the yacht charter business. In many resorts, it's possible to get a job or a free ride as a crew member on a yacht. A book entitled *Go Boating Safely* is published by the Australian Government Publishing Service.

Yacht racing is popular in all areas, including 18-foot skiff (an Australian invention) races, which are staged in Sydney Harbour on most Saturdays during the summer. One of Australia's major sporting events is the Sydney to Hobart yacht race (run annually since 1945), which starts on 26th December. It's a handicap race over 630 nautical miles and attracts competitors from all over the world.

Scuba Diving & Snorkelling

Australia is a Mecca for scuba divers and snorkellers, particularly the Great Barrier Reef (see below), and diving shops abound in resort areas and the major cities. Divers in Australia need a Professional Association of Diving Instructors (PADI) certificate. To obtain a PADI certificate in Australia you usually require a doctor's certificate that you're fit to dive and you must usually show that you can tread water for ten minutes and swim 200m to be accepted on a course. Tuition in Australia is among the cheapest available in tropical waters and a PADI certificate course lasts five days for beginners and costs between $350 and $550.

There are diving schools in many coastal towns in Queensland, among the most popular of which are Airlie Beach, Cairns and Townsville. Shop around and ask about courses and avoid cheap 'cowboy' operators, as beginners have occasionally died after receiving poor tuition from these. Some diving clubs offer free introductory lessons in a local pool. Not all courses offer good value and with the cheaper courses you're likely to spend most of the time in a classroom or pool. A good mix is two days in the classroom and pool, a day trip to the coast (ideally, the Great Barrier Reef), and perhaps a further two days at sea, spending the night on board.

Great Barrier Reef

The Great Barrier Reef (2,000km/1,240mi in length) offers some of the world's best diving and is one of the natural wonders of the world, with some 400 different types of coral and around 1,500 species of fish. Experts enthuse about the diving on the outer reef wall and you can rent underwater photographic equipment (some boats even offer on-board film processing). You can also wreck dive on the reef, which is the graveyard of over 500 ships.

Many diving boats operate out of Cairns and other towns on the northern Queensland coast (boats are licensed to operate from around 20 sites). A day trip from Cairns costs around $115 for snorkellers and $155 for scuba divers, which includes two tank dives. Full snorkelling gear can be hired for around $30 a day, although some day trip organisers provide it free. During the wet season (January to March), however, floods

Blue jellyfish

can wash mud out into the ocean, seriously reducing viability. There are rules regarding where you can dive on the reef and what you can do (e.g. spearfishing is prohibited most places).

It isn't necessary to be a scuba diver or snorkeller to enjoy the Great Barrier Reef, which you can view from a glass-bottomed boat.

Other Locations

Although the Great Barrier Reef is the main destination for divers in Australia, there are interesting alternatives, including Fly Point at Port Stephens (north of Newcastle, NSW) and Ningaloo Marine Park (extending for 260km/160mi along the western side of the Northwest Cape in Western Australia), which is a smaller, more accessible version of the Great Barrier Reef (in places it's only a few hundred metres offshore). In some areas there are 18th century wrecks (e.g. off Rottnest Island near Perth, WA) and Second World War wrecks, which make interesting dives.

Surfing & Windsurfing

Surfing is a way of life rather than just a sport in Australia, where surfers (variously known as seaweed munchers, shark-suckers, surfies and waxheads) are mocked for their fanaticism. A number of international surfing competitions are staged in Australia, which has many professional surfers (Australian Mark Richards, who won the world title four times from 1979 to 1982, is considered the greatest competitive surfer of all time).

There are surfing schools in all major (and many minor) surfing areas, which run beginners' courses usually lasting three to seven days. It's best to have a few lessons before buying your own board to see whether you take to it (surfboards can be hired for around $35 per hour and some resort hotels allow guests to use them free of charge). A wetsuit is usually necessary in winter. Some schools operate surfing 'safari' trips, where you camp in remote locations and learn how to surf, fish and look after yourself in the wild. Surfing variations include surf mats, surfoplanes and boogie boards (small boards that you lie on while learning to master a proper surfboard). Boogie board users comprise a large proportion of those rescued by lifesavers; some aren't. Surfers must keep to the designated surfing areas off beaches; if you fail to comply, your board may be confiscated.

The best surfing is usually in NSW and Western Australia. The best beaches in Sydney are on the south shore, including Bondi, Coogee, Maroubra, North Narrabeen and Tamarama. Cronulla, south of Botany Bay, is also popular, and there are many beaches between Manly and Palm Beach on the North Shore. Byron Bay in northern NSW is considered one of Australia's best surfing areas. If you live in Canberra, the nearest good surfing beach is around 160km (100mi) away at Batemans Bay. The best surfing close to Melbourne is found at Mornington peninsula on the Great Ocean Road. Anglesea, Bells Beach, Jan Juc, Lorne and Torquay are also popular surfing venues in Victoria. In South Australia you need to travel to Pondalowie for the state's most reliable and strongest waves. Tasmania has some good surfing beaches, the best of which is Marrawah on the west coast, although the sea is very cold. Surfing conditions are poor north of Brisbane, and Surfers' Paradise doesn't live up to its name. Cottesloe and Leighton are popular surfing venues in Perth, although the best surf is found at Yallingup further south.

In some areas, you can call a number to find out where the best waves are, although local surfies can be protective of their patch and may discourage newcomers. Surf carnivals are held in popular surfing resorts during the season (December to April). Enthusiasts may wish to buy a copy of *Surfing Australia* by Mark Thornley (Periplus Publishing).

Windsurfing is popular throughout Australia, and windsurfing schools abound in beach resorts and on inland lakes (you probably learn faster on an inland lake than on coastal waters). Tuition costs around $175 for two half-days with a wetsuit included; windsurfer hire costs around $65 per day.

Rowing, Canoeing & Rafting

Rowing is a serious sport in Australia (Australia was fourth in the Olympic medal table in Athens in 2004), and there are rowing clubs in all major cities and towns. Canoeing is popular on rivers and lakes, where there are numerous clubs offering courses, equipment hire and tours (the *Canoeing Guide to NSW* is published by Australian Canoeing, ☎ 02-8116 9727, 💻 www.canoe.org.au), and Australia has a number of world champion canoeists.

White-water rafting is popular in Australia, with its many excellent rapid rivers graded from 1 (easy) to 6 (heeelp!!!!!). Among Australia's wildest rivers are the Franklin and Gordon in Tasmania. The Caltex Avon Descent is Australia's greatest (or, depending on your point of view, most appalling) whitewater experience, covering 133km (83mi) on the Avon River in Western Australia from Northam to Perth.

Melbourne from Williamstown, VIC

Victorian shopping arcade, Melbourne, VIC

17.
SHOPPING

Australia isn't one of the world's great shopping countries, either for variety or for bargains. Although the choice and quality of goods on offer has improved considerably in the last decade, they're still limited compared with Europe and North America, and many new products aren't available in Australia or cost a fortune (top-branded, imported goods are much more expensive in Australia than in many other countries). However, there's a reasonable choice of chain, department and international stores in the major cities, and exclusive boutiques and chic stores abound in arcades and shopping centres.

Australia doesn't exactly have a free and open retail market, and there are many cartels, monopolies, protected industries and tariffs, although competition reforms have been introduced in recent years. Consequently, consumers don't always get the best deal and often pay higher prices than in other countries. In the case of expensive and luxury items, you may be better off buying them overseas by via the internet (see page 151). However, the price of many consumer goods such as cameras, computers, electrical apparatus, household appliances and TV and stereo systems has fallen dramatically in recent years.

In stark contrast to the cities, small country towns are likely to have only a general store and a few other shops. Prices are also necessarily higher in rural areas owing to freight costs, and most people who live in the country stock up on goods and buy expensive items when visiting a city or large town, or shop by mail-order or on the internet.

There are many small, family-run stores in Australia, particularly in rural areas, small towns and the suburbs of major cities, although Australia's shopping scene has been transformed in the last few decades with the opening of numerous large shopping centres (malls) and vast supermarkets. Following the trend in most developed countries, there has been a drift away from town centres by retailers to out-of-town shopping malls, which has left some town centres run down and deserted. However, in some areas too many shopping malls were built for too few customers and some are now being redesigned, redeveloped, reinvented or even demolished. Towns are turning to 'street-scaping', i.e. reviving streets by landscaping, installing traffic 'calming' (speed bumps) or pedestrianising them. Australian cities invariably have excellent shopping centres, many housed in fine period buildings and pedestrianised streets, although parking can be a nightmare.

There's generally no bargaining or bartering in Australia, although if you intend to spend a lot of money or buy something expensive, you shouldn't be reticent about asking for a discount (except in department and chain stores and supermarkets, where prices are usually fixed). Many shops will match any genuine advertised price, although often reluctantly. Taxes are usually included in advertised prices, although for some items goods and services tax (GST – see page 312) may be added to the marked price. Since the demise of one and two cent coins, prices have been rounded up or down to the nearest five cents. Always shop around before buying, but make sure that you're comparing similar goods or services, as it's easy to 'save' money by purchasing inferior products.

Goods made in Australia often have a green and gold symbol to distinguish them from less expensive (and supposedly inferior) goods made in Asia.

In general, Australian-made products are of high quality, although they're often more expensive than similar imported goods.

A wealth of quality arts and crafts are sold in Australia, including ceramics, embroidery, glassware, handbags, hand-woven and knitted woollen garments, hides and skins (particularly sheep- and lambskin products), jewellery (e.g. diamonds, gold, opals and pearls), leather goods, paintings, rugs, traditional Australian 'outback' clothing, and woodwork. Aboriginal art (of which there are many styles produced by different tribes) is popular and is best purchased directly from artists' co-operatives or Aborigine-owned shops rather than from tourist shops. It's cheapest in Alice Springs, Darwin and outback towns, although genuine Aboriginal art can be expensive. Aboriginal Arts Australia (AAA) was established by the government to market Aboriginal and Torres Strait Islander arts and crafts, through its shops in Alice Springs, Darwin and Perth. Much 'Aboriginal' artwork is mass-produced junk, and cheap 'fake' Aboriginal souvenirs are also made in Asia,

so before buying anything always check where it was made.

Most shops accept major credit and debit (EFTPOS) cards, although you may be asked for proof of identification. Personal cheques aren't usually accepted, and some shops don't even accept cash, in order to deter robbers. In major cities and tourist areas you **must** be wary of pickpockets and bag-snatchers, particularly in markets and other crowded places. **Don't tempt fate with an exposed wallet or purse or by flashing your money around.**

Many retail outlets require customers to allow staff to search their bags (excluding very small bags such as handbags) when paying or leaving a shop. This is usually shown by a sign; by entering a shop you consent to having your bags searched (no sign, no checks). If you have any questions about your rights as a consumer, contact your local citizens' advice bureau, consumer affairs office or fair trading bureau. Most retailers, particularly department and chain stores, exchange goods or give a refund without question, but smaller shops aren't so enthusiastic. The quality of service and assistance in shops ranges from excellent to poor, depending on the type of shop, although generally Australian shopkeepers aren't renowned for their service. Shopping guides are available in many areas, including the essential *Bargain Shoppers* guides to Melbourne and Sydney (published by Universal Magazines, Unit 5, 6–8 Byfield Street, North Ryde, NSW 2113, 🖳 www.universalmagazines.com.au) and *Shopping in Exciting Australia and Papua New Guinea* by Ronald Krannich (Impact Publications). Many shops, particularly department and chain stores, provide free catalogues at Christmas and other times of the year. If you're looking for a particular item or anything unusual, the yellow pages

Consumer confidence has fluctuated in recent years, and the retail sector has been relatively flat since the recession in the early '90s. While many Australians have become bargain hunters, deserting department stores for no-frills retailers and discount stores such as Big W, Harris Scarfe and Kmart, upmarket department stores such as David Jones and Myers are also flourishing.

There's a lively second-hand market in Australia for almost everything, from antiques to motor cars, computers to photographic equipment. With such a large second-hand market there are often bargains to be found, particularly if you're quick off the mark. Many towns have a local second-hand or junk store and charity shops (e.g. Salvation Army or Vincent de Paul), selling new and second-hand articles for charity, where most of your money goes to help those in need. There are a number of national and regional weekly newspapers devoted to bargain hunters such as the *Trading Post* in Sydney.

Classified advertisements in local newspapers are also a good source of bargains, particularly for furniture and household appliances. Shopping centre (mall) and newsagent bulletin boards and company notice boards may also prove fruitful. Expatriate club newsletters are a good source of household items, which are often sold cheaply by those returning home. Car boot (trunk) sales are gaining popularity in Australia, and garage sales, where people sell their surplus belongings at bargain prices, are also popular. Sales may be advertised in local newspapers and signposted on local roads (they're usually held at weekends).

Another place to pick up a bargain is at an auction, although it helps to have specialist knowledge about what you're buying (you'll probably be competing with experts). Auctions are held in Australia throughout the year for everything from

can save you a lot of time and trouble (and shoe leather). Shopping Tours have become popular in recent years, whereby shoppers are guided round mainly discount and warehouse shopping in Sydney (e.g. Shopping Spree Tours ☎ 02-9360 6220), Melbourne (e.g. Shopping Spree Tours, ☎ 03-9596 6600) and Adelaide (e.g. Adelaide Shopping Tours, ☎ 1300 137 897).

SALES & BARGAIN SHOPPING

Most shops hold sales at various times of the year, the largest of which are in December/January and July. The most popular sales are the post-Christmas (or end-of-year) sales, which traditionally start on 26th December, when savings of up to 60 per cent are possible. Some shops seem to have a permanent sale, although retailers aren't permitted to advertise goods as reduced when they've never been advertised or sold at a higher price.

antiques and paintings to motorcars and property. Local auctions are widely advertised in newspapers and via leaflets.

There are antique shops and centres in most towns, and street markets and fairs are common in the major cities (where you can pick up interesting items – but you must get there early to beat the dealers to the best buys). For information about markets, ask at your local tourist office or library.

SHOPPING HOURS

Shopping hours in Australia vary with the city or town, the state or territory and the day of the week, but generally are among the most liberal in the world.

Shopping hours have been extended in recent years, and in some states (e.g. Victoria) shops can now open 24 hours a day, seven days a week, apart from a few public holidays (e.g. before 1pm on ANZAC day, and at any time on Christmas Day and Good Friday).

Most large stores and many smaller shops are open from 9 till 5 or 6 on Sundays.

In the major cities, many shops are open for up to 12 hours a day (some are even open 24 hours) and on Sundays, and many remain open all day on Saturdays. Department stores may open on Sundays (e.g. from 10am to 4pm) and some open earlier on sales days, e.g. at 7.30 or 8am. City chemists', delicatessens and newsagents' usually open on Sundays (e.g. from 8am until 8pm), and chemists' may open up to 24 hours a day. There are Food Plus shops and 7–11 stores (modelled on the eponymous American stores) in the major cities which, despite their name, open 24 hours a day and may have a petrol station 'attached'.

Harbourside shopping centres in Sydney (such as Darling Harbour) are open from 10am to 9pm, Mondays to Saturdays and from 10am to 6pm on Sundays. Many city bookshops are open during the evenings and throughout weekends. Even shops which aren't open all day and all night usually open until 9 or 9.30pm one evening per week, generally on Thursdays or Fridays.

In some areas, shops stay open an hour later in summer than in winter. Most shops in resorts such as the Gold and Sunshine Coasts are open at weekends and on public holidays as well as late at night. Normal shopping hours in country areas are usually from around 8.30 or 9am to between 5 and 6pm, Mondays to Fridays, and from 9am until noon on Saturdays.

DEPARTMENT & CHAIN STORES

Australia has a number of excellent department and chain stores. For the uninitiated, a department store is a large store, usually on several floors, which sells almost everything and may also include a food hall. A chain store is a store with a number of branches, usually in different towns, e.g. Kmart, Target and Woolworths. There are dozens of chain stores in Australia, selling everything from books and clothes to electrical and household goods.

In department stores, each floor is usually dedicated to a particular type of goods, such as furniture and furnishings or women's or men's fashions. Some stores have departments where engraving, key cutting and shoe repairs are done while you wait. Some stores are housed in beautiful art-deco or Victorian buildings and many are air-conditioned with a restaurant or cafeteria, telephones and toilets. The floor at street level is designated the ground floor in Australia, the floor above the ground floor is the first floor and the floor below the ground floor is usually called the basement.

The major department store chains in Australia include Coles Myer and David Jones. Adelaide, Brisbane, Canberra, Melbourne, Sydney, have both, Sydney boasting two David Jones stores, one with an excellent international food hall. Coles Myer's store on Bourke Street Mall in Melbourne is the largest department store in the southern hemisphere and one of the ten largest in the world. Other department stores Fosseys in Canberra, Fitzgerald's in Hobart, and Ahern's in Perth. Department stores have struggled in recent years, under pressure from no-frills retailers and discount stores, although some have been revitalised and are making a strong comeback.

Many department and chain stores provide customer accounts and allow the account balance to be repaid over a period of time, although this isn't usually wise, as the interest rates are high. Many department and chain stores offer gift vouchers, which can be redeemed at any branch. Department stores (and many smaller shops) provide a gift wrapping service, particularly at Christmas time, and deliver goods locally or send them by post/courier, both within Australia and worldwide.

SHOPPING CENTRES

In the last few decades, numerous vast indoor shopping centres (called malls after their American counterparts) have sprung up in out-of-town areas throughout Australia. Malls usually contain a huge selection of shops, including a large department store and many of the most popular chain stores, and are open seven days a week. The main attractions are one-stop shopping and free parking, which usually means you can simply wheel your trolley full of purchases to your car. The largest malls incorporate a wide range of leisure attractions, including children's play areas, cinemas, food halls, fun parks, games arcades and a variety of cafes, pubs and restaurants.

> ⚠ **Caution**
>
> **Most towns and cities have covered shopping centres, although parking is often expensive and difficult in city and town centres, particularly on Saturdays, and parking areas may be located some distance from shops.**

Among the most famous city shopping centres are the vast Melbourne Central (home to around 300 shops) and the Centrepoint Shopping Complex, MLC Centre, Queen Victoria Building (around 200 shops) and Strand Arcade in Sydney. Many city malls are housed in restored period buildings (such as the converted GPO building in Sydney, now the New

Mall), which are often connected by tunnels and walkways to other shops and centres.

MARKETS

Most small towns have markets on one or two days a week, and in major cities and towns there may be a market (or a number) on most days of the week. Markets are cheap, colourful and interesting, and are often a good place for shrewd shoppers to pick up bargains, although you need to be careful what you buy (beware of fakes). Items commonly for sale in markets include arts and crafts, books, clothes, fish, fruit and vegetables, household goods, jewellery and meat. Markets are the best place to buy fresh food, where the quality and variety rivals that of any country. Arts and craft markets are common in major cities and resort towns, where artisans can often be seen at work. Flea markets are popular in the major cities and sell second-hand goods, including antiques, books, bric-a-brac, clothes and records. Some towns have permanent covered or indoor market places where markets are held from Mondays to Saturdays, and in some cities there are also popular outdoor Sunday markets. Check with your local council, library or tourist office for information (guides are available to markets in some states, e.g. Victoria).

FOOD

The quality and variety of food in Australia are superb and the equal of any country in the world. Food outlets include delicatessens (delis), ethnic food shops, general and corner shops, markets (where the freshest fish, meat and other produce are usually available) and, of course, supermarkets. There's a wealth of gourmet food shops in the major cities offering everything from bread and cheese to fruit and vegetables, from cakes and pastries to coffee and tea. You can buy almost any ethnic food and ingredients somewhere in Australia, and in the major cities there are shops specialising in imported American and British foods, although prices can be high. Australia still maintains the quaint British tradition of delivering milk to homes in many towns and cities (home bread deliveries are also made), and many shops deliver groceries, either free or for a small fee.

Australians have been eating more healthily in recent years, consuming less red meat (although they're still big meat eaters) and alcohol, and eating more fruit and vegetables. Meat is reasonably priced and of excellent quality, as generally is fresh fish and seafood (although it can be expensive). Most supermarkets have reasonable fruit and vegetables, owing to the high turnover of stock (although you should avoid packaged produce, which may be stale or over-ripe as well as being more expensive). Many supermarkets bake their own bread on the premises and most

have cheese, fresh fish and meat counters as well as their own delicatessens. Home cooking is one of the casualties of modern living and most Australians don't have enough time to shop and cook elaborate meals. Consequently, prepared, oven-ready meals, microwave food and take-away meals are increasingly popular, and all supermarkets cater for this lucrative growth market.

Food prices in Australia vary according to the city, the shop and the season. Brisbane has the lowest cost of living in the country, followed byAdelaide and Melbourne, while Darwin is the most expensive, as most food must be transported from outside the territory. The current prices of selected foods in Australia's capital cities are listed in the monthly *Australian Outlook* newspaper (see **Appendix B**).

Australians by most of their groceries in supermarkets, which are (not surprisingly) among Australia's most profitable retailers. However, despite increasing pressure from the major supermarket chains, independent grocers are expected to survive by providing locally-oriented products and personal service.

Supermarkets

Woolworths has over 1,400 stores throughout Australia, including a chain of Metro supermarkets, and employs some 140,000 Australians (around one in every 100 Australians of working age is employed by Woolworths!). Woolworths was the first Australian supermarket to introduce food shopping on the internet (see page 151), a service it calls 'Homeshop'. Minimum orders are $30 and deliveries are available in Canberra, Melbourne and Sydney (in 2006). Coles Myer also has Coles Express stores in city centres stocking around 13,000 products and offering up-market deli products, gourmet take-home meals, a home catering service and personalised cakes (e.g. for office celebrations).

Supermarkets carry some 45,000 products in their major outlets, although they've reduced the less popular brands in recent years.

> The biggest supermarket chains in Australia are Woolworths and Coles Myer, which together account for nearly 70 per cent of the market, the remainder being split between a few smaller players and independents.

Supermarkets may have in-store bank kiosks and petrol stations, and they also have plans to introduce news agencies and pharmacies. Major supermarkets open seven days a week and in some cities remain open until midnight. They provide trolleys, which usually require a deposit of 20 cents; some stores insist that customers use a trolley or basket even when they're buying only a few items. Nearly all supermarkets provide free plastic carrier bags and boxes, and provide staff to help you pack your purchases.

All supermarkets in Australia use computerised (electronic point-of-sale) pricing systems where a bar code is included on the labels of goods and is read by a laser reader at the checkout. Always check your receipt carefully, as customers are frequently overcharged, particularly on special offer items. In most supermarkets, if an item is scanned at a higher price than advertised (or displayed), you're usually entitled to it free under the voluntary code of practice of the Australian Supermarket Institute. Self-scanning, where customers scan their own goods, has been introduced in some supermarkets in recent years. Under this system, which reduces the time spent at checkouts, spot checks are made to deter cheats. In future, all supermarkets are expected to offer this option, although they won't do away with checkout staff (known as 'laser ladies') and will still offer the regular checkout service for those who don't wish to do their own scanning (and those who like a modicum of personal service).

Labelling

Many manufacturers make unsubstantiated and wild claims for their products, particularly 'health' foods and environmentally-friendly 'green' products, which are deliberately misleading and often illegal. You usually pay a premium for anything with a claim to be 'free-range', 'low calorie' or 'low fat', many of which are bogus, although stricter guidelines on food labelling have been introduced in recent years and claims such as 'high fibre', 'light', 'low cholesterol', 'low fat' and 'sugar-free' must meet specific standards.

There are also regulations concerning the vitamins and minerals that can be added to food and new rules about where food is produced. All highly perishable goods (e.g. dairy produce, fresh foods and prepared foods) must have a 'use by' date, after which their sale is illegal (perishable goods are usually discounted a day or two before the use by date). Use by dates are widely ignored in country areas. Regulations regarding the handling and storage of food have also be tightened in recent years to curb outbreaks of food poisoning, which is estimated to make thousands of Australians sick each year. All food is sold by the metric measure in Australia (see **Appendix C** for imperial comparisons).

CLOTHES

Good quality clothes are expensive in Australia, as there are high tariffs on imported clothing and footwear. The good news is that the mild climate for much of the year means that most people don't need an extensive wardrobe.

It used to be said (with some justification) that fashions arrived in Australia a decade after they had swept Europe and North America, although this is certainly no longer the case. Today, Australian clothes shops offer a wide range of attire, from traditional made-to-measure clothing to the latest ready-to-wear fashions, with prices ranging from a few dollars to several thousand. Top quality and exclusive (i.e. expensive) international women's and men's fashion shops abound, and all the leading international labels are available in the major cities. In addition to department and chain stores), all towns and cities have a wealth of independent shops covering the whole fashion spectrum and all price brackets. Bush clothes (or 'bush chic') can be purchased at specialist shops, including R M Williams (whose clothing has achieved cult status) and the Thomas Cook Boot and Clothing Company in Sydney. Bush clothes include leather belts, moleskins (trousers made of closely woven cotton), oilskin raincoats (e.g. Drizabone), riding boots, sheepskin coats, wide-brimmed Akubra hats and work shirts.

Although Australia's once thriving clothing manufacturing industry has largely disappeared, the country has a number of celebrated designers, some of whom have received international acclaim. Nowadays, most clothes are imported from Asia and many aren't of the same quality as is common in Europe and North America. However, although the quality of foreign-made clothes may occasionally be suspect, you usually get what you pay for.

☑ **SURVIVAL TIP**

Shopping malls and markets are the best place to shop for reasonably priced clothes, and mail-order fashion offers (in newspapers and magazines) usually provide good value.

Reasonable clothes can also be purchased at huge savings from factory outlets, which also sell 'designer' clothes (although you should try them for size and check for faults). There are vintage and second-hand clothing shops and markets in most Australian cities, plus clothes hire shops, where you can hire anything from a ball gown to a wedding dress, a morning suit to an evening dress.

The sizing of clothes in Australia follows the American rather than the British system – i.e. 'medium' is usually on the large side (see **Appendix D** for a comparison of sizes). Women's clothing manufacturers usually base their sizes on the average size 12, and many women find it difficult to locate fashionable clothes that fit. Most shops provide a tailoring or alteration service (for a small fee) and many also provide a made-to-measure service.

ALCOHOL

The average Australian family spends around $25 per week on alcohol (liquor), which can only be purchased from licensed bottle shops (also called grog shops), pubs and restaurants (it is never sold in food shops or supermarkets). There are drive-in bottle shops (possibly with 'express' and 'browse' lanes) in major cities, where the biggest and cheapest chains include Liquorland and Liquor Mart. The largest single liquor shop in Australia is Dan Murphy's Cellar in Melbourne with some 8m bottles of wine (enough to throw a **really** good party!). Opening hours vary with the state or territory, e.g. from 8.30am until 8.30pm, or 10am until 10pm, Mondays to Saturdays. There are reduced opening hours on Sundays. Wine can also be purchased in Australia by mail-order (e.g. from Cellarmaster Wines), and Australians buy some 15 per cent of all bottled wines by mail-order (compared with less than 2 per cent in most other countries). You must

be aged over 18 to buy alcohol or consume it in a public place.

Wine

Although part of the 'new world', Australia isn't a newcomer when it comes to wine production; vines were first imported in 1788 and commercial production started in the 1820s in New South Wales (NSW) and Tasmania, and in the 1840s in South Australia, Victoria and Western Australia. Until 1960, some 80 per cent of Australian wine was fortified wine. Today, over 90 per cent of Australian wine is table wine and the country has around 1,800 wineries. Only a dozen years ago, Australia imported more wine than it exported, but wine is currently one of the country's fastest growing exports: the industry has an ambitious long-term strategy known as Vision 2025, by which date Australian wine is expected to be worth $4.5bn in annual sales and the industry to be the world's most profitable and influential. Exports are made to nearly 100 countries, the biggest markets in the early 21st century being the UK, the US, Canada, New Zealand and Germany. However, while exports have soared, home sales have fallen in recent years, the average annual consumption per head being around 20 litres – Australians are increasingly choosing quality over quantity and drinking more premium wines, some of the best Australian wines rarely reaching foreign markets.

Australia makes good sparkling wines (both red and white), which are produced by the *méthode champenoise* (fermented in the bottle), although they may no longer be called champagne. An excellent sparkling wine can be purchased for $14 to $20.

Australia is also noted for its fortified wines, although they aren't well known overseas. These include brandy, madeira, muscat, port (red and white), sherry and tokay (the last having little in common with the Hungarian wine after which it's named), the best of which are world-beaters. Port, which is made in Victoria, is particularly popular in Australia, the best vintages selling for $80 to $100 per bottle (and a match for the best that Portugal has to offer), while a good non-vintage (such as Hardy's Tall Ships Tawny Port) can be purchased for around $15.

Australian wines have earned an increasing international reputation and respect in recent years, with their distinctive, deep fruity flavour, full-bodied character and consistency. In fact, Australian wines have been astounding the judges and competitors at international wine exhibitions for over a century – one story tells of an Australian wine winning a competition in France in the 19th century and promptly losing it again when it was discovered where the wine was produced! Australian winemakers have a pragmatic approach and are quick to introduce the latest technology; vineyards are noted for their high yields and low production costs.

Producers aren't afraid to experiment; indeed many go out of their way to introduce new grape varieties and create exciting new blends (they threw out the rule book decades ago). The climate, modern equipment, soil and techniques, allied to the Australians' freedom from tradition and love of experimentation, combine to produce some of the best and most original wines in the world.

> ⚠ **Caution**
> Australian wines are noted for their high alcohol content, which for reds can be up to 14.5 per cent.

Regions

South Australia produces around 45 per cent of Australia's wine, NSW (including the Australian Capital Territory – ACT) 27 per cent, and Victoria 22 per cent, the remainder being shared between Tasmania, Western Australia and Queensland, with a small area of production around Alice Springs in the Northern Territory. The most famous wine regions are the Barossa Valley, Clare Valley and Coonawarra in South Australia; the Hunter Valley in New South Wales (famous for its white wines, particularly chardonnay); the Geelong area, Mornington Peninsula, Rutherglen/Milawa (port and muscat) and Yarra Valley, where sparkling wines are produced, in Victoria; and the Margaret River and Swan River Valley in Western Australia.

Although each region is noted for a particular style of wine and specific grape varieties (varietal wines – most famously from cabernet sauvignon, shiraz and chardonnay), there's also a lot of experimentation and blending of grapes between regions. The top five wine producers are Hardy Wine Company, Southcorp, McGuigan Simeon, Orlando Wyndham and Beringer Blass (although a spate of mergers and acquisitions has made it difficult to keep abreast of who's who). There are also many small independent producers, sometimes called boutique vineyards, making high-quality wines.

Australia has no national wine appellation or quality control scheme, and buyers need to rely on the reputation of individual producers, which is generally an excellent guide, as there's little year-on-year variation in quality.

Wineries

Many wine producers welcome visitors and provide tastings, although you may need to make an appointment at the smaller wineries, which are often more attractive than the larger, more commercialised establishments. Some wineries charge a fee of a few dollars (to deter freeloaders), which is refunded if you buy. Wine at wineries isn't necessarily cheap, however, and can be more expensive than at bottle shops. Some wineries have restaurants where you can sample local food and wines at the same time. Most wine regions have a visitors' centre, e.g. the Barossa Valley Visitors' Centre, which is open from 9am to 5pm, Mondays to Fridays and from 10am to 4pm at weekends and on public holidays.

Prices

The price of Australian wine has been increasing steadily over the years and the best are now among the more expensive in the world. Prices have increased owing to a shortage of quality grapes (although there was a grape glut in 2005, which should curb further increase in the short term). A reasonable bottle costs around $8 to $12, while $18 to $25 buys an excellent bottle. Imported wines are available in Australia, but are expensive compared with similar quality local wines.

Australia invented the wine box ('chateau cardboard') in 1974; it consists of a plastic

bag in a box with a built-in tap. Some two-thirds of all wine sold in Australia is sold in boxes (flatteringly referred to as casks). Wine boxes are good value (but no longer the bargain they once were) and cost from $10 to $15 for three or four litres, up-market wines costing around $12 for a two-litre box.

Information

There are many books about Australian wine, including *Australian Wine - A Pictorial Guide*, *The Penguin Good Australian Wine Guide* by Huon Hooke and Mark Shield (Penguin), which contains ratings for all of Australia's premium wines, *The Wines of Australia* by Oliver Mayo (Faber & Faber), and James Halliday's *Australian Wine Companion* (Harper Collins).

Beer & Other Drinks

Before the Second World War, Australia was largely a beer-drinking country, and Australians still consume far more beer than wine – over 100 litres per head annually. Beer is sold in 375ml bottles (stubbies), 750ml bottles and 375ml cans. The cost of a dozen 750ml bottles is around $35 to $45. Most beer bottles have twist off caps, so no bottle-opener is required. Canned beer costs around $1.75 for single cans (375ml) reducing to around $1.35 per can when you buy a case of 24. 'No name' beers cost around 20 per cent less than the market leaders and don't taste significantly different. There's no longer a refund on beer cans, which should be recycled. For more information about Australian beer see **Bars & Pubs** on page 338.

> Australia's most famous spirit is rum, of which the Bundaberg ('Bundy') brand is the national spirit (there are also 'over-proof' rums, which are lethal).

Australians don't drink a lot of spirits such as whisky and gin (around a litre per head, per year). A bottle of 'cheap' Scotch whisky or London gin costs around $25 to $30.

NEWSPAPERS, MAGAZINES & BOOKS

Australians read more newspapers per head than most other nationalities and some 600 are published, including national, state, city, regional and suburban newspapers. In general, the Australian press is fairly parochial and provides scant coverage of foreign news (unless it's a major news item), and you shouldn't expect unbiased political reporting in Australian newspapers, which often reflect the political bias of their owners. Most major newspapers are owned by News Corporation (run by Rupert Murdoch) or John Fairfax Holdings. The law regarding cross-media ownership is restrictive (foreign ownership is limited to 15 per cent) and has led to clashes between the government and media interests.

Daily and Sunday newspapers range from the broadsheet 'quality' newspapers for serious readers and the popular tabloids. There are just two national dailies, *The Australian* (including *The Weekend Australian* on Saturdays) and *The Australian Financial Review* (Mondays to Fridays only). *The Australian* is Australia's foremost newspaper and is printed simultaneously at six sites around the country from Mondays to Fridays. Other major newspapers are either published state-wide or limited to one city. Those with the largest circulation are *The Herald-Sun* (Melbourne), *The Daily Telegraph* (Sydney), *The Sydney Morning Herald*, *The West Australian* (Perth), *The Courier Mail* (Brisbane), *The Age* (Melbourne) and *The Advertiser* (Adelaide). Most large regional cities have daily newspapers, and smaller towns publish weekly newspapers (there are also suburban weeklies in capital cities).

Most dailies publish larger Saturday editions, which usually sell around 50 per cent more copies than the weekly editions and may include weekend supplements, e.g. *The Weekend Australian* and *The Sydney Morning Herald*. The major Sunday newspapers include *The Sunday Telegraph* (Sydney), *The Sunday Mail* (Brisbane), *The Sun-Herald* (Sydney), *The Sunday Herald-Sun* (Melbourne), *The Sunday Times* (Perth) and *The Sunday Mail* (Adelaide). Most Sunday newspapers are tabloids and aren't as good quality as the weekday newspapers. Most cities also have evening newspapers.

The circulation figures of Australian newspapers are relatively small by international standards, for example (in 2006) 131,500 for *The Australian* and 702,000 for *The Sunday Telegraph*.

There's an active foreign-language press in Australia catering to immigrants of many

high cost of distribution. Most cafes and tea rooms provide free newspapers for customers to read on the premises, and newspapers can also be read in public libraries and at newspaper offices.

Australians are avid magazine readers, and around 1,000 titles are published every month, plus a further 700 trade publications. Foreign magazines are also popular and widely available in the major cities (particularly British and American magazines). Popular Australian political and business magazines include the *Business Review Weekly*, *My Business* and *The Bulletin* (Australia's leading weekly news and current affairs magazine). Women's magazines abound and include *Family Circle, Good Housekeeping, New Idea, The Australian Women's Weekly* (which is actually published monthly and sells around 1m copies) and *Woman's Day* (which is a weekly). There are also Australian editions of many international women's magazines, including *Cosmopolitan*, *Marie Claire* and *Vogue*.

All Australian cities have a wealth of book shops (with luck all selling this book). Angus & Robertson's Bookworld and Dymocks are the largest chains of book shops and are represented in most major cities (Dymocks in Sydney claims to be the largest book shop in the southern hemisphere). Many department stores and supermarkets also have book departments. Melbourne is reckoned to be the best city for book shops in Australia, with Sydney not far behind. Many book shops are open during the evening (some until midnight) and at weekends in major cities. Several also offer internet sales sites where you can purchase new and used books.

There are specialist book shops in major cities covering topics such as antiquarianism, art, backpacking, children's subjects, feminism, gay and lesbian interest, the new age and travel. In many towns there are 'remainder' or

different nationalities and producing around 150 publications in 40 languages. Foreign newspapers are available from international news agencies in cities and cost around $6, or $10 for the larger Sunday editions, although they're usually a few days old when they arrive in Australia. They're also available in some (e.g. state) libraries.

Newspapers of particular interest to British expatriates include the *Guardian Weekly, International Express, UK Mail* and *Weekly Telegraph*, all of which are published weekly and contain a summary of the week's most important news; they're available on subscription.

Newsagents in the ACT, NSW, Queensland and Victoria have a monopoly on newspaper distribution to convenience stores, homes and milk bars. Newsagents are open long hours in cities and also on Sundays. Prices are generally higher in remote areas and states other than where a newspaper is published, owing to the cut-price book shops, and in the major cities there are second-hand bookshops for collectors and bargain hunters. Many large book shops in cities also have a selection of foreign-language books, and there are ethnic book shops in some areas. Government publications can be purchased at Commonwealth Government Book Shops in the major cities or by post from the Australian Government Publishing Service, PO Box 84, Canberra, ACT 2601.

⚠ Caution

Books aren't sold at fixed prices in Australia, and books published locally are typically sold at a 10 per cent discount. However, imported books can be expensive and are usually marked up by 25 to 50 per cent.

Book tokens are sold and accepted by most book shops. Many organisations and clubs run their own libraries or book exchanges and public libraries usually have an excellent selection of books.

FURNITURE

Furniture is usually good value in Australia, where there's a wide choice of modern and contemporary designs in every price range, although (as with most things) you generally get what you pay for. Exclusive imported furniture is available (with matching exclusive prices), although imports also include reasonably priced quality leather suites and a wide range of cane furniture from Asia. Among the largest furniture chain stores in Australia are Freedom Furniture and Harvey Norman. The major department stores offer a wide range of top quality Australian-made and imported furniture. The Swedish giant Ikea currently has

seven outlets in Australia, with more planned.

When ordering furniture, you may have to wait weeks or months for delivery. Try to find a shop which has what you want in stock or which can give you a guaranteed delivery date (after which you can cancel and receive a full refund if you wish). A number of manufacturers sell direct to the public, although you shouldn't assume that this will result in huge savings and should compare prices and quality before buying.

There are also shops specialising in beds, leather, reproduction and antique furniture, and a number of companies manufacture and install fitted bedrooms and kitchens. Fitted kitchens are an extremely competitive business in Australia and you should be wary of 'cowboy' companies specialising in shoddy workmanship.

It costs around $10,000 to furnish an average three-bedroom home, although second-hand furniture is widely available.

Furniture can also be rented for around $225 to $300 per month for an average home. If you want reasonably priced, quality, modern furniture, there are a number of companies (e.g. Ikea, see above) selling furniture for home assembly (which helps keep down prices). Assembly instructions are generally easy to follow (although some people think Rubik's cube is easier) and some companies print instructions in a number of languages (some of which are unrecognisable). Retailers often assemble furniture for you, although this increases the price. Some shops offer you $100 or $200 for your old suite when you buy a new one from them. This may not be much of a bargain, however, particularly if your suite is worth more than the amount offered, and you should always shop around for the best price and quality.

Furniture and furnishings is a competitive business in Australia, and you can often reduce the price by some judicious haggling, particularly if you're spending a large amount of money. Some shops will match a competitor's price rather than lose a sale. Another way to save money is to wait for the sales. If you cannot wait and don't want to (or cannot afford to) pay cash, look for an interest-free credit deal. Check the advertisements in local newspapers and national home and design magazines such as *Australian Interiors, Better Homes and Gardens* and *home Beautiful*. See also *The Bargain Shoppers* guides to Melbourne and Sydney. All large furniture retailers publish catalogues, which are generally distributed free of charge.

HOUSEHOLD GOODS

Large household appliances such as cookers and refrigerators are usually provided in furnished rented accommodation and may also be fitted in new homes. Many homeowners include fitted kitchen appliances such as a cooker, dishwasher, refrigerator and washing machine when selling their house or apartment, although you may need to pay for them separately. Dishwashers are still something of a luxury item in Australia and aren't usually found in rented accommodation. There's a wide range of household appliances available in Australia, from Australian and foreign manufacturers. Some makes of certain appliances, e.g. refrigerators, cost twice as much to run as others (choose those with a high energy efficiency rating), and refrigerators/freezers in Australia are normally 'tropicised' or fan-assisted to cope with the high average temperatures.

If you wish to bring large appliances with you, such as a dishwasher or washing machine (it's illegal to import a refrigerator), note that the standard Australian unit width isn't the same as in other countries. Check the size and the latest Australian safety regulations before shipping these items to Australia, as they may need expensive modifications. On the other hand, if you already own small household appliances, it's worthwhile bringing them to Australia, as usually all that's required is a change of plug (but check first). If you're coming from a country with a 110/115V electricity supply (e.g. the US), you need a lot of expensive transformers (see **Electricity** on page 123).

> ☑ SURVIVAL TIP
> **Don't bring a TV to Australia as it won't work (see page 197).**

A huge choice of home appliances is available in Australia, where smaller items such as electric irons, grills, toasters and vacuum cleaners aren't expensive and are usually of good quality. It pays to shop around, as prices, quality and reliability vary (the more expensive imported brands are usually the most reliable). Before buying household appliances, whether large or small, it may pay to check the test reports in *Choice* magazine (see **Consumer Rights** on page 387) at your local library.

If you need kitchen measuring equipment and cannot cope with decimal measures, you must bring your own cups (American and Australian recipe cups aren't the same size), jugs, measuring scales and thermometers (see also **Appendix D**). Australian pillows and duvets aren't the same size or shape as in many other countries.

HOME SHOPPING

Mail-order catalogue shopping has long been popular in Australia, particularly among people living in remote areas, and has recently become increasingly popular thanks to fax and the internet (see below). Direct retailing is fairly common in Australia, particularly for computers, financial and insurance services, and office equipment and supplies. It's big business in Australia and direct retailers and their suppliers employ over 660,000 Australians (according to the Australian Direct Marketing Association). In addition to dedicated mail-order companies, most major department stores also provide mail-order catalogues.

TV shopping is also becoming increasingly popular and products sold through 'infomercials' have had a huge success. Shopping channels include TVSN, broadcasting 24 hours per day and offering an unconditional money-back guarantee and quick delivery.

Australian mail-order companies should be members of the Australian Direct Marketing Association (ADMA), which has a code of conduct and offers assistance to consumers (☎ 02-9277 9400, 🖳 www.adma.com.au). The

ADMA also offers extensive advice on e-commerce.

DUTY-FREE ALLOWANCES

Visitors or migrants are permitted to import the following goods duty free:

- 2,250ml (2.25 litres) of alcoholic drinks, including beer, wine or spirits, per person over 18 years of age;
- 250g of tobacco products (for customs purposes, 250 cigarettes are equal to 250g) per person over 18 years of age;
- all personal clothing and footwear (excluding furs);
- articles for personal hygiene/grooming such as toiletries but excluding perfume concentrate;
- articles taken out of Australia on departure, but excluding articles purchased duty and/or sales tax-free in Australia (any duty/tax-free goods are counted against your duty-free allowance);

- any other articles (except alcohol and tobacco) obtained overseas or duty and sales tax-free in Australia, up to a total purchase price of $900 per person aged 18 or over ($450 for under 18s) – this includes goods intended as gifts or received as gifts, whether personal or carried on behalf of others.

Members of the same family travelling together may combine their individual duty-free allowances. Duty must be paid on any goods above the duty-free allowance, excess articles being valued for duty on the price paid for them, converted to Australian dollars. However, duty up to $50 is waived on goods in excess of duty-free concessions, provided that the goods are declared as excess to concessions and aren't for commercial purposes. If purchase receipts aren't available, alternative methods of valuation may be used. Some items (such as jewellery) are subject to high rates of duty. Payment of duty can be made in cash, by international credit card and by travellers' cheque (in A$). Information can be obtained from state customs offices (see **Appendix A**) or the Australian Customs Service (🖳 www.customs.gov.au).

As well as duty-free shops at Australian airports, there are city duty-free shops where you can buy duty-free goods (upon presentation of a valid international air ticket) before going to the airport to catch your flight. Check the prices here first as they're usually lower than at airports. Purchases must usually be taken from the shop in a sealed bag (marked 'Important – Duty-Free Goods in Possession') that you must keep intact until you've boarded your flight. Alcohol, cigarettes, jewellery and perfume must be purchased within ten days of your departure and kept sealed until you've left Australia. However, some goods such as cameras, most electronic goods, film and watches can be used as soon as they're purchased.

> **Caution**
>
> **The maximum permitted value of purchases is $900, and these are listed on your ticket and must be shown to customs officers at airports, so you must take them with you as hand luggage when leaving the country.**

One unusual feature at Australian airports is in-bound duty-free shops where you can buy alcohol and tobacco products and a limited range of perfumes and cosmetics before you reach immigration and customs.

GST Refunds

A GST refund on goods to the value of over $300 is available to tourists leaving Australia (known as the tourist refund scheme or TRS). In order to obtain the refund, the goods must be bought at a registered shop or business, where a tax invoice must be obtained, and must be exported within 30 days of purchase. When you leave Australia, you should present to a customs officer the tax invoice and you may also be required to present your departure documents (e.g. airline ticket), your passport and the purchased goods. If the amount refundable is less than $200, you usually receive it in cash. If the amount is larger, you must lodge a payment authorisation with instructions on how you wish the money to be repaid to you (by cheque, by credit card or by payment to an Australian bank account). GST refunds can be reclaimed only at airports or seaports with a TRS verification facility, and GST isn't refundable on duty-free goods.

CONSUMER RIGHTS

If you buy something which is faulty, damaged or doesn't work or measure up to the manufacturer's or vendor's claims, you

can return it and obtain a replacement or your money back. Extended warranties and money-back guarantees don't affect your statutory rights as a purchaser, although the legal status of a warranty may be unclear. Some shops offer an unconditional refund or exchange of goods, which isn't required by law, although this guarantee is usually only for a short period and goods must be returned unused and as new.

You have the right to a refund or replacement goods if you buy a faulty product (with the exception of goods purchased at auction). Signs such as 'all care but no responsibility taken', 'goods left for repair at your own risk', 'no refunds given' and 'no responsibility for loss or damage' are meaningless and unlawful under state and federal laws. All goods must be of 'merchantable' (reasonable) quality and fit for the purpose for which they were sold, and it's illegal for sellers to include a clause in the conditions of sale that exempts them from liability for defects, lack of care or product faults. Most traders back down once you show that you know

the law and are determined to obtain your rights.

There are a number of consumers' organisations in Australia, including citizens' advice bureaux, consumer affairs bureaux, fair trading bureaux, ombudsmen and small claims tribunals (see also **Legal System & Advice** on page 405). A consumer affairs bureau gives general advice over the telephone, but won't usually take any action on a complaint unless it's made in writing or in person. If you make a complaint, the bureau gives you advice and writes to the trader concerned on your behalf, or may refer your complaint to another government or consumer body to investigate. However, callers are often given poor or incorrect advice. If you're unable to resolve a dispute with a trader or tradesman, you can take a dispute to a small claims or consumer claims court or tribunal for a small application fee. Claims are limited to between around $2,000 and $6,000, depending on the state. Traders who fall foul of the Trade Practices Act can be fined, usually up to a maximum of around $225,000, but much more in extreme cases.

The consumers' champion in Australia is the Australian Consumers' Association (ACA, ☎ 02-9577 3333, 🖥 www. choice.com.au), which publishes a number of magazines for consumers, including *Choice* (their general consumer magazine), *Choice Money and Rights*, *Computer Choice, Consuming Interest* (a quarterly magazine about consumer issues) and *Health Reader*. The ACA also publishes and distributes a wide range of consumer-oriented books. *Choice* contains independent tests of products and services and is essential reading when buying major household goods. Magazines are available only on subscription and not from newsagents. The ACA also provides a Consumer Information Service ☎ freecall 1800-069552).

18.

ODDS & ENDS

This chapter contains miscellaneous information, in alphabetical order. Although all topics aren't of vital importance, most are of general interest to anyone planning to live or work in Australia, including everything you ever wanted to know (but were afraid to ask) about tipping and toilets.

ABORIGINES

The ancestors of the Aborigines are thought to have travelled from south-east Asia and arrived in Australia at least 45,000 years ago, although some experts believe it could be over 60,000. When the first Europeans established a colony in New South Wales (NSW) in 1788, there were thought to be some 300,000 Aborigines living in Australia in tribes, either semi-nomadic or sedentary. Like many tribal peoples, the Aborigines have always lived in harmony with their environment, making the most of the adverse climatic and geographical conditions.

In spite of the Aborigine presence, the European settlers treated their new home as *terra nullius* (no man's land) and refused to recognise Aborigine land rights. Over the next two centuries Aborigines were driven from their land, systematically slaughtered or forced to do low-paid agricultural work, as well as suffering vast casualties from imported European diseases such as influenza and smallpox. In the early 20th century, most Aborigines were confined to government reserves or Christian missions. Australia then introduced its now infamous 'assimilation policy', under which the federal government had complete

jurisdiction over Aborigine lives, including legal custody over Aborigine children, many of whom were taken away from their families and put into foster homes or training centres. This generation of Aborigines is now referred to as the 'stolen generation'.

It was not until 1976 that the first Aborigine Land Rights Act was passed in the Northern Territory, where about half of all land is now under Aborigine jurisdiction, including Uluru (or Ayers Rock). Nevertheless, Australia's record in trying to improve the living standards of its indigenous peoples over the last 25 years is among the worst in the developed world. In the rest of the country, very little land has been returned to the Aborigines, who live in squalor and at serious disadvantage.

> Aborigines have a life expectancy of 20 years less than white Australians and an unemployment rate four times higher, as well as numerous other problems such as alcohol and substance dependency.

Amnesty International regularly launches scathing attacks on Australia's treatment of

Aborigines, and many decent Australians are appalled by the plight of many Aborigines and most want them to receive a better deal (provided it doesn't cost them any money or land). Although attitudes are improving, much is still left to be done to reconcile the two societies.

CITIZENSHIP

Immigrants are eligible for Australian citizenship after just two years' residence in the previous five years, but this must include a total of 12 months in the two years immediately before making a citizenship application, which costs $120. Applicants must be at least 18 years of age, have a basic knowledge of the English language, be capable of understanding the nature of their citizenship application and understand the responsibilities and privileges of Australian citizenship, be of good character, and be likely to live permanently in Australia or maintain a close and continuing association with Australia. The ability to speak English doesn't apply to people over 50, and those over 60 aren't required to understand the responsibilities and privileges of Australian citizenship. However, a more stringent 'citizenship test' has recently been proposed, which would include up to 200 questions about Australia to be answered in English.

Exceptions to the above rules apply to armed forces personnel (who need only to have served for three months), former Australian citizens (who need only to have been resident for 12 months in the last two years), permanent residents not present in Australia but engaged in activities beneficial to Australia, spouses, widows, widowers of Australian citizens (who normally need to have been resident only for the 12 months prior to their application) and various others. In certain cases, such as that of spouses/widows/widowers of Australian citizens, applicants must show that they would suffer significant hardship or disadvantage if they weren't granted citizenship.

Most people born in Australia before 26th January 1949 automatically became Australian citizens on that day, and those born between 26th January 1949 and 20th August 1986 automatically became Australian citizens unless one of their parents was a foreign diplomatic or consular official. Since 20th August 1986, citizenship has been acquired if, at the time of a person's birth in Australia, at least one parent was either an Australian citizen or a permanent Australian resident. Those born overseas to an Australian citizen can apply for registration as an Australian citizen by descent if they meet certain criteria. A child who's a permanent resident and legally adopted in Australia (after 22nd November 1994) automatically acquires Australian citizenship if at least one parent is an Australian citizen at the time of the adoption.

New citizens must make the following 'pledge of commitment': "From this time forward, under God, I pledge my loyalty to Australia and its people, whose democratic beliefs I share, whose rights and liberties I respect, and whose laws I will uphold and obey." (The words 'under God' may be omitted). The benefits of citizenship include the right to run for public office and to enlist in the defence and police forces, and undertake certain other public service jobs, the right to be protected under Australian diplomatic arrangements overseas, the right to claim full welfare benefits, the right to register children born overseas as Australian citizens and the right to vote, which is in fact an obligation, as Australian citizens are not only obliged to enrol on the electoral register, but obliged to vote in general elections as well! If you're granted Australian citizenship, you can retain your foreign passport (provided the country of issue permits dual nationality) and obtain an Australian passport. Once you're an Australian citizen, you must use your Australian passport to enter and leave Australia.

Over 70,000 people are granted citizenship each year, although only around one in ten immigrants becomes an Australian citizen (despite the fact that some 80 per cent of immigrants interviewed within six months of their arrival claim they will take out citizenship).

British immigrants are the least likely to become Australian citizens.

In 2001 the government launched a citizenship 'drive' coinciding with the Federation Centenary Year to try to persuade permanent residents to become citizens. For further information, consult the comprehensive Australian citizenship website (www.citizenship.gov.au).

CLIMATE

The biggest attraction of Australia for many immigrants, particularly those from the northern hemisphere, is its temperate climate and the lifestyle it affords. Australia has climates to suit everyone, although it broadly has just two climatic zones. To those from the northern hemisphere, Australia is an 'upside down' country (weather-wise), with the warmest part (nearest the equator) at the top and the coldest at the bottom. Some 40 per cent of Australia lies in the tropical zone, while the remaining regions (south of the Tropic of Capricorn) are in the temperate zone. The tropical zone has two seasons: wet (November to April) and dry (May to October), while the temperate zones have four seasons: spring (September to November), summer (December to February), autumn (March to May) and winter (June to August).

Australia's seasons are also the opposite of those in the northern hemisphere, i.e. when it's summer in Europe it's winter in Australia and vice versa. Australia is less prone to climate extremes than other continents of comparable size because it's surrounded by oceans and has few high mountain masses. The most pleasant seasons in most of Australia are spring and autumn, with the exception of Tasmania where summer is the most enjoyable season.

The average hours of sunshine per day in Australia's capital cities ranges from five in Hobart to eight in Perth. January is the hottest month in most southern regions, while February is hottest in Tasmania and southern Victoria. Average summer temperatures in January range from around 17°C (63°F) in Hobart to 29°C (84°F) in Alice Springs and Darwin. Temperatures exceed 30°C (86°F) in most areas during summer, and temperatures occasionally soar to 45°C (113°F) or higher. The hottest place in Australia is Marble Bar (WA), where the temperature from October to March usually averages 40°C (104°F) or more. The highest recorded temperature in Australia is 53.1°C (127°F), measured at Cloncurry (QLD) in 1889. If you cannot stand extreme heat, choose to live in Adelaide, Hobart, Melbourne or Sydney rather than Brisbane, Darwin or Perth.

Australia has the lowest rainfall of any continent after Antarctica. Average annual rainfall for the capital cities varies from 1,536mm (60.4in) in Darwin, which is in the monsoon region, to 530mm (21in) in Adelaide. During the wet season in the north (particularly from January to March), roads can quickly become impassable as tracks turn into raging rivers after a downpour. In contrast, large arid inland areas get less than 250mm (10in) of rain per year. In winter, temperatures can fall below 10°C (50°F) on winter nights in most regions, and sleet can fall on the urban areas of Hobart and even in Adelaide and Canberra. Snow is rare except in the Australian Alps, straddling the New South Wales/Victoria border,

where it's possible to ski between June and October (see page 361).

Approximate average daily maximum/minimum temperatures for Australia's major cities are shown below in centigrade and, in brackets, Fahrenheit.

The weather forecast is available in daily newspapers, via the internet and TV teletext services, and on TV and radio broadcasts. Warnings of extreme weather conditions affecting motoring are broadcast regularly on ABC national and local radio stations. Many newspapers devote a full page (often in colour) to the weather, and news programmes on radio and TV are usually followed by detailed weather forecasts and analyses. Forecasts are usually accurate, not least because of Australia's generally stable weather patterns.

Australia is frequently hit by frequent natural disasters, including bush fires, cyclones, droughts, floods and tropical storms, and occasionally by earthquakes. Periodic droughts are a way of life and a constant worry for farmers. In many rural areas, rivers are sucked almost dry by the demand for water for irrigation, causing many to slow to a trickle and the water to become polluted by toxic algae (rivers are

Average Temperature High/Low °C (°F)

City	Spring	Summer	Autumn	Winter
Adelaide	22/11 (72/52)	28/17 (82/63)	22/12 (72/54)	16/8 (61/46)
Alice Springs	30/14 (86/57)	35/21 (95/70)	18/13 (82/55)	20/7 (68/45)
Brisbane	26/16 (79/61)	29/21 (84/70)	26/16 (79/61)	21/10 (70/50)
Cairns	29/21 (84/70)	31/24 (88/75)	29/22 (84/72)	26/18 (79/64)
Canberra	19/6 (66/43)	27/12 (81/54)	20/7 (68/45)	12/1 (54/34)
Darwin	33/24 (91/75)	32/25 (90/77)	32/23 (90/73)	30/20 (86/68)
Hobart	17/8 (63/46)	21/12 (70/54)	17/9 (63/48)	12/5 (54/41)
Melbourne	20/9 (68/48)	25/14 (77/57)	20/11 (68/52)	14/7 (57/45)
Perth	22/12 (72/54)	29/17 (84/63)	24/14 (75/57)	18/9 (64/48)
Sydney	22/13 (72/55)	26/18 (79/64)	22/14 (72/57)	17/9 (63/48)

Cyclones (known as 'blows') are fairly common in the summer months (between November and April) in the northern regions of Australia (from Western Australia to Queensland). In 1974, Cyclone Tracey flattened Darwin with gusts of up to 280kph (174mph). It killed 66 people and destroyed more than 5,000 homes, leaving fewer than 500 intact in what was the worst natural disaster in Australia's modern history. The city has since been completely rebuilt to 'withstand' cyclones. More recently, Exmouth in Western Australia was devastated by Cyclone Vance in 1999. Violent tropical and electrical storms are common in the north of Australia, particularly northern Queensland. In January 1998, for example, torrential rains in Townsville caused widespread flooding when 500mm (20in) of rain fell in just 12 hours.

Greenpeace Australia Pacific predicts that the Australian climate will become more in extreme in the 21st century. The average temperature of much of the country is expected to rise by up to 2°C by 2030 and by up to 6°C by 2070. Australia, already the world's second-driest continent (after Antarctica), is also expected to become even drier. High temperatures and this increasing dryness combined in 2003 to cause severe bushfires which burned for 59 days, a sign of what is to come. Rainfall in south-west Australia could decline by up to 60 per cent by 2070, and much of Australia can expect storms with greater maximum wind speeds and more sudden and extreme rainfall (but with a reduction of total rainfall).

Earthquakes are rare in Australia, although in 1989 one struck Newcastle (NSW), killing 13 people, injuring 160 and causing damage costing $1.7bn.

Australian Capital Territory & Canberra

The Australian Capital Territory (ACT) has an average of seven hours sunshine per

also polluted by salt and some are dying). There are frequent (sometimes permanent) water restrictions in most regions of Australia, even in the major cities. The Australian weather is periodically affected by *El Niño*, an ocean warming phenomenon where prevailing cold water currents along the west coast of South America become warmer, thus upsetting weather patterns and leading to floods in North and South America and droughts in Australia.

Bush fires are a constant threat in country areas (mainly in summer), which are often caused by lightning strikes, although many are started by people. They often threaten country towns and occasionally major cities, and deaths among fire-fighters and homeowners are frequent (some people needlessly lose their lives because they refuse to abandon their homes). Lighting fires in a bush fire zone is strictly forbidden; even where it's permitted, you must ensure that every spark is extinguished before leaving and must **never** throw cigarette butts out of car windows.

day and summer temperatures average around 27°C (81°F). Canberra has four distinct seasons, with hot, dry summers and cold winters. It's situated inland, so the climate isn't moderated by the ocean as in Australia's coastal cities. Canberra is the coldest capital city in winter, with temperatures plunging to around freezing at night, although it rarely snows. Winter mornings are frosty but most days are bright and sunny, temperatures averaging around 12°C (54°F). Annual rainfall is low at around 660mm (26in).

> Canberra is noted for its clean air and isn't prone to pollution in summer.

New South Wales & Sydney

New South Wales (NSW) has a variety of weather, although it generally has an agreeable climate. Sydney's rainfall is higher than average for an Australian city at 1,140mm (45in), which is spread fairly evenly throughout the year, including summer. In Sydney it rains on some 150 days a year, the wettest months being April to June. It has mild winters, when daytime temperatures rarely fall below 10°C (50°F) and can reach 17°C (63°F). Summer temperatures average around 25°C (77°F), although the humidity sometimes makes the weather feel oppressive, particularly from January to March. Occasionally, the temperature in Sydney exceeds 40°C (104°F) and can still be 30°C (86°F) at midnight, although this is rare, as cool sea breezes help lower temperatures during heat waves. Sydney frequently has high pollution levels in summer.

Northern Territory, Darwin & Alice Springs

The Northern Territory has a tropical climate with just two seasons: wet from November to April (also known as the 'green' season) and dry for the remainder of the year. The weather is generally as hot as hell all year, with average daily temperatures in Darwin between 20 and 33°C (68 and 91°F) and reaching over 40°C (104°F) for weeks on end in the central desert regions (and Alice Springs). Rainfall is almost non-existent in Darwin from May to September, which is more than compensated for between December and March, when it's between 250 and 380mm (10 and 15in). The heat and humidity are often oppressive, with humidity as high as 95 per cent just before the start of the wet season. The Northern Territory is prone to cyclones and violent thunderstorms. Alice Springs has an average of 9.5 hours of sunshine a day, with warm winters and hot, dry summers. Summer evenings can be cool, while in winter the temperature often falls below freezing at night. Alice has low annual rainfall, with an average of around 40mm (1.5in) falling between December and February.

Queensland & Brisbane

Queensland has a sub-tropical climate in the south and is tropical in the north,

Sydney, NSW

with wet and dry seasons. Summer is the wet season, when rainfall averages around 1,000mm (40in), particularly in the north, where violent thunderstorms and floods are common. The state has the wettest town in Australia, Tully, with over 4,000mm (160in) of rain per year (four times that of Brisbane). Extremes of flood and drought are common in country areas. Brisbane is one of the sunnier cities in Australia, with an average of over 7.5 hours per day and mild, sunny winters. Average temperatures are between 10°C (50°F) and 21°C (70°F) in winter and between 21°C (70°F) and 29°C (84°F) in summer. Summer temperatures can, however, exceed 38°C (100°F), and humidity can be very high, although it's usually tempered by cool sea breezes in coastal areas.

South Australia & Adelaide

South Australia is the driest state and its northern regions are mostly desert. The inhabited parts, however, have an almost Mediterranean climate, characterised by long, dry summers and short, mild winters, and are said to have the best year-round climate in Australia. Adelaide is noted for its low rainfall (the lowest of any state capital) at just 530mm (21in), which falls mainly between April and October. It isn't too cold in winter, when average temperatures are between 8°C (46°F) and 16°C (61°F). There's an average of four hours sunshine per day in winter and seven hours in summer. Summers are hot with maximum temperatures averaging over 27°C (81°F), although nights aren't usually too hot and there's low humidity. It's very hot in the northern desert regions, where summer temperatures are frequently over 40°C (104°F).

Tasmania & Hobart

Tasmania has a temperate climate, with four distinct seasons, but is without the extremes of the mainland states. It's the coldest part of Australia and is occasionally hit by icy southerly winds from Antarctica,

although it's still relatively mild by northern European standards. Nights can be cool throughout the year, although winters aren't as cold as in Canberra and Alice Springs. The average winter temperature in Hobart is between 5°C (41°F) and 12°C (54°F). It has around 620cm (25in) of rain per year (half that of Sydney and Brisbane), rain falling on around 180 days per year, mostly between July and October. In the west, rainfall is around four times that of Hobart. Hobart enjoys an average of around five hours of sunshine per day, maximum summer temperatures averaging around 21°C (70°F).

 Caution

Water temperatures in Tasmania are much lower than in the rest of Australia, and it's generally too cold for sea bathing.

Victoria & Melbourne

Victoria has a generally mild climate, somewhere between maritime and continental, although it can have very hot and cold periods. The weather in Melbourne can be extremely changeable, and it's said that you can experience all four seasons in one day. Melbourne experiences cold, wet and windy weather in autumn and winter, although temperatures rarely fall below 5°C (41°F), with highs of around 14°C (57°F). Mountainous regions have snow in winter, when temperatures remain below freezing for long periods. Melbourne has low rainfall of around 660mm (26in), half that of Sydney and Brisbane, and this is fairly evenly spread throughout the year (June and July are the wettest months). The city has mild autumns (the most pleasant season) and hot summers, when temperatures average 25°C (77°F) and occasionally soar to 40°C (104°F).

Western Australia & Perth

The southern areas of Western Australia enjoy a Mediterranean climate, while northern areas have a tropical climate with dry and wet seasons. Perth is the sunniest capital city in Australia with an average annual temperature of 18°C (64°F) and over eight hours' sunshine per day. Spring and autumn are the most pleasant seasons. The average rainfall is low at 914mm (36in) per year (although it's over 1,500mm/60in on the south-west coast) and it falls mainly between April and October. The northern and eastern regions have very low rainfall and consist mostly of desert. Winters in Perth are mild and sunny but wet, with average temperatures of between 9°C (48°F) and 18°C (64°F), although frost is common away from coastal areas. Summers are very hot, with daytime temperatures frequently between 30°C (86°F) and 40°C (104°F) and hot nights, although it's a dry rather than humid heat. The summer heat is mitigated by cool breezes that blow in off the sea from Fremantle (west of Perth); the breeze is called the Fremantle Doctor for its soothing effect (some enterprising locals bottle it and sell it to tourists!).

CRIME

Australia is a safe country by international standards, however, it's important to take the usual safety precautions that you would in any country and to bear in mind that Australia has become a more violent place in the last decade. Crime rates vary from state to state: the ACT and the Northern Territory are the most dangerous places to live, while Tasmania and Victoria are the safest. Burglary is rife in Australian cities, particularly Sydney, and nearly 500,000 cases are reported each year. Car theft is also widespread in cities, although the incidence is decreasing. Beware of pickpockets and opportunist thieves such as bag snatchers in major cities and crowded places, and keep a close eye on your belongings when travelling on public transport and when staying in hotels or hostels. 'Ramraiding' used to be widespread in Australian cities but has fallen off since retailers stopped displaying valuable goods in their windows.

Although basically honest, many Australians delight in 'beating the system', including cheating their employers (bludging), fiddling their income tax (e.g. by not declaring income) and not paying motoring fines – unpaid fines total $millions annually. Many people take their lead from officials, the police and politicians, among whom corruption is widespread. Organised crime is rife in Australia's major cities, where much crime is linked to Asian gangs. It's estimated that crime costs Australia some $32bn annually, including white-collar crime (e.g. false pretences, forgery and fraud), which is the country's largest crime cost (it's also the biggest crime growth area and the hardest to prosecute). Around $13bn (of the $32bn mentioned above) per year is spent on public and private crime prevention.

Violent crime is still rare in Australia, although it has increased considerably in the last decade or so (as in most other developed countries).

 Caution

There has been a huge increase in armed robbery in the last decade, and assaults, murders and rapes have all increased dramatically, although muggings are still relatively rare.

Violent crimes by the young have soared (many children and youths are totally out of control) and gun (see below) and knife culture is widespread. Armed robbery is becoming fairly common in Australia, where banks, petrol stations and retail outlets are the most common targets (particularly all-night shops and petrol supermarkets). As a result, some outlets have stopped accepting cash and many are considering closing at night. Women should avoid travelling alone at night, and hitchhiking is dangerous for both sexes (there have been a number of murders of backpackers in recent years, many involving a serial killer, thankfully now behind bars).

Central government, local authorities, police forces and security companies all publish information and provide advice on crime prevention. Police forces have local crime prevention officers whose job is to provide free advice to businesses, homeowners and individuals. See also **Legal System & Advice** on page 405 and **Police** on page 411.

Drugs

Illegal drug use and trafficking is a vast and growing problem in Australia, although the authorities in some states have taken a more enlightened view of the use of 'soft' drugs such as cannabis and marijuana in recent years, and there are nationwide moves to liberalise laws prohibiting their use.

Smoking cannabis (pot) and marijuana is widespread in Australia, where around a third of the adult population uses or has used the drugs, and growing cannabis/marijuana plants is a vast cottage industry. The law regarding their use varies considerably. They've been decriminalised for minor possession and growing offences in the ACT, the Northern Territory and South Australia, where there's a fine for possession or production but no conviction is recorded. However, possession is still a criminal offence in NSW, Queensland, Tasmania and Victoria, where possession and/or production can result in a fine of up to $500,000 (Queensland) and/or up to 25 years in jail (Victoria). Victoria has introduced a

'cannabis cautionary scheme' for first-time offenders, who receive a formal caution and are then referred to a drug treatment centre (police forces around the country are watching the scheme with interest and in some states are considering introducing a similar scheme for heroin offenders), while in Western Australia, since 2004 the possession of small amounts of cannabis or marijuana is usually subject to a fine rather than a conviction. Unlike hard drugs, there's little crime associated with cannabis or marijuana use.

Hard drugs are responsible for a large proportion of crime in Australia, including over half of all thefts in the major cities (which are committed by drug addicts to finance their habit). It's also estimated that heroin trafficking is involved in some 40 per cent of serious crime. Some officials would like to decriminalise all drug use and treat users as victims rather than criminals, although this is unlikely to happen in the near future in Australia.

Guns

Like Americans, Australians have a fascination for guns and there are millions of legal and illegal guns in private hands. However, the incidence of gun crime is remarkably low considering the number of weapons in circulation (only some 25 per cent of murders involve the use of guns). Following the Port Arthur massacre in 1996 (when 35 people were shot dead when a gunman went on the rampage), the government instituted a buy-back of automatic and semi-automatic guns (including pump-action shotguns and self-loading rifles) financed by a Medicare levy. Owners were given 12 months to hand in guns but, when the amnesty ended in 1997, it was conservatively estimated that a million people held guns illegally. There has been compulsory registration of firearms since 1st July 1997 and owners must be aged over 18, undergo a training and safety course and have a good reason to own a gun, such as belonging to a shooting club. New penalties for possessing illegal firearms include a $6,000 to $24,000 fine and up to four years' imprisonment, depending on the type of firearm. However, Australia's gun laws are still among the most liberal in the world.

Prisons

Australia has a tough sentencing and prison regime (including controversial private prisons), and the prison population has more than doubled since 1990 (prison violence is widespread). The Northern Territory has the highest prison population.

Many people are held on remand for up to 12 months in prison cells where conditions are often appalling, and around half of them are acquitted by the courts. A disproportionate number of Aboriginal and Torres Strait Islander people are convicted of crimes: these comprise just 2 per cent of the population but make up 20 per cent of prisoners in some states. Deaths in custody (including suicides) are high and include a disproportionately high number of Aborigines.

> Tougher sentences have been introduced in recent years in many states, and sentence-reducing or remission have been abolished, although neither policy has had much effect on crime rates (the main reasons for crime are drug use, family breakdown, poverty and unemployment – particularly among youths).

GEOGRAPHY

Australia is one of the world's oldest land masses (some of its rock was formed over 3bn years ago) and the largest island. Separated from other land masses, it evolved in partial isolation, resulting in its unique flora and fauna, and the development of the Aboriginal race, with a civilisation stretching back between 40,000 and 60,000 years. The country extends 3,200km^2 (1,988mi^2) from north to south and 4,000km (2,485mi^2) from east to west, covering an area of 7,682,300km^2 (2,966,144mi^2), including Tasmania, with a coastline of 36,738km^2 (22,826mi^2). It's the world's sixth largest country (after Russia, Canada, China, the US and Brazil) and is around the same size as continental US (minus Alaska), one and a half times the size of Europe (excluding Russia) and more than 30 times the size of the UK.

Australia lies in the southern hemisphere, south-east of Asia and between the Indian and Pacific oceans. Its nearest neighbour is Papua New Guinea, which is some 200km^2 (125mi^2) north of Cape York in the north-west. Bali and other Indonesian islands lie off the north-west coast, and the French island of New Caledonia is situated to the north-east. New Zealand is around 1,700km^2 (1,050mi^2) from the

covers most of Western Australia, a large part of the Northern Territory and South Australia, and part of Queensland. East of the plateau are the Central Eastern Lowlands, extending from the Gulf of Carpentaria in the north to eastern South Australia and the western Victorian coast. The Great Dividing Range (or Eastern Highlands) follows the east coast southwards from northern Queensland to southern Tasmania, separating a narrow fertile strip of land on the coast from the vast, flat, arid inland plain, which is broken only by a few low mountain ranges such as the Flinders and Macdonnell Ranges and the Olgas, and by Uluru (Ayers Rock). Uluru is the largest rock on earth, 9.4km (5.8mi) in circumference; if you're tempted to climb it, bear in mind that it's Aboriginal sacred ground and many people have died of heart attacks in the attempt! Other mountain ranges include the Hamersley Range, the Kimberleys and the Stirling Range in Western Australia, and the Snowy Mountains (in the Australian Alps) in Victoria, where Mount Kosciusko is the highest point (2,230m/7,316ft) in Australia.

Australia has the lowest rainfall of any continent after Antarctica (see **Climate** on page 393) and evaporation exceeds rainfall in 70 per cent of the country. Surface water is scarce and most lakes and rivers are dry most of the year (Lake Disappointment is appropriately named!). The country's longest rivers are the Murray, Darling, Ord and Swan. The main river is the Murray which, with the River Darling, has a catchment area covering NSW, Queensland and Victoria.

south-east coast, and to the south lies Antarctica. Australia is surrounded by four seas (Arafura, Coral, Tasman and Timor) and three oceans (Indian, South Pacific and Southern). Almost 40 per cent of the country lies north of the Tropic of Capricorn.

The Great Barrier Reef lies between 50 and 300km^2 (31 to 186mi^2) off the north-east coast and stretches from the Torres Strait to Gladstone. It's the largest coral reef in the world, extending some 2,000km^2 (1,260mi^2) and encompassing an area of around 200,000km^2 (77,226mi^2). The reef is the world's largest living entity and an important marine ecosystem containing many rare life forms (it has been declared a World Heritage site).

Australia is the world's flattest continent, with an average elevation of less than 500m (1,640ft) – the world's average is 700m (2,296ft) – and only around 5 per cent of it is more than 600m (1,968ft) above sea level. The Great Western Plateau

Severe salting has occurred in recent years due to indiscriminate land clearing for agricultural use, which has reduced irrigation potential and lowered the quality of drinking water (if nothing is done, the Murray-Darling basin will be dead in 40 or 50 years).

Lush forests are found only on the east coast, particularly in the far north.

Much of the centre and west of the country consists of barren terrain (some 1.5m km^2/579,195mi^2) – a third is desert or arid lands, around two-thirds semi-arid and shrub lands – and only around 6 per cent is cultivated for crops or used for grazing. Australia has three main deserts – the Great Sandy, the Great Victoria and the Gibson – and several smaller ones.

Australia is divided into six states (New South Wales, Queensland, South Australia, Tasmania, Victoria and Western Australia) and two territories (the ACT and the Northern Territory). The island of Tasmania (also called the Apple Isle) is larger than Denmark or the Netherlands and was founded by the Dutchman Abel Tasman in 1642 and originally named Van Dieman's Land (changed to Tasmania in 1856). External territories include the

Australian Antarctic Territory, Christmas Island, the Cocos (Keeling) Islands and Norfolk Island (the territory of Ashmore and Cartier Islands). Macquarie Island (around 1,600km/994mi south-east of Tasmania) is administered by Tasmania.

GOVERNMENT

The Commonwealth of Australia was formed on 1st January 1901, when the states gained their independence from the UK, prior to which each state was an independent colony. Australia has a parliamentary system of government based on the British system, while the (written) constitution and federal structure are based on the US model. The powers of the Commonwealth parliament (the legislature) are laid down in the constitution, which can be amended only by a referendum carried by a majority of voters in a majority of the states, as well as an overall majority. The Australian constitution provides for a division of power between the Commonwealth and the states. The sovereign head of the Commonwealth of Australia is the UK's Queen Elizabeth II, who's represented in Australia by the Governor-General and state governors (see **Republic Debate** on page 405). Australia has a three-tiered system of government: Commonwealth, state and local.

Commonwealth Government

Like Washington DC in the US, Canberra is the purpose-built capital city and capital of the Australian Capital Territory (ACT). The ACT was created as a compromise when New South Wales (NSW) and Victoria couldn't decide between them whether Sydney or Melbourne should be the capital of Australia. In 1911 the ACT, located roughly half way between Sydney and Melbourne, was acquired from the NSW government. The Northern Territory was transferred from the state of South Australia to Commonwealth administration in the same year. The Commonwealth government first convened in Canberra in 1927, before which Melbourne was the seat of federal government. A new Parliament House was inaugurated in 1988 on Capitol Hill.

The Commonwealth government has constitutional power over Australian territories (the ACT and the Northern Territory) and can overturn laws made there, e.g. the controversial euthanasia law enacted in the Northern Territory in 1995. It's responsible for banking, currency, customs and excise, defence, foreign affairs, immigration, income and sales tax, intellectual property (copyrights, patents and trademarks), international trade and commerce, postal services and communications, and social services in all states and territories. The Commonwealth government controls around 80 per cent of total government spending.

The Australian parliament is bicameral (consisting of two houses): the House of Representatives and the Senate (see below).

House of Representatives

The house of representatives (lower house), whose principal role is as legislator (maker of laws), is elected every three years and its 150 members (MHRs) make up the government of the day. Each MHR is elected by and therefore represents a constituency with approximately the same population. The number of members allocated to each state and territory is proportionate to the number of residents, as follows: New South Wales (49), Victoria (37), Queensland (28), Western Australia (15), South Australia (11), Tasmania (5), the ACT (2) and the Northern Territory (2). Mathematicians might notice that the total of the states' representatives is 149, not 150, but the figures are from the government

website – it's a concern that the people running the country cannot add up!

Senate

The senate (upper house) represents state interests and reviews legislation passed by the lower house; its approval is required before proposed legislation can become law. The senate is composed of 12 senators from each state and two from each territory, making a total of 76. Senators are elected for a six-year term (except for the ACT and Northern Territory senators, who serve for three years) by a system of proportional representation. In senate elections, the whole state constitutes the electorate.

State & Territory Government

The lower house is called the Legislative Assembly or the House of Assembly and is usually elected for four years, while the upper house is usually called the Legislative Council and elected for twice the period of the lower house. The ACT, the Northern Territory (self-governing since 1978) and Queensland have a single house (the Legislative Assembly). The head of the largest party in the ACT and NT is called the chief minister, and the Queen's representative is called the administrator.

> Each state has its own parliament (with upper and lower houses, except for Queensland, which abolished its second house in 1922), a cabinet headed by a premier, a governor (who's the Queen's representative) and its own constitution.

State governments have control over Aboriginal welfare, community services, conservation, education, forestry, health, housing, infrastructure, justice, mineral resources, police, roads, tourism, transport and water. The states receive the bulk of their funding from the Commonwealth government, although they also levy stamp duty and charges on banking and other financial transactions, plus various other duties and taxes. They're continually in conflict with the Commonwealth government over funding for services such as healthcare and law enforcement.

State parliaments are generally elected under a preferential voting system for the lower house and by a variety of other systems for the upper house. Under the preferential voting system, voters must place number 1 against their first choice and 2, 3, etc. against the other candidates in order of preference. If nobody secures a majority from the first preference, the second is used. If nobody secures a majority from the second, the third is used, and so on.

State government was long noted for its corruption and nepotism, although this is generally considered to be no longer the case. Many state politicians do hardly

anything, and in some states (e.g. Victoria) the upper house rarely sits (upper houses are essentially just a 'rubber stamp' for the lower house).

Local Government

Local government, which comprises various councils, is responsible for a number of services, including community services, the construction and maintenance of local roads and other infrastructure, libraries, parks and recreation grounds, public health, refuse (rubbish) collection, sports and community centres, swimming pools, town planning, water and sewerage, and weights and measures. Councils (including city, municipal, shire and town councils) provide services to their communities and control local matters, such as property zoning. There are some 717 councils in Australia, whose powers and responsibilities vary from state to state, consisting largely of elected representatives who usually act in an honorary capacity. Although generally well run, some councils have built up huge debts, often through building and acquisition programmes. Councils are largely funded by business taxes, property taxes (council rates), supplemented by federal and state funds. Local government departments and officials are listed in telephone directories under 'Local Government'.

Political Parties

Australia has six main political parties: the Australian Democrats (AD), the Australian Labor Party (ALP), the Country Liberal Party (CLP), the Independent Party (IND), the Liberal Party (LP) and the National Party of Australia (NPA). Some parties are regional parties and stand in only one or two states (among them, despite its name, the NPA), and Australia essentially has a two-party system, comprising the 'liberal' and 'national' parties (right wing), who traditionally form a coalition, and the

ALP (left wing, but a much more moderate party than it was in the '60s and '70s), with the AD and the IND minor players. The party with a majority of seats in the House of Representatives generally forms the government (although, if it has no overall majority and cannot find coalition partners, it could find itself in opposition). The leader of the largest party (or the largest party in a coalition) becomes the Prime Minister (currently Kevin Rudd), who presides over a cabinet of ministers.

The Labor Party held power from 1983 until 1996, since when the Liberal/National coalition has been the dominant force – until November 2007, when the Labor Party was re-elected. All Australian citizens must vote in Commonwealth elections or face a fine (although there's a move to change to voluntary voting). Only Australian citizens over 18 years of age and British subjects who were resident in Australia and on the electoral roll on 25th January 1984 may vote.

Republic Debate

The sovereign head of the Commonwealth of Australia is Queen Elizabeth II, the Queen of England, who's represented in Australia by the governor-general (G-G) and the state governors. The G-G is nominated by the Commonwealth government and appointed by the Queen, and acts on the advice of ministers in virtually all matters. However, this system led to a major political crisis in 1975, when the G-G dismissed the elected Labor government of Gough Whitlam and called a general election after the government failed to pass the budget bill (this has, in fact, occurred six times in Australia's parliamentary history). There's a huge gulf between republicans and monarchists, and a referendum was held in November 1999. In spite of previous indications that the republicans would win, 55 per cent of Australians voted against the republic.

Only the ACT and Victoria voted clearly for a republic. Therefore, for the time being, Queen Elizabeth remains Australia's head of state.

> There's an ongoing debate in Australia over whether the country should become a republic and replace the Queen by an elected president.

LEGAL SYSTEM & ADVICE

Australian law is based on English common law, which it resembles closely. This is divided into statute law, enacted by legislature, and common law, which is developed by the courts, both of which continually evolve as a consequence of precedents set by the courts. There's also a clear distinction between criminal law (acts harmful to the community) and civil law (disputes between individuals). If there's a dispute between Commonwealth and state law, Commonwealth law takes precedence.

Less serious criminal cases are heard by magistrates or justices of the peace, while serious criminal and civil cases are held before a judge and jury (e.g. in a district or county court) consisting of 12 people in criminal cases (fewer in civil cases). There's no capital punishment in Australia. Many minor offences incur fines, including drinking under age, littering, smoking where it's prohibited, taking alcohol on to Aboriginal lands, and topless and nude bathing (where prohibited) – laws regarding these and other activities differ from state to state.

Each state or territory has its own court system, consisting of magistrates' courts, intermediate district or county courts and supreme courts. There are also state children's courts, courts of petty sessions, family courts (which handle divorce cases and the custody of children), industrial courts (which hear claims concerning industrial relations law) and small claims courts. Some disputes, such as family disputes and disputes between neighbours, can be resolved by mediation. Most criminal cases in Australia are heard in state or territory courts. There are huge delays in hearing cases, and local courts are hugely over-burdened, some magistrates courts processing up to 60 cases per hour. In serious cases, the accused are held in prison on remand for up to a year before their cases are heard; when the accused is on bail, cases can take up to 18 months to come to court.

A federal system exists to deal with matters over which the Commonwealth government has jurisdiction. The highest court in the land is the High Court of Australia (created in 1976), which is the country's final court of appeal from the states' supreme courts. It's presided over by the chief justice and six other justices, all of whom are political appointees. In recent years, there has been an acrimonious relationship between the High Court and politicians (at stake is the balance of power between the judiciary and the government). Other federal courts include the Federal Court of Australia and the Family Court of Australia, both of which handle specialised cases involving federal law.

In 1986, Australia changed the constitution to prevent the UK making laws in Australia or having any government responsibility, thereby removing the ultimate legal appeal to the British Privy Council. At federal and state levels, the office of ombudsman deals with a variety of citizens' complaints against government administration. Administrative Appeals Tribunals hear appeals in cases involving freedom of information, immigration, pensions and tax.

If you're arrested, you aren't required to give your name or address and are permitted to contact a friend or lawyer (called solicitors in Australia) before answering any questions. The police provide an interpreter if you're arrested and cannot speak English. It's best to say nothing until a lawyer is present and even then you have the right to remain silent (although this may change under a government review). Your country's consulate or embassy in Australia (see **Appendix A**) can usually provide you with a list of local lawyers, if necessary speaking your native language. If necessary, the police provide a duty lawyer. In some states, interrogation is recorded on video. If you're charged with an offence, you may be released on bail (a surety) or remanded in custody (foreigners may have their passports confiscated to prevent them leaving the country).

Each state has a legal aid commission, and you may be able to obtain legal aid if you cannot afford a lawyer, although it's subject to a means test and is becoming increasingly difficult to obtain as a result of cuts; people are often refused help unless they're facing jail or a fine of over $1,000. Information about legal aid can be obtained from local courts.

☑ SURVIVAL TIP

Free legal advice is also available in all states and territories (there's a fee of $2 in Western Australia) from various organisations, including citizens' advice bureaux, community legal or justice centres and legal aid commissions.

As in most countries, civil liberties are constantly under threat, although Australia remains one of the most free and open countries in the world. For information regarding civil liberties in Australia, contact the Australian Civil Liberties Union (ACLU, ☎ 03-9347 8671, 🖳 http://go.to/aclu), which publishes an annual booklet, *Your Rights*, containing information about your legal rights in various situations. The booklet is available from ACLU and from newsagents for $6.50. See also **Consumer Rights** on page 387.

MARRIAGE & DIVORCE

As in most developed countries, Australians are marrying later – on average around 27 years of age for women and 29 for men. Many people choose to remain single and there's an increasing number of single, childless women, although the annual number of marriages has been increasingly slightly since the low of 2001. Some 70 per cent of Australian adults are married, around 15 per cent are lone parents and some 8 per cent live in de facto marriages (an unmarried couple living together as husband and wife). De facto couples don't have the same inheritance rights as married couples and should therefore ensure that their wills reflect their wishes.

Weddings may take place anywhere, and an increasing number (currently around 45 per cent) don't take place in a church. Anyone planning to marry must complete a *Notice of Intention to Marry* and give it to the person (e.g. a minister or civil marriage celebrant) who's conducting the marriage. Notice must be given between one and three months before the planned date of the marriage. Both parties must provide their birth certificates and a divorce decree or death certificate if they've been divorced or widowed. A man must usually be 18 to marry and a woman 16, although anyone aged under 18 must have their parents' consent to marry and permission from a judge or magistrate. A marriage must be witnessed by two people aged over 18. A legal marriage that takes place overseas is almost always recognised in Australia. A woman usually takes her husband's surname when she marries, although it isn't obligatory and she can retain her maiden name.

Australia has one of the highest divorce rates in the world, marriages lasting an average of less than eight years (there's around one divorce for every two marriages). The year 2001 saw the highest number of divorces (55,300). Under the Family Law Act, the only grounds for divorce in Australia are the irretrievable breakdown of a marriage; 'fault' (e.g. adultery, cruelty or desertion) no longer constitutes grounds for divorce. Under the law, a marriage has irretrievably broken down if a couple has lived apart for one year and there's no reasonable likelihood of a reconciliation. It's also possible for these conditions to be met when a couple lives separately and apart in the matrimonial home, although it's difficult to prove. If a couple have been married for less than two years, they must usually have considered reconciliation with the assistance of a marriage guidance counsellor before a court will hear divorce proceedings.

be granted. After one month, a decree becomes absolute and the parties are free to re-marry. Although the law varies with the state, generally when a *de facto* marriage breaks up after two years, either party can apply for custody of children, division of property or maintenance as if they were formally married.

MILITARY SERVICE

The Australian Defence Force (ADF) comprises three services: the Australian Army, the Royal Australian Air Force and the Royal Australian Navy. The combined strength of the ADF (including reservists and civilians) is around 105,000 (51,819 permanent service personnel, 26,927 reservists and the remainder civilians). Some 13.3 per cent are women, who are eligible for 99 per cent of navy and air force positions and around two-thirds of army positions (women are banned from carrying combat arms). In recent years, there has been an exodus from the services, and the armed forces are finding it difficult to recruit.

> There's no conscription (draft) in Australia, where all members of the armed forces are volunteers

The average cost of a divorce in court fees alone (excluding your solicitor's fees) is around $2,500, with a fee of $639 payable simply to file an application. Extra fees apply to obtaining court orders on access to and custody of children and property orders. For further details, visit the website of the Family Court of Australia (⌨ www.familycourt.gov.au).

One of the Family Court's main duties is to protect and promote the welfare and rights of dependent children. Both parents have joint custody of a child under Australian law, although one parent can ask for and be granted sole custody, in which case the wishes of the child are taken into consideration. Before maintenance is granted, the age, financial resources and obligations, and health of each party are taken into consideration (the same applies to the division of matrimonial property). Matters concerning the custody of children, division of property and maintenance must be decided before a divorce can

All soldiers initially enlist for a minimum of four years under the Open Ended Enlistment Scheme and after four years can apply for discharge by giving six months' notice. Applicants for the ADF must be Australian citizens or be eligible for grant of citizenship or must undertake to apply for citizenship when they become eligible. They must be aged at least 17 and under 35 (42 if they have a particular skill) and must be at least 152cm (5ft) tall. Reservists serve a minimum of 26 days a year (14 full-time). In recent years, a new form of reserve service has been introduced. Under the Ready Reserve programme, members serve full-time for 12 months and then train for 50 days per year for four years. Soldiers may also transfer from the regular army or army reserve to the Ready Reserve, in which case they're committed to five years' part-time training.

Australia is a signatory to a number of defence treaties, including the Five Power Defence Arrangement (FPDA) with Malaysia, New Zealand, Singapore and the UK, and the ANZUS alliance with New Zealand and the US. The country also has a close military relationship with Indonesia, with whom it conducts combined exercises. Australian troops were deployed in East Timor during 1999 and 2000, and were responsible for most of the evacuation of UN personnel and the restoration of calm. Australia sent around 2,000 troops to help with the invasion of Iraq in 2003. Australia spends some $14bn per year on defence (2.8 per cent of its GDP) and there are plans to modernise the defence forces over the next ten years at a cost of $5bn.

PETS

Certain pets can be imported into Australia from most countries, although there are rigorous controls and it's expensive. The importation of birds and small mammals such as hamsters is also prohibited. Certain breeds of dog that are considered dangerous aren't eligible for importation, including dogo Argentino, fila Brazileiro, Japanese tosa and the pit bull terrier or American pit bull.

All imports are subject to quarantine (see below), and an import permit must be obtained before shipment. Applications should be made at least two months before the intended date of importation, to the Australian Quarantine and Inspection Service (AQIS, 🖳 www.daffa.gov.au/aqis) in the state where you'll be living. The

application fee is $280 for the first animal and $60 for any subsequent animals. An import permit takes up to four weeks to be issued and is valid for two months. Imported dogs and cats must meet the following criteria:

- be aged at least 12 weeks at the time of export;
- be identified by a microchip;
- have been continuously resident for six months (or since their birth if less than six months old) in the country of origin immediately prior to shipment to Australia;
- have not been in quarantine or under quarantine restrictions during the 30 days before export;
- have current vaccinations (see below).

Dogs must have vaccinations for distemper, hepatitis, para-influenza and parvovirus, and must also test negative for canine brucellosis, canine tropical pancytopenia and leptospirosis within 30 days of export. Cats must have vaccinations for calicivirus, feline enteritis and rhinotracheitis. Vaccinations must have been given at least 14 days before shipment and not more than 12 months previously. All dogs and cats must be treated for internal parasites within 14 days of shipment and for external parasites within 96 hours of export, and must pass a clinical examination within 48 hours of shipment.

⚠ Caution

If dogs and cats exported to Australia don't meet all the pre-export and post-arrival testing, and certification, health and vaccination requirements, they may need to be re-exported, treated or destroyed, or remain in quarantine until any disease concerns have been resolved.

All dogs aged over three months old must be registered annually with the local council. If your dog has been 'desexed', the charge is $20; if it still has its reproductive organs intact, you must pay $60!

Shipment

Pets must be shipped by air to Australia in an International Air Transport Association (IATA) approved container, available from pet shipping agents such as Airpets Oceanic (UK ☎ 01753-685571 or ☎ freephone 0800-371554, 🖥 www.airpets.com) and Moving Abroad – Pet Shippers (UK ☎ 0845-408-0298 or ☎ 0113-239-7287, 🖥 www.moggies.co.uk) in the UK. Animals are inspected at airports by a veterinary surgeon before shipment and can only arrive at the following airports in Australia: Kingsford Smith Airport (Sydney), Perth Airport and Tullamarine Airport (Melbourne). Other entry points require AQIS (see below) consent.

Quarantine

Dogs and cats from the Cocos (Keeling) Islands, New Zealand and Norfolk Island aren't required to undergo quarantine. Dogs and cats from approved rabies-free countries and territories, including Cyprus, Hawaii, Ireland, Japan, Malta, Norway, Singapore, Sweden, Taiwan and the UK, are quarantined for 30 days. Dogs and cats from countries and territories where rabies is considered to be well controlled (including Austria, Belgium, Canada, Denmark, Finland, France, Germany, Greece, Hong Kong, Israel, Italy, Luxembourg, Malaysia, the Netherlands, Portugal, Spain, Switzerland and the US) are quarantined for a minimum of 30 days and a maximum of 120. Pets from certain other approved rabies-free countries (mostly Pacific islands) must spend 60 days in quarantine. The import of dogs and cats from countries and territories where dog-mediated rabies is endemic is permitted only indirectly via an approved country, where the animal must have been resident for at least six months prior to export to Australia.

On arrival in Australia, dogs and cats are quarantined in an approved animal quarantine station at Byford (Western Australia), Eastern Creek (NSW) or Spotswood (Victoria). Quarantine costs are around $15 per day for a cat and $18 for a dog. Weekly visits are permitted during the quarantine period. Other charges include around $27 for document clearing, $70 for the examination of the animal and $95 or $120 for transport (depending on the time of day).

Many pet owners decide that the cost and strain of quarantine on their pets (and themselves) is too much to bear and find their pets new homes, acquiring new pets on arrival in Australia. For further information contact the Australian Quarantine Inspection Service (AQIS, 🖥 www.daffa.gov.au/aqis), which publishes a leaflet, *The Importation of Dogs and Cats into Australia* (AQIS information sheet 2), as well as having comprehensive information and forms online.

POLICE

Each state and the Northern Territory has an independent police force, and there's an Australian Federal Police (AFP) force, which is the Commonwealth government's primary law enforcement agency. The AFP is responsible for protecting federal property and enforcing federal laws such as those concerning counterfeiting, drug trafficking, fraud, illegal immigration, money laundering, organised crime and terrorism. The AFP also provides community police services in the ACT and in Australia's external territories. The National Crime Authority (which deals with organised crime) also has a policing role. Most state police forces have special squads to handle VIP protection and specific crimes such as armed robbery, drug trafficking and use, fraud and homicide. There are also water police in cities and coastal areas.

All police in Australia are armed and in addition to guns carry other 'weapons' to pacify 'dangerous criminals', such as extendable batons and capsicum (pepper) sprays (used by NSW officers to disable armed attackers). Police officers in NSW have been issued with semi-automatic pistols (15-shot, .40 calibre) in order to confront armed gangs and Victoria police are pressing for similar weapons. General police policy if threatened is to shoot first and ask questions afterwards, although this is changing after a number of 'accidental' deaths in recent years. There have been frequent incidents where police have shot dead unarmed assailants or even innocent bystanders (the Australian police shoot more innocent people than crooks). The number of deaths in custody has also risen

alarmingly in recent years, including many Aboriginals (black people are around 20 times more likely to die in custody than white people).

Police in some states (e.g. Victoria) have stopped attending routine calls (such as security alarms, the vast majority of which are false) in an effort to redirect resources to fighting crime. In some areas the police have drastically reduced the number of incidents they visit in order to cut their workload and allow more police to patrol the streets. Instead of sending a car, they may ask callers to report minor incidents by telephone or go to a police station.

> ⚠️ **Caution**
>
> **There are an increasing number of complaints by the public against the police in some states, and Australian police generally have a poor public image and are often seen as a law unto themselves.**

There have been numerous police corruption scandals in recent years in Australia, which, if the allegations are true, has some of the most corrupt police forces in the developed world. After investigations in NSW, for example, some 200 police officers were found to have criminal records. Corruption varies from minor infringements such as accepting free food and drinks and tipping off repair companies in return for a commission, to assaults and sexual harassment, extortion, fabrication of evidence, involvement in organised crime, selling confiscated drugs, selling inside information to criminals, stealing goods and money, and taking bribes. Freebies and kickbacks are considered to be a legitimate perk of the job by many officers.

An almost impenetrable police culture protects crooked officers, and the authorities find it virtually impossible to obtain convictions (and, in any case, don't like to wash their dirty linen in public). Whistle-blowers who shop their colleagues or don't 'play the game' are likely to be hounded out of the force or transferred to the 'back of Bourke'. The anti-corruption record of the Police Integrity Commission (PIC) has been described by some politicians as a joke.

Sexism and racism are widespread in Australia's police forces, and female officers generally have poor promotion prospects compared with male officers.

Details of your rights regarding arrest, detention by the police, questioning and statements are explained in the ACLU publication *Your Rights* (see page 387). The police emergency number varies with the state – if in doubt, call the operator on ☎ 1234 or the national emergency line on ☎ 000. See also **Legal System & Advice** on page 405.

POPULATION

The population of Australia is growing at around 1.4 per cent per year and reached 21m on 29th June 2007 (at 9.42pm, to be precise). Nevertheless, Australia has a declining birth rate (1.73 births per woman – less than half the birth rate in 1961), as women are generally choosing to marry later and have fewer children. Some predictions put the population at 28m by 2050, although other projections show a decline to 20m. For the statistically minded, Australia currently reports a birth every 1 minute and 56 seconds, a death every 3 minutes and 59 seconds and a net gain of a migrant every 3 minutes and 11 seconds, leading to an overall population increase of one person every 1 minutes and 44 seconds.

As in most other developed countries, the last 20 years have witnessed a huge rise in the number of people aged over 65 (who now account for almost 15 per cent of the population) and in particular those aged over 85. By 2020 the over 65s are expected to comprise around 16 per cent of the population. The average age in Australia is almost 37 years.

The indigenous Aboriginal and Torres Strait Islander population of Australia is around 300,000, over half of whom live in NSW and Queensland. The Aboriginal population was estimated at between 200,000 and 750,000 when Australia was colonised by the English in 1788, although it was reduced dramatically in the 19th and early 20th centuries, since when it has recovered. See **Aborigines** on page 391.

Australia is a country of immigrants and is the second most polyglot, multicultural nation in the world (after Israel), with large ethnic communities and migrants from over 125 nations. Before the Second World War, Australian migrants were predominantly from the UK and Ireland; even 40 years ago, when Australia would take virtually

anyone and even offered a £10 assisted passage scheme, the UK dominated Australia's migrant intake. The UK has provided over 2m migrants since 1945 and over 7m in total. In the first three years of the 21st century, only around 10 per cent of new migrants were British, although the UK remained the largest source of skilled migrants, but in 2004, the number of British migrants jumped to around 20 per cent of the total, and forecasts point to increasing numbers of Britons wanting to move to Australia, keen to escape the UK's bad weather, high crime levels, long working hours and inflated housing market.

Since the war, there has been an influx of migrants from continental Europe, including large numbers of Greeks and Italians, plus Lebanese, Turks, Yugoslavs and various others. All major cities contain suburbs with predominantly 'foreign' communities and atmospheres, including Chinese, Greek, Italian, Lebanese and Yugoslav. Sydney is home to more New Zealanders than most cities in New Zealand, and Melbourne's Greek population is the third largest in the world (after Athens and Thessalonica).

Since the end of the official 'white Australia' policy in 1973, Australia has admitted large numbers of Asian immigrants, including many refugees from Indochina. There are also significant numbers of immigrants from Central and South America, the Middle East, the Pacific and South Africa. An estimated 91 per cent of the population is currently of European descent, 5 per cent Asian and 1.5 per cent Aboriginal. Nevertheless, around 75 per cent of the population is Australian born.

> Within the next 50 years, around 25 per cent of Australia's population is likely to be of Asian origin.

Among current citizens, 23 per cent are foreign born, around 1m in the UK or Ireland, 350,000 in New Zealand, 220,000 in Italy, 155,000 in Vietnam, 150,000 in countries of the former Yugoslavia (Serbia, Montenegro, Croatia and the Republic of Macedonia), 143,000 in China, 116,000 in Greece, 108,000 in Germany, 104,000 in the Philippines, 95,000 in India, 83,000 in the Netherlands, 71,000 in Lebanon and 20,000 in Thailand.

Today, Australia has a multicultural migration policy and settlers are encouraged to retain their ethnic artistic traditions, languages and lifestyles – although there's increasing pressure on them to learn English and 'integrate'. However, some Australians are alarmed about what they call the progressive 'Asianisation' of Australia's immigration policy. In recent years, debate has centred on how migration affects employment, an increasing number of people believing that it increases unemployment (they claim that Australia's low unemployment rate would be even lower without immigrants). Some analysts see this as a knee-jerk reaction to make migrants the scapegoats for Australia's economic woes and say that no link has been established between migration and unemployment.

It isn't all one-way traffic. Around 5 to 10 per cent of Australians have emigrated to other countries, and over 30,000 people leave Australia each year. Many immigrants return home after a relatively short period (around 20 per cent of new arrivals in the last decade have left again).

Australia is a highly urbanised society: around 85 per cent of Australians live in urban areas (up from just over 60 per cent in 1921) and the population of the eight capital cities is growing faster than that of rural areas. Brisbane, Darwin and Perth are Australia's fastest-growing cities. Over 70 per cent of the population live in the major cities, which are situated on or near the coast, over 40 per cent in Sydney and Melbourne alone. Some 80 per cent of Australians live within 30km (20mi) of the coast, 35 per cent in NSW, over 60 per cent of whose population lives in Sydney and its suburbs.

The average population density in Australia, where vast areas are virtually uninhabited, is just two people per km (compared with 85 people per km^2 in Asia). The capital, Canberra, has a density of just 20 people per km^2 or around a tenth of the population density of most European cities. Victoria is the most densely populated state. The population of states and territories and their capital cities in 2004 (the latest statistics published by the Australian Bureau of Statistics, 🖥 www. abs.gov.au) was as shown below.

The long-term population shift away from the south-east to the west and the tropics has continued unabated in the early 21st century. Victoria has lost thousands of people to other states in the last decade or so, although by the late '90s the exodus had slowed to a trickle (most people move from Victoria to Queensland). South Australia and Tasmania have been losing the most people in recent years (Tasmania recorded a net loss in 1999) and the ACT is also losing residents at a high rate. And in recent years, Australians have been fleeing the arid interior and clinging to the coast with more enthusiasm than ever.

Queensland is the fastest-growing state (most new arrivals are interstate migrants, many moving there on their retirement),

although the flood of migrants, which increased by 30 per cent in the '90s, has slowed in recent years. Nevertheless, Queensland is expected to replace Victoria as the second most populous state by around 2025. Rapid population growth in some areas of Queensland has placed a huge burden on the infrastructure such as hospitals, roads and schools, and is also having detrimental environmental and ecological consequences in some areas.

Some environmentalists believe that Australia already has more people than its natural resources can sustain, despite the huge size of the country and the low population density, while others argue that the country can sustain a much larger population. (the post-war slogan of 'populate or perish' has been changed to 'populate **and** perish' by those who would like to see immigration drastically reduced.)

RELIGION

Australia has a tradition of religious tolerance, and every resident has total freedom of religion without hindrance by the state or community. In fact, Australia is a secular society and has no official state religion, although around 70 per cent of the population are Christians, at least nominally, and 25 per cent of Australians claim to have no religion. Churches (particularly the Catholic Church) play

State	Population	Capital
ACT	323,000	Canberra (320,000)
NSW	6.75m	Sydney (4.2m)
NT	198,000	Darwin (100,000)
QLD	3.85m	Brisbane (1.75m)
SA	1.6m	Adelaide (1.2m)
TAS	480,000	Hobart (198,000)
VIC	4.9m	Melbourne (3.6m)
WA	1.975m	Perth (1.4m)

church, Hunter Valley, NSW

a large role in education, most private schools being partly church-funded, but church attendance is low in Australia. In general, Australians are fairly laid-back about religion and there are few religious zealots and bible-thumpers, as are common in the US and some other countries.

Most Protestant churches have merged to become the Uniting Church, although the Anglican Church has remained independent. Roman Catholic (4.8m) and Anglican (3.9m) are the two main religions, followed by the Uniting Church (1.3m), Presbyterian (675,000), Orthodox (500,000), Baptist (295,000), Lutheran (250,000) and Pentecostal (174,000) churches. There are also sizeable Buddhist, Jewish and Muslim communities in the major cities. During the last decade, mainstream Christianity (apart from Catholicism) has declined (only the Orthodox Church thrives in Australia, particularly in Melbourne and Sydney),

while 'nature-based' religions such as druidism, paganism and witchcraft have proliferated. Eastern and minority religions have also gained in popularity, including Japanese Mahikari, Shinto and Taoism. There's no recognised Aboriginal religion, although the Aboriginal people have many sacred sites throughout the country.

Every town and city has an Anglican and a Catholic church, and Uniting churches are also common. Religious centres for all the world's major religions are found in the major cities, and details of church and religious services are published in local newspapers throughout the country.

SOCIAL CUSTOMS

All countries have particular social customs and Australia is no exception. Australians are generally very informal in their relationships and won't be too put out if you break the rules, provided your behaviour isn't outrageous. On the other hand, in some circles, eccentricity is much prized and you may be invited to some social functions **only** if you act disgracefully (but make sure you don't confuse the vicar's tea party with the local wife-swapping club). However, bear in mind that Australia is a multicultural society, and many people retain the same customs as their forefathers in their 'home' country, even when their family has been in Australia for generations. As a foreigner you may be forgiven if you accidentally insult your host, but you may not be invited again. The following are a few Australian social customs:

● When introduced to someone, you should generally follow the cue of the person performing the introduction, e.g. if someone is introduced as Bruce you can safely call him Bruce; however, if someone is introduced as the Reverend Piddleton, it might not be wise to address him as 'Piddles' (unless he asks you to). After you've been introduced to someone, you usually say something like 'hello', 'pleased to meet you' or even 'g'day mate' and shake hands. Even total strangers are often called mate (even women), particularly in working class circles (so don't be surprised if your plumber calls you mate). Note that 'mateship' (which roughly equates to the American term 'buddy') is a different thing altogether: it applies only to men and to be someone's life-long mate is considered an honour and a big compliment.

☑ SURVIVAL TIP

Among friends, it's common for men to kiss ladies on the cheek (or once on either cheek). Men don't usually kiss or embrace each other in Australia (although it depends on their nationality and sexual orientation).

- Australians are a lot more direct in asking questions and voicing their opinions than their British or European cousins (like Americans). Don't be surprised if an Aussie gives you the 'third degree' when you meet for the first time. It's nothing personal – they're just being curious and are genuinely interested in strangers.

- Australians are usually friendly and hospitable to strangers, and often go out of their way to help you. If you're travelling around Australia, don't hesitate to use your contacts to obtain a free bed (Australians you meet may offer to put you up or volunteer their friends and family). It's considered quite normal to take people up on these offers, even if they're total strangers.

- It's common for neighbours to invite newcomers around for a cup of tea (or something stronger), although in cities (where people often live next to each other and remain strangers) you may have to go out of your way to meet your neighbours. A good way to meet the locals is to hold a barbecue (barbie) and invite all your neighbours. If you're invited to a barbie, it's common to take a bottle of wine or some beer and you may be asked to bring your own meat (or whatever else you wish to eat). Some invitations ask guests to bring along a 'plate', e.g. a buffet dish from which everyone can help themselves. Men and women tend to congregate separately at social occasions such as parties or barbies. You are, however, permitted to fraternise with members of the opposite sex.

- Australians tend to dress casually, e.g. to wear shorts to the office in summer, and it isn't usual to wear a suit or tie unless you're a high-powered manager or a salesperson. Smart casual dress is adequate for most informal occasions, e.g. when visiting restaurants and nightclubs. When going anywhere that may be formal (or particularly informal), it may be wise to ask in advance what you're expected to wear. On the rare occasions when dress is formal, such as evening dress or dinner jacket, it's stated in the invitation and you're unlikely to be admitted if you turn up in the wrong attire. If you're invited to a wedding, always enquire about the dress, unless you want to stick out like a sore thumb. In Australia, black or dark dress is usually worn at funerals.

- Guests are normally expected to be punctual, with the exception of certain society parties, when late arrival is *de rigueur* (unless you arrive after the celebrity guest), and at weddings, when the bride is always late. Anyone

who arrives late for dinner or, horror of horrors, doesn't turn up at all, should expect to be excluded from future guest lists (unless he has a **very** good reason).

TIME DIFFERENCE

There are three different time zones in Australia, which is one of the few countries in the world to have a zone that isn't a whole hour ahead of or behind its neighbours (CST).

To add to Australia's temporal confusion, all states and territories except the Northern Territory, Queensland and Western Australia operate 'daylight saving' in summer, when clocks are advanced one hour. All except Tasmania change their clocks at 2am on the last Sunday in October and the last Sunday in March. In Tasmania, daylight saving starts a month earlier and ends up to a month later! This creates no fewer than five different time zones in summer, e.g. when it's 9am in Western Australia, it's 10.30am in the Northern Territory, 11am in Queensland, 11.30am in South Australia noon in the ACT, NSW and Victoria and either 11am or noon (depending on the month) in Tasmania. Not surprisingly, attempts are being made to rationalise summer time zones. Time changes are announced in local newspapers and on radio and TV.

Australia hasn't converted to the 24-hour clock, and times in many timetables are given using the 12-hour clock (i.e. am and pm), with before noon times printed in light type and afternoon times printed in bold type.

In view of the huge time difference between Australia and many other continents (e.g. there are 10 or 11 hours' difference between Western Europe and EST), you should always check the local time when making international calls (one sure way to upset most people is to wake them at 3am). The time difference between Australia and most countries is listed at the back of the white pages under 'Telstra 0011 International and Telstra Faxstream 0015 International'. The table below gives the time in a selection of cities when it's noon (in winter) in Sydney:

TIME ZONES

Zone	GMT+	States/Territories
Western Standard Time (WST)	8 hours	WA
Central Standard Time (CST)	9.5 hours	NT, SA
Eastern Standard Time (EST)	10 hours	ACT, NSW, QLD, TAS, VIC

INTERNATIONAL TIME DIFFERENCE

SYDNEY	LONDON	CAPE TOWN	TOKYO	LOS ANGELES	NEW YORK
Noon	1am	3am	10am	5pm*	8pm*

* previous day

TIPPING

Tipping isn't a general practice in Australia (Americans please note!), although you may wish to leave a tip when you've had exceptional service or have received good value. However, tips are regarded by some Australians as patronising or even insulting. People almost never tip taxi drivers in Australia. However, it's common practice to round up taxi fares to the nearest dollar, although a cab driver may round the fare down rather than give you change. Cloakroom attendants, garage staff (who clean your car's windscreen or check its oil or tyre pressures), hairdressers, hotel staff and porters (who usually have set charges) also don't expect to be tipped (but won't complain if they are). It isn't customary to tip a barman in a bar or pub, although many people leave their small change. Tipping in hotels depends where you're staying – it's unnecessary in tourist or medium class hotels, although staff in grand establishments are used to receiving tips from their wealthy clients. Otherwise, service charges aren't usually added to bills by hotels and restaurants.

One of the few exceptions to the 'no tipping' rule is top class restaurants, where it's customary to tip waiters up to 10 per cent of the bill for good service. Restaurant tips can be included in cheque or credit card payments or given as cash. The total on credit card counterfoils may be left blank to encourage you to leave a tip, so don't forget to fill in the total before signing it, or the waiter may enter his own 'tip'.

TOILETS

Public toilets in Australia are usually free and generally clean. They're commonly found in bus and train stations, council and tourist offices, department stores, parks and shopping centres. The most sanitary (even luxurious) toilets are found in department stores, hotels and restaurants, and are usually only for customers. Clean toilets are also found in airports, (near) beaches, car parks, museums and galleries, petrol stations, and public and private offices. Pub toilets vary from 'no-go areas' to spotless.

Australians don't use the terms bathroom, powder room or washroom when referring to a toilet, but use a variety of (often colourful) names, including ablutions, bog, crapper (after Thomas Crapper, who invented the WC), dunny (an outside toilet in country areas, often consisting of a wooden hut with an earth floor), ladies' or gents' (room), lavatory (lav), loo, privy, public convenience, thunder box, toot and WC (water closet).

Some toilets have nappy (diaper) changing facilities and facilities for nursing mothers, and there are also special toilets for the disabled at airports, bus and railway stations and in shopping centres in major cities. Roadside pubs in country areas (roadhouses) have toilets and showers. When using a public toilet, make sure you use the correct one, as it's sometimes difficult to tell the difference between the stylish male and female signs.

tea plantation, QLD

19.
THE AUSSIES

Who are the Australians? What are they like? Let us take a candid (and totally prejudiced) look at the Australian people, tongue firmly in cheek, and hope they forgive my flippancy or that they don't read this bit (which is why it's hidden away at the back of the book).

The typical Aussie is amusing, an anarchist, arrogant, a beach bum, boorish, brave, bronzed, a carnivore, casual, chauvinistic, classless, cosmopolitan, fiercely competitive, a cricket and footy fan, crude, delinquent, down to earth, eccentric, egotistical, a foreigner, frank (to the point of bluntness), friendly, a compulsive gambler, garrulous, generous, handsome, hedonistic, homophobic, honest, hospitable, idealistic, inebriated, informal, insular, irreverent, jingoistic, laid back, loud, macho, materialistic, matey, naive, an 'ocker', open, optimistic, outspoken, parochial, a philistine, proud, relaxed, a republican, sincere, sociable, sophisticated, a surfie, tardy, tough, an inveterate traveller, unambitious, unpretentious, unreliable and xenophobic.

You may have noticed that the above list contains 'a few' contradictions (as does life in Australia), which is hardly surprising as there's no such thing as a typical Australian and few people conform to popular stereotypes. Australia is one of the most cosmopolitan and multicultural countries in the world and a nation of 'foreigners' (except for a few hundred thousand Aborigines), who have as much in common with each other as Icelanders with Africans or Tibetans with South Americans.

However, despite its diverse cultural and racial mix, Australia isn't a universal melting pot, but a potpourri of ethnic splinter groups living separate lives with their own clubs, customs, neighbourhoods, newspapers, restaurants, shops, sports, and even TV and radio stations.

Australians pride themselves on their lack of class-consciousness and don't have the same prejudices and pretensions common in the 'old world', although Australia has never been an egalitarian society and is far from being a classless country. Status is as important here as it is anywhere else, although it's usually based on money and character rather than birthright. Australia generally has no 'old school tie' barriers to success and almost anyone, however humble his origins, can fight his way to the top of the heap (although colour barriers aren't so easy to overcome). Despite the fact that the vast majority of Australians are misplaced Britons and assorted Europeans on the wrong side of the world, modern Australia has more in common with the US in its ambitions, attitudes and lifestyle than with the UK or Europe.

Australians are noted for their insularity (which is hardly surprising when your nearest neighbours are thousands of miles away) and xenophobia – no doubt due to being inundated by foreigners, many of whom cannot (or won't) speak English. Nobody knows better than the Aussies that foreigners were created solely to be detested and loathed (Australians have a wealth of derogatory terms for immigrants), and transmit exotic diseases – which is why their planes are fumigated before they're allowed to set foot on Australian soil. Many Australians are prejudiced against all foreigners, who only come to Australia to steal their jobs and 'bludge' (scrounge) off the state, and they don't care much for anyone who isn't a dinky die Aussie (newcomers are derisively called 'new Australians'). The culture gap is widest between Australians and Asians (the White Australia policy was officially abandoned in 1973 – but not in the nation's psyche), who are better educated, more hard-working **and** often more intelligent – enough to incense anyone. However, for better or worse, the country has belatedly (and reluctantly) concluded that its future lies in trading with its Asian neighbours rather than maintaining its traditional ties with the UK.

⚠ Caution

The natives have a particular abhorrence for the ubiquitous British (Poms) and New Zealanders (Kiwis), both of whom are the prime culprits in stealing Aussie jobs (when not dole bludging on Australian beaches).

Kiwis have free access to Australia and wash up on Australian shores in vast numbers (Bondi Beach is the 'home of the NZ government in exile'); not surprisingly, they're the butt of many Australian jokes. However, Aussies reserve a special place in their hearts for the British, endearingly referred to as whinging Poms or Pommy bastards, to whom they're inexorably drawn by mutual antipathy. Making fun of the Poms is a popular pastime and has given rise to a surfeit of Pommy jokes (e.g. Q. What's the difference between a 747 and a Pom? A. When you switch off the engines, a 747 stops whining.). The Aussies cannot bear to be constantly reminded of their convict ancestry, while the Poms are mortified that they gave the Aussies free passage (admittedly brig class) to their land of sunshine and plenty while they stayed at home in the cold and rain. Aussies are an ungrateful shower and don't appreciate what the Poms have done for them, such as teaching them how to play cricket and rugby, introducing them to British culinary delights, and generally educating them on how to behave in polite society (admittedly this hasn't been an unqualified success – but what can you expect from 'Neanderthals' who live at the end of the earth, thousands of miles from the nearest civilisation?).

Australia is a hotbed of ethnic friction, although, apart from a small minority, most Australians **aren't** racist or even xenophobic. If it's any consolation to foreigners, Aussies don't get on too well with their fellow countrymen and delight in abusing their neighbours at every opportunity. All Australians look down on those from other states and love to make fun of them. The inhabitants of Australia's two major cities have a shared loathing for the 'other lot' and the only thing that's (sometimes) worse than a whinging Pom to a Sydneysider is a Melbournite (and vice versa). Interstate rivalries, particularly between Victoria and New South Wales, have been a brake on economic progress for decades. To outsiders, Sydney is full of crooks, homosexuals (it's one of the gay capitals of the world), posers and yuppies; it's always raining in Melbourne (Bleak City), where the locals are staid and snobbish and consist mostly of Greeks and Italians (called Mexicans by those from

NSW, as they're 'south of the border'); Queenslanders (banana benders) are red-necked fascists and uncivilised ockers; Canberra has been described as 'the ruination of a perfectly good sheep station' and is a deadly boring place (it's often likened to a cemetery) inhabited by civil servants and politicians (enough said) – if you develop a yearning to live in Canberra, you should seek immediate psychiatric help; Adelaide is conservative and dull and inhabited by prudes and killjoys (wowsers) – South Australians are disparagingly termed crow-eaters after the eating habits of the early settlers; Western Australians (sandgropers) are aliens, backward and country bumpkins who inhabit a different planet (Perth is the most remote city in the world); Northern Territorians (topenders) are Crocodile Dundee types, drunks and primitives, who are either

paid to stay or cannot afford to leave; and Tasmanians (taswegians) are dimwits (all that in-breeding), puritans and radical conservationists, descended from convicts and still living in the 19th century.

Being (relatively) intelligent people, Australians have a *laissez-faire* attitude to business and work, which lag well behind having a good time. They down tools at the drop of a spanner (Australia has some of the more militant trade unions in the world) and think nothing of having a day off work (sickie) when they've something better to do, which is most of the time. If Australians worked as hard as they played (particularly at sport), they'd put even the Japanese to shame. Contrary to the widely held misconception that 'hard work never did anyone any harm', Aussies know only too well that hard 'yakka' is bad for your health and can prove fatal. They prefer to make (or more often lose) their fortune at gambling, the only acceptable way to get rich, and bet on almost anything, including bingo, casinos, football pools, general elections, horse and greyhound racing, lotteries, poker machines (pokies), toad, cockroach and lizard races, which politician will get caught next with his hand in the till, or even (in desperation) two flies climbing a wall. Gambling on sporting events is a national obsession.

Australians are passionate about sport ('life be in it'), which is an integral part of Australian culture. The country is highly successful in international competitions, particularly swimming, which isn't surprising as training includes trying to out-swim a great white shark! Australians can be found in their natural state on a beach or anywhere where there's water (when not in a pub). However, with the exception of those who spend their time boxing kangaroos, racing water buffalo or wrestling crocodiles, the nearest most Australians get to working up a sweat is their TV.

Nevertheless, when achievements are measured against population, Australia is the foremost sporting nation in the world (but don't tell the Aussies – they're conceited enough as it is). Australia has fierce sporting rivalry with its neighbour New Zealand (particularly at rugby), although the most popular sport is Pommy bashing, which reaches its peak in the customary humiliation of the Poms at cricket. However, although they're sports fanatics, Australians believe in fair play and love to support the underdog – unless it's the English, in which case they yearn to see them ground into the dust.

> Despite the popular image of Australians as bronzed, muscular lifesavers and bathing beauties, the majority are overweight and unfit – a popular 'sport' in the outback is 'whammying', where fatties attempt to knock each other over with their beer bellies!

It's a common misconception among foreigners that Australians speak English – amazingly some people even go to Australia to **learn** English! However, don't expect Australians to speak British English or even American English (the Mad Max movies had to be dubbed for American audiences). The only people who speak proper English in Australia are the foreigners – apart, that is, from the million or so migrants who hardly speak a word of it. Australians converse in a secret language (slanguage) called 'strine', full of blasphemy, fun, profanity, rhyming slang, strange words and ungrammatical phonetic spelling (Aussies have some of the most colourful abuse in the world). Aussies routinely abbreviate everything, as it's usually too hot to say the whole word (and opening your mouth lets the flies in); most syllables are omitted to save energy – besides which, enunciating clearly is difficult when you're pissed.

Which brings us to the Aussies' favourite pastime – boozing. The Aussies' natural habitat is a pub (preferably close to a beach), where they spend their waking hours between visits to the dole office and the meat pie van. Their favourite tipple is ice-cold beer, otherwise know as amber nectar, a cold one, neck oil, etc., or a glass of Chateau Chumbawumba for the wimps. Aussies are passionate about their local beers and aren't particularly complimentary about brands brewed in other states (outside Queensland, XXXX stands for CRAP). In truth, Aussies don't really care much for beer, which is just an excuse for a good vomit (big spit, chunder, kark, laugh at the ground, shout for Ruth, technicolor yawn, etc.). However, despite their awesome reputation as a nation of drunks, Aussies consume less alcohol per head than the inhabitants of many European countries (which is best not mentioned in your local pub in Oz). Recent figures published by World Drink Trends showed Australia languishing in an ignominious 20th place.

Australia has long been famous for its 'cultural cringe' and is still occasionally typecast as a land of mutton-eating philistines, although it's no longer the cultural desert some would have you believe. It may come as a surprise that not all Aussies are beer-swilling, loud-mouthed, uncultured yobbos and some have even been known to visit theatres and listen to classical music (Australia even has an opera house!). Nowadays Australians export their culture in the guise of art, films, music and TV programmes, which are disseminated around the globe. It's even possible to take a degree in Australian studies, which lasts for **a whole week** and includes an in-depth study of barbies, the Bee Gees, the bush, Clive James, cricket, Crocodile Dundee, Dame Edna Everage, footy, Fosters, Germaine Greer, Kylie, Mad Max, Neighbours, Olivia Newton John, Rolf Harris, Skippy, surfing, and the Sydney Opera House.

⚠ **Caution**

However, although they have a sharp (crude) sense of humour, the Aussies are somewhat lacking in mirth when it comes to attacks on their culture, and newcomers should tread warily.

Aussies are infamous for their macho image and a peculiar Aussie male bonding called mateship (similar to American buddyship). Australian men are men's men, and mainstream males have no time for limp-wristed gays. However, rumour has it that Australian men are becoming more sensitive (heaven forbid!), that ockerism is dead and Aussie men are now new age guys – although anyone who believes that is a few snags short of a barbie (a sensitive Aussie is an oxymoron). The Australian lifestyle magazine *Ralph* (Responsible And Lovable Piss-Head) is much nearer the mark and is targeted at the ubiquitous incorrect bloke interested mainly in beer, boys' toys, humour, motors, sex, sport and trivia (not necessarily in that order – some Aussies actually prefer sex to beer, but most have a bigger capacity for booze).

Aussie males are rampant chauvinists (not surprisingly, women's lib passed Australia by), and some of their more flattering terms for women include bush pigs, swamp hogs and maggots – a good looking woman (Sheila) is a 'glamour maggot' or 'glam mag'. Paradoxically, Australia was the one of the first countries in the world to give women the vote, although they were still banned from the pub (not that most women would have been seen dead in one). When attending social functions, men traditionally congregate at one end of the room (or garden), usually where the booze is, and the Sheilas at the other (attending to the food). Despite their ocker image, many Australians are apparently (according to a recent 'survey') considerate lovers when sober, although they're also among the world's fastest performers (they don't want to waste valuable drinking time). To the average Aussie male, foreplay is 'hey Sheila, you wanna ****?' and sex drive is doing it in the back of a panel van. (While on the subject of sex, readers may wish to know that if they go to their corner shop and ask for some Durex, they're likely to end up with a roll of sticky tape).

Australian politicians (pollies) are world leaders in mismanagement and some of the most hilarious and entertaining in the world (you have to laugh, otherwise you'd cry). In a less liberal country they'd all be locked up, although this would deprive Aussies (not to mention a legion of broadcasters, cartoonists, journalists, etc.) of their best source of jokes. Whatever momentous events are happening elsewhere in the world, you can always rely on Aussie politics for some amusing diversions such as defections, lurks and perks, party infighting, rorts (scams), sackings and scandals, although strangely there are very few sex scandals – could they all be gay? When not junketing around the world (or abusing their official credit cards, etc.), pollies spend their time (well at least a few days a year) hurling personal abuse at each other in parliament (not surprisingly, there are relatively few women politicians in Australia). Aussies have a healthy disrespect (contempt) for their politicians and need to be forced to vote under the threat of fines. The seat of government (Canberra) is appropriately located in the wilds of New South Wales – well away from civilisation.

Immigration has undeniably made Australia a culturally richer, more diverse and infinitely more interesting country. However, today's Australia is closed to many of the immigrants who have made Australia one of the best countries in the world. (First you were transported for free, then you had to pay £10 and now they won't even let you visit without a visa – if you want to stay, you need to be under 30, speak fluent English, and have a couple of university degrees and ten years' work experience). However, if you're rejected, try to look on the bright side. The Australian Dream isn't always what it's cracked up to be, and surveys have found that almost half of recently arrived migrants believe they were better off at home (admittedly most were unemployed and without access to social security).

Australia's problems include child poverty, drug abuse, a high divorce rate, high suicide and crime rates, high unemployment (plus job insecurity), homelessness, pollution, a shameful record on preserving its environment, animal life and indigenous peoples (see **Aborigines** on page 391), and endemic welfare dependency. Many Australians have little optimism, particularly the young, many of whom are in a desperate plight and have been largely abandoned by politicians and business.

> In the last decade or so, the country has been ravaged by high unemployment, which together with the burgeoning number of single-parent families and low pay, is increasingly creating two Australias: the haves and the have-nots.

Poverty is blamed for causing domestic violence, family breakdowns and lawlessness. Many Australians work too hard, travel too far, arrive home too late, and have kids who go to schools too far away. These problems are by no means unique to Australia in today's ever-competitive world and are shared by most developed countries. However, how Australia faces up to them and the challenges of the 21st century will shape its future for generations to come.

Australians were profoundly shocked by the recession in the '90s, which destroyed the myth of economic security and eternal prosperity. In the '90s, Australians were under siege from all sides, with many of their traditional beliefs and values swept away by events largely beyond their control (such as Asia's economic meltdown). In recent years, Australia has appeared to be retreating from the rest of the world (the great leap backwards), introverted and inward-looking, unable to come to terms with its past, frightened by the future, and with political 'leaders' who lack strategy or direction. Many people consider that the current Liberal-National coalition government represents the old (widely discredited) conservative approach, and not the brave new world and opportunities that Australia needs to grasp in order to establish itself as a dynamic force in the modern world.

And now for the good news! Australia is one of the most liberal, open, stable and tolerant societies in the world. It has a strong economy, with abundant natural resources, political stability, a skilled workforce, steady population growth, and substantial domestic and foreign capital investment. It's renowned for its superb beaches, rugged beauty, wonderful climate, creativity, cultural diversity, freedom, outdoor lifestyle, excellent local government, friendly people, fine restaurants (and barbecues), open spaces, extensive sports facilities, good transportation and healthcare, and unique wildlife.

Australia is rated as one of the top countries in the world for its quality of life, and Sydney was ranked fifth and Melbourne 12th in a 2004 survey of the 'best' cities in the world by Mercer Human Resource Consulting; Adelaide, Brisbane and Perth also appeared in the top 25. Some say that Sydney is like America before the innocence faded, a truly cosmopolitan, international city. Australians rank among the world's most contented people and are generally happy with life, although paradoxically many people reckon that life is getting worse. Australia is nothing if not a land of contradictions and, despite the gloomy predictions from some quarters, most Australians have remarkable faith in themselves and optimism for the future, although newcomers should be aware that 'she'll be right' is code for 'everything that can go wrong will', and 'no worries' means 'it has screwed up again'.

Newcomers should also be sure never to compare Australia unfavourably with their home country (the worst sin is to say repeatedly, 'we do it like this/better at home'). However, if you really want to rile

the Aussies, you could complain about their boring blue skies and tell them their beer's too cold and their wine's too warm, the sun's too hot (and gives you cancer), there are too many flies and bugs, their birds squawk instead of sing, much of the wildlife is out to eat or kill you, and everywhere you turn there are smiling, friendly Aussies.

Aussies are casual (relaxed to the point of sleep), informal and straight talkers ('tell it as it is'), and expect you to be open and friendly also. One of the things that endears Aussies to foreigners is their outrageous sense of humour and ability to poke fun at themselves and everyone else. Australians generally take people as they find them and, if you're friendly and make an effort to adapt to their way of life, they may even take to you.

Although immigrants may criticise some aspects of Australian life, relatively few seriously consider leaving and most are proud to call themselves Aussies. In fact, immigrants from a vast range of backgrounds firmly believe that Australia is the best country in the world. Few other nations offer such an irrepressible and exciting lifestyle. For sheer vitality and *joie de vivre*, Australia has few equals and, for the fortunate few who are lucky enough to secure a residence visa, it's a land where you can turn your dreams into reality. Australia remains a country of great opportunity, although perhaps no longer the Lucky Country (if it ever was – you make your own luck in Oz through hard yakka). Provided you maintain a sense of humour about everything, you too may find that 'she will indeed be all right'!

Long Live Australia! God Save the Queen! Up the Republic!

20.
MOVING HOUSE OR LEAVING AUSTRALIA

When you're moving house or leaving Australia, there are many things to be considered and a 'million' people to be informed. The checklists contained in this chapter are designed to make the task easier and with luck prevent an ulcer or a nervous breakdown, provided of course you don't leave everything to the last minute (only divorce and bereavement cause more stress than moving house). See also Moving House on page 102 and Relocation Companies on page 104.

MOVING HOUSE

When moving house within Australia, you should consider the following:

- If you live in rented accommodation, you must give your landlord notice (the period depends on your contract). You may need to remain until a minimum period has elapsed and, if you don't give your landlord sufficient notice, you're required to pay the rent until the end of your contract or for the full notice period. This also applies if you have a separate contract for a garage or other rented property, e.g. a holiday home. If you're renting, make sure that your bond is returned.

- If you're a homeowner and are moving to a new council area, you should inform your present council when you move and re-register in your new council area after arrival. When moving to a new area or state, you may be entitled to a refund of a portion of your property taxes (council rates).

- If you have an Australian driving licence or an Australian registered car, give your local state traffic authority (see **Appendix A**) your new address as soon as possible after moving.

- Also inform the following:

  - your employer;

  - your electricity, gas and water companies;

  - your telephone company (or companies);

  - your accountant, bank or credit union, building societies, businesses where you have accounts, credit and charge card companies, insurance companies (for example car, health and home), post office, solicitor, stockbroker and other financial institutions;

  - your family dentist, doctor and other health practitioners. Health records should be transferred to your new dentist and doctor, if applicable.

— your children's schools. If applicable, arrange for schooling in your new area. Try to give a term's notice and obtain a copy of any relevant school reports or records from your children's current schools.

— all regular correspondents, friends and relatives, professional and trade journals to which you subscribe, and social and sports clubs you belong to. Give or send them your new address and telephone number. Arrange to have your post redirected by Australia Post (see **Change of Address** on page 138).

— your local consulate or embassy, if you're registered with it (see page 95);

☑ SURVIVAL TIP

Terminate any outstanding hire purchase, lease or loan contracts and pay all outstanding bills (allow plenty of time, as some companies may be slow to respond).

● Return any library books and anything else borrowed.

● Arrange removal of your furniture and belongings by booking a removal company well in advance. If you have only a few items of furniture to move, you may prefer to do your own move, in which case you may need to hire a van.

● Arrange for a cleaning company and/or decorating company for rented accommodation, if required.

● Cancel milk and newspaper deliveries.

LEAVING AUSTRALIA

Before leaving Australia permanently or for an indefinite period, the following items should be considered **in addition** to those listed above under **Moving House** above:

● Give notice to your employer, if applicable.

● Check that your family's passports aren't out of date.

● Check whether any special requirements (e.g. inoculations, permits, visas) are necessary for entry into your country of destination by contacting your local embassy or consulate in Australia. An exit permit or visa isn't required to leave Australia.

● Book a removal company well in advance. International shipping companies usually provide a wealth of information and may also be able to advise you on various matters concerning your relocation. Find out the exact procedure for shipping your belongings to your country of destination from the relevant embassy in Australia (don't rely entirely on your shipping company). Forms may need to be completed before arrival. If you've been living in Australia for less than a year, you're required to re-export all personal effects, including furniture and vehicles that were imported tax and duty-free.

● Arrange to sell anything that you won't be taking with you, e.g. car, furniture and house. If you sell a second home in Australia, you may need to pay capital gains tax on any profit made on the sale (see page 309).

● Claim any rebate on your tax payments to which you're entitled.

● If you're leaving Australia permanently and have been a member of a superannuation scheme, your benefits won't be paid until you reach the 'preservation' age. Contact your employer's personnel office or your superannuation company for information.

- If you have an Australian-registered car which you're exporting permanently, you should ask your local state traffic authority to de-register the vehicle, and register it in your new country of residence on arrival (as necessary).

- Depending on your destination, your pets may require inoculations or may need to go into quarantine for a period.

- Arrange health, travel and other insurance as necessary (see **Chapter 13**).

- Depending on your destination, you may wish to arrange dental and health check-ups for your family before leaving Australia. Obtain a copy of all your dental and health records and a statement from your health insurance company noting your present level of cover.

- Check whether you're entitled to a rebate on your car and other insurance. Obtain a letter from your Australian motor insurance company stating your number of years without claim.

- If you aren't selling your property, arrange to let it through a friend or a letting agency (see **Chapter 5**).

> ☑ SURVIVAL TIP
>
> **Check whether you need an international driving permit or a translation of your Australian or foreign driving licence for your country of destination.**

- Give friends and business associates in Australia a temporary address and telephone number where you can be contacted overseas.

- If you're travelling by air, allow plenty of time to get to the airport, register your luggage and clear security and immigration.

- Buy a copy of the relevant *Living and Working* book before leaving Australia. If we haven't written it yet, drop us a line and we will get started on it right away!

Have a safe journey!

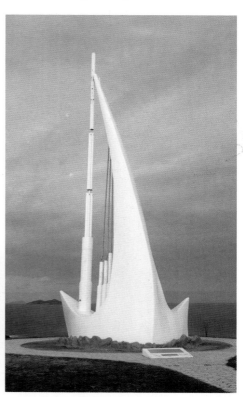

Singing Ship monument, Emu Park, QLD

Kookaburra

APPENDICES

APPENDIX A – FURTHER INFORMATION

Embassies & Consulates (Canberra)

A selection of embassies in Canberra is listed below. A full list of embassies and consulates in Australia is available from the Department of Foreign Affairs and Trade's website (💻 www.dfat.gov.au – go to 'Embassies'). Business hours vary considerably and all embassies close on their national holidays as well as on Australian public holidays. Always telephone to check opening hours before visiting.

Austria: 12 Talbot Street, Forrest, ACT 2603 (☎ 02-6295 1533, 💻 www.austria.org.au).

Belgium: 19 Arkana Street, Yarralumla, ACT 2600 (☎ 02-6273 2501, 💻 www.diplomatie.be/canberra).

Bulgaria: 33 Culgoa Circuit, O'Malley, ACT 2606 (☎ 02-6286 9711, 💻 www.bulgaria.org.au).

Canada: Commonwealth Avenue, Canberra, ACT 2600 (☎ 02-6270 4000, 💻 www.canada.org.au).

China: 15 Coronation Drive, Yarralumla, ACT 2600 (☎ 02-6273 4780, 💻 http://au.china-embassy.org).

Czech Republic: 8 Culgoa Circuit, O'Malley, ACT 2606 (☎ 02-6290 1386).

Denmark: 15 Hunter Street, Yarralumla, ACT 2600 (☎ 02-6270 5333, 💻 www.canberra.um.dk).

Finland: 12 Darwin Avenue, Yarralumla, ACT 2600 (☎ 02-6273 3800).

France: 6 Perth Avenue, Yarralumla, ACT 2600 (☎ 02-6216 0100, 💻 www.ambafrance-au.org).

Germany: 119 Empire Circuit, Yarralumla, ACT 2600 (☎ 02-6270 1911, 🖥 www.germanembassy.org.au).

Greece: 9 Turrana Street, Yarralumla, ACT 2600 (☎ 02-6273 3011).

Hungary: 17 Beale Crescent, Deakin, ACT 2600 (☎ 02-6282 3226).

India: 3-5 Moonah Place, Yarralumla, ACT 2600 (☎ 02-6273 3999).

Indonesia: 8 Darwin Avenue, Yarralumla, ACT 2600 (☎ 02-6250 8600, 🖥 www.kbri-canberra.org.au).

Ireland: 20 Arkana Street, Yarralumla, ACT 2600 (☎ 02-6273 3022).

Israel: 6 Turrana Street, Yarralumla, ACT 2600 (☎ 02-6215 4500, 🖥 http://canberra.mfa.gov.il).

Italy: 12 Grey Street, Deakin, ACT 2600 (☎ 02-6273 3333, 🖥 www.ambcanberra.esteri.it).

Japan: 112 Empire Circuit, Yarralumla, ACT 2600 (☎ 02-6273 3244).

Malaysia: 7 Perth Avenue, Yarralumla, ACT 2600 (☎ 02-6273 1543).

Netherlands: 120 Empire Circuit, Yarralumla, ACT 2600 (☎ 02-6220 9400, 🖥 www.netherlands.org.au).

New Zealand: Commonwealth Avenue, Canberra, ACT 2600 (☎ 02-6270 4211, 🖥 www.nzembassy.com/australia).

Norway: 17 Hunter Street, Yarralumla, ACT 2600 (☎ 02-6273 3444, 🖥 www.norway.org.au).

Papua New Guinea: 39-41 Forster Crescent, Yarralumla, ACT 2600 (☎ 02-6273 3322, 🖥 www.pngcanberra.org).

Philippines: 1 Moonah Place, Yarralumla, ACT 2600 (☎ 02-6273 2535, 🖥 www.philembassy.au.com).

Poland: 7 Turran Street, Yarralumla, ACT 2600 (☎ 02-6272 1000, 🖥 www.poland.org.au).

Portugal: 23 Culgoa Circuit, O'Malley, ACT 2606 (☎ 02-6290 1733).

Russia: 78 Canberra Avenue, Griffith, ACT 2603 (☎ 02-6295 9033, 🖥 www.australia.mid.ru).

Singapore: 17 Forster Crescent, Yarralumla, ACT 2600 (☎ 02-6271 2000).

Slovakia: 47 Culgoa Circuit, O'Malley, ACT 2606 (☎ 02-6290 1516, 🖳 www.slovakemb-aust.org).

Slovenia: Level 6, 60 Marcus Clarke Street, Canberra, ACT 2601 (☎ 02-6243 4830).

South Africa: Corner State Circle and Rhodes Place, Yarralumla, ACT 2600 (☎ 02-6272 7300, 🖳 www.sahc.org.au).

Spain: 15 Arkana Street, Yarralumla, ACT 2600 (☎ 02-6273 3555, 🖳 www.embaspain.com).

Sweden: 5 Turrana Street, Yarralumla, ACT 2600 (☎ 02-6270 2700, 🖳 www.swedenabroad.com/canberra).

Switzerland: 7 Melbourne Avenue, Forrest, ACT 2603 (☎ 02-6162 8400, 🖳 www.eda.admin.ch/australia).

Thailand: 111 Empire Circuit, Yarralumla, ACT 2600 (☎ 02-6273 1149).

United Kingdom: Commonwealth Avenue, Canberra, ACT 2600 (☎ 02-6270 6666, 🖳 www.britaus.net).

United States of America: Moonah Place, Yarralumla, ACT 2600 (☎ 02-6214 5600, 🖳 www.canberra.usembassy.gov).

Australian Customs Service

The Australian Customs Service has a nationwide telephone number (☎ 1300-558 287 within Australia only) and a website (🖳 www.customs.gov.au) for general information. State and territory offices are as follows:

ACT: Customs House, 5 Constitution Avenue, Canberra, ACT 2601.

NSW: 10 Cooks River Drive, Sydney International Airport, NSW 2020.

NT: 21 Lindsay Street, Darwin, NT 0800.

QLD: Terrica Place, 140 Creek Street, Brisbane, QLD 4000.

SA: 220 Commercial Road, Port Adelaide, SA 5015.

TAS: 1st Floor, MBF Building, 25 Argyle Street, Hobart, TAS 7000.

VIC: 1010 Latrobe Street, Melbourne Docklands, VIC 3001.

WA: 2 Henry Street, Fremantle, WA 6160.

Consumer Affairs & Fair Trading

The government consumer service (🖳 www.consumer.gov.au) provides general information with state and territory services offering more comprehensive advice:

ACT: Office of Fair Trading (☎ 02-6207 0400, 🖳 www.fairtrading.act.gov. au).

NSW: Office of Fair Trading (☎ 02-9895 0111, 🖳 www.fairtrading.nsw.gov. au).

NT: Consumer Affairs (☎ 08-8999 1999, 🖳 www.caba.nt.gov.au).

QLD: Office of Fair Trading (☎ 07-3405 0970, 🖳 www.fairtrading.qld.gov. au).

SA: Office of Consumer & Business Affairs (☎ 08-8204 9777, 🖳 www. ocba.sa.gov.au).

TAS: Consumer Affairs & Fair Trading (☎ 1300-654 499 – within Australia only, 🖳 www.consumer.tas.gov.au).

VIC: Consumer Affairs (☎ 1300-558 181 – within Australia only, 🖳 www. consumer.vic.gov.au).

WA: Department of Consumer and Employment Protection (☎ 1300-304 054 – within Australia only, 🖳 www.docep.wa.gov.au).

Motor Vehicle Registration Authorities

ACT: Road Transport Authority, PO Box 582, Dickson, ACT 2602 (☎ 02-6207 7000, 🖳 www.rego.act.gov.au).

NSW: Roads and Traffic Authority, PO Box K198, Haymarket, NSW 1240 (☎ 02-4920 4159, 🖳 www.rta.nsw.gov.au).

NT: Motor Vehicle Registry, PO Box 530, Darwin, NT 0801 (☎ 1300-654 628 – within Australia only, 🖳 www.nt.gov.au/transport).

QLD: Queensland Transport, PO Box 673,Fortitude Valley, QLD 4006 (☎ 13-2380 – within Australia only, ⌨ www.transport.qld.gov.au).

SA: Vehicle Standards, Transport SA, PO Box 1, Walkerville, SA 5081 (☎ 08-8348 2222, ⌨ www.transport.sa.gov.au).

TAS: Registrar of Motor Vehicles, PO Box 936, Hobart, TAS 7001 (☎ 1300-135 513 – within Australia only, ⌨ www.transport.tas.gov.au).

VIC: Vic Roads, PO Box 1644, Melbourne, VIC 3001 (☎ 03-9854 2666, ⌨ www.vicroads.vic.gov.au).

WA: Department of Transport, Licensing Division, PO Box R1290, Perth, WA 6844 (☎ 08-9427 6404, ⌨ www.dpi.wa.gov.au/licensing).

Miscellaneous

Australia Travel & Tourism (⌨ www.australia.com).

Australian American Association, PO Box 869, Randwick, NSW 2031, Australia (⌨ www.australianamerican.org.au).

Australian-Britain Society, National Office, PO Box 9088, Deakin, ACT 2600, Australia (⌨ www.aust-britsociety.org.au).

Australian-British Chamber of Commerce, Level 15, 3 Spring Street, Sydney, NSW 2000, Australia (☎ 02-9247 6271, ⌨ www.britishchamber.com).

Australian Bureau of Statistics (☎ 02-9268 4909, ⌨ www.abs.gov.au).

Australian Embassy, 1601 Massachusetts Ave., NW, Washington, DC 20036, USA (☎ 202-797 3000, ⌨ www.usa.embassy.gov.au).

Australian High Commission, Australia House, Strand, London WC2B 4LA, UK (☎ 020-7379 4334, ⌨ www.uk.embassy.gov.au).

Australian Taxation Office, PO Box 9990 in the capital city of state or territory, Australia (☎ Excise Inquiry Line (☎ 13-2861 – within Australia only, ⌨ www.ato.gov.au).

Foreign Investment Review Board, Department of the Treasury, Langton Crescent, Parkes, ACT 2600, Australia (☎ 02-6263 3795, ⌨ www.firb.gov.au). Provide information about buying property in Australia for non-residents and retirees.

United Kingdom Settlers' Association (UKSA), PO Box 707, South Yarra, Victoria 3141, Australia (☎ 03-9787 3112, ⌨ www.geocities.com/endeavour_uksa).

APPENDIX B: FURTHER READING

Magazines & Newspapers

A directory of Australian publications by state and territory, with links to their websites, is available from ⌨ www.nla.gov.au/npapers.

The Advertiser – Adelaide (⌨ www.adelaidenow.news.com.au). Adelaide's leading daily newspaper.

The Age – Melbourne (⌨ www.theage.com.au). Mebourne's quality newspaper.

Australia and New Zealand Magazine, Merricks Media, 3 Riverside Court, Lower Bristol Road, Bath BA2 3DZ, UK (☎ 01225-786 850, ⌨ www.merricksmedia.co.uk). Monthly lifestyle, property and travel magazine.

The Australian – National (⌨ www.theaustralian.news.com.au). Australia's only national newspaper and the most authoritative.

The Australian Financial Review – National (⌨ http://afr.com). Australia's daily financial newspaper.

Australian Outlook, Consyl Publishing, 13 London Road, Bexhill-on-Sea, East Sussex TN39 3JR, UK (☎ 01424-223111, ⌨ www.consylpublishing. co.uk). Monthly subscription newspaper for prospective migrants.

The Bulletin (⌨ http://bulletin.ninemsn.com.au). Australian news magazine affiliated with the American *Newsweek* magazine.

The Canberra Times – ACT (⌨ http://canberra.yourguide.com.au). Canberra's leading daily.

The Courier Mail – Brisbane (⌨ www.thecouriermail.news.com.au). Brisbane's best-selling daily newspaper.

The Daily Telegraph – Sydney (⌨ www.dailytelegraph.news.com.au). A leading Sydney newspaper.

Emigrate Australia Newspaper, Outbound Publishing, 1 Commercial Road, Eastbourne, East Sussex, BN21 3XQ, UK (☎ 01323-726040, 🖥 www.outboundpublishing.com). Monthly subscription newspaper for prospective migrants.

The Herald-Sun – Melbourne (🖥 www.heraldsun.news.com.au). Melbourne's best-selling newspaper.

The Mercury – Hobart (🖥 www.news.com.au/mercury). Tasmania's leading newspaper.

National Library of Australia (🖥 www.nla.gov.au/npapers). Provides a comprehensive list of all Australia's national, state and local newspapers.

The Sydney Morning Herald (🖥 www.smh.com.au). Sydney's best-selling newspaper.

TNT Magazine, 14-15 Child's Place, Earls Court, London SW5 9RX, UK (☎ 020-7373 3377, 🖥 www.tntmagazine.co.uk). Free weekly magazine for expatriate Australians in the UK, but of interest to anyone planning to live in Australia.

The West Australian – Perth (🖥 www.thewest.com.au). Western Australia's best-selling newspaper.

Books

A selection of books about Australia is listed below; the publication title is followed by the name of the author and the publisher's name (in brackets). Some of the books listed are out of print, but you may still be able to find a copy in a bookshop or library.

Aboriginal Australia

Aboriginal Art, Wally Caruana (Thames & Hudson)

Aboriginal Myths, Legends & Fables, A.W. Reed (Read Natural History)

Australian Dreaming, Jennifer Isaacs (New Holland)

The Aborigines, R.M. Gibbs (Australia in Print)

Mutant Message Down Under, Mario Morgan (Thorsons)

My People, Kath Walker (Jacaranga Wiley)

My Place, Sally Morgan (Virago)

The Other Side of the Frontier, Henry Reynolds

Seeing the First Australians, Ian & Tamsin Donaldson (Allen & Unwin)

The Songlines, Bruce Chatwin (Picador)

Triumph of the Nomads, Geoffrey Blainey (Macmillan)

Wandering Girl, Glenys Ward (Virago)

Culture

Australian Sport: Better by Design? (Routledge)

Culture Wise Australia, David Hampshire & Martin Kidd (Survival Books)

The Little Book of Etiquette, Patsy Rowe (New Holland)

The Pocket Book of Aussie Patriotism, Brendan Gullifer (Black Inc.

What Australia Means to Me, Bob Carr (Penguin)

Who We Are: A Snapshot of Australia Today, David Dales (Allen &Unwin)

Xenophobe's Guide to the Aussies, Ken Hunt & Mike Taylor (Oval)

History

Australia's Immigrants 1788-1978, Geoffrey Sherington (Allen & Unwin)

Australia, the People (Lands, Peoples & Cultures), Erinn Banting (Crabtree)

The Commonwealth of Thieves: The Story of the Founding of Australia, Thomas Keneally (Chatto & Windus)

Divided Nation: Indigenous Australians in Australian Political Culture, Tim Rowse & Murray Groot (Melbourne University Press)

The Fatal Shore, Robert Hughes (Pan)

A History of Australia, Manning Clark (Penguin)

The Lucky Country: Australia in the Sixties, Donald Horne (Angus & Robertson)

The Oxford Companion to Australian History (OUP)

The Penguin History of Australia, John Malony (Penguin)

The Road to Botany Bay, Paul Carter (Faber & Faber)

A Secret Country, John Pilger (Vintage)

The Tyranny of Distance: How Distance Shaped Australia's History, Geoffrey Blainey (Pan Macmillan)

What Happened When?, Anthony Barker (Allen & Unwin)

Language

Australian Language & Culture, Paul Smitz (Lonely Planet)

Australian Phrasebook (Lonely Planet)

Australian Sign Language, Trevor Johnston & Adam Schembri (CUP)

Cambridge The Cambridge Guide to Australian English Usage, Pam Peters (CUP)

The New Dinkum Aussie Dictionary, Crooked Mick (New Holland)

Wordbook of Australian Idiom: Aussie Slang, Kerrin P. Rowe (Trafford)

Living & Working

The Australian Immigration Book (Made-To-Measure)

Buying & Renting Houses & Apartments, Jimmy Thomson (The Age/ SMH)

The Cost of Living and Housing Survey Book (Commonwealth Bank of Australia)

Living and Working in Australia, David Hampshire (Survival Books)

Outback

Australian Bushcraft, Richard Graves (Taylor-Type)

Bushwalking in Australia, John Chapman (Lonely Planet)

Bush Tucker: Australia's Wild Food, Tim Low (Angus & Robertson)

Dangerous Creatures of Australia, Marty Robinson (New Holland)

Discover Australia by 4WD (Hema Maps Pty Ltd)

How to Survive Australia, Robert Treborlang (Major Mitchell Press)

Outback Australia (Lonely Planet)

Outback Australia? No Worries!, Peter Wearing Smith (Omni Travel)

Safe Outback Travel, Jack Absalom (Five Mile Press)

Stay Alive, A Handbook on Survival, Maurice Dunlevy (AGPS)

People

12 Edmondstone Street, David Malouf (Penguin)

The Australian People, Craig McGregor (Hodder & Stoughton)

The Australian People, James Jupp (ANU)

The Australian Dictionary of Biography (MUP)

The Australians, In Search of an Identity, Ross Terrill (Bantam)

Christina Stead, Hazel Rowley (William Heinemann)

Contemporary Australians (DW Thorpe)

A Fortunate Life, Albert Facey (Viking)

From Strength to Strength, Sara Henderson

More Please, Barry Humphries (Penguin)

Patrick White: A Life, David Marr (Vintage)

Robert J Hawke, Blanche D'Alpuget (Penguin)

Unreliable Memoirs, Clive James (Picador)

Wild Card, Dorothy Hewett (Virago)

Tourist Guides

Australia (Lonely Planet)

Australia: Eyewitness Travel (Dorling Kindersley)

Australia: Insight Guide (Insight Guides)

Australia: The Rough Guide (The Rough Guides)

Australia and New Zealand on a Shoestring (Lonely Planet)

Australia & New Zealand, Travellers Survival Kit, Susan Griffith & Simon Calder (Vacation Work)

Berlitz Pocket Guide to Australia (Berlitz)

Bicycle Touring in Australia, Leigh Hemmings (Mountaineer Books)

Cycling in Australia, Nicola Wells (Lonely Planet)

Discover Australia, Ken Bernstein (Berlitz)

Essential Australia (Automobile Association)

Globetrotter Australia, Bruce Elder (New Holland)

Insider's Australia Guide, Harry Blutstein (MPC)

Let's Go: Australia (Pan)

Maverick Guide to Australia, Robert W. Bone (Pelican)

Sydney Time Out Guide (Penguin)

Travel Literature

At Home in Australia, Peter Conrad (Thames & Hudson)

Australia: True Stories of Life Down Under (Traveler's Tales)

Daisy Bates in the Desert, Julia Blackburn (Minerva)

Down Under/In a Sunburned Country, Bill Bryson (Doubleday)

In The Land Of Oz, Howard Jacobson (Penguin)

Outdoor Traveller's Australia (Stewart, Tabori, Chang)

A Ride in the Neon Sun, Josie Dew (Little, Brown & Company)

The Ribbon and the Ragged Square, Linda Christmas (Penguin)

The Road from Coorain, Jill Kathryn Conway (Vintage)

Sean and David's Long Drive, Sean Condon (Lonely Planet)

Sydney, Jan Morris (Penguin)

Tracks: A Woman's Solo Trek Across 1,700 Miles of Australian Outback, Robyn Davidson (Vintage)

Miscellaneous

The 100 Things Everyone Needs to Know About Australia, David Dale (Pan McMillan)

The Aussie Fact Book, Jenny Hunter (New Holland)

Australia (Commonwealth of Australia)

The Book of Australia (Watermark Press)

Everything You Didn't Need to Know About Australia, Adam Ward (Sanctuary)

How to Be Normal in Australia, Robert Treborlang (Major Mitchell Press)

The Little Aussie Fact Book, Margaret Nicholson (Penguin)

Wine Atlas of Australia, James Halliday (Mitchell Beazley)

APPENDIX C: USEFUL WEBSITES

A selection of websites is listed below by subject (in alphabetical order) and isn't intended to be exhaustive. Websites relevant to specific aspects of living and working in Australia are listed in the appropriate section.

Commonwealth Government

Australian Bureau of Statistics (🖥 www.abs.gov.au) – a wide range of statistics on Australia's economy, environment, industry, population and regions.

Australia Council for the Arts (🖥 www.ozco.gov.au) – the Australian government's arts funding and advisory body.

Australian Customs (🖥 www.customs.gov.au).

Australian Department of Foreign Affairs and Trade (🖥 www. dfat.gov. au/travel).

Australian Government (🖥 www.australia.gov.au) – useful information for, among others, jobseekers, migrants, retirees, students and women.

Bureau of Meteorology (🖥 www.bom.gov.au) – information about all aspects of Australia's climate.

Department of Foreign Affairs and Trade (🖥 www.dfat.gov.au/aib) – Australia in brief.

Department of Immigration & Citizenship (🖥 www.immi.gov.au/immigration.htm) – everything you need to know about visas and immigration.

Invest Australia (🖥 www.investaustralia.gov.au) – Australia's national inward investment agency.

Office for Women (🖥 http://ofw.facs.gov.au/index2.htm) – the government website of the Office for Women.

Study in Australia (🖥 www.study-in-australia.org) – the official Australian government site for international students.

Culture

Australian War Memorial (🖥 www.awm.gov.au) – national museum commemorating the sacrifice of Australians in war.

Convict Creations (🖥 www.convictcreations.com) – the hidden story of Australia 's missing links.

Immigration Museum (🖥 http://immigration.museum.vic.gov.au) – the history of Australian immigration from the 1800s to the present day.

National Gallery of Australia (🖥 www.nga.gov.au) – details of collections, events and exhibitions.

National Library of Australia (🖥 www.nla.gov.au) – the website of Australia's largest reference library.

National Museum of Australia (🖥 www.nma.gov.au) – details of collections, events and exhibitions.

National Wine Centre of Australia (🖥 www.wineaustralia.com.au) – part of the University of Adelaide, the NWCA provides information about winemaking and all aspects of Australia's vibrant wine industry.

Education

Adult Learning Australia (🖥 www.ala.asn.au) – a body concerned with adult education in Australia.

Australian Government Education Portal (🖥 www.education.gov.au/goved/go). Gateway to over 5,000 websites proving information about education and training in Australia.

Australian National University (🖥 www.anu.edu.au) – one of the world's foremost research universities.

Study in Australia (🖥 http://studyinaustralia.gov.au) – a government site with advice on studying in Australia.

Living & Working

About Australia (🖥 www.about-australia.com) – one of Australia's longest established information portals containing information about business, lifestyle, towns and regions, and what's on.

Australian Lifetips (💻 http://australian.lifetips.com) – miscellaneous information about life in Australia.

Blackstump (💻 www.blackstump.com.au/all.about.australia.htm) – comprehensive information and portal about Australia.

British Expat Australia Forum (💻 www.britishexpat.com/expatforum/australia) – a forum where you can read and post messages on Australia-related matters.

City of Melbourne (💻 www.melbourne.vic.gov.au/info) – the official Melbourne local government website.

City of Sydney (💻 www.cityofsydney.nsw.gov.au) – the official Sydney local government website.

Come on Aussie (💻 www.comeonaussie.com.au) – internet services directory.

Living in Australia (💻 www.livingin-australia.com) – useful information for immigrants.

Newcomers Network (💻 www.newcomersnetwork.com) – Australia's first network for newcomers.

Working Today (💻 www.workingtoday.com.au) – advice for working people.

Media

Australian Newspapers Online (💻 www.nla.gov.au/npapers) – a complete directory of Australian publications by state and territory, with links to their websites.

The Australian (💻 www.theaustralian.com.au) – Australia's leading newspaper.

Australian Broadcasting Corporation (💻 www.abc.net.au) – Australia's public radio and television company.

Radio Australia (💻 www.radioaustralia.net.au/australia).

Sydney Morning Herald (💻 www.smh.com.au) – Sydney's leading newspaper; a useful source of Australian and international business, entertainment, news, sport and technology.

Miscellaneous

Australia Institute (🖥 www.tai.org.au) – develops and conducts research and policy analysis.

Best Restaurants of Australia (🖥 www.bestrestaurants.com.au) – Search for restaurants by location, cuisine, price, features and more.

Charles Sturt University Guide to Australia (🖥 www.csu.edu/au/australia) – a useful collection of links on many topics, including culture, education, geography, tourism, towns and cities, trade and commerce, and travel and communications.

Housing Institute of Australia (🖥 economics.hia.com.au) – analysis and forecasting of Australia's housing industry.

Indigenous Australia (🖥 www.dreamtime.net.au) – information about Australia's indigenous peoples.

Insurance

National Women's Justice (🖥 http://nwjc.org.au/womensorgs.html) – promotes women's equality.

Ninemsn (http://ninemsn.com.au) – a joint venture between Microsoft and Australia's leading media company, Publishing and Broadcasting Limited (PBL), ninemsn is Australia's number one interactive media company.

Online Opinion (🖥 www.onlineopinion.com.au) – e-journal of social and political debate.

Relationships Australia (🖥 www.relationships.com.au) – an organisation offering help to couples, families and individuals.

Wikipedia (🖥 http://en.wikipedia.org/wiki/Portal:Australia) – the Australian encyclopaedia.

Yellow Pages (🖥 www.yellowpages.com.au) – online business telephone directory.

State Government Offices

ACT: Government of the Australian Capital Territory (🖥 www.act.gov.au).

NSW: New South Wales Government Trade and Investment Office (🖥 www.nsw.gov.au).

NT: Government of the Northern Territory (⌨ www.nt.gov.au).

QLD: Agent-General for Queensland (⌨ www.qld.gov.au).

SA: Agent-General for South Australia (⌨ www.sacentral.sa.gov.au).

TAS: Government of Tasmania (⌨ www.tas.gov.au).

VIC: Agent-General for Victoria (⌨ www.vic.gov.au).

WA: Government of Western Australia (⌨ www.wa.gov.au).

State Tourism Offices

ACT: Tourism Canberra (⌨ www.canberratourism.com.au).

NSW: Tourism New South Wales (⌨ www.visitnsw.com.au).

NT: NT Tourist Commission (⌨ www.ntholidays.com).

QLD: Tourism Queensland (⌨ www.queenslandholidays.com.au).

SA: SA Tourist Commission (⌨ www.southaustralia.com).

TAS: Tourism Tasmania (⌨ www.discovertasmania.com.au).

VIC: Tourism Victoria (⌨ www.tourism.vic.gov.au).

WA: Tourism Western Australia (⌨ www.westernaustralia.net).

Travel

About Australia (⌨ www.about-australia.com) – Digests of each state and a wealth of information for travellers.

Austravel (⌨ www.austtravel.com.au) – Australian travel emporium.

Go Australia (⌨ http://goaustralia.about.com) – information for visitors.

Images Australia (⌨ www.imagesaustralia.com) – photographs and general information about Australia.

Flight Centre (http://www.flightcentre.com.au) – A good website for flights, hotels and other travel arrangements, both in Oz and abroad.

Lonely Planet (⌨ www.lonelyplanet.com) – Australia's leading publisher of travel books.

Melbourne Online ( www.melbourne.com.au) – what's on in Melbourne.

Picture Australia (www.pictureaustralia.org) – a service hosted by the National Library of Australia, providing access to the digitised picture collections of a range of cultural institutions.

Sydney Online (www.sydney.com.au) – what's on in Sydney.

Tourism Australia (www.australia.com) – the organisation responsible for marketing Australia, containing information about all aspects of visiting and living in the country.

Travel Australia (www.travelaustralia.com.au) – accommodation and travel in Australia.

Up From Australia (www.upfromaustralia.com/reallyaussie.html) – Aussie browsing and shopping.

White Hat (www.whitehat.com.au) – information about Melbourne and Australia.

APPENDIX D: WEIGHTS & MEASURES

Australia uses the metric system of measurement. Those who are more familiar with the imperial system of measurement will find the tables on the following pages useful. Some comparissons shown are only approximate, but are close enough for most everyday uses. In addition to the variety of measurement systems used, clothes sizes often vary considerably with the manufacturer. The following websites allow you to make instant conversions between different measurement systems: 💻 www.omnis.demon.co.uk and 💻 www.unit-conversion.info.

Women's Clothes

Continental	34	36	38	40	42	44	46	48	50	52
Aus/UK	8	10	12	14	16	18	20	22	24	26
US	6	8	10	12	14	16	18	20	22	24

Pullovers

	Women's						Men's					
Continental	40	42	44	46	48	50	44	46	48	50	52	54
Aus /UK	34	36	38	40	42	44	34	36	38	40	42	44
US	34	36	38	40	42	44	sm	med	lar	xl		

Men's Shirts

Continental	36	37	38	39	40	41	42	43	44	46
Aus/UK/US	14	14	15	15	16	16	17	17	18	-

Men's Underwear

Continental	5	6	7	8	9	10
Aus/UK	34	36	38	40	42	44
US	sm	med		lar	xl	

Note: sm = small, med = medium, lar = large, xl = extra large

Children's Clothes

Continental	92	104	116	128	140	152
Aus/UK	16/18	20/22	24/26	28/30	32/34	36/38
US	2	4	6	8	10	12

Children's Shoes

Continental	18	19	20	21	22	23	24	25	26	27	28	29	30	31	32
Aus/UK/US	2	3	4	4	5	6	7	7	8	9	10	11	11	12	13
Continental	33	34	35	36	37	38									
Aus/UK/US	1	2	2	3	4	5									

Shoes (Women's and Men's)

Continental	35	36	37	37	38	39	40	41	42	42	43	44
Aus/UK	2	3	3	4	4	5	6	7	7	8	9	9
US	4	5	5	6	6	7	8	9	9	10	10	11

Weight

Imperial	Metric	Metric	Imperial
1oz	28.35g	1g	0.035oz
1lb*	454g	100g	3.5oz
1cwt	50.8kg	250g	9oz
1 ton	1,016kg	500g	18oz
2,205lb	1 tonne	1kg	2.2lb

Length

British/US	Metric	Metric	British/US
1in	2.54cm	1cm	0.39in
1ft	30.48cm	1m	3ft 3.25in
1yd	91.44cm	1km	0.62mi
1mi	1.6km	8km	5mi

Capacity

Imperial	Metric	Metric	Imperial
1 UK pint	0.57 litre	1 litre	1.75 UK pints
1 US pint	0.47 litre	1 litre	2.13 US pints
1 UK gallon	4.54 litres	1 litre	0.22 UK gallon
1 US gallon	3.78 litres	1 litre	0.26 US gallon

Note: An American 'cup' = around 250ml or 0.25 litre.

Area

British/US	Metric	Metric	British/US
1 sq. in	0.45 sq. cm	1 sq. cm	0.15 sq. in
1 sq. ft	0.09 sq. m	1 sq. m	10.76 sq. ft
1 sq. yd	0.84 sq. m	1 sq. m	1.2 sq. yds
1 acre	0.4 hectares	1 hectare	2.47 acres
1 sq. mile	2.56 sq. km	1 sq. km	0.39 sq. mile

Temperature

°Celsius	°Fahrenheit	
0	32	(freezing point of water)
5	41	
10	50	
15	59	
20	68	
25	77	
30	86	
35	95	
40	104	
50	122	

Notes: The boiling point of water is 100°C / 212°F.

Normal body temperature (if you're alive and well) is 37°C / 98.6°F.

Temperature Conversion

Celsius to Fahrenheit: multiply by 9, divide by 5 and add 32. (For a quick and approximate conversion, double the Celsius temperature and add 30.)

Fahrenheit to Celsius: subtract 32, multiply by 5 and divide by 9. (For a quick and approximate conversion, subtract 30 from the Fahrenheit temperature and divide by 2.)

Oven Temperatures

Gas	Electric	
	°F	°C
-	225–250	110–120
1	275	140
2	300	150
3	325	160
4	350	180
5	375	190
6	400	200
7	425	220
8	450	230
9	475	240

Air Pressure

PSI	Bar
10	0.5
20	1.4
30	2
40	2.8

Power

Kilowatts	Horsepower	Horsepower	Kilowatts
1	1.34	1	0.75

APPENDIX E: COMMUNICATIONS MAP

The map below shows the main airports, roads and railways in Australia. A general map of Australia is shown on page 6.

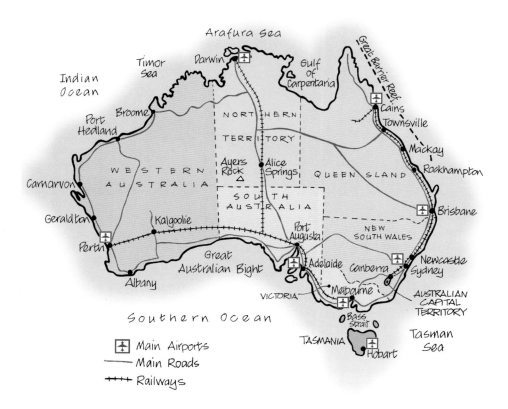

Brighton Jetty, Adelaide, SA

INDEX

Second Valley, Fleurieu Peninsula, SA

Survival Books

Essential reading for anyone planning to live, work, retire or buy a home abroad

Survival Books was established in 1987 and by the mid-'90s was the leading publisher of books for people planning to live, work, buy property or retire abroad.

From the outset, our philosophy has been to provide the most comprehensive and up-to-date information available. Our titles routinely contain up to twice as much information as other books and are updated frequently. All our books contain colour photographs and some are printed in two colours or full colour throughout. They also contain original cartoons, illustrations and maps.

Survival Books are written by people with first-hand experience of the countries and the people they describe, and therefore provide invaluable insights that cannot be obtained from official publications or websites, and information that is more reliable and objective than that provided by the majority of unofficial sites.

Survival Books are designed to be easy – and interesting – to read. They contain a comprehensive list of contents and index and extensive appendices, including useful addresses, further reading, useful websites and glossaries to help you obtain additional information as well as metric conversion tables and other useful reference material.

Our primary goal is to provide you with the essential information necessary for a trouble-free life or property purchase and to save you time, trouble and money.

We believe our books are the best – they are certainly the best-selling. But don't take our word for it – read what reviewers and readers have said about Survival Books at the front of this book.

Order your copies today by phone, fax, post or email from:
Survival Books, PO Box 3780, Yeovil, BA21 5WX, United Kingdom.
Tel: +44 (0)1935-700060, email: sales@survivalbooks.net,
Website: www.survivalbooks.net

Buying a Home Series

Buying a home abroad is not only a major financial transaction but also a potentially life-changing experience; it's therefore essential to get it right. Our Buying a Home guides are required reading for anyone planning to purchase property abroad and are packed with vital information to guide you through the property jungle and help you avoid disasters that can turn a dream home into a nightmare.

The purpose of our Buying a Home guides is to enable you to choose the most favourable location and the most appropriate property for your requirements, and to reduce your risk of making an expensive mistake by making informed decisions and calculated judgements rather than uneducated and hopeful guesses. Most importantly, they will help you save money and will repay your investment many times over.

Buying a Home guides are the most comprehensive and up-to-date source of information available about buying property abroad – whether you're seeking a detached house or an apartment, a holiday or a permanent home (or an investment property), these books will prove invaluable.

Living and Working Series

Our Living and Working guides are essential reading for anyone planning to spend a period abroad – whether it's an extended holiday or permanent migration – and are packed with priceless information designed to help you avoid costly mistakes and save both time and money.

Living and Working guides are the most comprehensive and up-to-date source of practical information available about everyday life abroad. They aren't, however, simply a catalogue of dry facts and figures, but are written in a highly readable style – entertaining, practical and occasionally humorous.

Our aim is to provide you with the comprehensive practical information necessary for a trouble-free life. You may have visited a country as a tourist, but living and working there is a different matter altogether; adjusting to a new environment and culture and making a home in any foreign country can be a traumatic and stressful experience. You need to adapt to new customs and traditions, discover the local way of doing things (such as finding a home, paying bills and obtaining insurance) and learn all over again how to overcome the everyday obstacles of life.

All these subjects and many, many more are covered in depth in our Living and Working guides – don't leave home without them.

The Expat's Best Friend!

Culture Wise Series

Our **Culture Wise** series of guides is essential reading for anyone who wants to understand how a country really 'works'. Whether you're planning to stay for a few days or a lifetime, these guides will help you quickly find your feet and settle into your new surroundings.

Culture Wise guides:

- Reduce the anxiety factor in adapting to a foreign culture
- Explain how to behave in everyday situations in order to avoid cultural and social gaffes
- Help you get along with your neighbours
- Make friends and establish lasting business relationships
- Enhance your understanding of a country and its people.

People often underestimate the extent of cultural isolation they can face abroad, particularly in a country with a different language. At first glance, many countries seem an 'easy' option, often with millions of visitors from all corners of the globe and well-established expatriate communities. But, sooner or later, newcomers find that most countries are indeed 'foreign' and many come unstuck as a result. **Culture Wise** guides will enable you to quickly adapt to the local way of life and feel at home, and – just as importantly – avoid the worst effects of culture shock.

Culture Wise – The Wise Way to Travel

The essential guides to Culture, Customs & Business Etiquette

Other Survival Books

Investing in Property Abroad: Essential reading for anyone planning to buy property abroad, containing surveys of over 30 countries.

The Best Places to Buy a Home in France/Spain: Unique guides to where to buy property in Spain and France, containing detailed regional profiles and market reports.

Buying, Selling and Letting Property: The best source of information about buying, selling and letting property in the UK.

Earning Money From Your Home: Income from property in France and Spain, including short- and long-term letting.

Foreigners in France/Spain: Triumphs & Disasters: Real-life experiences of people who have emigrated to France and Spain, recounted in their own words.

Making a Living: Comprehensive guides to self-employment and starting a business in France and Spain.

Renovating & Maintaining Your French Home: The ultimate guide to renovating and maintaining your dream home in France.

Retiring in France/Spain: Everything a prospective retiree needs to know about the two most popular international retirement destinations.

Running Gîtes and B&Bs in France: An essential book for anyone planning to invest in a gîte or bed & breakfast business.

Rural Living in France: An invaluable book for anyone seeking the 'good life', containing a wealth of practical information about all aspects of French country life.

Shooting Caterpillars in Spain: The hilarious and compelling story of two innocents abroad in the depths of Andalusia in the late '80s.

Wild Thyme in Ibiza: A fragrant account of how a three-month visit to the enchanted island of Ibiza in the mid-'60s turned into a 20-year sojourn.

**For a full list of our current titles, visit our website at
www.survivalbooks.net**

CULTURE WISE
AUSTRALIA

Traveller's often underestimate the depth of cultural isolation they can face abroad, even in a country where English is spoken. To many people, Australia may seem an 'easy' option, with it's long history of immigration, multicultural society and millions of annual visitors. However, sooner or later, most newcomers find certain aspects of Aussie life alien - and some come unstuck as a result!

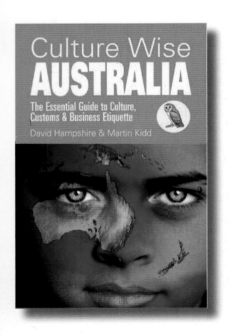

PRINTED IN COLOUR!

Inside you'll discover:

◆ How to overcome culture shock

◆ The historical and political background to modern Australia

◆ Australian attitudes and values - at home and at work

◆ Do's, don'ts and taboos

◆ How to enjoy yourself in Aussie style

◆ Business & professional etiquette

◆ Australia's spoken & body language

◆ How to get around Australia safely

◆ Shopping the Aussie way

Culture Wise Australia will help you understand Australia and it's people, and adapt to the Aussie way of life. Most importantly, it will enable you to quickly feel at home.

Buy your copy today at www.survivalbooks.net

Culture Wise - The Wisest Way to Travel

BUYING A HOME IN AUSTRALIA

Buying a Home in Australia is essential reading for anyone planning to buy a home in Australia (previously published as *Buying a Home in Australia & New Zealand*), and is designed to guide you through the property maze and save you time trouble and money! Most importantly, it is packed with vital information to help you avoid disasters that can turn your dream home into a nightmare!

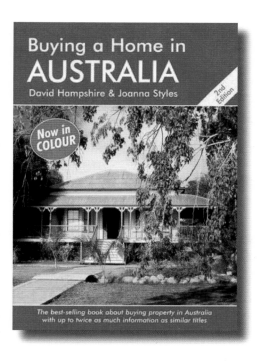

Buying a Home in
AUSTRALIA
David Hampshire & Joanna Styles
2nd Edition

Now in COLOUR

The best-selling book about buying property in Australia with up to twice as much information as similar titles

PRINTED IN COLOUR!

Inside you'll discover:

- ◆ Major Considerations
- ◆ Finding the Best Place To Live
- ◆ Funding Your Dream Home
- ◆ Money Matters
- ◆ The Purchase Procedure
- ◆ Moving House
- ◆ Taxation
- ◆ Insurance
- ◆ Letting
- ◆ Miscellaneous Matters
- ◆ Useful Addresses, Further Reading
- ◆ Useful Websites and Maps

Buying a Home in Australia is the best-selling and most comprehensive book available for foreigners planning to buy property in Australia.

Buy your copy today at www.survivalbooks.net

Survival Books - The Expats' Best Friend

Photo Credits

www.shutterstock.com

16 © Dmitriy Shironosov, 22 © Marten Czamanske, 24 © Dasilva, 26 © Courteney Keating, 28 © Innocent, 31 © Phillip Minnis, 35 © Rene Jansa, 37 © Glen Jones, 38 © Sandy Maya Matzen, 42 © Ximagination, 44 © Francois Etienne du Plessis, 48 © János Gehring, 50 © GeoM, 53 © Ingrid Balabanova, 57 © Pavel Bortel, 59 © Dimitrije Paunovic, 61 © Matthew J. Brown, 62 © Styve Reineck, 64 © John Austin, 67 © Francois Etienne du Plessis, 68 © Thorsten Rust, 70 © Aaron D. Settipane, 72 © Lee Torrens, 75 © Tatiana53, 82 © Chee-Onn Leong, 88 © Pavel Losevsky, 92 © Anyka, 94 © Dhoxax, 97 © Kwest, 103 © Neale Cousland, 105 © Bob Denelzen, 109 © Walter Quirtmair, 111 © Colin & Linda McKie, 119 © Olivier Le Queinec, 121 © Rob Marmion, 123 © Gelpi, 125 © Sklep Spozywczy, 127 © Johnny Lye, 129 © Christopher Meder, 130 © Pres Panayotov, 133 © Thomas M. Perkins, 136 © Stuart Taylor, 142 © Christopher Meder, 144 © Stephen Coburn, 147 © Max Blain, 149 © Kurhan, 150 © Andriy Rovenko, 156 © Ronen, 159 © Jason Stitt, 160 © Colin & Linda McKie, 163 © Colin & Linda McKie, 167 © Phil Morley, 169 © Alex Brosa, 173 © Leah-Anne Thompson, 174 © Buida Nikita Yourievich, 179 © Deborah Reny, 180 © Gelpi, 183 © Andresr, 188 © Tijmen, 194 © Gibsons, 196 © Milan Vasicek, 200 © Doxa, 204 © Maarten Wagemans, 207 © GeoM, 213 © Colin & Linda McKie, 217 © Stieglitz, 227 © Tomasz Trojanowski, 239 © Ashley Whitworth, 243 © Iofoto, 248 © Marcin Balcerzak, 251 © Feng Yu, 252 © Beerkoff, 254 © Olena Kucherenko, 257 © Kurhan, 261 © Chee-Onn Leong, 265 © Chee-Onn Leong, 266 © Leah-Anne Thompson, 269 © Sandra G, 275 © Stephen Coburn, 284 © Johnny Lye, 289 © Filaphoto, 300 © EHO, 305 © Robyn Mackenzie, 317 © Colin & Linda McKie, 326 © Eric Isselée, 328 © Jenny Solomon, 332 © Aaron D. Settipane, 335 © Carlos Sanchez Pereyra, 345 © Chee-Onn Leong, 346 © Robyn Mackenzie, 348 © Sebastien Burel, 351 © Max Blain, 352 © Stephen Finn, 359 © John Barry de Nicola, 361 © Neale Cousland, 362 © Galina Barskaya, 364 © Lee